European Politics

Visit the companion website for this
text at:
http://www.palgrave.com/politics/bale

COMPARATIVE GOVERNMENT AND POLITICS
Founding Series Editor: The late **Vincent Wright**

Published

Rudy Andeweg and Galen A. Irwin
Government and Politics of the Netherlands (2nd edition)

Tim Bale
European Politics: A Comparative Introduction

Nigel Bowles
Government and Politics of the United States (2nd edition)

Paul Brooker
Non-Democratic Regimes: Theory, Government and Politics

Robert Elgie
Political Leadership in Liberal Democracies

Rod Hague and Martin Harrop
Comparative Government and Politics: An Introduction* (6th edition)

Paul Heywood
The Government and Politics of Spain

B. Guy Peters
Comparative Politics: Theories and Methods
[Rights: World excluding North America]

Tony Saich
Governance and Politics of China (2nd edition)

Anne Stevens
The Government and Politics of France (3rd edition)

Ramesh Thakur
The Government and Politics of India

Forthcoming

Judy Batt
Government and Politics in Eastern Europe

Robert Leonardi
Government and Politics in Italy

* Published in North America as **Political Science: A Comparative Introduction (4th edition)**

Comparative Government and Politics
Series Standing Order
ISBN 0–333–71693–0 hardback
ISBN 0–333–69335–3 paperback
(*outside North America only*)

You can receive future titles in this series as they are published by placing a standing order. Please contact your bookseller or, in the case of difficulty, write to us at the address below with your name and address, the title of the series and an ISBN quoted above.

Customer Services Department, Macmillan Distribution Ltd
Houndmills, Basingstoke, Hampshire RG21 6XS, England

European Politics

A Comparative Introduction

Tim Bale

First published 2005 by
PALGRAVE MACMILLAN
Houndmills, Basingstoke, Hampshire RG21 6XS and
175 Fifth Avenue, New York, N.Y. 10010
Companies and representatives throughout the world

PALGRAVE MACMILLAN is the global academic imprint of the Palgrave
Macmillan division of St. Martin's Press, LLC and of Palgrave Macmillan Ltd.
Macmillan® is a registered trademark in the United States, United Kingdom
and other countries. Palgrave is a registered trademark in the European
Union and other countries.

ISBN-13: 978–14039–1870–3   hardback
ISBN-10: 14039–1870–8   hardback
ISBN-13: 978–14039–1871–0   paperback
ISBN-10: 14039–1871–6   paperback

This book is printed on paper suitable for recycling and made
from fully managed and sustained forest sources

A catalogue record for this book is available from the British Library.

A catalog record for this book is available from the Library of Congress.

10 9 8 7 6 5 4 3 2 1
14 13 12 11 10 09 08 07 06 05

Printed in China

To Jackie, Javier, Belén and Jack,
who helped me stay sane enough to commit this irrational act

Contents

List of illustrative material

Boxes

Maps

Country profiles

List of abbreviations and acronyms

General terms

ACP	African, Caribbean and Pacific
ADB	*algemene bestuursdienst* (Netherlands)
AMS	Alternative member system
ASEAN	Association of South East Asian Nations
ASEM	Asia-Europe Meeting
CAP	Common Agricultural Policy
CEEP	European Centre of Enterprizes with Public Participation and of Enterprizes of General Economic Interest
cefic	European Chemical Industry Council
CET	Common external tariff
CFSP	Common Foreign and Security Policy
CIS	Commonwealth of Independent States
CoE	Council of Europe
CoR	Committee of the Regions
COPA	Committee of Agricultural Organizations
COREPER	Comittee of Permanent Representatives (EU)
COSAC	Conference of Community and European Affairs Committees
DDR	(Communist) East Germany
DG	Directorate General (of the European Commission)
DOM	*Departement d'Outre-Mer* (French Overseas Department)
EBA	'Everything but Arms'
EC	European Community
ECB	European Central Bank
ECHR	European Convention for the Protection of Human Rights and Fundamental Freedoms (European Convention on Human Rights)
ECJ	European Court of Justice
ECOFIN	Economic and Financial Affairs Council
ECSC	European Coal and Steel Community
EDC	European Defence Community
EEA	European Environmental Agency
EEC	European Economic Community
EFPIA	European Federation of Pharmaceutical Industries and Associations
EFTA	European Free Trade Area
EMU	European Monetary Union
ENP	European Neighbourhood Policy
EP	European Parliament
EPC	European Political Co-operation
ESDP	European Security and Defence Policy
ETA	*Euskadi Ta Azkatasuna* (Basque Homeland and Liberty – paramilitary organization)
ETUC	European Trade Union Confederation
EU	European Union
EU-15	European Union of fifteen member states (1995–2004)
EU-25	European Union of twenty-five member states (2004–)
EVS	European Values Survey
FDI	Foreign direct investment
FRG	Federal Republic of Germany (West Germany)
FPP	First-past-the-post
FSU	Former Soviet Union
FYROM	Former Yugoslav Republic of Macedonia
G-8	Group of the world's richest industrialized countries (Britain, Canada, France, Germany, Italy, Japan, Russia, US)
GATT	General Agreement on Tariffs and Trade
GDP	Gross domestic product
GDR	German Democratic Republic (Communist East Germany)
GHGs	Greenhouse gasses
GM	Genetically modifed/modification

GNP	Gross national product
ICT	Information and communication technology
ID	Party ID (party identification)
IMF	International Monetary Fund
IRA	Irish Republican Army
IRU	International Romani Union
IT	Information technology
JHA	Justice and Home Affairs
LDC	Less-developed country
M&A	Mergers and acquizitions
MEDEF	*Mouvement des Entreprizes de France* (French employers' organization)
MEP	Member of the European Parliament
MMP	Mixed member proportional
MP	Member of Parliament
NATO	North Atlantic Treaty Organization
NELF	New European Left Forum
NFU	National Farmers' Union
NGO	Non-governmental organization
NIS	Newly independent states
NPM	New Public Management
ODA	Overseas development assistance
OPZZ	Ogólnopolskie Porozumienie Związków Zawodowych (All-Polish Alliance of Trade Unions)
OSCE	Organization for Security and Co-operation in Europe
PFI	Private Finance Initiative
PPC	Permanent Partnership Council (EU/Russia)
PPP	Purchasing power parity
PR	Proportional representation
QMV	Qualified majority voting
R&D	Research and development
RRF	Rapid Reaction Force
RSPB	Royal Society for the Protection of Birds
SEA	Single European Act
SEM	Single European Market
SGP	Stability and Growth Pact
SIS	Schengen information system
SME	Small and medium-sized enterprizes
SOE	State-owned enterprize
SSA	Sub-Saharan Africa

STV	Single transferable vote
TACIS	Technical Assistance to the CIS (EU)
TEU	Treaty on European Union (Maastricht Treaty)
TOM	*Territoire d'Outre-Mer* (French overseas territory)
UK	United Kingdom
UN	United Nations
UNHCR	United Nations High Commissioner for Refugees
UNICE	Union of Industrial and Employers Confederations of Europe
USSR	(Union of Soviet Socialist Republics) Soviet Union
WEU	West European Union
WMD	Weapons of mass destruction
WTO	World Trade Organization

Political parties

AN	*Alleanza Nazionale* (Italy)
AOV	*Algemeen Ouderen Vorbond* (Pensioners' Party – Netherlands)
AP	*Alianza Popular* (Popular Alliance – Spain)
AWS	*Akcja WyborczaSolidarność* (Solidarity Electoral Action – Poland)
C	*Centerpartiet* (Centre Party – Sweden)
CDA	*Christen Democratisch Appèl* (Christian Democratic Appeal – Netherlands)
CDC	*Convergència Democrática de Catalunya* (Democratic Convergence of Catalunya – Spain)
CDS/PP	*Centro Democrático Social /Partido Popular* (Social Democratic Centre/Popular Party – Portugal)
CDU	*Christlich-Demokratische Union* (Christian Democratic Union – Germany)
CiU	*Convergència i Unió* (Convergence and Union – Catalunya, Spain)

CSSD   *Česká strana sociálné demokratická* (Czech Social Democratic Party)

CSU   *Christlich Soziale Union in Bayern* (Bavarian Christian Social Union – Germany)

CU   *ChristenUnie* (Christian Union – Netherlands)

D'66   *Democraten 66* (Democrats 66 – Netherlands)

DC   *Democrazia Cristiana* (Christian Democracy – Italy)

DF   *Dansk Folkeparti* (Danish People's Party)

DUP   *Democratic Unionist Party* (Northern Ireland)

DS   *Democratici di Sinistra* (Democrats of the Left – Italy)

FDP   *Freie Demokratische Partei* (Free Democratic Party – Germany)

FN   *Front National* (National Front – France)

FpL   *Folkpartiet Liberalerna* (People's Party Liberals – Sweden)

FPO   *Freiheitliche Partei Österreichs* (Austrian Freedom Party)

FrP   *Fremskrittspartiet* (Progress Party – Norway)

GL   *Groen Links* (Green Left – Netherlands)

K   *Kristdemokraterna* (Christian Democrats – Sweden)

KESK   *Suomen Keskusta* (Finnish Centre)

KSČM   *Komunistická Strana Čech a Morava* (Communist Party of Bohemia and Moravia – Czech Republic)

LN   *Lega Nord* (Italy)

LPR   *Liga Polskich Rodzin* (League of Polish Families)

LPF   *Lijst Pim Fortuyn* (Pim Fortuyn List – Netherlands)

M   *Moderata Samlingspartiet* (Moderate Rally Party Sweden)

MP   *Miljöpartiet de Gröna* (Green Environmental Party – Sweden)

ÖVP   *Österreichische Volkspartei* (Austrian People's Party)

PCF   *Parti Communiste Français* (French Communist Party)

PCI   *Partito Comunista Italiano* (Italian Communist Party)

PDS   *Partito Democratico della Sinistra* (Democratic Party of the Left – Italy) or *Partei des Demokratischen Sozialismus* (Party of Democratic Socialism – Germany)

PiS   *Prawo i Sprawiedliwość* (Law and Justice – Poland)

PS   *Parti Socialiste* (Socialist Party – France)

PP   *Partido Popular* (Popular Party – Spain)

PSL   *Polskie Stronnictwo Ludowe* (Polish Peasants' Party)

PSOE   *Partido Socialista Obrero Español* (Spanish Socialist Workers Party)

PvdA   *Partij van de Arbeid* (Labour Party – Netherlands)

SAP   *Arbetarepartiet-Socialdemokraterna* (Social Democratic Labour Party – Sweden)

SGP   *Staatkundig Gereformeerde Partij* (Political Reformed Party – Netherlands)

SLD   *Sojusz Lewicy Demokralycznej* (Democratic Left Alliance – Poland)

SLDP   *Social Democratic and Labour Party* (Northern Ireland)

SP   *Socialistische Partij* (Socialist Party – Netherlands)

SPD   *Sozialdemokratische Partei Deutschlands* (German Social Democratic Party)

SVP   *Schweizerische Volkspartei* (Swiss People's Party)

UCD   *Unión Centro Democrático* (Union of the Democratic Centre – Spain)

UDF   *Union pour la Démocratie Française* (Union for French Democracy)

UPM   *Union pour un Mouvement Populaire* (Union for a Popular Movement – France)

V   *Vänsterpartiet* (Left Party – Sweden)

VVD   *Volkspartij voor Vrijheid en Democratie* (People's Party for Freedom and Democracy – Netherlands)

VB   *Vlaams Blok*, now *Vlaams Belang* (Belgium)

Introduction

Why European politics?
Why this book?
Keeping it real – and up to date
Where is it going?
Getting started

It is perhaps ironic that a book introducing you to the politics and governance of Europe was conceived as far away from the place as anyone can get. While teaching European politics in New Zealand between 1998 and 2003, I was never quite happy with the textbooks I was using. Basically, there were two types to choose from. The first was the country-by-country approach. As a student, this arrangement has the merit of teaching you a great deal about a few very important countries. But even the best of such books (and there are some very good ones) sometimes leave you not knowing that much about how politics works in the continent as a whole. The approach makes it hard to compare and contrast because it cannot help but stress particularity. The second kind of textbook on offer, organized not by country but by theme, gets over this problem by being explicitly comparative. But this can leave you feeling both overloaded and a little detached from the living, breathing Europe that less abstract country-by-country texts are better able to evoke and convey.

What was needed, I thought, was something that combined the strengths of both approaches – something which did not lose sight of the wood for the trees or the trees for the wood; something that captured *commonality* but also *diversity*. The time had also come, I thought, to treat both the European Union (EU) and Central and Eastern Europe (CEE) as integral, rather than stranding them in separate chapters from those on the west European Countries. This book is the product of that critique and that thinking.

Why European politics?

Any undergraduate textbook is judged by what must be one of the world's most critical audiences. Students have less time and less money to waste than ever before. A new book needs to appreciate this and therefore has to make a good case for itself – and for its subject matter – in what can sometimes be a crowded market. Unless both content and format have a rationale, they will not command – and will not deserve to command – the attention of those at whom they are targeted. This book is intended to be user-friendly enough for the general reader but is aimed at those studying politics for their degree or as part of their degree. According to one recent definition, studying politics is about:

> developing a knowledge and understanding of government and society. The interaction of people, ideas and institutions provides the focus to understand how values are allocated and resources distributed at many levels, from the local through to the sectoral, national, regional and global. Thus analyses of who gets what, when, how, why and where are central, and pertain to related questions of power, justice, order, conflict, legitimacy, accountability, obligation, sovereignty and decision making. Politics encompasses philosophical, theoretical, institutional and issue-based concerns relating to governance (QAA, 2000).

Those who study politics, are supposed to be able, among other things, to:

> demonstrate knowledge and understanding of different political systems, the nature and distribution of power in them; the social, economic, historical and cultural contexts within which they operate, and the relationships between them (QAA, 2000).

Studying European politics is clearly one way of doing this. Europe also provides us with comparative material on political institutions, processes and issues – the kind of things that anybody with an interest in politics *per se* is naturally going to be keen to find out more about. Even if you are primarily interested in your own country, you can hardly avoid making comparisons, even if you do it only implicitly. Political science is inherently comparative because it has pretensions to building and testing theories (if not laws) that work *across time and space*; even when its focus is the unique, it attempts generalizable (and therefore) comparative explanations.

But the rationale for studying European politics goes wider than the intellectual. It may, for instance, be quite practical: even those readers who do not currently live or work in Europe may well do so at some time in the future. At the very least, they may pursue careers that involve some passing contact either with European companies or even European governments and the EU. Knowing what makes the continent tick politically, and having some handle on the social and economic issues that preoccupy it, is culturally and practically useful. Nor should we necessarily play down the emotional reasons. Having lived and taught outside Europe for five years, I am as aware as anyone that more and more of us are born and/or brought up outside our family's 'country of origin'. If that country is European, then studying the continent helps achieve a sense of connection to your roots. This obviously applies to students in the so-called 'settler societies' – the US and Canada, Australia and New Zealand, Israel, and South Africa. But it can just as easily apply if, say, you were born and brought up in one European country but your family (or a part of it) has its origins or still lives in another.

There is also a democratic and, if you like, political purpose to studying the politics of other countries. Wherever we live, we are generally given to believe by our own politicians that the way things are done in our country are either in tune with what goes on elsewhere, or probably even better. But when we look abroad we soon realize several things. The first is that 'it doesn't have to be this way': governments that do things differently to the way your own government does them do not necessarily go to hell in a handcart. Second, many of the challenges faced and the solutions offered by the politicians you voted (or did not vote) for bear a remarkably strong (and only sometimes depressing) resemblance to the challenges faced and the solutions offered by their European counterparts. And, third, wherever you are, the picture of European and EU politics painted by the media is almost guaranteed to be highly partial – in both senses of the word. Ample reason, then, to dig a little deeper.

Why this book?

Persuading you that European politics is something worth studying in general is one thing. Persuading you that this book in particular is worth using is another. One reason why it might be is because it takes seriously the argument that students who study politics need to learn how to 'gather organize and deploy evidence, data and information from a variety of secondary and some primary sources' and get into 'critical reading of a wide range of texts including documents, monographs, scholarly articles, statistics, newspapers ... and sources on the internet' (QAA, 2000). This book not only encourages you to do all that (more of which later), but it also tries to do exactly that itself. The final reason why this book might be worth using is because it is founded on experience in the classroom, and because it is based on what works.

What works is providing you with a good balance of breadth and depth, simplicity and complexity, overview and detail. In other words, providing you with a book that will tell you not only what you need to know but also introduce you to issues that you might like to find out more about. A book that communicates the enthusiasm of the author but does not blithely assume you share it – at least at the outset, anyway! A book that you can understand but refuses to talk down to you. A book that avoids jargon when it is unnecessary but is not afraid to use it and explain it (either in the text or in the definitions **emboldened** in the text) when it is. A book that does not pretend that absolutely everything can be broken down into predigested, bite-sized chunks, but which also realizes that it needs to be accessible. A book that uses bang-up-to-date examples from the real world of European politics, allowing and encouraging you to make connections between what you study in the classroom or the library and what you watch, listen to and read in the media. A book that realizes that, unless it helps you better understand and function in the world as you perceive it, then education – an increasingly expensive commodity – is pretty pointless.

The media has a considerable advantage over an academic work, of course. It may be more simplistic and one-sided, but it is a good deal less time-consuming and even less time-bound. It rarely tells us more than we need to know – even if sometimes that is not quite enough. It is almost always well crafted and presented, with the accent on the visual and a style that aims to grab the attention of busy people who, by and large, can take it or leave it. Paradoxically, the media may also be quite influential: it helps to construct a common wisdom that by definition many of us buy into whatever our political convictions – assuming we have any in the first place. This book also works because it is unapologetic about seeking to question at least some of that common wisdom. Part of its point, without trying to sell you a particular world view, is to interrogate some of the popular assumptions – be they conservative or right-on and radical – about European politics and Europe's politicians. That will almost certainly include some of the truths you yourself hold to be self-evident, whether they concern, for instance, the supposed iniquity, inevitability and impact of globalization, the apparently all-pervading electoral power of the media, or the much-trumpeted shortcomings and sell-outs of self-interested politicians.

You should expect, then, to disagree – and anyone who is teaching you to disagree – with quite a bit of what this book says. At the very least, it may make you think twice. Even if you do not change your mind, your opinions are likely to be the stronger for being tested. Maybe – indeed probably – you can prove me wrong. Time itself might well do so, too. Part of the mix of fascination and frustration of studying politics is that things never stand still. However hard you try as an author, some of what you write is almost certainly past its sell-by date even before it hits the shops, let alone the shelves of the library.

Keeping it real – and up to date

This unavoidable built-in obsolescence can be tackled in two or three ways. The first is to minimize the number of examples used. But because that disconnects you from what is really going on, it is not really an option. This book is full of tables and figures that, hopefully, will give you some helpful facts at your fingertips. Even though each chapter mentions all sorts of countries, focusing here and there on particular states that seem particularly relevant to the discussion in hand, I have made the decision to concentrate in the tables and figures on just nine countries. These run from the north through Sweden, down through the UK, the Netherlands, France, and Spain, then over, via Italy, to Germany, and east through the Czech Republic and Poland. Each country is given its own profile, providing an overview of its history, economy and society, governance and foreign policy, plus some further reading. Some headline statistics are also provided but, since absolute numbers for things like area, population and GDP can easily be found elsewhere (e.g. Turner, 2005 or http://www.odci.gov/cia/publications/factbook/), I have tried to add comparative value by expressing each as a share of the EU-25's total.

These countries are chosen because they are some of the biggest and because they represent variety. They can never, of course, represent every country in Europe. But there is always a trade-off in terms of focusing on a manageable core and doing everything. I have chosen the former, well aware that in so doing I am bound to disappoint some people who hoped to see more of their favourite countries – or at least the ones on which they had decided (or been asked) to write an essay or term paper. Not everybody who seeks to improve European understanding is faced with such a choice. Each of the seven banknotes that make up Europe's single currency, the euro (€), contains a picture of a bridge (the images and their rationale can be explored by going to http://www.ecb.int/bc/banknotes/looks/html/index.en.html). Like the bridges on the front cover of this book, the intention is to emphasize links and communication between the different countries of Europe and between the continent and the rest of the world. Unlike those on the front cover, however, the banknote bridges, though apparently prompted by actually existing structures, are imaginary. They represent, if you like, an attempt to inspire without offending those who are left out. On the other hand, they avoid the sometimes messy reality which this book – admittedly a slightly lesser project than the epochmaking switchover to the euro! – tries to encompass and make sense of.

To that end, this book is also full of boxes. They are not there just to break up the text, though if they help do that, all well and good. They are there to provide you with vignettes designed to provide (hopefully) vivid examples of the points the surrounding paragraphs are trying to make. You do not actually have to look at them if you do not want to. But if you do, they should add a lot not just to your enjoyment, but also to your understanding and your ability to recall what you have read – something that can make all the difference when you are in the exam room or trying to pull that essay or dissertation together from scratch. Think of the boxes like hyperlinks on a webpage. You do not have to click on them but it is often worth it when you do; and even when it turns out not to be, you can get back to where you were by hitting the Back button, or in this case just by turning over the page.

This brings us to the second way of keeping things current; namely, the use of the web and other electronic and print media. This book refers to websites and has one of its own (http://www.palgrave.com/politics/bale) which, in addition to providing the 'questions for further discussion' provided by most textbooks, will provide selective update material and function as a gateway to other websites. Some of them may be academic: indeed, it never ceases to amaze me how much time we all waste on search engines when a quick look at the electronic contents pages of a few politics journals (many of which offer free, downloadable articles via libraries) would get us what we need much quicker (and with more quality control). With the electronic subscriptions so many campus libraries now hold, many of the journals mentioned in the Bibliography are as easy to access as the internet itself. Often the best way to find them is via the databases that most of the same libraries subscribe to (IBSS is a good

example): you can get to these (and many other more direct resources) from a library homepage or by going to what is undoubtedly the best academic jumping-off point; namely http://www.sosig. ac.uk/politics/. Using these databases, you can often search all the journals at once, get the citations and very often click straight on to what you want to read, normally in pdf, should you want to print it off and maybe write all over it.

But back to the web. Other useful sites for European politics are set up by NGOs, pressure groups, parties, and governments both within and without Europe. I have no qualms, for instance, about recommending the CIA's World Factbook (http://www.odci.gov/cia/publications/factbook/) if you need basic (and more detailed) information on individual countries. And do not forget the European Union (http://europa.eu.int/): for instance, the EU's *Eurobarometer* surveys are easy to get hold of online (http://europa.eu.int/comm/ public_opinion/standard_en.htm) and they provide a great way of taking the temperature of public opinion in all the member states. Other useful sites will be run by the enthusiasts who do so much to make the web such a great resource for all of us: anyone even faintly interested in elections can while away hours in the company of Wilfried Derksen (www.electionworld.org/) or Wolfram Nordsiek (www.parties-and-elections. de/indexe.html), both of whom deserve some kind of medal for their services to hard-pressed comparativists who need those election results yesterday! Also very useful, especially if you want comparisons, is the *Nationmaster* website (http://www. nationmaster.com): you can use it to pull up (and even construct your own) graphs and bar charts on all sorts of social, political and economic indicators very quickly indeed – just remember to credit them in your footnotes and/or bibliography!

Still other websites will be run by media organizations who make it their business to keep us informed and are becoming increasingly good at providing searchable archives. Some of them, it is true, shut you out just when things get interesting. If you are studying at a university or college, however, you are very likely to find that your library actually gives you free and full access to the premium content that others who are less fortunate would have to pay for. Again, if you use a database (*LexisNexsis* is one, but there are others) you can search many newspapers and news magazines at once and save time doing it. Even if you are not at college or university right now and cannot take advantage of the reduced prices often offered to students, you might want to think about a trial subscription to a news magazine like *The Economist*. Notwithstanding its slightly off-putting title (and, for some, its off-putting editorial line!), it has to be one of the best (and definitely the best-written) concise sources on European (and indeed global) political developments. Subscribing also gives you access to its very useful archive on the web.

Time Magazine, which is also a good source for in-depth articles on aspects of European society and politics, has a similarly useful searchable archive online – again, a subscription (or campus access) helps. So, too, does the fully-accessible BBC News website (http://news.bbc.co.uk/), which is good for keeping up with day-to-day developments in European politics and often does in-depth special features on subjects of interest. Another great site for day-to-day reports is the World News Network (www.wneurope.com/) which gets you into newspapers but also newswire services. Another site which does something similar and is helpfully grouped by country is http://www.europeunie.com. Particularly good on the EU (but also on European political developments more generally) is the portal http://www.euractiv.com. If you want to go a bit deeper into debates in and about Europe (and indeed politics more generally), check out www.openDemocracy.net. All this indicates that, even (or perhaps especially) when you are pressed for time and that essay is due in tomorrow, there is more to life than Google – great though it is.

The third way to keep a textbook current is by publishing new editions. This will be made all the easier – and all the better – by getting your feedback. Use the website to let me know where you think I get things wrong and maybe even where I get them right. What would you like to see more of? What should go to make way for it? When do I miss the point? When am I – as I hope I am at least once or twice – spot on? What does and does not work in terms of content and format?

Where is it going?

But all that is for the future. The task now is to give you a broad overview of how the book is organized and to explain why it is done the way it is. What is needed is a route-map, a rationale and a taster all rolled into one.

This text does not assume any prior knowledge of European history. Rather, it starts by providing a brief but systematic overview intended to help both the novice and the person who just needs to fill in a few gaps to appreciate how we got where we are today. It also stresses the need to get to grips with contemporary Europe economically, demographically and sociologically – and with where it might be heading on all three counts.

Once it gets into the politics, this book takes a distinctive approach. Most textbooks begin, very democratically but perhaps rather idealistically, with citizens and then take readers on up through groups, parties, elections, parliaments, governments until they reach the top, the state itself. This book, however, begins at the top. After all, before there were citizens who could vote and groups they could belong to and parties they could vote for, before there were parliaments those parties could sit in and elected governments they could hold to account, there was the state. So, the state – historically if not always logically prior to other democratic institutions – is our starting point. As we show, though, it is an increasingly problematic one, under attack, as some would have it, both from below and from 'above' in the shape of the EU – a body we introduce early on but whose institutions and influence are deliberately woven throughout the chapters on the grounds that they are now woven throughout European politics. This **Europeanization** is an overarching theme and persistent concern in this book.

Europeanization is a recent and much contested field of enquiry in political science, and there are ongoing arguments concerning its definition and scope (for brief guides to such matters, see Buller and Gamble, 2002 and Mair, 2004; see also Börzel, 2002, Cowles, Caporaso and Risse, 2001 and Featherstone and Radaelli, 2003). Consonant with the working definition supplied above, the following chapters look not for convergence on some imagined 'European model', although many of them find evidence of patterned variation which often allows us usefully to group states. Rather, they look for evidence (and sometimes explanations) of this process of incremental and interactive influence – a process that is always mediated by national variations in political economy (Chapters 1 and 9), public policy (Chapter 3) and, of course, politics, be they bureaucratic politics (Chapter 3), parliamentary politics (Chapter 4), party politics (Chapter 5), mediated politics (Chapter 7), pressure group politics (Chapter 8), or international politics (Chapter 11). The same interactive influence can be seen in the two chapters that concentrate on particular issues: one (Chapter 9) on the oft-noted (but not always accurate) extent to which 'the left' in Europe has moved so far to the right that people have trouble telling them apart; the other (Chapter 10) on what the media often see as one of the biggest concerns facing European politics – immigration.

> **Definition**
> **Europeanization** is an observable process – ongoing and contested, more or less voluntary, but neither inevitable nor uniform – by which the policies, institutions, norms, goals and actors of the EU and/or other European countries have a perceptible and significant impact on those of individual European countries; policies, institutions, norms, goals and actors can be 'uploaded' to Europe, just as those from Europe are 'downloaded' to and by individual countries.

The way politicians are handling these and other issues, and the way the institutions they work within and create seem to be moving, involves what is sometimes called **multilevel governance**. This, like Europeanization, is also a persistent theme in this book. The idea of multilevel governance originated in academic work on European integration (see Hooghe and Marks, 2001). It combines two things. First, it comprises criticism of academic work that explains integration as the product either of bargaining between self-interested governments or, in contrast, the role of EU institutions. Second, it contains insights derived from research into individual states on the fragmentation of formerly top-down government.

Like Europeanization, multilevel governance is thus a portmanteau – and not altogether uncontested – term, but one that arguably describes – and perhaps even helps to explain – the complex reality created by decentralization and the impact of the EU. Unlike Europeanization, the extent of which perhaps varies much more according to the institutions and issues under discussion (indeed, part of understanding European politics nowadays is about getting some idea of where the EU matters more and where it matters less), we are likely to see multilevel governance in evidence in almost all the areas that we explore.

> **Definition**
> **Multilevel governance** refers to the fact that the allocation of resources, the delivery of services, and the making of law and policy in Europe is characterized – perhaps increasingly so – by a dispersal or diffusion of power, a multiplication of (sometimes overlapping) sites of authority and policy competence, as well as a mixture of co-operation and contestation between tiers of government that would formerly have been considered more separate and hierarchically ordered.

Getting started

Every chapter, then, is self-contained, but – to the extent that they are relevant in each case – each one touches on Europeanization and multilevel governance. Also, every chapter hopefully follows its predecessor in a more or less logical manner. Each one also contains lots of references to the other chapters so you can (to pursue the hyperlink metaphor one more time) click (or in this case flick) from one to the other. In other words, this is a book that can be read cover-to-cover, but one that realizes this is not normally the way things work. If you, or your lecturers, instructors and tutors are anything like me, you are pretty much guaranteed to create your own order to fit either the way your particular course runs or the way your own mind works. Use the contents pages, the definitions, tables, figures, boxes, as well as the index, and the sub-headings and the summaries contained at the beginning and end of the chapters, to help you 'pick and mix'. Take a look, too, at some of the suggestions in the learning resources section which concludes every chapter. And maybe check out some of the citations in the references in the back of the book: most of them are there not just to acknowledge the author (although that is always important in academic work, including student essays and term papers!), but also because I think they are worth chasing up. The web is all very well, but it cannot give you the depth and range provided by the experts who commit their words to the printed page (even if that printed page may be available electronically too). Much of what I cite is chosen with an eye to approachability.

So, there you have it. A book that tries to be a one-stop shop if that is all you want it to be, but also one that provides you with a gateway to other, more detailed and sophisticated takes on European politics. You can use it just for self-directed study. But more likely you will use it as part of a course that someone else has designed. If so, it hopes to sit neatly between the general overview that lectures are normally intended to give you and the more detailed stuff you will discuss in small group classes and (if the books are not still somewhere on the re-shelving trolley or lying in a 'must read sometime soon' pile on someone's floor or desk) read in the library. Hopefully, it will give you enough of what you need, something you might even like and, if you are of an argumentative cast of mind, something you can disagree with as well. If so, neither my time nor your time will have been entirely wasted. And nor will the time of all those whose work, support and generosity has helped me over the years. There are way too many of them to mention by name (and most of them will in any case see their work cited in the bibliography); special thanks, though, should go to my colleagues at Sheffield, Victoria University of Wellington and Sussex, to my publisher, the near-legendary Steven Kennedy, and, most of all of course, to my family.

Chapter 1

Europe: a continent in the making

People into empires
Empires into nations
Nations into states
States into blocs
The new Europe
Europe's economy: rich in variation
Society: class and gender still matter
In theory if not in practice: religion
   in Europe
Composition and identity: multi-ethnic,
   multinational – and European?

Covering around ten million square kilometres or just under 4 million square miles, Europe is the second smallest of the world's seven continents. But it is number three in terms of population: over 725 million people live there, some thinly spread in the cold of the far north or the heat of the far south, but most packed closely together in towns and cities. That population density, combined with centuries of international trade and the fact that it was the home of the industrial revolution, has made Europe one of the richest and most powerful parts of the globe. Historically, it was also one of the most violent. Its turbulent history was crowned in the twentieth century by two world wars, after which it was divided during nearly fifty years of Cold War into the capitalist 'West' and the communist 'East'. With the collapse of the latter, however, Europe now contains more genuinely democratic states than any other continent on earth.

But Europe, like most continents, is not just a place, a geographical container for those states. It is also an *idea* and an *identity* (see Pagden, 2002). Indeed, because of this, it is actually quite difficult to define it as a place. Our notions of where it begins and ends are fuzzy: they change to suit our conceptions of who should be in and who should be out. The Europe covered in this book is as much of a conventional and convenient fiction as any other. For instance, it excludes some states like Russia, Ukraine, Georgia and indeed Turkey, despite the fact that all of them pop up in the European section of newspapers and news magazines and despite the fact that they could claim (and in the case of Turkey are claiming) to be sufficiently European to join the EU. The Europe covered here basically encompasses those states located between the Mediterranean in the south and Arctic in the north, and between the Atlantic in the west and the Urals and the Caspian Sea in the east. Most of our focus will be on the twenty-five states that make up the EU, as well as inveterate non-joiners like Norway and Switzerland, and soon-to-be-admitted Bulgaria and Romania. This means there is less focus on the Balkan countries of the former Yugoslavia – although, as we shall see below, they have played a dynamic part in European history and provide an extreme example of what can happen when, as is the case in several European countries, multiple nations and/or ethnicities are obliged to live together in just one state.

The first aim of this chapter, however, is to provide some historical background to those concerns. It hopes to show not just how Europe got where it is today, but how some of what happened to it along the way still resonates with and helps to structure the contemporary continent. The latter then becomes the chapter's main focus as it explores what Europe looks like now and how is it changing – economically, demographically and sociologically. All three aspects play a huge part in political processes, preoccupations and possibilities, not least because they help structure what political scientists call **cleavages**.

Definition
To a political scientist, **cleavages** are splits or divisions in a society that give rise to conflicts that may well be expressed in political form – often, though not necessarily, via the formation

of opposing parties representing people on either side of the split. The most obvious example is the so-called 'owner–worker' cleavage between those who make their living from the skilful use of capital and those they employ – the cleavage that gave rise to the left–right division that still does much to structure politics today. More recently, some political scientists have identified cleavages that are less sociological than they are values-related. One example would include a split between those happy with a more cosmopolitan and multicultural society and those opposed to such developments. Another (possibly related or overlapping) cleavage would be the split between the majority for whom their standard of living is important and a minority who, once their basic needs are met, are more concerned about a whole host of issues to do with equality, peace and justice: this is the so-called 'materialist–postmaterialist' cleavage (see Chapters 5–7).

Exploring the 'then and now', and indeed the 'where next?' helps us to question and qualify some of the common wisdom surrounding social and economic (and so, perhaps, political) change: for instance, the welfare state appears to be alive and well, education has not brought about the classless society as yet and women are not doing as well as some of their mothers and grandmothers might have hoped. The chapter shows that European countries, and the people who live in them, may be growing a little less unlike each other. But it also gives us little reason to think that either Europeanization (which we defined in the Introduction) or *globalization* (discussed in Box 1.1), necessarily entail convergence, let alone homogenization. Europe may be coming together literally as well as figuratively in the guise and under the umbrella of the EU. As a result, it is already more than simply the sum of its parts. But, at the beginning of the twenty-first century, the contrasts and contradictions between those parts – contrasts and contradictions that emerged over hundreds and thousands of years of often overlapping development – are not disappearing quite as fast as we might think.

BOX 1.1
Globalization or globaloney?

Globalization has got to be the biggest buzzword of the 21st century so far. But like many buzzwords its meaning is a little fuzzy and the evidence for it not always as solid as those who bandy it about often assume. In short, the fact that the concept is used so often – as well as blamed or praised for almost all the woes and the wonders of contemporary life – does not make it true or mean that it explains that much.

As far as meaning goes, there are many versions (see Scholte, 2001). But the most popular ones are encapsulated in the following definitions:

'The intensification of worldwide social relations which link distant localities in such a way that local happenings are shaped by events occurring many miles away and vice versa' (Giddens, 1990: 64).

'A process (or set of processes) which embodies a transformation in the spatial organization of social relations and transactions – asssessed in terms of their extensity, intensity, velocity and impact – generating transcontinental or inter-regional flows and networks of activity' (Held *et al.*, 1999: 16).

'A social process in which the constraints of geography on economic, political, social and cultural arrangements recede, in which people become increasingly aware that they are receding and in which they act accordingly' (Waters, 2001: 5).

Apart from this apparent collapse of time, space and national and regional difference, other writers see globalization as western capitalist imperialism by another name (see Hardt and Negri, 2000) and/or as heralding the end of the nation state and the rise of transnational states (see Sklair, 2000).

As far as evidence goes, there are, however, many analysts who are sceptical, claiming the rhetoric surrounding globalization may be more important than the reality, which is nowhere near as all-encompassing and transformative as many of us now routinely and casually assume (see Hay, 2000, Hirst and Thompson, 1999 and Mann, 1997).

People into empires

People have been around in Europe since the first Stone Age. From around 6000 BC nomadic hunter-gathering began to give way to farming. And by the time the first 'Indo-Europeans' began arriving in the southern and western part of the continent after 2500 BC, people were already working bronze, trading and practising religious rites. Early civilizations included the Minoans of Crete and the Indo-European Mycenaeans, who by 1500 BC not only controlled most of Greece but had also supplanted the Minoans. In more central parts of Europe, a rapidly expanding population was beginning to work iron and had already begun to form (language) groups with which we are still familiar today. Celts lived at the western borders of the continent, Slavs in the east and the Germanic peoples in the north. In the south, the Greeks had recovered from the decay of the Mycenaean culture and now formed a number of powerful city-states. They were also expanding into what we now call southern Italy – a land whose northern half was peopled by the Villanovans and then the Etruscans, who, soon after it was founded, took control of Rome.

In the fifth century BC, however, it was the city-state of Athens which, after fighting off Persia (modern-day Iran), was the foremost power in Europe. It was also home to many of the classical political philosophers, such as Aristotle and Plato, whom we read even today. Its ambitions proved too strong for its own good, however. Greece descended into a series of wars between the various cities, the devastating consequences of which made it relatively easy prey for Macedonia, to the north. Macedonia's Alexander the Great then proceeded to forge an empire from both Greece and Persia. By the middle of the second century BC, however, that empire was controlled by the Romans. Previously they had taken not only all of Italy, but also that part of Europe that bordered the Mediterranean sea, as well as much of North Africa and the Middle East. Although Greek culture was allowed to thrive by the Romans, they insisted that all those living under their protection become citizens of Rome and encouraged the use of the Latin language. This, and their commit-ment to building a transport infrastructure, facilitated trading and other contacts among the peoples of Europe (and North Africa and the Middle East). This helped usher in a period of prosperity and economic development throughout the continent.

Despite a series of civil wars, the Roman Empire, persisted into the fourth century AD. By then, Christianity had become what amounted to its 'official religion', and the political and administrative centre of gravity had shifted east to Constantinople (now Istanbul). By the fifth century, however, Germanic peoples such as the Franks, the Visigoths and the Vandals (famous for their sackings of Rome) had first undermined and then destroyed the western part of the empire. What they did not undo, though, was the widespread use of Latinate languages and Christianity, with the latter increasingly under the sway of the head of the Roman Catholic church, the Pope. By the beginning of the ninth century AD, this religious power combined to mutual advantage with the military and political power of the Franks to form what became known as the 'Holy Roman Empire', under Charlemagne.

Empires into nations

This new empire, however, was a rather loosely coupled affair with overlapping authority exercised by various kings and princes. It also proved no more immune to invasion and division than its Greek and Roman predecessors. The Vikings came from Scandinavia and settled in mainland Europe, including the northernmost part of France, eventually producing a duke, William of Normandy, who became the conqueror of England in 1066. Elsewhere, too, monarchs other than the emperor, as well as lesser nobles, monastic orders such as the Benedictines, and eventually the papacy itself, dominated their own territories, wherein the 'feudal system' (the granting, from the king downwards, of land and rights in exchange for military and political support) gradually took hold. At the same time, Europe's economy and population expanded prodigiously, as did the towns and cities which, despite the power of the feudal nobility who often continued to live in less urban areas, became centres of commerce, religion and education. These developments provided the resources and the rationale for the Christian Crusades in the Holy Land (now the Middle East) of the eleventh, twelfth and thirteenth centuries. They also financed the overseas voyages of exploration to more far-flung continents, all of which were to provide new sources of wealth and raw materials and eventually empire and colonies.

The earliest beneficiaries of overseas expansion were Portugal and, in particular, Spain. Since the expulsion of the Moors of North Africa in the late fifteenth century and the subordination of the country's component kingdoms to that of Castile, Spain had become a firmly Christian country. It also became the foremost upholder of Roman Catholicism against the threat posed to it by what became known as Protestantism. This dissenting movement – aided by the invention of the printing press and the ambitions of German princes who chafed against the Holy Roman Empire – had grown up in central and northern parts of Europe at the beginning of the sixteenth century in both spiritual and political opposition to what it saw as the corrupt papacy. This role as defender of the faith helped put Spain on a collision course with its commercial rival, England which, after breaking with Rome over the Pope's refusal to acquiesce in its king's divorce plans, had adopted a non-Roman Catholic hybrid known as Anglicanism as a state religion. Spain's Armada, a sea-led invasion fleet, was defeated, and the country slipped into its long-term decline, its apparently endless access to the gold of South America stymieing economic dynamism. The religious question in the British Isles, however, was by no means decided and, as it did all over Europe, played a part in politics in the run up to and long after the country's civil war in the 1640s (see Map 1.1).

Nations into states

In fact, religious conflict and political self-interest and expression combined to cause wars not only between but also within countries throughout late sixteenth- and early seventeenth-century Europe – and not just in the west. Hungary, for example, had been one of central Europe's strongest powers but spent much of its strength on successive wars against the Islamic Ottoman empire, centred in what we now call Turkey. By the sixteenth century, however, its former rulers, the Habsburg dynasty of Austria, who also held the crown of the rather fragmented Holy Roman Empire, took advantage of Hungary's weakness to restore Roman Catholicism to a country that had – officially anyway – become Protestant. Struggles such as this culminated in the so-called Thirty Years' War. Fought between 1618 and 1648, it brought the Scandinavian countries into a prolonged armed conflict that also involved the kings and princes of central and western Europe. It also saw France emerge not just as mainland Europe's strongest rival to British power, but arguably also as the world's first modern state. Power was centralized in Paris under a large state bureaucracy, and a military maintained to fight wars, many of them aggressive rather than defensive, in what was supposedly the national interest.

Definition

The **balance of power** is an equilibrium existing between states (or groups of states) when resources – especially military resources – are sufficiently evenly distributed to ensure that no single state can dominate the others. The concept was an essential part (and, indeed, aim) of European diplomacy and warfare from at least the seventeenth century onwards.

This model was copied by other European states, so France's pioneering role did not grant it predominance for long. By the late eighteenth century, Europe was characterized not by one 'hegemonic' (all powerful) nation but by a so-called **balance of power** between countries such as France, Britain, Austria (and its unstable empire in Hungary and elsewhere) and Prussia, part of what we now know as Germany. By the nineteenth century, Europe was also characterized by a mixture of monarchies and republics. France had become the most famous of the latter. But, after what amounted to ten years of permanent revolution from 1789 onwards, it succumbed to the dictatorship of Napoleon Bonaparte. Napoleon declared himself emperor and proceeded to

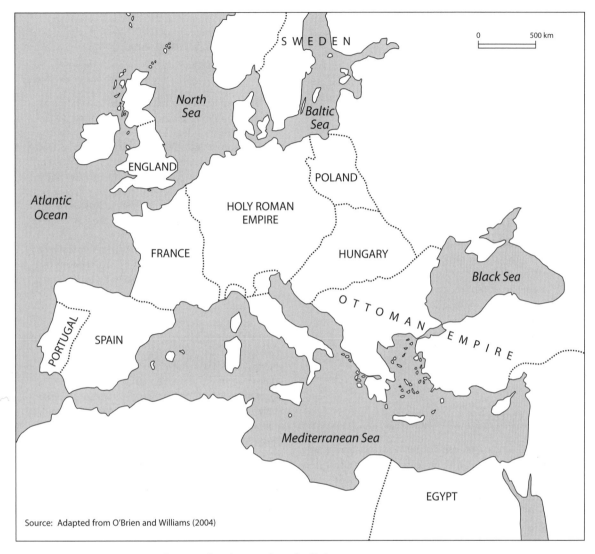

Source: Adapted from O'Brien and Williams (2004)

Map 1.1 Europe c.1500: on the eve of two centuries of religious wars

centralize the French state even further. He also unleashed a succession of aggressive military campaigns against other countries, onto which he attempted, quite successfully, to graft the French administrative model. That was until he over-reached himself in Russia and was defeated by the combined might of Britain and Prussia at the battle of Waterloo in 1815, in what is now Belgium.

The nationalism, in part inspired by the Napoleonic wars, spread throughout Europe. Hungary continually chafed at its Austrian domination; Bulgaria tried (with the help of Russia) to break free of the Ottoman empire; and Romania actually succeeded in winning its independence from not just the Ottoman but also the Russian empire. Nationalism was soon competing, however, with demands on the part of the public of many European countries for political participation commensurate with what liberals suggested were their rights and what they themselves argued was their economic contribution. Such demands grew stronger among workers to whom industrialization and urbanization now afforded the concentrated power to organize collectively to press their case. In continental Europe, a series of failed proto-socialist revolutions in the mid-nineteenth century in the end gave way to politically more successful (if socially less radical) efforts to achieve representation by democratic means. By the beginning of the twentieth century, universal (or near-universal) male suffrage had been adopted in many European countries. Nationalism, however, continued apace, and Europe entered the twentieth century with the hitherto fragmented Germany and Italy now unified nation states, bringing the number of states on the continent to around twenty-five, compared to the 500 or more that had existed in 1500 (see Tilly, 1975). To a greater or lesser degree, all these turn-of-the-century states assumed an increasingly active role in the national economy, not least in order to raise the tax revenue that could be used to boost military strength, as well as to improve control over the increasingly industrialized population, be it through coercion through an expanded police apparatus or through education, much of which aimed at the reinforcement of national identity (see Tilly, 1993).

States into blocs

As Germany began to use its new-found unity to claim an overseas empire, Europe's always fragile balance of power began to harden into the military alliances that ended up driving the continent into the First World War. Germany's ambitions were opposed by its imperial rivals, France and Great Britain. They allied with Russia, a country whose association with Slavic national independence movements in Serbia set it on a collision course with Germany's ally, Austria-Hungary. Other countries were sucked into the war once it broke out in 1914: Italy, Japan and, eventually, the US on the side of the self-styled 'Allies' (Britain, France and Russia); Bulgaria, and Turkey's Ottoman empire, on the side of Germany and Austria-Hungary. Only Scandinavia, Spain and Portugal, and Switzerland (which had pursued a policy of neutrality since it came together as a confederation in the early sixteenth century) escaped involvement. For most of the four years which followed, the combatants fought each other to a standstill at the cost of millions of human lives

BOX 1.2
The Soviet Union and communism

The Union of Soviet Socialist Republics (USSR) was established in 1922 by the *Bolshevik* regime that came to power under its first leader, Lenin, during the Russian revolution of 1917. The Bolsheviks were communists, believing in a state supposedly run on behalf of the working class and with equality and social justice for all. It was dominated by Russia, but also came to include the republics to Russia's south, including Georgia and Ukraine, and the Baltic states of Latvia, Lithuania and Estonia (now EU members). Under the leadership of Lenin's successor, Stalin, it undertook the industrialization of vast swathes of Eastern Europe, as well as the collectivization of its agriculture – projects that delivered economic growth but at a terribly high price: tens of millions died, most from starvation but also as a result of forced labour and the political repression needed to maintain the dictatorial regime. Millions of people also lost their lives during the desperate fight against Germany in the Second World War. The postwar period, during which the nuclear-armed Soviet Union faced off but never actually fought against the capitalist West, offered some respite, though the communist regime remained essentially intact until the late 1980s. With its collapse came the collapse of the Soviet Union, and its population of nearly 300 million people found themselves living in either Russia (population 145 million) or what are routinely referred to as the Newly Independent States (NIS).

lost or blighted. But such a war of attrition eventually favoured the side with the greatest resources in terms of men and matériel. True, the Allies suffered a loss when, in 1917, Russia was seized by Communist revolutionaries under Lenin, who saw the war as benefiting only the old ruling class and its capitalist allies and ended Russia's participation accordingly. Nevertheless, in the autumn of 1918, Germany and Austria-Hungary were basically starved into to signing an armistice.

After the World War, the map of Europe was literally redrawn. Firstly, came the creation of the *Soviet Union* (or USSR), through which Russia extended its empire (Box 1.2). Secondly came the

BOX 1.3
Fascism and socialism

European fascism of the 1920s and 1930s was in many ways defined by its opposition to communism, and to socialism or 'social democracy', which believed in achieving public ownership and redistributionary policies and seemed destined to win over many working-class voters. Although fascism was also about the supremacy of the ethnically exclusive state over the interests and rights of individuals, the private sector was allowed to profit from its activities. Fascist leaders promised easy solutions to the worldwide economic depression of the 1930s – solutions based not just on totalitarian politics and increasingly racist, anti-Semitic policies, but also on the sort of military rearmament and an aggressive, expansionist foreign policy that socialists and social democrats (some of them pacifists as well as 'internationalists') abhorred.

Treaties of Versailles and Trianon. The Austro-Hungarian and Ottoman empires were broken up and Turkey forced out of Europe. Hungary lost territory to the new states created for Slavic peoples in the artificially constructed states of Czechoslovakia and Yugoslavia, the latter created not just at the behest of Slav nationalists, but also to provide Serbian protection to small countries such as Slovenia and Croatia against larger powers such as Italy (which despite territorial gains continued to believe it had been short-changed). Further north, Germany – now a republic – lost territory to France and Poland and was forced not only to admit guilt for the war but also to pay financial compensation ('reparations') to France. The resentment thus created was cleverly exploited by nationalistic, fascist dictators, such as Hitler and Mussolini (see Box 1.3).

Other states, also coping with the economic depression, proved unable or unwilling to quash fascism's territorial ambitions, despite the existence of the 'League of Nations' (the forerunner of the postwar United Nations). Emboldened by its success in grabbing back Austria and much of Czechoslovakia, and determined to act before potential enemies such as Great Britain and France could fully prepare themselves, Germany signed a non-aggression pact with the Soviet Union. This pact basically delivered the Baltic republics of Estonia, Latvia and Lithuania to Russia, along with half of Poland. In September 1939, Germany invaded Poland to take its half, thereby provoking war with Britain, France and, in the end, also the Soviet Union. The US, which was attacked by Germany's ally, Japan, at Pearl Harbor in 1941, joined the fight against the so-called 'Axis' powers (Germany, Japan and a not altogether enthusiastic Italy) in the same year.

It took the use of nuclear weapons to bring Japan to surrender in the summer of 1945. But the Second World War ended in Europe with the occupation of first Italy and then Germany in the spring of that year. However, if anyone thought that the continent's problems were solved, they were sadly mistaken. Although spared a re-run of the postwar influenza outbreak that had killed millions in the aftermath of the 1914–18 conflict, Europe was on its knees. Millions of Jews, as well as political opponents, Roma (gypsies) and other minorities, had been put or worked to death by the Nazis – a tragedy now known as the Holocaust. In addition, the physical destruction and economic misery wrought by six years of total war involving civilian populations as well as armed forces was calamitous.

Any chance that the victorious Allies would continue their co-operation in peacetime was quickly dashed. The Soviet Union was determined to maintain a military presence in the eastern part of the continent and used its occupation to facilitate the seizure of power by Communist parties in Poland, Czechoslovakia, Hungary, Romania and Bulgaria. Only Finland was allowed to remain free, and over time it became a fully integrated part of a Scandinavia that included neutral Sweden as well as Denmark and Norway, occupied in the war by Germany. In the face of the developments in central Europe, the US quickly reverted to the strongly anti-communist stance that it had pursued since the Russian revolution and had softened only during the war. It took steps to ensure that the Soviet 'sphere of influence' (the area where its dominance could not be challenged) would not expand to include the western part of Germany, which was now divided into two states: the liberal capitalist Federal Republic of Germany (FRG), which most

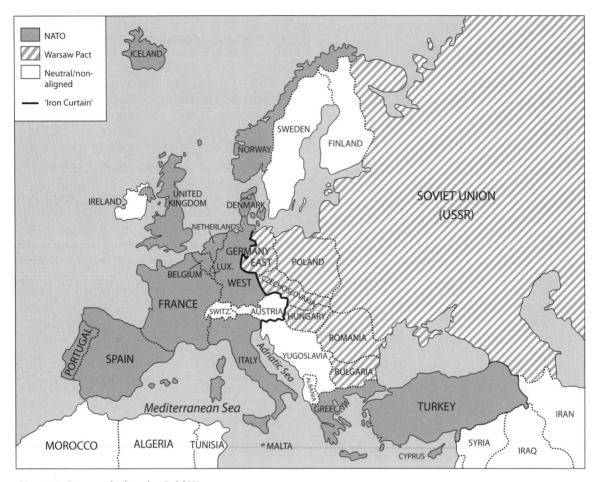

Map 1.2 Europe during the Cold War

outsiders called West Germany, and the communist German Democratic Republic (GDR), routinely labelled East Germany. By the same token, the US put considerable effort (and cash) into ensuring that the homegrown (but Soviet-aided) Communist parties did not take power, even by ostensibly democratic means, in Italy and Greece (which endured a short civil war) (Map 1.2).

The other side of this anti-communist, anti-Soviet 'containment' strategy included the establishment of NATO (Box 1.4) and the stationing of American military capability throughout Europe. This included bases in Spain, which, like Portugal, had succumbed to right-wing authoritarian dictatorship in the interwar period but had remained neutral between 1939 and 1945. Another important part of the strategy was economic, with the US

'Marshall Plan' (named after the former general who initiated it) providing much-needed aid to most countries in its sphere of influence. European democracies spent it not just on American goods, but also on redeveloping their industrial base, on establishing welfare states and, in time, participating in the consumer booms of the 1950s and 1960s.

US efforts to secure a peaceful western Europe as a bulwark against Communist expansion and as a prosperous trading partner also led it to support moves among some European governments to create a mechanism for increasing interstate co-operation that would lock in their economic interdependence and, along with unity in the face of the Soviet Union, make war between western European powers a thing of the past. These moves began in 1952 with the European Coal and Steel

---

BOX 1.4
NATO and the Cold War, 1948–89

1948   West European democracies sign Treaty of Brussels, pledging themselves to common defence should one of them come under attack. Soviet blockade of American and British controlled West Berlin encourages negotiations with the US.

1949   Creation of the North Atlantic Treaty Organization (NATO), involving most of western Europe, plus Canada and the US.

1950–55   Korean War (1950–53) pitting US-backed South against Chinese-backed North. Greece and Turkey, and then West Germany join. Soviet Union and its Central and Eastern European (CEE) satellite states form the opposing Warsaw Pact. NATO gets a permanent command structure. European countries fail to realize European Defence Community (EDC) plans for an integrated military force after they are vetoed by French Parliament in 1954. Countries opt for looser co-operation under the West European Union (WEU).

1956–70   US stymies Franco-British attempt to seize back the Suez Canal, nationalized by Egypt: the failed colonial adventure arguably precipitates European countries' withdrawals from their colonies during the next decade; but it also confirms UK politicians in their belief that the US must in future be kept onside at all costs and contributes to France withdrawing from NATO's military command (though not the treaty) in 1966. Liberalizing communist governments in Hungary (1956) and Czechoslovakia (1968) overturned by Soviet troops. The US and Soviet Union narrowly avoid nuclear war over the Cuban Missile Crisis (1962). Tension and 'proxy wars' (fought by and in other countries but financed by the Americans, Russians and Chinese) in the Middle East, Africa and South East Asia (including Vietnam). Europe deadlocked and divided, but peace preserved.

1970s   Begin with period of so-called *détente* (or easing of tension) between the US, China and the USSR. EEC members (which from 1973 include the UK) begin halting moves toward foreign policy co-ordination under EPC (European Political Co-operation), which includes meetings of foreign ministers. Decade ends with USSR's invasion of Afghanistan – an expensive failure which contributed not just to instability in the region (and the rise of the Taliban regime), but also to the downfall of the bankrupt Soviet system.

1980s   Poland's trade union and Catholic Church-inspired reform movement crushed by communist leadership afraid of Soviet invasion. Newly elected US President Ronald Reagan helps persuade European NATO members to host intermediate-range nuclear missiles. Soviet leadership, already reeling from expensive and failed invasion of Afghanistan, cannot afford to match such high defence spending. Newly selected leader Mikhail Gorbachev lets satellite states know that the era of Soviet interference in their affairs is over. Communist regimes in East and Central Europe collapse.

Community (ECSC) and eventuated in the founding of the European Economic Community (EEC) by the Treaty of Rome in 1957. Having played a massive part in helping to preserve peace and, for the most part, prosperity, it has since relabelled itself the European Union, commonly known as the EU. In 2004, it expanded to take in a total of twenty-five members, including former dictatorships in Southern and Central and Eastern Europe that are now functioning market democracies (see Map 1.3).

Notwithstanding the EU's importance, it was by no means the only thing that helped western Europe become such a secure and prosperous place. Other factors helped, too. A generation of politicians was determined not just to avoid the mistakes of the interwar period but also to prove that liberal capitalism was better than communism. They also presided over a withdrawal from what had become costly overseas entanglements, with Britain, France and smaller countries such as Belgium, the Netherlands and Portugal letting go of the bulk of their colonial empires (see Chapter 10). The American-led postwar boom (Box 1.5), and the fact that consumers were kept spending both by vastly expanded leisure and mass media markets and the extension of the welfare state, meant that, compared to the prewar period, even the bad times were good. Nor, as Box 1.5 also shows, were they as bad as we might think (at least when it came to the essentials) in what became known as the 'Soviet Bloc'.

CEE countries, in fact, were transformed during the postwar period from agricultural backwaters into modern industrial economies in which income inequalities were narrow and access to health, welfare and education was impressively wide. For all this, however, it remains true that instead of 'burying' capitalism, as one Soviet leader had famously promised, communism proved incapable of matching either the technological progress, the prosperity or the freedom enjoyed by those living under liberal capitalism in 'the West' – an 'imagined community' (Anderson, 1991: 5–7) which seemed to stretch beyond western Europe through North America and down to Australia and New Zealand. The problem was there seemed to be nothing that those who lived in Eastern and Central Europe could do about it. Any time they came close to trying to liberalize their regimes, reformists were crushed by Soviet tanks.

The new Europe

Yet at the same time as it looked as if things would never change in Europe, something had to give. The Soviet Union found itself financially unable both to deliver its population a basic standard of living and to compete with the Americans militarily – particularly if it meant holding on as firmly as ever to its satellites in eastern Europe. This analysis persuaded Mikhail Gorbachev, who took over the leadership of the Soviet Communist Party in 1985, to signal to those countries that they could pursue their own course without fearing military action on his part. Gorbachev clearly hoped that this would mean merely a reform of the existing system, in whose basic principles he still believed. But it rapidly became clear that his famous policies of *glasnost* (openness) and *perestroika* (restructuring)

BOX 1.5
The postwar boom – east and west

To many in western Europe, the years 1950–73 represented a kind of 'golden age'. Economic growth averaged over 4 per cent a year, with catch-up countries such as West Germany, Spain and Greece making up for relatively poor performers such as the UK and Belgium. Inflation was present, but rarely rose above 3–4 per cent. Europe's unemployment rate was only 3 per cent in the 1950s and dropped below 2 per cent in the 1960s. European countries began to catch up technologically. Energy was also very cheap. Moreover, consumer demand, already pent-up during the war, was boosted by governments willing to spend to avoid a return to 1930s-style depression and to meet the military challenge of Soviet and Chinese communism. The American-supervised system of stable exchange rates also provided liquidity within a secure institutional framework for international trade, while the EEC helped to facilitate trade between member states.

Interestingly, the economy of Communist Europe actually grew even more rapidly (7 per cent p.a.) in the 1950s and 1960s than that of the capitalist west. As the Soviet bloc countries transformed themselves from largely agricultural economies to essentially modern, industrial nations, national income quadrupled and industrial output in 1970 was seven times that of 1950! An overemphasis on heavy industry, however, as well as the inefficiencies inherent in central planning, meant a poor environmental outlook, a continued curtailment of human rights, and only a very poor range and quality of consumer goods. However, Eastern Europeans did enjoy heavily subsidized housing, essential foods and other goods. And unemployment was 'abolished' or at least heavily disguised.

---

gave the populations of Central and Eastern Europe the green light to overthrow Communist dictatorships in favour of democracy and market-based economies.

The year 1989 saw revolutions all over Eastern Europe, symbolized for many by the fall of the Berlin Wall that had for so long and so cruelly kept apart those living in the capitalist and communist halves of the city. Fortunately, most of these revolu-

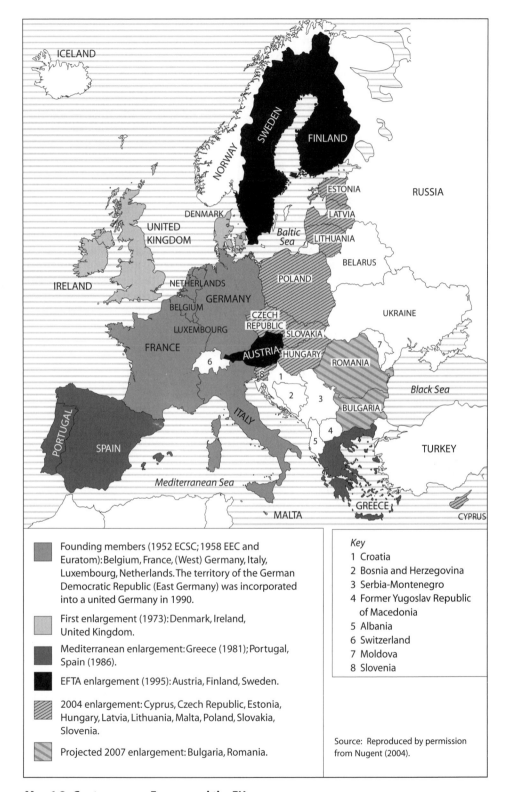

Founding members (1952 ECSC; 1958 EEC and Euratom): Belgium, France, (West) Germany, Italy, Luxembourg, Netherlands. The territory of the German Democratic Republic (East Germany) was incorporated into a united Germany in 1990.

First enlargement (1973): Denmark, Ireland, United Kingdom.

Mediterranean enlargement: Greece (1981); Portugal, Spain (1986).

EFTA enlargement (1995): Austria, Finland, Sweden.

2004 enlargement: Cyprus, Czech Republic, Estonia, Hungary, Latvia, Lithuania, Malta, Poland, Slovakia, Slovenia.

Projected 2007 enlargement: Bulgaria, Romania.

Key
1 Croatia
2 Bosnia and Herzegovina
3 Serbia-Montenegro
4 Former Yugoslav Republic of Macedonia
5 Albania
6 Switzerland
7 Moldova
8 Slovenia

Source: Reproduced by permission from Nugent (2004).

Map 1.3 Contemporary Europe and the EU

tions, barring the one in Romania and the events which followed the break up of Yugoslavia (see Chapter 2), were mercifully peaceful. Yugoslavia aside, border changes in what was now post-Cold War Europe were limited to the surprisingly swift reunification of Germany in 1990, and the slightly more drawn out and not entirely amicable 'velvet divorce' of the Czech and Slovak republics. The biggest changes on the map actually occurred in the former Soviet Union, which itself dissolved in 1991, after a failed coup by Communist hardliners. What became the Russian Federation, under Boris Yeltsin, initially tried to hold on to its regional hegemony by getting even large former Soviet republics like Georgia and Ukraine to join the so-called 'Commonwealth of Independent States' (CIS), although it soon became clear that the CIS would not allow it to exert anything like the control Russia had in the Soviet era (see Malgin, 2002 and Olcott, Åslund and Garnett, 2000). Moreover, Russia failed to exert any control whatsoever over the former Soviet republics of Estonia, Latvia and Lithuania, all of which joined the EU and NATO in 2004.

To those so-called 'Baltic states', and to the other CEE postcommunist countries who joined the EU (and NATO) alongside them, accession was a symbolic 'coming home'. As we have seen, for centuries up until the end of the Second World War they were intimately connected to those countries which, as the Cold War wore on, sometimes forgot that they were part of the same continent. Now that they have assumed their rightful place, Europe has in effect reassumed the shape it had for hundreds, even thousands, of years. And it has done so in a manner that seems likely to forestall the kind of intra-European (and indeed intercontinental) warfare that characterized so much of its history, but also helped make it what it is today. It is to the task of describing what it is today – economically, demographically and sociologically – that we now turn.

Europe's economy: rich in variation

Resources

Europe is the home of most of the world's great trading nations. As the industrial revolution that began in the UK in the late eighteenth century gained momentum all over Europe, these nations imported raw materials from the rest of the world in order to manufacture finished goods for export, as well as for the burgeoning home market. Yet Europe is by no means devoid of natural resources of its own. Norway, Finland and Sweden all have large forests. France and Sweden were traditional sources of iron ore. Coal could be found in quantity in Britain, Germany, Poland and even (no doubt to the surprise of many who do not know it) in Spain. The North Sea between the UK and Scandinavia contains oil and natural gas fields. Europe has also been more than self-sufficient in most agricultural products for many decades. Although mixed farming predominates, the further north one goes, the more meat and dairy feature; the further south, the more citrus, olives and grapes one finds; the further east, the more cereal and other arable crops there are.

Size

The differing extent to which Europe's states are blessed with access to this or that natural resource, however, combines with differing access to international trade routes and areas of expertise and comparative advantage, to make for a great deal of economic variation between their economies. Size matters, too. A quick glance at Figure 1.1 shows us that Germany's Gross Domestic Product (GDP) dwarfs not only that of the neighbouring Czech Republic (as one would expect) but is also nearly three times the size of Spain's, even though its population is only twice as great. Germany, of course, has the biggest population of any country in Europe, at 82 million people. But even taking this into account by looking at GDP per person – or, to use the jargon, *per capita* – the Germans as a whole are still among the continent's best-off inhabitants (Figure 1.2).

At the other end of the scale are the postcommunist countries whose GDP *per capita* means that, while they are clearly much better off than those living in developing or 'Third World' nations, they do not enjoy anything like the living standards of many of their fellow Europeans. Certainly the gap between the richest and the poorest EU member states is considerably greater than is the gap

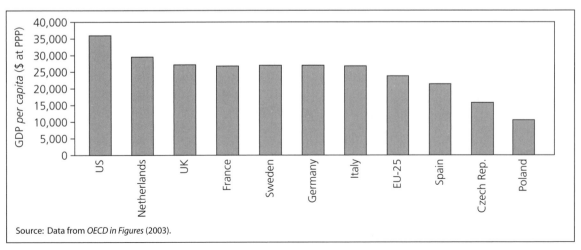

Notes: 1 GDP (Gross Domestic Product) is the overall market value of goods and services produced in a country during the year. It comprises the country's consumer, investment and government spending, along with the value of everything the country exports, minus the value of what it imports. It is the generally accepted measure of a country's economic worth.
2 PPP stands for Purchasing Power Parity and takes into account what money can buy in each country in order to make a more meaningful comparison.

Source: Data from *OECD in Figures* (2003).

Figure 1.1 Overall GDP by country, 2003

between, say, the richest and the poorest states of the US: Mississippi's GDP per capita is around 50 per cent of Connecticut's, but Latvia's is only around 20 per cent of super-rich Luxembourg or 34 per cent of Ireland (the two richest member states in 2003). For the most part, this relative poverty is a characteristic of former communist countries, particularly Bulgaria and Romania which, due in part to their comparative backwardness, did not join the EU with their fellow applicants in 2004. However, there are also differences between traditionally 'western' countries, with Portugal and especially Greece lagging some way behind their fellow EU members and in danger, in time, of being 'overtaken' by postcommunist countries such as the Czech Republic and Slovenia.

Behind the figures, however, lie all sorts of other measures of how well or badly a country is doing, many of which impact more directly on the public, who will be only dimly aware of things like GDP.

Source: Data from *OECD in Figures* (2003).

Figure 1.2 GDP per capita, 2003

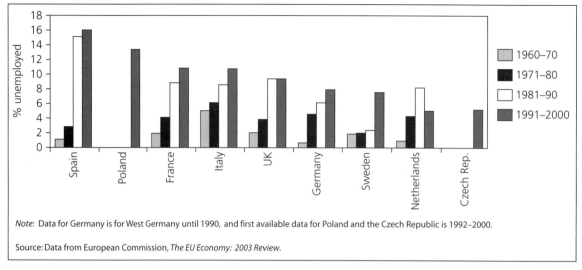

Note: Data for Germany is for West Germany until 1990, and first available data for Poland and the Czech Republic is 1992–2000.

Source: Data from European Commission, *The EU Economy: 2003 Review*.

Figure 1.3 The return of chronically high unemployment in Europe, 1960–2000

The most obvious of these are *inflation* (a measure of rising prices, normally expressed as an annual percentage) and of course *unemployment*. During most of the postwar period, European (and American and Australasian) governments operated on the assumption (labelled 'Keynesian' after British economist John Maynard Keynes) that there was a trade-off between the two. In other words, if economic demand outstripped supply, then there would probably be plenty of jobs around (so-called 'full employment') but inflation would rise; if, however, government acted to reduce demand (by, say, reducing its own spending or that of consumers and business by raising taxes or the interest rates at which banks charged people for borrowing money) then inflation would fall but unemployment would rise. This so-called *Phillips Curve* (named after the economist who came up with the graph that expressed the relationship) seemed to operate until the late 1960s–early 1970s, when most advanced industrial economies suffered 'stagflation' – high inflation and higher unemployment.

From the late 1960s onwards, a number of influential 'neo-liberal' or 'monetarist' economists persuaded many governments that trying to boost demand to tackle unemployment was making the situation worse. Their answer was to stop allowing trade unions to use full employment to bid up wages, to stop subsidizing loss-making industries

and generally to leave things like monetary policy (i.e. interest rates) to the free market. As governments moved towards these policies, there was what was euphemistically called a 'shake-out' of inefficient manufacturing firms (especially those involved in or connected to 'heavy industries' such as steel, shipbuilding, mining, etc.). This accelerated the end of the postwar boom and heralded the return of the kind of mass unemployment that postwar generations had assumed was a thing of the past. This unemployment is 'structural' as much as 'cyclical' (i.e. it will not all disappear in times of economic growth), and is still in many European countries today – in marked contrast to the so called 'golden age' of the 1960s (see Figure 1.3). GDP figures, then, do not tell the whole story.

Regions

Just as importantly, there are big regional variations between different parts of the same country (see Box 1.6). Germany, for instance, contains some of the richest regions of Europe; but, having absorbed the formerly Communist East Germany (GDR) in 1990, it also contains some of the poorest. It is by no means alone in this, for these national and regional variations are inherent in the very different ways in which the economies of

BOX 1.6
Poverty amid plenty: Europe's huge regional variations in wealth

Before the accession of ten new member states in 2004 there were, according to Eurostat (the EU's statistical division), just under fifty regions in EU member states whose per capita GDP was below 75 per cent of the EU average. Not surprisingly, nearly all the regions of Greece, Spain and Portugal were among them, as were the regions that made up the former East Germany. Also included were southern regions of Italy, and three in the UK. Taken as a whole, just under 70 million people (nearly 20 per cent) of the total population of the EU-15 (the EU of fifteen countries prior to 2004) live there. Yet they live alongside other regions that are far wealthier than the average. Indeed, many of the larger western European countries outside Scandinavia show huge regional disparities. In seven of the former EU-15 states, including Germany, the UK and Italy, the highest regional GDP per capita is more than double the lowest. Estimates for the EU's newest members show fewer regional differences within countries, though a great deal of poverty compared to the West. One of only two regions above an EU average recalculated to include the new members was the Czech capital, Prague. But the rest of the country was not much better off than other CEE regions: the regional GDP of Prague, indeed, was 2.5 times higher than the poorest region of the Czech Republic.

European states are structured. Traditionally, wealth and development were associated with industrialization which, after the Second World War, was concentrated in Southern Scandinavia (Gothenburg, Malmö and Copenhagen), England, Eastern France, Northern Italy, Belgium and the Netherlands, Germany, the Czech and Slovak Republics and Poland. In the latter half of the twentieth century, however, this relationship began to break down as wealth became more closely connected with services.

'Postindustrialism'?

Most European states, such as the US and other advanced countries, can be labelled 'postindustrial' because the service sector has overtaken the manufacturing sector as the biggest employer in the economy, with agriculture shrinking still further (Table 1.1). This is not, however, to deny that the label may be a little misleading in view of the fact that many so-called 'service jobs' are no less routinized, low-status, low-skilled and low-paid than the production-line jobs traditionally associated with industrialization (see Wilensky, 2002: 186–190). Nor should we forget, that some European nations still have large farming sectors. In the west, Greece and Portugal still have 17 per cent and 12 per cent, respectively, employed in agriculture, but this is nothing compared to the situation in some of the continent's more easterly, often post-communist states. Some of these resemble their counterparts in western Europe: the

Table 1.1 Towards the postindustrial economy in Europe?

% EU population employed in:	1975	1985	1990	1994	1999	2002 'EU-15'	2002 States joining EU in 2004	2002 'EU-25'	% EU-25 GDP 2002	% US GDP 2002
Agriculture	11.1	8.3	6.7	5.5	4.4	4.0	13.4	5.5	2.0	1.4
Industry	39.5	34.4	33.3	30.7	29.3	28.2	32.1	28.8	27.0	20.1
Services	49.4	57.3	60.1	63.7	66.3	67.8	54.5	65.8	71.0	78.6

Source: Data from European Commission, *Employment in Europe, 2000*; Eurostat: *Living Conditions in Europe* (2003); *News Release*, 36/2004; *The Enlarged European Union* (available online at http://www.eu-datashop.de/download/EN/sonstige/allgm/may2004.pdf)

Czech Republic, Hungary, Slovakia, Slovenia and Estonia all have under 10 per cent of their work-force employed in agriculture. But in Romania the figure is around 35 per cent, and in Bulgaria 25 per cent. Poland, may not lag quite so badly, but a figure of 19 per cent of such a large population represents a lot of farmers! This was a major issue in negotiations to join the EU, since the then fifteen member states could not countenance extending the financial assistance afforded by the EU's Common Agricultural Policy (CAP) to so many marginal producers. For one thing, it would have breached their commitment to do no more than maintain the absolute level of agricultural spending, which takes up almost half the EU's total (see Chapter 2), thereby reducing it over time. For another, it would have involved subsidizing (and perhaps ensuring the continuation of) an industry badly in need of rationalization. Although there are exceptions, a large agricultural (or primary goods) sector tends to be associated with poorer states.

In the decades following the Second World War, there was also a strong association in Europe between wealth and industrial development. With the rise of the service sector in most advanced economies, however, this relationship began to break down. Nowadays, with the exception of Germany, which still benefits from its traditionally high-quality industrial base, Europe's wealthiest countries are those in which services – be they predominantly private (and profit-generating) or public (and welfare-creating) – are strongest.

Transition

One factor, then, in the disparity between western Europe, where two-thirds now work in services, and Central and Eastern Europe, where fewer of the workforce are similarly employed, is the fact that much of the latter has yet to move into the postindustrial age. At a regional level in the west, it is those parts of a country historically associated with primary production, mining and/or heavy industries such as steel-making or shipbuilding which, after the agricultural regions, are least pros-perous. This means that Eastern and Central Europe, where these sectors were key to Communist postwar modernization right up until the late 1980s, are at a big disadvantage.

The economic backwardness associated with communism is not a disadvantage that can be over-come overnight. It will take decades – at least. Nevertheless, the so-called 'transition' economies of postcommunist Europe have made considerable progress. That progress has not, of course, been even. Some countries were already closer to the West to begin with. And, although most decided early on that capitalism was where they wanted to go, there has been considerable variation in the route chosen to get there. Hungary, for instance, which actually had already begun market-style reforms under its communist regime, pursued a fairly cautious strategy. Poland, and to a lesser extent the Czech Republic, chose to move more quickly: both devalued their currencies to a real-iztic level, removed price subsidies and tolerated a degree of unemployment and (what they hoped would be) short-term contraction in order to achieve manageable inflation and respectable growth in the long term.

Privatization, too, was clearly important in Europe's postcommunist countries. But, like other policies, it was emphasized more by some govern-ments than it was by others. Governments also went about it in slightly different ways and at different speeds: the Czech Republic, for example, was particularly keen (Hopkins, 1998), but perhaps too keen. By the late 1990s, some three-quarters of the economy was in private hands after the government gave ordinary people vouchers that then became tradeable. But it had also become apparent that managers of the privatization funds that held their investments had been systematically stealing from them. Managers of newly privatized firms had also been appropriating their assets and obtaining state bank loans under false pretences and that successful bidders for privatized firms were involved in the party financing scandal that forced the resignation of the then Prime Minister (and now President) Václav Klaus (see Chapter 4). Poland, despite its reputation in the early 1990s for adopting what some economists labelled 'shock therapy' took things more slowly against a back-ground of public scepticism (Klich, 1998). But like most postcommunist governments it was sensible enough to vary the mode of sale: assets were (and are still being) divested via trade sales, sometimes to foreign companies, as well as by allotments to employees, transfers to pension funds and public holding companies.

All this meant that, with the exception of Romania and Bulgaria, most CEE countries largely managed to avoid the overnight creation of a semi-criminal oligarchy that occurred in Russia. Still, the process was not without its problems (see Iatridis and Hopps, 1998). Governments did little to dampen expectations early on and, especially in Poland, they suffered a backlash as the public caught on to the fact that privatization would make very few people wealthy and a lot of people unemployed. They were also so keen to get rid of state assets that they not only failed to realize their true-value, but, in selling off rather than breaking up dominant firms, they also failed to create truly competitive markets. There were undoubtedly cases where entrepreneurs obtained profitable parts of state-owned enterprizes (SOEs) with large market share at knock-down, never-to-be-repeated prices. And legitimate criticisms can be made of the extent to which the 'creative destruction' of some of communism's industrial inheritance was really that creative, even (and perhaps especially) in East Germany.

Generally, however, to have transferred so much in so short a time without causing utterly unbridled corruption, mass poverty or disruption to the supply of goods and services has to be seen as a major achievement. Given that speed and the creation of a viable market economy were by far the most important priorities of early postcommunist governments (much more so than preserving a relatively equitable distribution of wealth, for instance), then privatization in the region has to be judged a success on its own terms. In the Czech Republic, Poland and Hungary, by far the bulk of the economy is now in private hands. Because there is a lot of catching-up to do (and a relatively large amount of foreign direct investment (FDI) coming in) growth is or is likely to be slightly higher than in the former West. Inflation (the rise in the cost of living) is similarly low. Unemployment, however remains a persistent problem, especially in Poland, Slovakia and (to a lesser extent) the Baltic states (Latvia, Lithuania and Estonia). Meanwhile, Slovenia, formerly part of Yugoslavia – always rather closer to the West than countries in the Soviet bloc – boasts the best-performing economy of all the postcommunist states. The wooden spoon goes to Bulgaria and Romania, where reform was slow until economic crisis finally galvanized change in the latter half of the 1990s.

Globalization and/or Europeanization?

The economic picture in Europe, then, is complex, and even in some cases quite negative, at least in the short term. Some accounts make it seem even bleaker by suggesting that jobs in manufacturing and even services are leaking away to developing countries, leaving Europe destined to be 'overtaken' by growth economies such as China and other East and South Asian economies. According to this view, Europe's corporates will, like their American counterparts, benefit from globalization, but its population will end up as victims. In fact, there is as little evidence to support this pessimistic view, however fashionable, as there is to support some of the more ambitious versions of globalization itself. Both of them buy too heavily into the idea that things are fast changing beyond recognition and that space, time, existing patterns and cultural inertia may not matter much any more. Arguably, however, they do. Even if we ignore the obvious argument that a great deal of European countries' economic activity is (as it is in the US) domestic, and concentrate on the international sector, it is (a) not clear that European countries are doing badly and (b) obvious that all of them spend more and more time and more and more money with each other than with anyone else.

Take, for instance, the argument that industry, and therefore jobs, will abandon Europe in favour of the 'Tiger' economies of South East Asia. Statistics do show that, like the US, some European nations (often traditional trading nations such as the UK and the Netherlands) seem to be running large deficits in manufacturing trade with NICs such as Korea and Taiwan. But they also show that others, notably Italy and Sweden, export far more goods (at least in terms of value) to those countries than they import from them. And, bluntly, none of this may matter if a country's 'comparative advantage' is in services rather than in manufacturing (as is undoubtedly the case with the UK). Moreover, despite the common fallacy, there is no finite number of jobs out there in the world that means if one country loses them, it cannot grow them again: a high- or low-tech plant in Shanghai or yet another call-centre in Mumbai does not spell the end of the road for Europe. In any case, rising trade with the rest of the world – which, if it were done fairly, should help all concerned – is not half so important as the steady rise in the extent to which European countries, especially those within the EU, trade with each other (Table 1.2). The myriad connections this trade is built on are long-standing (centuries old, indeed) and increasingly institutionalized by EU membership and co-operation. At the very least, then, 'Europeanization is sufficiently deeply embedded to act as a filter for globalization' (Wallace, 2000: 381).

National and patterned variation

But just because European countries trade with each other and are all moving towards postindustrial economies, albeit at varying rates, we should not take Europeanization to mean some kind of uniformity. History matters in economics as much as it does in politics and policy. Obviously, there are some basic similarities. Notwithstanding some of the postcommunist outliers, European countries have relatively advanced and – compared to, say, the US – relatively 'mixed' economies. Within a largely capitalist framework that sees most goods and services produced by the private sector, there is public sector involvement in areas such as defence and law and order, education and welfare provision and, not uncommonly, in the ownership of utilities and other industries. Even where state involvement is relatively low, it is probably crucial to the continued health of a nation's economy. The state, whether local or national, is a big customer for many private firms. Moreover, by maintaining transport and networks, and building and staffing schools and hospitals, it helps supply the infrastructure and the human resources those firms need. Its welfare payments help to ensure that as many consumers as possible have money to buy the goods and services produced by the private sector. Its stewardship of the economy, via tax and spending decisions and the legal and regulatory framework it maintains, contribute to the creation of an environment in which, hopefully, business will thrive.

But the distinctions between Europe's mixed

Table 1.2 The growth and current importance of intra-European trade

	% growth in trade with rest of the world 1960–2000	% growth in trade with other EU countries 1960–2000	Current trade with EU-25 countries as % of country's total trade (2004)
Czech Rep.	n/a	n/a	78
France	743	1666	67
Germany	755	902	65
Italy	1166	1720	60
Netherlands	862	1485	68
Poland	n/a	n/a	74
Spain	1909	2591	71
Sweden	1043	711	65
UK	342	1000	57
EU	734	1221	66

Sources: Data from Badinger and Breuss (2003); Eurostat (2004).

economies are arguably every bit as important as the similarities. This need not mean we give up the search for some kind of patterned variation, however. Hall and Soskice (2001), for instance, put together a stimulating case that (west) European countries' economies can be characterized as 'liberal' (UK, Ireland) or 'co-ordinated' (Germany, Scandinavia and Benelux) or hybrids where the state is still quite a prominent actor (France, Greece, Italy, Portugal and Spain). Analysts also routinely draw distinctions between Europe's welfare state regimes (see Box 1.7)

It is still to soon to place Europe's postcommunist countries precisely and firmly into such schemas. But the early signs are there. After seeming to take their initial inspiration from the US, via the recommendations of the International Monetary Fund (IMF) and the World Bank (see Ferge, 2001) many of them (notably the Czech Republic) are moving toward a less residual and more government-regulated 'European' model – often one which seems to pick and mix elements of both the social democratic and the 'corporatist' or 'conservative' model (see Deacon, 2000). As one

BOX 1.7
Europe's various welfare state regimes

Stressing variations in the extent to which political and trade union representatives of ordinary working people were able to wring concessions from states that were essentially pro-capitalist, Swedish expert, Gøsta Esping-Andersen (1990) posited the existence of the following three 'worlds of welfare'.

Social-democratic: Extensive high-quality services, open to all irrespective of income; generous (and income-related) transfer payments to those out of or unable or too old to work; strong public support; exemplified by Scandinavian countries such as **Sweden**.

Liberal, Anglo-Saxon: Basic services, many available only via means-testing; limited transfer payments; safety net for the poor so middle-class use and support is limited; both the **UK** and Ireland are examples, but (compared to, say, the US) only imperfect ones because they have been influenced by the other traditions.

Conservative, corporatist: Insurance-based welfare schemes, many of which are administered by unions and employers; strong bias towards support for traditional family structures; Austria, **Germany**, **the Netherlands** and the other Benelux countries fit neatly into this category, though **France** and **Italy** (and rather less easily **Spain**, Portugal and Greece) can also be included.

observer, after judiciously sifting through the impassioned arguments and the mixed evidence concerning postcommunist social policy, concludes, any border that still exists between Western and Central and Eastern Europe is most definitely not one that demarcates 'two essentially different types of welfare regime', not least because there are so many types in each region. In short, 'East-Central European welfare regimes are muddling through to achieve some degree of normalcy by an average of Western standards' (see Kovács, 2002: 176, 196). As Wagener (2002: 170) points out, it is crucial to remember this lest we allow '[a]ll the horror stories about transformation-induced alco-

holism, falling life expectancy, deteriorating health status and appalling income inequalities' – phenomena that in the main affect the former Soviet Union (and therefore to some extent the Baltic states) – to give us a totally misleading view of welfare in the mainly Central European states that joined the EU in 2004.

The fact that some of Europe's postcommunist states are tending toward at least some aspects of Esping-Andersen's conservative or corporate welfare regimes, relying as they do on social insurance rather than tax-funded welfare, may not be a good thing for their populations, especially those who are unemployed. In March 2004, for instance, some 19 per cent of Poles were out of work, with the figure for under-25s double that. Rhodes (2002) notes that in west European countries whose welfare states rely on social insurance paid by employers and to a lesser extent employees (such as France, Germany, Italy and Spain), employers are reluctant to take on new (and that often means young) workers when the costs to them are so high, especially if what they see as 'red-tape' (but others see as worker protection) makes them difficult to offload if things do not work out. At the same time, as Rhodes also notes, their relative generosity to pensioners places a much greater burden on those in work than is the case in other countries. These residual 'Anglo-Saxon' welfare states, such as the UK or egalitarian 'Scandinavian' welfare states such as Sweden, are not only a little less generous to pensioners but load more of the burden of taxation onto the individual (via income tax) and their consumption, since they regard insurance-based levies as 'a tax on jobs' which hurts those looking for one.

If Europe's new democracies do adopt this insurance aspect of the conservative or corporatist (some use the term 'Bismarckian' after the founder of the system in Germany) welfare regime (see Wagener, 2002), it might mean that once the comparative advantage they enjoy over western economies in terms of cheap labour wears off they, too, run into some of the same problems. On the other hand, because that advantage is likely to last for at least a decade or more, they have plenty of time to adjust, and adjustment clearly is possible. Given a certain amount of political will (and perhaps a perceived 'fiscal crisis'), European states can and have moved from one category to the other or at least turned themselves into hybrids. The restructuring of social security in the Netherlands, which in the 1980s seemed to be trending to the 'welfare without work' model, shows that, even faced with public opposition (over one million joined street protests in 1991), politicians are capable of turning things around (Green-Pedersen 2001 and see van Kersbergen, Hemerijck and Manow 2000). Whether they have turned them round enough – and whether the so-called 'Dutch model' is really one to be followed – is another matter (see Keman, 2003).

Debates about *how* European countries should best finance their welfare states should not, however, obscure the main point that they do still finance them! There is a lot of hype surrounding 'the end of the European welfare state', but it is not well supported by the facts. Since the mid-1970s, governments in most European countries have been keen to stress their commitment to 'reigning in spending' and 'shrinking the state'. But, as we suggest in Chapter 9 where we discuss the relationship between rhetoric and reality on this matter in more detail, there is little evidence that they have succeeded. European governments recently appear to be spending slightly less of their countries' wealth,

but this would seem to be more a case of re-establishing control rather than relentlessly driving down spending to American levels (see Table 1.3). Nor do they seem to be spending any less on education and welfare (see Figure 1.4 and Crouch, 1999: 368–74), with only slight (though not altogether insignificant) variations in what each country spends its money on. For instance, France and Germany spend (per capita) a little more than most on health, but Sweden spends (per capita) more than other countries on education; postcommunist countries do not spend significantly more or less (at least per capita) than the rest; all spend a good deal on the elderly – and will continue to do so (see Box 1.8).

Society: class and gender still matter

Whatever happened to 'the classless society'?

In both the former West and East, however, there are systematic differences in the distribution of employment, income and wealth. This, many analysts would suggest, is because European soci-

---

Table 1.3 Government expenditure as a percentage of GDP, 1961–2005

	1961–73	*1974–85*	*1986–90*	*1991–5*[1]	*1996–2005*[2]
Sweden	n/a	57.5	57.9	63.8	59.8
France	36.7	n/a	51.4	54.0	54.0
Czech Rep.	n/a	n/a	n/a	61.0	51.4
Italy	32.3	43.9	52.2	55.6	49.3
Germany	n/a	46.6	45.0	48.6	48.4
EU-15	n/a	45.5	47.5	50.0	48.0
Netherlands	37.1	53.2	54.9	54.3	47.7
Poland	n/a	n/a	n/a	49.8	44.5
UK	35.7	49.2	42.5	44.9	40.8
Spain	n/a	31.0	41.0	45.4	40.5
US	30.5	34.1	35.8	36.2	33.8

Notes: 1 Data for Czech Republic and Poland is 1992–5.
　　　　 2 Data after 2003 are projections.

Source: Data from European Commission, DG Economic and Financial Affairs, *European Economy, Statistical Annexe* (Spring 2004), available online at http://europa.eu.int/comm/economy_finance/publications/europeaneconomy_en.htm.

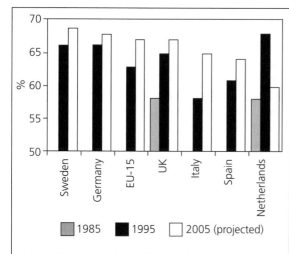

Note: Social transfers include both 'transfers in kind' (eg. free healthcare, housing subsidies, daycare) and cash benefits.

Source: Data from European Commission, DG Economic and Financial Affairs, *General Government Data (by Country)* (Spring 2004), available online at http://europa.eu.int/comm/economy_finance/indicators/general_government_data/government_data_en.htm Unfortunately no comparable figures are available for Central and Eastern Europe or for France.

Figure 1.4 Proportion of government spending devoted to social transfers, 1985–2005

eties remain (or in the case of postcommunist countries are becoming) 'class societies'. There is plenty of room for argument about the precise make-up of these classes. Sociologists disagree and different countries employ different means of categorization, and it may be true that the traditional categories are becoming somewhat blurred (see Crouch, 1999: Chapter 5). There is also considerable dispute, as we shall see in Chapter 6, about the precise and changing impact of class on political behaviour. However, it is difficult to refute the general proposition that the circumstances into which a child is born and the work an adult finds him or herself doing (or, in the case of the unemployed, not doing) strongly influence his or her income, life-style and life-chances.

In Europe, the manual working class – at nearly a third to almost a half of European countries' populations – is still the largest group (especially if we were to confine our figures to men). It is, though, in decline as jobs in manufacturing and mining decrease relative to jobs in the often non-

BOX 1.8
Births, deaths: and a lot more in between

Europe has probably reached its peak as far as population is concerned. This is primarily because after a postwar boom its birth rate has declined to just 1.5 per woman (only 1.15 in Spain and Italy), which is way below the 2.2 replacement rate required to keep numbers stable. in 1950, 548 million people lived in Europe and this increased to 727 million by 2000. But by 2050, Europe's population will have declined to 580 million. On the other hand, life expectancy is expected to increase. Life expectancy at birth in Europe between 1995 and 2000 stood at 73.2; by 2045–50 it will be 80.8.

Putting these two things together leads to the obvious conclusion that Europe has an 'ageing population'. Take the median age – the age you would pick in order to divide a country's population into two equal halves. In 1950, this would have been 29.2, in 2000 it would have been 37.7 and in 2050 it is expected to be 49.5! In fact, Japan aside, it is in Europe where population ageing is at its most advanced. The proportion of children in Europe, for instance, is projected to decline from 17 per cent in 2000 to 14 per cent in 2050, while the proportion of older people (those over 60) will increase from 20 per cent in 1998 to 37 per cent in 2050. By then, there will be 2.6 older people for every child and more than one in every three people will be aged 60 years or over.

Italy, Switzerland, Germany and Sweden currently have median ages of 40 years each. But in 2050, Spain is projected to have the oldest population, with a median age of 55 years. Italy, Slovenia and Austria, (54 years) will not be far behind. In Germany, Greece and Italy, there are already at least 1.5 people aged 60 or over for every child, and by 2050 Italy and Spain are each expected to have nearly four older people for every child. The old are also getting older! In 2050, Austria, Belgium, Finland, France, Germany, Greece, Italy, the Netherlands, Norway, Slovenia, Spain, Sweden, Switzerland and the UK are all projected to have at least 10 per cent of their population aged 80 years or over.

Source: Data from UN Population Division.

manual service sector. Because many of the jobs in the latter are not necessarily well paid (especially if they are occupied by women) the so-called 'growth of the middle class' has not, however, been accompanied by a trend toward growing equality of incomes or wealth. Indeed, quite the opposite (see Figure 1.5).

In many – though not all – European countries, including the postcommunist states and the UK (which along with Italy, Ireland, Spain and France was historically one of the continent's most unequal societies), inequality actually increased from the 1980s onwards. In East Central Europe, this increase began slightly later and occurred because of the collapse of the communist economic system and the move toward marketization; it has, however, been notably less extreme than in the countries of the former Soviet Union (FSU), and at

least some governments – and here the Czech Republic would seem to be in advance of its counterparts in Hungary and Poland (see Ferge, 2001) – are taking the problem of poverty seriously. In the west, the increase in inequality was largely because (with the exception of the late 1980s/early 1990s when some workers lost out as unemployment affected them directly or indirectly by lowering wages), the rich got richer (as they benefited from more deregulated economies) rather than because the poor got poorer. The rise in inequality even occurred in egalitarian bastions like Sweden, although that country, with its Nordic neighbours, nevertheless remains one of the most equal in Europe. Nowhere in Europe, however, is inequality as evident as it is in the US or, closer to home, Russia (see Figure 1.6).

The extent and growth of income inequality differs between European countries. But its continued existence would seem to contradict the claim that the so-called 'classless society' has finally arrived, brought about, ironically, not by communism but by the capitalism it set out to destroy. But inequality does not stop at income. Take education, which is said by many to be one of the factors contributing to the blurring of class distinctions. Throughout Europe, an individual's progress and performance is influenced most not by the school she attends but by the educational attainment (and to a lesser extent the socio-economic position) of her parents. Like the US, though later on, Europe has seen a massive expansion in university and other tertiary education provision. But research suggests that across the continent the main – or at least the first – beneficiaries were those sorts of families who were already consumers of such provision. Rather than lots more working-class children going on to university, for example, places have been found for the siblings whose gender or limited ability would have ruled them out in the more sexist and selective days of old. In short, while there has been a considerable closing of the gender gap (and in many European countries the opening of a new one as more women gain degrees than men) education is as much influenced by class distinctions as ever. It is therefore unlikely to have as big an impact on eroding such distinctions as some optimistic advocates suggest (see Crouch, 1999: 238–41).

	Early/mid 1970s– mid/late 1980s	1980s	Mid/late 1980s– mid/late 1990s
Czech Rep.	n/a	n/a	↑↑↑
France	↓	↔	↑
Germany	↓	↑	↑
Italy	↓↓	↑	↑↑
Netherlands	↔	↑	↑↑
Poland	n/a	n/a	↑↑
Spain	n/a	n/a	n/a
Sweden	↓	↑	↑
UK	↑↑	↑↑↑	↑↑

Key:
↑ = modest rise in income inequality, ↑↑ = rise,
↑↑↑ = significant rise.
↔ = no real change
↓ = modest fall in income inequality, ↓↓ = fall,
↓↓↓ = significant fall.

Source: Adapted from Smeeding (2002).

Figure 1.5 Growth in inequality, 1970s–1990s

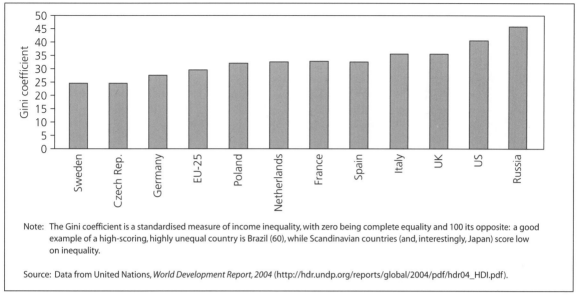

Note: The Gini coefficient is a standardised measure of income inequality, with zero being complete equality and 100 its opposite: a good example of a high-scoring, highly unequal country is Brazil (60), while Scandinavian countries (and, interestingly, Japan) score low on inequality.

Source: Data from United Nations, *World Development Report, 2004* (http://hdr.undp.org/reports/global/2004/pdf/hdr04_HDI.pdf).

Figure 1.6 Inequality in Europe compared

Nor should too great a faith be placed in the capacity of social policy more generally to reduce inequality. There is some evidence to support the idea that reductions in inequality in former dictatorships such as Spain, Portugal and Greece may have had something to do with big increases in social spending (particularly in the last two countries). We can also say that efforts to curb welfare spending in the UK, which in the 1980s saw it swing toward the 'Anglo-Saxon' model and away from the social democratic one, probably exacerbated its relatively high level of poverty. At the other end, of the scale, however, the Scandinavian countries that consistently emerge as having the most equal societies do so not just after, but also before, we take taxation and transfers into account – though this is not to discount completely the redistributionary effect of their welfare states. Interestingly (and perhaps surprisingly to those who argue that, as in the US, inequality and national wealth go hand-in-hand), this is a reminder that in Europe there appears to be a positive correlation between how rich and how equal a country is (see Conceição, Ferreira and Galbraith, 2001).

Glib predictions about the coming of the classless society, then, are at the very least premature. On the other hand, this should not prevent us from acknowledging that the proportion of the population that can be called, or calls itself, working class is on the decline. In short, while there are just as many workers on wages or salaries out there, far fewer of them are wearing blue collars and far more are wearing white. This is partly because, as we go on to discuss, more of them are wearing skirts, too. But it is also because of a move away from large-scale extraction and industrial production and into services. Fewer mines and large factory settings means fewer places where large numbers of (traditionally) male manual workers work, live and play together and in so doing sustain a sense of themselves as having different (and competing) interests to those who employ them. As we shall see in Chapters 5 and 6, this has had a major impact on voting and party politics, posing particular problems for parties of the left, for whom such people were historically their core supporters.

Women – working but not yet winning?

If class remains an important source of differences between people, so too does gender. This is despite the fact that one of the clearest European social trends of the latter half of the twentieth century was a move into the paid workforce by women, particularly married (or, increasingly, cohabiting)

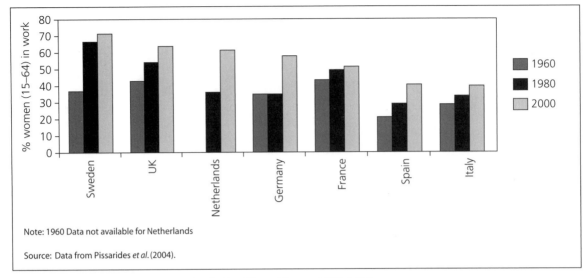

Note: 1960 Data not available for Netherlands

Source: Data from Pissarides *et al.* (2004).

Figure 1.7 More and more women in the (paid) workforce, 1960–2000

women. As we can see from Figure 1.7, the rate at which this move has occurred actually varied between countries. Some western European nations, particularly those such as Italy and Spain, in which the Roman Catholic church exercised a strong influence, historically had low levels of female participation in the paid workforce: the increase in the latter may seem impressive, but rates overall are still lower. Although comparable figures are not available, some former communist countries deliberately and successfully encouraged women to enter the workforce by providing easily accessible childcare and promoting gender equality as official policy. They therefore started from a high base.

The so-called 'feminization' of the workforce is relative as well as absolute. The increase in female participation in paid employment has occurred alongside a decrease in the proportion of men working. This decrease is mainly explained by the steep rise in unemployment experienced by almost all European countries as the 'long' or 'postwar' boom came to an end at the same time as technological advance really began to impact on jobs. Much of this unemployment is long-term, affects the less skilled, is often geographically concentrated and occurs in the manufacturing sector. The service sector, however, has remained very much a growth area, and it is clearly this sector that has

provided the bulk of the jobs that women, in increasing numbers, have moved into. Many of these jobs are part-time. There are, though, considerable national variations in the supply of, and demand for, this kind of work: it is popular in the Netherlands, Norway, Denmark and the UK, for instance, but less so in, say, in France and Southern Europe. Perhaps as a result women in these countries are more likely (in Spain twice as likely!) to be unemployed than men.

In some European countries, most notably in the Nordic countries, many of these jobs are also in the public sector, particularly in welfare (although men, it should be noted, continue to dominate the higher grades even here). There, so many women work that their need for childcare – a responsibility few European men seem willing to take on – cannot be met informally (through family or friends) and instead is met by the state. Those whom the state employs to perform that and other tasks (such as looking after the elderly) are mainly women. More women therefore work, and so on in circular fashion. Whether this circle is 'vicious' or 'virtuous' is a moot point. Some see emancipation and empowerment. Others see the traditional segregation of male and female roles simply transferred from the domestic to the paid economy, with Europe's women no less exploited and, because they still do far more domestically than men, weighed down by the 'dual burden' of work and family.

Responses to this burden vary, but they may include an avoidance or at least a postponement of marriage and childbearing and/or childrearing. Certainly, there are strong trends in European countries (trends often led by Scandinavia and picked up last in Southern Europe) toward having fewer children and having them later on in life and toward later marriage or no marriage at all (though headline figures here can be misleading because of the rise of cohabitation). Divorce is also on the rise in Europe, although, outside the UK and Scandinavia, it is nowhere near the levels seen in the US. Indeed, in countries with a Roman Catholic (and Orthodox) tradition, it is still low, internationally speaking. This, though, may begin to change as religious constraints on the legal (i.e. divorce) regime, as well as on the thinking and behaviour of the population begin to decline.

Clearly, however, there are areas in which papal prohibitions on contraception have long since lost their influence. Two strongly Roman Catholic countries, Spain and Italy, have the lowest birth rates in the world, and are therefore doing nothing to prevent the remorseless ageing of Europe's population (see Box 1.8) Interestingly, birth rates in the Nordic countries, where women participate more fully in the labour force, are at least at replacement level. This is possibly because childcare and other welfare provision is easily accessed by working women in Scandinavia. It may also be because, as surveys consistently show, people in Southern Europe continue to place a higher priority on family obligations. Since they are committed to carrying out what they see as their duties (which, more often than in the north, also include looking after resident elderly relatives as well), they are more careful about adding to them. There are still few women who have no children, but many more who have just one. On a lighter (but by no means entirely frivolous) note, the low birth rate may also be a function of the fact that in Southern Europe (and particularly in Italy and Spain), adult children increasingly live with their parents far longer (i.e. well into their late twenties and thirties) than would be deemed 'normal' or even 'healthy' in other European countries!

In theory if not in practice: religion in Europe

Even this brief excursion into European demography reveals the extent to which some of the broad distinctions we can make between countries, or groups of countries, are influenced by religion. Since, as later chapters show, democracy would appear to be similarly influenced, no survey of Europe would be complete without exploring the continent's religious life a little more deeply. First and foremost, until very recently at least, Europe has been a bastion of Christianity. Yet the history of each country has been profoundly shaped according to which branch or branches of the Christian faith were important within its territory (see Table 1.4). The earliest divide in the Christian church was the eleventh-century breach between Roman Catholicism and the Orthodox church, which split Europe in an East–West fashion from (Catholic) Poland in the North down to (Orthodox) Greece in the South. This split left most modern states on one side or the other. In the

Table 1.4 Religious adherents in Europe, 2000

	Catholic (%)	Protestant (%)	Jewish (%)	Muslim (%)
Czech Rep.	40	3	–	–
France	82	2	1	7
Germany	35	37	–	4
Italy	97	1	–	1
Netherlands	35	27	–	4
Poland	92	1	–	–
Spain	98	0	–	1
Sweden	2	95	–	2
UK	10	53	1	2

Notes: 1 Percentages are given only if the proportion of the population identifying with a particular religion reaches 1 per cent; the absence of a figure does not mean the total absence of a community (the Jewish community is a good example).
2 Note also that, because of the methodology used, Protestants in predominantly Catholic countries may be slightly underrepresented. The figure for Protestants in the UK includes Anglicans.

Source: Data from Barrett *et al.* (2001).

sixteenth and seventeenth centuries, Protestantism either overcame (as in Lutheran Scandinavia) or (as in the UK, Germany, Switzerland and the Netherlands) came to exist alongside Roman Catholicism. The latter continued to dominate the Irish Republic, Belgium, Austria, France and, of course, Italy, Spain and Portugal.

In some countries, the influence of the dominant branch of Christianity went beyond society and was reflected at the level of the state. In the postwar period, of course, things changed, especially in the east where communist states displayed various levels of hostility towards organized religion, ranging from the obstructive (Bulgaria, Hungary, Romania and Poland) to the overtly antagonistic (Czechoslovakia). In the west, however, most states continued to provide subsidies to churches, whether direct or indirect (for example, by funding faith-based schools and hospitals).

In the middle of the twentieth century, Europe still seemed to be a religious place. Although regular attendance could be patchy, the church continued to play a part in the life of most Europeans as the place where rites of passage – births, marriages and deaths – were marked. As the new millennium approached, things had changed, but perhaps less than might be imagined. Research (see, for example, Halman and Riis 2002 and Norris and Inglehart, 2004) suggests that the numbers of people who in censuses and surveys declare themselves adherents of no religion has increased, particularly in France and Belgium (where Roman Catholicism has been the big loser) and in the Netherlands (where Protestantism lost even more heavily than Catholicism). In addition, although religious baptism and marriage are still the norm for most western Europeans, there has been a continental decline in the former and a decidedly mixed picture as regards the latter. Eight out of ten couples still have a church wedding in Italy, Spain, Portugal, Greece and Finland – the 'western' states which historically took longest to move from the agricultural into the industrial age. But only around half of couples in other western states do the same. Moreover, while there is still a tendency to 'marry in' rather than 'marry out', it is very small – far smaller than among, for instance, some of Europe's non-Christian ethnic communities.

As for church attendance, problems with obtain-

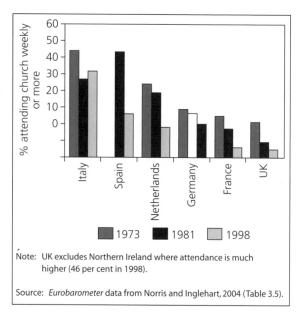

Note: UK excludes Northern Ireland where attendance is much higher (46 per cent in 1998).

Source: *Eurobarometer* data from Norris and Inglehart, 2004 (Table 3.5).

Figure 1.8 The west European decline in church attendance, 1973–98

ing accurate information from either churches or their parishioners make it difficult to say anything conclusive or precise about change over time. However, the evidence we do have both from World Values Surveys and the big opinion polls regularly conducted by the EU known as *Eurobarometer* surveys suggests a general decline in western Europe (see Figure 1.8). Until recently we might have had the confidence to say that Roman Catholics, at least outside France, were much better at actually going to the church than Protestants, particularly those Protestants belonging to the official state churches of the UK and Scandinavia. Recently, however, there are reports that attendance even in bastions of Roman Catholicism such as Ireland and Italy, though still relatively high, is in rapid decline. On the other hand, participation in the EU members like Malta and Poland seems not to have dropped off, and in many CEE countries, attendance seems to be on the increase now that the state does nothing to discourage it. Interestingly, judging by surveys, years of communist anti-clericalism seems to have had only limited impact on a seemingly natural tendency for most people to believe in some kind of higher power. Outside the former East

Germany, atheism (believing that no spirit or God or life force beyond mankind exists) is not noticeably higher than in 'western' countries such as Denmark. Similarly, agnosticism (not knowing either way) would appear from surveys to be widespread. Generally, though, there appears to be no evidence that either atheism or agnosticism is on the rise. And, despite all the above, the number of people still identifying with one religion or another is still significant (see Table 1.4).

What some label 'secularization', then is real, but it can be overstated or misunderstood. What cannot be overstated, however, are the considerable similarities between Europeans (east and west) on religion, and on its role in society and politics. These are neatly summed up by one researcher, who concludes (Laitin, 2002: 77) that:

> there is a EU-wide consensus in support of a secular Christianity, a respect for national churches than do not meddle in political life, and a recognition as well of minority religious groups as long as the religious expression of these groups is contained within that community.

This last aspect of the 'consensus', however, may lead to problems, not least because of the growth and increasing visibility of the continent's other main religion, Islam. Up to 13 million people in Europe are Muslim, around 4.5 million of whom live in France, with around 3.5 million in Germany and 2 million in the UK. Unlike most of their Christian compatriots, many of them are relatively new immigrants and members of ethnic minorities. This makes them far more prone to discrimination, as well as to poverty. Many European towns and cities, however, contain mosques. And the stereotype of non-integration in the face of supposedly decadent western values, on the one hand, and reactionary moral and doctrinal conservatism, on the other, is just that – a stereotype (see AlSayyad and Castells, 2002, Haddad, 2002, Nielsen, 2004, Pauly, 2004 and Ramadan, 2003). That the stereotype is stronger than ever, however, is clearly down to the events of the terrorist attacks in New York in 2001 and Madrid in 2004. But it merely builds on what one writer, in view of the crusades and expulsions touched on above, justifiably calls 'a thousand years of myth making in Europe' (see Reeves, 2003).

On the other hand, there are increasing media reports of European Muslim involvement in an apparent rise in anti-Semitic attacks – attacks on Jews or Jewish property – especially in France, which along with the UK has Europe's largest Jewish community. There are Jewish communities in other countries but, as Table 1.4, indicates, they are very small relative to the population. In absolute terms, of course, there are large numbers of Jewish people living in Germany (96,000) Italy (34,000), the Netherlands (25,000), Sweden (16,000) and Spain (13,000). In Poland and the Czech Republic the population is no more than a few thousand, due mainly to the Holocaust. To give some idea of scale, the Jewish community of the US is five times bigger than the Jewish community of all the countries listed in Table 1.4. In contrast, the Muslim community in the US is only just over a third of that living in the European countries listed. This may or may not help explain some of the foreign policy differences we explore in Chapter 11.

Composition and identity: multi-ethnic, multi-national – and European?

But if the proportion of people in European countries who can be clearly and conventionally identified as religious, or working class, is shrinking, there seem to be increasing numbers whose self-definition now includes some element of nationality and/or ethnicity (distinctive group characteristics rooted in history and/or race). In fact, Europe provides plenty of opportunity for people to feel and claim multiple and divided loyalties because, as we explore in more detail in Chapters 2 and 10, the continent contains far more ethnic groups than states. Many people, even those who may be officially classified as citizens of one or other country, think of themselves as belonging (either solely or simultaneously) to some other entity or identity. Because of the way the map of Europe has been drawn and redrawn over the centuries, and because of migration, there is almost no country that is completely unaffected by such currents, or by the backlash against them.

BOX 1.9
Politically significant ethnonational minorities in Europe

Belgium 60 per cent Dutch-speaking Flemish in the north; 30 per cent French-speaking Walloons in the south: considerable rivalry (see Chapter 2).

Bulgaria 10 per cent Turkish; 8.5 per cent Roma (gypsies).

Czech Rep. Moravians (13 per cent), but most identify as Czech; 2 per cent Roma.

Cyprus 12 per cent Turkish minority, living in officially unrecognized independent state.

Estonia Formerly part of the Soviet Union: 30 per cent Russians, 4 per cent Ukrainian and Belarusian.

Finland 6 per cent Swedish.

France Mediterranean island of Corsica. On mainland, sizable ethnic and racial minorities from former African colonies, many of whom are of Arab descent and practising Muslims.

Germany Some regional identity in former East Germany. Large immigrant community, made up of various European groups plus Turks (2.5 per cent).

Hungary 4.5 per cent Roma, 2.5 per cent German, 2 per cent Serb, 1 per cent Slovakian.

Italy Two small linguistic minorities: German-speaking *Alto Aldige*, and French-speaking *Valle d'Aosta*. Significant North v. South divide.

Latvia Formerly part of the Soviet Union: 30 per cent Russian, 7 per cent Ukrainian and Belarusian.

Romania Collection of very small minorities from surrounding states, plus 6.5 per cent Roma, as well as 7 per cent Hungarian concentrated in Transylvania.

Slovakia 10 per cent Hungarian, 9.5 per cent Roma.

Spain Several more or less self-conscious regions, two of which (Catalunya and *Euzkadi* or the Basque country) see themselves as separate nations (see Chapter 2). Small Roma population.

Switzerland Patchwork of largely German-speaking and French-speaking areas, but no separatism.

UK Sizable national minorities in Scotland and Wales, though separatism is non-violent and not as intense as in Northern Ireland where a large proportion identify with the Irish Republic to the south (see Chapter 2). Significant ethnic minorities from former colonial possessions in the Indian subcontinent (4.4 per cent) and the West Indies (2 per cent).

Source: Data from CIA *World Factbook* and Barany (2002: 160).

But some are more affected than others (see Box 1.9).

Given their reputation, and their media, it may come as some surprise that British people are not, relatively speaking, particularly nationalistic. According to the European Values Survey (EVS) of 1999/2000, half of all British respondents claimed they were 'very proud' of their country, and 40 per

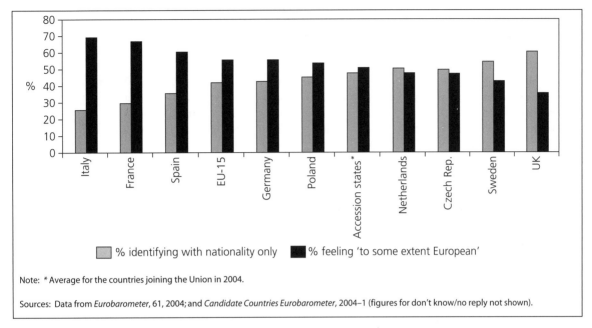

% identifying with nationality only % feeling 'to some extent European'

Note: * Average for the countries joining the Union in 2004.

Sources: Data from *Eurobarometer*, 61, 2004; and *Candidate Countries Eurobarometer*, 2004–1 (figures for don't know/no reply not shown).

Figure 1.9 Mixed feelings: European and national identity

cent were 'fairly proud'. This may put them above people from Belgium, Germany and the Netherlands. But it only puts them on a par with people in Austria, Finland, Slovenia and Spain. Pride in one's country, however, is stronger in Ireland, Malta, Portugal and Poland, the latter being somewhat unusual in postcommunist Europe, where national pride is generally lower than in western Europe.

Interestingly, there is no consistent connection, however, between the level of national pride in a country and any tendency among its people either to identify with, or be antagonistic to, Europe and/or the European Union. Surveys continue to show that while outright hostility is low, there is little evidence that the populations of the continent's various countries are developing an explicitly (let alone an exclusively) European identity. On the other hand, many people seem comfortable with both national and European identity. *Eurobarometer* surveys consistently suggest that just over half of people in the EU member states feel 'to some extent European', while under half identify exclusively with their own country. The demographic analyses show that people who left full-time education at the age of twenty or older, those

who are still studying and managers are most likely to feel 'to some extent European'. They are also most likely to feel 'proud to be European'. Retired people and people who look after the home are most likely to identify with their own nationality only. In other words, education, class (and age) make quite a difference. Breaking things down by country, however, reveals even bigger differences (see Figure 1.9).

People in some countries are clearly much more willing than others to identify with something called 'Europe'. The fact that some people are quite reluctant Europeans while others are comfortable with multiple or 'nested' identities (local, regional, national and supranational) is interesting. But it could also prove politically problematic: it may divide an educated cosmopolitan elite from an undereducated parochial mass. There are clearly national differences which may have their origins in the extent to which European identity is portrayed in public debate as a threat or a complement to national identity (see Díez Medrano and Gutiérrez, 2001 and Smith, 1992). In other words, there is no simple 'zero-sum' game between Europe and the nation: sometimes they are seen as opposed; in other places the one is constitutive of the other (see Kriesi *et al.*, 2003 and Stråth, 2001). This interaction and debate is destined to continue. As we suggest in Chapter 2, 'Europe' can no longer be thought of as existing outside or even above the state, while state and nation are no longer as commensurate as some countries tried to pretend they were.

But we need to be careful not to think that low, or at least variable, levels of identification with an abstract called 'Europe' means that Europeans do not share some – or at least enough – attributes in common. In fact, recent research suggests that they do (see Fuchs and Klingemann, 2002). It is true that one can draw systematic distinctions between groups of European countries with regard to democratic and liberal values (e.g. self-responsibility and work ethic, solidarity with the disadvantaged and trust in others, ethnic tolerance, support for and confidence in democracy and the political system, rejection of violence). And it is true that these differences may be traceable to countries' religious and imperial histories, as well as their level of economic development. But it is also true that there seem to be systematic differences between (broadly speaking) the countries that currently make up the EU-25 and, on the one hand, the US and, on the other, countries further to the east (i.e. the FSU). And it is true that the differences between the old and new member states of the EU are nowhere near as significant as we sometimes think – indeed, in the realms of religion, ability to speak English as a *lingua franca*, and popular culture, there are often more differences between the fifteen member states that made up the EU before 2004 than there are between those fifteen and the states that joined in that year (see Laitin, 2002). As Fuchs and Klingemann (2002: 52) put it, 'Between the countries of Europe there is little difference in the political values and behaviours that are essential to a democracy'.

Learning resources

Histories of Europe abound: the best reads are Davies (1998) and Mazower (1998). By far the best work on the sociology and economics of western Europe – and one which has helped inform this account – is Crouch (1999), but see also Hall and Soskice (2001). A concise overview of the progress of the postcommunist countries is Lavigne (2000); up-to-date and well-presented information on economic and other issues in postcommunist Europe, is provided by the UN Economic Commission on Europe, online at http://www.unece.org/ead/survey.htm. A stimulating – and stimulatingly short! – essay on Europeanization and globalization is provided by Wallace (2000). On the ethnic minorities of Europe, by far the best up-to-date reference book is Cordell and Wolff (2004). On values, by far the best primary source is Halman (2002), while for analysis see Arts, Hagneaars and Halman (2004). On religion, see Halman and Riis (2002), Inglehart and Baker (2000) and Norris and Inglehart (2004). An informative, non-academic guide to the state of the Christian religion in Europe is Chu (2003). As for websites, easy-to-follow maps of Europe and its countries, plus basic information and links to other websites are available at http://www.worldatlas.com/webimage/countrys/eu.htm; more detailed facts and figures on individual countries can be found at http://www.odci.gov/cia/publications/factbook/, as well as in Turner (2005).

EXECUTIVE SUMMARY

- Europe has a conflict-ridden history that has seen the passing of sometimes global empires, religious wars, the rise of states whose borders do not always coincide with nations and, until the collapse of Communism, the artificial division of the continent into 'East' and 'West'.

- As one would expect in a continent whose countries vary so much in size and historical development, the European economy is characterized by variation. Postcommunist and (to an extent) southern European states are less well-off, but in most cases only relatively so. There are also big differences between regions in the same country.

- Europe is an important part of the wider global economy but the growth of intra-European trade is just as important. Europe's economy is not heading downhill, but it has a stubborn – though not equally distributed – unemployment problem.

- Despite most economies being 'postindustrial', there are persistent and patterned variations between the kind of capitalism in operation in individual countries, and similar variation characterizes Europe's still relatively large welfare regimes. Postcommunist countries may be developing into hybrids of these styles and regimes but few are going down the 'American' road toward a more minimal state.

- Class, income and gender inequalities also remain persistent.

- Europe's population is ageing faster than in any other part of the world outside Japan.

- Though not quite as much as in the US, and despite a big drop in church attendance, religion still matters in Europe. An increase in the number of Muslims also means that Europe is far from an entirely secular society.

- Because of long-term migration, Europe has become racially more diverse, although there have been ethnic minorities in many countries for hundreds of years.

- The extent to which people think of themselves as 'European' varies according to social characteristics but also across countries.

- People in the former 'East' and 'West' may show statistically significant variations in politically relevant values, but nowhere near significant enough to prevent us from considering a once-divided continent in its entirety once more.

Chapter 2

The end of the nation state? Federalism, devolution and the European Union

As we saw in Chapter 1, the late nineteenth and early twentieth century confirmed Europe as a continent of states. These were constructed on the basis – sometimes firm, sometimes more fictional – that they were the institutional embodiment of a nation, of a community living (and in most cases born) in a territory and amongst other people with whom they felt a binding affinity. These **nation states** were presumed to be *sovereign* in the sense of exercising supreme political authority within their territorial boundaries and remaining free from hindrance from outside bodies.

Definition
A **nation state** is a country where the boundaries of the political and administrative system are presumed – rightly or wrongly – to coincide with those that contain a population with a supposedly shared culture, history and (probably) language.

In fact, the reality has rarely matched the presumption – especially in the second half of the

twentieth century, but also long before that. There are two reasons for this. First, many European countries contain 'stateless nations' (Keating, 2001). These are minorities that consider themselves to be, or to belong to, nations other than that on which the state claims to be founded. In recent years, many have become politicized and, as we shall see below, have obliged states to respond to their demands. Second, few states could claim complete freedom from outside 'interference' Those in Central and Eastern Europe formerly (if not formally) controlled by the Soviet Union are only the most blatant example. Many of their western counterparts, by joining what is now the EU, have also compromised (if not actually surrendered) their **sovereignty**.

Definition
The possession of **sovereignty** implies the ultimate right, free from external hindrance, to decide and control how a state will be run and the direction it will take.

This chapter explores, in turn, both facets of what some are bemoaning as the end of the nation state in Europe. It begins by looking at how the phenomenon of **minority nationalism** is helping to make historically unitary states (in which sub-national government traditionally enjoyed no real power) look more like those

---

Definition
Minority nationalism is the feeling on the part of one community within a state that they belong to a separate nation that should therefore be accorded some kind of autonomy, special rights or even independence.

---

federal states where local autonomy has long been important. And it asks whether the hybrid forms they have taken on will be enough to save them from eventual break-up. Secondly, it looks at how the nation state is apparently being undermined both 'from above' and even 'from within' by the European Union.

Stateless nations

Some Europeans have an emotional attachment – sometimes only latent or dormant, sometimes vociferously and even violently manifest – to a nation that is different from the state in which, officially, they live. In some European countries there is a clear territorial, as well as historical, cultural (and possibly linguistic) demarcation between these 'national minorities' and the majority population, even if the minority is effectively surrounded in its 'enclave' (a smaller territory within, yet distinct from, a larger territory) by the majority. In other places, the minority may assert there is a clear territorial demarcation, but so many people from the majority live inside what they claim to be their 'borders' that the pattern is in fact complex and confused. Complexity and confusion can also arise when a minority in one state sees itself as part of a nation, but the majority of their fellow 'nationals' live in a neighbouring state – a situation which can give rise to 'irredentism' (the pursuit of reunification with the homeland). This situation occurs (outside Northern Ireland, anyway) far more frequently in Central and Eastern Europe than in the west: the Hungarian populations of Slovakia, Serbia and Romania mentioned in Chapter 1 are obvious examples. In the west (again, with the exception of Ireland), states that could have laid claim to some common identity showed no interest in interfering in the politics of their neighbours: examples include the Swedish with Swedish-speaking Finns, or the Austrians with German-speaking Italians, or the Netherlands with Dutch-speaking Belgians.

That said, European history provides plenty of examples of the bloody consequences of minority nationalism. As we saw in Chapter 1, the First World War itself was sparked by Serbian national-ists anxious to throw off what they saw as the yoke of the Austro-Hungarian empire. Ironically, however, the treaties that followed the war were so intent on dismembering the latter that they established artificial borders that, in Central and Eastern Europe, often left linguistic minorities stranded in a state they did not regard as their own. This was not something the architects of the peace after the Second World War did much about, the exception being their complicity in the forcible repatriation of the (Sudenten) German minority in Czechoslovakia, one of the many 'artificial' states created in the aftermath of the 1914–18 conflict. After 1945, an already broad consensus on borders in Western Europe was effectively locked into place by the need for collective solidarity against the threat from the Soviet Union. This threat also ensured that Spanish dictator Francisco Franco would be given free rein to suppress those 'Spaniards' who insisted on asserting the ancient autonomy of their regions. Moreover, the rush to join in the consumerist prosperity that seemed to be the natural accompaniment to peace and democracy also seemed to have helped reconcile minorities to living alongside the similarly materially preoccupied majority. Meanwhile in the east, communist regimes that were widely thought of as permanent seemed to have effectively kept the lid on and perhaps extinguished any lingering disputes between and within the member states of what became the Warsaw Pact (see Chapter 1).

Partly as a result, few texts on European politics written in the three decades following the Second World War considered 'minority nationalism' of sufficient contemporary interest to bother affording it much, if any, space. As a cleavage it was a has-been, a relic of a bygone age. Like that other formerly important cleavage, religion, it would supposedly slip into history. Yet the loyalty and identity we call nationalism, the need to belong to an 'imagined community' with whom we feel meaningfully connected (Anderson, 1991: 5–7) only appeared to have burned itself out. In fact, the embers could quite easily be fanned into life. Whatever states did to 'deal with' such loyalties – trying to ignore them (France), gradually acknowledging them (the UK and Belgium), or forcibly repressing them (Spain) – clearly did not deprive them of the oxygen they needed to exist, even if only in latent rather than in manifest form.

The transition of minority nationalism from latency to relevancy seems to have resulted, in the main, from two developments. On the one hand, the concept of democracy itself seems to have undergone considerable stretching from the 1960s onwards. It began to include notions of 'subsidiarity' (decisions being taken at the lowest appropriate level) and participation, not least as a response to the idea that 'big government' was bad government and that the political system was suffering from 'overload' (see Chapter 3). Instead of trying and failing to keep up with and balance too many demands by too many people wanting too much money (especially in 'lame duck' peripheral regions), states would be better advised to let them get on with it themselves. Such advice applied as much to their treatment of national minorities as any other group. On the other hand, democracy, or voting at least, seemed gradually to have less and less to do with class identity (see Chapter 6). Clearly, there is no necessary trade-off between class and ethnic and/or regional identity, but as the intensity of one declined, the intensity of the other seems to have increased.

This is partly explained by politics and economics as much as by sociology. For instance, in the UK the Scots' increased sense of themselves as distinct is likely to have been influenced by the imposition of unpopular policies by a largely English Conservative government during the 1980s. That decade saw 'London' widely blamed for an economic recession that hit Scotland's heavy manufacturing base hard – and all this as nationalists (increasingly prepared to stand candidates in all electoral contests) were claiming that Scotland's oil wealth, among other things, could make it a viable independent state within the EU. In Spain and Belgium, too, the desire for more autonomy on the part of at least some of the nations that made up those states was likewise driven by a mixture of politics and economics. And it, too, developed in a context where European integration seemed to offer the chance for small states to prosper.

But material interests and institutions do not explain everything. Nowadays, only the most antediluvian Marxist or 'institutionalist' zealot would claim that people's identity, political or otherwise, can be 'read off' from their position in the market place or the political structures in which they are embedded. Clearly, we are all social and emotional as well as economic actors and are capable of storing, accessing and displaying multiple loyalties – not necessarily at will, but certainly when inspired by events, or at least the construction put on those events by inspirational and/or demagogic leaders. And the consequences of such politicization can be tragic. In the early 1990s in the former Yugoslavia, latent minority nationalism was so whipped up by gangster politicians that it spilled over into civil war and the murder and forcible removal euphemistically called 'ethnic cleansing' (Box 2.1).

The terrible events in the Balkans in the early 1990s seemed to provide proof of this tendency, and heightened fears that in East and Central Europe states might celebrate their release from imperial bonds by attempting the kind of centralizing, majority nation-building that characterised Western Europe in the nineteenth century. The kind of nation-building, in other words, that ignored the wishes of often quite substantial minorities by privileging 'ethnic nationalism' over the sort of 'civic nationalism' that may have originated with a dominant ethnic core but saw it more or less peacefully co-opt first the elites and then the people of more peripheral regions (see Péteri, 2000, Schöpflin, 1995 and Smith, 1991). Fortunately, such fears were not in the main borne out.

There were certainly some concerns, especially in the early 1990s, about the Baltic states (Estonia, Lithuania and especially Latvia), which were understandably reluctant, after winning their freedom from the Soviet empire by precipitating its collapse, to think much about the rights of the many Russians that had settled there during the previous half-century. Attempts to restrict their rights – particularly in the field of language and education – did not, however, survive a combination of pressure from the newly-formed Russian federation and the EU, which made it crystal clear that any state with a poor record on minority rights might as well forget trying to join. Elsewhere, individual politicians and parties have tried to make capital by harking back to a time when all their 'countrymen' were united in the one homeland,

BOX 2.1
Break up in the Balkans

Yugoslavia was created by the victorious powers of the First World War not only to finish off the Austro-Hungarian empire, but also to contain those Balkan nations whose rebellion against the empire had helped spark the conflict in the first place. Though a Communist country from the end of the Second World War, Yugoslavia maintained its independence from the Soviet empire. It was also a federal state consisting of six republics. These were Bosnia and Herzegovina, Croatia, Macedonia, Montenegro, Slovenia and Serbia, which also contained two autonomous provinces (Kosovo and Vojvodina) with non-Serb populations (Albanian and Hungarian respectively). After the end of the Cold War, multiparty elections were held in the republics in 1990. They were all won by non-communist nationalist parties, except in Serbia and Montenegro where the Socialist Party (the successor to the communists) was elected on an aggressively nationalistic platform. Slobodan Milosović, the Serbian leader, had already withdrawn the autonomous status of Kosovo and Vojvodina, thus raising fears that Serbia would move to stamp its authority on the other republics.

Sensing a window of opportunity, Slovenia and Croatia declared independence in June 1991, followed by Macedonia in November. In Slovenia and Macedonia, the Yugoslav army (the JNA) made little or no attempt to stop them. Croatia, however, descended into a six-month civil war, during which Serbs living in Croatia, supported by the JNA, achieved control of around a third of the fledgling state. Early the following year (in March 1992), Bosnia and Herzegovina declared independence, an act that led to a three-way civil war between Bosnian Serbs and Bosnian Croats (both backed by the armies of their respective states) and Bosnian Muslims. Even though they asked the USA to let them come up with a solution, European states were, from the outset, split over what to do. None of them was keen to get involved, and many even blamed Germany's recognition of Croatia for sparking the war in the first place. Because they could not (or would not) back up diplomatic initiatives with military force (particularly against Serbia), such initiatives proved fruitless. Fighting came to an end only in 1995 after the credible threat of US armed intervention, by which time hundreds of thousands were dead or wounded and millions made refugees. Many were the victims of what became known as 'ethnic cleansing' – the forcible removal (and, in some cases, the systematic rape, assault and murder) of populations in order to ensure areas were purely Serb (or, to a lesser extent, Croat and, to a much lesser extent, Muslim).

The Dayton Peace accord brokered by the USA did little more than recognize the situation on the ground in Bosnia. The republic is now split into three largely ethnically homogeneous sections, with the Serbs the biggest winners and the Muslims the biggest losers. When, however, the Milosović regime attempted, four years later, to 'ethnically cleanse' Kosovo of its Albanian population, the Americans and the Europeans – working together as NATO – acted rather more rapidly, bringing the Serbian campaign to a halt by aerial bombardment between March and June 1999. Their action also hastened the fall of the Milosović regime, which was replaced in 2000 by politicians keen to end their country's isolation.

particularly in Hungary. Politicians in Slovakia (where many ethnic Hungarians live) also began the 1990s with a line in both exclusionary rhetoric and public policy decisions, though, as in the Baltic states, such populism was forced to soften in the face of their own possible exclusion from the EU (see Tesser, 2003). Just as importantly, perhaps, most of Europe's newest democracies could see for themselves that their western counterparts were beginning to accommodate rather than ignore or suppress what seemed to be a resurgence of minority nationalism from the 1960s onwards. This is a strategy that we now go on to explore in more detail.

Belgium: federal solution or slippery slope?

It used to be easy to sort European states into two categories. The majority were centralized, **unitary** states – a category which included, first, former

Germany (Deutschland)

Area: 9.0% of EU-25
Population: 18.2% of EU-25
GDP: 19.3% of EU-25
Joined EU: Founder member 1957
Capital city: Berlin

History: Present-day Germany has its origins in the Holy Roman Empire that, a thousand years ago, covered much of central Europe. It developed into a loose collection of principalities that, in the sixteenth century, spawned the religious break-away from Roman Catholicism that became known as Protestantism. These small states, plus the much larger states of Prussia and Austria, were melded into the German Confederation in the early nineteenth century and finally united, minus Austria, as one country (initially known as the German Empire) in 1871. Germany became a constitutional monarchy with a parliament under its Chancellor Otto von Bismarck, a statesman famous both for building the rudiments of the modern welfare state and maintaining a balance of power in Europe that, for a few years at least, saved the continent from an all-encompassing war.

With its large population and industrializing economy, Germany rapidly threatened to overtake the UK and France as Europe's most powerful state – a challenge that helped to bring about the collapse of Bismarck's balance of power and usher in the First World War (1914–18). The harsh peace settlement embodied in the Treaty of Versailles, along with the rise, re-armament programme and imperial dreams of Adolf Hitler's dictatorial

Nazi regime, precipitated the Second World War just two decades later. Once again, the Germans (in alliance this time with the Italians and the Japanese) were pitted against the French, the British and, in time, the Americans. As well as inflicting (and suffering) enormous casualties in what became known as 'total war' (especially on the 'Eastern front' with Russia), Germany shocked the world by systematically putting to death some 6 million Jews across occupied Europe in what became known as the *Holocaust*. The country's total defeat in 1945 saw it divided into the liberal capitalist Federal Republic (FRG, known as West Germany), with its capital in Bonn, and the communist Democratic Republic (GDR, known as East Germany) with its capital in the divided imperial city of Berlin.

Although East Germany was (relatively speaking anyway) one of communist Europe's success stories, it was easily eclipsed by the 'economic miracle' that saw its much bigger western counterpart become the powerhouse of the European economy from the 1960s onwards. In 1990, just a year after the fall of the communist constructed wall that had separated them for decades, the two states were reunified – or more, accurately, East Germany was re-absorbed by the Federal Republic. This new Germany was governed by the centre-right Christian Democrats, under Helmut Kohl, until 1998, and then by a 'Red–Green' coalition led by the centre-left SPD.

Economy and society: Since reunification, western Germany has not only extended its very generous welfare state to the east, but poured billions of euros into its economic development. Yet the east still remains comparatively depressed, with very high unemployment. Germany as a whole has seen its formerly world-beating economy run into trouble in recent years, yet it is still one of Europe's richest countries: in 2003 its 82 million people (nearly 2 million of whom are Turks drawn into the country during the boom years) had a GDP per capita around 8 per cent above the EU-25 average. Some

regionalist sentiment is evident in eastern Germany, as well as in the predominantly Roman Catholic region of Bavaria in the south.

Governance: Germany is a parliamentary democracy, elected under proportional representation (PR). It is also a federal system, with considerable autonomy granted to its regions or states (called *Länder*) by the constitution which is policed by a powerful federal constitutional court. The federal government is presided over by a prime minister (called the Chancellor), elected by a majority in parliament. The latter, which also elects a president as a ceremonial head of state, is divided into two houses: the popularly elected *Bundestag* and a second chamber, the *Bundesrat*, made up of *Länder* representatives, which (unusually in Europe) has the power to make or break most legislation. Outside parliament, there is an extensive network of consultative bodies – involving regional government, employers and trade unions – that regulate the social and economic life of the country

Foreign policy: Germany spent most of the second half of the twentieth century persuading its neighbours that they had no need to fear a repeat of the first half. It placed a great deal of emphasis on the country's membership of multilateral organizations such as the UN and NATO and, until the latter's military intervention to remove Serbian troops from Kosovo in 1999, was very reluctant to send its armed forces abroad, even on peace-keeping missions. Also, crucially important to Germany's rehabilitation was its membership of what is now the EU, in which the country effectively ceded political leadership to France in exchange for the right to be able to rebuild economically. This fraying 'Franco-German axis' was somewhat revived by the two countries' shared opposition to the US invasion of Iraq in 2003.

Further reading. Conradt (2004), Padgett, Paterson and Smith (2003) Schmidt (2003).

imperial powers and their ex-colonies; secondly, the then communist countries; and thirdly, Scandinavian states. Traditionally, only a handful of European states were **federal** states (Germany, Austria and Switzerland) although such a bald distinction always had its critics, not least because the federalism of Germany is very different to the federalism of, say, the USA and also different to the federalism of Switzerland (see Chapter 3). But recently, the distinction has become even more blurred as some former unitary states underpressure from minority nationalism, even where the justification and support for it is weak (see Box 2.2), are adopting federal or quasi-federal forms in response. The question is, in the long term, whether this will save them from break-up.

In one former unitary state, Belgium, federalism is now fully fledged, even if (as in other federal states in Europe) it is not federalism US-style. Ever since it was, to all intents and purposes, conjured up by foreign powers in 1830, the country was linguistically divided between the Walloon, French-speaking, south and the Flemish, Dutch-speaking, north. However, well into the postwar period its government and administration was conducted in French, even if many of those who

Definitions
Unitary states are those in which local government is really only local administration of centrally determined (and often financed) services, and where any power exercised by local government is ultimately dependent on the consent of the central state.
Federal states are those in which territorial sub-national government enjoys constitutionally guaranteed autonomy and functional competence – in other words; local government really is government and is not simply administration under delegated authority from the centre.

ran it were from Flanders, their main link with their Walloon counterparts being Roman Catholicism. The capital, Brussels, although located in the Flemish region was (and continues to be) predominantly French-speaking. This French-speaking control was facilitated not just by an essentially Francophone monarchy, but also by the fact that the more industrialised Wallonia provided the greater part of the nation's wealth. But the decline of heavy industry from the 1950s

---

BOX 2.2
Padania?

Italy's *Lega Nord* (Northern League) is a political party that has been in centre-right national governments and is also renowned for its xenophobic rhetoric. For almost a quarter of a century, its leaders have been arguing for increased autonomy for some of the richest of Italy's regions, such as Lombardy, Piedmont and Veneto. Although the grounds for their claim to independence seem in the main to be economic (resentment at the supposed drain on dynamism caused by the South's relative poverty), they have tried to bolster it by dreaming-up a nation, *Padania*, that is supposedly united by history and culture. Few seem persuaded by such claims: they certainly seem less genuine than those of Italy's five existing 'special regions' (Sardinia, Sicily, Val d'Aosta, Trentino-Alto Adige and Friuli-Venezia) that have been accorded a degree of autonomy since the 1970s. But the *Lega*'s usefulness as a coalition partner, and the threat it poses to the votes and ability to govern of other political parties, has lent momentum to a rather less ambitious campaign for a federal Italy – a state which, after all, did not exist until 1870. It was no surprise, then, that reforms were passed in 2002 devolving power over health, police and schooling to the regions, although they still had little power (unless granted permission) to raise their own revenue, and could have any legislation they passed overturned either by the centrally appointed commissioner appointed to each region, or by parliament. In 2004, the centre-right government moved further, with proposals to elect the Italian Senate (see Chapter 4) on a regional basis. Some of these moves have support across the political spectrum, especially since a cross-party parliamentary commission in 1997 made not dissimilar suggestions. *Padania* may be more fiction than fact, and Italy is not yet a federal country. But it may be moving in that direction.

onwards reversed the situation and turned the political tide: as the Flemish north began to outstrip the French-speaking south economically, its people and their representatives began to demand autonomy from a community that, in their view, had not only dominated them unfairly for over a hundred years but was now also a drain on their resources. They were not, however, alone: a number of Walloon politicians believed their region would be better off without the Flemish. By 1993, this push for autonomy resulted in Belgium becoming a federal state, albeit one rendered unconventional because the ensuing **devolution** involved the transfer of powers not just to three geographical regions – *Wallonie*, *Vlaams* and *Brussel* or *Bruxelles*) but also to three 'communities' – French-, Dutch- and German-speaking.

What is significant is that when the process of disaggregation began as far back as the early 1960s, it started out as a way of defusing tensions, not as a conscious first step on the road to federalism. Yet Belgium seemed to slide inexorably towards the latter. Laws passed in 1962 and 1963 defined the boundaries of the linguistic groups. Constitutional

---

Definition

Literally, **devolution** is the transfer of competences from national to sub-national government. However, it has taken on a particular meaning in the UK where it is used in order to make it clear that the transfer of powers is not the forerunner of federalism, let alone complete independence for Scotland and Wales.

---

reform in 1970 set up linguistically based communities with responsibilities in 'cultural' areas such as broadcasting and education. Further constitutional reform in 1980 not only granted executive status to these communities (which were given additional responsibilities in health and welfare), but also gave executive and legislative powers to the regions of Wallonia and Flanders in economic planning, environment and transport, as well as setting up a court to arbitrate disputes between the regions, the communities and central government. More reforms in 1988 and 1989 added to the powers and responsibilities already devolved, and granted the same to Brussels. Equally significant is the fact that 1993 did not bring an end to the process: further

pressure from Flanders led to even more devolution of powers to the regions in the so-called 'Lambermont Accord' of June 2001, to the extent that, beyond taxation, social security, the monarchy, sports and the location of Brussels in Dutch-speaking Flanders, there seems to be little holding the country together. Belgian parties had long since split into Dutch- and French-speaking organizations, although for the moment they agree to abide by an agreement that the federal government should be linguistically balanced.

In fact, there is a recent European precedent for a state splitting in two. In 1993, the Czech Republic and Slovakia underwent a largely uncontested, 'velvet divorce', ending a federation that had first been put into place in 1969, some fifty years after the state's creation after the First World War. The divorce came about more as the result of the people accommodating the politicians rather than the latter finally agreeing to give the former what they appeared to want, whereas in Belgium politicians have arguably reflected popular will as much as they have shaped it. Also, things were made easier for the erstwhile Czechoslovaks than they would be for the disgruntled Belgians because each region had its own recognised capital. Another difference with the Belgian case lies in the fact that the main impetus for the break-up of the state came from the smaller, poorer and economically backward region, Slovakia, where politicians did their best to whip up fears over (among other things) language concessions to its Hungarian-speaking minority. By and large, Czech politicians were initially reluctant to dissolve the federation and consented only when it became clear that progress on other fronts would be blocked by the Slovaks until they did so. Given the often turbulent nature of politics in Slovakia in the 1990s, and the much slower economic progress it made relative to the Czech Republic, it seems clear who got the best of the deal.

'Asymmetrical' federalism: Spain

The lesson from Belgium, surely, is that decentralization, rather than satisfying calls for more autonomy, can whet the appetite for even more. Yet this has not discouraged politicians in other European

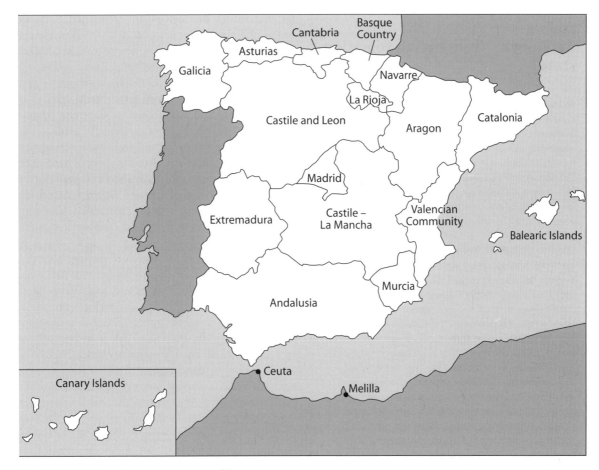

Map 2.1 Spain's autonomous communities

states – most notably in Spain, the United Kingdom and more recently Italy (see Box 2.2) – proffering devolution as some kind of 'solution' to the 'problem' of minority nationalism (Map 2.1).

Since its emergence from authoritarian dictatorship at the end of the 1980s, Spain has transferred increased powers and competences to its *Comunidades Autónomas* (literally, autonomous communities or regions). Many of these continued, as historic kingdoms, to maintain a sense of themselves as distinct, despite forming part of what for hundreds of years was one of the most centralized unitary states in Europe. However, this transfer of powers has proceeded on a piecemeal (or at least evolutionary) basis depending on negotiations between the central government and each of the seventeen autonomous communities established under the 1978 constitution, all of which now have

an elected assembly and government. According to the statutory agreement each community has made with the state, each has a unique range of powers on issues excepting defence and foreign policy, key aspects of social security and macroeconomics, all of which are reserved for the centre. They can exercise these powers in any way they see fit provided they do not conflict with the constitution which, although it created what some see as a hostage to fortune by acknowledging and guaranteeing 'the right to autonomy for the *nationalities* and regions' (author's italics), also committed itself to 'the indivisible unity of the Spanish Nation'.

However, not all of Spain's autonomous communities have chosen (or been able) to assert their autonomy to the extent seen in, say, the Basque country (see below) and Catalunya (see Box 2.3). This has led to Spain being labelled as a

---

BOX 2.3
Catalunya – from nation to nation state?

Along with the Basque country, Catalunya, whose capital in Barcelona is one of Europe's most widely admired cities, is at the forefront of claiming and exercising its rights as an autonomous community. Its wealth, linguistic differences (6 million speak Catalan as well as Spanish) and history of independence give it a good claim to nationhood – or at least to special treatment compared to other autonomous communities whose poverty, history (and the fact that they speak *Castellano* – the Spanish spoken all over the country) mean they are far more dependent on Madrid. As a trip to its English language website (http://www.gencat.net/index_eng.htm) shows, Catalunya takes its independence very seriously: the *Generalitat* – its government – not only promotes the Catalan language and negotiates some agreements direct with the EU, it also conducts its own 'foreign relations' with other governments. Critics would say that the only way the alliance that has run Catalunya for over two decades, *Convergència i Unió*, has managed to achieve all this is by cynically lending the support of those members of parliament (MPs) it sends to the national parliament in Madrid to governments of both right and left . But cynical or skilful, the strategy has been successful to the point that Catalunya enjoys more power and prestige than many regions in formally federal states, and (much to the concern of some Spaniards, especially on the political right) is likely to want to institutionalize its independence still further – perhaps even to the point, in the long term, of breaking up the Spanish state.

---

practitioner of 'differentiated' or 'asymmetrical' federalism (see Agranoff, 1996). Under this hybrid system, most of the country still seems to operate as a unitary state, albeit with some devolution to the regions. But at the same time, there are parts of the country that look, to all intents and purposes, as if they are part of a federal state, or even independent nations. Theoretically (that is to say, constitutionally) Spain is not a federal state – the powers enjoyed by some of its regions, some might argue, are not defined as such by the constitution. But the idea that they can be taken back or that, as

far as many in the regions are concerned, they are not actually inalienable rights, is fanciful to say the least! The question now is not so much whether Spain is or is not federal or on the way to federalism, but whether the latter – hybrid or pure – will be enough to prevent its eventual break-up.

In the three and a half decades since the Basque separatist organization, *Euskadi Ta Azkatasuna* (ETA), first began its campaign of violence against the Franco dictatorship, over 800 people have been killed. Millions of euros have also been paid out by businesses in what is one of Spain's wealthiest regions in protection money, extorted as a 'revolutionary tax' by an organization whose less high-profile *kale borroka* or 'street struggle' has also caused millions of euros' worth of damage to property. ETA demands the independence of what Basque speakers call Euskadi and Spanish speakers call *el País Vasco*, with its most ardent supporters subscribing to a 'catastrophist' belief that unless it is achieved, the Basque 'race' will be wiped off the face of the earth by a 'genocidal' Spanish government. This has conditioned a revolutionary strategy, whereby terrorism will supposedly tempt the authorities into repression that will engender support for more violence until eventually the cost to Spain becomes too great to bear. Accordingly, the hope that the coming of democracy would see the end of ETA was a pipe-dream. The Basque country may have its own parliament and police force, it may control education and even taxation, but in relative and not just absolute terms, far more killing has gone on since Franco's death than before it, and now includes 'soft targets' such as local politicians and foreign holiday-makers.

To the Spanish government, however, secession is not an option. The region may be an autonomous community with a unique cultural heritage, but it is home to hundreds of thousands of people who identify themselves either solely or (like the majority of the region's population) jointly as Spanish (see Box 2.4). It is also, Madrid maintains, but one part of an indissoluble state – notwithstanding the fact that the 1978 constitution failed to achieve majority support in the Basque country after calls for a boycott by peaceful nationalist parties. These parties continue to do much better than the extremists in regional elections and to prevent candidates from the local branches of the

BOX 2.4
Multiple identities: the evidence – and the way forward?

Research seems to suggest that fewer and fewer people in Spain's most autonomous 'nations' see themselves as Spanish or 'more Spanish' than, say, Catalan or Basque. In Catalunya, there has been growth in those who feel Catalan or 'more Catalan', and the number of those who see themselves as both has stayed the same. In the Basque country, it is the number of Basque or 'more Basque' identifiers that appears to have remained constant, while the number of those feeling equally Basque and Spanish has increased, presumably because fewer see themselves as Spanish or 'more Spanish'. Interestingly, the detailed figures vary considerably from year to year. For instance, 1992 (the year of the Barcelona Olympics, the Sevilla World Fair and the five hundredth anniversary of the European discovery of America) saw a temporary increase in those claiming to feel equally Spanish and Basque or Catalan!

	1979 (%)	2001 (%)
I feel:		
Only Basque or more Basque than Spanish	50	50
Equally Basque and Spanish	25	35
More Spanish than Basque or only Spanish	25	10

	1979 (%)	2001 (%)
I feel:		
Only Catalan or more Catalan than Spanish	25	40
Equally Catalan and Spanish	35	35
More Spanish than Catalan or only Spanish	35	20

Source: Adapted from Martinez-Herrera (2002), percentages rounded to nearest 5 per cent.

ists, during a short-lived ceasefire in 1998 and 1999, showed themselves willing to contemplate negotiations with ETA and even work with its political wing, *Herri Batasuna* (the leader of an electoral alliance called *Euskal Herritarrok* or Basque Citizens). September 11 2001 reinforced the then Spanish government's hard-line stance, and possibly prevented it capitalizing on internal disagreements among extremists and hopefully achieving a split in the *Batasuna* ranks.

In the summer of 2002, the Spanish government achieved cross-party support for legislation allowing the banning of parties that seek to justify or excuse terrorism and in so doing outlawed *Batasuna*. In August of that year, in the wake of *Batasuna*'s failure to condemn a car bomb that killed a six-year-old girl, high-profile Spanish 'superjudge' Baltasar Garzón (see Chapter 3) slapped a three-year ban on political activity on the organization. On the same day, the lower house of the Spanish parliament, the *Cortes*, overwhelmingly approved a request by the government, under a June 2002 law allowing the banning of parties that seek to justify or excuse terrorism, to petition the supreme court to ban *Batasuna* indefinitely, notwithstanding its 1,000 elected representatives at various levels of Basque government.

While opinion polls indicated a majority in favour of the move, many commentators both inside and outside Spain were either outraged at what they considered an offence against democracy, or concerned that the move would prove counterproductive. On the other hand, the ban could be presented as the final tightening of the noose around ETA, which was finding it harder and harder to get away with, and even mount, terrorist attacks as the Spanish and French police arrested more and more of its activists. In March 2003, the Supreme Court unanimously banned *Batasuna* and then banned 241 political groups that its elected representatives had set up in order to get around the ban in time for the local elections in May of that year. *Batasuna*'s response was to issue its supporters with their own ballot papers, and some 10 per cent of voters in the region stuffed these into ballot boxes instead of the official papers. The EU's response, much to the delight of Spain, was to add *Batasuna* to its list of proscribed organizations.

national parties governing the region, much to their irritation. That irritation, not to say outrage, was rendered even greater when moderate national-

Meanwhile, the moderate nationalists, the PNV, in the Basque assembly and government united to block the suspension of *Batasuna* assembly members and to call for what Madrid immediately labelled an illegal referendum on plans for some form of looser 'free association' with Spain, with the Basque country being nominally ruled by King Juan Carlos but conducting its own foreign policy and possessing its own legal system. August 2003 saw the leak of a more definite plan on the part of the PNV for an amendment to the 'statute of Guernica' (the law governing the relations between the Basque region and the Spanish government) so as to create 'a free state associated with Spain'. This would then supposedly be presented for approval by the Spanish parliament and then, in a referendum, by the Basque region's voters. Polls released at the same time suggested that, while many of the latter knew nothing about the plan, they were keen on the idea of a referendum, but that only a fifth were definitely pro-independence, with one-third against and one-third for whom it would depend on the conditions. Madrid immediately reminded the Basque government that there was no chance of any Spanish parliament accepting such an amendment and that the Constitutional Court (see Chapter 3) would be asked to (and in all likelihood would) annul it. Outrage was not the only emotion, however. Some saw Madrid's rejection of these calls for 'shared sovereignty' as hypocritical given that this is precisely the solution it currently favours for the British colony of Gibraltar on the Southern coast of Spain – a territory it continues to lay claim to in spite of the clear preferences of its population to remain British – and at the same time Spain insists it has every right to maintain its own possessions (Ceuta and Melilla) in Morocco.

Spain's concern over Catalunya is not surprising. In autumn 2002, in the wake of moderate Basque nationalists' demands for a referendum on shared sovereignty, Artur Mas, the new leader of Catalunya's nationalist alliance, *Convergència i Unió* called for Catalunya to be recognized as 'a nation' by the rest of Spain. The latter, he claimed, should enter negotiations on a new framework that would see a single administration in Catalunya which, in addition to the control it already has over education, culture, health and policing, would have the final say on public finances and be represented separately from Spain in the EU and at other international bodies. Madrid immediately rejected his ideas, but that was under a right-wing government. The Socialist PSOE government elected in 2004 may prove slightly more accommodating, not least because it is a minority government reliant on the support of some nationalist parties, one of which has already shocked observers by admitting it has conducted talks with Basque hardliners.

The government, like its predecessor, will also have to decide how it handles the fact that further privileges handed to so-called 'fast-track' autonomous communities (the 'nationalities' of Catalunya, the Basque Country and Galicia) will prompt further demands for equal treatment by what were originally considered mere 'regions' (such as the Canary Islands and Andalusia). If these demands are acceded to, then (a) Spain could end up fully federal; and/or (b) the 'nationalities' may, in the event that they enjoy no more autonomy than the 'regions', demand independence. On the other hand, given the numbers of people living in the 'nationalities' who are clearly comfortable with being Spanish as well as Basque or Catalan, and so on (see Núñez, 2001: 22–5), there is no reason to suppose support for independence would be sufficient to secure it even if a vote were allowed.

The UK: another hybrid

The only European country outside the Balkans that rivals Spain in terms of the potential for violence associated with minority nationalism is the UK, and in particular Northern Ireland. It, too, has taken considerable steps towards a quasi-federal solution under which different regions are accorded different rights. We deal with Scotland and Wales below, but begin with Northern Ireland (Map 2.2).

The UK province of Northern Ireland (or Ulster) came into being because, although Ireland achieved independence from Great Britain in the 1920s, the majority Protestant population of the northeasternmost six counties of the island remained committed to the Union. Northern

Map 2.2 The British Isles: the UK and Ireland

By the mid-1980s, it had become clear to many republicans that, despite the huge cost to the UK in terms of loss of life, security and, above all, taxpayers' money, the 'armed struggle' was not going to kick the 'Brits' out of Northern Ireland as long as the majority of its population remained committed to the Union. Meanwhile, the commitment of the Irish Republic and the UK to put an end to violence resulted first in the 'Anglo-Irish Agreement' (1985) and then in the 'Downing Street Declaration' (December 1993), which sought to institutionalize intergovernmental and cross-border cooperation, and created a new *quid pro quo*. London (declaring it had 'no selfish strategic or economic interest in Northern Ireland') now recognized the possibility of a united Ireland, while Dublin acknowledged that this could come about only with the consent of the majority in the North. These confidence-building measures, although they alarmed hard-line unionists, were enough to tempt the what is widely regarded as the political wing of the IRA, Sinn Féin, into talks with the British – talks that eventually led to a ceasefire and to the creation (backed up by a referendum, by the release of paramilitary prisoners and by a promise on the part of the IRA and others that they would 'decommission' their weapons) of an elected Northern Ireland Assembly and an executive on which all parties would serve depending on their share of the vote. The peace process has proved to be a halting one, and the Assembly and the executive had to be suspended several times as a result of Unionist dissatisfaction with the pace and extent of decommissioning.

As for the population of Northern Ireland, opinion polls reflect relief that the ceasefire is holding but little confidence that the present political settlement can bring a permanent solution to 'the troubles'. Depressingly, but not perhaps surprisingly, the sectarian divide between Protestants and Catholics – always a matter not so much of doctrinal nitpicking as cultural identity and social networks – has deepened over the last three or four decades, and been reinforced by the decline of mixed neighbourhoods and intermarriage.

The deepening of, rather than the decrease in, hostility is reflected at the political level, with support for the more hard-line Democratic

Ireland had its own government and parliament but, its largely Protestant 'unionist' population insisted, it was nevertheless very much part of the UK. Only a small minority of Roman Catholics thought the same way, with most looking forward, as 'nationalists', to 'a united Ireland' in the long term. The pursuit of this goal by violent means by the Irish Republican Army (IRA), however, attracted little support until the late 1960s and early 1970s when, following sectarian violence triggered by attempts to address the civil rights grievances of Catholics, the British government initially sent in troops and then imposed direct rule from London. There followed two decades of high-profile terrorist attacks in the province and on the mainland (in part funded by republican sympathizers in the USA), as well as lower-profile (but seemingly relentless) sectarian 'tit-for-tat' killings, not only by the IRA but also by Protestant paramilitary organizations – some allegedly with the collusion of the official security forces.

Unionist Party (DUP) and Sinn Fein growing at the expense of the official Ulster Unionists and Social Democratic and Liberal Party (SDLP), respectively. But it is also reflected at the day-to-day level. Incidents like that at Holy Cross (Box 2.5) are a warning to us not to buy into the comforting notion that, if only a malicious minority of extremists on either side would stop spoiling things for everyone else, ordinary people would be living together in harmony. The malicious minority of populist politicians and paramilitaries on both sides does nothing to help. But nor are they utterly unrepresentative – either of the unionism that understandably fears being 'sold-out' by the British and losing its majority status to the expanding Catholic population, or of the republicanism intent both on defending Catholics from Protestant attacks and bringing about a united Ireland sooner rather than later. Interestingly, 'the troubles' have clearly taken a toll on the UK population outside Northern Ireland, too. If opinion polls are to be believed, the majority blames both sides of the sectarian divide for the problem, and support for a united Ireland, while not quite reaching a majority, is considerably higher than that favouring keeping the province part of the UK indefinitely.

Such views are not replicated, however, when it comes to Scotland, which was granted a parliament in 1997 – partly, some argue, in order to head off calls by nationalists for an end to the 1707 Act of Union. Support for independence in Wales (which was absorbed much earlier and which could never really establish such a clear claim for itself as a self-governing nation) has always been much lower, evidenced by the very narrow majority (on a very low turnout) that, in 1997, approved the setting up of an assembly without the tax-varying powers granted to Scotland's new legislature. Interestingly, there is as yet little evidence (certainly when compared to Belgium and Spain) that these measures represent a 'slippery slope' toward a more thorough-going federalism and possible threat to the British state itself. There have been calls for the devolved legislatures and the executives to be given more powers – particularly in Wales, where politicians at least would like to see themselves on a par with their Scottish counterparts. At the moment, unlike the Scots, the

---

BOX 2.5
Street-level hatred in Northern Ireland

In September 2001, television viewers all round the world were treated to pictures of snarling, jeering and jostling Protestant residents attempting to prevent Catholic parents walking their children by the shortest available route to Holy Cross School in the Ardoyne area of North Belfast. There, in microcosm, was the bitterness between two communities living side by side but who have grown up with violence since they, too, were school children. The Catholic community, increasingly numerous, is now more assertive about its rights to go about its normal business in areas that were once, even in broad daylight, no-go areas. At the same time, it is determined not to allow Unionists to parade their supposed superiority by marching down streets in Nationalist areas. Unionists see this as a double standard. They also resent the help given to the Catholic community by a police force they once regarded as their own. And they fear, in the long term, being 'out-bred' and becoming a minority themselves – a position that could lead to them being outvoted in a future referendum on the constitutional status of 'their' province. The walls built in the past to separate the communities can do nothing to halt the demographic trends, nor the flight of Protestants out of neighbourhoods that even a decade or so ago could still be regarded as 'their territory'. But, some argue, burning churches and intimidating school children are unlikely to help the loyalist cause much either.

Welsh have no executive power over the legal system or penal policy and policing, no primary legislative powers at all (Scotland has them for most bread-and-butter matters including health, education, social services and transport) and no right to vary taxation.

The parties in both Scotland and Wales have also been keen to distance themselves from their counterparts at Westminster. But these developments have arguably been overshadowed – at least in the media – by concerns about public apathy and the excessive costs of constructing the new parliament and government buildings. Moreover, if the purpose of devolution from the Labour Party's point of view was to stop nationalist parties like the Scottish Nationalists (SNP) and the Welsh *Plaid Cymru* from 'stealing' votes from it at Westminster elections, so far it seems to have worked: while both parties have done much better in elections to their devolved legislatures, their support at general elections has indeed declined. Meanwhile, fears that devolving power to Scotland and Wales would spark a serious 'English backlash' – perhaps in protest at Scottish (and Welsh) MPs at Westminster voting on legislation (such as variable tuition fees for university students) that did not actually affect their own constituents – do not seem (yet, anyway) to have been born out in practice.

The prospect, then, of a fully federal Britain with separate parliaments for each of the nations currently seems a long way off – especially given the absence in the UK of a written constitution (and pressure for one) that could guarantee the existence and rights of those parliaments. On the other hand, as in Spain, it would be equally far-fetched to think that, merely because the national parliament (i.e. Westminster) is still technically sovereign and therefore able to take back any rights and powers it has granted to sub-national legislatures and executives, it would be politically feasible for it to do so except (as with the deadlocked Northern Ireland Assembly) from those devolved bodies that are so divided amongst themselves that they cannot function. Given this, it is not surprising that some constitutional experts argue that the UK is now a quasi-federal system (albeit one operating Spanish-style 'differentiated' or 'asymmetrical' federalism) and may eventually 'go all the way'.

France: no longer quite so indivisible

In view of this risk, those who wish to preserve the nation state intact sometimes look to France – supposedly *une et indivisible* (one and indivisible) – for inspiration. Despite movements for more independence for historic nations such as *Bretagne* (Brittany) in the west, *Occitanie* (modern-day Languedoc) in the south and *Pays-Basque* (Basque Country) in the south west (see Map 2.3), France continues to protest its indivisibility – even to the extent of preserving the myth that its overseas

possessions (in, for example, the South Pacific) are simply extensions of mainland France. Closer to home, however, France has recently had to be rather more flexible. Nationalists on the Mediterranean island of Corsica have not resorted to large-scale violence to anything like the same extent as their Irish and Basque counterparts, which possibly accounts for the relatively low profile of their struggle. The latter may also have something to do with the fact that in Corsica the relationship between nationalist terrorism and organized crime, by no means unimportant in Northern Ireland and Euskadi, is so close: violence there tends to be more surgical than spectacular, with hundreds of small incendiary explosions a year damaging (mainlanders') property and the line between mafia-style and apparently political assassinations very blurred. Due to this, perhaps, and to the awareness that the island depends economically on the mainland for tourism and aid, there would appear to be rather less support for full-blown independence among Corsica's quarter of a million inhabitants than in, say, the Basque country. Certainly, peaceful nationalist parties do less well in elections than their Basque counterparts.

Yet, following the murder of its prefect (local governor) in 1999, the French government made a bold move to break with its self-image as 'one and

Map 2.3 France

indivisible', putting together a staged autonomy package known as the 'Matignon Accords'. The island would be granted greater self-government and allowed to place greater emphasis on the teaching and use of its own language in return for progress on law and order that, if secured, would see a constitutional revision allowing for PR elections and an assembly and executive with (albeit limited) law-making powers. Predictably, critics on the nationalist side declared that the Accords had not gone far enough, while critics in Paris declared it could be a Pandora's box that would lead not just to independence for Corsica, but encourage claims for more autonomy by mainland regions. Nevertheless, the plan was adopted by the Corsican Assembly in July 2000 and given an initial green light by the National Assembly in May 2001. Notwithstanding a truce declared by the Corsican National Liberation Front, the murderous feuding between separatist organizations continued. Opinion polls also seemed to suggest that far from dampening enthusiasm for independence, the Matignon Accords may well have encouraged it and, as in the case of British attitudes to Northern Ireland, the number of 'mainlanders' happy to see the back of the island is also rising.

With the election of a centre-right government in 2002, hopes of action on the Accords looked as if they had been dashed, as the new government's rhetoric suggested a reassertion of the Gaullist unitary state tradition. But while the new prime minister withdrew his predecessor's promises of a tailor-made autonomy package for Corsica, he sweetened the pill considerably, first, by making it clear that Corsica could be at the cutting edge of plans for limited decentralization throughout France and, secondly, by not reneging on the previous government's promise of almost €2 billion in development aid over the next decade-and-a-half. By July 2003, the government's devolution plans – which centred on a merger of the island's multiple elected bodies into one in return for enhanced powers – were ready to put to the islands voters in a referendum. Some of the largest separatist parties, such as *Corsica Nazione*, were prepared to go along with the plan as the first step; others rejected it as inadequate. Frustratingly for the French government, and those prepared to give it a chance, the plan was narrowly rejected. Quite where the island goes from there is unclear, especially since the situation was inflamed in April 2004 by the arrest, on racketeering charges, of Jean-Guy Talamoni, leader of the pro-independence party *Unione Nazionale*.

The European Union and the end of sovereignty?

An argument put forward by those campaigning for the independence of nations with aspirations to statehood in twenty-first-century Europe is that it is rendered more feasible than ever by the existence of the EU. It may have been true, once upon a time, runs the argument, that Scotland or Catalunya (to take two of the most obvious examples) would have found it difficult to survive, given the costs of mounting, for instance, an independent foreign and trade policy. Now, the argument continues, so many of these expensive tasks can, in effect, be 'contracted out' to the EU. To some observers, the latter already promotes a degree of autonomy, via a 'Committee of the Regions' (COR), which advises (though it cannot compel) other EU institutions on policy and legislation that affect local or regional government. More importantly, the EU operates an 'internal market' which supposedly guarantees that even the smallest state (Malta, Cyprus or Luxembourg, for example) can survive economically.

The irony is, of course, that while some who aspire to independence look to the EU to underwrite it, many of the latter's existing member states worry about the EU undermining the independence they currently enjoy! This final part of the chapter explores the extent to which the EU in general and some of its institutions, policies and processes in particular, may be impacting negatively on the sovereignty of its member states.

Origins and enlargement

The forerunner of the EU, the European Economic Community (EEC), began life in 1958 after the signing of the Treaty of Rome by six Western European nations: France, Germany, Italy, the Netherlands, Belgium and Luxembourg.

All had been co-operating with each other since the USA had encouraged them in the late 1940s to work together to make the most of the aid granted to the continent by what became known as the Marshall Plan. The 1950s had seen that co-operation reinforced by the formation in 1952 of the European Coal and Steel Community (ECSC) – a project which aimed, by locking together those industries across the different member countries, not only to boost their economic fortunes but to tie them together in the hope that this might prevent yet another European war. Success in the economic and industrial realm contrasted with the failure of an ambitious attempt to bring together former enemies in defence cooperation. Economic co-operation was also limited somewhat by the reluctance of the UK to become involved on the basis of its perception that its interests were global rather than regional and that both its sovereignty and freedom of action might be put at risk. Joining the EEC committed 'the six' to very practical measures such as a customs union with a 'common external tariff' (CET), and a 'common agricultural policy' (the now infamously expensive CAP) to ensure both plentiful food and a reasonable standard of living for farmers by providing them with a mixture of subsidies, protective tariffs and guaranteed prices.

The Treaty of Rome, building on ECSC structures, also set up the *European Commission* and the *European Court of Justice (ECJ)* (see Box 2.7). Both were supranational rather than intergovernmental institutions (see Box 2.6) and, as such, were to prove instrumental in the drive to what the Treaty called 'ever closer union.' This notwithstanding, the UK soon changed its mind about joining, realizing quite quickly that it would suffer economically if it stayed out. After the failure of two applications in the 1960s, it became a member in 1973, along with Denmark and Ireland. Although global recession in the early 1970s took some of the shine off the initially impressive economic performance of the EEC, further expansion followed, most recently with the admission of eight former Communist countries (see Figure 2.1). The political security reasons behind expansion are dealt with in more detail in Chapter 11. The economic arguments are also important. A bigger union provides a bigger and, over time, a wealthier market for European

BOX 2.6
Balancing the intergovernmental and the supranational

Most international organizations are *intergovernmental*: those states that belong to them co-operate in search of better outcomes but reserve the right and maintain the power to block or at least ignore decisions that they feel are contrary to their interests. Such intergovernmentalism has always been one side of the story of European integration. But there is another, *supranational* side. This is the agreement on the part of member states, on some matters at least, to forgo the right to a veto and be bound by decisions with which they do not always agree. Arguably, the history of the EU is the history of the tension between *intergovernmentalism* and *supranationalism*. It is also a tension embodied in (if not always effectively tamed by) its institutional structure. No EU body is completely and utterly intergovernmental or supranational in both composition and role, but (as Boxes 2.7 and 2.9 suggest) all display a bias one way or the other.

6
(1957: Belgium, France, Germany, Italy, Luxembourg, the Netherlands)

+3
(1973: Denmark, Ireland, UK)

+1
(1981: Greece)

+2
(1986: Portugal, Spain)

+0
(1990: East Germany absorbed by reunified Germany)

+3
(1995: Austria, Finland, Sweden)

+10
(2004: Czech Rep., Cyprus, Estonia, Hungary, Latvia, Lithuania, Malta, Poland, Slovakia, Slovenia)

= 25

Figure 2.1 From the EEC Six to the EU-25: enlargement, 1957–2004

BOX 2.7
The EU's supranational institutions

These bodies may be appointed by governments or elected by their voters, but those who are chosen go on to work for the EU, not for member states. They include:

European Commission
Based in Brussels, with a staff of some 20,000 people, the Commission is headed by a President and Commissioners appointed by member states. It is made up of over twenty Directorate Generals (DGs) which report to those commissioners and are charged with preparing and administering policy in a particular area – agriculture, environment, internal market, regional policy, etc. Most EU law is based on proposals from the Commission, which are then discussed and adopted (or not!) by the Council of Ministers (see Box 2.9), and increasingly the European Parliament (EP), too (see below). The Commission is also heavily involved in implementing laws and ensuring that the laws (and the Treaties more generally) are obeyed in and by member states. This task sometimes involves the Commission in initiating legal proceedings against states, and sometimes commercial concerns as well, for non-compliance. As a result – and as a result of its role in ensuring that the European market is truly competitive and therefore free of subsidies and monopolies – the Commission is often in the news and often accused (as meddling 'Brussels Bureaucrats') of unwarranted interference. Less often commented on, but just as important, is the Commission's role as the sole trade negotiator for all EU states at the World Trade Organization (WTO).

European Court of Justice
Based in Luxembourg, the ECJ is staffed by judges appointed by member states. It hears cases involving disputes between member states and the Commission and also cases referred to it by domestic courts for clarification of European law which may or may not be relevant to cases those courts are trying. Early on its life, the ECJ successfully persuaded member states (or at least their courts) that European law was supreme and could enjoy 'direct effect' within them. This led to a body of case law that has had important ramifications within member states, most obviously with regard to the free movement of goods, services and labour, and sex discrimination. As with the Commission, the ECJ is often in the news because it says things that companies and governments do not want to hear. Even worse, because there is no higher court, it can legally oblige them to go along with its rulings. Not surprisingly, then, the ECJ is seen as one of the EU's most supranational institutions. Its critics argue that, because it has to adjudicate disputes in the light of treaties designed to promote 'ever closer union', it has a built-in bias toward integration. They also complain that this bias, along with the fact that it often has to operate

---

goods and services; it should also encourage the kind of mergers and acquizitions (MaAs), and economies of scale, that will allow European business to compete more effectively across the globe.

The EU also provides a limited degree of redistribution from Europe's richer to Europe's poorer states. It gets approximately 15 per cent of its revenue from tariffs and duties, 35 per cent from a share of the value added tax (VAT) receipts of member states, and 50 per cent of it from member states who contribute a fixed proportion of their GNP. The EU then spends this money (equivalent to only around 1.1 per cent of the GNP of all its members or less than 5 per cent of all their govern-

ment spending put together) on, among other things agricultural support (which accounts for around 45 per cent of spending) and structural funding (help for poorer regions, which takes up about 35 per cent of spending). This spending, particularly on poorer regions (see Chapters 1 and 3), as well as spending on countries that are hoping to join the EU, effectively takes money from the richer parts of the Union and gives it to their poorer counterparts. This is clearly not simply an act of generosity: in the longer term, making the backward regions better off should provide those that currently help fund them with more lucrative markets for their goods and services.

continued

where no court has gone before, leads it not so much to interpret as actually make law. As we see in Chapter 3, however, this accusation is increasingly levelled against national courts as well.

European Parliament
Since it was first directly elected in 1979, the EP (which meets in both Brussels and Strasbourg, France) has been transformed from a body that was merely consulted to one that – at least in certain circumstances – really counts. Not only is its approval required for the EU's budget and accounts to be accepted, under the 'co-decision' procedure it now has equal say with the Council of Ministers on most legislation. The Commission has to pass an investiture vote in the EP and this is no longer a forgone conclusion. In September 2004, objections to a Conservative Catholic nominee forced him to stand down and delayed matters considerably. The EP also has the power to dismiss the entire Commission – a possibility that prompted that body's resignation in 1999 after corruption allegations. Individual commissioners, the European Central Bank (ECB) and the European Council have to appear before and report to the EP, although practically there is little it can do if it dislikes what it hears. The EP tends to be seen as a supranational institution for three reasons: most of those who work in it are broadly in favour of European integration; they do not continually seek to uphold the views of the states from which they come; and they have an institutional interest in seeking to reduce (or at least match) the power of the body that most obviously represents those member states, the Council of Ministers. Members of the European Parliament (MEPs) are elected country-by-country (see Chapter 6), but they sit (and for the most part vote) in party groups based on ideology not nationality: the Party of European Socialists, for instance, contains members from all Europe's socialist and social democratic parties; the European People's Party is its centre-right equivalent (see Chapter 4). The problem all MEPs face, however, is that, despite their getting more and more power, those whom they claim to represent – the citizens of Europe – are less and less interested in them: as we show in Chapter 6, turnout at European elections is at spectacularly low levels and has declined over time.

European Central Bank
The ECB, based in Germany's financial capital, Frankfurt, is possibly the EU's most supranational institution. It sets an interest rate which applies across the member states that operate with the Euro, irrespective of whether it is as high or as low as they or their populations would like or need it to be. But the ECB is, to all intents and purposes, beyond the reach of individual member states: they may appoint its president and executive board and the national central bank presidents that make up its governing council, but that council is not practically accountable to them or to any other European institution.

Increasing integration and institutional reform

After a decade of relative inactivity after the recession of the mid-1970s, European integration got going again in the 1980s. The case law of the ECJ, the activism of the Commission and fears that, without an end to intra-European trade barriers and the encouragement of bigger companies, Europe would lose out to Japan and America, all combined to produce the Single European Act (SEA) of 1986. The SEA was an intergovernmental treaty which committed what became known as the European Community (EC), and then (after 1991) the EU, to further legislation enshrining the 'four freedoms' of goods, services, capital and labour.

The European project aimed from the outset to give its member states access to a common market. Member states also become part of a customs union, charging a CET on goods coming from outside the EU, although these are often moderated or even removed as a result of trade deals, most obviously with those countries belonging to European Free Trade Association (or EFTA); namely, Iceland, Liechtenstein, Norway and Switzerland (see http://www.efta.int/), which are unwilling to join the EU on the grounds that the political integration entailed by full economic integration is too much for them. Not joining may not mean much of a loss in trade terms, but it does mean that they are unable to take advantage of any of the financial support on offer from the EU for things such as farming or the development of poorer regions. On the other hand, EFTA members, as relatively well-off countries, would in all likelihood join the ranks of the EU's net contributors (see Figure 2.2), so it is understandable if such incentives pale beside the costs of membership. These are not only financial but logistical, legal and political. For instance, as the 2004 accession states found, any state wishing to join has to bring its administrative and legal system into what is known as the *acquis communautaire* – the corpus of legislation in force in the EU that is binding on member states, either directly or indirectly, via national laws that must be passed to give it expression. Largely because of the renewed push by the EU to make the common (or single) market a reality, the number of laws making up the *acquis* doubled between 1983 and 1998 (see Maurer, Mittag and Wessels, 2003: 57).

Just as importantly, the SEA introduced procedural changes, such as the expansion of Qualified Majority Voting or QMV (see Box 2.8) in one of the EU's most important and most intergovern-

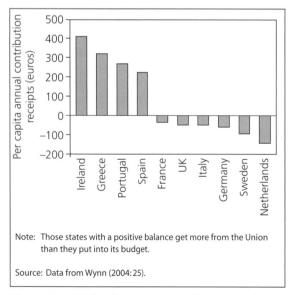

Note: Those states with a positive balance get more from the Union than they put into its budget.

Source: Data from Wynn (2004: 25).

Figure 2.2 EU budget: net contributors and recipients per capita, 2002

BOX 2.8
QMV

If every piece of European legislation had to be passed unanimously, the Council of Ministers – effectively the EU's most powerful 'legislative chamber' even though it is not a parliament (see Box 2.9) – would be continually prone to deadlock or blackmail as member states exercised or threatened to exercise their veto. On the other hand, simple majority voting – where each member state was accorded one vote – would risk the possibility of legislation being passed against the wishes of governments representing the bulk of Europe's population. To guard against this possibility at the same time as lessening the chances of deadlock, the SEA established the system known as Qualified Majority Voting (QMV). A great deal of legislation is still passed by consensus, not least because of the threat of losing a majority vote. Indeed, the council ends up voting on only around 10 per cent of legislation and even then dissent is often limited to one or two countries (see Mattila, 2004). QMV was adjusted (largely at the expense of medium-sized countries) by the Nice Treaty of 2000 in order to reassure larger member states that they would not be overwhelmed by the increased number of small states after the accession of 2004.

The system relies on each member state being allocated, out of a total of 321, a certain number of votes roughly (very roughly say some larger states!) according to their population as follows: Germany, the UK, France and Italy (29); Spain and Poland (27); the Netherlands (13); Greece, the Czech Republic, Belgium, Hungary and Portugal (12); Sweden and Austria (10); Slovakia, Denmark, Finland, Ireland and Lithuania (7); Latvia, Slovenia, Estonia, Cyprus and Luxembourg (4); and Malta (3). In order to pass, a piece of legislation needs to obtain a so-called 'triple majority': at least 232 (or just under three-quarters) of the 321 votes on offer; a majority of the member states; and support from member states accounting for at least 62 per cent of the EU's population. This complexity and continuing worries among the bigger states that, should one or two of them defect to the cause of smaller states, they can be overcome by the latter, has led to calls for reform. No reform can change the underlying truth, however: on those issues where it applies (and some are still beyond its reach), QMV means that a state, and arguably therefore its sovereignty, can be overridden.

BOX 2.9
The EU's intergovernmental institutions

These bodies, in which member states are directly represented by national governments and civil servants, exist to ensure that the interests of those states play an important role in the decisions and direction of the EU.

Council of Ministers
Rather confusingly, the Council of the European Union (to give it its formal title) is in fact made up of a number of different councils, each dealing with a particular portfolio and each of which is attended by the relevant minister from each member state: hence transport, for instance, is dealt with by the transport ministers who meet regularly (around five times per year) in Brussels with their counterparts. Some sets of ministers meet much more regularly than others: for instance, those in charge of foreign affairs (the so-called 'General Affairs' council and economics and finance (dubbed ECOFIN) meet thirteen or fourteen times a year, whereas those in charge of education and health (subjects the EU is largely kept out of) meet only two or three times. At council meetings, ministers debate and amend, approve or reject proposed legislation from the European Commission, although often this is done on the nod after agreement has already been reached in COREPER, the committee made up of each member state's permanent representative (a senior diplomat each appoints) to the EU. The Council is, then, the EU's legislature. Although this is increasingly a role it shares with the EP under the co-decision procedure, the Council remains more powerful because it grants final approval on legislation under other procedures in which Parliament's wishes can be overridden. It also plays an influential role in initiating proposals, even in those areas for which the Commission supposedly has the sole right of initiation. The Council is often thought of as a bastion of intergovernmentalism, although recent developments in voting procedures (see Box 2.8) mean that member states are not always in a position to block unwelcome developments.

European Council
Although it got going only in the early 1970s, this originally informal meeting of heads of government and foreign ministers from the member states can lay claim to being the most powerful body in the EU. It is, for instance, free from any of the quasi-constitutional checks and balances that, because they were set up by treaties, constrain the other institutions. Over the years, the European Council has developed into an institution that sets the overall political direction of the EU, determining, for instance, that there should be monetary union and enlargement, or deciding that, for example, migration and the promotion of deregulation and economic dynamism should be key goals. Its summit meetings (which occur at least twice a year) also deal (though not always satisfactorily) with those issues that have proved too difficult to solve within the EU's formal structure, such as CAP and constitutional reform. The power of the European Council symbolizes to some the fact that, ultimately, the member states control the EU rather than the other way around.

---

mental institutions, the *Council of Ministers* (see Box 2.9). The ostensible aim of such changes may have been to ensure the swifter passage of that legislation. But they also had the effect of undermining the ability of individual member states (at least on anything that could be said to affect the internal market) to veto proposals that they objected to. According to 'Eurosceptics' – the nickname given to those who want to reverse or slow the pace of integration – this seriously, even fatally, undermined or at the very least compromised state sovereignty.

Some member states, notably (but not exclusively) the UK and Denmark, were sensitive to what they saw as a diminution of their sovereignty. Their concerns fed into the agreement which turned the EC into the EU – the Maastricht Treaty (or 'Treaty on European Union', [TEU]) signed in 1991. Maastricht narrowed the range of topics on which a state could veto a proposal from the Commission. But it also attempted to 'ring fence' those issues that most directly touched on sovereignty. It did this by assigning them to the second and third of what was to become known as the 'three-pillar' structure. Broadly speaking, the first 'European Community' or EC pillar would include economics and trade and be subject to 'community procedures' that in the main ruled out a veto; the second ('Common Foreign and Security Policy', CFSP) and third pillars ('Justice and Home Affairs', JHA) would remain intergovernmental rather than supranational. This would allow any single member state to prevent progress on an issue if it objected. Matters deemed to be part of the second and third pillars would also be excluded from the jurisdiction of the ECJ. This lessened the chance that member states would see their preferences and their domestic legislation, on those matters at least, overridden by European law.

These concessions to intergovernmentalism were, however, somewhat balanced by Maastricht giving the supposedly more supranational *European Parliament* (see Box 2.7) much more say in law-making. Previously it had been very much the inferior of the Council of Ministers, in which each member state was represented equally and that alone could pass or block new laws proposed by the Commission. Henceforth (at least in some areas), the EP would have the right of 'co-decision' with the Council of Ministers. The EP was further empowered a few years later when, in 1997, the Amsterdam Treaty (much of which was an attempt to codify and simplify previous treaties) expanded the range of issues to which the co-decision procedure would apply.

Integration via economics: EMU

Probably the most important move made at Maastricht in 1991, however, was the establishment of a timetable for 'European Monetary Union' (EMU) – a process which, in 2002, saw the twelve of the then fifteen members give up their separate currencies in favour of a single currency, the euro (€). The economic arguments for the move were not necessarily clear cut (see Chapter 9), but the political rationale and ramifications are clearer (see Jones, 2002). First and foremost, Germany gave up its currency, the *Deutsche Mark* – at the time, by far the strongest and most stable currency on the continent – for the cause of integration. This acted to calm concerns (especially in France) that it would demand a role in European and global affairs to

match its increased size after unification in 1990 (see Chapter 11).

Second, EU member states had agreed to not just a symbolic but very substantial loss of political control over their economies – and arguably their destinies. True, control of interest rates had often been a matter for central banks in each member state. But governments had ways of exerting leverage over their decisions. The *European Central Bank* or ECB (see Box 2.7), however, is presumed to be immune to political pressure – certainly from individual member states, for whom the Europewide interest rate may be so low it encourages inflation or so high that it chokes off growth and (by making the Euro too strong against, say, the US dollar) renders exports uncompetitive. Individual governments can (and, as we see in Chapter 9, do) still employ fiscal measures (tax and spending) to help control their economies. But some observers argue that such measures need to be co-ordinated with other member states, creating a pressure for the Europeanization of fiscal policy (tax and spending) as well as monetary (mainly interest rate) policy.

Given all this, it is hardly surprising that those states traditionally less enthusiastic about further integration have chosen not to participate. Denmark, Sweden and the UK have strong traditions of parliamentary sovereignty and (in the case of the latter) governments that do not wish to surrender any more control of their economies than some argue they already have done (see Chapter 9). Their self-imposed exclusion, however, poses a problem for the EU as a whole. Most obviously, they are in a position to veto progress toward the kind of co-ordinated fiscal policy (beginning with, for example, the harmonization of taxation regimes) that some argue is necessary. Moreover, the fact that they have been allowed to 'opt out' and have not suffered economically as a result sends a message to the EU's newest member states that they can – and perhaps would be well advised to – do the same. Clearly some of the latter will want to, and be allowed to, adopt the single currency. But if some do not, it may prevent the Euro becoming quite as much of a force for political and economic integration as many of its advocates – more or less openly – expected it to be.

Integration by law

Europe's newest member states already had first-hand knowledge of the extent to which the EU could override domestic practices and preferences even before they joined. In order to do so, after all, each had to demonstrate that they were capable of adopting the so-called *acquis communautaire* – EU **directives**, **regulations** and the **case law** of the ECJ. Since the 1960s, the Court's decisions not only have 'direct effect' (i.e. they do not need to be embodied in domestic legislation before being enforced by government and the courts) but are also 'supreme'. This means that in the event of a conflict between the existing law of a member state and European law, the latter will be upheld. Moreover, domestic courts, even at a low level, can go direct to the ECJ for a ruling, effectively bypassing the normal national hierarchy of courts and courts of appeal. Even more so than in the economic sphere, then, it is obvious that the sovereignty of member states, inasmuch as it involves the right to make the ultimate decision (via parliament) on its own laws, has been compromized.

Definition

The EU's **acquis communautaire** is the accumulated laws currently in force that must apply in every member state if the EU is to function properly as a legally based and regulated community. Laws include **directives** (rules that must be turned into, or 'transposed' into, domestic law in national parliaments), **regulations** (which are automatically binding on all member states without any parliamentary discretion on their part as to their precise form) and the **case law** of the ECJ.

An EU constitution?

In June 2004, the member states, following tough negotiations on a draft produced by a Convention including national delegations and EU institutions, finally agreed on the text of a *Treaty Establishing a Constitution for Europe*. Their ostensible aim was to provide a single document to replace the various treaties (Rome, the SEA, Maastricht, Amsterdam, Nice, etc.) that over time have laid down how the EU is to be governed. The proposed constitution gets rid of the 'three-pillar' structure set up by the Maastricht Treaty in 1992, although there are still special procedures for foreign, defence and security policy. It also reduces the number of ways in which EU law can be made, tries to streamline the institutions (by, for instance, reducing the number of European Commissioners), and creates an EU minister of foreign affairs, chosen by the member states, who will sit in both the Commission and the Council of Ministers. In addition, it augments the role of the EP by extending the 'co-decision' procedure (renamed the 'ordinary legislative' procedure) to around 95 per cent of all legislation, as well as attempting to improve decision-making in the Council of Ministers by extending QMV (see Box 2.8) and changing its rules slightly. Out goes the system of weighted votes: ordinarily, a qualified majority is defined as at least fifteen of the member states representing at least 65 per cent of the EU's population, with any 'blocking minority' requiring at least four member states; in more sensitive areas (such as justice and home affairs, economic and monetary policy or the withdrawal and suspension of a member state) a qualified majority will be 72 per cent of the Council's members. Member states who are outvoted, however, have the option of applying an 'emergency brake' and trying to persuade the European Council that their vital national interests must be protected. Other notable innovations include the following:

- Explicit provision for 'enhanced co-operation' (especially on foreign and defence policy, and on matters affecting those countries using the Euro) by member states who wish to push integration further than others (who will nevertheless have to consent to them doing so)
- A full-time 'President of the European Council' chosen (by QMV) by the European Council to oversee the agenda and work of the EU, thereby providing more continuity than the current 'rotating presidency' held by each member state for six months
- The opening up of the Council of Ministers' legislative deliberations to the public

▸ A procedure whereby a petition signed by 1 million European citizens from a significant number of member states can invite (though not, apparently, oblige) the Commission to submit proposals to the Council and the EP

▸ A procedure whereby one-third of national parliaments can demand a review of a Commission proposal

▸ The granting to the EU of a 'legal personality' allowing it to negotiate international treaties and agreements on behalf of its members, providing of course they are happy for it to do so

▸ An acknowledgement that leaving the EU is possible and an outline procedure should a member state wish to exercise this 'exit option'

▸ The formal adoption of a 'Charter of Fundamental Rights', including the right to life and liberty, and the right to take industrial action.

Although the Constitutional Treaty makes it clear that the power of the EU is derived from member states and that it can act only where they cannot achieve an objective acting on their own, the document is, to some, yet another worrying extension of EU competence. Of particular concern is the extension of QMV to asylum and immigration and also the Charter of Fundamental Rights. Versions of the latter, however, are included in a number of countries' national constitutions, not least in postcommunist Europe, and more often than not are regarded as goals to aim for rather than as legally actionable and enforceable guarantees (see Procházka, 2002 and von Beyme, 2003). To others, however, it fails to go far enough, representing some kind of victory for the UK and other less 'integrationist' member states who were determined not to let the exercise do much more than codify and tidy up existing procedures. This debate will presumably be replayed as the member states go on to try to ratify the treaty – something that is by no means guaranteed, especially now that at least eight states (including Denmark, France, Ireland, Luxembourg, the Netherlands, Spain, Portugal, and the UK) look likely to hold referendums (see Chapter 6) on the issue.

The end of the nation state?

Given what we have learned about both minority nationalism and the EU, it is easy to present a picture of Europe's historical nation states menaced, on the one hand, by sub-national pressures that may one day lead to the creation of new nation states and, on the other, by European integration. Indeed, as we have already noted, there is a sense in which the two threats to state integrity and sovereignty are complementary. National minorities take control of cultural and educational affairs and service delivery, while the EU handles (among other matters) monetary policy, agriculture, trade and the environment, supposedly leaving little for the state to do. But this is too simplistic.

For one thing, by no means the majority of European states find themselves under pressure from national minorities, and are unlikely to institute changes that undermine their status as relatively homogeneous unitary states. Scandinavia is an obvious example, notwithstanding the autonomy granted by Nordic countries to Greenland and the Faroe Islands (Denmark), the Swedish-speaking Aaland Islands (Finland) and the Sami (Laplanders). Moreover, the collapse of communism has brought back into the European fold a handful of countries that, at first glance, are both unitary and linguistically homogeneous and unlikely to want to compromise a sovereignty that was so long suppressed by Soviet domination. Any list would include on it Poland and the Czech Republic, as well as the much smaller Slovenia.

That said, however, the new members of the EU also include countries, such as Slovakia and Hungary and the Baltic states that contain minorities who (like Northern Ireland's nationalist community, although less violently) may feel more loyalty to neighbouring states. Whether, though, they will allow them more autonomy is another matter. Instead of following the UK, Spain and Belgium down the (quasi-) federal or devolutionary route, they seem more likely to follow France's example and cling to the constitutional ideal of being 'one and indivisible' in spite of the historic claims of certain regions for more autonomy. But they need to be careful. For one thing, as we have seen, France is not quite as inflexible as it presents itself. For another, France can get away with more because it is a country with clout. New EU members, and particularly those still wanting to join, like Romania and Bulgaria (with Turkish minorities), may well be pressured to make more accommodation than they might like. On the other hand, pressure on such matters can prove counterproductive: Greek Cypriots clearly felt 'bounced' by the EU and the UN into accepting a federal solution to end the partition of their island and bring the Turkish-occupied north into Europe with them, and promptly voted 'no' to the plan in a referendum in April 2004.

We should also remember that while the EU boasts many of the outward symbols we traditionally associate with a state – a flag, a passport, an anthem and perhaps even a constitution – it lacks a good deal of the substance. The EU's parliament is not sovereign, executive authority is blurred and it fails to command the primary loyalty of those it likes to call citizens. On the other hand, anyone supporting European integration can point, on the evidence of this chapter, to the fact that many member states, too, fail to inspire loyalty or affection among all those living within their borders. And, as we shall see in Chapters 3 and 4, few European states can boast a genuinely independent or powerful parliament – or, for that matter, an executive whose competence is clear, unencumbered and unchallenged.

Yet, even if there is no clear 'pincer movement' against Europe's historical nation states, they are no longer quite what they were. Only some of them are under threat from below; but all of them have ceded the final say in some areas of policy and law to the European Union. Indeed, such is the reach of the EU into the economics, policy-making (see Chapter 3) and particularly the legal life of its member states, that it cannot be said merely to present a threat from above. Instead, it is embedded within the nation state. Whether, however, this represents an end to sovereignty is a moot point. Practically, European states that join the EU no longer have complete control or freedom of action. On the other hand, there is as yet nothing – beyond the enormous costs that would presumably be involved – to stop them, if they so wished, from leaving and reasserting whatever control and freedom they feel they have lost.

But while in many European countries the nation state as an institution is under threat, if not siege, it continues to exercise considerable cultural sway over many, perhaps even the majority, of Europeans. As we have seen in Chapter 1, people still see themselves as Czech or German or Dutch or Swedish or even (though in increasingly lesser numbers) Spanish or British or Belgian. This sense of identity is reinforced daily, not just by politics but, perhaps more powerfully by the 'banal nationalism' (Billig, 1995) of linguistic and spatial familiarity and popular culture, be it sport or prime-time television (see Chapter 7). The challenge for Europe is to reconcile its population's persistent attachment to nation states with its movement toward a 'multilevel governance' that, institutionally anyway, can override and undermine those states. Failure to do so risks delegitimizing democratic politics as a whole. Success might help pave the way for the co-existence of national and European identity that some experts on nationalism argue is by no means impossible (see Smith, 1992).

Learning resources

On the nation state and minority nationalism, the first port of call would be Keating (2001) and Guibernau (1999). Also useful are Ishiyama and Breuning (1998), Jenkins and Sofos (1996) and MacIver (1999). See also Panayi (2000) and, if you want to know more about Europe's minority languages, try the website http://www.ethnologue.com/country_index.asp?place=Europe. Work on the EU is voluminous to say the least. A justifiably popular introductory text is McCormick (3rd edn. 2005) and good ways into more complex and contemporary debates are Cowles and Dinan (2004) and Rosamond (2000). An excellent advanced, but very approachably presented, guide is Hix (2004). Another good way into the EU is via its own website http://europa.eu.int, and for both news and debate on the EU, it is difficult to do better than the portal http://www.euractiv.com. Finally, O'Leary (2003) and Schmitter (1996) provide typically stimulating essays on some of the issues raised here.

EXECUTIVE SUMMARY

- Several European states – big and small, ancient and modern, though mainly western rather than eastern – are under pressure from minority nationalism, some of which is expressed violently.

- Many have responded by granting more autonomy to regions, sometimes to the extent that they seem to be turning themselves from unitary into federal states. It is unclear whether this devolution strategy will prove sufficient to prevent further undermining of the states employing it.

- Most European states in any case have compromised (though not ultimately abandoned) their sovereignty, by joining (or even just by trading heavily) with the EU, which has expanded to cover nearly all European states outside of the former Yugoslavia and the former Soviet Union (FSU).

- The EU is influential because states, in return for the security and material benefits they derive from membership, have gradually granted it legal powers over them, extended the competence of its institutions and integrated their economies into a single market with (for some of them) a single currency.

- There exists a perennial tension in the EU's organization and processes between supranationalism (power and institutions that can encourage or compel member states to recognize a common interest) and intergovernmentalism (the continued capacity of member states to protect and promote national interests in the policy and governance of the Union).

- The EU's proposed new constitution – like the treaties that have gone before it – is both a 'tidying up exercise' and a potential opportunity for deeper integration.

- The nation state will be around for some time, but not necessarily in its traditional form.

Chapter **3**

From government to governance: running the state, making policy and policing the constitution

Pushing things out to the periphery: decentralization

'More control over less': central government reform

Policy-making: sectors and styles

The booming third branch of government: the judicialization of politics

In Chapter 2, we looked at challenges to the supposed integrity and the impermeability of the traditional European nation state. We discovered that the latter was under pressure from both within and without. Not every country was affected by minority nationalism, but all had conceded important powers to the EU, not least in the economic and legal domains. Those worried by such developments can perhaps derive some comfort, however, from the fact that, notwithstanding such concessions, each country still retains its unique constitution. This formal legal framework sets out the rules of the game for politicians, citizens and the institutions by which they govern and are governed. The fundamental feature of most of these is a so-called **separation of powers** between the legislature, the executive and the judiciary.

This chapter focuses primarily on the bureaucratic side and the policy-making of the second of the 'three branches', the executive. This is the body that traditionally 'runs the country' or 'governs', albeit under the supposed direction of democratically elected politicians who form the government of the day and who are themselves meant to be under the watchful eye of parliament (see Chapter 4). But this chapter also considers the increasing importance of the third branch – the judiciary and the courts. It has two main themes. The first is that, once again, we see some commonalities, but also the persistence of national differences.

The second main theme is that governing in Europe, in as much as it was ever easy, is not as easy – or as easy to describe – as it used to be. Like that of the nation state, the scope and even the size of the executive is everywhere questioned. Authority, even where it is accepted, is more diffuse or spread out. What we used to talk of simply as govern*ment*, it seems, is giving way to what is now termed gover*nance* (see Peters and Pierre, 2000). The former conjures up an image of institutions run by or on behalf of the state delivering, in more or less

---

Definition

The political philosopher Charles de Secondat, Baron de la Brède et de Montesquieu (1689–1755), known to us simply as Montesquieu, published his *On the Spirit of Laws* in 1748. In it he famously argued that the 'checks and balances' required to safeguard a country against tyranny were best embodied in the **separation of powers** between the following 'three branches of government'. These were a legislature to pass laws and agree taxation, an executive to administer those laws and take decisions where appropriate and a judiciary to broker disputes. In his time, Montesquieu believed that this division of labour was best exemplified by England. Since then it has become better entrenched – albeit with a rather more active executive than Montesquieu may have envisaged – in the US. It also helps structure politics in Continental Europe, and is an important part of an ideal that emerged in German constitutional theory but spread throughout the continent, namely the *Rechtsstaat* – a state whose acts must conform with laws enshrining fundamental rights.

top-down fashion, those public goods which citizens (and the groups we examine in Chapter 8) are presumed to need. The latter implies a more complex process by which executive institutions – public and private, central and local – combine more or less smoothly to deal with the demands of increasingly less deferential individuals and interests. It is this, when combined with the growing impact of the EU, that has led political scientists to talk of the spread throughout Europe of the multi-level governance we defined in the Introduction – namely, the dispersal of power, a multiplication of sites of authority and policy competence, and a mixture of co-operation and contestation between tiers of government that would formerly have been considered separate and hierarchically ordered.

This chapter begins by looking at how and why power has allegedly passed downward toward lower levels or tiers of government – a process often labelled 'devolution' (see Chapter 2) or 'decentralization' or more specifically 'regionalization'. It then returns to the topmost level – to the so-called **core executive**. It explores whether (and if so why) the core executive has shrunk, yet also possibly gained in strength, via measures to improve co-ordination between a formerly more fragmented bureaucratic machine. Have recent developments such as the establishment of arm's-length 'agencies' (running things on behalf of government but not run by government) helped to 'hollow-out' the state (Rhodes, 1997) to a degree that undermines one of the key branches of government? Or have they simply allowed it 'more control over less'? The chapter then goes on to show how the authority of the executive (and possibly parliament) is now constrained by the activism of the judiciary to such an extent that we should perhaps see the latter, too, as a part of the multilevel governance emerging across the continent.

Definition
The **core executive** is a label given by political scientists to the heart of government. It comprises both the political part of the executive – normally Cabinet and Prime Minister – and its bureaucratic support, as well as key civil servants from the most important departments, ministries and intelligence chiefs. The core executive normally operates out of the national capital.

Pushing things out to the periphery: decentralization

In Chapter 2, we referred to the classical distinction between unitary and federal states (see Elazar, 1997) and noted that it was breaking down as some former unitary states moved toward federalism. This move between classical categories, however, has been made only by the handful of countries we discussed; namely Belgium, Spain,

---

BOX 3.1
Alpine exceptionalism: the Swiss confederation

Each of the twenty-six cantons that make up the *Confoederatio Helvetica* (CH) or Switzerland is linguistically homogeneous. They comprise German speakers (who make up 65 per cent of the population) or French speakers (18 per cent) or Italian speakers (10 per cent). Each tends as well to be dominated by either Protestants (who make up 40 per cent of the population) or Catholics (who make up 45 per cent), though by no means all German-speaking cantons are Protestant, nor all French-speaking cantons Catholic. Little surprise, then, that the state forged from this religious and linguistic patchwork is federal rather than unitary. Survey evidence suggests that, in contrast to Germans, who do not feel much emotional attachment to their *Länder* (regional states), the Swiss root both their cultural and political identity in their canton rather than in the state. Why else, one could argue, would they tolerate a federal government that has places all but reserved for a handful of the biggest parties, pretty much irrespective of results, with senior politicians almost automatically getting a turn to be president? The federal government may control more areas of day-to-day life than some suppose. But its growth is limited by the constitutional requirement that any new powers must be agreed by the cantons, as well as referendum of all citizens, Switzerland being one of the world's biggest fans of *direct democracy* (Chapter 6). Cantons largely determine their own taxes. They have a big say in federal legislation, too. Not only do they have an 'upper house' of parliament all to themselves, but this *Council of States* knows that its veto cannot be overridden in the lower house, no matter how many MPs are ranged against it.

	% of total revenue taken by federal/central taxes	% of total revenue raised by state taxes	% of total revenue raised by local taxes
Germany	30.6	22.0	7.3
Switzerland	34.1	23.8	16.6
Belgium	35.5	24.0	4.6
France	41.8	0	9.3
US	43.7	19.4	12.3
Czech Rep.	44.8	0	10.6
Spain[2]	47.5	0	16.5
Poland	51.5	0	18.3
Sweden	56.2	0	30.8
Italy	58.6	0	12.2
Netherlands	59.4	0	3.5
UK	77.3	0	4.1

Table 3.1 The central/state/local split of taxation, 2001[1]

Notes: 1 Note that the remainder of taxes are taken by social security funds.
2 Spain's autonomous communities would appear to be treated by the OECD as local government, but one could make the argument that they should be treated as states.

Source: Data from OECD *Revenue Statistics, 1965–2002*.

the UK and (possibly) Italy. Apart from Germany, Austria and Switzerland, all the others remain unitary states. Yet that binary distinction between unitary and federal has always been as much analytical as real. In 'unitary' Scandinavia (especially Denmark, for instance) local government has long collected (relative to other non-federal states) a large proportion of state revenues (see Table 3.1). It has also been quite a big spender and runner of services, all of which has allowed room for regional variation. And even outside Scandinavia, local authorities in Europe are responsible for a raft of things that in some countries would be the preserve of central government (or private companies). These include public housing, public utilities, welfare and health. Consequently, even if they do not collect much of their country's revenue, they account for quite a high proportion of its spending: in Spain, in 1979, for instance, central government accounted for 90 per cent of public spending and town councils 10 per cent. By 2000, the figures were 59 per cent and 14 per cent, respectively, with the increasingly powerful autonomous communities (see Chapter 2) accounting for 27 per cent and

destined to account for even more with the transfer to them of responsibility for health services (Colomer, 2002: 196–7).

Spain, as we saw in Chapter 2, is not a 'normal' federal country, but even the supposedly more conventionally federal Switzerland (see Box 3.1 and Church, 2004) and Germany are by no means replicas of US-style federalism. German *Länder* (regional states) have less power and autonomy than their American counterparts (see Box 3.2), though they do have considerable influence on national politics via the *Bundesrat* (the upper house of parliament) and on political outputs more generally because (along with local government and insurance funds) they control two-thirds of Germany's budget. In Switzerland, the competence of the federal (i.e. central) authority has been growing. The Swiss states (called cantons) are still the prime source of identity and the ultimate authority when it comes to giving more power to the centre. But they are too fragmented to deliver all services and functions efficiently or effectively.

But if those countries moving toward federalism (full-blown or otherwise) are in the minority, they

---

BOX 3.2
Germany's Länder: not quite as autonomous as they look

Under the 1949 Basic Law (Germany's constitution) every one of its sixteen *Land* governments is accountable to a separate parliament, elected in different ways, and operates according to its own constitution. The split with regard to responsibilities is broadly as follows:

	State (Land)	Federal (Bund)
Exclusive responsibility	Broadcasting	Defence
	Transport	Foreign and trade policy
	Police and judiciary	National budget
	Education (incl. curriculum)	
Shared responsibility	Environmental policy, business and labour market regulation	

However, the federal government also has the ultimate say on anything judged to require uniformity throughout the country. The federal government also delegates a good deal of the implementation and administration of the policy areas in which it has competence. Interestingly, the *Länder* can deal direct with the European Commission on issues for which they have competence and, following arguments over ratifying the Maastricht Treaty, they have a constitutionally guaranteed right to a say on any transfer of sovereignty that may affect them. They are also allowed to make their own agreements with foreign states – but only with the consent of the federal government.

In short, there is a good deal more functional overlap than there is in, for example, the US and therefore plenty of room for disputes. These, ultimately, must be adjudicated by the Constitutional Court (see Table 3.3, p. 76). Recently, there have also been tensions over the *Finanzausgleich* – the constitutionally backed obligation on the most wealthy *Länder* to subsidize their poorer counterparts (especially those in the former East Germany). Potentially, these tensions have the capacity to undermine the hold of the *Länder* over the federal government by making it more difficult for them to coalesce (or gang up) against it in the very powerful second chamber of Germany's bicameral parliament, the *Bundesrat* (see Chapter 4).

---

are by no means alone in pursuing decentralization. A variety of political, economic and institutional pressures have pushed – or are likely to push – all but the smallest European states in the same direction. From at least the 1970s onwards, central government finances in many unitary states were coming under pressure as the postwar boom began to tail off. This prompted the idea that they were suffering from 'overload' – too much responsibility for too many aspects and activities (see King, 1975). Policy makers wanted to offload some of this overload (and some of the blame for cutbacks to services) onto lower tiers of government. But they were nevertheless aware that efficient and effective service delivery and economic planning were just too big a job for the lowest level of local administration (normally called 'the commune' or district in Europe) – a level that is notoriously fragmented (Italy and France, for example, have over 8,000 and 36,000 communes, respectively). They were also coming to terms with the fact that development aid from the EU was increasingly targeted at the level of the region rather than the state (see Keating and Hooghe, 1996): indeed, the move toward regionalization arguably provides some of the most concrete evidence of Europeanization we have.

This combination of ideological change and institutional pressure (domestic and European) drove a rationalization of central and local government. It also led to the setting up or strengthening of so-called 'meso-level' or regional government,

---

BOX 3.3
EU regional funding in Central and Eastern Europe

More than 35 per cent (€213 billion in 2000–06) of the EU budget is transferred to its poorer regions. There are two sources of funding: the *Cohesion Fund* (which helps finance projects relating to the environment and transport networks in member states with a GDP below 90 per cent of the EU average) and the larger *Structural Funds*. Those states in western (or more properly southern) Europe which were the poorest members of the EU before the 2004 enlargement – namely Portugal, Greece and Spain – have hung on to some of their funding, at least for a transitional period. But now Poland is by far the biggest beneficiary, with the wealthier Czech Republic in third place (after Hungary). Despite the initial reluctance of some politicians in the Czech Republic, who were cagey about any hint of federalism after their experience with Slovakia, these countries have divided themselves into regions as follows:

	Number of Regions	Eligible under Objective 1	Structural Funding (2004–6) € (billion)	Cohesion Funding (2004–6) € (billion)
Poland	16	16	8.3	4.2
Hungary	7	7	2.0	1.1
Czech Rep.	8	7	1.7	0.9

Source: Data from http://europa.eu.int/pol/reg/index_en.htm.

---

which in many (though not all) countries has progressed from being appointed to being elected (see Keating, 2000). Partly because it has been influenced (though by no means wholly driven) by EU membership, this incremental trend toward 'functional decentralization' (the parcelling out of tasks and competences previously assumed by central government) first affected western Europe, including some of its administratively most centralized states. France, for instance, began by setting up appointed regional authorities to co-ordinate economic investment and planning in the 1970s, and the twenty-two in mainland France became elected bodies in 1986 as part of a general process of *déconcentration* (decentralization) pursued by governments of both left and right (see Box 3.5). Likewise, Italy moved away from a system of provinces overseen by prefects who reported directly to Rome to a system of twenty popularly elected councils representing its historic regions. The situation in the Netherlands is rather more complicated (see Andeweg and Irwin, 2005). The country maintains its system of twelve provinces, with elected governments and legislatures, dealing mainly with transport and environ-

mental matters; these are much smaller than most European regions, hence a not-altogether-convincing recent attempt to group them into four 'Euro-sized' *landsdelen* or 'country-parts' which at the moment have no real domestic function.

As far as Central and Eastern Europe goes, many states (except for the very small ones) may find themselves prodded – as was Greece, for example, in the 1980s and 1990s (see Sotiropoulos, 2004: 417) – by the regional bias of EU funding mechanisms (see Box 3.3) towards decentralization. This is despite the fact that, outside Poland, there is little tradition of strong sub-national government, and few signs that, left to their own devices, post-communist politicians would be interested in decentralization. Such a move might, after all, erode the power of states which are often perceived not as too strong but rather as too weak to do their job properly (see Bruszt, 2002: 136). In this respect, multilevel governance (or at least the belief that it may be the way of the future) is less of a feature in the region than it is in the former 'West'.

We should be cautious, however, not to overstate the case for 'regionalization'. For one thing, as Table 3.1 makes clear, money does not follow structure in any simplistic way. Central governments in many countries – even those such as the UK or Spain that have supposedly devolved power to regions – continue to keep a tight hold on sources of revenue and, where possible, spending. Politicians running central governments are aware of the impact on the macroeconomy (and perhaps their electoral chances) if they cede control of revenue-raising to sub-national government. It would also appear, rather interestingly in view of the common wisdom that European integration is a force for regionalization, as if they are using the advantages afforded to them by their greater presence and involvement in decision-making in Brussels to maintain a gate-keeping role between the EU and regions – the clear exceptions being Belgium and Germany (though not similarly federal Austria, see Falkner, 2000a) where regions/states have been adamant about their right to direct contact (see the various country studies in Wessels, Maurer and Mittag, 2003).

Nor is regionalization the whole story when it comes to decentralization. Beneath the level of the region there have also been significant developments in local government whose service delivery role still dwarfs that of regions. Most notable in this respect is the extension – on the grounds of improving both management and accountability – of personalized political control (see Box 3.4). 'Regionalization' also masks the potential for conflict between local and regional authorities: in Italy, for instance, regions took over some of the supervision of local authorities from centrally appointed prefects. This, and the failure of the regions to devolve some of their powers to the local level, has caused considerable tension. Indeed, some larger European towns and cities (especially in Italy) have even tried to bypass the regions by forming a more direct relationship with central government.

We should note, however, that this kind of local–regional (and central) conflict is not endemic in Europe. True, in countries with more adversarial styles of politics (such as Spain, the UK, France and Italy) parties in opposition at the national level use their occupation of local or regional office to 'grandstand' against the government. But in countries with more consensual political styles (e.g. Germany, the Netherlands and the Nordic countries) co-operation tends to win out over conflict. In Sweden, for example, decentralization is taken for granted and runs relatively smoothly, albeit not utterly without tensions. Each of its twenty-four counties has an elected council, but also a governor appointed from the centre. He or she leads an administrative board, but one made up of members chosen by the county council. The administrative board fulfils a planning role alongside not only the county councils but also the municipal authorities. The municipalities look after day-to-day service delivery according to goals set for them by government agencies. But they also raise a relatively large amount of their own revenue (see Table 3.1, p. 59) and have a fair amount of discretion to decide how exactly they spend their centrally determined bloc grants (see Pierre, 1995: 153). Meanwhile in Germany, the fact that the *Länder* and the federal government, irrespective of party differences effectively have to work together, via the *Bundesrat* (the upper house of parliament) in order to avoid gridlock (see Chapter 4) also means that when conflict does flare up it eventually gives way to co-operation. This does not always happen in Spain (see Chapter 2) where the autonomous communities play only a minor role in Spain's upper house, the *Senado*.

'More control over less': central government reform

Although many of its functions (and at least some of its funding) have been devolved downwards to regional and local authorities, the central state in Europe has by no means withered away. Many analysts, however, suggest that it has been 'hollowed out' (Rhodes, 1997). According to them power has passed upwards (to the EU), outwards (via the privatization we deal with in Chapter 9) and downwards (to arm's-length agencies, for example). At the same time as pushing things to the periphery, central governments across Europe have, to a greater or lesser degree, been changing how they do the things that are left. Influenced in part by New Public Management (**NPM**) ideas, many have sought to separate policy-making and setting (the advisory and supervisory function) from policy implementation (the administrative

---

BOX 3.4
The trend toward direct election in European local government

In June 2004, Ken Livingstone was elected for the second time as Mayor of London, the first directly elected mayoralty in the UK. London has since been joined by a handful of other towns and cities. Moreover, other local councils have moved away from the traditional system of an appointed chief executive overseen by committees of elected councillors toward a system of a council leader with a cabinet (see Wilson and Game, 2002).

But the UK has a long way to go to catch up with Italy. There, as in France and Germany, there is a stronger tradition of an individual (elected or not) exercising administrative powers on behalf of the state. Since 1993, any of Italy's eight thousand *communi* (local councils) with a population of more than 15,000 can hold direct elections for their mayor. Some local authorities have also been able to take advantage of a new property tax, the rate of which they can determine, to enhance their autonomy.

On the other hand, both the UK (which, in the jargon, is traditionally a *monist* country, emphasizing collegial, elected and local supervision of council activities) and Italy (a Napoleonic or *dualist* country where elected bodies traditionally worked alongside an individual executive answerable to the state) are part of a European trend (see Borraz and John, 2004). The rest of Germany has been catching up fast with the southern *Länder*, which have a strong tradition of directly elected executive mayors. Meanwhile the countries of Scandinavia, as in Britain, have been experimenting with more powerful council leaders and cabinets, and even directly elected mayors. In the Netherlands, mayors were traditionally appointed by the government, but this is no longer obligatory – a move which may pave the way for direct election.

The aim has been to increase the responsiveness of services to local demands, and hopefully to offset declining voter turnout. Doubtless, direct election will enhance the prestige (and perhaps the accountability) of mayors and council leaders, especially in the biggest cities, *vis-à-vis* regional and national government. However, the extent to which greater powers for the locality have accompanied this enhanced prestige is less easy to gauge.

---

function). But they have also taken steps to offset the potential fragmentation involved in this effort. This has been done by maintaining and indeed improving political control of the non-elected part of the core-executive.

The extent to which NPM ideas are seen as common sense in a particular country is, research suggests, heavily dependent on cultural and institutional traditions (see Wright and Hayward, 2000). For instance, in Germany public service is more about administering according to legal procedure than managing service delivery, while the power of the *Länder* in the *Bundesrat* (see Chapter 4) has always meant that rapid change is difficult to achieve politically. Not surprising, then, that Germany has not proved particularly fertile soil for those hoping to sow the seeds of the new public management (see Pollitt and Bouckaert, 2000: 91–2). On the other hand, the British civil service values pragmatism, bargaining and flexibility; nor

is it either compartmentalized or governed by a separate civil service law. This, and the relative absence of constitutional and legal constraints on a majority government means that NPM could be imposed relatively effectively from the late 1980s onwards (see Pollitt and Bouckaert, 2000: 47). Interestingly, there appears to have been little attempt by outside agencies (such as the IMF or the Organization for Economic Co-operation and Development, OECD) or the EU to make the adoption of NPM (as it did with privatization) a condition of assistance to the new democracies of East Central Europe (Goetz, 2001).

National history, tradition and culture, then, play a big role in governance. Indeed, it can sometimes seem that the only structural feature that European executives share is the tendency (particularly when it comes to the civil service and particularly at the highest levels) for them still to be staffed almost exclusively by white, largely middle-class and usually highly-educated, middle-aged men! While there may be a common thrust, and even common pressures (fiscal, political and otherwise), each country adapts to them in ways that – unlike, say, their parties and party systems (see Chapter 5) – do not always fit obvious patterns. For example, we cannot simply fall back (as the media often does) on easily assumed differences between the practices and responses of 'Northern' and 'Southern' Europe: differences do exist, but only some of them (the 'Mediterranean' tendency towards large-scale political appointments to civil service jobs and the 'over-production' of formalistic regulations) can be said to be systematic (see Sotiropolulos, 2004). And the national stereotypes that inform not only journalistic but also academic analysis are only sometimes useful (see Box 3.5). Comparative research on public administration rightly lays great stress on the strength and explanatory power of national traditions. But we should not allow this to trap us into automatic acceptance of outworn stereotypes that caricature countries rather than capture a more complex and dynamic reality.

The fact that comparison in this area is difficult may explain (and to some extent be caused by) the relative paucity of truly cross-national research in public administration (though see Weller, Barkis and Rhodes, 1997, Peters, 2001 and especially Pollitt and Bouckaert, 2000 for honourable exceptions), even though there are several useful collections of single-country descriptions (see Bekke and van de Meer, 2000; Bevir and Weller, 2003; Page and Wright, 1999; Peters and Wright, 2000; Pierre, 1995; Verheijen, 1999). Many of these

---

> **BOX 3.5**
> ## France: plus ça change; perhaps not
>
> France is routinely portrayed (and sometimes ridiculed) as one of the most inveterately centralized, 'statist' (and, indeed, elitist) states in Europe, or perhaps the world. This portrayal always needed some qualifications. Centralization, for example, was traditionally mitigated by the fact that so many of France's national politicians held (and continue to hold) elected positions (for example, as mayors) at the local level, guaranteeing that state policy took sub-national needs into account. But the portrait is also increasingly inaccurate. True, its civil servants or its politicians have not rushed to embrace what they see as the neo-liberal tenets of NPM. But there has been a concerted attempt by governments of both right and left, beginning in the early to mid-1980s to transfer powers from Paris (and its agents, the *préfets* or prefects) to local and regional government, which now controls almost half of government expenditure. These lower tiers of government have responded positively to being given extra responsibilities, and governments have seen fit to add to them over the years. Nor have civil servants at the centre, as well as at local level, resisted reform completely (see Clark, 1998 and Rouban, 1995). Generally, reform has tended to accelerate when both president and prime minister are from the same side of the political spectrum: just as federalism slows what little enthusiasm there has been for NPM in Germany, *cohabitation* tends to do the same in France (see Pollitt and Bouckaert, 2000: 49).

> *Definition*
> **NPM** (New Public Management) is as much an ethos as a doctrine. It rests on the notion that the public sector cannot only learn a lot from the private sector in terms of its competitive focus on efficiency, value for money and responsiveness to clients or customers, but that it should actually be re-structured to resemble a market wherein, ideally, the purchasers of a service are split from its providers, with managers given more autonomy but also clearer targets.

begin by estimating the number of 'civil servants' employed by each state. But even a cursory glance makes it clear that using these to compare the size of central states or core executives is highly problematic, because what counts as a civil servant varies so much between countries. What does emerge, however, is the fact that since the 1980s civil service numbers across Europe seem to have stopped expanding. This is especially the case if we accept the assertion that employees transferred, say, to regional governments or to bodies that used to be part of the central state but now exist at arm's length from it (in agencies) are no longer, strictly speaking, civil servants.

The state that regards itself as the pioneer of separating policy-making and policy implementation was the UK. Since the late 1980s the British government has been steadily 'hiving off' operations and delivery to what are known as 'agencies'. There are now around one hundred employing around three-quarters of what would traditionally have been called civil servants. Perhaps the most visible example is the 'Benefits Agency' which is responsible for social security payments and employs tens of thousands of people all over the country. Each agency is a more or less (see Gains, 2003) autonomous unit responsible for a particular function or service. It is headed by a chief executive reporting to a minister who, advised by senior civil servants, determines the agency's resources and goals.

Both fans and critics of 'agencification' in Britain point (either in sorrow or sceptically) to the fact that the model has not been enthusiastically adopted elsewhere in Europe, with the exception perhaps of Denmark and more recently the Netherlands. Yet they miss an important point. In fact, the 'hiving off' of policy implementation has long been taken for granted in many other countries, notwithstanding the fact that few of them had much sympathy for the NPM ideas that held sway in Britain (see Box 3.6). In Germany and the Netherlands, for instance, the delivery (and to some extent, via their collection of insurance premiums, the funding) of much of the welfare state has traditionally been left with so-called 'parastatal' or 'parapublic' bodies. The Federal Employment Service (*Bundesanstalt für Arbeit*) in Germany, for instance, runs most of the country's job centres, while most healthcare is provided via insurance premiums collected by its *krankenkassen* – bodies organized either by sector or by geography and with the involvement of unions and employers. In the Netherlands, many of the institutions that originated in the days when the country was divided along the lines of its religious subcultures continue to deliver services (often organized regionally), albeit in a much more secular age.

Spain, it must be said, has less of an 'agency' tradition, and has been too preoccupied with territorial decentralization to develop one along NPM lines. Nor has there been much enthusiasm in France for agencies. On the other hand, they have

---

BOX 3.6

Neither new nor neo-liberal: government agencies in Sweden

The hiving-off of government business from ministries to agencies is often associated with Thatcherite Britain in the 1980s. In fact, social democratic Sweden was the pioneer of the notion that the formulation of policy should be institutionally separated from its implementation. Indeed, the separation is formalized in its constitution, which charges government departments (overseen by cabinet ministers) with policy formulation while implementation rests with around eighty legally autonomous agencies (*ämbetsverk*). This means ministers cannot be held accountable for bureaucratic mistakes, but it also means that, potentially, they have much less control than some of their counterparts in other countries (for example, the UK) over what is done in the name of the government by agencies (see Ziller, 2001). In fact, ministers are able to exert influence via informal contacts between civil servants and, more formally, via the *Riksdag* (the Swedish parliament), which can vote to reorganize agencies and which determines their budgets. Interestingly, these have shrunk in recent years as agencies' service delivery roles have passed to local government. The response of agencies has been to turn themselves into supervisors rather than providers of local services (see Pierre, 1995).

---

always played a part in Italy – some would say too big a part: their proliferation as means of providing patronage opportunities for politicians and bureaucrats alike has done nothing to ameliorate the unimpressive reputation of its public servants (see Box 3.7 overleaf).

Hiving off the job of implementation has its potential downsides. The most obvious is that the creation of more structures (and arm's length structures at that) will make it harder for the government of the day to co-ordinate, let alone control, policy and delivery (see Wright and Hayward, 2000). This task is already rendered difficult in some states owing to a tendency toward compartmentalization on the part of ministries and departments (see Box 3.8, p. 67). Partly in response, to these problems, potential and actual, Europe's politicians have recently looked for ways to help

---

Living up to the stereotype: the civil service in Italy

Lazy, offhand and wedded to interminable bureaucratic procedure which will be set aside only if you know him personally or pay him if you do not. Such is the stereotype of the Southern European civil servant. Unfortunately, it is a stereotype that many familiar with the byzantine world of the Italian civil service would argue holds true (see Lewanski, 2000). Historically, many civil servants saw their posts not so much as a passport to progression or a vocation but as a slowly rising means of subsistence that could be supplemented either by kickbacks or by holding down another job outside of the notoriously short opening hours. The administrative culture is highly legalistic, which ensures that there are myriad opportunities for those involved to charge a private premium for anyone wanting to move things along. Of course, all this applies most to 'street-level' bureaucrats. But the senior levels of Italy's civil service also comes in for criticism (see Cassese, 1999) for excessive legalism, reform-resistant culture (though see Lewanski, 1999) and a tendency towards little empires ruled over by men who are there because of their staying-power and social networks rather than their talent. Traditionally, none of this mattered too much because – in a manner which in some ways paralleled the situation in Communist East Central Europe before 1989 – the grip of Italy's political parties on society was so strong: politicians could effectively by-pass the civil service in order to get things done. Since the collapse of the old party system in the early 1990s, however (see Chapter 5), this is no longer the case, strengthening the case for reform.

rather than dry-as-a-bone administrators (see Pierre, 1995: 207 and also Aberbach Putnam and Rockman, 1981 and Rhodes and Weller, 2001). This may explain why, despite it being increasingly possible to do so, not that many top civil servants are parachuted in from the private sector. Second, this notwithstanding, politicians seem ever keener to appoint to senior positions people they can trust.

No European country has anything like the 'spoils system' that sees incoming administrations in the US make wholesale and overly partisan changes at the top of the civil service. But Greece and (to a slightly lesser extent) Spain come some way towards it (see Sotiropoulos, 2004: 410): newly elected governments in 2004 (one right-wing, one left-wing) made fairly sweeping changes at the top of the civil service and even in corporations where the state still has some involvement. And there are other states which are more accepting of party involvement than some. In Austria and Belgium, for example, it has long been a convention that political parties were granted a number of positions according to their relative strength to which they would appoint their members. At the other end of the spectrum lie countries such as the UK and Sweden, where there is a strong cultural norm toward neutrality. Here, top civil servants are expected to switch seamlessly from outgoing to incoming governments of a different stripe. Indeed, it is by no means easy (especially in the UK) for a minister to replace staff whose attitudes he or she does not find conducive with those to whom he or she is better disposed. It is, however, increasingly accepted (as it is in the Netherlands) that ministers will supplement existing staff with a handful (and no more) of people who are acknowledged to be political appointments but join the civil service as temporary 'special advisors'. Often they provide political or media management advice that would be considered beyond the pale for permanent civil servants.

Other countries lie along this spectrum. In Germany and the Netherlands, openly political appointments to senior civil service posts, especially by new governments, are increasingly common. In France, ministers, in addition, to the departments they run, are allowed what is called a *cabinet* – a group of, at the very least, ten high-

them at least steer their state machinery, even if – because of the fragmentation inherent in functional and territorial decentralization – they can no longer control it. It is this that explains what those who cling to the ideal of a neutral civil service believe is a damaging trend toward the politicization of bureaucracy. This trend encompasses two things. First, there is an increased willingness on the part of senior civil servants to acknowledge that they need to be politically sensitive networkers

BOX 3.8
Joined-up government: compartmentalized civil services

The compartmentalized rule

NL: Highly autonomous departments with own specialized recruitment; consequent lack of joined-up government has given rise to reforms, among them the ABD (*algemene bestuursdienst*) designed to improve horizontal mobility among senior civil servants.

Germany: Very specialized departments with own career patterns.

Sweden: As in most Scandinavian countries, the civil service is highly sectoral.

Spain: Departments and ministries colonized by particular and specialized professional associations, called *cuerpos*, which seem to have survived an attempt by centre-left governments in the 1980s to loosen their grip.

Italy: Notoriously fragmented; low mobility.

Poland and **Czech Republic**: Little central recruitment or horizontal mobility.

The interdepartmental exceptions

UK: Emphasis on centrally recruited generalists; good horizontal mobility; cross-ministerial committees.

France: generalist administrators with good networks often based on highly-sought after membership of a *grand corps* (professional association), shared educational background in one of the *grandes écoles* and movement between departments, ministerial staff, and in and out of politics.

Sources: Bekke and van der Meer, 2000; Page and Wright, 1999; Verheijen, 1999.

fliers, some of whom will be plucked from departments and some of whom will come from outside the civil service altogether, to help them supervise and drive their ministries. France's powerful president (see Chapter 4) also has a *cabinet*, in addition to his own general secretariat of civil servants who co-ordinate the work of the government. The practice of appointing advisory *cabinets* has been institutionalized in Poland, but not in the Czech Republic. This is in spite of the fact that governments in both countries, like many who now run former Communist states (see Goetz, 2001 and Meyer-Sahling, 2004), are faced with rather plodding bureaucracies. These were 'politicized' in the sense that who you knew helped you get the job, but not in the sense of being responsive to changes in priorities occasioned by changes in governments. Compounding their difficulties, some

argue, is the fact that civil servants in the postcommunist states seem to have adopted the highly legalistic approach typified by Germany. This is precisely the system that in some countries, Italy being the most notorious example, slows the bureaucratic system down so much that people try to by-pass it in ways that would be frowned on as improper in, say, the UK, the Netherlands or Sweden.

Once again, then, cultural and institutional differences seem set to persist. Although we can identify a European tendency toward trying to tighten political control over a state machine that is now more 'loosely coupled', there is no such thing as conformity. But what of one potentially crucial force for such conformity; namely, the need to improve the 'fit' between national and European administrative structures (see Cowles, Caporaso and Risse, 2001)?

It is certainly common to hear suggestions (from both federalists and anti-federalists alike) that the differences between East and West, and North and South, and between individual countries, will gradually grow smaller as their executive structures are somehow brought into line by the demands of dealing with the European Union.

Clearly, there is evidence of Europeanization in this respect: for instance, the *grands corps* (high-ranking civil service organizations) in France have arguably lost some of their self-confidence and grip on the policy process in recent years as a result both of European integration and the way reformers have used it to bolster their case (see Cole and Drake, 2000: 29–30). More generally, member states have had to develop mechanisms for interministerial and departmental co-ordination, not an easy thing given the extent to which civil servants can make direct contact with their functional counterparts in other countries, often via the some 1,000–1,500 EU working groups and committees operating at any one time. The member states have done this, however, in strikingly different ways. Traditionally centralized states such as the UK and France have tried (not altogether successfully) to maintain central co-ordination of the European involvement of ministries, often via *ad hoc* committees, while other states – Sweden is an example – prefer a more formalized co-ordination and decision-making process that takes place at cabinet level. Meanwhile, some traditionally more fragmented, less streamlined states find co-ordination on issues with a European dimension more of a trial (see Maurer, Mittag and Wessels, 2003: 69 and the individual country chapters in Wessels, Maurer and Mittag, 2003).

This divergent response to a common adaptational challenge is confirmed in a useful summary of the research on the issue in western Europe; Klaus Goetz (in Hix and Goetz 2000) observes that 'the gap between expected adaptive reactions and the often rather modest effects that empirical analyses uncover' is wide. Most studies, he notes, testify to 'the importance of national context and the capacity of national administrative traditions to modify, accommodate … and, perhaps, even neutralize European pressures'. The signs, Goetz goes on, are little different in the newer members

of the EU from East Central Europe – and anyway the impact of Europeanization would be difficult to disentangle from the effects of the wider changes that postcommunist countries have undergone. More generally, as Page and Wouters (1995) observe, the survival of profound differences in structures and procedures in the bureaucracies of the component states of the US – a fully federal system – should make us very cautious about predicting that the EU will somehow make Europe's state bureaucracies look more like each other.

Policy-making: sectors and styles

As for structures, so for policy-making – in other words, what actually goes on in those structures and emerges out of them? As Wessels, Maurer and Mittag (2003: xv–xvi) conclude from their comparative study of all fifteen states that made up the EU until May 2004, although 'the head of government, governmental administrations and interest groups … have increased their role as strong and active multi-level players' compared to 'weak adaptors' like parliaments (see Chapter 4) and (interestingly) regional administrations, '[f]undamental patterns of national policy-making have not changed'.

> *Definition*
> A state's **policy style** can be defined as the interaction between a characteristic problem-solving approach covering each stage of the policy cycle – initiation and formulation, implementation, evaluation and review – and a characteristic relationship between those involved, including (though not exclusively) politicians, bureaucracy and those groups affected by and/or seeking to effect change (see Richardson, Gustafsson and Jordan, 1982: 13).

This firm rejection of the idea of 'Europeanization-as-convergence' when it comes to policy-making raises the question of what those patterns are in the first place. Is it possible to talk about each European state having some kind of identifiable **policy style**? To which our answer is probably, but not without considerable qualifica-

France

Area: 13.8% of EU-25
Population: 13.1% of EU-25
GDP: 15.2% of EU-25
Joined EU: Founder member 1957
Capital city: Paris

History: Present-day France is composed of various regions centralized in the seventeenth century by a monarchy that was then overthrown in a revolution which began in 1789. In the following two decades, the country emerged (under dictator Napoleon Bonaparte) as an imperial power occupying territory all over Europe as well as overseas. After Napoleon's defeat by the British and the Prussians (modern-day Germans) at the Battle of Waterloo in 1815, the monarchy was restored, only to be overthrown once again in 1848. Following two decades of dictatorship and the loss of a war with what (partly as a result of victory) promptly became Germany, France finally settled, albeit fractiously, into democracy, although under this 'Third Republic', it rapidly began to lose its status as a world power.

This loss of great power status was confirmed by the Second World War, during which the northern half of France was occupied by Germany, while the southern half (so-called 'Vichy France') was ruled by a collaborationist regime under Marshal Pétain. After an initially unstable period (the so-called 'Fourth Republic') during which both its constitution and its colonial policy were called into question, France pulled itself together under

its famously imperious president, Charles de Gaulle. De Gaulle resigned following student and industrial unrest in the late 1960s, but the centre-right held on to power in what was known as (and still is) the 'Fifth Republic' until 1981, when François Mitterrand constructed the first fully centre-left government since the 1930s. Its radical economic programme soon came unstuck, however, forcing a policy U-turn. Since then, government has alternated between multi-party blocs of the left (which includes a much weakened Communist Party and the Greens, as well as the more mainstream Socialists) and the right (made up of conservatives and liberals who, for the moment, continue to shun the potentially powerful far-right National Front).

Economy and society: France is still one of Europe's most powerful economies, and a notable exporter of agricultural as well as industrial goods. Able to afford a generous, insurance-based welfare state but plagued by relatively high unemployment, France's 60.5 million people enjoy a GDP per capita in 2004 around 13 per cent above the EU-25 average. Paris, indeed, is one of the richest cities in Europe, although some of its suburbs are notoriously blighted by crime and poverty. Some 4.5 million people in France are Muslim (most of whom have their origins in France's former colonial possessions in North Africa). There is some regionalist sentiment in the West and South, but it is only serious (and separatist) in the Mediterranean island of Corsica.

Governance: France is unusual in a number of ways. Its elections are fought, unlike anywhere else in Europe, under a two-ballot, majoritarian system rather than under PR: the only other country which shuns the latter is the UK. France is also Europe's only 'semi-presidential' system. Its president is directly elected every five years and then appoints a prime minister and cabinet who are accountable to a

notoriously weak parliament. This means that the French sometimes experience divided government if parties other than those who support the president win the parliamentary elections. In that case, the president has little choice but to appoint political opponents as prime minister and to cabinet. This so-called *cohabitation* may, though, become less common now that parliamentary elections are somewhat more likely to follow hard on the heels of the presidential contest. France's Constitutional Court is an increasingly powerful player in the political process, and potentially important interest groups include (despite their small membership) the public sector trade unions and the farmers. Notwithstanding its reputation for being one of the continent's most 'statist' countries, France has pursued a policy of decentralization for more than two decades. Its national and its local politics are, in any case, intimately connected by virtue of many national politicians – again, unusually in Europe – continuing to hold positions as local mayors or heads of regional government.

Foreign policy: After 1945, France dedicated itself to locking its old enemy Germany into Europe via an integration process that it was determined to lead and exploit. It has also attempted (much like the UK) to hang on to the vestiges of its great power status: France may have lost most of its overseas possessions by the 1960s (including, most bitterly, Algeria), but it still has far-flung colonies in the Caribbean and the South Pacific, still has its own nuclear weapons, and (along with the UK, US, China and Russia) is still one of the five permanent members of the UN security council.

Further reading: Bell (2002), Elgie (2003), Guyomarch *et al.* (2001), Stevens (2003).

tions. The first of these is the extent to which policy-making in nearly all advanced societies is 'sectorized', with each area engendering its own, more or less permeable, **policy network** involving, at the very least, government and those interest groups trying to get it to do something that may benefit them or prevent it from doing something that they see as detrimental (see Chapter 8 for more detail on such groups). This means that there may be more in common between the making of, say, energy policy between two countries than there is between policy-making in, for instance, health and education within the same country, making generalizations misleading if not meaningless.

Definition

A **policy network** is a range of actors (including, for instance, organized groups, national and European civil servants, regulators, academics) that interact, more or less systematically, in a given policy area. In **policy communities** interaction between the interest group or groups involved and the state is close and continual, with a premium placed by both sides on mutual and largely confidential co-operation that is both formal and informal and may well extend into implementation as well as setting of policy. An **issue network** is a looser arrangement that corresponds rather more closely to what pluralism is in some ways supposed to be about; that is, government setting policy but having due regard to a variety of sometimes discordant voices – a situation that, rather in the manner of a free market, is theoretically supposed to provide the best outcome.

The second qualification to the idea of national policy styles is that the reality of policy-making may differ considerably not just from the 'ideal type' or simplified model analysts use to understand it (the same is true for policy networks, as we note in Chapter 8), but also from the 'standard operating procedures' or 'norms' that those involved might prefer to adhere to – or, alternatively, might need to appeal or resort to if a deal cannot be worked out (see Hayward, 1982). Three examples of this – historical principles acting as a fallback, if you like – spring immediately to mind.

First, there is the tradition of the state overriding objections in the public interest in France. Secondly, there is the insistence on 'parliamentary sovereignty' (a majority of the House of Commons ultimately trumping any intransigence by, say, interest groups) in the UK. Thirdly, there is the *Rechtsstaat* tradition in Germany, whereby anyone proposing a policy, even on a relatively unimportant topic, should be able to show it is consonant with the constitution.

The point, though, is that on a day-to-day basis these principles are not brought into play: most of the time consultations and negotiations lead to deals. We therefore need to be careful about using these normative traditions to characterize (or caricature) a country's policy style. This still happens, as one of the examples just given illustrates: we now have ample evidence that French policy-makers are no longer elitist apostles of *dirigisme*, directing things from the top because they assume they have all the answers as well as the right to do so; instead, they work with (and are sometimes severely constrained by) interest groups and local and regional governments (see Guyomarch *et al.*, 2001). Yet it is still not uncommon to see the country labelled, indeed almost dismissed, as 'statist'. The potential, and possibly the propensity that has always existed for such statism may still be there, but it is rarely drawn on lest it waste political capital which politicians and bureaucrats might need in future policy-making

This brings us to the third qualification to the idea of national styles, one which opens up a classic debate in political (and all social) science; namely, the relationship between 'structure' (institutions, procedures, processes and norms) and 'agency' (individual and group action). The paradigmatic European example of agency triumphing over structure is the Conservative government under Margaret Thatcher that governed the UK in the 1980s and early 1990s. Possibly some of those triumphs were as rhetorical as they were real, but they ruthlessly exposed the fact that the policy style widely associated with that country (and, indeed, that party) before it came to power in 1979 – pragmatic, consultative, compromising – was in some ways misleading, relying on what had been done before, not on what could be done if politicians were determined enough. Ironically, it also demonstrated that the notion of 'parliamentary sovereignty' alluded to above might indeed be important when comparing the UK with other countries where political circumstances, culture, processes and institutions made this kind of untrammelled power highly unlikely (see Table 3.2). Then again, parliamentary sovereignty can tell us little about how UK governments (in fact, all European governments) have fared when dealing with matters that demand policy but on which parliament plays only a bit part, such as economic policy – which is why, incidentally, one cannot really cover policy-making by drawing a few standard diagrams of 'how a bill is passed' in various countries' legislatures. Nor does the concept (or the diagrams) help us much when it comes to governments having to deal with crises that demand immediate administrative action rather than parliamentary process – whether these crises are real (such as the floods in central Europe in 1998 or the spike in petrol prices that occurred in September 2000) or one of the less tangible matters that temporarily achieves prominence in the media-primed 'issue attention cycle' (Downs, 1972 and see Chapter 7).

Even the strongest 'agents', then, may find themselves undone by structures not of their own making (the oil markets) or by sheer contingency (the weather). Or, as we have suggested, they may sometimes find it convenient to recall an idealized version of their role in policy-making rather than act, as they do on most days, more prosaically. Or, as we have also said, different 'standard operating procedures' may apply in different policy sectors. Nevertheless, it may still be worth essaying some broad generalizations about individual countries' policy styles. These should take into account the institutional influences on them (i.e. the other actors governments must deal with) and the normative influences on them (i.e. their problem-solving approach), since, as a valuable recent study found (Héritier *et al.*, 2001), they help to explain how essentially similar policy goals often produce sharply differing outcomes. The generalizations are illustrated in Table 3.2, the aim being to provoke discussion and promote comparison rather than to present an all-encompassing account.

An all-encompassing account of policy-making in Europe would prove impossible anyway, given the very little we know as yet about policy-making styles in East Central Europe. In fact, these styles are probably still very much in the making, just as they have been in older 'new democracies' like Portugal, Greece and Spain (on which see Magone, 2004). An exhaustive account would be equally difficult owing to the caveats already discussed above. Any comparative schema or shorthand characterization will inevitably fail to explain exceptions to what, in any case, are tendencies rather than rules.

For instance, the incrementalism and 'interconnectedness' that the Germans label *politikverflechtung* does not rule out major reforms being pushed through, often in the face of considerable doubts and opposition. One only has to think of the decision during reunification to allow East Germans to swap their weak communist currency one-for-one with the powerful Deutsche Mark then used in West Germany or, more recently, the Schröder government's 1999 reform making it easier for 'foreigners' to claim citizenship. On the other hand, one could argue that both examples show the dangers of departing from the norm: currency union is included in a fascinating comparative study of European 'policy disasters' (see Gray and t'Hart, 1998), while the political arm-twisting required to get the citizenship law saw it rapidly struck down by the Federal Constitutional Court. Compare this with the Schröder government's equally contentious policy of phasing out nuclear power: the negotiations were tortuous, with both sides having to accept hard-to-swallow compromises, but the decision looks set to stick.

In other words, just as policy styles that potentially brook no compromises need not preclude them, styles that emphasize consensus are equally capable of fostering innovative solutions. Indeed, because they eventually achieve 'buy-in' from all concerned, they may even be better at producing policy that works and lasts. The welfare reforms in the Netherlands and Sweden that we touch on in Chapter 9 are good examples. The latter country's policy system is famously consensual to the point of being cumbersome. Governments wanting to do something routinely appoint a state commission (*statsutredningar*) composed of experts, interest groups, agencies and representatives of (other) parties to examine their ideas and produce a report. At the same time, a wide variety of opinion is

Table 3.2 Policy styles and their institutional and normative influences

	France	Germany	Italy	Netherlands	Spain	Sweden	UK
Limits to action:							
Federal states/devolved regions?	No	Yes	No (may change)	No	Some (increasingly)	No (but decentralized)	Some
Accessible/assertive constitutional court?	Can be	Yes	No	No	Not often	No	No
Relatively powerful parliament?	No	Yes	Potentially	No	No	Yes	No
Institutionalized interest group participation?	Some	A lot	Some	A lot	Little	A lot	Little
Powerful coalition partners?	Rarely	Always	Always	Always	Rarely	Rarely	Never
Coalition agreement that really counts?	No	Yes	No	Yes, very much so	No	No	No
Interest groups required for implementation?	Sometimes	Often	Sometimes	Often	Sometimes	Often	Sometimes
Fragmented departments?	Occasionally	Often	Often	Often	Often	Often	Sometimes
Procedure over flexibility?	No	Yes	Yes	No	Yes	Yes	No
Intervention over 'hands-off'?	Yes	Yes	Yes	No	Yes	Depends	No
Consensus over majority rule?	No	Yes	No	Yes	No	Yes	No
Overall policy style characterized by:	Consultation within limits, then action	Interconnection and incrementalism, risking immobilism	Disconnection and heavy-going	Consensus where possible, action if not	Consultation within limits, then action	Consultation without immobilism	Consultation within limits, then action

canvassed under the pre-legislative *remiss* consultation procedure. All these views feed into legislative proposals that are then intensively debated in parliamentary committees, often resulting in cross-party agreement. Yet for all this, Sweden is one of the few countries in western Europe that has 'grasped the nettle' on the pension reforms that many think Europe's ageing population make vital (see Chapters 1 and 8). France, with its more 'heroic' policy style has achieved some reform, but more will be needed – and will probably occasion more of the protest that occurred first time around.

Amid all this talk of national variations, what of Europeanization, as defined in the Introduction? Is policy-making right across the continent increasingly interconnected, with state and non-state actors 'downloading' the prescriptions of the EU and/or other European countries at the same time as seeking to 'upload' their own? Studies seem to suggest a good deal of variation, with two things standing out as important. The first is the extent to which involving or invoking EU institutions and initatives presents opportunities to domestic actors to speed up or slow down change as they see fit (see Héritier *et al.*, 2001: 288). In other words Europeanization occurs or does not occur in part because its occurence or non-occurence suits policy-makers: it need not be an unstoppable force but can just as often prove a valuable resource.

The second thing determining the extent of Europeanization is whether the EU has policy competence in the policy area concerned (see Zeff and Pirro, 2001 and especially Wallace and Wallace, 2000). So, for instance, policy-making on agriculture and fisheries, or on the environment, does, of course, go on at the domestic level, but those involved (across all member states) exhibit a 'co-ordination reflex' which means they are attuned to and involved in (and therefore thinking of the consequences for) the policy process at the EU level. Perhaps, for instance, they participate in an EU *groupe d'expert* (preparatory committee) and therefore meet fairly frequently in Brussels with their sectoral counterparts from other countries – the kind of activity that, incidentally, makes it harder and harder for Foreign Ministries to maintain their gatekeeping and co-ordinating role over the interaction of supposedly 'domestic' departments. In other areas – including, say, health and

education where governments have not ceded much to the EU – policy-makers may well be learning from other countries, and they may well have a special 'desk' that deals with European affairs, as well as a man or woman on the ground in Brussels (in the government's Permanent Representation if they are a civil servant or, if they work for an interest group, at its office in the city). But they are not looking over their shoulders at other countries or seeking to anticipate their actions in anything like the same way. It is because of this variation between policy areas that we need to be careful before we assume that Europeanization necessarily disrupts or undermines the traditional (if informal) hierarchy that means some ministries tend to be seen as more important than others.

The booming third branch of government: the judicialization of politics

Talk of 'disruption' and 'undermining' brings us rather neatly to the extent to which the executive's job in Europe is made more difficult these days by the role of what in the US is traditionally a powerful 'third branch of government': the judiciary. Theoretically its role is not just to enforce criminal sanctions, but also to adjudicate disputes by applying the civil law to particular cases. These might be between private parties, or between individuals and the state, or perhaps between central and local government. In so doing, the judiciary is meant to provide another 'check and balance' by ensuring that government and the state operate under the rule of law and do not exceed their powers and/or violate fundamental liberties laid out in the constitution.

All European states have written constitutions with the exception of the UK, which prefers the flexibility of tradition and precedent. At least in the eyes of the ordinary citizen, these constitutions – even though they are almost all the product of regime change and new-found independence – rarely attain the status enjoyed by the US constitution. Historically, in any case, they have never been so sanctified nor so sacred. In fact, they have often been amended or even replaced by new, improved versions. They are nonetheless important, helping as they do to structure politics by laying down the powers and roles of the various institutions (president, government, parliament, regions, etc.) involved in running a country. Many political 'rules of the game' can be rewritten pretty easily by the players; constitutions less so. They may not be totally fixed objects around which the executive is obliged to work, but they are seriously heavy pieces of scenery – very difficult to shift, and best not bumped into too often.

The UK is not only unusual in that its constitution is unwritten (though some documents are vital to it) but also because (with the exception of Scotland) its legal system is based on what are called 'common law' principles, whereas the rest of Europe (including Scotland) operates systems based on 'Roman' or 'code' law. In England and Wales, and also Ireland (and to some extent former dependencies like Malta and Cyprus), statutes passed through parliament are important (especially for criminal law), but so too are precedents set by judges' decisions in past cases. These establish principles – based on notions of equity and individual rights (for example, to free enjoyment of property) that are binding on lower courts

In other European countries, however, civil law is much more likely to be 'codified' – systematically written down so it can be applied to particular cases by judges. These judges therefore enjoy rather less discretion than their counterparts in the common law system and are often seen (and, indeed, recruited and trained) as highly specialized civil servants rather than lawyers who have served their time arguing before other judges before going on to become one themselves. Roman law systems are generally less adversarial (and more 'inquizitorial') than common law systems. They also tend to have more of a division of labour between various specialist courts set up to deal with, for instance, criminal, financial or administrative law (although we should note that over the last two or three decades, the British legal system has also developed a network of more specialized administrative tribunals).

This is not to suggest that all Roman law systems are the same. For instance, Germanic countries (and now most CEE countries) place more stress on a logical progression from general principles – the *Rechtsstaat* idea we referred to when defining

separation of powers – than do 'Napoleonic' countries (France, the Benelux countries, Italy, Portugal and Spain). In Scandinavia, codes are slightly less rigid and detailed, but process is important. Nor should we fail to note that many countries are hybrids – Poland and Greece, for instance, sit somewhere between the Germanic and the Napoleonic style, while Scotland even mixes in common law influences. Generally, though, the distinctions between Roman and common law systems have traditionally been more important than the differences within them.

> **Definition**
> **Judicial review** is the process by which legislation, regulations and administrative acts of the state are examined by the judiciary in order to check, among other things, that they are in accordance with the constitution and other law, and that neither the executive nor the legislature is going beyond its powers, breaking its own procedural rules or acting unreasonably. Review can make use of a particular case (concrete review) or not ('abstract review' which may take place before the law comes into force).

Anyone with a nodding acquaintance with US politics will be familiar with the idea of a Supreme Court that provides the ultimate insurance against government, be it central or local, undermining the rights guaranteed to citizens by the constitution. Similar courts exist in many European countries. The obvious exceptions are Britain, the Nordic countries and the Netherlands, though this by no means guarantees that politicians are free from judicial constraints (see Box 3.9). Where such courts do exist, the main difference between Europe and America is that in the US, any judge in any court, can declare a law or government action or decision unconstitutional. This ruling can then be tested in other courts right up to and including the Supreme Court. In Europe, this kind of **judicial review** has traditionally been rejected on the grounds that ultimate power rests with the people and is therefore invested in a democratically elected parliament rather than in appointed judges.

BOX 3.9
What, no constitutional court?

Just because they do not have a constitutional court does not make politicians in the UK, the Netherlands and Sweden immune from legal intervention – or, just as importantly, the fear of it. Although judicial review is only rarely resorted to in Sweden, the 'Council on Legislation', made up of senior judges, can be asked by the government or by a parliamentary committee to rule on government proposals. This usually takes place prior to the bill being brought before the *Riksdag*, which also appoints *ombudsmen* to protect citizens' rights to due process. In Britain, Acts of Parliament cannot be overturned by judges, but the actions of the authorities can be challenged on the grounds that they are taken without due authority, or are irrational and unreasonable, or not in accordance with proper procedure. And while it is true that no court can actually strike down a statute as unconstitutional, it has for some time been open to a judge either to rule illegal the executive action required to carry it out or to declare that parts of it are unlawful to the extent that they deprive an individual (or company) of their rights under EC law. Indeed, after the passing of the Human Rights Act of 1998, a judge can now declare a statute incompatible with the European Convention on Human Rights (ECHR). This also holds true in Sweden and in the Netherlands. The Dutch constitution may explicitly deny the courts any right to constitutional review, but has not prevented them considering many matters that many would consider political, most famously euthanasia and (more mundanely) employment issues (see Andeweg and Irwin, 2005).

Alongside this belief in the supremacy of statutes, however, runs an enthusiasm for constitutionally backed rights, freedoms and principles which – logically, anyway – would seem to constrain and take priority over parliament. Many countries have resolved this potential contradiction by setting up special constitutional courts that are – supposedly, at least – 'above politics' (see Table 3.3). Countries that have set up such courts include Germany, France and Italy and, more recently, Spain, Poland and the Czech Republic (see Procházka, 2002), all of which emerged from dictatorship wanting an extra bastion against any return to arbitrary rule. Italy and Germany were of course in a similar position in the 1940s, and the latter would in any case have needed some kind of umpire to settle disputes between federal and state authorities.

However, unlike the US Supreme Court, which sits at apex of the ordinary court system and is, in effect, that system's final court of appeal, Europe's constitutional courts sit outside that system (the only exception being Ireland, where the High Court does the job of a constitutional court). It is possible in most countries that have a constitutional court for that court to hear cases referred to it by ordinary courts concerning laws that are already in force – a process known as 'concrete review'. But it will also spend much of its time (and, in the French case, all of its time), responding to requests by politicians (local or national) to decide on the constitutionality of laws that have already been passed by parliament but that are not yet in force. This process – because no particular case is involved – is known as 'abstract' review.

From sometimes small beginnings, these constitutional courts have expanded the role of the third branch of government. For the most part, the expansion was largely unforseen and, because it crept up on politicians only gradually, went largely unnoticed. In France, for example, the Court was seen as a tool of or prop for the executive and few made much of its 1971 decision henceforth to take into account the wide-ranging preamble to the constitution. This decision, along with a constitutional amendment in 1974 that extended the right to refer matters to the court to any sixty members of either legislative chamber, paved the way for a massive (and creative) increase in its competence and importance. Now, it may well have taken on a self-sustaining momentum of its own (see Stone Sweet, 2000). The use by opposition politicians of abstract review to try to strike down legislation and policy that they are unable to vote down in parliament is increasing. In France, virtually every contentious bill (and budgetary measure) is re-fought in this way and, because it takes time for judges appointed by previous administrations to be replaced by those more favourable to the present government, such bills

Table 3.3 Europe's constitutional courts

Country/Name	Membership	Reputation	Role	Record
Germany: Federal Constitutional Court	16 members (half appointed by *Bundestag*, half by *Bundesrat*, both needing a two-thirds majority).	Highly regarded as 'above politics' or at least balanced.	Considers constitutionality before and after legislation has come into force. Pre-legislation ('abstract review'), applied for by federal or *Länder* governments, or one-third of MPs, and can therefore be a means by which oppositions try to overturn a parliamentary defeat. 'Concrete' (i.e. *post hoc*) review initiated by courts or, most commonly, by individuals claiming violation of rights by a public body. Adjudicates between federal government and *länder*, and civil liberties/human rights.	1990 forces changes to East German electoral system; 1993 rejects challenge to Maastricht Treaty, but stresses limitations on EU's power; 1992 lowers state funding to political parties; 1993 makes publicly funded abortion harder; 1994 clears way for German military participation overseas; 1998 clears way for Germany to adopt the euro; 2001 grants equal legal treatment of 'gay marriages'; 2002 forces government to rethink liberalization of citizenship law; 2002 upholds military conscription; 2003 rejects legal ban on neo-Nazi parties.
France: Constitutional Council	9 members (3 each chosen by President, National Assembly and Senate), including many former politicians.	Highly partisan: appointees of right-wing governments tend to oppose left-wing successors and vice versa.	Can consider constitutionality only before legislation comes into force (i.e. abstract but not concrete review possible) on request of the President, presidents of the two chambers of parliament, or 60 MPs. Lower courts cannot refer cases to it. Covers wide range of issues, but rarely involved in human rights cases. Seen by many as almost a third chamber, given the propensity of opposition parties, having lost the votes in parliament, to refer virtually all important bills and budgets to it.	1982 insists on adequate compensation for nationalizations; 1982 strikes down an attempt to boost the number of women candidates in local elections; 1984 blocks Left's plans to regulate media ownership; 1986 interferes with Right's plans to deregulate media; 1993 limits Right's attempts to tighten immigration and asylum regime; 1998 overturns Socialist by-election win over National Front because of media bias; 1999 grants same-sex couples full legal rights

	Composition	Perception	Review powers	Significant decisions
Italy: Constitutional Court	15 members (5 chosen by President, 5 by parliament and 5 by judges in higher courts).	Only moderately partisan, and normally reasonably balanced between partisans of the various parties.	Carries out pre-legislation abstract review (usually on the initiative of national or regional government) and concrete review (i.e. post hoc referrals from courts). Wide range of activity but particularly active as gatekeeper for requests for referendums.	1971 allows sale of and information on contraception; 1970s strikes down sexist adultery laws; 1970–74 upholds constitutionality of divorce liberalization; 1976 breaks up government monopoly of media.
Czech Rep.: Constitutional Court	15 members, appointed by President and parliament.	Seen to favour government's estabishment of liberal capitalism, notwithstanding social costs; early clashes with centre-left.	Abstract and concrete review – the former initiated by the President, or government or parliament, the latter by courts or individuals.	1993 upholds retrospective punishment for crimes under Communist regime and right to restitution of property, but strikes down criminal prosecution for i defamng political institutions; 1997 forces immigration authorities to allow appeals in person; 2000 strikes down rent controls.
Poland: Constitutional Tribunal	15 members, appointed solely by parliament.	Seen initially as subserviant to parliament and government's liberalizing agenda, but beginning to be more assertive.	Before 1999 it could be overriden by two-thirds majority in parliament, but now its say is final. Very accessible - abstract review on the initiative of political institutions at the national and local level, judges and even on its own initiative. Concrete review via referrals from courts.	1989–94 strikes down some of Poland's 'shock therapy' economic reforms; declares President's attempts to extend powers unconstitutional; upholds rights of former regime officials to pensions; upholds rights and privileges of the Roman Catholic church; upholds anti-abortion laws.
Spain: Constitutional Tribunal	12 members, 2 each appointed by the judiciary and the government and 8 by parliament.	Partisan appointments (especially under Socialist governments), but not sufficiently so as to undermine its legitimacy.	Abstract review on application by Prime Minister, president of parliament, 50 parliamentarians, regional governments, ombudsman. Concrete review via referral from court or requests by ombudsman or individuals. Can also rule on the text of international treaties.	1983 counteracts legislative move to slow down (for fear of antagonizing conservatives) granting of regional autonomy and declares that state law prevails over regional law; 1993 strikes down key provisions of the government's internal security reforms (minister resigns).

stand a 50:50 chance of being declared in some way unconstitutional. Governments and parliaments, in the face of possible defeat during what amounts to an extra final reading of bills, and knowing that changes to constitutions require big majorities (especially if the article covers basic rights), are already obeying what political scientists call 'the law of anticipated reactions'. They are watering down their legislation to improve its chances of either avoiding or passing judicial scrutiny – something that calls into question the idea of a separation of powers.

Also being called into question are the differences between Roman and common law systems – a development that provides considerable potential for, as well as evidence of, Europeanization. Concrete review – whereby courts (and sometimes individuals or ombudsmen) can ask their national constitutional court for a ruling which they can then apply to their particular case – is blurring the formerly hard and fast distinction between ordinary courts and constitutional courts which, as a result, are arguably becoming more like a US-style Supreme Court. And the increasing stress on the interpretation of constitutional principles (as opposed to merely applying a code) may not differ that much from the use of precedent and the notion of the supremacy of decisions of higher courts that are already associated with common law systems. At the same time, common law systems, by developing specialized administrative tribunals and increasingly taking into account codified EC law, are becoming more like Roman law systems.

Law is one area in which Europeanization is without doubt important. True, there are big differences in the extent to which European countries transpose European law into domestic legislation, and in the frequency with which they are hauled up in front of the ECJ for lagging behind or non-observance (see Table 3.4). And national politicians will often go for the most flexible interpretation of EU rules. They will also try to square the Commission, which is responsible for policing them and referring cases to court: government provision of 'state aid' to ostensibly private firms (which we touch on in Chapter 9) is a good example. But, as the decline in state aid can be said to show, the fact is that, for the most part,

Table 3.4 Persistent offenders: ECJ judgements on member states' 'failure to fulfil their obligations'

	Average from date of joining until 2000*	Average 20001–3
Italy	9	17
France	5	16
Spain	6	12
Germany	3	9
Netherlands	2	4
UK	2	7
Sweden	1	1

Note: * Average is lower than recent yearly figures because there were fewer laws to infringe on earlier!

Source: Data from ECJ, *Annual Reports* (2001–3) (figures represent infringements declared).

compliance eventually occurs. This is because, as we noted in Chapter 2, both national politicians and national courts have accepted the supremacy of European law and, where appropriate, acknowledged that it has direct effect on their countries without needing transposition. Indeed, the alleged enthusiasm of some national courts (especially lower courts) for the ECJ – combined with the willingness of businesses, individuals and pressure groups to bring actions based on European law (see Chapter 8) – has been a major factor in blunting any incipient resistance to its power on the part of national politicians. At least in those areas where their predecessors have granted competence to the EU, then, Europe's elected politicians and the states they run find their room for manoeuvre restricted by non-elected judges.

While Europe's politicians do not like being 'named and shamed' via the ECJ, they do not always object to being bound by European-level law. ECJ decisions, like those of domestic courts, can sometimes provide political opportunities as well as constraints. A good example would be the series of decisions that helped build momentum for the Single European Act (SEA) (see Chapter 2), which accelerated progress on the single market (see Chapter 9) – something most of Europe's politicians (even reluctant Europeans such as the UK's Margaret Thatcher) were keen to see. Another would be the ECJ's ruling that pension ages for men and women should be the same – something that allowed European governments to raise the age of entitlement for women which will, in the long-term, save them money. States also exploit the power of the ECJ in disagreements they have with each other: ECJ rulings (backed up by the possibility of large fines) were said to be instrumental in getting France to drop what the UK claimed was an illegal ban on the import of British beef. In judicial matters as in many other aspects of European politics, then, the EU 'lives' inside as well as outside the state and can be an opportunity and not just a threat.

Some claim to see in both domestic and EU affairs, and the blurring of the boundaries between them, the beginnings of a slide down a slippery slope they call the 'judicialization' of public life and politics. At the bottom lies a homogenized European legal system that, they argue, takes no account of national traditions which, supposedly at least, are culturally appropriate and have done the job well enough for centuries. Parliamentary government, they claim, is giving way to 'rule by judges' who owe their positions partly to their professional colleagues, mostly to politicians and not to the supposedly sovereign people. We should be careful, though, before we assume that this development necessarily goes against the wishes or the interests of either politicians or people in general. A number of the issues the courts deal with, such as anti-discrimination and the right to life, are seen by the former as 'too hot to handle' and by the latter as best kept free of partisan party politics. The same may be true of disputes between central, local and regional government, which will undoubtedly become more frequent with the popularity of decentralization, devolution and even federalization (hybrid or otherwise). In dealing with them, the judicial branch of government is, in effect, doing everyone a favour. It is also contributing a great deal to the governance not only of each country, but, especially with regard to EC law and the ECHR, Europe as a whole. Meanwhile, polls suggest that

people trust judges, though only few of them could be called household names (see Box 3.10), more than they trust politicians. It is to the latter, in their related roles as the representative side of the executive and as the legislators who help oversee it, that we now turn.

BOX 3.10
'Super-judges'

Apart from disputes and decisions about the legality of administrative actions, about the balance of power between central and local government, and about the constitutionality of legislation, there are two other ways in which the judiciary has been active in European politics in recent years. The first is mundane but can have big political implications. This is when judges are asked by governments and parliaments to undertake commissions of inquiry into political contentious matters that require independent, though not legal, investigation: the Hutton enquiry in the UK in 2004 is a good example (see http://www.the-hutton-inquiry.org.uk/). The second is guaranteed an even higher profile. The early 1990s saw major financial (and other) scandals involving politicians in several countries – most notably in Italy, but also in Spain. In those countries, disillusion with the political class elevated some investigating judges to celebrity status. Italian magistrates like Giovanni Falcone and Paolo Borselino (murdered by the Mafia), Antonio di Pietro (who went on to enter politics) and Francesco Borrelli (whose disputes with Prime Minister Silvio Berlusconi helped lead to a judges' strike in June 2002) became heroes during the *mani pulite* ('clean hands') investigation of Italian politicians that hastened the collapse of the party system they operated (see Chapter 5). Spanish judge Baltasar Garzón, who became famous throughout Europe when he attempted to extradite former Chilean dictator General Pinochet from the UK, was similarly revered for his role in the so-called 'GAL' affair, which revealed politicians' roles in the illegal killings of terrorist suspects. Their actions are testament to the continuing capacity of the judiciary not only to be a thorn in the side of the executive, but also to reflect the popular will as much as any parliament.

Learning resources

For a discussion of governance, see Peters, and Pierre (2000). On regions, see Keating (2000). On the central state in Western Europe, see Bekke, and van der Meer (2000), Page and Wright (1999), and, above all, Pollitt and Bouckaert (2000). On the bureaucracy in post communist Europe, see Goetz (2001) and Verheijen (1999). On the extent to which Europe and the domestic have (and have not) become enmeshed both bureaucratically and in terms of policy, see Wessels, Maurer and Mittag (2003). On policy-making in the EU, the first port of call must be the incomparable Wallace and Wallace (2000). For selected countries, see Compston (2004). On the interface between law and politics, especially in those countries operating constitutional courts, see Stone Sweet (2000). On constitutional courts in former communist countries, see Procházka, (2002). On the ECJ and its influence see Wincott (1999) for an overview, and, for a more detailed study, Alter (2001).

EXECUTIVE SUMMARY

- The executive in Europe no longer thinks that it knows best or at least that it should do everything – though this has always been the case in Europe's federal states, and in some of its unitary states, too. Accordingly, it has contracted out some of its work (though perhaps less of its power and its money) to regions and/or agencies

- These bodies now form part of a not-altogether tidy network of policy-making and service delivery. But while most countries have arrived at what some observers call 'multilevel governance', they have taken many cultural and institutionally different roads to get there and by no means look the same when they do.

- All over Europe, however, attempts have been made to offset any resulting loss in politicians' capacity to steer state activity, often via political appointments at the top level of the civil service. The latter varies considerably between countries, although none escapes co-ordination problems and 'sectorization' completely.

- This sectorization, plus the difference between 'norms' and 'behaviour' and the relationship between 'structure' and 'agency' make it difficult but not impossible to posit national policy styles.

- These styles seem to have survived and adapted to greater involvement in the EU, whose effect on policy varies according to the role granted to it in different sectors.

- For all these differences, European states share a tendency, via both their homegrown constitutions and (just as importantly) the EU, toward what some might regard as unwarranted interference in their prerogatives on the part of the second branch of government, the judiciary.

Chapter 4

Governments and parliaments: a long way from equality

Chapter 3 looked at governance, but, in addition to looking at policy-making, it concentrated mainly on the changing architecture of the state and the non-elected people who help to run it, be they civil servants or judges. Now we turn to governments – the representative part of the executive. The elected government in almost all European countries must enjoy 'the confidence of parliament', normally expressed in a vote when it takes office – a vote it has to win or, at the very least, not lose. Europe's parliamentary governments are led by a prime minister and a group of colleagues which political scientists call a **Cabinet**. The fact that cabinet members very often sit in, and in all cases are responsible to, parliament blurs the distinction between the executive and the legislature that constitute two parts of the classical three-part 'separation of powers' that we outlined in Chapter 3. This clear division of labour is considered sacrosanct by some Americans, yet its blurring in Europe does not seem to exercise many Europeans. Conversely, Americans see nothing strange in the head of state and the head of government being one and the same person; namely, the President. However, nearly all European countries,

more or less successfully, keep the two functions separate.

> **Definition**
> **Cabinet**, which may be known in particular countries by a different name (for instance, in France it is called the Council of Ministers) is the final democratic decision-making body in a state. In Europe, the cabinet is made up of party politicians who are, more often than not, chosen from the ranks of MPs and are collectively (as well as individually) responsible to parliament.

This chapter begins by looking at the largely attenuated role of the head of state in European countries. It then focuses on governments, and in particular cabinets. Who and what are they made up of? Do they always command a majority in parliament? How long do they last? How is it decided who controls which ministry? What do they spend their time doing? Next, the chapter turns to Europe's parliaments. Most European legislatures have two chambers: we look at whether it makes much difference. The chapter then moves on to the basic functions of legislatures – hiring and firing governments, making law, and scrutiny and oversight. It explores whether and why some of Europe's parliaments are weak and some are stronger. The chapter ends by asking why, despite the fact that some parliaments are relatively powerful, they are rarely a match for governments.

The head of state

All European countries have a head of state. In the continent's monarchies (Belgium, the Netherlands, Denmark, Norway, Sweden, Spain and the UK), the head of state will be the king or queen. In republics, it will be a president, either elected directly by the people (as in Austria, Bulgaria, Cyprus, Finland, France, Ireland. Lithuania, Poland, Portugal, Romania, Slovakia and Slovenia) or 'indirectly' by the parliament. The title of 'president', however, does not mean the post holder is, like the US President, both head of state and head of government. In Europe – with the sole exceptions of Cyprus (where the government is fully presidential) and France (where it is 'semi-presidential', see Box 4.1) – the two roles are kept separate. Outside France and Cyprus, Europe's presidents, like Europe's monarchs, do not wield executive power but are instead supposed to be above day-to-day politics. As such, they are trusted not just to represent the state diplomatically but also neutrally to carry out vital constitutional tasks such as the official appointment of a prime minister as head of government, the opening of parliament and the signing of its bills into law.

It is tempting to write off Europe's presidents and monarchs as playing a merely legitimating and/or symbolic role. They are a reminder to people (and, more importantly, to elected governments) that, underneath the cut and thrust of inevitably partisan politics, something more steady and solid endures. And, like the flag and certain unique traditions, they can be rallied round by all sides in times of trouble. But heads of state – particularly when elected – do constitute an alternative locus of potentially countervailing power that can constrain the actions of governments seeking to push their mandates a little too far or promote their friends inappropriately: examples would include refusing to ratify the appointment of an unsuitable candidate to a ministerial post, delaying the signing of legislation or petitioning a constitutional court to examine it.

This countervailing power – often as much to do with words as deeds – is supposed to be used sparingly and for the good of the country. But it does leave those heads of state who use it open to the accusation that they are simply trying to undermine or obstruct an elected government with whom they (or their party) have policy disagreements. This happened early on in several postcommunist countries, notably Poland, Hungary and Romania. In recent years, however, the situation

BOX 4.1
Monsieur le President: France's executive head of state

Under France's 'semi-presidential' system (see Elgie, 1999), the president has executive (and especially emergency) powers that go well beyond those given to other heads of state in Europe. Not only is he head of the armed forces and the negotiator of international agreements, he can also dissolve parliament for fresh elections without consultation and can call a referendum on policy put forward by parliament or the government. Very often, he is also in charge of domestic policy – but not always. As in most other European countries, the French president appoints a prime minister who must command the confidence of the lower house of parliament, l'Assemblée Nationale. The prime minister and cabinet ministers are then collectively and individually responsible to parliament, which is what differentiates semi-presidential from full-blown presidential systems. This means that French presidents can exercise anything like full executive power only when the prime minister and cabinet are drawn from his or her own party, or (as is often the case in France) alliance of parties. Since the mid-1980s there have been several periods (1986–88, 1993–95, 1997–2002) where this has not been the case, obliging the president to 'cohabit' with a prime minister and cabinet drawn from a party or parties on the other side of the political fence. While the tension and conflict arising from *cohabitation* has not always been as bad as it might have been, the situation certainly obliges the popularly elected president to take more of a back seat – though less so in foreign and defence policy and diplomacy than in domestic policy. Now that French presidential elections have been re-timed to take place every five years, and in all likelihood just before parliamentary elections, it may be that *cohabitation* becomes much more rare.

appears to have resolved itself in favour of the elected parliamentary government. Poland's 1997 constitution, for instance, significantly scaled back or curtailed the powers of the president as regards vetoing legislation and dissolving parliament. Not that the spats in the region have stopped completely: Václav Klaus, for instance, was prime minister of the Czech Republic from 1992 to

1997, during which time he had to put up with what he regarded as unwarranted interference and sniping from the much respected former dissident, Václav Havel. In 2003, after rehabilitating himself from the corruption scandals surrounding privatization that led to his fall from office, Klaus became Czech president, since when he has been more than happy to let people know when he disagrees with the government! Verbal sparring aside, there is no doubt, though, that in times of crisis, the role of president can be especially important – and can be far more influential than a quick glance at its limited formal powers would suggest (Box 4.2).

Prime minister, cabinet and parliamentary government

In all European states except France and Cyprus, the person formally charged with the running of the country is clearly the prime minister. He or she is normally the leader of (or at least one of the leading figures in) a political party that has sufficient numerical strength in parliament to form a government, whether on its own or (more usually) in combination with other parties.

Because of this relationship with parliament, European prime ministers arguably enjoy less autonomy than, say, an executive who is also head of state, such as the President of the US. This is not to say they are powerless. Far from it. Prime ministers may well have a great deal of say in the appointment of their cabinet – the group of people who are tasked both with running particular ministries and co-ordinating government policy as a whole (see Blondel and Müller-Rommel, 1997). Moreover, the fact that they typically chair cabinet meetings means that they can wield considerable influence on what cabinet does and does not discuss, as well as over the conclusions and action points emerging from those discussions. Ultimately, too, most of them have the power to hire and fire cabinet colleagues, the exceptions being the Dutch and French Prime Ministers. The latter, though he can force ministers to resign, can also have ministers all but forced on him if operating under a president from the same party.

In general, prime ministers also have power-bases in their party and may be so popular with the

---

BOX 4.2
The Italian presidency comes into its own

The scandal-fuelled collapse of the Italian party system in the 1990s left a vacuum that the country's presidents stepped in to fill. As his own Christian Democratic Party imploded, President Francesco Cossiga earned himself a reputation for outspokenness and even overstepping the mark. He made it clear that, like the public, he thought little of some of his fellow politicians and supported electoral system change and fresh elections. He then surprised people by stepping down early. His successor, Oscar Luigi Scalfaro, played an even bigger role: in 1994 he refused to dissolve parliament at the request of Silvio Berlusconi (whose first attempt at being prime minister ended after just a few months), having earlier prevented him from appointing his choice of Minister of Justice. Scalfaro consequently went on to appoint a non-party 'technocratic' administration which lasted just over a year until it was no longer able to command the support of parliament. Scalfaro was succeeded by former central banker, Carlo Azeglio Ciampi in 1999. Ciampi, too, has not been content simply to sit back. When Berlusconi became prime minister again, Ciampi imitated his predecessor by objecting to a proposed ministerial appointment. In December 2003, he provoked the outrage of Berlusconi by exercising his right to veto a bill passed by parliament which many claimed gave Berlusconi *carte blanche* for a media monopoly in Italy (see Chapter 7). He was, however, constitutionally barred from vetoing the bill a second time when a slightly amended version was passed in April 2004.

---

general public that ministers dare not risk deposing such a figure, even if they feel that his or her treatment of them verges on the dictatorial. Ministers are also at a comparative disadvantage because it is the prime minister, by dint of his or her co-ordinating function, who knows – in as much as any one person can know – what is going on across the whole range of government activity. This does not necessarily allow the prime minister to interfere as much as he or she might like to in the business of the ministry – indeed, in Germany, for instance, there are strict conventions precluding such interference, notwithstanding an equally powerful convention (also included in Germany's, constitution, the *Grundgesetz* or 'Basic Law') concerning the Chancellor's right to set the overall direction of government policy. But the prime minister's overview does allow him or her to play one minister (or set of ministers) off against another. His or her prominence in the media may also be a source of power, and is one more thing that leads some to argue that European countries are undergoing what they call 'presidentialization' (see Poguntke and Webb, 2004).

Notwithstanding all this (and to a much greater extent than is the case with an executive president) a European prime minister must also engage in collective decision-making with his or her cabinet – even if this often takes place outside and prior to the cabinet formal meeting which is then used simply to formalize decisions. Ultimately, he or she cannot function (or, indeed, continue in office) without its collective consent to his or her being *primus inter pares* or 'first among equals'. In as much as it exists in its own right, then, 'prime ministerial power' is constrained not just by contingencies of time and chance and personality, but the multiple and mutual dependencies between the prime minister and his or her cabinet.

This is not to say, of course, that the extent of this interdependence is the same in all European countries (see King, 1994). It clearly varies according to political circumstances: for example, Polish prime ministers have frequently been far more than *primus inter pares* because they (and their staff) were the anchor in what (in the postcommunist period) have often been highly unstable cabinets; yet on one or two occasions they have been merely the frontmen for the party leadership (Sanford, 2002: 156, 161–2). Historical tradition and how much control a prime minister has over government appointments are also crucial. The UK prime minister, presiding over a single-party government and armed with the traditional prerogatives of the Crown, is more powerful, for instance, than his or her Dutch counterpart. This is because the latter is hemmed in by both a closely worded coalition agreement with other parties and a tradition of ministerial equality.

The relative lack of personal autonomy enjoyed by the prime minister of a European country,

---

BOX 4.3
The Netherlands' non-parliamentary executive

In the majority of European countries, ministers are also parliamentarians, though in only a few (the UK and Ireland are good examples) do they, in effect, have to be. The Netherlands, like France, Sweden and Norway, is more unusual in the sense that, there, members of the *Tweede Kamer* are constitutionally obliged to give up their seats once they become ministers. Their place is taken by substitutes from their own party so as to maintain the balance of party power in parliament. They can still appear in parliament to answer questions – and do so much more frequently than their cabinet counterparts in the US, for example. Interestingly, though, this formally enhanced separation between executive and legislature seems to do little to increase the willingness of the latter to stand up to the former: the *Tweede Kamer* is not seen as one of Europe's more assertive legislatures.

---

however, has its upsides. Compared to, say, a US President whose hold over the legislature may be tenuous or even non-existent, the prime minister and the cabinet of a European country can generally feel confident that their decisions will, where necessary, be translated into legislation. European governments are, above all, party and parliamentary governments. The political face of the executive more or less accurately reflects the balance of power between the parties elected into the legislature and will often (though not always) be a multi-party coalition. The ministers who make up the cabinet formed from that coalition may or may not be MPs (Box 4.3). But they are there first and foremost because they represent a political party whose presence in the government is required in order to secure an administration able to command – at least for the time being and on crucial pieces of legislation (such as budgetary matters) – what is routinely referred to as 'the confidence' of parliament. Although confidence is understood by most people in 'Anglo-Saxon' or 'majoritarian' democracies such as Britain (see Lijphart, 1999) to mean a stable majority of the MPs in parliament, this is by no means always the case.

Table 4.1 Which type of government occurs most often in which country, 1945–2003[1]

Single-party majority (%)	Minimal winning coalition (%)	Minority government (%)	Oversized coalition (%)
UK[2] (100)	Germany (70)	Sweden (70)	France (70)
	Netherlands[3] (50)		Italy (60)
			Netherlands[3] (50)

Notes: 1 Figures rounded to the nearest 10 per cent.
2 Note that the UK had one very brief single-party minority government in the 1970s.
3 The Netherlands appears twice because it has had almost as many minimal winning as oversized coalitions.

Source: Calculated from Gallagher, Laver and Mair (2001) and author's own records of governments post-1999.

Many European governments do indeed command such majorities, some even when they are made up of just one party. But, as Table 4.1 shows, a significant number qualify as minority governments, i.e. administrations made up of one or more parties which together control less than half (plus one) of the seats in parliament. Such a prospect would be anathema in some countries, inside as well as outside Europe. But in others it is a far from frightening prospect. To understand why, we need to look a little deeper into the process of government formation.

Permutations of parliamentary government

Minimal (connected) winning coalitions

Few political scientists, even when conducting thought experiments, think of democratic politicians as purely 'office-seekers', interested in power either for its own sake or because of the personal profile, wealth, comfort and travel opportunities it can bring them. However reluctant the fashionably cynical among us might be to acknowledge it, the fact is that most people prepared to represent a political party are also 'policy-seekers'. They want to see some real progress (however limited) made toward realizing their vision of the good society. Even if we forget all the other aspects that may be involved (from the psychology of bargaining to the personal relationships between party leaders), this dual motivation is enough to ensure that government formation is very rarely simply a matter of putting together what political scientists call a **minimal winning coalition**. True, around one in three governments in postwar western Europe have been minimal winning coalitions, while only around one in ten have been single-party majorities. But most of these coalitions have also been what political scientists call **minimal connected winning coalitions** (see Table 4.2 for an example).

Given that in most countries such a coalition would be theoretically, and often practically, possible, how then do we account for the fact that so many parties in Europe hold office, either singly or together, as **minority governments**? In fact, the answer is quite simple: they do it because they can.

Minority governments

In some countries minority government is difficult, if not impossible. These are countries that operate what political scientists call 'positive parliamentarism'. This refers to the fact that their governments have to gain at least a plurality (and sometimes a majority) of MPs' votes before they

> *Definition*
> A **minimal winning coalition** is a government made up of parties that control as near to just over half the seats in parliament as they can manage in order to combine their need to win confidence votes with their desire to have to share ministerial portfolios between as few claimants as possible.
> **Minimal connected winning coalitions** are made up of parties with at least something in common ideologically, even if governing together means having more parliamentary seats than would be strictly necessary and/or could be formed by doing deals with less like-minded parties.

Table 4.2 A minimal connected winning coalition: the Netherlands

SP	GL	PvdA	D66	CDA	VVD	LPF	CU	SGP
Left	Left/Green	Soc.Dem	(Soc) Lib	Ch. Dem	(Neo) Lib	Far-right	Relig.	Relig.
9	8	42	6	44	28	8	3	2

Notes: 1 Shading indicates government.
2 Seats required for overall majority = 76 (eg PvDA, D66, VVD).

are allowed to take office – something that is normally tested in what is called an 'investiture vote' on a potential government's policy programme and cabinet nominations. Examples include Germany, where minority government is made less likely still by a rule that insists that no government can be defeated on a vote of no confidence once it has been allowed to form unless the majority voting against it is ready to replace it immediately with another government. Other examples of countries insisting on investiture votes include Belgium, Ireland and Italy. So, too, do Poland and Spain which, like Germany, have a 'constructive' vote of confidence, where a successor government has to be ready to take over before one can be called. But Spain also reminds us that 'politics' can often trump 'institutions': after the 2004 general election, the social democratic PSOE managed, in spite of the rules and conventions, to construct a minority government!

Other European countries, however, are characterized as operating 'negative parliamentarism'. Governments do not need to undergo an investiture vote or, if they do (Sweden, where the prime minister rather than the government has to step up to the plate, is an example), they are not obliged to win the vote, merely not to lose it. In other words, they can survive as long as those voting against them do not win over half the MPs to their cause. Likewise, the government has to be defeated rather

than actually win on motions of no confidence. This makes it much easier for minority governments to form and to stay in power once they have formed. It therefore comes as little surprise that a list of countries operating negative parliamentarianism includes (as well as Finland, Portugal and the UK), countries such as Sweden, Norway, and Denmark, where minority government has, since the 1970s, become the norm.

These countries are all the more likely to experience minority government because elections, historically anyway, have often produced what political scientists refer to as 'strong' parties. These may well be the largest party in the parliament. Moreover, they are 'pivotal' in the sense that any minimal connected winning coalition would have to include them, and would, if you filled all the seats in parliament in left–right order, have one of its MPs occupying the middle seat (and therefore known in the jargon as the 'median legislator'). Pivotal parties are always at an advantage, even if they are not large: for example, the liberal FDP in Germany managed to turn its position midway between the Social Democrats and the Christian Democrats into almost thirty-one years of government in the forty-nine years between 1949 and 1998. But when a pivotal party is also parliament's largest, it is often in a great position to run a minority government. This is particularly the case when, as in Scandinavia, parties on their immediate flank (say, ex-communist or green parties in the case of the social democrats or a far-right or zealous market-liberal party in the case of the conservatives) would not dream of teaming up in government with parties on the other side of the left–right divide or bloc. Unless these smaller, less mainstream parties are willing to increase what political scientists refer to as their 'walkaway value' by, say, threatening to

---

Definition

A **minority government** is made up of a party or parties whose MPs do not constitute a majority in parliament but which nevertheless is able to win – or at least, not lose – the votes of confidence that are crucial to taking office and/or staying there.

Table 4.3 A minority government: Sweden

V	MP	SAP	C	FpL	K	M
Left	Green	Soc. Dem	Centre	Liberal	Ch. Dem	Conservative
30	17	144	22	48	33	55

Notes: 1 Shading indicates government.
2 Seats required for overall majority = 175.

support the other side or precipitate a new election, they become, in effect, 'captive parties', whose support (or, at least, abstention) in confidence motions can be pretty much guaranteed (see Table 4.3).

In any case, life as what political scientists refer to as a 'support party' rather than a coalition partner, might suit all concerned. This is especially the case if it involves (as it increasingly does in Scandinavia) some kind of written contract – an understanding that may fall short of a full-blown coalition agreement but provides some promises on policy and consultation (see Bale and Bergman, forthcoming). The bigger party can still be in government and affect a 'respectable' distance from what might be a rather distasteful bunch of extremists. The smaller party can go into the next election hopefully combining a claim to contributing to political stability with a claim not to be responsible for all those things the government did that voters disliked! That election, or future elections, may deliver them more seats by which time they will not only be more experienced but better able to drive a hard bargain with a potential coalition partner.

There is another reason why minority governments are more common than we might first suppose, and more common in some countries than in others (see Strøm, 1990). It is that in some systems being 'in opposition' is not nearly so thankless a task as it is in others, notably the UK. As we go on to show, some parliaments – particularly those with strong committee systems – offer considerably more scope for politicians whose parties are not in the government to influence policy and legislation. Again, it is the Scandinavian countries that experience frequent minority government where this so-called 'policy influence differential' between government and opposition is smallest. Finally, it is probably also the case, that once a country has experienced minority government on a number of occasions and has lived perfectly well to tell the tale, it is more likely to embrace the possibility in the future.

In short, the tendency toward minority or majority government has to be seen as cultural, as well as mathematical. There are few institutional barriers to minority government in the Netherlands, for instance: even though the government has to get parliament to approve the often very detailed policy agreement the coalition parties spend months negotiating, there is no formal investiture vote, for example. Yet minority government continues to be almost unthinkable to the Dutch – possibly a hangover from the historical need to form governments that were sufficiently broad-based to include representatives of both the Protestant and Catholic churches that traditionally were so important to people's identity. Conversely, and rather uniquely in a PR system, Spain's two main political parties seem to be so wedded to the idea of single-party government that, if it also means minority government, then so be it! This almost certainly has something to do with not wanting to court accusations that they are 'selling out' the unity of Spain to the regional parties with which they would have to coalesce in order to form a majority administration. Cultural 'hangovers' and cultural realities also help to explain a tendency in some countries toward the last type of parliamentary government, **oversized** or **surplus majority coalitions**.

Oversized or surplus majority coalitions

The traditional home of **oversized or surplus majority coalitions** in Europe is Finland. Because of its delicate proximity to the old Soviet Union,

> *Definition*
> **Oversized** or **surplus majority coalitions** are governments that contain more parties than are needed to command a majority in parliament, to the extent that if one (or possibly more than one) party were to leave the government, it might still control over half the seats in the legislature.

the country got used to putting a premium on national unity, on consensus and on including the left so as not to anger its bigger neighbour. So entrenched was the mindset that, until 2000, legislation that in most countries would have required only a simple majority in parliament required two-thirds of MPs to vote for it. In Italy, too, there were institutional reasons for oversized coalitions. Until parliament stopped voting – at least, routinely – by secret ballot, governments needed a stockpile of extra votes because they could not trust enough of their highly factionalized MPs to toe the party line! The tradition of including more parties than a coalition really needs also built up over decades during which the main aim of most parties was to stand together in order to prevent the Communist Party sharing power. It will probably take longer to die, not least because a new electoral system encourages parties to do deals with each other before elections that need honouring afterwards, which is why the centre-right coalition that took power in 2001 was bigger than it needed to be. France's electoral system, though different, encourages similar behaviour and that country, too, looks likely to sustain its tendency toward surplus majority government (see Table 4.4).

None of this is to suggest, however, that such governments are impossible or even unlikely in other countries. Under certain circumstances over-sized coalitions can turn out to be the best, or even the only, option. A case in point is Belgium. There, the contemporary need to ensure a balance of parties from both the Dutch- and French-speaking communities may make oversized coalitions increasingly necessary. But other classic 'institutional' reasons also come into play: the federalization of the country we explored in Chapter 2 requires two-thirds votes because it entails changes to the constitution. This reminds us that a country's 'preferred solution' to government formation can change over time as institutions and cultures change. Another example of the latter is the Netherlands. True, it still prefers majority governments, but as the differences have blurred between religious and ideological groups – differences that traditionally encouraged broad-based coalitions – then the country has moved from preferring oversized to minimal winning coalitions: prior to 1975, the latter made up only one-fifth of postwar Dutch governments; after 1975, over two-thirds (see Keman, 2002: 230).

Government duration and stability

Much of the fear of minority government in countries with a more or less institutionalized preference for majorities results from the conviction that it is somehow less stable. In fact, this does turn out to be the case, but with important qualifications. A useful rule of thumb is that single-party majority governments last longest, generally one year more than minimal winning coalitions and twice as long as minority governments. Also important, however, is the ideological affinity or 'connectedness' of the various parties that go to make up a government. A government composed of those who are politically close will be more stable than

Table 4.4 An oversized or surplus majority government: France

PCF	Verts	PS	UPM	UDF	Other
Left	Green	Soc. Dem.	Conservative	Liberal	Various
21	3	140	357	29	27

Notes: 1 Shading indicates government.
        2 Seats required for overall majority = 289.

one which is not. Nor, of course, should we forget the influence of institutional rules. For instance, the rules we have already mentioned on votes of no confidence are bound to make a difference. Governments will often last longer where these are hard to lose or (as in Germany, Spain and Poland with their 'constructive' confidence votes) hard to stage in the first place. On the other hand, political culture or system traditions are also important. For example, minority governments in Sweden and Norway last longer than minority governments in Italy or Belgium. Also important is the existence or absence of comprehensive and more-or-less binding coalition agreements. In some countries (for example, the Netherlands) these work well. In others where they are uncommon (such as Italy) they might actually undermine stability by removing the flexibility that particular system seems to demand.

Another qualification is that the 'durability' of European governments to some extent depends on the number of parties that actually make up (or potentially could make up) a coalition. A parliament with a large number of small parties presenting each other (and larger parties) with multiple options can mean that relatively minor shocks caused by policy or personality conflicts are enough to precipitate a collapse of the government. This is especially the case when such a collapse does not necessarily entail fresh elections. All this holds true for Italy, and explains in part, why (until very recently when governments have begun to last longer) it has 'enjoyed' so many more governments than other European countries. On the other hand, Italy's impressive postwar economic performance suggests there is no easy relationship between apparent 'instability' and poor (or at least socio-economically unsuccessful) government!

Dividing the spoils: 'portfolio allocation'

Putting together a coalition, of course, entails coming to some agreement both on policies and on the division of ministerial rewards. 'Who gets what, when and how?' is one of the classic political questions, and no more so than when it comes to what political scientists call 'portfolio allocation' – deciding which party gets which ministries. Except in the case of single-party governments, which in Europe tend to be the exception rather than the rule, this happens in two stages. First, the parties haggle over which ministries and departments they will occupy in the coalition cabinet. Next, they decide who in the party will take up the portfolios they manage to get. Actually, of course, the two stages are not quite so separate: which ministries a party wants may well be conditioned in part by the need to accommodate particular politicians.

In theory, there are basically two methods governing the first stage of portfolio allocation: according to *bargaining strength* or according to some kind of rule of *proportionality*. In the first instance, parties that are part of the coalition can use their importance to that coalition as leverage with which to gain the highest number of seats around the cabinet table as possible – even if this number is disproportionate to the number of MPs they bring to the government benches. The other way is simply to give each party in the coalition the number of cabinet places that best reflects the proportion of MPs with which it provides the coalition. For instance, a party which provides 30 per cent of the MPs on the government benches should entitle it to claim around a third of the cabinet positions.

In the real world, both these systems of allocation operate, but other factors come into play as well. For instance, it is often the case that certain parties have certain favourite ministries. For example, a party representing agricultural interests might ask for, and almost always get, the Agriculture portfolio. Likewise, social democrats tend to want health and social security and greens the environment. This risks sclerosis, as the party in control has little incentive for fresh thinking. On the other hand, it does avoid damaging policy swings and can give the party a chance to make a difference. This is not something that seems to be that easy (as we go on to explore in much more detail in Chapter 9). Yet, there does seem to be some link between which particular party in a coalition controls a particular ministry and the policy direction of that ministry. Political scientists Ian Budge and Hans Keman (1990) looked at labour and finance ministries and found, for instance, that they tended to pursue policies to avoid unemployment more strongly when they were controlled by social democrats rather than conservatives, who in turn were more interested in reducing the role of the state.

Governing

The formation of a government via the naming of a cabinet and the swearing-in of ministers to whom particular portfolios have been awarded is, of course, merely 'the end of the beginning'. Most politicians in Europe, even the most mainstream centrists, see themselves as having a particular job to do, above and beyond merely keeping the state ticking over. Normally, this involves the translation of policy into practice. More precisely, it involves ministers overseeing the drafting of legislation and the progress of civil servants in implementing the policies that have made it through the government formation process – the policies that are included in the coalition agreements that are becoming an increasingly common phenomenon in Europe (see Müller and Strøm, 2000). This, as we suggested in Chapter 3, has become more difficult. Most European states are no longer simply 'top-down' affairs although, as we also saw in Chapter 3, steps have been taken to tighten the hold of politicians over non-elected parts of the 'core executive'.

Ministers also have to meet with and take on board (or, at least, absorb) the views of pressure groups, particularly those on whom they may rely to some degree for the implementation of policy (see Chapter 8). In addition to interest groups and parties, another source of policy (and possible trouble) is the European Union. As we noted in Chapter 2, ministers in some departments may spend two or three days a month consulting with their counterparts in the other member states. In these consultations, they are assisted both by their home departments and by their country's Permanent Representative in Brussels. This 'ambassador to the EU', along with his or her twenty-four colleagues on the intergovernmental committee routinely referred to as COREPER, works to achieve compromises that will protect and promote the 'national interest' and, quite frankly, ease the burden of work for ministers.

Not everything can be 'fixed' beforehand, however. A trip to Brussels can often, therefore, involve ministers trying to get something done or, alternatively, trying to stop something happening. This might be at the behest of other departments, whose civil servants meet in interdepartmental committees with those of the department concerned. Or it might come from pressure groups or the cabinet or even, in Denmark, parliament (see Box 4.7, p. 97). Ministers therefore play a vital linkage role between the national and the 'supranational'. Indeed, they are the embodiment of the blurring of the boundaries between them that is so important a part of contemporary European politics.

In Europe's parliamentary systems, ministers, even when they are not themselves MPs, also play a vital linkage role between citizens and the state by being individually answerable and, in most cases, collectively responsible to parliament. Being individually answerable means that they can, at least theoretically, be held to account for the actions of their department. This is vital if there is ultimately to be democratic control of the state, although not all countries follow Poland, for example, and allow parliament to officially vote 'no confidence' in an individual minister, thereby forcing him or her to resign. Being 'collectively responsible' means that ministers are expected to support government policy or else resign. This cabinet collective responsibility is also important in democratic terms because parliaments express their confidence (or at least their lack of no confidence!) in the government as a whole. The fiction that ministers are all pulling in the same direction has therefore to be maintained, in order to preserve the political accountability of the executive in a system where the buck stops not with one individual (as it does in presidential systems), but with government as a whole.

This supposedly constitutionally necessary convention does not, in fact, hold everywhere: Belgium's cabinet ministers, for instance, are under no such obligation (Keman, 2002: 229) and, notes one expert (Sanford, 2002: 165), their Polish counterparts certainly *feel* under no such obligation! Nor, of course, even where the convention has developed, does it preclude genuine and sometimes bitter disagreement

United Kingdom

Country Profile 4.1

Area: 6.1% of EU-25
Population: 13.1% of EU-25
GDP: 15.7% of EU-25
Joined EU: 1973
Capital city: London

History: The United Kingdom of Great Britain (England, Wales and Scotland) and Northern Ireland took some time to assume its present shape. Wales was all but assimilated into England in the 1540s. But the union of the two with the kingdom of Scotland, long an ally of France, was not achieved until 1707 and not assured until after a Civil War. This conflict, even after the monarchy returned after a short-lived republic, established the supremacy of parliament over the crown. By then, after centuries of religious dispute that began in the sixteenth century when the English king broke with the Roman Catholic church, Britain was a largely Protestant country.

Across the sea, however, the island of Ireland, which Britain had conquered but found hard to subdue, was predominantly Catholic. There was, however, a Protestant minority in Ulster (the name it gave to its stronghold in the north) – one deliberately transplanted there (mostly from Scotland) in order to strengthen colonial power. When, in the wake of the First World War (1914–18), Ireland began to regain its independence, this minority rejected a place in what (in 1948) finally became the sovereign Irish Republic. Instead, it insisted on retaining its links with Great Britain. By the beginning of

the twentieth century, Britain had become the world's greatest commercial and imperial power. Having been forced out of the US in the eighteenth century, it had spent the nineteenth century fighting the French in Europe and using the wealth generated by its pioneering role in the Industrial Revolution to establish control of huge swathes of the Indian subcontinent and Africa.

This imperial expansion helped put the country on a collision course with the up-and-coming industrial power of Germany. Although the ensuing First World War resulted in a British (and French) victory, it proved a big drain on the country's resources, just as its other ally, the US, began to supersede it economically. The Second World War (1939–45), from which Britain also emerged victorious, confirmed this relative decline, as did its inexorable surrender of its overseas empire. On the domestic front, however, the aftermath of the war saw the building by the country's first majority Labour government of a comprehensive welfare state. Since then, power has alternated between Labour, on the centre-left, and the Conservatives, on the centre-right, with the former, under Tony Blair, winning a landslide victory in 1997 after eighteen years out of office.

Economy and society: After decades of being a relatively poor performer, the UK economy – which underwent severe restructuring under the free market policies of Conservative prime Minister Margaret Thatcher during the 1980s – has undergone something of a renaissance in recent years. As a result, the country's 60 million people – around 6.5 per cent of whom came (or their parents or grandparents came) as immigrants from the Caribbean and the Indian subcontinent – enjoy a per capita annual income of about 20 per cent above the EU-25 average (2003). The south-east of the country around London, however, is notably better off than some of the more peripheral regions.

Governance: The UK is unusual in that, like the US, it employs not a PR but a 'first-past-the-post' electoral system to elect MPs to its Westminster parliament. This almost always results in single-party majority governments and makes things difficult for the third largest party, the Liberal Democrats. It does, however, afford representation at Westminster to nationalist parties from Northern Ireland, Scotland and Wales. As a result of the Labour government's pursuit of decentralization and 'devolution', these components of the UK now have their own legislatures, elected under more proportional systems. The Northern Ireland Assembly, however, has failed to function as planned due to disputes over the 'decommissioning' of terrorist weapons.

The UK government likes to think of itself as at the cutting edge of new approaches to governance, contracting out civil service work to public agencies not directly controlled by ministers. It also pioneered the privatization of formerly state-owned utilities.

Foreign policy: The UK proved reluctant to join in European integration until the late 1950s, when it realized its days as a world power were numbered and that its economy was stagnating. After several rebuffs (from France), it finally joined what was then the EEC (now the EU) in 1973. It retains its reputation as 'an awkward partner' in the EU, and has chosen so far not to adopt the euro. EU membership is not seen as contradicting either the country's continuation of its self-styled 'special relationship' with the US (with whom it retains close defence, intelligence and trade links) nor its contacts with its former colonies via the British Commonwealth.

Further reading. Budge *et al.* (2003), Dunleavy *et al.* (2003), Gamble (2003) and Richards and Smith (2002).

within Cabinet. Studies of cabinets across western and eastern Europe suggest that many governments (though not all governments, Sweden being an obvious exception) employ networks of cabinet committees to pre-cook and filter out issues different departments can agree on so as not to disrupt Cabinet itself – although this technique cannot always prevent Cabinet from becoming a court of last resort between disputatious ministers rather than a collegial and collective decison-making enterprize. But those same studies also show that cabinets themselves are mostly still meaningful forums: their deliberations actually change policy (Blondel and Müller-Rommel, 1997, 2001). The extent to which cabinets actually control ministers and prevent them from 'going native' (becoming more interested in protecting their departments than the interests of the government as a whole), however, is another matter (see Andeweg, 2000).

It is also one that feeds into another thorny issue – the extent to which cabinets made up of politicians from different parties, as is the norm in many countries, can actually work together. In fact, co-ordination often takes place outside the cabinet room itself. In an increasing number of countries, the formation process produces a written agreement which is used to bind the coalition partners (and their ministers) into a common programme: the most detailed study we have comes from the Netherlands, and suggests it is quite an effective technique (see Thomson, 2001). In a few countries, the cabinet as a whole is encouraged to 'bond' by spending time with each other (whether they like it or not!) at 'working lunches' and the like – this is famously the case in Norway, for instance.

More often, co-ordination involves not just ministers but other party political actors. Sometimes this kind of co-ordination goes on in so-called coalition committees: the Red–Green coalition that took power in Germany in 1998 for instance quickly established a *koalitionsausschuß*. But more often than not, it occurs informally. This might involve bilateral contacts by ministers or their political appointees to the civil service. In the case of disputes that are harder to resolve, it could involve troubleshooting by the prime minister and deputy prime minister who are very often from different parties. But it may also involve meetings between party leaders, especially when, as occurs surprisingly often in Europe, those leaders do not actually play a formal role in government or even parliament (see Gibson and Harmel, 1998). In Belgium, for example, party chairmen meet frequently (often weekly) with 'their' ministers (see Keman, 2002: 228) and thus exercise a kind of 'outside' influence on Cabinet that would be considered intolerable in a country such as the UK, for example.

Excessive ministerial autonomy (or 'departmentalitis') and intra-coalition co-ordination are not, however, the only problems facing the political part of a state's executive branch. Limited time is clearly a major – if largely overlooked – constraint. And a government's capacity to do what it wants to do may be constrained by events beyond its control such as war, terrorism, recession and opposition from important interest groups such as trade unions or business representatives, often backed by the media. One would also expect, on both a strict interpretation of the separation of powers doctrine and the assumption that they owe their very existence in most European countries to parliament, that governments would be constrained by the second 'branch of government', the legislature. Interestingly, however, the influence of Europe's parliaments over their executives – their governments – is widely dismissed as illusory. According to common wisdom, they are (or have over time been reduced to) talking shops and rubber stamps, while the prime minister and the cabinet call the shots. Is this really the case? Or – considering the variation in both the structure and the operation of parliaments around Europe that we now go on to discuss – is it rather more complicated than that?

Parliaments: one house or two

In most European countries, as in the US, the legislature is 'bicameral', with an 'upper house' that sits in addition to a 'lower house'. A minority – especially in small unitary states (the Scandinavian and Baltic states being a good example) – are 'unicameral'. They have only one chamber, although some (such as Norway) have developed

Table 4.5 Overwhelmingly bicameral, but on what basis: Europe's parliaments

Unicameral	Bicameral	Basis of upper house
	Czech	Directly elected
	France	Electoral colleges of mainly local politicians, and overseas territories
	Germany	Delegates from state governments (*Länder*)
	Italy	95% directly elected; 5% life-time appointments
	Netherlands	Elected by provincial councils
	Poland	Directly elected
	Spain	85% directly elected; 15% indirectly elected by regional authorities
Sweden		N/a
	UK	80% appointed for life; 15% hereditary; 5% church

ways of dividing into what amounts to two chambers in order to scrutinize legislation better. In bicameral systems, the lower house (as the sole chamber in unicameral systems) is filled by MPs or 'deputies' who are directly elected by all adults entitled to vote. Upper houses, on the other hand, are not always directly elected (see Table 4.5). A couple have appointed members, including the British 'House of Lords'. Many are composed of democratically chosen representatives from local, regional – or, in federal countries, state-governments and can therefore be considered 'indirectly' elected.

With the exception of Germany (Box 4.4), and to some extent Italy (see Boxes 4.4 and 4.5, pp. 94–5) and Romania, there is no doubt that in bicameral systems it is the lower house that is the more powerful, and therefore the focus of public attention. On the vast bulk of legislation, the power of upper houses lies primarily in their ability to amend and/or delay, rather than actually to block, bills passed by the lower house. However, in some countries even this power is very limited. This might be because the lower house has the ability to bring things decisively to a head, as in France, where the senate can be overruled. Or it may be because the power is little used since the party composition of the upper house is so similar to that of the lower house, as in Spain. Despite this relative weakness, however, there seems to be no movement to dispense with them altogether in favour of unicameral systems: even in the Czech Republic,

where debate about the need for such a body and its composition was initially so heated that it almost failed to get off the ground, people seem reconciled to its existence, if not exactly enthusiastic.

However, upper houses are not powerless. The power of delay is not necessarily to be sniffed at. Moreover, on proposed constitutional changes supported by the lower house, many of Europe's upper houses possess a power of veto. This makes sense given that their *raison d'etre* – especially in federal systems – is often to protect the rights and interests of sub-national government. And even where such a role is denied them, one can argue that upper houses still, potentially at least, have a valuable role to play. For instance, they provide a forum that, because it is less of a focus for media attention, is somewhat less charged and therefore somewhat more conducive to clear-headed consideration of issues. The UK House of Lords, for example, may be ridiculed as a bastion of entrenched conservatism, but its European Union Committee is acknowledged as performing a useful role in scrutinizing EU legislation that will impact the UK.

Parliaments: hiring and firing

Generally, however, when most Europeans think of parliament, they think of the directly elected lower house. This is the place that not only passes laws, but makes and breaks – and in between hope-

BOX 4.4

The upper house with the upper hand? The German Bundesrat

Germany's upper house, the *Bundesrat*, is made up of sixty-eight members belonging to delegations from the governments of each of the Federal Republic's sixteen states (*Länder*), with delegations varying in strength from three to six members depending on the size of the state. These representatives of the *Länder* have quite a large role in the passing of federal (i.e. national) legislation. The *Bundesrat* has veto power over legislation impacting on states – which means that over half of all legislation has to be voted on and approved there. And even when a bill does not fall into this category, it is open to the *Bundesrat* to reject it. This obliges the lower house, the *Bundestag*, to produce a 'yes' vote as big as the *Bundesrat*'s 'no' vote in order to overrule it. The extent to which this makes things awkward for the government depends, more than anything, on whether the party controlling it also controls the upper house. As in the US, this depends on it being able to win those state elections that take place in between federal elections. If the opposition win these (and they very often do as the government bears the brunt of 'mid-term blues'), the party composition of one or more states' delegations changes, causing the government to lose its control of the *Bundesrat*. When this happens, 'divided government' prevails and the upper house comes into its own. Perhaps through negotiation in the *Vermittlungsausschuß* (the mediation committee formed by representatives from both houses), the *Bundesrat* often obliges the government in the lower house to modify those aspects of its legislative programme that opposition parties do not support. It is this need to take account of the views of opposition parties that makes Germany's parliament (and perhaps its politics in general) so consensual. According to critics, though, it also makes radical reform practically impossible (see Chapter 9). Frustration on both sides led to the setting up in 2003 of a bicameral commission to look into modernizing the federal structure, possibly via a deal that sees the *Länder* get the right to determine things at local level in return for a reduction in their ability to block measures at the federal level.

fully scrutinizes – governments. As we have seen, running European countries rests on a party or a coalition of parties being able to command a majority in confidence and supply votes in parliament. Ultimately, then, parliaments are theoretically the most powerful branch of government. When it comes to the crunch, it is they who retain the right to hire and fire the executive, thereby translating the results of elections into a government and forcing that government to account to those whom electors elect, and perhaps the electors themselves. But how powerful does this make them in practice?

Hiring is indeed crucial, as we have suggested when looking at government formation. But it normally pits one party or collection of parties against another rather than the legislature as a whole against the executive. Moreover, once the task is complete, the power is essentially 'used up' until next time. Similarly, the power granted by the right to fire the executive lies more in the threat to use it than its actual use. The fact that it is a 'nuclear option' probably explains why, although the right of dismissal exists, it is surprisingly rarely used and few European governments are actually brought down by votes of no-confidence. This is partly, of course, because some of them choose to go before they are formally pushed. Others are sufficiently adaptable to avoid the kind of policies that would offend the MPs that originally supported their formation. Still others, when this cannot be done, are sufficiently prescient to have arranged alternative sources of support.

In a handful of cases, institutional rules make votes of no-confidence even more unlikely. In Germany, Spain and Poland, as we have seen, a government can be defeated only by a 'constructive' vote of no-confidence, which demands that the opposition already has an alternative government ready to take over immediately. In many countries, a government defeat in the house can – although it does not always – lead to new elections that can come as a merciful release after a period of political crisis or legislative gridlock. But in Norway, where elections can be held only every four years, this option is unavailable. This makes no-confidence motions a less attractive way of 'solving' a supposedly intractable parliamentary problem. The fact that a government defeat on a motion of confidence can lead to fresh elections in other countries points to the fact that parliament's right to defeat the executive is, in any case, normally balanced by the executive's right to dissolve (or request the head of state to dissolve) parliament – a right that exists in all European democracies outside Norway, Switzerland and Finland. If, as an MP, your party is not likely to do well in a snap election, you are unlikely, however dissatisfied you are with the government, to stage a vote of no-confidence and thereby risk cutting off your nose to spite your face.

Parliaments: the production of law

Parliament's other most important function is the making (or at least the production) of law – the consideration and passing of legislation. There is provision in most countries for so-called 'private members bills'. But by far the bulk of the proposals (and certainly the bulk of proposals that stand an earthly chance of actually ending up on the statute book) will come from the government that, as we shall suggest, can pretty much rely on party discipline to get its way. Consequently, it is all too easy to buy into the caricature of European legislatures as merely 'rubber stamps' or 'talking shops' – or, worse, 'sausage machines' into which the executive shoves its bills, cranks the handle, makes mincemeat out of the opposition, and smiles as its statutes pop out at the other end. Without going too far the other way, it is fair to suggest that such metaphors disguise a good deal of variation, but once again it is patterned variation.

Broadly, one can divide parliaments in western Europe into two groups that correspond to Lijphart's distinction between majoritarian and consensual systems (see Lijphart, 1999). In the former group, one would include the UK, and probably Spain, along with Ireland, Greece and France. In these countries, the government pursues its agenda with little regard for the input of other parties, which are more often than not clearly regarded as the opposition. This opposition knows that government is almost guaranteed to get its

---

BOX 4.5
The Italian Senato: powerful or pointless?

With the exception of a handful of senators-for-life, the vast bulk of the Italian *Senato* is directly elected to an upper house that has equal standing with the lower house, the *Camera dei Deputati*. Italy therefore would appear to have one of the most powerful second chambers anywhere in the world. But, as in Spain, because elections to the two houses take place simultaneously the party complexion of each is remarkably similar. Consequently there is far less of the partisan friction witnessed in Germany (see Box 4.4). This does not, however, prevent disagreements between the two chambers on particular pieces of legislation, not least because local and national interest groups lobby both assiduously. Because both houses have equal power, some bills can be batted back and forth between them for so long that they perish when new parliamentary elections are held. Given this tendency to delay legislation, Italians can be forgiven for wondering quite what the point of bicameralism is in their country. On the other hand, Italy seems headed toward a more majoritarian and yet also a more devolved future, and it seems as if the *Senato* may now be given a regional basis, and therefore the unique constitutional function it currently lacks. Both these developments may see it emerge as more of a genuine countervailing force.

---

way. And anyway, it is likely to be sympathetic to the theory that its winning of the election gives it a mandate to do so. Therefore, opposition parties can do little more than offer the kind of criticism that (a) will allow them to say 'I told you so' at the next election, at which hopefully the mandate will pass to them; and (b) hopefully undermine the government's popularity in the meantime. Parliament, in terms used by some political scientists, is an 'arena' rather than a truly 'transformative' institution – and one that reacts to, and can do little or nothing to stop or even seriously slow up government initiatives (see Box 4.6).

The same can be said of 'consensual' parliaments, such as those in Germany, the Netherlands

---

BOX 4.6
France's feeble parliament

Most observers agree that the *Assemblée Nationale* is one of Europe's weakest legislatures. Its members do themselves no favours by often staying away in order to attend to the affairs of local government, in which many continue to hold elected office and have their main power-base. The government controls parliament's agenda. It can insist on it taking a yes/no 'package vote' on a bill in its unamended state. It has nothing to fear from unwieldy, oversized committees. And it has at its disposal a host of procedural techniques to over-come any residual power of delay. Parliament, constitutionally, can legislate only in certain prescribed areas outside of which government can issue what amount to decrees. The censure motion necessary to oust any government determined to insist on treating a particular bill as a matter of confidence is difficult to employ. Moreover, parliament is constitutionally unable to pass a non-governmental bill or amendment that would involve lowering state revenues or increasing expenditure!

Fortunately, France's constitutional court (see Chapter 3) has recently made decree laws subject to much greater constraint. In addition, regulations can be amended by the Assembly. Theoretically, it also gets to subject all bills to committee scrutiny before the plenary session and now even gets to meet all year round, not just the six months initially allotted to it. But the picture painted is nonetheless one of weakness. This came about by design rather than by chance: the framers of the 'Fifth Republic' that began in 1958 were reacting – some might say overreacting – to a history of governments that were often powerless in the face of an Assembly riven by ideological and geographical disputes.

---

they may be institutionally supported. For instance, parliament's agenda might require the unanimous (or near-unanimous) consent of all parties (as in Scandinavia, and the Germanic and low countries, as well as Spain and Italy) rather than being decided by the government majority (as in the United Kingdom, Ireland, France, Greece and Portugal) – something frequently used as an indicator of the overall power of parliament (see Table 4.6).

The parliaments of Central and Eastern Europe are harder to locate in such a schema. At first, a combination of volatile party systems, arguments between presidents and prime ministers, and weak bureaucratic support for the executive seemed to suggest that parliaments in the region had, if not the upper hand, then rather more power than in the more established democracies (see Kopecký, 2003). Certainly, the Polish *Sejm* (which, it must be said, has a proud history stretching back over centuries) could claim to be one of Europe's more independent legislatures: it has a powerful committee system (a generally accepted indicator of strength, as we see below) whose members can initiate legislation, up to half of which (a very high proportion in relative terms) passes (see Sanford, 2002: chapter 5). Yet, it is hard to know how much of its strength is institutional and how much derives from the difficulties Polish governments face because of the unusually large number of parties and 'party-hopping' by Polish MPs, all of which makes things difficult for governments. Across the region as a whole, however, decreasing turnover among, and increasing professionalization of, MPs and the declining number of parties in most of its parliaments, have made them easier to manage. Also important in strengthening governments' hands have been the fast-track procedures brought in to ensure that parliaments could get through the huge body of legislation needed to meet the requirements of accession to the EU. It will be interesting to see whether such procedures are used for other purposes now that the accession process is complete.

The differences between consensual and majoritarian parliaments are visual as well as rule-based. Some countries even have seating systems designed to take some of the heat out of the more adversar-

(and Belgium), Sweden (and other Scandinavian countries) and Italy, but not without some qualification. While they are still essentially 'reactive' (at least when compared to the US Congress) parliaments in these countries tend to feature more constructive criticism and operate at least sometimes in 'cross-party' rather than always 'inter-party' mode (King, 1976). These tendencies are, or have become, culturally ingrained, though

Table 4.6 European parliaments: the strong and the weak								
Strong parliament (Sets own agenda; strong committee system)					*Weak parliament* (Government sets agenda; weak committees)			
Germany	Sweden	Italy	Poland	Netherlands	Czech Rep.	UK	Spain	France

ial aspects of parliamentary politics: Sweden, for example, makes its MPs sit in regional blocs rather than according to party, and many parliaments in Europe avoid the adversarial layout of the British House of Commons (see Andeweg and Mijzink's chapter in Döring, 1995, for the layout of European legislatures). Perhaps most important, however, for both the facilitation of cross-party activity and the overall power of parliament is the existence of powerful legislative committees. These are especially prevalent in Scandinavian parliaments (see Box 4.7), in Germany and in some of the newer democracies in Central and Eastern Europe, especially Poland. In many countries in those regions, such committees get to make amendments to (and in some cases redraft) bills before they are debated on the floor of the house by all interested MPs in what is known as 'plenary session'. In majoritarian systems, committees usually get to go over the bill only once it has received at least one, and possibly two, readings in plenary, by which time party positions have already hardened up and legislation is more 'set in stone'. Unlike in their consensual counterparts, committee membership in these systems may not even be distributed according to each party's share of seats. In more consensual systems, proportionality is taken as given and (especially where there are minority governments) increases the chances of committees taking an independent line.

BOX 4.7
Power outside the plenary: Danish parliamentary committees

Although other Scandinavian parliaments – and Germany and Poland – boast influential committees, and although some Italian committees traditionally had the right of final assent on some minor legislation, experts agree that the Danish *Folketing* possesses Europe's most powerful parliamentary committees. It has twenty-four standing (i.e. permanent) committees, each with seventeen members, with membership roughly proportional to the party distribution of seats in parliament. Most committees cover the work of one particular ministry. When a minister proposes a bill, he or she can expect a flood of written questions by committee members and may well be asked to appear in person, too. Delay is not advisable because any bill that does not make it through all its stages in the parliamentary session in which it is introduced will have to start all over again. The committees' report on the bill outlines the parties' positions and amendments that they hope to see adopted in the second reading. In many parliaments that would be it, but in Denmark an MP can demand that the bill go back to committee after the second reading for a supplementary report!

All *Folketing* committees are potentially powerful because, as in other Scandinavian countries, minority government is so common, meaning that the executive will rarely have a majority in committee. But the two most powerful are, without doubt, the Finance Committee, whose say on the budget is much greater than its counterparts in other legislatures, and the European Affairs Committee, which is able to dictate to the country's ministers the stand they must take on certain issues when voting in Brussels. Ministers are first answerable to the Committee, and only then to their colleagues for their EU-related actions. This loss of executive autonomy is seen as a price worth paying by governments keen to ensure that rows over 'Europe' do not break them apart or cause other parties to withdraw their support.

Parliaments: scrutiny and oversight

MPs, and therefore parliaments, can exercise the crucial role of scrutiny and oversight over the executive via parliamentary questions, written or oral. The use of this technique, once a hallmark of 'Westminster', majoritarian systems, is now ubiquitous and rising throughout Europe, not least because of the realization, particularly by opposition parties, that hard-hitting questions and possibly inadequate replies are eagerly picked up on by the media. The latter (as we shall see in Chapter 7) is always looking to focus on the controversial and the dramatic in order to hold consumers' interest in a subject that they fear may otherwise cause them to change channels. In many countries, questions can lead direct to a special debate on the reply. These so-called 'interpellation' debates serve to keep the spotlight on the government for even longer, even if, critics argue, they tend (like many of the goings-on in parliament) to generate more heat than light.

The main way, however, that Europe's parliaments perform scrutiny and oversight on the executive is via the committee system. Interestingly, in some countries where committees play a relatively weak role in legislation, they play a much bigger role in holding ministers to account for the work of their departments. For instance, the UK parliament's 'select committees' are more specialized, have long-term membership and can instigate and take evidence in their own enquiries; they therefore offer far more of a challenge to the executive than the much larger, *ad hoc* 'standing committees' that are charged with examining legislation. Conversely, committees in Sweden are less active in this respect than they are in law-making, where they frequently (and successfully) make changes to legislation.

It is unusual for Europe's legislators to carve out a powerful niche for themselves as committee specialists in the manner of their US counterparts. But being seen to do a good job in this area can boost the chances of promotion into the ranks of government, although whether, as a government backbencher, 'a good job' means giving ministers a hard or an easy time is a moot point! Committee work also gives MPs a chance to bring to bear their own professional experience on questions of national importance: those with, say, a military or a medical background may be valuable on the Defence or Health Committee. But such work does more than merely pad out MPs' résumés. It can throw the spotlight on issues the executive would rather remain obscure.

Moreover, with the increasing impact of EU legislation on domestic affairs, committees can arguably go some way to closing the so-called **democratic deficit**. Germany's constitution, the Basic Law, for instance, obliges its government to inform the *Bundestag*'s EU Affairs Committee (attended by both MPs and MEPs) of impending European legislation before it becomes 'set in stone'. Indeed, national parliaments all over Europe – though more slowly in the weaker parliaments, perhaps (Dimitrakopoulos, 2001) – are waking up to the fact that, in order to have any influence at all on European legislation, they have to assert a right to examine and express their opinions on proposed EU law much sooner than governments would otherwise like them to (see Maurer and Wessels, 2001 and Raunio and Hix, 2000). Indeed, they can now invoke a protocol to the Amsterdam Treaty that obliges governments (though not, note, in urgent cases!) to give them a minimum of six weeks between notifying their national parliaments of a proposal and it coming to the Council of Ministers for a decision.

On the other hand, six weeks is hardly adequate, and, as a closer look at the German example shows (see Holzhacker, 2002), partisan considerations – protecting or damaging the government – are often

> **Definition**
> The EU's **democratic deficit** is the gap between the powers and competences assumed by the EU and the ability of European citizens to determine the make-up of those institutions and oversee the exercise of those powers and competences. It arises from the tendency of member states, via treaty or treaty-based legal decisions, to cede legislative and executive functions that would hitherto have been the preserve of elected parliaments and governments to unelected bodies (such as the Council of Ministers and the Commission) that the EP cannot effectively hold to account.

only just below the surface in the work of European affairs committees. In any case, paying them too much attention can distract us from an arguably much more profound truth; namely, the fact that, because they continue to take the leading role in the relationship between states and the EU, governments (and, indeed, the executive) in general enjoy a profound institutional and informational advantage over their legislative 'colleagues' – an advantage they have always enjoyed with regard to diplomacy and foreign policy (see Putnam, 1988). To the extent that an increasingly important EU continues to rest, ultimately, on intergovernmental bargaining and to exclude national legislatures from that part of its governance which can be called 'supranational' (see Chapter 2), then Europe's parliaments look set to lose out even more to its governments (see Moravcsik, 2001). As a fascinating case study of the Austrian parliament shows (Falkner, 2000a), this includes even those parliaments that thought they had negotiated extra safeguards against marginalization prior to their country joining the EU. And it may even include parliaments in those countries that are not EU member states: a recent study of Switzerland, for instance, illustrates that when (as often happens) the country has to undertake legislative change so as to ensure that it remains roughly in line with what is going on within the EU itself, the executive wields more power than it would do on purely domestic legislation (see Sciarini, Fischer and Nicolet, 2004).

Parliament and government: the European level

It is perfectly possible to slot into our discussion of the functions and strengths of parliaments, and their relationships with governments, mention of the institution that, more than national legislatures, is supposed to help close the 'democratic deficit' – the European Parliament (EP). Indeed, recent academic work on the latter has argued strongly that the EP (and, in fact, the EU in general) be analysed, not as *sui generis* (constituting a unique class of its own), but using the same tools of analysis (coalition theory, disaggregating the various roles and functions of different parts of the

system, etc.) that comparative politics uses to examine other political institutions (see Hix, 2004). This is not merely an analytical imperative, but a normative one, too: as we have suggested above, national parliaments find it hard to play much of a role in European law-making, while links with each other and with the EP through bodies such as COSAC (the Conference of Community and European Affairs Committees; see Corbett, Jacobs and Shackleton, 2003: 282–5) seem unlikely to lend them that much leverage. This makes it all the more vital for democracy in Europe that we understand the workings of the EP, using what we already know about legislatures more generally to help us.

For instance, one can argue that the EU has what amounts to a bicameral legislature along the lines of some federal parliaments. The increasing use of the co-decision procedure (see Chapter 2), for instance, gives equal power on some legislation to the two 'chambers', the EP and the Council of Ministers – particularly now that the two have to resolve their differences in a conciliation committee (not unlike the German parliament's *Vermittlungsausschuß* mentioned in Box 4.4: p. 94) in order for legislation not to fail. On the other hand, at least until co-decision becomes the norm for every piece of EU legislation, one can argue that there remains a big difference in that, in the EU, the chamber representing the people (the EP) is weaker than the one representing the states or regions (the Council). And the dissimilarities do not, of course, end there. For instance, the Council of Ministers, despite its reputation as a 'bastion of intergovernmentalism' (see Chapter 2), often co-operates with the supposedly 'supranational' Commission (in its role as the 'executive' of the EU) on the rejection of amendments by the EP (see Tsebelis *et al.*, 2001); and, unlike any other legislative chamber in Europe, the Council gets to hold its debates in secret! The other big difference between the EU and its member states is that, in the EU, the 'executive' or 'government' (such as it is) is not formed by a majority in the legislature. Instead, it is divided between the Commission and the European Council, made up by the heads of government of the member states.

This means that there is a relatively (indeed, a very) indistinct relationship between the results of elections to the EP (see Chapter 6) and the political direction of the EU. Even if (as was the case immediately after centre-right parties did well in the EP elections of 2004) one side of the political spectrum, can occasionally claim what amounts to a 'majority' in the Commission, the Council of Ministers and the EP, it rarely lasts long. And it may not be that significant: national governments change, and there is no hard and fast relationship between commissioners' and ministers' party affiliations and the policy line they take. Moreover, while the EP can withhold its approval of the president and its commission and can (and has on rare occasions, such as 1999) help to effect their removal, its role in 'hiring and firing' the executive is, again, rather less direct than its counterparts in the member states.

Another key difference between many national parliaments and the EP is that voting in the latter often proceeds along cross-party lines. Often this is because, in order to realize its potential legislative strength *vis-a-vis* the Council of Ministers, the EP needs to cobble together an absolute majority of all members, notwithstanding the fact that, as members of national parties, nearly all of them belong to increasingly consolidated European Parliamentary Groups (see Figure 4.1). This kind of majority is practically impossible unless the two biggest parties, the social democratic PES and the Christian Democrat/conservative EPP–ED, vote together (see Kreppel, 2000, 2002). Given they are often joined by the relatively large liberal grouping, the ALDE, this means that the EP is often dominated by a kind of 'grand coalition' that marginalizes the smaller, less centrist groups. The party line-up may, then, may resemble that of, say, the Netherlands or Germany (see Chapter 5), but unlike those countries (and others) it shows little sign of moving from cosy centrism to more bipartisan competition between right and left (see Chapter 9). Of course, we should not forget that cross-party voting also goes on in some of Europe's more consensual parliaments, such as the Swedish *Riksdag*. There, it is largely the product of a lawmaking process in which parliamentary committees play an important role. Given that committees also play a similarly vital role in the life of the EP, this is one way in which it can be said to demonstrate significant similarities with national parliaments. Another is the attempt by the EP to improve its scrutiny and oversight of the Commission (see Corbett, Jacobs and Shackleton, 2003: 241–68).

Arguably, in fact, MEPs have more incentives than MPs to play the scrutineer and the overseer. Unlike at least some of their national counterparts (and even US Congressmen to some extent), they have no partisan interest in protecting the executive, which allows them more freedom to range across party lines in their criticisms. That said, we need to be very careful not to think that parties (or technically party groups) are not that important in the EP. If anything, they are becoming increasingly important. True, national parties, where issues are

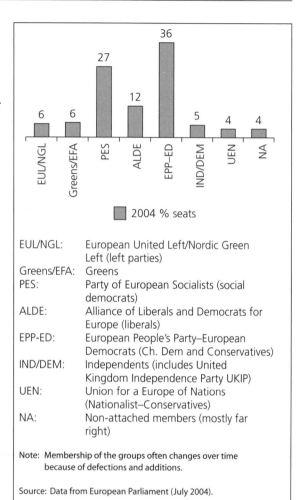

EUL/NGL: European United Left/Nordic Green Left (left parties)
Greens/EFA: Greens
PES: Party of European Socialists (social democrats)
ALDE: Alliance of Liberals and Democrats for Europe (liberals)
EPP-ED: European People's Party–European Democrats (Ch. Dem and Conservatives)
IND/DEM: Independents (includes United Kingdom Independence Party UKIP)
UEN: Union for a Europe of Nations (Nationalist–Conservatives)
NA: Non-attached members (mostly far right)

Note: Membership of the groups often changes over time because of defections and additions.

Source: Data from European Parliament (July 2004).

Figure 4.1 Party groups in the EP following the 2004 elections

thought to be sufficiently important, can occasionally request (and normally rely on) their MEPs to vote differently to the EP group to which the party belongs (see Hix, 2002). But the extent to which MEPs now vote along party group lines (called 'cohesion' in the jargon) is higher than ever, and at nearly 90 per cent is much closer to European than to US levels; meanwhile the bigger groups appear to be competing more often along predicable ideological lines (see Hix, Kreppel and Noury, 2003; see also Faas, 2003).

Parliament, power and parties

Talk of cohesion and voting along party lines brings us back to the reasons why legislatures in Europe are generally relatively weak. While the patterned variation that emerges between consensual and majoritarian democracies can be summed up graphically (as in Table 4.6: p. 97), we should be careful not to think things are that simple. Because government in Europe is parliamentary and party government, there is no clear, US-style separation between the executive and the legislature. This means that the conflicts between the two branches are likely to pale into insignificance alongside conflicts between the government majority and the 'opposition'. Moreover, the power of parliament is as contingent on parliamentary arithmetic (and therefore electoral fortunes) as it is on constitutional conventions or internal organization. Even in consensual countries, an executive made up of a majority coalition or single-party majority will encounter fewer problems with the legislature than a minority government. In any case, schemas of strong and weak parliaments risk relying too much on comparisons of formal powers when, in fact, the strength or weakness of the institutions may lie elsewhere. A clue to where this 'elsewhere' might be comes in the observation made about the UK by French political scientist Maurice Duverger (see Duverger, 1954: 46): 'Parliament and Government,' he noted, 'are like two machines driven by the same motor – the party.'

How hard do most European governments have to work to command the votes of their MPs? In most countries, the answer – normally, anyway – is not terribly hard at all. Levels of party discipline are very high in most of Europe's parliaments. Parliaments in the newer democracies of Central and Eastern Europe initially experienced higher turnover of MPs and more party splits – something that, along with their role as constitutional founders made them appear rather stronger than they really were, constitutionally speaking. But, with the notable exception of Poland, turnover and defections – labelled 'party tourism' (see Millard, 2004: chapter 6) – have in general dropped. Nowadays, all over Europe, most members in most parliaments stay loyal. They have more in common ideologically with their own party than with others and, even in Central and Eastern Europe, they are becoming evermore professionalized, full-time politicians. As such, they are evermore dependent on the party to whom they owe their (re)election, their salary, their staff (such as it is: US congressmen are far better resourced), their privileges, and their chance of executive office

Europe's MPs, then, may have some vestigial loyalty to their home-base or perhaps the profession or pressure group with whom they were associated before they came into parliament. But in general it will weigh relatively lightly with them compared to, say, their counterparts in the US Congress. The same is even true for members of the EP, for whom domestic concerns, while still important, are giving way more and more to loyalty to what appear to be increasingly competitive party groups. Moreover, in as much as the links between national parliaments and the EP have increased over the years – and it is easy to overplay the extent to which even timetabled joint sessions of committees constitutes significant growth – any meaningful co-ordination in the future will probably need to take place at the intra-party as much as at the interparliamentary level (see Messmer, 2003).

All this means that the key to the executive dominance demonstrated in both the consensual and majoritarian democracies of Europe, is to be found inside parties – forums that, sadly, political scientists, although they can make educated guesses (see Heidar and Koole, 2000), are almost never allowed into. But it also means that the power of the executive can at least potentially vary over time according to the hold it has on its own 'backbenchers'. This might depend, say, on the selection

---

BOX 4.8
Europe's unrepresentative representatives?

As the political theorist Edmund Burke argued, parliamentarians are not delegates but representatives: their job is not simply to parrot the views of their parties, but to exercise their judgement in the best interests of their constituents and the country as a whole. Should they therefore be literally representative of its population? If 5 per cent of citizens, for instance, are of Arab descent, should 5 per cent of MPs also be Arabs? If 40 per cent are working-class, should parliament reflect the same proportion? And given that women make up at least half the population, then should not every other MP be female? Anyone answering 'yes' to all these questions is likely to be disappointed. Parliaments in Europe are notoriously unrepresentative of racial minorities. They are also becoming ever more middle-class: social democratic and other left-wing parties no longer see it as their mission to bring 'workers' into parliament, and the communist aspiration that parliaments should reflect ordinary people has long been abandoned by most parties in East and Central Europe, who now also largely field candidates drawn from the professions (see Millard, 2004: 156–83).

As for gender, the invaluable (and constantly updated) 'league table' on women in parliament maintained by the Interparliamentary Union (http://www.ipu.org/wmn-e/classif.htm) shows huge variation across the continent, as the following summary indicates:

▶ *Good* (over one in three MPs are women): Sweden, the Netherlands, Spain.

▶ *Fair* (almost a third): Germany, the EP.

▶ *So-so* (one in five, or less): Czech Republic, Poland, UK.

▶ *Could do better* (as in the US, not much over one in ten): France and Italy

Note that the same patterned variation is replicated at cabinet level, according to figures produced by the Council of Europe in 2002 (http://www.coe.int/t/e/Human_Rights/Equality/). There may be a link between PR (see Chapter 6) and greater representativeness, but it seems to depend on the precise system used and may be less important than the tendency of left-wing parties to promote women more heavily (an example would be the Spanish government elected in 2004). Yet any trend toward parliamentary gender equality is hardly impressive across the continent! Generally, women are best represented in those countries where they can expect to enjoy greater equality (in practice as well as in theory) in other areas of life. Rules to encourage 'parity' do not always work: they were introduced for the 2002 elections in France, but many parties simply paid the fines involved rather than change the habits of a lifetime (see Baudino, 2003).

---

processes of the parties that form the government, as well as on what those backbenchers think are its chances of re-election. Put bluntly, a government that (a) looks likely to suffer at the next election and (b) is made up of one or more parties that can do little to stop the reselection of recalcitrant MPs is probably going to have to pay attention to those MPs (and therefore parliament). One that is polling well, and maintains firm and centralized control over who gets to go where on the party list next time around, is likely to have fewer problems.

We should, of course, avoid allowing the question of who is weaker and who is stronger, the govern-ment or parliament, to completely overshadow our thinking on these 'branches of government'. After all, although politics is about power, it is also about function. Parliaments hire and fire, produce laws, scrutinize the activities of the executive and its bureaucracy, but they also play a vital role in legit-imizing (if not necessarily popularizing!) rule by a necessarily smaller set of people over a much larger group of us. Moreover, they perform a recruitment role by launching the political careers of that smaller set of people – though whether they do it very well (at least when it comes to being represen-tative) is another matter (see Box 4.8). Even if parliaments are just 'talking shops', as some cynics allege, they would still be performing the function of a forum for interests (organized or otherwise), as well as expressing and channelling people's views to those whom they choose, more or less willingly, to contract out governance.

On the other hand, one of the main messages of this chapter is that anyone searching for evidence of the power of parliaments and governments in Europe needs to look behind closed doors. They will not find it by focusing on the kind of open confrontation that sometimes occurred between, say, kings and queens and their parliaments in times past or that still occurs between executive presidents and their legislatures outside Europe. Instead, they will find it, as Duverger implies, in institutions that, while they attract their fair share of criticism these days, nevertheless continue to play a crucial part in politics in Europe. It is to these institutions, the political parties, that we now turn.

Learning resources

On Europe's presidents, see Elgie (1999). For an overview of cabinet structures and norms, see Blondel and Müller-Rommel (1997, 2001). On the supposed 'presidentialization' of Europe's parliamentary and party democracies, see Poguntke and Webb (2004). The obvious starting-point on parliamentary, coalition governments is Müller and Strøm (2000). Also useful are Strøm, Budge and Laver, (1994) and De Winter (2002). A good first port of call on parliaments and governments would be the contributions to Döring (1995) and Norton (1998). Also useful is Müller and Saalfield (1997). For an invaluable attempt to get at what goes on behind closed doors, see Heidar and Koole (2000). For Central and Eastern Europe, see Kopecky (2003). On the EP, there are three ideal places to start: Corbett, Jacobs and Shackleton (2003), Hix and Scully (2003) and Judge and Earnshaw (2003). On the distinctions between 'consensual' and 'majoritarian' democracies, see the incomparable Lijphart (1999). Parliaments are well represented on the net: the best gateway is http://www.ipu.org. See http://www.idea.int/women/parl/toc.htm for more on women in parliament. Also interesting are Davis (1997) and Freeman (2002). Millard (2004: 223) not only provides an account of the situation of women in postcommunist parliaments, but a good introduction to the issue of female representation more generally.

EXECUTIVE SUMMARY

- Unlike their American counterpart, nearly all Europe's presidents are – like Europe's monarchs – largely ceremonial figures, even where they are directly elected by the people.

- Governments in Europe are instead headed by a prime minister, who with his or her cabinet of ministerial colleagues, derives authority from, and is collectively responsible to, parliament. Most owe their office to deals done between the parties that are elected to it. The distinction between the executive and the legislative branches of government is therefore blurred.

- Most parliaments are bicameral. Governments in Europe have to be able to command a majority in the lower house of parliament, but only on crucial confidence votes. The incidence of minority government is much higher than is generally assumed.

- The duration and stability of governments varies according to the size of their majority, but cabinets (and cabinet ministers) share similar challenges across Europe, even if some are more collective enterprizes than others.

- Few parliaments in Europe are anything like as powerful as, say, the US Congress, though some are less weak than others, particularly those with a strong committee system and/or an upper house with the ability to block legislation.

- The EP differs from other European legislatures because it does not produce governments, but is becoming more like them with regard to party politics. It is relatively weak compared to other EU institutions, although this is beginning to change.

- At the domestic level, governments get their way sooner or later, however. This is largely because of the continued cohesion and strength of political parties.

Chapter 5

Parties: how the past affects the present, and an uncertain future

What are parties and what are they for?
Organization
Party systems and party families
The bases of party systems: social and institutional, luck and skill
Party system change?
Are parties in decline?
The Europeanization of parties and party systems?

In Chapter 4 we suggested that parties are the key to understanding how the executive in Europe dominates the legislature – how the government, in other words, controls parliament. In fact, parties are crucial to the government and politics of European countries, more generally. Without them representative democracy could not function. In this chapter we explain what parties are, and how they came to be. We also look the ways they organize, and at the way political scientists have tried, by looking at their ideas and their origins, to sort them into meaningful categories that they call 'party families', most of which are represented in almost every individual country's **party system**. We go on to look at these systems and at how political science tries to classify them, and ask whether, why, how and how much they are changing. Finally, we touch on debates on how parties should be funded and explore the popular notion that parties – unpopular with the public and struggling for members – are on the way out.

What are parties and what are they for?

Although they have been around for some 200 years, **political parties** still sometimes seem easier to recognize than to pin down. We have made an attempt to come to a workable definition, but it is

> **Definition**
> A country's **party system** is the more or less stable configuration of political parties which normally compete in national elections. It is normally characterized by how many parties there are, what they stand for and their relative strengths. In more sophisticated definitions (see Mair, 1996) it is also characterized by the extent to which competition between parties is predictable or unpredictable, and post-election changes in government tend to be marginal or wholesale. A country's party system is not the same as its electoral system – which is merely the means by which votes are turned into seats – though it may be influenced by it. It can also be affected by other institutional arrangements (constitutions, parliaments, etc.) and tends to be rooted in long-standing social conflicts.

necessarily qualified. The qualification 'for the most part' is necessary because there are parties, for instance, that refuse either to contest elections at all or, if they do, make it clear that their eventual aim is not to work within the system but to dismantle it. Others exist only for their own (and hopefully others') amusement. 'More often than not' is also a necessary caveat because there may be no clear link between a party's ideas and certain interests and/or values. Its ideas may reflect the personal predilections of a charismatic leader. A party's ideas may

> **Definition**
> **Political parties** are organizations that, for the most part, recruit candidates to contest elections in the hope that they can then participate in government, or at least push it in the direction of their own ideas – ideas that, more often than not, reflect the socio-economic interests and/or moral values of those who support them.

also owe more to historical hangovers than current concerns.

As far as functions go, a hypothetical job description for parties would include, at a minimum, the following:

▶ Representing socially or culturally significant interests at the same time as 'aggregating' (lumping together and packaging) their sometimes contradictory preferences
▶ Recruiting, selecting, socializing and providing material and ideological support to candidates and elected politicians who will do the representing, often at both national and sub-national level
▶ Structuring an otherwise bewildering array of choices available to voters at parliamentary and local elections, which, by their very presence, they render competitive
▶ Facilitating the formation of governments that produce relatively co-ordinated and coherent policy responses to perceived and real problems
▶ Effectively mediating between millions of citizens and a state that otherwise might act exclusively in the interest of those it employs and those whose economic clout could give them a disproportionate say in its direction.

Organization

As with ideas, so with organization (see Box 5.1). The structure of most parties, as well as being influenced by both electoral competition and the political philosophy the party claims to represent, is heavily constrained, if not wholly determined, by both their history and changes in their environment – an environment they can only do a little to help shape.

On a superficial level, accounts of modern party organization do not depart much from the common wisdom found in the media. This portrays parties as basically in the hands of leaders determined not to allow their more zealous supporters to scupper their electoral chances by remaining true to whatever cause the party was set up to promote or defend. In fact, however, when we look more closely, that portrait – and therefore the common wisdom – is far from describing the

reality for many, if not most, parties. Repeated investigation by political scientists of what is sometimes called the 'law of curvilinear disparity' (the idea that leaders and voters are routinely less 'extreme' and more electorally-minded than activists) suggests that it is no more a law – or at least a universally applicable one – than is Michels's so called 'iron law of oligarchy' (see Box 5.2).

In other words, many party supporters and members are just as interested in winning elections as leaders. And, as we suggested in Chapter 4 when we looked at government formation, many, if not most, of those leaders care deeply about what policies they pursue.

There is a tendency for parties in European democracies to conform to 'common-sense', essentially hierarchical, norms of organization that apply across a variety of social, government and commercial sectors. Whether or not this so-called 'isomorphism' (or fit) obeys the 'iron law' outlined in Box 5.2 is, however, a moot point. After all, the extent to which they conform to those norms varies considerably. For instance, the Italian party *Forza Italia* was founded in the early 1990s by continental media magnate and now Italian Prime Minister, Silvio Berlusconi (see Chapter 7). But it began very differently from traditional parties, being arguably little more than a hollow holding company and marketing organization for the ideas and interests of its charismatic leader (see Hopkin and Paolucci, 1999). A sharp contrast to the 'business firm model' represented by *Forza Italia* is provided by Green parties. Despite modifying the 'flat' (i.e. non-hierarchical), ultra-participative structures that they brought with them from their beginnings in social movements, green parties still stress membership consultation, consensus, and limitations on leadership (Burchell, 2001).

Party systems and party families

When it comes to parties, history matters, often far more so than the media's treatment of day-to-day political events would sometimes have us believe. It certainly influences what political scientists refer to as the party system. Most political scientists employ a dual approach to classifying party

BOX 5.1
The evolution of political party organization

Cadre parties (Duverger, 1954) were clearly controlled by an elite *caucus* (or small group) commonly consisting of parliamentarians and local notables, with the addition later on of a national organization to deal with members who were expected not so much to decide policy but simply to contribute funds and campaign at elections. Examples include **nineteenth-century Liberal and Conservative parties**.

Mass parties (Duverger, 1954) were founded by those who did not enjoy political power (at least to begin with) and tended to adopt a 'branch' structure in which members, as well as providing financial and campaign resources, could hope to contribute to policy. This meant that party leaders enjoyed rather less autonomy from the centre than their counterparts in the cadre parties. Examples include **early twentieth-century Socialist parties**.

Catch-all parties (Kirchheimer, 1966) seek to broaden their base beyond their traditional support and attract the 'floating voter' and interest group backing. Such parties downplay ideology in favour of pragmatism, and cede considerable autonomy and control to the leadership over the active membership. In the age of mass media, such parties may become **electoral professional parties** (Panebianco, 1988) – dominated by career politicians employing experts to track public opinion and market the party accordingly via resources derived not from membership subscriptions but from interest groups and the public purse. Examples include **mid-twentieth-century Social Democratic and Christian Democratic parties**.

Cartel parties (Katz and Mair, 1995) arguably become so reliant on public subsidies and so distant from their largely symbolic membership that they have become not so much brokers between society and the state as components of the latter. Organizationally, such parties shift or maintain the balance of power away from parts of the party that might be captured by activist members, such as the national, extra-parliamentary, organization (*the party in central office*) towards the parliamentary wing (*the party in public office*). The latter is controlled by the leadership, which communicates over the heads of activists with the rest of the largely passive membership (*the party on the ground*) and potential voters via direct mail and the mass media. Examples suggested include **most twenty-first-century mainstream parties**.

Anti-system parties are a reaction to the collusive consensus which arguably results when established parties join a cosy, only superficially competitive, cartel. Examples suggested include **1980s Green Parties and 1990s far-right parties**.

systems. Following the Italian political scientist Giovanni Sartori, who pioneered work in this area, they give equal weight to a consideration of the number of parties present in parliament (referred to as the degree of 'fragmentation') and the ideological distance between them (referred to as the degree of 'polarization'). Both of these can be seen as dimensions that can be plotted against each other on a graph. Countries can then be located on the graph according to how they score on each dimension (see Figure 5.1). Doing this reveals similarities and differences between countries. Taking our core countries, we find only one – the UK – that has few parties and (relatively) little

distance between significant parties on the left and the right – a situation we call 'moderate two party-ism'. There are rather more countries (Germany, Sweden, the Czech Republic and Spain) where the distance between right- and left-wing parties may not be that great, but where there are more of them – a situation we know as 'moderate multipartyism'. The rest (Poland, France, Netherlands, Italy) are all illustrations of 'polarized multipartyism' – lots of parties and a big difference between the most left- and right-wing parties.

These classifications are interesting because they provoke predictions and hypotheses that can be tested. One obvious hypothesis involves the rela-

---

BOX 5.2
Michels' iron law of oligarchy

To an early theorist of party organization, Robert Michels, the adoption by mass, left-wing parties of elitist or cadre-style organization (and the concomitant watering down of their radicalism) was wholly predictable. According to his 'iron law of oligarchy', a combination of bureaucratic necessity, the inevitability of specialization, the trappings of office and the submissiveness of supporters would eventually ensure that power would pass from the membership to a leadership more interested in survival than social change (Michels, 1962). A later theorist like Angelo Panebianco may qualify the extent to which this necessarily implies a decline of ideological distinctiveness and question the existence of a truly cohesive leadership (Panebianco, 1988). But he, too, notes that party survival rather than the implementation of its founding philosophy becomes the name of the game.

---

tionship between party systems and the kind of party competition that occurs within them. For example, in a system with few parties and a narrow range of ideological difference (i.e. one that exhibits moderate multipartism or two-partyism), we might predict that parties will tend to campaign in the centre ground rather than emphasizing their left and right credentials. Party competition will, in other words, be 'centripetal' (tending toward the centre) rather than 'centrifugal' (tending toward the extreme). This is the case, for instance, in the UK. Under conditions of polarized multipartyism we are likely to see more centrifugal competition as a number of the parties aim to occupy niches along the entire political spectrum.

These classifications of party systems, however, in some ways beg the question. How did countries' systems come to be the way they are? Many political scientists believe that party systems are rooted in social (or, increasingly, values-based) conflicts, which they call cleavages. Most of these were those already in place at the end of the nineteenth century and the beginning of the twentieth century, when democracy (or at least the vote for all adult males) was introduced. Indeed, one of the most famous theses in comparative politics holds that, as a result, they helped to structure – or even freeze – Europe's party system for decades to come (see Lipset and Rokkan, 1967). Some, of course, have developed since, while others have declined in salience or, as in Central and Eastern Europe, had their development arrested, either temporarily or permanently (see Zielinski, 2002). The extent to which a cleavage was more or less important in a

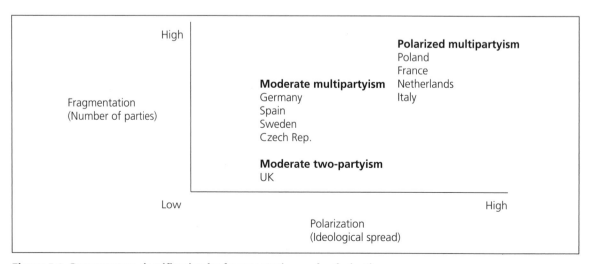

Figure 5.1 Party system classification by fragmentation and polarization

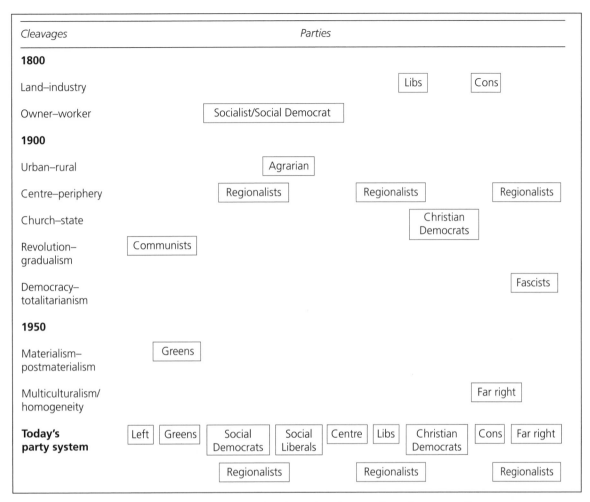

Figure 5.2 The evolution of Europe's party families, from the nineteenth to the twenty-first century

particular country helped to determine which parties (or, comparatively speaking, representatives of the various party families) were present, as well as which were stronger or weaker. So, too, did the extent to which existing parties were able to adapt in order to mobilize on that cleavage as well as the one that gave birth to them. Figure 5.2 shows the evolution of a hypothetical party system containing all the main cleavages and therefore all the party families we will go on to discuss. But clearly not all countries will, in reality, have been affected by all cleavages and will therefore contain representatives of only some rather than all the party families.

We can go through what is, of course, a stylized diagram in Figure 5.2 from the top down. The different interests of landowners and those who were beginning to make money from industry or the professions had led around the middle of the nineteenth century to the foundation of, on the one hand, *conservative* parties and, on the other, *liberal* or *radical* parties. These parties stood on either side of the *land–industry* cleavage. The increased need and willingness among wage-earners to express their own interests gave rise, as the nineteenth century drew to a close, to *socialist* or *social democratic* parties, which then spawned *communist* parties that believed in a more revolutionary route to power. These mobilized one side of the *owner–worker* cleavage and reinforced the basic division between what we have come to call 'right' and 'left'. The rise of the city (especially in Scandinavia) saw the creation of *agrarian* parties dedicated to defending the interests of farmers (the *urban–rural* cleavage). Another conflict that influenced politics was the *church–state* cleavage that, in time, saw the creation of conservative *Christian democratic* parties opposed to the secularism, as well as the progressive social and economic policies, of the left in particular. Meanwhile, the *centre–periphery* cleavage encouraged, in some countries, the formation of *regionalist* parties which defended the autonomy of communities with separate identities (and possibly languages) against state centralization. More recently, agrarian parties have become *centre* parties, and (with the end of the Cold War) some communist parties have become *left* parties. Even more recently, cleavages seem to have opened up around more values-based *post-materialism* (see Chapter 6 for a full definition): this focuses on matters such as the environment and multiculturalism, giving rise to *green* parties and possibly helping to give a new lease of life to *far-right* parties.

The relationship between cleavages (or more precisely the conflictual 'issue dimensions' they give rise to) and parties can, incidentally, be used to predict the number of parties in a system. This is done with a simple formula produced by influential Dutch political scientist Arendt Lijphart (whose distinction between 'majoritarian' and 'consensual' systems we have already referred to in Chapter 4). More often than not, there is a relationship between the number of issue dimensions and the number of parties. This can be expressed as $N = I + 1$, namely the number of parties will equal the number of issue dimensions, plus one. So, for example, in the Netherlands, the issue conflicts are religious, socio-economic and post-materialist, which means (at least) four parties. Of course, this does not always hold exactly, and requires that one ignore very small parties that may well be influential at certain times or on certain issues – as the United Kingdom's and Spain's regional parties are, for instance. The number of parties may also change as issue dimensions become more or less important. Nevertheless, it is probably one of the more robust formulas in political science.

Even more political scientists are in broad agree-

ment with the idea that countries that had cleavages in common tended to contain similar parties, even if their names were slightly different. Political scientists interested in comparison and generalization often group these parties into 'party families' (see Mair and Mudde, 1998), on the basis that, while some national variation is inevitable, what each party stands for tends (historically, at least) to 'run in the family'. We now look at each party family in turn, not in order of foundation (as in Figure 5.2) but instead in broad order of contemporary political importance. We also provide examples of each, partly to show that, although generalizations are useful, membership of the family does not always involve direct lineage.

Socialist and social democratic parties

These parties first began to emerge in the last quarter of the nineteenth century as those on one side of the owner–worker cleavage began to agitate not merely for political rights, such as the vote, but also for an economy and a society run in the interests of the many rather than the few. Such demands were obviously anathema to conservatives. But liberals were divided into those who wanted to work with (and ideally retain control of) any progressive forces in politics and those who regarded socialism as a threat to private property and individual freedom. Many socialist parties allied with the increasingly powerful trade union movements. Partly as a result, and partly because many radicals departed to form communist parties following the Russian revolution (1917), it became clear that these parties aimed not to overthrow capitalism but to mitigate and even dynamize it. This they hoped to do by using the state: through the ownership (or at least the regulation) of key industries and utilities, the use of progressive taxation and redistributionary government spending, governments would co-operate with trade unions (and hopefully employers, too) to deliver full employment and social security, health and education for all (see Box 5.3).

The postwar period saw the implementation of key planks of the social democratic programme across western Europe. This was initially by social democrats themselves, but then also by parties of the centre-right who recognized that opposition

---

BOX 5.3
Modernization over Marxism: two social democratic parties

It is often said that the British Labour Party originated 'from the bowels of the trade union movement' rather than the philosophical beliefs of impractical ideologues. Its original purpose was to ensure that laws passed by parliament did not unfairly hinder unions in their role as protectors and promoters of the interests of ordinary working people. Once the bulk of those people became entitled to vote, it quickly became clear that Labour would become one of the UK's two main parties. Despite *Clause IV* of its constitution, committing it, in theory, to extending public ownership of the economy, Labour in practice came to be associated not so much with the more radical Marxist diagnosis and prescriptions that characterized continental social democratic parties, but with redistribution via progressive taxation, the welfare state and the sort of 'nationalization' of key industries that made sense in the 1930s and 1940s but was seen by many as outdated by the 1950s. The very vagueness of Clause IV, and fear of the infighting that would greet any attempt to replace it, meant that it was only in the 1990s that the party finally equipped itself with what its leadership argued was a more relevant, realistic 'mission statement'.

All this is in marked contrast with other European social democratic parties. Despite close relationships with the trade unions (particularly in Scandinavia), these parties were not so financially nor so organizationally dependent on them. Nor were they so uninterested in ideological direction and debate. In their early years they were heavily influenced by the writings of Marx and his followers. Initially, indeed, the really significant difference between them and the more radical *Communists* (many of whom started out as social democrats) was their commitment to a peaceful and parliamentary road to socialism – even if the plan originally was to refuse (unlike the British Labour Party) to get involved in government until an electoral majority for their cause had been won. Ironically, it was their stress on social analysis – and frustration with ruling themselves out of government despite their relative electoral strength – that made these parties more open to change in order to adapt to new circumstances. One of the best examples is the German SPD, originally founded in 1875. At its famous *Bad Godesburg* congress in 1959, the party announced its abandonment of old-style, Marxist, socialism and its embrace of the 'social market economy', setting itself on a path toward both catch-all party status and, quite soon afterwards, coalition government.

---

presented electoral difficulties. During this period, social democrats had the support of at least a third (and in the UK, Sweden and Austria considerably more) of the electorate. When the postwar boom came to an abrupt end in the mid-1970s (see Chapter 1), social democratic parties with the misfortune to be in government – whether or not they or their policies were to blame (and with the exception of Austria and Sweden) – bore the brunt of public displeasure. Conversely, the social democratic success stories of the 1980s were in Spain, Portugal and Greece, where socialist parties turned out to be the main beneficiaries of the collapse of dictatorships (see Merkel, 1992). The French *Parti Socialiste*, having won a historic victory in 1981, however, ran into far greater difficulties when, unlike its Mediterranean counterparts, it attempted to buck, rather than adapt to, the trend

toward economic liberalism. Its radical programme of nationalizations and public spending quickly ran into trouble (not least with the financial markets) and it was forced to execute a U-turn toward austerity (see Ross, Hoffman and Malzacher, 1987). This trauma, and ongoing defeats of sister parties in the UK and Germany, led some commentators to predict 'the death of social democracy', its ideology outdated and its core support (the manual working class and trade unions) shrinking. A process of policy renewal and reaching out to middle-class voters, plus a series of electoral 'come-backs' in the late 1990s seemed to have put paid to such pessimism for a while. But the first elections of the twenty-first century have not been so positive (see Chapter 9).

In the postcommunist democracies of Eastern Europe, the performance of, and prospects for, social democratic parties are better than some might have predicted – particularly when one considers that for the most part they began as the means by which Cold War communist parties attempted, almost overnight, to establish their newly moderate, democratic, credentials. In most countries in East Central Europe, social democratic parties have already made it into government on one or more occasions and either are, or are close to being, the largest single party.

While the likeness may not be exact, the newest members of the social democratic family, then, bear some resemblance to those in the West that have been around much longer. New or old, most social democrats, as we argue in Chapter 9, continue to believe in using the power of public initiative and the public purse to (at the very least) protect the less fortunate and, in the long term, reduce their numbers via strategies promoting equality of opportunity. All, however, realize that this power is constrained by what is deemed prudent by international financial markets and reasonable, taxwise, by their electorates. To them, the state still has an economic as well as a welfare role, but it is as a regulator or framework-setter as opposed to an owner or driver. And while not immune to both differences of emphasis and internal division on the issue, all are basically in favour of a European Union that aims to liberalize and increase trade – though not at the expense of social provision or labour standards, commitment to which is reinforced by continuing close links with the union movement. On issues of morality, conscience and sexuality, social democratic parties are firmly in the secular liberal tradition.

For all these reasons, and because in northern if not in southern Europe (see Astudillo, 2002) they continue to be closely linked to trade unions, Europe's social democrats may perhaps be more comparable than ever with the US Democrats. Those looking for a single 'European equivalent' of the Republican Party, however, will have a harder time. In their enthusiasm for a strong defence of the nation, no-nonsense policies on crime and punishment, and a low-tax, no-meddling government, the Republicans share much in common with Europe's conservative parties. But in their rhetorical commitment to 'compassionate conservatism' and their anti-permissive stance on family values and personal (and especially sexual) morality, they have strong affinities with Europe's Christian Democrats. These are the party families we go on to look at next.

Conservative parties

Europe's conservative parties were formed in order to co-ordinate the defence of the socio-economic privileges of the traditional, mainly landed, hierarchy against what were seen as the pretensions of the rising liberal middle-class. Where liberals were supposedly motivated by theory, enthused by international free trade, obsessed with the individual and possessed of an off-putting earnestness, conservatives declared themselves to be more pragmatic, more patriotic, more paternalistic and yet also more fun! In the UK, for instance, they were backed by brewing and agricultural interests, as well as the dominant church. They were able to survive the granting of universal suffrage – firstly by poaching middle-class voters who were put off by liberalism's identification with sectarian, urban and (increasingly) radical politics and, secondly by appealing to the nationalism, the traditionalism and the respectable aspirations of newly enfranchized working-class voters.

The second challenge for conservative parties was the advent of the welfare state. Although conservative parties were paternalistic, they argued that the less well-off were best protected by a thriving private sector and a mixture of self-help and charity. State intervention should be limited largely to policing law and order and providing for the defence of the realm. However, the obvious popularity of increased social provision and what, at the time, seemed the inevitability of public involvement in key sectors such as transport and energy, meant they concentrated their efforts for most of the postwar period on limiting rather than 'rolling back' state spending and activity. Following the economic difficulties encountered by European nations in the 1970s, when countries such as Germany and the UK were governed by the centre-left, the opportunity arose to pursue a more aggressive attack on the state (see Chapters 1 and 9). This was taken furthest in the UK, where the emphasis was on cutting state subsidies to industry, reducing the role of the trade unions and selling off state

---

BOX 5.4
From nowhere to somewhere to nowhere: two conservative parties

The Spanish *Partido Popular* (PP) began life in 1976 as the *Alianza Popular* (AP), a home for high-ranking members of the Franco dictatorship who wished to pursue their conservative politics in the new, democratic Spain. This did nothing to harm the prospects of the social democrats (PSOE) who cruised from victory to victory under their younger, more charismatic leader, Felipe Gonzalez. Finally, in 1990, the centre-right, at the same time as reforming under the single banner, *Partido Popular* (PP), found a leader from a new generation of conservatives too young to be tainted by association with the authoritarian past. Although less charismatic than his socialist opponent, José María Aznar was able to exploit his image as a reliable, pragmatic, centrist – and, above all, clean – politician to his advantage. After a disappointing setback in the elections of 1993, PP finally overhauled PSOE in 1996, when it assumed office as a minority government with the support of smaller regionalist parties. This gave it the chance to demonstrate to any who still doubted it that it had no intention of turning the clock back on democracy or on a constitution that granted considerable autonomy to many Spanish regions. Nor was PP about to deconstruct the country's fledgling welfare state or indulge in over-zealous neo-liberal reform of an economy that has been an impressive performer (except on unemployment) over two decades. Such reassurance, and especially the support of young people for whom PSOE (rather than Franco) was the representative of monolithic, old-fashioned, corrupt politics, helped PP win itself an overall majority (in a PR system) in the general election of 2000. It seemed about to win again in 2004 when the Madrid train bombings carried out by Islamic terrorists blew everything off course.

The British Conservatives, on the other hand, seem stuck in a rut. After years of success (it governed the UK for the vast bulk of the twentieth century, and for a good deal of the nineteenth, too), the party has been in crisis since the early 1990s. For most of its life, the Conservative Party was a pragmatic operator, using its status as 'the natural party of government' and its unashamed nationalism to ensure that any concessions to social democracy (such as public ownership and the welfare state) were kept within limits. It was not until 1979, with the coming to power of Margaret Thatcher, that the Conservatives attempted – with some success – to roll back these concessions in pursuit of a more ideological free-market approach. Helped by the weakness of its Labour opponent, the party stayed in power for eighteen years, but the price of longevity proved high: by 1997 it was faction-ridden, sleazy, and had even managed to blow the reputation for economic competence that had allowed it to overcome suspicions about its supposed lack of social compassion. It had also adopted a hostile attitude to the European Union that, while it may appeal to the nationalism of the electorate, does not appear to do so anywhere near sufficiently to boost it electorally. Meanwhile the party is seen as old, out of touch, and (ironically) too ideological.

---

assets. Although welfare provision suffered, there were electoral constraints on how much could be cut.

This was in keeping with the fact that Europe's conservative parties have historically been careful not to allow their ideological instincts to sway them too far away from the centre of the political spectrum (Box 5.4). This may well be due to the fact that they are strongest in countries that display two characteristics. First is the tendency among the country's voters, irrespective of the electoral system, to give power to one of two main parties (or blocs): a recent example would be Hungary, where over 80% of the vote at the 2002 election went to the two main competitors, one of which, *Fidesz*, had rapidly transformed itself into the region's most successful Conservative party (see Kiss, 2002). Second is the weakness or absence of a traditionally more centrist *Christian Democracy* (see below) in that country; instances include the UK, Malta, Spain, Greece and arguably, since the 1990s, Italy. Notable exceptions to the Conservative or Christian Democrats, but not both 'rule', however, include Sweden and the Czech Republic.

Christian democratic parties

These parties, especially those of Roman Catholic origin, were around in various forms by the beginning of the twentieth century (Box 5.5). But representatives of this centre-right party family really came into their own following the end of the Second World War (see Kselman and Buttigieg, 2003). While clearly opposed to the collectivist, class-based ethos of the left (and in particular the Communists), Christian democratic parties were markedly more positive about state and trade union involvement than some of their conservative counterparts (see Hanley, 1994 and van Kersbergen, 1995). Prizing social harmony above individualism and unfettered free markets, Christian democratic parties were instrumental in the development of 'corporatism' (see Chapter 8)

in Austria, and to a lesser extent Germany, in the second half of the twentieth century. The stress was on 'capitalism with a conscience' and on a role for the state in facilitating long-term, mutually beneficial and institutionally supported relationships between business and unions. But the collective good wasn't everything, as it supposedly was to parties on the left: individuals mattered, too. Yet they had to be seen not as the autonomous, primarily self-interested actors beloved of economic liberals, but as socially embedded contributors and beneficiaries of an organic whole (an idea known as 'personalism'). The stress was also on support for the family – especially the traditional family that was seen as the embodiment and transmission belt for Christian moral values. But while compassion and help for the less fortunate

---

BOX 5.5

Crossing classes and denominations: Christian Democratic parties

Germany's *Christlich Demokratische Union* (CDU) traces its roots back to the predominantly Catholic Centre Party of the interwar years. Indeed, Christian Democracy in Germany still attracts disproportionate support from Catholics, especially in Bavaria, the stronghold of the CDU's sister-party, the *Christian Social Union* (CSU). But its appeal in the postwar period has been non-denominational and to a great extent non-religious in character. The CDU began as a collection of local, anti-communist cadre parties knitted together to promote Konrad Adenauer who was Chancellor from 1949 to 1963, and who oversaw Germany's democratic consolidation and rapid economic recovery. During those years, it not only gained support from Protestants but also many working class voters, especially those among Catholics not recruited into the SPD-supporting trade unions. It became, in effect, one of Europe's archetypal 'catch-all' parties. Unlike its Bavarian sister-party, the CDU is not overtly nationalistic, nor morally or socially very conservative. Although it has been influenced since the 1980s by economic liberalism, it continues to see a place for government intervention, for consultation with trade unions and for a strong insurance-based welfare state (see Chapter 1). After dominating German politics in the 1980s and 1990s, the CDU then enjoyed rather less luck. Its initial success in attracting support in the former East Germany proved difficult to sustain; it has been mired in financial scandals. And it suffered from the recent weakness of its former coalition partner, the liberal Free Democratic Party (FDP). That said, it only narrowly missed winning the 2002 election, and its time as the country's 'natural party of government' is by no means over.

Norway's *Kristelig Folkeparti* – the model for the Christian democratic parties of Scandinavia – may be a member of the same party family as the CDU, but is different in many ways that may even challenge the notion that there is such a thing as a pan-European party family. Far from being a catch-all party, it relies on a core support of Lutherans, many of whom feel very strongly (and conservatively) on social issues (particularly on their opposition to alcohol and to abortion) and/or their right to hang on to their particular Norwegian dialect (*Nynorsk*). The party, which was founded in 1933, is also geographically highly concentrated, and attracts nowhere near the catch-all cross-class vote of the CDU. Its loyal support, however, has managed to prevent it from dropping too far below 10 per cent. In recent years, it benefited from the charismatic leadership of Kjell Magne Bondevik, who could claim the prime minister's post in centre-right governments even though his party was by no means the biggest in the coalition.

was important, tolerance and compromize had their limits when it came to issues such as abortion and divorce.

Although strong feelings on those issues are most associated with Roman Catholicism, it is important to emphasize the fact that, outside traditional strongholds like Austria, Belgium and (until the early 1990s) Italy, some Christian democratic parties (for example, in Germany and the Netherlands) came to appeal to Protestants as well. In fact, in almost uniformly Protestant Scandinavia, they could do little else. Ecumenical appeals, however, cannot completely insulate the Christian democrats from the decline in number of western Europeans who are practising Christians (see Chapter 1). On the other hand, Christian Democrats outside Scandinavia (where they continue to concentrate their appeal to people of faith), have, since the Second World War pursued a 'catch-all' strategy (see Box 5.1 p. 107): their centrist, pragmatic policies consciously appeal to as wide an audience as possible even as they begin to adapt more 'neo-liberal economic policies and, in so doing, start to look increasingly like secular conservative parties (see van Hecke and Gerard, 2004).

Recent elections in Austria, the Netherlands and Germany show that it is a strategy that can work. The situation in the new postcommunist democracies is less hopeful, however. With the exception of Slovenia, Christian Democratic parties seem to be in decline. This is true even in places like the Czech Republic and Hungary where they had a foothold in the first place, while in (still very Catholic) Poland, the obvious potential for a successful 'family member' has yet to be realized.

Liberal Parties

These parties were first set up to promote the interests of people who earned their living from commerce and the professions, and lived in the towns and cities that grew quickly in the Industrial Revolution of the nineteenth century (Box 5.6). Early on, they promoted the legal, property, political and religious rights of the individual in contrast to the arbitrary rule of a traditional, landed interest that was happy to see the state identify with a particular church. In the twentieth century, however, liberal parties seem to have gone one of two ways. The first, sometimes called 'neo-

---

BOX 5.6
Two variations on a liberal theme

The *Volkspartij voor Vrijheid en Democratie* (People's Party for Freedom and Democracy, VVD) may have been founded in 1948, but it benefited from a long list of liberal predecessors stretching back into the nineteenth century. During that time, politicians objecting both to the religious influences of Dutch conservatives and the statist inclinations of Dutch workers' parties were instrumental in progressive social reform and the expansion of civil and political rights. In the postwar period, the VVD grew to become the Netherlands' third largest political party and recently has commonly formed part of the government, usually in coalition with the Christian Democrats, but also with the Labour Party. Their focus has been on tax reductions and on decentralization. Both their participation and their focus seem to have earned them growing support. The man responsible for both, Frits Bolkestein, was appointed EU commissioner for the internal market and tax reform in September 1999.

D66 (*Democraten '66*) is the Netherlands' other liberal party. It is much closer than VVD to the Labour Party on welfare and economic policy, but it has distinctive stances on constitutional reform (it believes in 'bottom-up' and direct democracy) and is very committed to the freedom of the individual above and beyond the market place. It traces its roots back to the *Freethinking Democratic League* founded at the beginning of the nineteenth century. But it really got going in the late 1960s as a reaction to the seeming impasse between liberals and social democrats – an impasse that was allowing the Christian Democrats to rule yet ignore the need to modernize the country. D66's stress was on the need to bypass class and religious loyalties in favour of participatory democracy wherein all express their personal values – so much so that some see it shading into the 'postmaterialism' exemplified by the Greens. D66 has tended to support governments of the left, but in 2003 entered a centre right-coalition – along with VVD!

liberalism', prioritizes a commitment to the free market and opposition to state interference in the economy as well as in matters of morality – all of which distinguish it from centre-right parties belonging to the Christian democratic family. In very recent years, however, this brand of liberalism has been concerned not to appear too 'soft' (i.e. libertarian) on issues such as drugs and civil liberties issues, and has begun to incorporate a hard line on immigration into its platform. The second strand of liberalism, sometimes labelled 'social liberalism', has generally not abandoned its reputation for tolerance and the promotion of civil liberties. It is generally more sympathetic than the first strand toward government intervention in the economy and welfare policy, believing that it helps to ensure that people can actually benefit from the freedoms they should enjoy.

The UK Liberal Democrats are a good example of this second strand, although the country's electoral system constitutes a big (if not necessarily insuperable) barrier to them gaining office – or regaining it, since they began life as one of Britain's two biggest parties (see Chapter 6). Elsewhere in Europe, however, liberal parties, whether on the neo-liberal right or in the more 'progressive' centre, have been involved in government far more frequently. Sometimes this has been as part of a so-called 'bourgeois bloc' against social democracy (as in Sweden). At other times, they have been 'third parties' able to join either a right- or a left-wing government (as in Germany) or a wider 'rainbow coalition' (as in Belgium and the Netherlands). In western Europe, they now poll on average around 10 per cent, though the range is large: from around half of the average in Scandinavia to two or three times the average in the Benelux countries, Switzerland and, recently, the UK. The liberal party family is similarly well represented in some of Europe's smaller, newer democracies such as Latvia, Lithuania and Slovenia. There is also a small liberal party that broke away from the Conservatives in the Czech Republic.

Green parties

In Europe, the Greens began to take shape in the 1970s and 1980s as 'new social movements' (which are defined in Chapter 8) campaigning against the supposed unsustainability and exploitative nature of growth-oriented economic development sought parliamentary representation (Box 5.7). Their appeal was – and is – 'postmaterialist' (about quality of life rather than standard of living) or even anti-materialist. Although the environment (and particularly opposition to nuclear power) was the primary focus, it also encompassed anti-militarism and anti-discrimination, solidarity with the developing world, social equality and justice, and liberal tolerance of alternative life-styles. Greens also differentiated themselves from so-called conventional, 'grey' parties by their continued (if, over time, slightly diluted) commitment to participatory democracy and local autonomy – a commitment which typically saw them adopt much flatter organizational structures than other, generally hierarchically organized, parties.

Although not as successful as the far right, the Greens are clearly one of the 'success stories' of politics since the 1970s, having found what seems to be a secure footing in several major European countries. They have been in coalition government in the largest, Germany, but they have also served in Finland, Belgium, Slovakia and in France and Italy, despite their electoral performance in the last two countries being poorer than it is in Sweden, Austria and Switzerland. The relatively poor performance in France and Italy is probably explained in part by their more majoritarian electoral systems (see Chapter 6). But it may also reflect the fact that Green parties have found it hard to progress in southern Europe generally: their strength in Spain, Portugal and Greece is negligible. It is not much better, interestingly, in Norway or Denmark. There, the lack of Green success may be due to the fact that the general level of environmental consciousness is so high that mainstream parties factored it in to their own platforms at a very early stage. In Denmark, however, there is a very small Red–Green party, as there is in the Netherlands. As in Southern Europe, the level of environmental consciousness in the post-communist democracies, where material necessities are still very much the issue for the vast majority of the population, is very low. Consequently, the Greens are virtually non-existent in electoral terms in Central and Eastern Europe.

BOX 5.7
The difficult art of compromise: two Green parties

The first Green Party to make it into government in western Europe was the Finnish *Vihreä Liitto*, whose 6.4 per cent of the vote in 1995 was enough to earn them a cabinet seat in a so-called 'rainbow coalition' stretching all the way from the Left Alliance to the Conservatives. This was only eight years after the formation of the party in 1988, though Greens had been elected as MPs in 1983 and 1987. The coalition was returned to power, with the Greens improving their vote to 7.3 per cent and retaining the Ministry of the Environment. During their time in government, the Greens scored notable successes in extending conservation land and introducing more sophisticated environmental taxes. They were unable, however, to prevent a majority of MPs (most other parties were split on the issue) voting to begin work on a fifth nuclear reactor. In May 2002, the party met and decided to leave the government in protest. They made a point of saying, however, that they would be willing to enter coalition negotiations following the next elections in 2003. This magnanimous offer was, not surprisingly, turned down by other parties.

Europe's highest-profile Green Party, Germany's *Die Grünen*, has been around rather longer than its Finnish sister party, beginning formally in 1980. By the end of their first decade, they were polling an impressive 8 per cent, but seemed to lose steam as the 1990s progressed. However, their 6.7 per cent in 1998 was enough to make them the logical coalition partner for the incoming SPD and they began their spell in government. It was not always an easy time. There were severe internal disagreements over the gradual way in which nuclear power was to be phased out and over the transportation of atomic waste, as well as over the government's sending of troops overseas. As the election approached, however, a combination of floods blamed on global warming, anxiety about US militarism, and increased recognition of the Greens' achievements (on nuclear power, on widening citizenship, on the legal recognition of same-sex relationships, among others) lifted the party to 8.6 per cent and into a renewed coalition with a grateful SPD. There was, though, one sting in the tail, and it came from ordinary members. As a warning to the leadership not to rest on their laurels and move too far away from the grassroots democracy tradition, the party ignored the pleas of its biggest star, foreign minister Joschka Fischer, and forced their co-leaders to resign before they were allowed to take up the parliamentary seats they had won.

Far-right parties

Far-right or extreme-right parties were first founded as highly nationalist, conservative and militarist responses to the Communist revolution in Russia and the economic difficulties that followed the end of the First World War (Box 5.8). After that war, they seized power – sometimes after being elected to it – in several European nations including, most notoriously, Italy and Germany (see Chapter 1). The aggressively expansionist policies of those regimes, their blatant disregard for democracy and human rights and their ultimately genocidal theories of racial superiority, were largely discredited following their defeat in the Second World War. But this did not mean that some of the tendencies they managed to mobilize disappeared completely.

While few extreme right parties in the West actively celebrated their connection with the fascist past, some were still willing to play on similar themes in the postwar period. At first, they enjoyed little success. But more recently – as hostility to immigration has risen among Europeans (see Chapter 10) – this has changed. Along with its xenophobic (anti-foreigner) thrust, far-right rhetoric is characterized by 'populist' attacks on supposedly corrupt 'politics as usual' conducted by what is portrayed as a cosy cartel of mainstream politicians apparently more interested in their own survival than in the real needs or views of 'ordinary people' (see Taggart, 2000). Often led by a charismatic leader who promises to clear up the mess at a stroke, many far-right parties began the 1980s and 1990s by offering potential voters a mix of strong support for a low-tax, low-interference free-market economy, and conservative social values –

BOX 5.8
Different, but all here to stay: three far-right parties

Jean-Marie Le Pen goes down as one of Europe's most high-profile far-right leaders. A former soldier, active in extreme politics for decades and willing to flirt with Holocaust denial, he makes an ideal anti-hero for a media all too eager to associate the contemporary far right with the fascist past. There is no doubt that he deserves their attention, having taken his *Front National* (FN) from relative obscurity to what seems like a permanent place on the French political scene, where it can claim to enjoy around 10–15 per cent support nationwide – and much higher in certain regions in the East and the South of France. But there are limits to Le Pen's success. First and foremost, it tends to be more pronounced in presidential than parliamentary contests. In 2002, his charisma, combined with a poor campaign by his Socialist opponent and a large number of surprisingly successful fringe candidates, helped him to not much less than 20 per cent of the vote for president. But the FN could manage only 11 per cent in the parliamentary elections held a couple of months later – a performance that left it without a single MP owing to France's electoral system, which severely handicaps smaller parties who might do better under PR (see Chapter 6).

In other European countries, the far right is led by rather more modern, sophisticated leaders who, unlike Le Pen, enjoy the advantage of operating under PR and have worked hard to render themselves more acceptable to potential allies on the centre-right, in the hope that they will one day share in (or at least influence) government. A good example is Pia Kjaersgaard, whose *Dansk Folkeparti* (DF) took 12 per cent of the vote in the Danish general election of 2001 (up from 7.4 per cent in 1998) and helped a centre-right minority government to take power by acting as a support party in parliament (see Chapter 4). This position has given it considerable sway over immigration policy, but will perhaps help it avoid the fate suffered by another far-right party led by the best known of the new breed of leaders, Jörg Haider. In 1999, his Austrian Freedom Party (FPÖ) could claim to be the continent's most successful party of its kind, winning 27 per cent of the vote at that year's general election, after which it became a full coalition partner with the Austrian Christian Democrats (the ÖVP). But being in power proved rather more difficult than carping from the sidelines and the party almost disintegrated. Yet, the fact that it could still poll 10 per cent of the vote in 2002 and be retained as a coalition partner suggests that it, like other far-right parties, is likely to feature in European party systems for some time to come.

---

all of which appealed most to middle-class ('petit bourgeois') voters.

Recently, however, they have made big inroads into the working-class vote, focusing more on promises to cut immigration in order to cut crime and to ensure that the traditional welfare entitlements of the native-born are not compromized by allowing in foreigners with unrestricted access to them (an appeal known in the jargon as 'welfare chauvinism'). Because they are so opportunistic, and because most of them reject attempts to link them with interwar fascism, there is room for argument not just about which parties belong to this party family, but whether it can properly be called a 'family' at all. Some political scientists prefer, as a result, to draw a distinction between the old, fascist right and the new, populist or radical right that is less associated with the past. It

is this second strand that seems to have gained ground recently in Italy, in Switzerland, Denmark, Norway and, especially Austria. The far right also exists in most of the postcommunist democracies, although, with the possible exception of the Polish populist *Samoobrona* (Self-Defence) and ultra-conservative *Liga Polskich Rodzin* (League of Polish Families), who might possibly fit into this party family, it seems much further away from government.

Communist and Left parties

Communism provided an expression for those dissatisfied with the gradualism of social democracy and who believed that the replacement of capitalism by a collectivized, classless society could be achieved by rapid, revolutionary means (Box

---

BOX 5.9
Making the best of a bad job: four 'former' communist parties

Arguably the most successful former Communist Party in western Europe is the Swedish Left Party, which had its roots in the break-away from the Social Democrats by hopeful revolutionaries in 1917. The party remained loyal to the Soviet Union from the 1920s until the 1960s, when a newly independent stance led to a partial name change. The 'Communist' label was finally dropped in 1990. It has often acted as a support party for minority social democratic (SAP) governments (see Chapter 4). This responsible role has resulted in some concrete achievements on the issues it has made its own – gender equality and resolute defence of the welfare state. It has, however, eaten away at its support, which dropped from 12 per cent in 1998 to 8 per cent in 2002. Much of that support came from those active in or sympathetic to 'new social movements' (see Chapter 8). Whether it will prove possible to hold on to the opponents of globalization and US militarism while playing such a pivotal parliamentary role will be interesting to see.

Not all communist parties, however, have deserted the old cause and (in the West) transformed themselves into Left parties and (in the East) into social democrats. Nor does keeping the faith necessarily mean electoral oblivion. In the Czech Republic, the existence of the Social Democratic ČSSD effectively closed off the latter option for the KSČM. Instead, it stuck to its traditional ideas about state ownership and opposed market reforms and membership of NATO and the EU. It also tapped into nationalist fears about the reclaiming of Czech lands by dispossessed foreigners (especially Germans) and antipathy to economic restructuring on the part of those who had lost their industrial jobs as a consequence. The party made the most of its relatively large, disciplined membership to maintain a healthy share of the vote, particularly among older people. In 2002, these strengths, along with widespread dissatisfaction with the social democrats, the collapse of a nationalist alternative on the far right, and an eye-catching campaign involving topless models, delivered the Communists 18.5 per cent of the vote. Other parties continue, however, to rule out coalition with such an unreconstructed force.

The one relic of the past the KSČM did ditch was the Soviet-style hammer and sickle on its logo (now a rather jaunty couple of cherries). Even this concession to modernity, however, proved too much for the Italian *Rifondazione Comunista*, which proudly retains the old symbol, and continues to attract sufficient support (5 per cent in 2001) to make itself a considerable nuisance to the social democratic *Democratici di Sinistra* – essentially that part of the former Communist Party (PCI), which chose a more moderate path at the end of the Cold War.

5.9). In those countries that found themselves within the sphere of influence of the old Soviet Union, Communist parties were able to seize control in the fledgling democracies that briefly replaced the defeated dictatorships after the Second World War. The regimes they established resembled the Soviet Union's in that they were essentially party dictatorships that replaced the market with state planning, trading off political freedom and private property rights for near-universal (though low-level) economic and social security (see Chapter 1). In the West, however, the prospect of Communist parties winning power looked increasingly unlikely as the Cold War wore on. In Sweden and France, admittedly, the Communist Party supported social democratic administrations on more than one occasion. But in Italy, where the communists (the PCI) received significant electoral support, they were largely kept out of formal participation in government by an American-backed agreement on the part of other parties to form whatever coalitions were necessary to keep them out. This was in spite of their fairly flexible, forward-looking, democratic and less state-centric 'Eurocommunist' stance.

The end of the Cold War, however, has presented the radical left with a new opportunity. So, too, has the tendency of social democratic parties to back away, in word if not necessarily in deed (see Chapter 9), from state ownership, high taxation and generous social spending. In Sweden and Finland, for example, the former communists,

---

BOX 5.10
Insiders and outsiders: two successful regionalist parties

Europe's regionalist parties come in all ideological shapes and sizes. Among the most powerful is the *Convergència Democràtica de Catalunya* (CDC), the biggest partner in the Catalan nationalist union or CiU (see Chapter 2). Formed at the end of the Franco regime, it dominated politics in the province of Catalunya throughout the 1980s and 1990s, under its leader (and five-term head of the Catalan government, the *Generalitat*), Jordi Pujol. It also challenged the United Left (an alliance that, after all, covered the whole of Spain) for the position of third party behind PSOE and PP in the national parliament – a position it used to support the former and then the latter in government in 1993 and 1996, with ever-more autonomy for Catalunya as its price. It is able to do this partly because it is courted by the other parties but also because the size of the Catalonian population means it can win around 5 per cent of the nationwide vote just by fighting there. The politics of the CiU have been described as slightly to the right of centre, but above all pragmatic.

In Belgium, the *Vlaams Blok* (VB) campaigns not only for a fully independent Dutch-speaking Flanders (see Chapter 2) but also for the barring and even the repatriation of immigrants. Founded in 1977 by radicals impatient with the gradualist nationalism of other Flemish parties, it has a solid base in the biggest Dutch-speaking city of Antwerp and took 11.6 % of the vote in the 2003 general election, despite (or perhaps because of) the decision of Belgium's other parties to treat it as an extremist 'pariah' with whom they would have no dealings. Although this 'cordon sanitaire' continues, they clearly have to pay attention to the support VB gathers on issues such as crime and immigration, while fear of increasing its support has undoubtedly led to further concessions to Flemish demands for more autonomy. Attempts to ban VB in 2004 backfired when it reinvented itself as *Vlaams Belang* and attracted, if anything, even more support.

---

now calling themselves *Left* parties, look to have a secure hold on some 5–15 per cent of the vote. They consciously provide a home for those dissatisfied with social democrats' defence of the welfare state and labour market protection. But they also stress so-called 'new politics' (or postmaterialist) issues, such as anti-discrimination, aid to the developing world, environmental awareness, anti-militarism and, increasingly, anti-globalization, as well as opposition to what they claim is the neo-liberal agenda of the EU. The same can be said to a lesser (and it seems less successful) extent of the PCF in France and the former communists, the PDS, in Germany, who have a double identity as a regionalist party. These new politics values mean that many (western) former communist parties now have a lot in common with parties first set up in places such as Denmark and Norway in the 1960s to offer a radical alternative to both communism and social democracy. This makes it possible to talk of a Left 'party family'.

In the former communist countries of Eastern Europe, Communist parties – as we note above – have generally transformed themselves into social democratic parties. As in Italy, however, where the PCI became the Left Democrats (DS), a minority of supporters who see this tendency as a sell-out have remained 'true to the faith', albeit with a now avowedly democratic stance. Support for these 'hardliner' parties is, with the exception of the Czech Communists, the KSČM, small. It has some similarities with the support base of the more traditionally inclined former Communist parties of the West, like the one which dominates the United Left or *Izquierda Unida* in Spain. But it contrasts with that of the Scandinavian Left parties, which appeal to younger, more middle-class, urban and educated voters, as well as to the trade unionists that both kinds of former Communist Party try to target.

Regional and ethnic parties

Some parties exist to promote the cause of those who argue (see Chapters 1–3) that their group and/or region merits autonomy or even complete

---

BOX 5.11
Two farmers' parties: 'ecohumanists' and populists

The Swedish *Centerpartiet* was founded in the second decade of the twentieth century as the Farmers' Federation, and functioned essentially as a parliamentary pressure group until the 1930s, after which it worked closely with the social democratic SAP. Co-operation continued until the late 1950s when the Federation, sensing it no longer had a future if it continued to appeal purely to its rural constituency and to cosy up too closely to the SAP, changed its name to the Centre Party and began to take a more independent stance. This strategy proved highly successful for a while: in 1956 it had polled under 10 per cent, but by the end of the 1960s, the *Centerpartiet* could claim to be the biggest non-socialist party in the country. In 1976, it took almost 25 per cent of the vote and its leader became the first non-social democrat prime minister in forty years. It was not, however, the best time to be in office (the world economy was in a mess) and the party arguably became distracted by its strong opposition to nuclear power. It was not in office again until 1991, but by then only as the smallest party (scoring only 8.5 per cent) in a four-way non-socialist coalition that lasted only three years. Following that unhappy period, it helped keep the minority SAP government in power between 1995 and 1998. At the 2002 election, fighting on what it calls an 'ecohumanist' platform, mixing social liberalism with environmentalism, it took just 6.2 per cent of the vote.

Self-Defence (*Samoobrona*) started life as a Polish farmers' union in the early 1990s but – under the leadership of the charismatic populist Andrezj Lepper – soon turned itself into a political party and, in 2001, overtook the hundred-year-old Polish Peasant Party (PSL) with 10 per cent of the vote. Where the PSL, as a member of several coalition governments, has headed toward the mainstream, *Samoobrona* puts itself at the head of demonstrations and protests by Poland's large agricultural sector. But, by calling for greater government intervention in the economy, it has also broadened out beyond its agricultural base to express the concerns of the many Poles for whom the transition to capitalism has not been easy – the 'transition losers' (see Szczerbiak, 2003). It combines this 'economic populism' with calls to get tough on crime and corruption and, unlike most of Europe's centre and agrarian parties (see Batory and Sitter, 2004) has not yet reconciled itself to the EU.

---

independence from the state (Box 5.10). In some western European countries they play an important role in sub-national, and sometimes national, coalition governments. Most important are those in Belgium, where all parties in the families represented there are also regional, representing either Dutch-speaking Flanders or French-speaking Wallonia. Most numerous are those in Spain. The views of such parties on economic or social and moral issues vary considerably from left, through centrist to far-right. Regionalist parties also exist in the postcommunist democracies, where they sometimes represent national minorities who identify with another country, perhaps one just across the border. In Romania and Slovakia, Hungarian minorities (and in Romania plenty of other minorities) are represented in parliament, and indeed in government, by their own parties; so, too, is the Turkish minority in Bulgaria. Indeed, one of the successes of the transition from communism in such countries is the extent to which such parties have been included in coalition politics for reasons of both political necessity and ethnic stability (see Millard, 2004: Chapter 9).

Agrarian and Centre parties

Some parties were originally set up to defend and promote the interests of farmers – often small-scale producers and peasants – especially in Scandinavia (Box 5.11). This is still part of their identity but, as the declining proportion of people employed in agriculture has eroded their core support, agrarian parties have repositioned (and often renamed) themselves as *Centre* parties, moving, as it were, 'from farmyard to city square' (see Arter, 2001): currently the most successful example is the Finnish *Keskusta* (KESK) which took a quarter of the vote in the 2003 election. Centre parties target middle-class, often small-town, voters looking for a party that will moderate both the left and the right. Perhaps as a consequence, they cannot easily be pigeonholed ideologically. Private enterprise and traditional morality is important, but so, too, is generous welfare, agricultural support and in some cases environmental conservation. In postcommunist Europe – including Hungary where there was some early success – such parties barely exist, the one significant exception being Poland. There, agrarian parties reflect the suspicions of the still extensive (but often small-scale) agricultural sector that the larger, urban-based parties will sell out small producers to multinationals and the European Union.

The bases of party systems: social and institutional; luck and skill

Acknowledging that historical cleavages help structure present-day party systems need not blind us to the way parties may develop away from their original intentions and support. Nor does it mean downplaying the extent to which parties either enjoy or make their own luck. Often, a cleavage can be given political expression by a party founded on one side of another cleavage but sufficiently flexible to incorporate other concerns as well. From very early on, for instance, the British Labour Party managed to express the interests not just of the working-class (owner–worker cleavage) but also those of Wales (centre–periphery). But, by the same token, parties cannot rest assured that they have one or other side of a cleavage 'sewn up': to take the same example, Labour 'inherited' Wales from the Liberal Party, but now faces a threat to its monopoly from *Plaid Cymru*, the Welsh Nationalists (as it does in Scotland from the Scottish National Party, the SNP).

As well as the skill shown or the luck enjoyed by particular parties, their relative strength (or even their very presence) – especially at a parliamentary level – is explained not just by social conflicts but by man-made, constitutional arrangements. Those who take an 'institutionalist' (as opposed to a sociological) approach argue that the political 'rules of the game' shape party systems just as much as cleavages, and neither rules nor systems should be seen as mere reflections of socio-economic 'reality'.

The most obvious institutional influence on party politics is the electoral system used in a particular country. These systems are examined in more detail in Chapter 6, so here we will limit ourselves to just a few key observations about their potential affects. Parties from some of the smaller or more extreme party 'families' (such as the far right or the communists or the agrarians) may find it harder to win parliamentary seats in a country such as the UK. There, the electoral system does not award them seats according to the proportion of votes received, unlike a country such as Norway or Austria, where it does. On the other hand, a 'plurality' system with plenty of small constituencies, such as the UK's, may well make it easier for regional parties, whose share of the overall national vote might see them failing in a more purely proportional system to make it into parliament. But this effect, in turn, depends on the extent to which a proportional system has large or small constituencies or districts. The Netherlands' system treats the whole country as one district, offering little hope for regional parties. The Spanish system divides the country into regions, which makes it more likely that they will be represented at a national level.

Once again, however, it is important to stress that party systems are the product of both institutional arrangements *and* social forces – and that neither of these will necessarily prevent the emergence of a skilful or a lucky party or guarantee the survival of a short-sighted or unlucky one. Things are doubly complicated because parties are themselves involved in setting and changing the institutional framework in which they operate. All this is most obvious early in the life of the new democracies of postcommunist Europe. There, at a time when it was difficult to predict which social cleavages would become important or salient, those political parties which enjoyed initial success tinkered with thresholds and district magnitudes in order to ensure such success continued (see Bale and Kopecký, 1998). For some it did, but some have declined or even disappeared as they were rendered less relevant by more pressing social conflicts and outmaneouvred by other 'political entrepreneurs' (see Millard, 2004). As the Spanish UCD, which disappeared almost overnight after seeing the country safely into the democratic era,

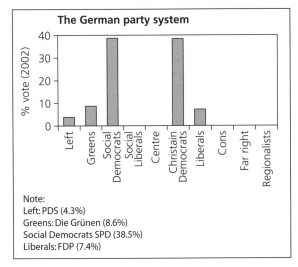

The German party system

Note:
Left: PDS (4.3%)
Greens: Die Grünen (8.6%)
Social Democrats SPD (38.5%)
Liberals: FDP (7.4%)

Figure 5.3 The German party system after 2002

could have told them, voters are not necessarily grateful once the job is done (see Hopkin, 1999).

And while postcommunist party systems still tend to be more fragmented or polarized than those of their 'never-communist' counterparts, in some countries (notably the Czech Republic, Hungary and Slovenia) they are now presenting voters with a familiar set of options rather than a bewildering array of choices – at least when it comes to parties that have a chance of getting into or influencing governments (see Millard, 2004: chapter 6). In many of Europe's new democracies (even those where party competition remains unsettled), a sizable social democratic party, sometimes flanked on its left by a smaller socialist or communist party, competes against a more or less fluid right, though there are still centrist (e.g. liberal) parties that may be willing to play a role in governments of either block. This pattern would, for instance, be readily recognizable to Scandinavian voters long used to this kind of basically *bipolar, two-bloc* competition. French (and, more recently, Italian and German) voters would recognise the pattern, too (see below).

Figure 5.3 illustrates the relative strength of the parties in the German party system mapping the actual parties' share of the vote in 2002 onto a graph of support for party families. Figure 5.4 does a similar mapping for the eight other 'core countries' considered in this book at the most recent

available elections. Although, there is always room for disagreement about which party belongs to which family, it emphasizes once again that although not every party family is represented in every country, a good many of them are, making generalizations about European party systems more than feasible. The 'exception that proves the rule', however, is Poland, whose politics is still in such flux that it is far harder to pigeonhole parties. Indeed, many analysts (see Millard, 2004) would question whether Poland can be said to have a party 'system' in the sense that there is no stable pattern of interaction or number of parties.

Party system change?

Interestingly, however, if the party systems of the continent's older and newer democracies are beginning to look more like each other, it may not simply be a matter of the former East 'catching-up' with the West – arguably a rather patronizing way of seeing things anyway. It could also be that politics in the latter is in flux – possibly, some would argue, because it is becoming detached from its historical roots. In other words, it could be that the Europeanization of party systems from West to East and North to South may be a two way-process. Voters and parties in the newer democracies may be taking time to discover where they stand. Meanwhile, in the older democracies both voters and parties are less and less likely to think, do or say things just because political custom and tradition dictates it.

This has led some political scientists to argue that, after years in which they were in effect 'frozen', party systems in western Europe since the 1970s are undergoing profound and accelerating change. The central features of this are an increase in fragmentation (the number of parties in the system), accompanied and in part explained by two things: **electoral volatility** and **dealignment**.

As we show in Chapter 6, the evidence that cleavage-driven voting has disappeared completely is weak: it might not necessarily be foolish, even now, to think we could predict a person's voting behaviour from his or her occupation or religion. However, we would, indeed, be less likely to make a correct prediction than we would have been

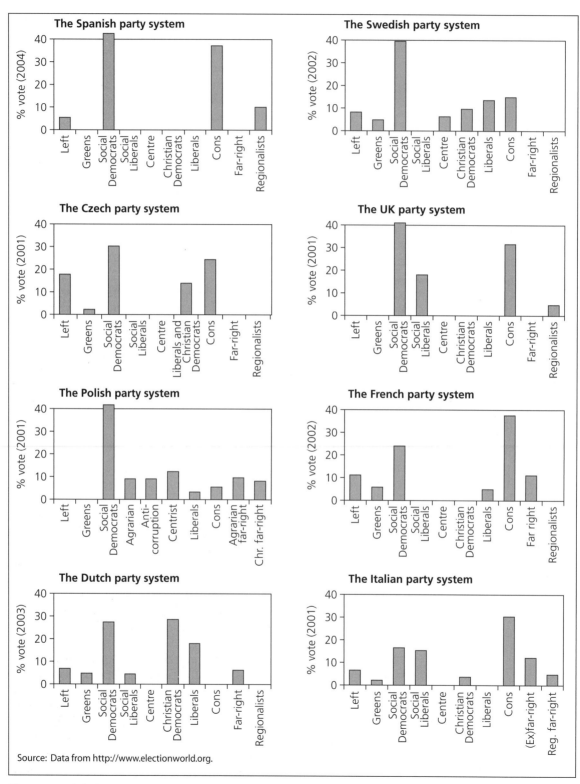

Source: Data from http://www.electionworld.org.

Figure 5.4 Eight European party systems, 2004

> *Definition*
> **Electoral volatility** occurs when voters switch their votes between parties from one election to another. **Dealignment** describes the way in which people's political preferences seem to be becoming less related to their location on one or other side of certain key cleavages than they used to be – preferences, in other words, seem to be increasingly individual and decreasingly collective, less fixed and more floating.

thirty, forty, or fifty years ago. It also seems, as we show in Chapter 6, that predicting how a person will vote based on how they voted last time is less easy than it was. In the 1990s, every west European country saw volatility rise compared to the 1980s – in many cases, to levels never reached before. Voters in Italy, the Netherlands and, to a slightly lesser extent, Sweden and Norway, seemed particularly willing to switch between parties (although not, interestingly, between the blocs of the left and right). Volatility in postcommunist countries remains very high and looks likely to stay that way (see Millard, 2004: chapter 5), defying comforting predictions that things would somehow inevitably settle down. If the new century picks up where the old one left off – and judging by some recent elections, it may do – then volatility may become the rule and not the exception across Europe.

What about *fragmentation*? Has all this switching of votes led to more parties? And are some of these new parties? Our answer – even if we exclude Italy, whose party system underwent an unusually complete transformation in the early 1990s once the corrupt Christian Democrats could no longer frighten voters with the spectre of a communist takeover (see Newell, 2000) – has to be 'yes'. But it should be a qualified 'yes'. There is no doubt that in many west European countries there has been – in contrast to the situation in many postcommunist countries in the east – a rise in the number of parties capable of making it into parliament. The increase, however, is by no means large. When it comes to new parties, there have indeed been many, but also many that have proved (such as the pensioners party, AOV, which suddenly made it into the Dutch parlia-

ment in 1994) to be what political scientists sometimes call 'flash parties', disappearing into obscurity as quickly as they appeared. Of course, the green, far-right and regionalist parties that first emerged in the 1970s have not only gatecrashed their way into the politics of many countries, but also look set, eventually, to become 'old' parties themselves.

Yet, even the impact of these successful new parties can be overstated. This is because for the most part, and sometimes in spite of their own efforts to retain their 'anti-system' or 'anti-party' reputation, they have quickly become identified with one side or other of the familiar left and right blocs. The far-right parties have ended up either joining (as in Italy) or effectively supporting (as in Norway and Denmark) coalitions led by more moderate conservatives. The Greens may have argued that they were 'neither left nor right but out in front', but few voters bought this line and they have gradually accepted their fate as part of the left. Regionalist parties, it must be said, are sometimes rather harder to pigeonhole, but even this can be exaggerated. Few were surprised, for instance, when the Catalonian nationalists (CiU) supported the then minority government of the conservative *Partido Popular* (PP) in Spain between 1996 and 2000.

In fact, if we look at the support for the two blocs, left and right, across Europe as a whole, it has remained remarkably consistent since the 1950s. If we include in the left bloc socialists (including former communists), greens and social democrats, it still commands around 40 per cent of the vote across Europe. The right, if we include not only conservatives, Christian democrats and the far right, but also liberals and agrarians, continues to poll around 55 per cent. In other words, we are seeing change, but just as importantly we are also seeing 'bipolarization' (see Bale, 2003 and Mair, 2001) – politics based around competition between left and right blocs rather than politics that gives the whip hand to potentially pivotal centre parties or even 'grand coalitions' between the main parties of the right and left. It may or may not be wrong to argue that that left and right are no longer any different in policy terms (see Chapter 9), but when it comes to voting and government formation, neither parties nor voters may be quite as 'promiscuous' as the common wisdom suggests.

Should we, then, conclude that western European party systems are no longer 'frozen' but thawing fast? Rather than being 'caught up' by unevenly consolidating East European party systems, will they not instead meet them coming the other way? Quite possibly, yes. However, three points need to be made.

▶ First, the apparently sharp increase in the pace of change in party systems should not blind us to long-term, albeit previously imperceptible, causes. These may well be sociological. The structural shifts in occupational, migration and family patterns discussed in Chapter 1 have almost certainly produced in every country a more heterogeneous and less tradition-bound electorate, for instance. But there will also be institutional causes. Mainstream centre-left and centre-right parties, for instance, may well have contributed to the partial 'de-coupling' of social class and voting (see Chapter 6) by their attempts to broaden their 'catch-all' appeal by stressing pragmatism and competence over ideology and particular interests (see Chapter 9).

▶ Second, it is possible that, in focusing on what, some argue, is after all only fairly marginal change to party systems, we may in fact be peering down the wrong end of the telescope. Perhaps, given the huge changes to European societies over the fifty years since the end of the Second World War, it is the lack of any correspondingly huge change in the continent's party systems that needs explaining! And here again, the danger of putting things down to *either* sociology *or* institutions becomes obvious. The lack of change in party systems may indicate, for example, that political scientists have always tended to overstate the links between those systems and social realities. Perhaps parties – and especially old parties – have found it easier to adapt to (and maybe even help shape) those realities than they are sometimes given credit for. Or perhaps the constitutional and electoral arrangements they had a hand in designing have served to constrain the kinds of party system change that a more sociological approach might have predicted.

▶ Third, the fact that, arguably, such change does now seem to be gathering pace need not mean that within a decade or so Europe's party systems will be subject to such volatility, fragmentation and dealignment that we may as well abandon the search for patterns and predictions and kiss goodbye to the whole notion of party systems and even to parties themselves! If the twentieth century is anything to go by, change is a constant but often a gradual process, and by no means always in the same direction. Even so-called 'earthquake elections' (contests which see many of the old parties losing seats to new competitors appearing out of nowhere) rarely end up changing the political landscape for good or rendering it unrecognizable (see Box 5.12). Party systems of the future will probably end up

---

BOX 5.12

Earthquake? What earthquake? Recent Dutch elections

The contest in the Netherlands in 2002 certainly looked like an earthquake, not least because of the dramatic entrance of a far-right party (the LPF, whose leader Pim Fortuyn was assassinated just before polling day). But the underlying story was the punishment voters meted out to parties involved in the coalition that governed the country before 2002. Each of its members (Labour, the Liberals and the Social Liberals) suffered badly. The LPF imploded very soon after it went into government with the Christian Democrats and the Liberals, and a second election was held soon afterwards. Things returned to something closely resembling 'normality' in 2003.

	1998	2002	2003
Labour Party	29.0	15.1	27.3
Christian Democrats	18.4	27.9	28.6
Liberal Party	24.7	15.4	17.9
Social Liberals	9.0	5.1	4.1
Green Left	7.3	7.0	5.1
Socialists	3.5	5.9	6.3
Christians	3.2	2.5	1.6
Far-Right	–	17.0	5.7

looking a little different from how they look today, but rarely completely so – just as how they look today is pretty close to how they looked three or four decades ago. Then, just as now, they will be the product of a subtle and reciprocal interaction of institutional arrangements and sociological realities, both of which will influence and be influenced by the behaviour of parties themselves.

Are parties in decline?

Whether party systems change profoundly or stay more or less the same, will many Europeans even care? Certainly few of them – especially in East Central Europe but also in the West – join parties or stay very long if they do (see Table 5.1). If ever there was a golden age for parties in the postwar period, it is over now. There are many other things that people with more leisure and money can now do with their time, and, for the politically inclined there are many single-issue groups that seem to offer a more direct (and possibly more enjoyable)

Table 5.1 Party membership in Europe, late 1990s		
	Total party membership	*% of electorate*
Sweden	366,000	5.5
Italy	1,1974,000	4.0
Czech Rep.	320,000	3.9
Spain	1,131,000	3.4
Germany	1,780,000	2.9
Netherlands	294,000	2.5
United Kingdom	840,000	1.9
France	615,000	1.6
Poland	326,000	1.1
Europe*	11,671,000	5.0

Note: * Europe includes twenty states: those above plus Austria, Belgium, Denmark, Finland, Greece, Hungary, Ireland, Norway, Portugal, Slovakia and Switzerland.

Source: Data from Mair and van Biezen (2001), with membership figures rounded to nearest thousand.

way to get what you want (see Chapter 8). Meanwhile, although there is evidence to suggest that members are useful to parties, in terms of finance or legitimacy or even campaigning (see Scarrow, 1994), they are able to cope without too many of them – especially if it means they will be free of the damaging impression that internal wrangling can cause in the media.

To many media pundits, and a few political scientists, high levels of anti-party sentiment and electoral apathy across the developed world are a recipe for the long-term decline of parties as genuinely representative institutions linking citizens to governments. Perhaps, suggest some analysts, parties were merely a stage democracy went through in the modern industrial era. Now they are increasingly hollow hulks or dinosaurs destined to extinction as the citizens of postmodern, postindustrial Europe turn to other more direct or more digital ways of doing politics (see Chapters 7 and 8) – or simply turn away from politics altogether. There may be some truth in these predictions, but we should not expect wholesale change – at least, not too quickly. There is a great deal of inertia around. The media may or may not help spread cynicism about parties, but they also rely on them to structure the reporting of what might otherwise be an unintelligible process of governance (see Chapter 7). Moreover, in the face of reduced membership income and donations that cannot always be relied upon (or relied upon to be strictly legal!), parties in many countries seem to have persuaded the states they help to run that they are worth subsidizing (see Box 5.13) .

There are plenty of arguments which supporters of state funding can point to. Parties are the least worst option when it comes to ensuring competitive elections and contestable national governance. This is because they are at base information-economizing devices for voters who would otherwise be confronted with a chaotic choice of alternatives and agents whom they could neither conceivably hope to know nor trust. Parties – especially established ones – offer a reasonably predictable set of diagnostically-based responses to both novel and perennial problems. They also offer – in extreme cases – some hope of bridging the gap between the majority and minorities who feel strongly enough to pursue armed struggle. They possess sufficient

BOX 5.13
How parties are financed: three regimes

	UK	Germany	Spain
State funding	No	Yes	Yes
Goes to	–	Parl. 'Head Office' Party foundations	Head Office
How allocated	–	Per vote, plus matching funding	Per parl. seat
Subsidies-in-kind	TV time, meeting halls, postage	As per UK	As per UK
Membership subscriptions	Relatively unimportant	Significant	Insignificant
Open donations	Significant	Relatively small	Not significant
Declarable above	€7,500	€10,000	–
Capped at	–	–	€44,000
Secret donations	Insignificant	Significant	Significant
Spending limits	€31 million	–	–
Scandals?	Few	Major	Some

Sources: Data from Nassmacher (2001).

democratic credentials – often exemplified in their own internal practices – to spare citizens the worry that those whom they choose to govern will turn around and deprive them of that choice next time around. Finally, they make it easier for those who did not get the government they wanted: if your team did not finish top, then at least it was beaten by an outfit or outfits playing roughly the same game under the same rules, and who you might hope to beat in the future.

Certainly, interest groups and protest movements may be better at expressing the direct material or identity needs of their participants (see Chapter 8). But they cannot fulfil this competitive function because they are not set up to play the same game, in the public eye (and with internally more or less democratic ways of doing things) year after year. When (like the environmental movement) they move, out of a sense of frustration perhaps, towards standing candidates in elections, they begin to turn into parties whether they like it or not. Sooner or later they will make the transformation by default or drop out. If they succeed in gaining ground and want to keep it that way, they will face media demands for positions on a range of issues. If they meet those demands they will (as greens all over Europe have found) be well on the way to the sort of interest aggregation that is the traditional function of the institution they will by then have become – a party. If they stick only to their original selective purpose, then they are unlikely to attract long-lasting or widespread attention, making continued electoral participation fruitless and a return to group status and other strategies considerably more attractive.

Supporters of the role of parties in a democracy also deny that other groups can fulfil a governing function because governing involves balancing various social claims for resources. By definition, those promoting one interest to the exclusion of most or all others are unable to do this, at least with any degree of efficiency and legitimacy. The idea that neutral, non-political state managers will be able to help them do so is patently false. As we note in Chapter 8, state bureaucracies sometimes fall victim to 'producer-capture' by well-funded and well-organized interests – even when overseen by parties with different concerns and constituencies. How much more likely and worse would this be without those parties around at all?

Supporters of parties are also sceptical about the only other possible check on too cosy a relationship between the state and groups – the so-called 'fourth estate', the media that we look at in more detail in Chapter 7. Any one hoping for a sudden increase in column inches or airtime devoted to investigative reporting of, say, corporate dominance, they argue, is likely to be sorely disappointed. Proprietors are reliant on those same interests for advertizing, and may even be part of the game themselves. Their journalists, as we suggest in Chapter 7, are reliant on their sources: without the parties as providers of information, balance and the ready-made personalization and dramatization of stories which turn them from mere events into what we think of as 'news', they would be lost.

This is not to say that parties are by any means perfect. They often talk as if they have a monopoly on good ideas, even though they know that they are heavily reliant on input from other players, including other parties – something which proportional systems that help facilitate coalition governments implicitly acknowledge. This, and other elements of their gamesmanship (and their salesmanship), can drive some citizens either to despair, or away, or both, as evidenced in recent British, Polish, Czech and European Parliament elections. But a great many others enjoy politics at least a little, and even if only as a spectator sport. There is

little evidence that those who stay at home would be any more actively involved by some other means of legitimately organizing the periodic and at least semi-public surrender of collective sovereignty to a handful of individuals. Parties may well be no more popular than (and just as stuck in the past as) other despised professions such as used-car salesman. But people will almost certainly continue to use them both for a very long time to come!

The Europeanization of parties and party systems?

Primarily because they contest national elections we tend to think of parties as national organizations, albeit with local branches and sections. But they also have an international and even transnational dimension, especially in Europe. Sheer proximity aside, the EU provides not only opportunities to persuade and learn from other parties of like mind but also a whole new electoral battleground and set of issues (organizational and ideological) with which to contend (see Ladrech, 2002 and Mair, 2000). As a result, we have to consider the effect on parties and party systems of Europeanization – the potential we identified in the Introduction for European integration to impact on the constraints, incentives, resources and influences experienced by hitherto 'domestic' political actors.

The impact on organization is immediately apparent. For instance, representatives of national parties elected to the EP need to work together, which they do by forming party groups in the EP (see Chapter 4). They may also be members of transnational federations outside the EP (see Table 5.2 and Johansson and Zervakis, 2002). Clearly, this transnational activity could lead to co-ordinated campaigning at EP elections – indeed, it has already done so in the case of the greens in 2004. The tendency for the various national leaders of the party families to caucus together before European summits may also both build on and facilitate transnational relationships that might have a policy impact at the European level, to the extent perhaps that centre-right leaders may, say, agree to co-ordinate a push for business deregulation.

But there is an awful lot of 'could', 'may' and 'might' about all this. Party politicians attend the

Table 5.2 Transnational party federations

Party family	Federation	Website
Left	New European Left Forum	n/a
	European Left Party*	n/a
Greens	European Federation of Green Parties	http://www.europeangreens.org/
Soc. Democrat	Party of European Socialists	http://www.pes.org/
Liberal	European Liberal Democrats	http://www.eldr.org/
Cons./Christian Dem	European People's Party	http://www.eppe.org

* Formed in May 2004, includes some members of NELF (such as the German PDS, the French PCF the Italian *Rifondazione Comunista*, the Soanish *Izquierda Unida*). It was also supposed to include more 'unreconstructed' communist parties, such as the Czech KSČM (see Box 5.9). Their presence explains the reluctance of other Left parties in NELF (especially those from Scandinavia) to participate in the new party, although, ironically, the KSČM stormed out of the inaugural meeting in protest at criticisms of the Soviet era!

European Council as heads of government and tend to push their national interests as much as their ideological positions. For example, centre-left leaders in Sweden, the UK and the Netherlands from 1997 onwards may have been interested in reforming the CAP but their counterparts in France and Germany did not stand shoulder to shoulder with them; and on liberalization of the European economy during the same period, the agenda was driven by an alliance between a centre-left prime minister in the UK and a centre-right prime minister in Spain. It is also doubtful in the near or medium term whether the increasing power of the EP will change the incentives parties have to keep their activities largely national. For one thing, organizational change not only disrupts vested intra-party interests (Panebianco, 1988) it also presents co-ordination problems at a time when many parties already have enough on their plates coping with sometimes inreasingly decentralized systems (see Deschouwer, 2003 and Hopkin, 2003). For another, parties are not so rich that they can devote significant resources to relationships between national parties, transnational federations and EP party groups (EU funding for which cannot legally be filtered back to the national party). Notwithstanding all this, we should remember that parties are above all adaptive organizations, and it could be that in future they will adopt a kind of 'franchizing' model, whereby (like many fast-food chains) the component parts of the organization will be allowed a good deal of autonomy as long as they use and promote the basic brand (Carty, 2004): this less hierarchical structure might facilitate within parties the kind of multilevel governance they are having to adjust to both at home and in Europe.

On the other hand, political cycles in European countries show little sign as yet of synchronizing and are unlikely to, given different constitutional arrangements. This makes working together across national borders difficult. And, as we saw once again in 2004, the EP elections themselves are still fought largely on national issues under national systems and are not seen to impact that strongly on the policy direction of the EU (either by parties or by voters). They also tend to see incumbent parties suffer, irrespective of the party family they represent, making co-ordination between the levels (for example, between parties in national government and EP groups) difficult and, arguably, pointless. A party may have sent a lot of MEPs to Strasbourg at the last election but if it is in opposition at home, its MPs may well be less enthusiastic than those MEPs are about European legislation, seeing it more as the product of a government they object to than the result of the hard work of their Euro-colleagues. Finally, there have been very few changes in party rules to allow those colleagues a greater say in the running of national parties.

None of this, however, should allow us to forget what should be apparent from almost every chapter in this book, namely, that the structures and issues that form the environment in which parties have to operate (either as governments or in terms of electoral competition) are affected – often increasingly so – by European integration. A major development since the 1980s, for example, is the extent to which social democratic parties have reoriented themselves towards a more 'pro-European' position as they recognize, first, that co-ordinated continental action may make more sense than the pursuit of the same goals at a purely national level and, secondly, that the latter is no longer clearly demarcated from the transnational anyway (see Ladrech, 2000). Left parties have also had to come to terms with Europe, recognizing that unless they engage positively in transnational politics in general and with the EU in particular that their fears about the latter 'locking-in neo-liberalism' (see Chapter 9) are more likely than ever to be realized (see Dunphy, 2004). Green parties, too, have learned to live with, if not completely overcome, their ambivalence. Indeed, more than that, a recent study suggests that 'Europeanization has accelerated both trends of professionalization of Green strategy and the mellowing of their ideological edge' (Bomberg, 2002: 45). In particular, success at EP elections has given the greens extra exposure, while perceived failure has helped speed up organizational reform (Bomberg, 2002, 34–5, 38). All of this indicates (Bomberg, 2002, 46) that 'Parties need not simply lie back and "let Europe happen to them": they can (and often do) actively engage and exploit European structures for their own party political gain.'

In keeping with this, we should reflect on other recent research which suggests that, despite the potential for 'Europe' to provoke internal tensions in some parties, most parties can, by and large, incorporate 'Europe' into existing and familiar modes of competition. Party (family) stances on European issues do more generally seem to be consistent with, rather than cutting across, their left–right (and their postmaterialist–materialist) positions. For instance, social democratic parties tend to favour a 'social Europe' that helps to correct market failures, while conservatives tend to favour a Europe that promotes the cause of economic liberalization and business deregulation – something that really worries left parties. Meanwhile, green parties appreciate the opportunities provided by the for environmental regulation, while far-right parties fear a loss of national sovereignty will undermine their ability to keep out immigrants and maintain a home-grown culture and welfare state (see Hooghe, Marks and Wilson, 2002 or Marks and Wilson, 2000).

Partly because of this and partly because of strategic and tactical imperatives, the pace, direction and extent of European integration is itself becoming an issue – if not always a central one, at least for mainstream parties – in national elections (see Gabel, 2000, Grzymala-Busse and Innes, 2003 and http://www.sussex.ac.uk/sei/1-4-2-8.html). Euroscepticism is now a potentially potent war cry not just in the UK and Scandinavia, where it has played a part in partisan competition for some time, but in elections all over the continent (see Szczerbiak and Taggart, 2005). It is these contests that are the focus of Chapter 6.

Learning resources

The standard text on political parties, Ware (1996), is excellent, though in need of updating. Mair and Mudde (1998) is useful, too. Good country overviews (and pointers to more detailed study) are available in Broughton and Donovan (1999) and Webb, Farrell and Holliday (2002). For the electoral performance of the main parties and party families in the postwar period, see Mair (2002). Most of the key conceptual readings are helpfully collected in Wolinetz (1997, 1998). Anyone particularly interested in parties should consult the following: Dalton and Wattenberg (2002), Gunther, Montero and Linz (2002) and Luther and Müller-Rommel (2002), Mair, Müller and Plasser (2004). Ladrech (2002), Mair and van Biezen (2001) and Yanai (1999) are also stimulating reads on decline, resilience and Europeanization, respectively. On the latter, so too are Gaffney (1996) and, especially, Mair (2000). For postcommunist states in particular see Bielasiak (2002), Kitschelt *et al.* (1999), Lewis (2001), Millard (2004) and Sitter (2003). Internet users can most usefully start at the http://www.electionworld.org/, where you can find out more by simply double-clicking on the party names, or go straight to http://www.electionworld.org/europeanunion.htm, which takes you to the transnational federations and then, via links, to national parties. For EP groups, go to http://www.europarl.eu.int/groups/default.htm.

EXECUTIVE SUMMARY

- Europe's political parties have gradually developed into institutions with the capacity not just to translate social and ideological cleavages and conflicts into workable compromises, but also to provide a voice for those who reject them and demand change.

- This essentially historical development means there are significant variations both between parties and over time in the way they organize and appeal to the electorate.

- The fact that many of the conditions in which they began and continue to compete are common to many countries means that parties in different states share certain worldviews.

- It also means that we can make meaningful comparisons not just between parties in different countries, but also between the party systems that their relative strengths and their patterns of co-operation and competition (along with different electoral arrangements) create. Some of these systems are ideologically polarized and/or fragmented, some less so.

- These systems are more or less in flux, mostly as a result of changes in the electorate, though the extent of this flux can be overstated. Moreover, parties are not passive victims of their environment: they adapt to and even help shape it. Because of this and because they are uniquely equipped to play their democratic role linking citizens with government, they are likely to be around for some time, whether we like them or not.

- Notwithstanding the creation of transnational federations and the impact of the EU on domestic politics and processes, parties seem likely – at least in the foreseeable future – to prioritize (and to organize at) the national rather than the European level.

Chapter 6

Elections, voting and referendums: systems, turnout, preferences and unpredictability

Europe's myriad electoral systems
Electoral systems and party systems
Turnout: decline and variation
Preferences: what makes people vote the way they do?
EP elections
Direct democracy: useful tool or dangerous panacea?

Democracy came to Europe in the late nineteenth and early twentieth centuries. But the process was far from complete even before it was set back for decades, first, by authoritarian dictatorships which began in the 1930s and, secondly, by the forty years of communist rule in East Central Europe which followed the Second World War. In France, Italy, Belgium and Greece, for instance, women won the vote only in the wake of that conflict, and in Switzerland they had to wait nearly another thirty years! On the other hand, in all European countries, the age at which people become entitled to vote (though not to stand as candidates) now matches the age at which they legally become adults, with some countries (such as the UK) either debating or even (as in Germany) experimenting with a reduction in the age.

If by 'democracy', however, we mean a chance for every adult periodically to vote on who runs the country, locally and nationally (see Box 6.1), Europe became 'democratic' only in the early 1990s. Democracy is an abstract that, like 'Europe', disguises a wealth of variation when it comes to the particular.

This chapter begins by looking at different electoral systems and their effects, including their interaction with the party systems we described in Chapter 5. It then goes on to examine the decline in turnout that some believe is coming to afflict all liberal democracies: is it happening, and if so, why? Next, it tackles the even thornier issue of electoral behaviour. Why do people vote the way they do? How influential are things such as class and, perhaps surprisingly, religion? And what about short-term factors? Do these matter more these days as people lose their loyalty to particular parties and are more inclined to switch their vote from one election to another? Finally, the chapter looks at so-called 'direct democracy' – referendums and the like. Are they a viable substitute for the representative democracy that all European countries still seem to prefer?

In all European democracies, the physical process of voting is still simple and similar. Notwithstanding some developments in electronic voting (either remotely or at the polling station),

---

BOX 6.1
The timing of elections

In most European countries, there is considerable flexibility with regard to when elections are held. Naturally, all have a maximum (generally four years, though five in France, Ireland and the UK), but only Norway (where elections can only be held every four years) has a minimum time between national contests. Sweden is also unusual in that it is committed to holding a general election every fourth September, irrespective of whether an early election has been held in between. Elsewhere, convention mostly has it that the government can decide when it wants to call an election providing that it is within the maximum permitted. In some countries (like Germany and, until recently, the Netherlands), however, this kind of 'cutting and running' is frowned upon.

most voters still enact the same ritual. They enter a private space with a ballot paper, mark it in some way to record a preference and then deposit it in a ballot box for counting later. Only then do things get complicated. The number and percentage of votes each party gets has to be translated into a number and percentage of parliamentary seats. The match between votes and seats is rarely exact in any country, but in some it is more exact than in others. The crucial mechanism is the electoral system.

Europe's myriad electoral systems

Europe's electoral systems can basically be split into two main groups: **plurality/majority**, on the one hand, and **proportional**, on the other. One can then split the first group into two – plurality and then majority – and the second group into three – list PR, mixed systems, and single transferable vote (which is used by only two countries, Ireland and Malta). Each of the systems is explained in more detail below. Table 6.1 (p. 137), which follows those explanations, indicates which system each of our common core countries uses for its general elections.

Definition
Plurality/majority systems use single-member constituencies or districts, with the candidate who gets a *majority* (more than half the votes cast) or a *plurality* (more votes than any other candidate) getting elected. **Proportional systems** – often known collectively as PR or proportional representation systems – make use of multimember constituencies or districts so that the seats a party gets in the legislature more accurately reflects its share of the vote.

Plurality and majority systems

Europe's simplest electoral systems are those that employ plurality and majority rules. These were also initially the most widely used systems, but they are now employed by so few countries that they may be more familiar to Americans than most Europeans. A 'plurality system', often called 'first-past-the-post' (FPP), is one in which the candidate who gets the most votes is elected. It is the system employed in the UK, with the exception of elections in Northern Ireland and elections to the Welsh Assembly, and the Scottish and European Parliaments. A 'majority system' is slightly different. It requires that the winning candidate get over half the votes, with the most common way of ensuring such an outcome being a second, 'run-off', election between the top two candidates. This method is employed in presidential but not parliamentary contests in Austria, Finland, and Portugal. France, like the UK, conducts its legislative elections in hundreds of single-member constituencies (also known by electoral systems experts as 'districts' or sometimes as 'electorates'). But French candidates who win a plurality but not a majority in the first round of voting must fight a second round a week later against all of his or her opponents who won 12.5 per cent or more in the first round. In the second round, the winner is the candidate who wins the most votes (i.e. a plurality), although often (because many second-round contests turn into two-horse races) he or she will actually win a full-blown majority. France's president is also elected under a two-ballot majority system, with only the top two candidates going through to the second round. This system seems to encourage voters to 'vote with their hearts' first time around, spreading their votes around a diverse variety of candidates from extreme left to extreme right, and finally 'with their heads', eliminating the candidate furthest from their own stance (often at the request of the defeated candidate for whom they voted in round one).

PR systems

In contrast to France and the UK, by far the majority of European countries use electoral systems that attempt to ensure that the share of seats a party has in parliament more or less reflects the share of the vote it received at the election. Indeed, Europe can be said to be the home of PR. However, there are many subtle variations in the systems used by each country, all of which affect just how accurately votes are converted into seats. Although the advocates of PR emphasize its 'fairness' when compared to FPP systems, most are aware that what are all too easily dismissed as dull, technical differences between proportional systems are actually crucially important in determining which parties are likely to do well, or at least better than their competitors.

That this is the case is not surprising, given PR's history. It did not replace FPP as the system used by most countries (beginning with Belgium in 1899 and Sweden in 1907) because it was universally acknowledged to be fairer or more rational. It actually started out – at least in part – as the means by which the various parties representing the privileged and the propertied hoped to survive the coming of universal suffrage, and thus the enfranchizement of the working classes. It was widely assumed that such parties would suffer if they stood in individual constituencies because – unless constituency boundaries were drawn so as to make some of them middle-class strongholds (as happened in the UK) – their better-off voters would always be in the minority. Ever since, parties of all stripes have played a major role in determining the 'rules of the game' and, unsurprisingly, have done their best to ensure that they are helped, or at least not disadvantaged, by the sophistication and the subtleties of those rules.

Before going on to look at some of those subtleties and sophistications, we should first understand the basic differences between PR systems. They can be conveniently be divided (following Lijphart, 1999) into three:

▸ List PR systems
▸ Mixed systems
▸ STV systems

List PR systems involve voters voting in multimember constituencies or districts for lists of candidates provided by political parties or alliances of political parties. When the votes are counted, each list is awarded seats in proportion to the votes cast for it. In the Netherlands, there is only one national constituency, which guarantees a proportional result overall. In other countries, however, regional variations could produce an overall result that is disproportionate. While some (like Spain) are prepared to live with such an outcome, others are not. A number of countries (including Sweden) reserve a certain proportion of seats (normally 10–20 per cent) in order to correct any such imbalance – the so-called 'higher-tier' seats. There is one more important difference between countries employing list PR. Some (e.g. Spain) employ 'closed' lists, in the sense that the party (or parties if they are fighting as an electoral alliance) determines the rank order of the candidates on the list: those voting for the list can do nothing to change that order. Others (such as Finland, Estonia and Poland) employ 'open list PR', where the candidates who make it into parliament off the list are determined by the voters who rank order or actually simply vote for the names on the list. Still others employ hybrids, whereby voters can express a preference. In some (e.g. Sweden and the Czech Republic) their preference can and does make a difference, with some popular candidates leapfrogging into parliament over those placed higher on the list by their parties. In others (e.g. the Netherlands) the rank order provided by the party nearly always determines things. Clearly, 'closed list' PR makes it more difficult for candidates who make themselves unpopular with their parties and therefore end up with a low list position, and thus strengthens the disciplinary capacity of party managers.

Mixed systems give voters two votes. They use one to vote for a candidate in their local constituency or district. They use the other to vote for a list in a multimember constituency (often covering a particular region). The list is 'compensatory': it is used to ensure that, whatever the results of the constituency contests, the overall result of the election is more or less proportional. Its ability to do this, however, is to some extent dependent on how many seats in parliament are constituency seats and how many are party or list seats. In Germany, about half of all parliamentary seats are non-constituency seats, a number adequate to produce a pretty proportional result: this is why its system, still sometimes called AMS (alternative member system), is increasingly labelled MMP (mixed member proportional). Strictly, speaking Italy probably does not merit the MMP label: there, only a quarter of parliament's seats are non-constituency seats, a number that is insufficient to compensate fully for a disproportionate result in the constituencies. This is also the case in a number of postcommunist democracies, whose systems are now given the label 'mixed-

Italy (Italia)

Area: 7.6% of EU-25
Population: 12.6% of EU-25
GDP: 13.4% of EU-25
Joined EU: founder member 1957
Capital city: Roma (Rome)

History: Italy was for centuries a collection of city-states, many of them ruled by foreign powers such as Spain and then Austria. It was also invaded by France at the end of the eighteenth century. In the nineteenth century, however, nationalists led by Garibaldi built on the achievements in the north by Cavour and, by 1870, had succeeded in unifying the country under a constitutional monarch. Italy held its first mass elections (though still denying women the vote) on the eve of the First World War, a conflict from which Italy emerged on the winning side.

From the 1920s onwards, Italy, like Germany, collapsed into authoritarian dictatorship (in its case under the fascist leader Benito Mussolini). Following its defeat in the Second World War, in which it allied itself with Germany, Italy became a republic. Its politics were dominated by the centre-right Christian Democratic party (DC), which benefited from an unwritten pact between most political parties to keep the powerful communist party (PCI) out of office at the national level. The DC's constant presence in every postwar administration until the early 1990s provided a kind of disguised stability for a system that saw forty-seven governments between 1947 and 1992. But it also relied on clientelistic corruption, as well as links with organized crime

and even terrorism. With the collapse of Communism, Italians were finally able to express their discontent, and the early 1990s saw the end of the Christian Democrats and a new, less proportional electoral system. The electorate divides its support between a fissiparous left-wing bloc based around the former PCI, now calling themselves Democrats of the Left, and an equally fissiparous right-wing bloc composed of a former fascist party (the now conservative National Alliance), a xenophobic regionalist party (the Northern League) and the dominant partner, *Forza Italia*, led by media mogul Silvio Berlusconi.

Economy and society: Interestingly, Italy's superficially chaotic politics did little to harm its economic revival after the Second World War, and the country remains one of Europe's economic powerhouses with a reputation for producing stylish, high-quality goods in demand all over the world. In 2003, its 58 million people had a per capita GDP around 7 per cent above the EU-25 average. However, there is a big gap on all social–economic indicators between the rich industrialized and service-oriented north and the poorer, more agricultural south (or *Mezzorgiorno*) that also includes the islands of Sicily and Sardinia. This has led to tensions, with people in the North feeling resentment at having, as they see it, to subsidize the South – a sentiment summed up in the catch-cry or slogan of the Northern League 'Roma Ladrona' (Rome, the thief). Partly because there is a relatively low level of identification with the nation state, Italians have historically been very pro-Union. Traditionally, they have also been among the most tolerant toward migrants, although this has changed in recent years, as foreigners have been attracted in substantial numbers into the vibrant northern economy. More are likely to join them, since Italy, along with Spain, has one of Europe's most rapidly ageing populations.

Governance: Italy is a parliamentary democracy elected, since 1994,

under a mixed, and not very proportional, system that has, however, failed to reduce the number of parties. Very unusually, both houses of the legislature have practically equal power. Also, in recent times Italian presidents, elected by parliament and supposedly with little more than ceremonial power, have shown themselves more willing than their counterparts in other European countries to criticize the government of the day. Italy's judiciary – and not just its constitutional court – is also renowned for its willingness to investigate its politicians and their actions. Relations became even more strained during Silvio Berlusconi's second period of office beginning in 2001. The prime minister not only faced criminal and civil cases against him as a result of his business dealings, but appeared willing to use his considerable media power to denounce his political and judicial opponents.

These high-profile spats, should not, however, obscure other fundamental developments in the governance of Italy, not least the move toward granting its regions much greater autonomy – a move designed to respond to the demands of the Northern League that Italy's rich north not be 'held back' by its poor south.

Foreign policy: Italy, like Germany, spent most of the latter half of the twentieth century atoning for its overassertiveness before 1945. A staunch member of the EU and NATO, it has, however, often been accused of not living up to the commitments it often seems to observe more in word than in deed. In recent years, Italy has modified its knee-jerk enthusiasm for European integration and, with the UK and Spain, its government (in contrast to its population) was a strong supporter of American intervention in Iraq.

Further reading: Ginsborg (2003, 2004), Newell (2000) and Pasquino (2002).

Table 6.1 Who uses which electoral system?

Plurality (FPP)	Majority (double ballot)	List PR	Mixed
UK	France	Czech Rep.	Germany
		Netherlands	Italy
		Poland	
		Spain	
		Sweden	

parallel' as opposed to 'mixed-linked', like MMP (see Millard, 2004: chapter 4). Hungary's hybrid system is, broadly speaking, a variant of MMP, though its subtle contortions mean that, strictly speaking, it is 'a mixed-linked, majoritarian-proportional, two-vote system, with two-round majority-plurality and regional PR list elements and a compensatory national list' (Birch et al., 2002: 60)!

In STV (single transferable vote) systems, voters in multimember constituencies or districts, are presented not with lists but with names of individual candidates (along with their party affiliations) which they are then invited to rank order. Candidates receiving a certain quota of first-preference votes are deemed elected, after which any of their votes over and above the quota are transferred (as if they were first preferences) in proportion to that candidate's voters' second choices. The same thing happens to the second-preference votes on the ballots of the weakest candidate. The transfer process continues until all the seats allocated to the constituency are filled by candidates reaching the quota. (For a full decription of this very complex process, see Farrell, 2001: 126–39.)

PR's subtleties and sophistications

The subtleties and sophistications mentioned above are myriad, but only two or three of them are worth focusing on here. The first two are features that impact on the proportionality of PR systems; namely 'thresholds' and 'district magnitude'. The third is the mathematical formula adopted to working out the allocation of seats. All

three can negatively impact on the proportionality of PR systems (see Anckar, 1997).

A threshold is a percentage figure of the vote that a party (or electoral alliance) has to score before it is awarded a share of seats in parliament or, if a higher-tier exists, a share of those seats. Thresholds exist in almost every country that employs PR, normally because of a desire to limit fragmentation (i.e. a large number of parties in parliament) for fear that this would threaten stable government – and, of course, the position of existing parties! Thresholds vary between a low of 0.67 per cent in the Netherlands and a high of 5 per cent in the Czech Republic, Poland and Germany, where avoiding a return to the extreme multipartism of the interwar years was uppermost in the minds of those who designed its electoral system. Basically, the higher the threshold, the higher the hurdle and the harder it is for small parties to make it into parliament. Given this, it is not entirely surprising that thresholds have been tinkered with in many European countries by those parties with a vested interest in preventing competition. This was a lesson quickly learned by the parties that initially did well in elections in the postcommunist democracies (Bale and Kopecký, 1998). After the 'velvet divorce' that saw Czechoslovakia split into two countries, for example, both new republics raised thresholds, particularly for parties that formed alliances to fight elections, and in 1999 the Romanian parliament voted to increase its threshold from 3 to 5 per cent, with electoral alliances needing to obtain an additional 3 per cent of the vote for every party belonging to it. On the other hand, such manipulative measures are rarely fool-proof, as the smaller parties in Poland quickly discovered (see Box 6.2).

BOX 6.2
The uncertain science of electoral engineering: Italy and Poland

In 1993, Italians voted in a referendum to abandon their country's relatively 'pure' form of PR in favour of an MMP system. This, they hoped, would bring political stability by making it harder for small parties to gain parliamentary representation. The latter effect, it was assumed by those who supported the system, would be achieved in two ways. First, they allocated only 25 per cent of seats to the (regionalized) 'higher-tier' (or list section), therefore reducing the ability of these list seats to compensate for a disproportionate result in the constituency contests (a move that would also provide governing coalitions with bigger majorities). Second, they insisted that parties would have to win at least 4 per cent of the national vote in order to qualify for list seats. However, the effect was partially undone by a fantastically intricate rule (the *scorporo*) brought in to buy off the resistance of smaller parties to the change. This rule has the effect of reducing the vote share of the larger parties in the list section and means that small parties stand a better chance of getting over the threshold! This, plus the willingness of parties to form electoral alliances to help them win seats in the constituencies, has meant the number of parties in parliament has not decreased anywhere near as much as many people expected.

This would come as no surprise to Poles. Poland undertook a number of changes to its electoral system in its first few years as a democracy, with larger parties insisting that a reduction in fragmentation – the number of parties in parliament – would be good for stability and good government (as well as, of course, reducing the competition). Many casual observers noted that these seemed to work: the number of parties in parliament reduced quite markedly. After the 1991 election, the *Sejm* contained eighteen parties (though, significantly, the senate, elected by plurality, afforded representation to thirty-one!). In 1993, with the introduction of thresholds of 5 per cent for single parties and 8 per cent for alliances, the number declined to just six. However, the extent to which this reduction was directly due to rule changes (rather than, say, to some kind of 'learning curve' according to which people began trying to avoid giving their votes to tiny parties with no parliamentary clout) is debatable. In any case, smaller parties were able to offset some of the negative effects of the rule changes by creative strategies, such as forming alliances that, for instance, they were careful to call 'committees' and not 'coalitions', thereby avoiding the higher threshold (8 per cent) imposed on the latter! Their efforts did not however, prevent, over a third of votes being 'wasted' on parties that failed to make it into parliament.

The number of MPs allocated to each constituency – known in the jargon as district magnitude – can make a significant difference to the proportionality of a PR system, especially where there is no second tier of seats to correct any disproportionality at the regional level. Basically, the lower the 'district magnitude' (i.e. the lower the number of MPs allocated to each constituency), the lower the proportionality of the overall result. This arithmetical relationship results from the fact that, as some of us may remember from primary school, dividing a relatively small number by a relatively large number entails a greater likelihood of a remainder. Proportionality is therefore pretty easy to achieve in the Netherlands where the whole country is treated as one constituency with 150 MPs. But it is much less likely in Spain. There, in addition to having strong regional differences, the country is split into fifty-two constituencies with an average of seven MPs per constituency. At the general election of 2000, this allowed the centre-right *Partido Popular* (PP) to form a single-party majority because its 44 per cent of the vote afforded it 52 per cent of the seats. The opposition PSOE could hardly complain, however, because it had taken advantage of the same sort of disproportionality in the 1980s and early 1990s!

Thirdly, the electoral system can be made to work to the marginal advantage of larger or smaller parties according to the mathematical formula used to allocate seats to parties in PR systems. Table 6.2 deliberately eschews a detailed discussion of the mathematical merits of each formula (on which, see Farrell, 2001), but summarizes their effects. Many countries use one formula for allocating constituency seats and another for the compensatory higher tier of list seats. This combination can cancel out the bias toward larger or smaller parties. Others, which generally employ a formula that favours larger parties, do not have a higher tier and therefore the bias goes uncorrected: Spain is an obvious example. While these matters can seem awfully abstruse to some of us, they matter a lot to parties. For instance, in Poland, prior to the election of 2001, various parliamentary parties on the right, fearing (correctly) that the more unified centre-left social democrats were about to win a big victory, got together to change the electoral formula from d'Hondt in favour of St-Laguë, which is thought to favour smaller parties: it may well be that the change did enough to deny the social democrats an outright victory that year.

Generally, we can say that the Netherlands (and Denmark) have the most proportional PR systems, with most others somewhere in the middle. The exceptions are Spain and Greece (and to some extent Portugal) where larger parties do better than, strictly speaking, they should. On the other hand, levels of disproportionality are still under half of that experienced by the United Kingdom and under a third of that experienced by France.

Electoral systems and party systems

It is easy in political and other social sciences to mistake correlation (some kind of relationship between two factors) for causation (suggesting that one causes the other). Doing so would lead us to think that, because countries with proportional electoral systems tend to have multi-party systems, the latter must be the result of the former or that two-party systems are explained by FPP – views sometimes associated with Maurice Duverger, one of the 'founding fathers' of comparative politics. There are two problems with such reasoning. First, it does not quite fit contemporary and historical reality. For instance, the most solid two-party system in Europe is in Malta, but Malta uses STV. On the other hand, France, with its plurality contests, is – for the moment, at least – very much a multiparty system. Historically, most of the countries that moved to PR just before or just after the First World War already had multiparty systems even under plurality rules – even if some of those parties did not get their fair share of parliamentary seats. And the move toward multiparty politics in, say, Austria and Ireland, occurred only recently despite decades of using PR systems. Italy's move towards a less pure proportional system has not, as people hoped, cut down on the number of parties in parliament – something Poles could have told them (see Box 6.2). Secondly, as we have already suggested in Chapter 5, treating the electoral system as the prime cause of party systems would be to place too great a weight on institutional factors and too little weight on the social factors that also help to shape things.

Table 6.2 PR electoral formulas and the parties they favour

Formula employed	Largest remainders	Modified St-Laguë	d'Hondt
Formula favours	Smaller parties		Larger parties
Countries using formula for constituency seat (first-tier) allocation		Sweden Poland	Netherlands Spain Czech Rep.
Countries using formula for list seat (higher-tier) allocation	Germany* Italy*	Sweden	

Note: * Germany and Italy (as mixed systems) use plurality systems for constituencies.

Source: Adapted from Birch *et al.* (2002: 27, 86), and Gallagher, Laver and Mair (2001: 310).

Obviously the electoral system plays a role, but it is not necessarily a determining one. If plurality systems really did create two-party politics and PR multiparty politics, how would we explain either the virtual duopoly that exists in Malta, which operates STV, or the range of parties on offer to French voters under their plurality system? Giovanni Sartori (whose work on party systems we referred to in Chapter 5) has persuasively argued (Sartori, 1997) that a plurality system cannot in and of itself produce a two-party system. This is because the existence of the latter also depends on limited polarization and on the absence of geographically concentrated minorities that are unwilling to be represented by either of two big parties (and therefore elect MPs from regionalist parties instead). On the other hand, Sartori suggests, if two-party competition does take hold, a plurality system will exert 'a brakelike influence' and 'a freezing effect'. By the same token, moving to PR (or a more 'pure' form of PR) will, of course, remove obstacles to new entrants. It may also encourage the splitting of old parties whose two wings previously had to put up with each other in order to avoid the electoral wilderness. But Sartori argues that this simply gives institutional expression to what was going on anyway – 'freedom to increase [the number of parties]', he writes, 'is no more the cause of increasing than freedom to eat is the cause of eating'. Given the extent of obesity in the developed world, however, one might be forgiven for wondering whether his argument holds water! Knowing you can walk out of the party taking some of your colleagues with you and/or start up a new party and still stand a chance at the next election surely might cause political actors to do something they otherwise might not even contemplate. Likewise, the consequent expansion of the alternatives on offer may well also encourage voters to vote in a way that would otherwise never have occurred to them. This goes beyond even the 'psychological effect' posited by Duverger (1954), who concentrated on the tendency of voters under FPP not to bother voting for smaller parties that (because of the 'mechanical effect' occasioned by their failure to win their fair share of seats) have no chance.

Academic disputes over the causal relationship (or lack of it) between electoral and party systems, however, pale in comparison to wider arguments about the relative merits of proportional and plurality systems. These are summarized in Box 6.3 and, given the perceived political effect of different systems, understandably generate considerable passion on either side. Ultimately the issue may be what some philosophers call 'an essentially contested question' – one involving so many underlying assumptions and motivations that it is unlikely ever to be satisfactorily answered.

Turnout: decline and variation

Recent elections throughout the democratic world have given cause for concern among pundits and politicians because the number of those eligible to vote who actually do so appears to be dropping – in some cases, like a stone (see Table 6.3, p. 142). In fact, as political scientists like Mark Franklin (2002) argue, the decline, while not insignificant (just compare some recent elections against long-term averages), is not as large as is often thought. Franklin also suggests we need to start taking the levels achieved in the 1950s as an unusual high point rather than as a norm from which we have now sadly departed. Nowadays, for better or worse, he argues, there may be fewer 'great causes', fewer profound disputes between labour and capital. And we need to remember that a handful of high-profile cases of low turn-out (most notably perhaps the UK election of 2001) do not necessarily constitute a trend so much as point to the importance of contingency in explaining variation over time within one country – something that is also stressed in a recent exploration of turnout in Central and Eastern Europe (Millard, 2004: 75–81). Franklin's analyses suggest that a shorter than usual period between elections, for instance and, more significantly still, a highly predictable result, both tend to depress turnout; so, too, does a feeling on the part of the electorate that, first, the differences between the alternatives on offer and, secondly, the connection between who is in power and the policies pursued, is vague.

More interesting and significant, perhaps, than an apparent decline in turnout are the variations in turnout between European countries (see Table 6.4). We know that the richer and/or more

BOX 6.3
PR or plurality: for and against

The case for plurality

Voters vote directly for governments and MPs: less horse-trading by parties forced to water down their election promises in order to become part of a winning coalition; better chance of calling to account or completely getting rid of governments and MPs, forcing the latter to take account of local feeling rather than simply toeing the party line.

Stronger, and very often single-party, governments: administrations can pursue mandated programmes instead of delaying or rendering them incoherent through compromise, allowing them to tackle problems properly rather than waste time on searching for a consensus; governments more stable and durable; not prone to being blackmailed into unpopular policies by small, fringe parties.

The case for PR

Fewer 'wasted votes' on the part of people who vote for parties or candidates that do not go on to get into parliament.

More representative parliaments: MPs come from right across the political spectrum in line with voter preferences, providing them with a real choice; more women and ethnic minority MPs because parties do not need to worry about the risk of putting up a female and/or an ethnic candidate in an FPP constituency when voters are assumed (rightly or wrongly) still to prefer white men.

More coalition governments: legislation and policy theoretically has the support of a majority of voters and not just a majority of MPs; the need to balance the interests of various parties necessitates and promotes consensus politics – and prevents an essentially unrepresentative executive inflicting its programme on the country even though a majority of voters did not vote for it; the increased likelihood of having to take account of ethnic parties promotes consensual solutions to ethnic conflicts.

Little or no opportunity for parties to tinker with electorate boundaries (redistricting) in the hope of giving themselves an advantage – something that occurs frequently in the US, and has occurred occasionally in the UK and Ireland.

Boosts electoral turnout – the proportion of people who actually go to the polls at a general election tends to be measurably and markedly higher under PR.

educated and/or more interested in politics a person is, the more likely he or she is to vote. But none of this really matters as much as the fact that he or she is from, say, Sweden (where turnout is generally high – 80 per cent in 2002) or from Poland (where it is much lower – 46 per cent in 2001). There seem to be several reasons behind these variations, as Franklin's work shows. Compulsory voting, postal voting and weekend voting and proportionality itself are significant, as is the extent to which one party or another is close to getting an overall majority. But by far the most important factor is 'electoral salience' (the extent to which elections are seen actually to impact on the complexion and conduct of government). Countries in which elections are seen to mean something boast turnouts up to 30 per cent greater than countries such as Switzerland, in which, 'whoever you vote for the government still gets in'. Compulsory, postal and weekend voting seem to increase turnout by just over 5 per cent each, while every percentage point closer to perfect proportionality a country gets is apparently worth around half a per cent in additional turnout. Countries that present voters with the possibility of voting for or against a party that is close (but only close) to

Table 6.3 Turnout in selected European Countries, 1945–2004: long-term decline or trendless fluctuation?

Year	Italy	Netherlands	Sweden	Germany	Czech Rep.	UK	France	Spain	Poland
1950s	94	96	79	87	n/a	80	80	n/a	n/a
1960s	93	95	86	87	n/a	77	77	n/a	n/a
1970s	91	84	90	91	n/a	75	76	73	n/a
1980s	89	84	89	87	n/a	74	72	77	n/a
1990s	85	76	85	80	83	75	69	78	48
2000s	81	80	80	79	58	59	60	73	46
Mean, 1945+	90	87	86	85	78	75	75	74	47

Note: n/a means not applicable because state was not a democracy at the time. All calculations based on registered voters only (which tends to give a slightly higher figure than figures based on age-eligible population). Mean is the average at all elections from 1945 onwards. Italy has (weakly enforced) compulsory voting. Source: http://www. idea. int/vt/index.cfm.

getting an overall majority seem to have turnouts around 5 per cent higher than those that do not. Smaller countries have higher turnouts, but the difference turns out to be minimal.

Clearly, things will not be set in stone. For instance, if Swedish voters begin to think that, whatever they do, the support of 'captive parties' like the Greens and the Left Party will keep the Social Democrats in power (see Chapter 5), they may begin not to bother. It is also important to note that we may be observing the beginning of a trend which is masked by doing long-run comparisons. Finally, we should note that turnout in CEE states is subject to similar variations and fluctua-tions, many of which we can explain, some of which we cannot (see Kostadinova, 2003 and Millard, 2004: 75–81). But turnout in postcommunist democracies does seem unlikely to reach the relatively high levels seen in some west European states. As Table 6.5 shows, Poland seems to suffer from chronically low turnout in parliamentary elections – a die that also seems to have been cast in the Baltic Republics of Lithuania and Estonia (but not Latvia). Turnout in the Czech Republic seems to be trending downward after an initial burst of enthusiasm, and (as in the UK, for instance) dropped alarmingly in 2002. Meanwhile, Slovenia, Slovakia and Hungary seem to have

Table 6.4 The European turnout league table, 1961–99

85% +	80–84%	75–79%	70–74%	65–69%	50–60%
Malta	Germany	Portugal	Spain	Estonia	Hungary
Belgium	Czech Rep.	Romania	Bulgaria		Switzerland
Italy	Greece	Finland	Ireland		Poland
Austria	Netherlands	UK			Lithuania
Iceland	Norway	France			
Luxembourg					
Sweden					
Denmark					

Source: Adapted from Franklin (2002).

relatively 'healthy' levels of turnout with around seven or eight out of ten people voting. Hungary, incidentally, is a good illustration that what goes down can come up! In 1998, turnout was 58 per cent, which all too predictably had media commentators claiming it would go the way of Poland. But in 2002, turnout in Hungary rose to just over 70 per cent – which should caution us not to write off, say, the Czech Republic.

Preferences: what makes people vote the way they do?

These cultural differences in voting behaviour between states are often more noticeable than they are explicable. Likewise, explaining why people vote the way they do has always been much harder than we would like. It is, if you like, the Holy Grail of that branch of political science called 'psephology' (a term for the scientific study of elections invented in the 1950s and based on the Greek word for the pebbles that were used by the ancients for casting their ballots). The reason is that there are so many possible factors that go into such a decision that it is impossible to control for all of them – certainly at the individual level.

This does not mean, however, that we cannot make educated guesses based on aggregate data – in other words, by using survey research to see if there is a correlation between certain characteristics (which become the 'independent variable', the thing doing the influencing) and voting for one party or another (the 'dependent variable', the thing being influenced). Decades of research in this area has traditionally accorded particular significance to three things: class and religion (both of which fitted quite neatly with Lipset and Rokkan's [1967] idea of 'cleavages' discussed in Chapter 5) and 'party identification' (the extent to which someone feels 'close to' a particular party). The problem is that the same research now suggests that the effect (or at least the predictive power) of all three has not necessarily disappeared, but has almost certainly declined. Indeed so much so, some argue, that we would have just as good a chance of predicting which party someone is going to vote for if we were to flip a coin instead of bothering to ask them which party they identify

Table 6.5 Turnout in two postcommunist democracies, 1990–2002

Year	Poland (%)	Czech Rep. (%)
1990		96*
1991	43	
1992		85*
1993	52	
1996		76
1997	48	
1998		74
2001	46	
2002		58

Note: * Figures relate to Czechoslovak elections.
Source: Data from IDEA international and http://www.election-world.org/.

with or about their social background and religious beliefs.

Party ID

The idea of party identification (often referred to simply as party ID) is often associated with the 'Michigan model' of voting (so-called because it was pioneered at the University of Michigan in the US). This model held that the majority of people were socialized into feeling closer to one party rather than another. Although this did not necessarily mean they would always vote for it – judgements about economic conditions or particular issues or candidates could play a part as well – normally they would. This 'homing instinct' made party identification a powerful predictor. Whether someone considered themself generally to be a Democrat or a Republican, whatever the reasons, would allow psephologists to make a pretty educated guess about which way they would vote in any given election. Those who study voting in Europe, however, have always been rather more sceptical (particularly outside the UK) on the grounds that a voter's primary identification might be to a social class or religious denomination or region and only then, in indirect fashion, to one of what might be a number of parties claiming to best serve its interests. They have also been doubtful that respondents to surveys are able to disentangle their current political preference from any long-term identification they may or may not have.

These conceptual and methodological objections do not mean that no work has been done on party identification in Europe – indeed some of the most cutting-edge work on voting argues strongly that the concept does travel well (Evans, 2004). For many analysts, though, much of the work that uses it fails to provide a convincingly clear-cut answer to the question, 'has there been a Europe-wide decline in party ID over time?' (see Schmitt and Holmberg, 1995). Any overall drop might be heavily skewed, for instance, by figures from Italy whose party system has undergone complete transformation. Even studies on individual countries do not always agree on the extent of change: for instance, some studies of Germany point to change (see Dalton, 1996), whereas some do not (Lohmann, Brady and Rivers, 1997). France is also a case in point (Evans, 2004). In the UK, to take another example, the picture is complex. Overall, it is easy to overdo decline, but perhaps significantly, the number of people saying they identify very strongly with a particular party is now only about a third of what it was in the 1960s, and the number who identify only weakly has risen (see Crewe and Thomson, 1999). Individual countries aside, by no means all cross-national studies (most of which exclude East Central Europe and should perhaps also exclude newer democracies like Spain and Portugal where time series data is limited), suggest there has not been any overall decline in party identification (van Deth and Janssen, 1994). On the other hand, some researchers are equally convinced that the evidence for decline is there (see Dalton, 2000).

In all probability, the debate over the decline or otherwise of party identification may simply take time to resolve. If cumulative research does indeed go on to show a downward trend, this will only leave us with another challenge – not simply showing that people are less attached to parties than previously, but explaining why. Two possibilities spring immediately to mind. One is to suggest that it is linked to public dissatisfaction beginning in the 1970s with the relatively unimpressive performance of their countries' economies. This

was transferred to the parties, which seemed to be incapable of doing much to make things better and which more recently have had their reputations badly damaged by scandals, financial and otherwise. The evidence for this is not particularly impressive, however. Those who are least partisan are not necessarily those who are most dissatisfied, and vice versa.

The other explanation for a decline in party identification links it to the increased educational capacity of most electors and the greater access they have to information supplied by the media rather than by parties (see Chapter 7). Taken together, these mean that people have less need to rely on instinct and loyalty and instead can make the kind of consumerist, individual choice they are increasingly used to in other areas of life. Linked to both these explanations is the suggestion – which seems to be borne out by the evidence – that decline in party identification feeds on itself. The new-found uncertainty of older generations means that younger generations, who to some extent take their cues from their elders, never develop identifications (strong ones anyway) in the first place. This point brings us naturally to the post communist democracies, where partisan identification has had little time to develop, is comparatively weak and, in the opinion of some analysts, is by no means logically bound to develop at all (see Vlachová, 2001).

The 'end of class voting' and the rise of values?

As Chapter 1 suggested, class has not disappeared, either as a useful categorization or as an identity that means something to many, perhaps even most, people. So we should be careful before we rush to write its obituary as an influence on voting – something that many commentators have been accused of doing (see Franklin, Mackie and Valen, 1992). On the other hand, there is some truth in the suggestion that, for too long, researchers influenced (even if not consciously and certainly not ideologically) by Marx and other nineteenth-century sociologists tended to let class overshadow other cleavages. In particular, they forgot about cleavages such as religion, language and ethnicity that are more cultural than economic, social or geographical (see Dogan, 2001). Perhaps we should ask first whether class is as important in some countries as it is in others, and then whether there is evidence that it has declined as an influence over time. On the first question, there is reasonably broad agreement that class voting (the extent to which, put at its most basic, the working class votes left and the middle class votes right) varies considerably across countries (see Table 6.6).

The second question – the decline (or not) of the influence of class on voting – is rather more controversial. What is *not* at issue is that, however measured, the proportion of the population that can be categorized (or thinks of itself) as working class has shrunk by around one third in the postwar period (see Chapter 1). What *is* at issue is the extent to which people vote in a certain way because they belong to (or at least can be labelled as) a certain class. Most research suggests that overall there has been a significant decline in such class voting from the late 1960s and early 1970s, though one that is more pronounced in some countries than others. For instance, Ireland and the Netherlands do not appear to have experienced a decline; Austria, Belgium, France and Italy have experienced a decline, but not as pronounced as that in Britain, Germany and above all Scandinavia, especially Norway.

All this certainly fits nicely with the tale told by most commentators and one often repeated in academic texts. Actually, however, there is considerable debate about its truth. Outside Norway and Sweden, where there does seem to be broad agreement on the decline of class voting (albeit from an unusually high level), some country-level studies would appear to contradict or at least severely qualify this conventional wisdom (see Evans, 1999). Even in countries where there are fluctuations, they argue, there is no firm trend, and what we are seeing, they suggest, is not so much 'dealignment' (class position becoming more weakly associated with voting, as touched on in Chapter 5) but of 'realignment' (certain social groups moving away from a predictable attachment to one party but (equally, but almost as predictably) latching on to another. There are of course plenty of country studies that do support the conventional wisdom: for example, work on the French party system (see Evans, 2002) shows very convincingly that the left-wing parties have lost whatever claim they had to be the party of the working class. On the other hand, it also suggests that many blue-collar workers (as in Austria, too) now vote for the far right (see Chapter 9) – evidence of both dealignment and a certain degree of realignment.

Even if we do accept the dealignment thesis, of course, we are still left with the task of explaining *why* class is now a less reliable predictor of vote. This is not an easy one, and explanations so far are deductive (based on theoretical speculation which may or may not fit data from a process that is still unfolding over time) rather than inductive (emerging from a clear body of evidence). These (largely sociological) explanations are summarized in Box 6.4 (see Evans, 1999: 6–7).

Table 6.6 The comparative importance of class voting

Low	Relatively low	More significant	Relatively high
US	France	Austria	Denmark
Postcommunist countries	Ireland	Belgium	Finland
	Italy	Germany	Norway
	Netherlands		Sweden
	Portugal		UK
	Spain		
	Switzerland		

Source: Data from Nieuwbeerta and DeGraf (1999).

BOX 6.4
Why people's class might no longer predict their vote

(1) As services supersede industry, creating so-called 'postindustrial societies' (see Chapter 1), other cleavages (such as gender, nationality, ethnicity) may be superseding class which, after all, had its roots in industrialization.

(2) The growth of education and an emphasis on individual over collective identities has increased people's ability to think for themselves and make more rational, calculating and issue-based political decisions.

(3) As most people now have met their basic material needs, some experts argue that they tend to think more in terms of values rather than interests: this postmaterialism cuts across class voting, encouraging, for example, many middle-class salary earners to vote for social liberal, new-left and green parties, while many workers gravitate toward the far-right.

(4) As the manual working class has declined as a proportion of a population (something not even those who are sceptical about the decline of class voting dispute), mainstream social democratic parties have had to – or at least convinced themselves that they have had to – extend their appeal to the middle classes. This 'catch-all strategy' has met with some success, but the downside is (supposedly) a loss of some disillusioned working-class supporters.

European societies may not be becoming classless in the sense that life-chances are no longer influenced by social background (see Chapter 1). Nevertheless, the distinction between hitherto poorly-paid manual work and traditionally better-paid clerical or administrative work has blurred considerably. Some skilled manual workers will earn more than some middle-class people who work in, say, the 'caring professions' or education, and the latter may have more of a vested interest in the election of a government committed to upholding the welfare state rather than trimming it to cut taxes.

These explanations were developed for the most part to explain the putative decline in class voting in western European countries. As such, they may be of limited use in helping us to understand the links between social structure and voting in other parts of Europe. One could argue that in post communist countries such as Poland and the Czech Republic, class will in fact increase its influence on voting, as 'marketization' since the early 1990s makes it clearer to people with which side of the left–right divide their material interests (perceived as much collectively as individually) lie (see Whitefield, 2002). Whether this is primarily because the electorate has taken its cue from politicians, or because politicians are reflecting the feelings of the electorate (in the jargon 'preference-accommodating' rather than 'preference-shaping') is very much a moot point – and one to which we return when we discuss the concept of volatility (first touched on in Chapter 5) below. On the other hand, not all analysts agree that class, any more than party identification, will necessarily come to take its 'proper place' as a cue for voters in CEE countries such as Poland and the Czech Republic (see Zielinski, 2002). Instead, it can be argued that a voter's self-placement on a left–right scale – one that is often more rooted in historical understanding and moral values rather than socio-economic issues – may continue to be a much better predictor of political preferences than, say, occupation (see Gijsberts and Nieuwbeerta, 2000, Mateju and Vlachová, 1998, and Szczerbiak, 2003).

Interestingly, a stress on the electoral importance of the values held by voters rather than their class position is not limited to those interested in East Central Europe. Not everyone agrees that older cleavages such as class and religion (see below) are paling into insignificance beside something we touched on in Chapter 5 in the context of green parties and go on to talk about in Chapter 8, namely, **postmaterialism**. Although the existence of such a trend is often taken for granted, and has even been used to help explain not just the rise of the greens but also that of the far right (see Ignazi, 2003: chapter 12), there are those who are highly sceptical (see, for instance, Wilensky, 2002: 191–207). Yet many analysts argue that 'value voting' is at least as important as 'cleavage' or 'structural' voting (see Knutsen and Scarbrough, 1995). Indeed, they would argue, in some particularly advanced industrial states (the United Kingdom, Germany and the Nordic countries) it is more important.

Definition

Postmaterialism refers to the supposed trend in advanced countries, once the basic needs of the educated and reasonably well-off have been met, for such people to eschew political beliefs and behaviour based on the defence or promotion of material interest in favour of an interest in 'quality-of-life' issues, self-expression and ensuring the rights and well-being of minorities and/or the less fortunate (see Inglehart and Rabier, 1986).

Yet, many of those who support the idea of 'value voting' (the tendency to cast one's vote according to a conception of 'the good life' held irrespective of one's occupation, religion, etc.) are by no means sure that it began in the 1970s. It may, they note, have been important (but unmeasured) in the 1950s and 1960s, helping to explain in part why party systems have not undergone the kind of change we might have expected given the huge changes in society in the postwar period (see Chapters 1 and 5). On the other hand, others do link the rise of value conflict to recent changes in social and occupational structures. In particular, they point, first, to the rise of a new (professional rather than managerial) middle class attracted to 'left-libertarian' values (broadly speaking postmaterialism plus, perhaps, a defence of redistribution and the welfare state) and, secondly, to the rise of an unskilled, under-educated and often under-employed group of workers – 'the underclass of losers in the current rat race to modernity' – attracted to the xenophobic values of the far-right (see Kriesi, 1998).

Religion: another death announced prematurely?

Just as some political scientists are beginning to challenge the common wisdom on the putative end of class voting in an era where individual values are supposedly coming to the fore, others are warning

that, likewise, we write religion off at our peril. Similarly, their criticisms do not involve an attempt to refute the obvious. Just as those who see a continuing link between class and voting do not try to argue, for instance, that there are just as many manual workers as ever there were, those who still see religion influencing votes do not contest the fact that fewer and fewer people go to church these days (see Chapter 1). What they argue, however, is that (a) religion impacts most on the voting behaviour of those who attend regularly, and (b) even many non-attenders still consider themselves to be believers/members of churches and that this continues to have at least some influence on their vote. This influence may be direct, in that they vote for, say, a Christian Democratic party. Or it may be indirect, in the sense that it encourages them to support a certain party because of the stances it takes on issues on which their opinions are in part shaped by their religious convictions.

So what about the evidence (see Broughton and Ten Napel, 2000 and Norris and Inglehart, 2004)? Certainly, there does seem to be evidence that in some countries differences between Christian denominations may matter less than differences between those who go to church and those who just think of themselves as members of one. In Germany, for instance, people are more likely to vote for the CDU–CSU if they are regular churchgoers, be they Protestant or Catholic. But things are complex. In a country such as France, for example, there is still a difference between denominations (Catholics still tend to vote for right-wing parties), though one reinforced by regular attendance (at least on the Catholic side) and, significantly, by higher social status. This is a warning to us of the risks of dismissing either class or religion simply because, investigated in isolation, they do not seem to make much of a difference! They also seem to be linked in Scotland (and to a lesser extent) England, where (unusually in Europe) Catholicism is associated with centre-left rather than centre-right voting. In the Netherlands, research seems once again to show that actually practising a religion rather than just feeling an affinity to it seems to make a difference: active Protestants vote disproportionately for explicitly religious – Protestant – parties and practising Catholics are most likely to vote for the CDA. But, like research on other countries, it lends little support to the suggestion that there might exist widespread indirect, 'issues-based' voting for particular parties owing to their stances on 'moral issues' such as abortion or marriage and the family. Indeed, in many European countries there has been a deliberate attempt by political elites of both the left and the right to place such matters outside party competition. A good example is Spain, where neither of the two main parties (PP and PSOE) now has a monopoly of Catholic votes. The same can be said for the parties (or blocs) that now dominate Italy's party system, although, again, there does seem to be a positive relationship between regular attendance and voting for the centre-right.

So, the right has traditionally benefited more than the left from the impact of religion on voting and still does so, not just in Europe but throughout the world (see Norris and Inglehart, 2004: chapter 9). But (as we saw in Chapter 1), fewer and fewer people are going to church regularly (if at all) nowadays. And the extent to which religious belief predicts one's political stance does appear (according to Norris and Inglehart's massive cross-national study) to be weakening over time, even if it remains a better predictor than other characteristics, including class. Hence, the value of this relationship to the right would appear to be a wasting asset (much as the decline in trade union density we consider in Chapter 8 may well harm the left). Accordingly, mainstream centre-right parties all over Europe have been attempting to reduce any reliance they may have had on religious voters – and not without success, even where they continue to call themselves Christian Democrats. On the other hand, secularization need not spell the death of parties making a specifically religious appeal. This does seem to have been the case in, say, France (where they were never strong) and in Belgium. But in Germany, support for the Christian Democrats has remained fairly steady, notwithstanding unification with the former East Germany, where levels of religious belief (let alone church attendance) are very low. Meanwhile, in the Netherlands and Austria, they seemed to have turned things around in recent years. In Scandinavia, the recent performance of some Christian parties might suggest a niche (though no more than a niche) audience worth pitching for in these supposedly more postmaterialist times. On the other hand, nowhere in Europe can match the US in terms of religiosity and therefore the potential impact of politics on religion.

This is especially true in CEE countries, many of which were (officially anyway) atheist under communism, but there are exceptions (see Whitefield, 2002), including one big one. This is Poland, where Roman Catholicism, and the extent to which it is actually practised rather than simply adhered to, continues not just to influence voting but (along with attitudes to the communist past) actually structures popular conceptions of what is and is not right- or left-wing (see Szczerbiak, 2003). Many parties on the right make a specific pitch for Roman Catholic voters, some quite successfully so. The Church's aggressive insistence on de-secularizing the country after the collapse of communism managed, among other things, to stymie the emergence of a large, moderate, Christian Democratic party (Szczerbiak and Bale, 2005). But its support over the years for various anti-communist groupings (accordingly thought of as right-wing) has proved important. In 2001, for example, the *Liga Polskich Rodzin* or League of Polish Families (LPR) had solid roots in Catholic institutions and the Catholic media and picked up many voters from the collapsed AWS Solidarity coalition. This is not to say that the relatively successful Social Democratic Alliance (SLD) has few Catholic voters – any party in staunchly Catholic Poland could not survive let alone thrive without them! But its voters are somewhat less likely than LPR's, for instance, to be frequent church goers. They are also more likely to separate their religious views from their political convictions – which mainly, it would seem, revolve around the need for economic competence and a desire to move on from the past toward a European future. The fact that SLD, at least in 2001, was able, however, to attract its fair share of practising Catholics to this centrist, pragmatic vision is possibly testimony to its having nuanced what was previously a more obviously secular stance. As a result, there seems little likelihood that Poland will any time soon seek to separate church and state or dogma and legislation quite as rigidly as most European countries.

Ethnicity: not much evidence

The fact that, as we noted above, Catholics in England tend to vote Labour, can be explained by the fact that Catholicism was the religion of (poorer) Irish immigrants. But this begs questions about whether the relationship in question is actually to do with religion or with ethnicity. The same goes for the fact that Britain's non-white population continues to vote overwhelmingly for Labour. Is it because they are non-Christian? Or is it because they are non-white and therefore suffer disproportionately from discrimination, are more likely to be in lower-paid occupations, and less likely to favour a party (the Conservatives) that (rightly or wrongly) has been perceived as tougher on immigration. The UK, however, would seem to be unusual: as in the US, there is one party (Labour in Britain, the Democrats in the US) that picks up the majority of the 'multicultural' vote. This does not seem to be the case elsewhere, though, in fact, there is very little research published – at least in English – on the voting patterns of ethnic (and particularly immigrant) minorities in Europe outside of the UK (see Saggar, 2000). This urgently needs remedying, especially given the growing presence of such minorities all over Europe (see Chapter 10). It may also be that a backlash against immigration is helping to create a new ethnic cleavage (see Dogan, 2001).

The rise of 'issue voting', 'judgemental voting' and volatile voting

Arguably, then, old cleavages, while by no means irrelevant as influences on voters' preferences, are less important relative to newer sources of conflict and loyalty. Possibly the 'individuation' of European society touched on in Chapter 1 has eroded collective identities of any sort at such a pace that cleavages old or new do not matter so much any more. People, as we suggest in Chapter 5, are thinking for themselves rather than letting their background do their thinking for them. Issues and images may have become much more important – possibly because of changes in media coverage of politics (see Chapter 7). 'Judgemental voting' – based on a one-off assessment of parties' policies and reputations, as well as guesses about

their ability to deliver what they promise – may be the reality for more and more voters in Europe.

This would certainly seem to fit with the rise in volatility (the extent to which people switch their vote from one election to another) that we have already addressed in Chapter 5. In fact, European electorates may be even more volatile than the headline figures suggest. This is especially the case if we draw a distinction between such figures, which are based on aggregates calculated from election results, and figures based on survey research that actually asks people how they voted. Research suggests that aggregate figures disguise, first, the extent of switching (between parties and between voting and non-voting) that goes on between one election and the next at the individual (or 'micro') level and, secondly, the extent to which such switching has risen (though not always in strictly linear fashion) from the late 1960s/early 1970s onwards. For instance, in 1960 only 7 per cent of those surveyed by the Swedish election study said that they had changed their vote from four years previously; in 1998 the figure was 31 per cent (see Dalton, McAllister and Wattenberg, 2002) – an increase seemingly replicated in other European countries where the question was asked (see Table 6.7, which uses a year-on-year average which has the effect of 'smoothing out' highs and lows in particular years caused by exceptional circumstances).

It also fits with figures from the same surveys which seem to indicate that voters are increasingly leaving their decision about which way to vote until nearer polling day. To use the Swedish example again, only 18 per cent made up their minds during the campaign in 1964; thirty-four years later, in 1998, the figure was 57 per cent. This may of course have been particularly high in the latter year because many social democrats defected (temporarily) to the Left Party in protest at the government's welfare squeeze (which may also explain the high level of volatility in that year). But, once again, compiling an average which 'smooths out' peaks and troughs in the data (see Table 6.7) suggests that there has been an increase over time – and not just in Sweden.

But knowing that Europe's voters are more volatile and make up their minds later does not mean we can establish beyond doubt *why* they are

Table 6.7 Switching votes and deciding later, 1970s–1990s

	Yearly increase in volatility	Period covered	Yearly increase in 'late deciders'	Period covered
Austria	0.6	1979–99	0.65	1979–99
Denmark	0.25	1971–98	0.03	1971–98
Germany	0.3	1961–98	0.3	1961–98
Netherlands	0.2	1971–98	0.95	1971–98
Norway	0.6	1969-1993	0.9	1969–93
Sweden	0.5	1956–98	1.1	1956–98
UK	0.1	1964–97	0.45	1964–97

Source: Data from Dalton, McAllister and Wattenburg (2002).

more volatile and put off their decisions. We can, though, make some educated guesses. For instance, quick fixes for Europe's economic difficulties – persistently high unemployment and sluggish growth – have eluded political parties on what some see (rightly or wrongly) as an increasingly hazy left–right divide (see Chapter 9). This may have eroded trust and encouraged voters to take their disappointment out on whomsoever is in power. A rather more benign interpretation might focus on how the growth of mass education (especially at the tertiary level) and mass (and now 24/7) media, combined with the erosion of traditional patterns of employment and family structure, have led to an electorate that votes according to more changeable but more rational judgements instead of relying on 'tribal instincts'.

In fact, we can meld the two interpretations together and posit some kind of feedback loop. As we saw in Chapter 5, Europe's parties (especially mainstream parties) can no longer rely on large numbers of members either to reflect back the views of the electorate to them or to spread their message to the electorate and keep some of it loyal. Acting increasingly on the basis of opinion polls and focus groups, and having to rely more and more on a media they cannot control (see Chapter 7), parties stress their 'catch-all' centrist pragmatism and emphasize their stances on so-called 'valence issues' – the things that every government is expected to deliver – rather than on the issues they traditionally (and generally still) 'own'. For instance, parties of the mainstream left and right will make more of their ability competently to run a stable and growing economy than they will of their intentions – albeit ones they still profess and even act on (see Chapter 9) – to, say, decrease taxation (the centre-right) or defend the welfare state (the centre-left). Europe's voters, taking their cues from the parties, begin to vote on the basis of the content and the credibility of the more specific offers being made to them – in other words, they vote ever more *instrumentally* than ideologically. The parties pick up on this consumerist response and adapt their appeals accordingly. Whether this is a vicious or a virtuous circle depends partly on your view of political marketing – the art of adjusting your political 'offer' in line with what you believe people want. For some, it brings policy closer to the preferences of the electorate – which is democracy. For others, it renders politics an inchoate mess where choice is as illusory as it is pointless!

EP elections

It is easy – but increasingly misleading – to apply, as do many media commentators, adjectives such as 'pointless' and 'illusory' to elections for the EP, which take place every five years. Their criticisms are understandable. Notwithstanding the increasing power of the EP in the EU's law-making system, turnout at the elections (which, note, are fought as simultaneous national contests not as one pan-European election) has dropped across the

Table 6.8 Turnout in EP elections, 1979–2004

	1979	1984	1987	1989	1994	1995	1999	2004	Prev. gen. election
Czech Rep.	–	–	–	–	–	–	–	28.3	58.0 (2002)
Poland	–	–	–	–	–	–	–	28.32	46.3 (2001)
Sweden	–	–	–	–	–	41.6	38.8	37.8	80.1 (2002)
UK	32.2	32.6	–	36.2	36.4	–	24.0	38.83	59.4 (2001)
Netherlands	57.8	50.6	–	47.2	35.6	–	30.0	39.3	79.9 (2003)
France	60.7	56.7	–	48.7	52.7	–	46.8	42.76	60.7 (2002)
Germany	65.7	56.8	–	62.3	60.0	–	45.2	43.0	79.1 (2002)
Spain	–	–	68.9	54.6	59.1	–	63.0	45.1	77.2 (2004)
Italy	84.9	83.4	–	81.5	74.8	–	70.8	73.1	81.3 (2001)
EU average	63.0	61.0	–	58.5	56.8	–	49.8	45.7	–

Source: Data from www.elections.eu.int.

continent in recent years (see Table 6.8). True, a modest recovery in some countries can be hidden by the average figure, which now includes very low turnout countries in Central and Eastern Europe. And, over the years, the average has also dropped with the inclusion of other less 'Europhile' countries, the position of the elections in national election cycles, the reduction in compulsory voting – and of course the trend toward turnout decline discussed above (see also Franklin, 2001a, 2001b). But the turnout difference between national and European elections is marked.

Although there is limited evidence to suggest that the potential exists for voters to fit European issues into their existing left–right and materialist–post-materialist orientations (see Gabel and Anderson, 2002), research since the EP was first directly elected in 1979 confirms again and again that European elections are what political scientists call 'second-order' contests (though see Blondel, Sinnott and Svensson, 1998). Like local and regional elections, they are often used by voters to send a message (often one of dissatisfaction conveyed by voting for small and/or opposition parties) to the national government of the day (see van der Eijk and Franklin, 1996). This means that EP elections seem unlikely, at least for now, to contribute much to the creation of a European identity among the citizens of the member states. Whether, though, this is because those citizens are

irretrievably nationally focused or whether they are encouraged to be so by parties who are neither ready nor willing to supranationalize their appeals or their focus, is a moot point (see van der Eijk and Franklin, 1996: 364–5).

This second-order status can give rise to co-ordination problems. Because EP elections are largely national contests and because of the tendency (particularly pronounced when national elections are a long way off) to punish incumbents, there are always likely to be 'mismatches' between member state governments (and maybe the commissioners they nominate) and the EP. These mismatches, given a legislative process relying on 'co-decision' between the EP and the Council of Ministers (representing national governments), could make European law-making more conflictual, especially if the EP begins – as it seems to be doing (see Hix, Kreppel and Noury, 2003) – to vote more on left–right (or at least party-bloc) lines. Whether this will mean that at least some national governments will be faced with more European legislation of which they do not approve, however, is another moot point. Hypothetically, a centre-right government which loses out in the Council of Ministers under QMV (see Chapter 2) may be able to rely on centre-right MEPs of whatever nationality to make the kinds of changes it desires at a later stage of the legislative process – changes which, if the EP carries on expanding the range of legislation over which it has some control, could have big (budgetary) implications.

Irrespective of these unintended consequences of EP elections, the latter play an important part in the domestic politics of member states (see Gabel, 2000). Both parties and voters use them (and their results) as signals and portents, which may then affect their subsequent behaviour. A party may finally realize, for instance, that it has to dump its underperforming leader, while a protest vote allows voters to register their dislike of the direction in which a particular party is travelling and/or provides an opportunity for catharsis, after which they return to the fold by the next general election.

BOX 6.5
The home of direct democracy

The Swiss confederation is famous for a century or more of referendums. Nationally, it takes just 50,000 of the country's 7.3 million citizens who so object to a law or policy that they want to see it struck down to sign a petition to force a binding referendum on the government. To win, they need to muster 'a double majority': Switzerland is made up of *cantons* (mini-states that enjoy a great deal of independence from the federal government at the centre); in order to pass at the national level, a referendum proposal has to win not just a majority of all those voting but also has to pass in a majority of cantons. Switzerland is also the only country in Europe to allow its citizens the right of initiative. As in California and other western US states, they can propose a new law, and if passed, it becomes binding on parliament. Getting a vote on a proposal, however, is more demanding than getting one that seeks to strike something down; 100,000 citizens must sign, and more often than not their proposal will be rejected. Frequently, though, the campaign (perhaps even before it has achieved all the signatures needed) will prompt the government into a counterproposal. Indeed, research suggests that the Swiss political class have become increasingly adept at doing deals in order to head off or at least control the effects of referendums (Papadopoulos, 2001). Whether this means that ultimately no one can beat politics-behind-closed-doors, or that those who conduct such politics are nonetheless more responsive to those outside the room is a moot point.

Or the effect of that vote is maybe to allow a new entrant onto the political scene who then stays around for good. For instance, EP elections – fought as they are under PR even in countries that ordinarily use majoritarian systems – gave the far-right *Front National* and the Greens an early boost. Similarly, EP elections have finally given voters in Europe's other majoritarian system, the UK, the chance to make a vote for a small party count; conceivably this may make them more willing to vote for smaller parties in other elections – a logic that also applies, incidentally, to the use of PR for elections to the Scottish Parliament and the Welsh Assembly, and could well spill over into increasing support to change the system at national level. These possibilities, however, probably pale into insignificance alongside the more immediate fact that European integration more generally (rather than the EP in particular) is increasingly part of domestic political disputes, either on its own or because hostility to it is becoming a now familiar favourite for populist politicians all over the continent (see Szczerbiak and Taggart, 2005).

Direct democracy: useful tool or dangerous panacea?

Representative democracy is not the only form of democracy in Europe: all of the continent's states, apart from Germany and the Netherlands, also have experience of **direct democracy** at the national level – most famously in Switzerland (see Box 6.5). The referendums used in the latter take various particular forms (see Table 6.9). But the issue is worth studying in general, not just because referendums look likely either to breath life into or scupper the chances of the proposed new EU constitution (see Chapter 2), but because direct democracy is sometimes put forward as an

---

Definition
Representative democracy is the election of parties and candidates to parliament where they then form governments and pass legislation on the people's behalf. By **direct democracy** we mean the holding of referendums in order to decide policy and/or constitutional changes.

Table 6.9 Types of referendums and where they can be used

Called by	'Law-controlling'	'Law-promoting'
Constitutional requirement	*Mandatory* (law in this area – normally constitutional) requires a referendum before coming into force). **Austria, Denmark, Estonia, Ireland, Latvia, Lithuania, Romania, Slovakia, Spain, Switzerland**	
Elected representatives	*Abrogative* (overturns laws already in force). **Italy, Switzerland** *Rejective* (overturns – normally constitutional – laws passed but not yet in force). **Austria, Bulgaria, Czech Rep., Denmark, Estonia, Greece, Ireland, Italy, Lithuania, Poland, Romania, Slovakia, Slovenia, Spain, Sweden, Switzerland**	*Ad hoc/optional* (called on a particular issue and may or may not be declared binding). **Austria, Belgium, Denmark, Finland, France, Greece, Hungary, Norway, Portugal, Slovenia, Sweden, UK**
Citizens	*Abrogative* **Italy, Switzerland** *Rejective* **Switzerland**	*Popular initiative* (draft law proposed by citizens which becomes binding if passed). **Hungary, Latvia, Lithuania, Poland, Romania, Slovenia, Switzerland**

Source: Adapted from Setälä (1999); entries for postcommunist states from Auer and Bützer (2001).

alternative, or a cure, for the supposedly moribund state of party-driven politics in Europe.

Supporters of direct democracy put forward a whole host of arguments. At the more fundamentalist or populist end of the spectrum lie claims that referendums have the potential to save democracy from parties that are portrayed as distant from the people and a distortion of, or even as parasites on, democracy. In the middle are claims, firstly, that referendums encourage participation and informed voting on crucial issues that would otherwise be subsumed in the packages of policies on offer at elections and, secondly, that parliaments make better laws if they know they risk being overturned. At the minimalist or pragmatic end of the spectrum lies the argument that they provide, first, a useful safeguard, particularly on constitutional issues that effect the political 'rules of the game' and, secondly, that they prevent particular issues paralysing the system.

This pragmatic argument for direct democracy certainly seems to reflect reality. In western Europe, the most widely used type is the ad hoc referendum and most referendums (of whatever type) have been used in order to decide questions that are considered too difficult (perhaps because they involve moral judgements on such things as abortion or divorce) or too crucial (normally because they touch on the constitution or on matters of sovereignty, particularly with regard to the EU, see Chapter 2) for parliament to decide for itself. This has been the case especially when an issue looks like splitting parties and/or when governments are hoping to insulate themselves from negative electoral effects it might have on them. The UK government's surprise announcement in 2004 that it would hold a referendum on any new EU constitution is typical.

Referendums on social or economic policy are not uncommon in the twenty-four US states which have citizen-initiated referendums. But (outside Switzerland) they are very unusual in Europe. Votes on moral issues – despite media interest in them – are also quite uncommon, especially outside Italy and Ireland. Three European countries have resorted to referendums on the divisive – and possibly postmaterialist – issue of nuclear power (Austria, 1978, Sweden, 1980 and Italy, 1987). All rejected it (the Italians voting to ban their country's activity in projects outside of Italy). Spain's socialist government in the 1980s used a referendum to legitimize its decision to remain in NATO, and Hungary held a referendum in 1997 before joining it – unlike Poland and the Czech Republic, neither of whom felt in necessary to hold one before doing the same thing. Referendums have also been held in Southern and East Central European states during their transition to democracy, not least as a way of gaining legitimacy for new constitutions.

Indeed, constitutional referendums are the biggest single group, closely followed now by EU referendums, not least because so many CEE states held referendums for both purposes. Some (the Baltic states and Slovenia) used referendums to declare themselves independent; significantly this was an option denied to the Czech and Slovak people by their politicians, who feared their plans for a 'velvet divorce' might be vetoed. With the odd exception, referendums on new constitutions have resulted in 'yes' votes. This stands in marked contrast to referendums on constitutional amendments that have sought to extend the power of one branch of government, normally the executive, or somehow seem to advantage the ruling party and do not have cross-party support (as was the case in Ireland in 1959 and 1968 when the *Fianna Fáil* party tried unsuccessfully to introduce FPP). The exception to the rule is provided by France, where Charles de Gaulle persuaded the people to back the creation of a directly elected president in 1962. But even this is only a partial exception: when de Gaulle tried to limit the powers of the Senate in 1969, his plans were rejected in a referendum and he resigned.

Most states limit such votes to those proposed by the legislature or the executive, though interestingly there are some grounds to think that they propose them more often in states where the judi-

ciary may be called on to oblige them to do so (as has happened in Ireland on three occasions in the postwar period; see Qvortrup, 2002: 105–7). However, two states – Switzerland and Italy – allow citizens themselves to call a vote on a particular question, requiring only that they gather sufficient signatures in to show that such a vote would be worthwhile holding. The relative ease with which this can be done, however, is balanced in both countries by safeguards designed to reduce the risk to minority rights by requiring that any vote be passed by a 'double majority'. In Switzerland this involves the cantons (see Box 6.5).

In Italy (where referendums can only repeal an existing law and where 500,000 signatures or five regional councils' support must be obtained first of all) they require at least 50 per cent of the country to actually turn up and vote and the repeal option has to gain majority support among those who do. After a golden period in the early 1990s when voters used referendums practically to oblige politicians to overhaul the electoral system, Italian referendums have failed to attract sufficient people to turn out and vote, rendering them – in the eyes of critics anyway – an expensive waste of time. The same has happened in Lithuania, which holds the record for the most referendums in Central and Eastern Europe, and in Poland, where the referendum turnout is even lower than at elections: in 1996 just 32 per cent turned out to vote on privatization, in 1997 only 43 per cent bothered on the constitution; however, turnout on EU accession improved to 59 per cent, higher than in other 'candidate countries' (in Hungary, for instance, it was only 45 per cent). Even countries where referendums are used sparingly can have trouble with turnout: the Portuguese government abandoned plans to liberalize abortion laws when the restrictionist case 'won' a referendum on the issue with a 1 per cent majority in 1998 but on a turnout of only 32 per cent despite weeks of high-intensity media coverage.

This falling-off of interest is not, of course, the only argument against direct democracy. Another is that, owing to the correlation between political participation and both affluence and education, those voting in referendums will be particularly unrepresentative of the electorate as a whole. Some critics also hold that they they risk the basest instincts and blinkered prejudice of the majority being whipped up by populist politicians who want to override the law and the rights of ethnic and other minorities – just as they were used by fascist regimes in the 1930s. Others believe that they discourage compromise, oversimplify complex matters and can produce contradictory laws and policies which are popular only because their wider context is not considered.

However, outside of Switzerland (where there is some evidence to suggest that poorer, less-educated voters are disproportionately less likely to vote in referendums) opponents of direct democracy have as yet produced no evidence to show that this is the case in other European countries or, if it is the case, that this underrepresentation is any worse than it is in parliamentary elections. The same goes for the suggestion that voters in referendums are ill-informed: again, this is unproven and, even if it were, the situation would probably be just as bad in parliamentary elections where some voters' knowledge of party and candidate positions (and names) is woefully poor. Advocates of referendums can point to evidence from Denmark and Switzerland that they actually help improve citizen understanding of the issues under consideration. This may affect not just the result of the referendum, but opinion on the wider issue of which it may be just one facet. For instance, those who know more about the EU tend to be more supportive of it: holding relatively frequent referendums on EU matters may then affect levels of support for the EU more generally, even perhaps if the referendum in question is 'lost'. That they are sometimes (though rarely) lost reflects a problem to which EU referendums are particularly (but not exclusively) prone; namely, that they become party political popularity contests rather than a carefully considered answer to a specific question – something which is even more likely if the governments that order them are obliged neither to obey the result nor to hold them in the first place (see Hug, 2002; see also Qvortrup, 2002: 76)

This raises another common criticism of referendums; namely, that governments more often than not pull the strings, holding them only if and when they think they can win. However, the accusation is not borne out by the record, which suggests that over three-quarters of referendums held in Europe

between 1945 and 1997 were not within their control. It also shows that just over a third did not turn out to be supportive of the government's stance on the issue in hand (see Qvortrup, 2002). Nor is there any evidence that national-level referendums in Europe have oppressed minorities. This is the case even in Switzerland, where some local referendums have produced some 'near-misses' for supporters of xenophobic measures: in September 2000, two-thirds of those voting rejected an initiative limiting immigration. The Swiss also overwhelmingly supported the decriminalization of homosexuality in 1992. Often, indeed, voters turn out to be surprisingly liberal. Referendums on moral issues are very rare outside Italy (where divorce was controversially permitted in 1974) and Ireland (which has had long debates on both divorce and abortion). But voters in these two Catholic countries have on several occasions surprised commentators by voting for the more liberal option – though in Ireland, it took a second referendum on both issues (abortion in 1992 and divorce in 1995) before this result was achieved.

Yet referendums vary rarely resolve an issue if it reflects deep-seated divisions within a society. For instance, in 1950 a majority of Belgians voted for the restoration of the monarchy, but only because of such strong support for the idea from the Flemish community; riots ensued (mainly involving French speakers from Wallonia) which forced the king to abdicate. More recently, the British government's ability to garner referendum backing for the Northern Ireland peace process in 1998 may well have helped prevent things slipping back into chaos, but it has not as yet enabled it to bring a lasting settlement appreciably closer. Meanwhile, the recent history of referendums in the Republic of Ireland, shows that those on the losing side of the argument (whether they be citizens or the government) do not necessarily give up; instead they go for another referendum: this happened on abortion in the 1990s and, more recently, the ratification of the EU's Treaty of Nice.

Demands for direct democracy are often a function of disenchantment with and distrust of 'politics as usual' and, as such, we might expect them to increase. But, going on the evidence, referendums are not a 'silver bullet' that can revivify ailing democracies. On the other hand, fifty years of experience suggest that they no longer need be tarred by association with the rigged 'plebiscites' of Fascist and Communist dictatorships. Instead the evidence suggests that, used sparingly, referendums can help democracy function more efficiently and, in some cases, provide a valuable reminder to politicians that getting elected every four or five years does not give them licence to ignore voters' views, particularly on issues of fundamental concern.

There is, however, one caveat, relating to a common criticism of direct democracy. The argument that 'special interests' can manipulate referendums can in part be dismissed by noting that it applies with equal force to parliamentary elections: indeed, one could argue that it is much easier for a wealthy interest group to 'buy' a small group of legislators than it is for them to 'purchase' the votes of millions of citizens. But the argument that the media may sometimes play a part in swinging the result one way or another may have some force, notwithstanding the fact that referendum results (as they did when voters in Sweden and Denmark rejected the euro) have often gone against the media consensus. As we go on to suggest in Chapter 7, fears of media influence on voting (if not on politics more generally) are often overplayed, yet they are not totally groundless, particularly when it comes to very close results. In most proportional systems such marginal 'distortions' will be spread across the parties. But in referendums, just as in two-horse races in FPP systems, media influence on just a few thousand voters can – just occasionally – mean the difference between winning and losing (see Siune, Svensson and Tonsgaard, 1994).

Learning resources

The arguments for and against plurality and the various PR systems are most effectively and accessibly detailed (in English anyway) at http://www.archive.officialdocuments.co.uk/document/cm40/4090/4090.htm. Also useful and clear is http://www.aceproject.org/main/english/es/. A fantastic global survey of turnout can be found at http://www.idea.int/voter_turnout/voter_turnout.html Anyone wanting accessible but reasonably in-depth analysis of European elections and – importantly – referendums, too, should go to http://www.sussex.ac.uk/sei/1-4-2.html, home of the European Parties and Referendums Network. For election results, go http://www.parties-and-elections.de/indexe.html or http://www.electionworld.org/. For the more academic arguments about the relationship between electoral and party systems, see Sartori (1997). Franklin (2004) discusses turnout and plenty more of interest besides. Electoral behaviour in (western) Europe, and particularly the decline (or not!) of class voting, is discussed from a wide variety of perspectives in Franklin, Mackie and Valen (1992) and Evans (1999). A refreshing, suggestive (and short!) critique is provided by Dogan (2001), while some of the difficulties surrounding political science's attempts to understand voting behaviour are admirably put by Dunleavy (1990) and tackled in more detail by Evans (2003). A stimulating discussion of some of the issues raised in this chapter is Pennings (2002). Anyone interested in exploring CEE voting patterns more closely should consult Tworzecki (2003). On referendums, the first ports of call should be Gallagher and Uleri (1996), Qvortrup (2002), Setälä (1999) and, on EU referendums, Hug (2002). An informative pro-referendum website is http://www.iri-europe.org; see also Kaufman and Waters (2004).

EXECUTIVE SUMMARY

- Nearly all European countries use PR systems, but for technical (though comprehensible) reasons, some are less proportional than they could be. Whether they should be is a more complex and contentious issue than it is sometimes made out to be.

- All systems have relatively (though not entirely) predictable effects, and therefore pros and cons. But PR does not always mean multiparty politics and government, any more than 'first-past-the-post' (FPP) guarantees a two-horse race.

- Social characteristics such as religion and especially class are becoming less reliable (though not yet completely hopeless) predictors of west Europeans' electoral preferences. Cleavages may now be rooted as much in conflicting values as in material interests.

- European voters are now more volatile, switching between parties and making up their minds later, according more importance to the perceived credibility, issue positions and government performance of parties, rather than falling back on tribal loyalties.

- This may mean that voters in the west are becoming more like voters in postcommunist countries, where there is only limited evidence of things 'settling down'.

- A Europe-wide decline in turnout may be occurring, but can be overstated: turnout varies considerably according to country and the circumstances surrounding each election.

- The decline is more obvious in elections for the EP, which continue to play a secondary – though not necessarily insignificant – role in domestic politics.

- Referendums are quite common in Europe, but there are significant (constitutional) limits on their use and impact. Most of the arguments against 'direct' (as opposed to 'representative') democracy are not borne out by the facts, but referendums are not a 'miracle cure' for discontent and disaffection.

Chapter 7

The media: player and recorder

Variations in usage and style
Structure and regulation
State and public service broadcasting
The changing coverage of politics
Bias and its effects
Pressure groups and populists
Cyberpolitics
The media and 'Europe'

Addressing a collection of political journalists, British Prime Minister Tony Blair's official spokesman – himself an ex-journalist – is said to have asked (Rose, 2001: 102): 'Explain to me just why I should waste my time with a load of wankers like you, when you're not going to write anything I tell you anyway?' A rhetorical question perhaps, and one that symbolizes the tension between that government – and perhaps any government – and those it seeks to exploit but ultimately cannot control. It is also a question with an obvious answer. Not wasting his time would have meant giving up one of the few ways in which politicians in a representative democracy made up of millions of people can hope to communicate even indirectly with those whose votes they rely on and whose welfare should be their main concern.

Even if many of those people are not listening, politics in Europe is still – and perhaps more than ever – an essentially mediated activity. The media may not control politics but it has 'come to create and constitute the space in which politics now chiefly happens for most people in so called "advanced" societies' like Europe (Castells, 1997). In as much as politics and the media operate as separate institutions – and the media is best seen as an institution since it persists over time with norms and rules that impact systematically on those who work in and deal with it (see Cook, 1998) – the membrane that separates them is highly permeable. The media in Europe does not simply observe but also helps drive politics and policy by setting agendas, as well as providing the main means of

contact between politicians and parties and electorates. It also operates in a highly politicized environment, subject to regulation by the state and continually coming in for criticism from all sections of society, not least political actors who spend a possibly increasing amount of time, money and effort trying to exploit it to their own advantage.

The media, of course, has its own interests. The core business of Europe's commercial newspapers, TV, radio stations and, indeed websites, is after all to make money – and possibly provide a degree of influence – for their owners. Yet the media is also supposed to exercise important functions in any democracy. It is a source (and on many matters practically the only source) of information and interpretation. It thereby produces and reflects what (admittedly rather loosely) we call 'public opinion'. It also acts as a 'watchdog'. It provides what those who conceive of it as a kind of 'fourth estate' see as a quasi-constitutional check and balance – particularly in systems where, for instance, parliament (and therefore political opposition between elections) is weak. Partly because it is recognized that the market might fail to perform these functions, the state in most European countries continues to own, or at least subsidize, public broadcasting. Rather less obviously (via lower rates of sales tax or postal/telecommunication rates), it also subsidizes the press (see Murschetz, 1998). State 'interference', however, does not stop there: the state – at both national and local level – regulates the media in myriad ways, from the granting of broadcast licences to the imposition of obligations towards political impartiality. In some countries, it goes even further, with the government of the day exerting a degree of control over output that in others would be regarded as illegitimate and even dangerous.

Given the state's concern to maintain a degree of control of the media – and we should never forget that in most countries broadcasting in particular was originally monopolized by states lest this frighteningly powerful new technology fall into the 'wrong' hands – it is hardly surprising that the Europeanization of media regimes has been slow. This does not mean that there are no similarities in the political role and impact of the media in individual countries. Indeed, it could be that the media – especially television – varies less across Europe than do many of the other institutions (governance, parliaments, parties, etc.) we have examined in previous chapters. There is of course some patterned variation, and this chapter begins by providing some general and country-specific material on media use which suggests significant regional differences. It then goes on to look at the structure of the media and the regulatory and ownership environment in which it operates across Europe, with a particular focus on the implications for government control and for the coverage of politics. Next, it explores how that coverage has changed in recent years, particularly with regard to the media's increased focus on personality-driven and 'presidential' coverage even in parliamentary systems and its move toward a less deferential style. It then deals with the difficult question of the media's effect on politics: is it overblown, can we measure it, and is it more about agenda-setting than directly influencing either voters or those for whom they vote? It goes on to explore the contribution of the media to the visibility and success of pressure groups and populist politicians. It finishes by examining the impact of new information and communication technology (ICT) on European politics and the contribution of the media, old and new, to European identity and integration.

Variations in usage and style

Broadly speaking, the further south and east you go in Europe, the less people read (or at least buy) newspapers (see Table 7.1). This is probably because mass education and democracies with entrenched freedom of the press came later to Spain, Portugal and Greece. Conversely, the further south you go, the more television people watch, the big exception to the rule being the UK. As McQuail (2001) notes, these regional variations also apply to media styles: for instance, the

Scandinavian media, despite its mass reach, takes its mission to inform and educate more seriously than most and, especially when it comes to local newspapers, is financially supported by the state for so doing (De Bens and Østbye, 1998: 14). This does not mean, however, that Nordic necessarily means high-minded. True, the UK tabloid press is even more heavily focused on entertainment than its equivalents elsewhere in Europe. But Sweden has its *Aftonbladet* just as Germany, where the 'tabloidization' of news has arguably proceeded at a slower pace than in, say, the UK (Esser, 1999), has its *Bild*. Elsewhere, tabloids quickly took hold in Poland, Hungary and the Czech Republic following the fall of communism (Gulyás, 2004: 84–5). Interestingly, it is newspapers in Southern Europe that are by and large relatively serious affairs bought by relatively few people, with most going to weekly magazines for the celebrity gossip that the British (and the Germans and the Swedes) get every day.

These variations, however, should not be allowed to disguise one very obvious trend throughout Europe, and that is the decline of circulation (see Papathanassopoulos, 2001: 111) and very probably daily newspaper reading. Irrespective of income and gender (which still matter in some countries, with the better-off and men reading more than the poor and women) and education (which

---

Table 7.1 Newspaper reading and TV watching: from high to low, north to south

Newspaper circulation: copies per 1000	Average TV viewing: minutes per day
Sweden 438	UK 228
UK 330	Spain 218
Germany 318	Italy 217
Netherlands 307	Poland 216
Czech Rep. 254	Czech Rep. 210
France 182	Germany 196
Poland 113	France 193
Italy 105	Netherlands 157
Spain 105	Sweden 149

Sources: Data from McQuail (2001) and Gulyás (2004).

interestingly is no longer a good predictor of read-ership anywhere), fewer people than ever are reading newspapers; and the problem is particu-larly acute among young adults, many of whom may never 'grow into' newspapers as their parents eventually did – a fact that may have a negative impact over time in overall interest in and under-standing of politics (see Lauf, 2001).

Another aspect of the media in Europe that is seemingly universal is 'news values' – the criteria that determine whether editors include or reject a story (see Palmer, 2002). All over the continent, stories have much more chance of seeing the light if they are visual, emotive, conflictual, intense, unambiguous, of majority relevance, unpredictable and apparently capable of some kind of 'common-sense' solution. Nevertheless, one can detect subtle national variations in journalistic methods and ethics (see Weaver, 1998), notions of objectivity (see Donsbach and Klett, 1993) and, more gener-ally, style: news programmes in Italy, Spain, and France, for instance, tend to carry more domestic news, longer items with fewer contributors and more studio-based content, whereas more 'Germanic' (as opposed to 'Romantic') news cultures, such as the UK and the Netherlands, go for short, sober, location-based reports (see Heinderyckx, 1993). Interestingly, there is little hard evidence that increasing commercial competi-tion in broadcasting has led to the 'dumbing down' of news provision, either when it comes to the privately owned channels themselves or to public broadcasters. Some detect 'divergence' – public broadcasting stays or gets even more 'serious') – while others observe 'convergence' – news on public channels becomes less 'serious' but commer-cial stations raise their game away from mere 'info-tainment' in order to compete (see Pfetsch, 1996, for a fascinating case study).

Structure and regulation

The extent to which media is national or more regionally based varies considerably in Europe, particularly when it comes to the press. We would be hard pushed in some countries to prove the exis-tence of a national newspaper market. The latter may exist in the UK, with the main division

between downmarket 'tabloids' and upmarket 'broadsheets'. But regional titles continue to play a big, if not bigger, part elsewhere. This is perhaps to be expected in a federal republic such as Germany, where many of the titles routinely cited in overseas press reviews (such as the *Frankfurter Allgemeine Zeitung* and the *Süddeutsche Zeitung*) are regional newspapers, albeit nationally distributed. Nor is it surprising in 'asymmetrically federal' Spain (see Chapter 2), where the combined circulation of the four top-selling national dailies is only a quarter of that of the regional press (Sanders with Canel, 2004: 199). Yet the same is true of supposedly centralized France where daily titles that are well known abroad (*Le Monde*, *Le Figaro* and *Libération*) sell predominantly in Paris; elsewhere regional papers rule the roost, to the extent that 'three out of four French citizens never read a daily national paper' (Kuhn, 2004: 26). The regional daily, *Ouest France*, for instance, has a higher circu-lation than any of its national competitors (De Bens and Østbye, 1998: 9).

While regional titles do cover national news, there is clearly less room for it, meaning that citi-zens in those countries where they predominate may be, first, more likely to think that what goes on in regional and local politics counts for something and, secondly, even more likely to turn to television for national-level political information. This serves to reinforce television's dominant role as most people's main source of political information, and hence the tendency of government and politicians to focus on broadcast (for which read television – see Box 7.1) rather than print media. The latter still has a place, though – both as a forum for elite-level, in-depth debate and, paradoxically, as creator of and conduit for populist opinion and political pres-sure. Unfortunately, the range of opinion and the direction of that pressure is not as diverse as it might be: the newspaper market in all European countries, with the partial exception of Scandinavia, has seen a fall in the number of titles, as well as increasing concentration of ownership of those that survive; the huge entry costs into the market also make it very difficult for newcomers to make it (De Bens and Østbye, 1998: 11). Owning newspapers is now a rich man's sport and rich men are not generally noted for their left-wing views. This does not, of course, mean that all Europe's

BOX 7.1
The agenda-setting Cinderella: radio and politics

Writing on Spain, Sanders with Canel (2004: 200–1) observe that radio is both 'a key source of political news' and 'the most unconstrained medium for the discussion of politics'; it is also, they note, an important agenda-setter, whose journalists are trusted more than their counterparts in TV and in the newspapers (an assumption confirmed in Figure 7.2, p. 175). Generally, however, there is little mention of radio in work on the media and politics in Europe, even though audience figures are actually quite high and the medium's possibilities still as endless as they ever were (see Hendy, 2000). This is partly because much of radio's output is music rather than speech, but also because surveys suggest the majority of people rely on TV for news (see Figure 7.1, p. 174). Yet most of those listening to music hear news bulletins on-the-hour-every-hour, and talk radio, (particularly the 'flagship' programmes made by public broadcasters that feature news and interviews with major political figures), often plays an important role in setting the day's news agenda. Appearing on those programmes is also a means by which those figures signal their positions and intentions to each other, as well as the audience. Since the advent of television, governments have paid rather less attention to radio, but this is perhaps changing. In a 24/7 news culture that continually seeks new angles in order to refresh and move a story on – and where there is considerable cross-ownership of radio, TV and print media – a radio story is more than capable of causing politicians headaches if they decide to take it seriously enough: witness the reaction of the British government in May 2003, to an item on 'Today' the 'flagship' news and current affairs radio show of the UK's public broadcaster, the BBC, even though it was broadcast just after 6 a.m. The fallout from this led to the so-called 'Hutton inquiry' (see http://www.the-hutton-inquiry.org.uk/) and the resignation of the BBC's chairman and director general. In addition, radio, more than television perhaps (see McNair, Hibberd and Schlesinger, 2002), can be a genuinely two-way, public-access medium: the phone-in 'talkback' show is nowhere near as developed or significant a format in Europe as it is in the US, but politicians ignore it at their peril.

newspapers are conservative or neo-liberal in persuasion: the logic of the market dictates that there is money to be made from papers that cater to the tastes of the millions of potential readers with a rather different outlook on life. But it does mean that those newspapers are unlikely to put themselves at the head of campaigns for, say, root and branch redistribution of wealth or a tax on international financial transactions.

Television may be dominant in Europe, but it has undergone considerable changes in recent years as technological progress (not least the arrival of digital and satellite) and free-market ideas have combined to turn what was once the fiefdom of a few (often state-run) terrestrial providers into a fragmented multi-channel world of round-the-clock choice. This poses major challenges for democracies and for the politicians and governments trying to run them. Deregulation of the broadcasting environment has if anything multiplied the tasks and the complexity of those charged with its oversight, albeit increasingly at arm's-length through 'independent' bodies that in a number of European countries (Germany and the Netherlands, for instance) contain representatives from supposedly important social interests.

Governments have to reconcile the demand for free speech with the fact that the market can potentially lead to monopolistic (and perhaps foreign-owned) media empires narrowing rather than widening the range of opinions on offer. This requires them to pass media laws that are often controversial, either because they are said to be overly restrictive or too lax – or sometimes because they attract accusations of political interference (see Box 7.2). But once these laws are passed this simply means an unending series of decisions to be taken on, say, awarding licences and on preventing or allowing takeovers. These decisions, rightly or wrongly, often draw flak from those who believe that they are influenced by the promise of political favours: successive Spanish governments of both left and right have been attacked, and even successfully challenged in both domestic and European Courts, by opponents for allowing sales to go through in contravention of rules on concentration (see Sanders with Canel, 2004: 201).

Most governments in Europe make an effort to avoid cross-ownership, overconcentration and, to a

---

BOX 7.2
Poland and political interference

Although not generally as bumpy as it has been in the Czech Republic and Hungary, the relationship between politicians and the media in Poland has never been plain sailing and still gives rise to controversies. In July 2001, the popular Justice Minister Lech Kaczynski was sacked after a documentary on the country's public service broadcaster, Telewizja Polska (TVP), accused him of fraud. But this was just the beginning. Kaczynski hit back at his critics and claimed the programme was politically motivated – claims that were backed by some TVP journalists. The public, too, seemed to take his side: the government from which he was fired went down to a catastrophic election defeat at the 2001 general election, while the anti-corruption party he set up in disgust, Law and Justice (*Prawo i Sprawiedliwoœæ* or PiS), came from nowhere to win 9.5 per cent of the vote! This incident pales into insignificance, however, when considered alongside the explosive events of Spring 2003 when the well-respected editor of one of Poland's top newspapers, *Gazeta Wyborcza*, Adam Michnik, claimed he had been offered a guarantee that a new law on media ownership would not scupper plans by the paper's proprietors to acquire a commercial TV station in return for a bribe of $17.5 million. Allegations were made of both prime ministerial and presidential involvement in the affair – dubbed *Rywingate* (after the alleged middle man involved) – which became even more complicated when it became apparent that Michnik had waited until the conclusion of Poland's EU accession negotiations before publishing the story, lest it damage the country's credibility in the eyes of the international community.

---

lesser extent, foreign ownership of broadcast and print media (see Box 7.3). But they may be fighting a losing battle as technological advances and free-speech arguments, plus the logic of the market – and in particular the single European market (SEM) – begin to overwhelm them.

True, states still have their own rules – dictating, for instance, the number of titles and channels in which a single firm is allowed to have a stake based on proportions of shares owned and/or audience share. Some even give this responsibility to lower tiers of government: public broadcasting in

---

BOX 7.3
Hungary: a case of (and perhaps for) foreign ownership

In most European countries, some foreign ownership of newspaper titles occurs. In Spain for instance the campaigning daily *El Mundo* is Italian-owned, while in the UK US-based News International owns a number of British titles. But it is actually quite uncommon (see De Bens and Østbye, 1998: 12). In postcommunist countries, however, it is by no means so unusual, not least because overseas interests were often able to buy into print media markets relatively cheaply; they also had more money to do so than domestic concerns. This was certainly the case in Hungary, where foreign-owned daily newspapers account for almost 90 per cent of circulation. But is this a bad thing? It can, of course, do little to prevent governments from favouring some titles and some owners over others by, for instance, directing their advertizing to particular papers or allowing contested takeovers. Nor has it been able to prevent circulation falling by a third between 1989 and 2001 – partly perhaps because cover prices rocketed. Meanwhile, time in front of the television, where political interference has been more obvious (see Sparks, 2000: 41) doubled. On the other hand, both the public and (significantly) journalists welcomed foreign owners on the grounds that they were less liable to pressure from domestic political groups and therefore better guarantors of editorial independence. Interestingly, right-wing politicians claim that Hungary's newspapers exhibit a left-liberal bias – not what one would expect from editors whose strings were being pulled by self-interested proprietors from abroad! More worrying perhaps is the degree to which ownership by the state has, in less than a decade, left newspapers in postcommunist countries, as in the West, in the hands of fewer and fewer proprietors.

Source: Gulyás (2003, 2004).

Germany may be controlled by a supposedly socially representative Federal Broadcasting Council, but most media regulation is done at the *Land* level. Yet, as Harcourt (2003) points out, EU member states have had to accept the principle, laid down by the ECJ (see Chapter 2), that broadcasting is not a cultural matter, and therefore under national control, but a tradeable service and therefore subject to European competition law. The ECJ also prevented states from blocking broadcasts from abroad into its domestic market, and, as Harcourt shows, has been a lever for liberalization. It has obliged governments in the Netherlands, Greece and Belgium to abandon legislative attempts to restrict competition. It has also limited the privileges of state-owned or subsidized public service broadcasting, even though the continued role of the latter received a vote of confidence and a measure of protection in an important protocol to the Amsterdam Treaty of 1997 (see Box 7.4).

Meanwhile, the Commission, in its role as regulator of the internal market, has had to get involved in the policing (and – especially in Germany and also in Spain – the prevention) of mergers and takeovers of media firms, many of which now have holdings in a number of European countries. Some governments have objected to such interference. But, interestingly, some have been grateful to Brussels, even if only privately: they find it very difficult to take on media empires for fear of alienating a potentially powerful political opponent (see Harcourt, 2003: 196) – a good example of a hard task being contracted out to the EU. On the other hand, there is of course a tension – as there always is – between allowing a degree of concentration in order to create European businesses which can compete effectively with large overseas conglomerates (one of the main drivers of the single market project, after all) and preventing monopoly at home. It is also increasingly difficult in such a fast-moving environment to use audience share (which changes all the time) or share ownership (which can be hidden by complex inter-business networks) as measures of market dominance (Trappel and Meier, 1998: 204).

That said, the EU is clearly a force, not just in terms of legal and competition decisions but in terms of setting the agenda for national regimes. Recent media legislation in the member states (including those who joined in 2004) and even in

---

BOX 7.4
The EU as protector of public service broadcasting

Governments and public service broadcasters were concerned that commercial concerns should not use EU competition law to try to undermine them completely on the grounds, say, that such broadcasting was an example of illegal state aids. They therefore inserted a protocol into the EU's Treaty of Amsterdam. This notes that 'the system of public broadcasting in the Member States is directly related to the democratic, social and cultural needs of each society and to the need to preserve media pluralism'. It goes on to note that nothing in the Treaty should be allowed to infringe on 'the competence of Member States to provide for the funding of public service broadcasting', although, it also observes, only 'insofar ... as such funding does not affect trading conditions and competition in the Community to an extent which would be contrary to the common interest'. The tension between cultural and economic logic, therefore, has not entirely disappeared (see Harrison and Woods, 2001)!

Switzerland shows significant signs of having been influenced by and redrawn to take account of the EU's 1989 and 1997 *Television Without Frontiers* Directives which (notwithstanding general moves toward liberalization) attempt to limit advertising and boost European content (see Harcourt, 2003: 201; also Wheeler, 2004). The latter aim does not go down well with the US, but the EU (especially under French pressure) has tried to hold the pass on the issue at international trade forums like the General Agreement on Tariffs and Trade (GATT) and the World Trade Organization (WTO).

State and public service broadcasting

In 1980, television in every European country, apart from Britain, Luxembourg and Italy, was public television, but by 2000 every country had allowed in commercial competition (Semetko, de Vreese and Peter, 2000: 123). But while public broadcasters may be under pressure, they have not disappeared. Outside Luxembourg there is no

European country without a state-funded or (if advertising revenue is permitted) at least a state-subsidized public broadcaster existing alongside commercial stations. True, the daily audience share of public broadcasters in postcommunist countries such as the Czech Republic and Hungary is low (around 30 per cent and 15 per cent, respectively), and some commentators question whether they can ever really emulate their western counterparts which, unlike them, had years to establish themselves (in terms of ethos and audience) before facing commercial competition (see Jakubowicz, 2004). In western Europe (including Norway, Sweden and the UK, where they are advert-free and rely largely on the licence fee), relatively embedded public broadcasters are not without their own troubles. But they can still boast considerable audience share (around 50 per cent or above), as well as the support of politicians who may be groping around for a new media policy paradigm but have not (yet) abandoned the public service model completely (see van Cuilenburg and McQuail, 2003).

European governments' support for public broadcasting – symbolized by both funding and by the common insistence that cable or digital services must include public channels in their subscriber packages – is driven by genuine concern to preserve national culture and a well-informed civil society. But it also stems from the belief – strengthened by fears of commercial concentration – that democratically elected politicians, and those who vote for them, should have access to at least one source of information and opinion that is insulated from the interests of this or that entrepreneur or enterprize, as well as bound by codes (some of them statutory) promoting political impartiality or at least 'balance'.

Politicians in Europe have had to get used to the fact that state ownership no longer provides them with direct access to quiescent cronies dedicated to serving the needs of the government of the day. The continued provision of public broadcasting nowadays rests on the need to promote diversity, protect minority interests and set a certain standard of impartiality and objectivity. But it has taken rather a long time (as well as public and legal pressure) to get some political players to recognize the fact. This is not only the case in new democracies

BOX 7.5
People power and Czech public broadcasting

In January 2001, the Czech capital Prague witnessed the biggest street protests since gatherings in Wenceslas Square brought down the country's Communist regime during the so-called 'velvet revolution' of 1989. People were demonstrating on behalf of journalists working for Czech television who were occupying their workplace, and broadcasting alternative news programmes, in protest against the appointment of Jiri Hodac as Director General. Hodac, the staff claimed, was the placeman of a Board of Governors who were themselves in the pockets of the two main parties, the Social Democrats and the Civic Democrats which at the time were running the country in what many voters (even their own) saw as something of an unholy alliance. Initially, the government took a hard line: the television centre was placed under virtual siege, forcing supporters of those inside to hoist food parcels (and at one stage chemical toilets) up through the windows to grateful staff. After a month, however, it became clear that many of the two parties' own MPs agreed with the protestors. The government promptly caved in under the pressure from within and without, and rushed a new media law through which allowed parliament to appoint a new, independent Director-General who would replace Hodac, who resigned 'on health grounds'. In early February, journalists agreed to remove the logo 'Strike' from the corner of the screens and signed (on live TV, of course) an agreement with a new interim Director General, who fired the Hodac-appointed station manager and news director. Another triumph for Czech 'people power', but hardly a ringing endorsement of postcommunist media policy!

(see Box 7.5), where state control, even if it was never as absolute or uniform as we might think (see Sparks, 2000: 37–40), was considerable. It is also true in countries that emerged from dictatorship over quarter of a century ago, such as Greece (see Box 7.6) and Spain (see Papatheodorou and Machin, 2003). Each incoming administration in Madrid gets to appoint a new Director General of public broadcaster TVE, whose news broadcasts

BOX 7.6
Greece: the battle against government control

In most European countries, surveys suggest that citizens trust television, be it public or commercial, to deliver them relatively unbiased political news and information. But Greece seems to be different: an opinion poll in 2000 revealed that not only did half of those questioned mistrust the political output of state TV, three-quarters of them regarded it as a mouthpiece for the government. This is not so surprising when one remembers that broadcasting in Greece began in earnest under a military dictatorship and that, although the democratic constitution of 1975 guaranteed a free press, it left broadcasting 'under the immediate control of the state'. This monopoly saw the government intervene again and again in both management and output on the grounds that, to quote long-time socialist prime minister Andreas Papandreou, 'impartiality and pluralism on state media were incompatible because this distorts government policy'. This monopoly lasted another decade and was brought to an end only when a corruption scandal involving the Papandreou government emboldened the mayors of Greece's biggest cities (all members of the main opposition party) to establish not only independent radio stations but also TV channels. Government attempts to use the courts to stop them were – significantly – stymied by the intervention of the ECJ, which, after a referral from the Greek courts, made it clear that the attempt to maintain a monopoly was 'ostensibly illegal'. The consequence was an almost overnight and relatively anarchic deregulation, and a media environment that is still heavily politicized and where government has on several occasions undermined the ESR – the supposedly independent regulatory body.

Sources: Chondroleou (2004) and Harcourt (2003: 185).

are widely criticized for favouring the government of the day – not only by the public but even by journalists who work there, some of whom have set up their own Advisory Council in order to counteract the impact of what they see as manipulation of their credibility.

Most other states in Europe (with the partial exception of France) try to avoid these problems by eschewing this 'politics-over-broadcasting systems' mode of governance. Instead, they operate the kind of 'formally autonomous systems' which exist in, say, the UK and Sweden, or the 'politics-in-broadcasting systems' (where governing bodies include representatives of political parties and interest groups) that still characterize Germany and the Netherlands (see Brants and Siune, 1998: 129). In the latter, this mode of media governance has led, following the introduction of commercial television in the late 1980s, to a system of three public service channels (one serving up supposedly family fare, one sports and entertainment and the third more 'cultural' and informative material). On each channel time is allocated (partly in accordance with their membership numbers) to eight not-for-profit associations of social and religious groups which make programmes reflecting their interests and points of view – a system that promotes considerable diversity (see van der Wurff, 2004). In Italy, the 'politics-in-broadcasting' mode was taken to its logical extent by giving control of each state channel to one of the main political parties. Recently, however, elite agreement on this *lottizzazione* system has broken down, with accusations from the left that the right-wing government of media magnate Silvio Berlusconi was not playing fair (see Box 7.10, p. 173).

The changing coverage of politics

Fragmentation

Just as Europe's politicians – or, at least, most of them – can no longer guarantee that state broadcasters will do their bidding, they can no longer rely on the fact that by speaking on two or three television channels they will get their message across to the majority of citizens. Admittedly, some futurologists oversell the pace of fragmentation: 'the true "break-up" of the "mass audience"' is, as McQuail (1998: 125), points out, not yet upon us. As in the rest of the developed world, most Europeans still rely on three or channels for the vast bulk of their viewing (see Curran, 2002: 190). This will continue to be the case while a stubborn but large minority refuses to pay directly for its television services and for the technology that makes digital services possible. It is also true that whereas over 20 per cent of households in western European countries presently have digital TV, the figure in some eastern European countries (though not all: in Poland the figure is similar) is lower. But the cost is coming down fast. It is also becoming a matter of a one-off payment rather than a long-term subscription, and may soon be unavoidable as analogue services are switched off.

The advent of on-demand services and 'narrow-casting' – the arrival of specialist channels providing an exclusive diet of, say, sport or music or wildlife or celebrity or life-style programmes – means that many people will be able to do what they always have wanted; namely, tune out politics and current affairs altogether. Political junkies, however, will increasingly have to search for what they crave (and perhaps pay for it via a subscription to a specialist channel) rather than being spoonfed for free. Given that the linkage between the public and parties has come to rely so much on mass rather than face-to-face communication, this development threatens to erode what is already a rather tenuous link even further. One can argue already that a market-driven media is unlikely to provide the kind of 'public sphere' or forum that is supposedly necessary for informed, democratic and hopefully rational politics and decision-making (see Habermas, 1989): whether any such space can be meaningfully said to exist when so many can contract out of it altogether is a moot point. In fact, contracting out is a feature of the non-digital environment, too, given the increased provision in recent years of regional and minority-language stations – something digitization will only make easier. It may be no accident, for example, that the difficulty countries such as Belgium and Spain – and possibly now the UK – have in holding themselves together has been accelerated by the opening up of 'sub-spheres' that allow minorities to cut themselves off from the rest of the state.

From 'party logic' to 'media logic'

Many European media outlets, and particularly broadcasters, are cutting down their coverage of politics and current affairs not just in between elections but also during them. For commercial broadcasters, this is largely on the grounds that elections and politics more generally do not deliver audiences and, therefore, advertizing revenue. But even public service broadcasters are backing away from what used to be thought of as a responsibility to inform and educate voters, irrespective of whether the low turnout at elections they use as justification for their shrinking coverage could conceivably also be a function of that shrinking (Semetko, de Vreese and Peter, 2000: 127–8). Programmers and editors, then, are less and less willing to allow politics and politicians to operate in some kind of 'reserved area' in which normal news values are suspended at crucial times (such as elections) in order to give people what they supposedly need as citizens rather than what they apparently want as consumers. Kuhn (2004: 35) notes, for example, that in the 2002 French presidential election, not only the commercial brand leader TF1, but also the main public service broadcaster, France 2, 'devoted significantly less time to election news and debates than in the previous presidential contest' and that 'frequently the election was not the lead story on television news'.

But this is not simply a question of a decrease in the time allotted to politics, but also the way in which it is treated. As one very prescient study of Italian election-time broadcasting put it, coverage has moved from 'party logic', where political institutions' right to set the agenda and occupy a prominent place in the schedules went unquestioned, toward 'media logic', where neither can be taken for granted (see Mazzoleni, 1987). There has for some time been a 'struggle for the agenda' between the media and politicians (see, for example, Asp, 1983, on its manifestation in Sweden in the 1970s). But, increasingly, normal news values – presumed topicality, obvious visuality, surprise and drama, easy intelligibility, personalization and negativity – are now applied to political stories. This means politics either falls out of favour or it becomes more entertaining – either by being more gimmicky or gladiatorial or, more subtly, by associating itself with the media's celebrity and lifestyle focus.

Gimmicks there are aplenty; but it is hard to identify a trend: perhaps fortunately, few European politicians followed a spate of Italian politicians who in the early 1990s appeared naked or semi-naked in order to court publicity and earn a repu-

Table 7.2 Ads and debates

	Paid election adverts?	Leaders' debates?
Czech Rep.	Yes	Yes
France	No	Normally (not last election)
Germany	Yes	Yes (at most recent election)
Italy	Yes	No
Netherlands	Yes	Yes
Poland	Yes	Sometimes (not last election)
Spain	No	Sometimes (not last election)
Sweden	Yes	Yes
UK	No	No
US	Yes	Yes

BOX 7.7

Ich oder der: Germany's Chancellor candidates go head-to-head

Germany's 2002 election threw up a number of memorable occasions: Chancellor Schröder did himself no harm at all by donning his boots to tour flood-stricken parts of the Federal Republic; his rival, Edmund Stoiber, tried to demonstrate that he was just as young and sporty as the incumbent by playing football and then having to apologize when his miskick hit a pensioner full-on in the face and broke her glasses (though fortunately not her nose). But the highlights were clearly the TV debates between the two men. This was the first time, some forty-two years after they began in the US, that these head-to-head debates had taken place in Germany: indeed, they may not have taken place at all had the Chancellor's party not been lagging behind in the polls and had the Chancellor not been widely considered more popular than either his party or his challenger! As in other countries, the instantaneous judgements of pundits and public alike were probably as important as the two debates themselves. In the first, the challenger was said to have shaded a fairly even contest. In the second, the incumbent was – according to polls and pundits – the clear winner in an ill-tempered affair, the reporting of which seems to have been dominated by boxing metaphors.

tation for liking a bit of good, clean fun (see Roncarolo, 2004: 113)! As for gladiatorial contests, although more and more parliamentary democracies seem to be going in for televised candidate debates (see Box 7.7), their place is not quite yet secure as it is in the US (see Table 7.2). The UK, for instance, has never staged one, and even those that have during one election have not at the next, largely because the incumbent resists taking part. This happened in Spain in 2004, where, despite polls showing that 75 per cent of the public wanted a debate, the man who expected to win the election, PP's Mariano Rajoy, refused to 'get into the ring' with the man who actually won it, Jose Luis Rodriguez Zapatero, around whom PSOE conducted a notably 'presidential' campaign. It also happened in France in 2002, where President Chirac refused to debate with the FN's Jean-Marie Le Pen not, he claimed, because he was scared of the latter laying into him over myriad corruption scandals but because he did not want to dignify an out-and-out racist with a platform.

How much longer candidates will be able to refuse debates without it counting against them, however, is another matter. Such behaviour, after all, runs counter to the trend that many political scientists claim to have identified toward the 'presidentialization' of not just campaigning (Mughan, 2000) but European politics more generally (see

Poguntke and Webb, 2004). Moreover, in the face of the common wisdom (see Chapter 9) concerning the ideological convergence of mainstream left and right (summed up nicely during the last presidential election in France by *L'Express* publishing a despairing article entitled *A la recherche du clivage perdu*) parties feel they must seek new ways to demonstrate that they are different. Given that politics, some claim, is no longer about big ideas but about competent and credible management, it makes sense for parties to try to embody their claim to such qualities by increasing the focus on their leaders. Ironically, however, as leaders become more important to party campaigns, it is not only competence and credibility that count: all-round personality seems to be becoming more important, creating a premium on candidates who can project personal warmth and charm irrespective of worthiness. Perhaps, as some seriously suggest they should (see Coleman, 2003), both those who do politics and those who cover it are learning from TV shows such as *Big Brother*, in which viewers get to decide by voting (often in bigger numbers than they do at EP elections!) which of the competitors gets to stay in the house.

Certainly, there does seem in some countries to have been a recent trend against candidates who are perceived as less friendly or human than their opponents. In 2002 both Jacques Chirac (against Lionel Jospin) and Gerhard Schröder (against Edmund Stoiber) made much of the contrast between themselves ('naughty but nice') and their rather austere ('worthy but dull') opponents. Indeed, notwithstanding the fact that the German Chancellor is indirectly elected by parliament rather than the voters (who vote for parties), the focus on the individual incumbent and challenger seems set to dominate election campaigns more than ever now that Germany has moved into the era of the TV debate (see Box 7.7).

What certainly seems to be embedding itself in political coverage, irrespective of gimmickry and gladiatorialism, is what Kuhn (2004: 34) calls 'the mediatization of intimacy' – the deliberate courting by politicians of appearances by themselves and often their wives (see Box 7.8) in supposedly non-political formats. These – the chatshow or the magazine portrait are the archetypes – purport to concentrate on the 'real' man or woman behind the public persona in the knowledge that in so doing they are (a) likely to reach voters who might otherwise be turning off and tuning out of politics; and (b) avoid hard questions by experienced and knowledgeable specialist journalists.

There is of course a flipside to all this. Since politicians have allowed the cameras into their lives in order to film friendly stories about just how like the rest of us they are, they are finding it increasingly difficult to prevent the media from exposing sides of them that might not go down so well. In many European countries there are strong privacy laws: France is a good example. But these are gradually being eroded as politicians who decide to live by the sword are deemed (often by the courts) liable to die by it, too (see Stanyer and Wring,

---

BOX 7.8
The politician's wife

With the focus shifting to the all-round (instead of the purely political) persona of the politician, the media in some European countries has taken (and been encouraged to take) more interest in his, or more unusually her, family members. Although, these have included (in Italy) mothers and aunts (see Roncarolo, 2004: 116) most cases this is limited to wives (and possibly to children). In the presidential campaign in France in 2002, both Bernadette Chirac (traditional, a lot of work for charity, and the patience of a saint) and Sylviane Agacinski (take-no-prisoners feminist married – in a thoroughly modern manner – to Lionel Jospin) went into bat for their husbands, the one helping to shore up his image as a loveable rogue, the other trying to persuade the public that he was rather more exciting than he looked. After their 'at home' spreads in the glossies and chatshow appearances, *Paris Match* – not known for its political content – published a poll which gave the *Les Jospin* the edge over *Les Chirac* as 'the couple who would best represent France' – not that it prevented at least one half of the first pairing crashing out of the presidential race after the initial round of voting (interestingly, there seems to have been no equivalent focus on M. Le Pen's domestic bliss). The UK may not be far behind: in 2004 the Conservative leader was, after all, married to a former fashion model; the Prime Minister, on the other hand, was married to a barrister whom the press seemed either to like or loath. Both 'Tony' and 'Cherie' (first names seem to be common currency in mediatized intimacy) seemed torn between trying to protect their children from the media spotlight and (like, say, Victor Orbán, the even more youthful and dynamic ex-prime minister of Hungary) profiting from their photogenic presence.

2004). And even if domestic law is still strong enough to prevent the emergence into the public domain of matters that many would regard as essentially private, the availability of many foreign newspaper titles on the internet and the advent of cross-border satellite broadcasting mean that it is almost impossible to keep things from anybody interested enough to find out (see Box 7.9).

BOX 7.9
The Media Chancellor sees red

Newspapers all over Europe had great fun when in April 2002 German Chancellor Gerhard Schröder, proved that he was indeed as image-conscious (though not quite as laid-back) as everyone thought. Schröder successfully sued a German news agency for quoting an image consultant to the effect that he dyed his hair. But there was less fun flying around when the Chancellor resorted to legal action in January 2003, ostensibly to protect the privacy of himself and his wife, of whom his re-election campaign had made extensive use the previous year. His use of Germany's relatively strict privacy laws to gag a couple of Germany's regional newspapers from repeating allegations concerning the state of his marriage might not have caused much trouble. But he sought to prevent the British *Daily Mail*, which published the story, from repeating it. Banking on the fact that the UK has no equivalent laws and on the fact that an injunction obtained in a German court could not be applied in England, the *Daily Mail* went ahead anyway – although it was careful not to sell those editions in Germany or to make mention of the story on its website. This did not, however, mean that the Chancellor had 'won' and that Europe's internal borders still counted for something in media terms – other news media in the UK reported the story about the story and their reports would have been available electronically in Germany for anyone who cared to look for them.

We need to be very wary, however, of thinking that packaging politics and politicians is a recent phenomenon in Europe. Kuhn (2004: 31) reminds us that, before he won the 1981 French presidential election, François Mitterrand underwent an 'image makeover'. So, too, did his British counterpart Margaret Thatcher before becoming Prime Minister in 1979, and she famously eschewed inquisitions by trained interrogators from the ranks of political journalism in favour of rather more cosy chats with sympathetic radio DJs. Even in the 1974 French election, Kuhn reminds us, 'the youthful Valéry Giscard d'Estaing presented himself as a man of the people by being photographed in a football strip and playing the

accordion (though not both simultaneously)'. He also famously floored his opponent, a then rather less media-savvy François Mitterrand, by reminding him (and the viewers) in a TV debate: 'You don't have a monopoly on compassion.' Holtz-Bacha (2004: 48–9) reminds us that a 1960s TV-ad for former Chancellor Willy Brandt sought to portray him as a man of the people by showing him driving himself to work through West Berlin, where he was mayor. Indeed 'personalization' seems to have been part of election campaigning and coverage in Germany as far back as 1949 and rather than there being an overall trend towards an increase, it tends to vary from election to election, often depending on the charisma of the candidates involved (Wilke and Reinemann, 2001: 301–2). We should also note that, in the UK, a *Times* newspaper editorial was already lamenting in 1970 the fact that people were being asked 'to vote not for a Member of Parliament, but for a Party; not for a Party but for its Leader; and not for its Leader but for a pre-packaged television presentation of what Market Research suggests the Leader should be'.

This is not to say that there is nothing new under the sun: simply that some developments we see as recent have being going on rather longer than we think. In any case, there are some changes in the media's coverage of politics that do stand out as genuinely novel – if not always welcome – developments. For instance, media providers throughout Europe are, especially during elections, crowding out their already limited discussion of policy issues and party programmes with a focus on speculation on who is winning (poll reporting and the 'horse race' aspect). Analysing Germany between 1980 and 1994, for instance, Brettschneider (1997) recorded a big increase (from 65 to 168) in the number of polls reported in the German media in the twelve weeks before federal elections. Broadcasters also seem to be 'dumbing-down' their coverage by forcing politicians into ever shrinking soundbites, at the same time, it must be said, as politicians themselves are moving away at election time from old-style party political broadcasts (a 5–10 minute lecturette from a talking head) to 2-minute spots that resemble the US-style adverts that many European countries now allow them to pay for in addition to publicly funded air-time.

It is also argued across Europe that, both during elections and between them, the media is allowing prediction, punditry and position-taking to crowd out the column inches and air-time devoted to the 'straight reporting' of political events, not least if those events are routine, complex and parliamentary (see Negrine, 1998). We need to be careful, however. The media in European countries may be spending less time on reporting parliament (and/or reporting only those parts of it that are dramatic and conflictual, such as question times), but they are still fairly reliant on it to provide a steady stream of the raw material for much of what still passes for news (policy conflicts, calls for legislation, airing of issues, and the like). What in the UK is called the 'silly season' – that period where news organizations struggle for stories as parliamentarians go on their long summer break – is testament to the ongoing (if uncomfortable) mutual dependency between politics and the media, between journalists and their sources (see Ericson, Baranek and Chan, 1989).

'Disdaining the news', or at least the parties

In the face of this ongoing dependency, there is a tendency by journalists in many European countries to assert their autonomy from politicians in the face of increasingly intense efforts on the part of the latter to control the news agenda and the way they are presented within it. Political parties all over the continent have professionalized their media relations (see Farrell and Webb, 2002) or at the very least adapted their practice (rarely as 'amateurish' as is often rather patronizingly suggested) to changing media technologies (see Negrine and Lilleker, 2002). At election time this has seen them seeking, first, to bully journalists into their version of what is and is not important and fair and, secondly, to spoonfeed them with neatly pre-packaged stories based on stage-managed 'pseudo-events' from the so-called 'campaign trail'. Notwithstanding a move towards stressing 'valence issues' such as economic competence (see Chapter 6), parties still aim, broadly speaking, to keep the focus of the campaign on the issues they 'own' or are associated with (for instance, health and welfare for social democrats or

smaller government for conservative parties). To do so, they are, it seems, employing greater use of 'spin doctors'. Although there are some exceptions, notably in the postcommunist democracies in Europe, where politics is still party- rather than candidate-centred, these almost iconic figures are rarely the roving consultants-for-hire or 'parajournalists' (see Schudson, 2003: 3) in the American mould (see Plasser and Plasser, 2002). Instead, they are partisans with considerable experience in the media who are either explicitly employed or simply relied on to get the party's message across (see Esser, Reinemann and Fan, 2000, for a comparative study of the UK and Germany).

As a response, journalists have taken to 'disdaining the news' (Levy, 1981) – undermining the efforts of politicians by pointing out to viewers the spinning and the strategic intent behind their statements and pseudo-events, and by revealing the tensions beneath the shows of unity and the fluster and flap beneath the calm and collected exterior. That this is an extension of 'media logic' triumphing over (or at least jostling with) 'party logic' is nicely illustrated by an interview given to a Dutch researcher looking at changes in public broadcasting's election coverage (see de Vreese, 2001: 170); a news editor observed that:

> The candidates are going to repeat ideas and central concepts from their program and election agenda. We will refrain from bringing reformulated views as news. Instead we will add content to the campaign by explicating and explaining party stand points. We are not going to be reactive, we will not let the parties determine our agenda … This implies that we will approach the campaign more analytically, we will expose campaign strategies and cover strategies rather than just registering events.

Journalists have also become less deferential and even aggressive, moving from the 'watchdog journalism' of earlier decades to the so-called 'attack-dog journalism' that seems to assume that all politicians are in it for themselves and out to put one over on the people (see Barnett, 2002). These developments have not, however, proceeded at the same pace throughout the continent. The populist 'disdaining', 'attack-dog' stance was first evident in

Spain (España)

Area: 12.7% of EU-25
Population: 9.1% of EU-25
GDP: 8.7% of EU-25
Joined EU: 1986
Capital city: Madrid

History: Modern Spain was created in 1479 by dynastic intermarriage. After defeating and expelling the last remnants of the Arab kingdom of Andalusia in the south in the name of Catholicism, its monarchs led the Counter-Reformation against Protestantism in Europe. Further intermarriage joined them to the Habsburg dynasty. For a while at least, this allowed Spanish monarchs to rule not just Spain, but also Austria and what was to become Belgium and the Netherlands, as well as parts of modern-day Italy, France and Germany. Meanwhile, the discovery of America gave Spain an empire (Florida, Mexico, part of the Caribbean and Latin America) and, of course, gold and silver.

By the eighteenth century, however, imperial decay had set in. Spain became a European backwater, ruled by a conservative aristocracy determined to preserve its own privileges, as well as Madrid's control of industrially and commercially more advanced regions such as the Basque Country and Catalunya. The nineteenth century saw Spain consumed by a series of wars between liberals and monarchists who were supported by the still-powerful church. This conflict witnessed the brief flowering of a federal republic before the return of the monarchy and a level of repression which radicalized both peasants and the growing urban working

class into anarchism and communism. Following a short-lived dictatorship in the 1920s, free elections ushered in a republic and then a left-wing government that threatened not just the privileges of the church and the propertied, but the very existence of the nation state. A military *coup* in 1936 led to three years of civil war that also served as a proxy conflict between Fascist Germany and Italy and Communist Russia.

The victor in the civil war, Francisco Franco, established an authoritarian dictatorship, backed by the Catholic church, that lasted from 1939 till his death in 1975. The early years saw thousands of opponents put to death, diplomatic isolation (notwithstanding Spain's neutrality during the Second World War), and the country's economic and social development all but arrested. In later years, Franco bought his country a place in the 'West' by allowing US air bases on Spanish soil. He also allowed millions of Spaniards to work abroad in northern Europe and eventually millions of tourists to make the trip south. This assisted economic development but also helped open up the country to foreign influences and the possibility of change. Following Franco's death, his anointed successor King Juan Carlos combined with reformists within the regime to restore democracy. After five years of centrist government, and a failed army *coup*, the Socialist Party (PSOE) assumed office and held on to it from 1982 to 1996, until it was finally overhauled by the centre-right Popular Party (PP). The latter won a bigger majority in 2000 and was forecast to win again in 2004 until, just days before the election, Islamic terrorists exploded bombs in Madrid, and the Socialists snatched a narrow victory.

Economy and society: Spain's 40 million inhabitants have seen their standard of living increase markedly since the end of the Franco era as the economy has become more fully integrated into Europe and boosted by EU funding. Few Spaniards need to work abroad any more. Indeed,

the country now imports labour, mainly from North Africa, to do the jobs that many Spaniards – despite the fact that unemployment is relatively high – will not do, especially in agriculture. However, the latter, along with fishing (Spain has easily the largest fleet in Europe) has become less important as the economy has diversified, particularly in the more industrial and commercial north. Annual per capita income in 2003 stood at just 5 per cent under the EU-25 average. Other big changes since the advent of democracy include a steep decline in the influence of the (Catholic) church, vast improvements in health, welfare and education, and in the position of women, who (not coincidentally perhaps) now have one of world's lowest birthrates.

Governance: Spain is now a solid parliamentary democracy, with both houses of parliament elected by a PR system that favours the two largest parties and parties from the country's regions. Under the 1978 constitution these 'autonomous communities' have been granted so much power that the country now resembles a federal state. This has not been enough, however, to end calls for independence from some regions, especially in the Basque country (where the terrorist movement ETA operates) and, to a lesser extent in wealthy Catalunya.

Foreign policy: Spain, initially concentrated on 're-joining' western Europe, via NATO (1982) and the EU (1986). Since then, it has tried to persuade its fellow member states to take Europe's relations with North Africa more seriously and, before it pulled its troops out after the Madrid bombings, angered many of them with its pro-American stance over Iraq.

Further reading. Closa and Heywood (2004), Colomer (2002), Magone (2004).

the US and it is therefore no surprise that it spread first to the UK. Other media cultures have been slower to adopt it – at least wholesale. A recent study of election coverage in (admittedly quality) newspapers in Germany from 1949 onwards did find that journalists tended to do more of their own interpreting rather than simply reporting what politicians said and did – a trend also identified in the Netherlands (see de Vreese, 2001: 172). But its authors could find 'no overall trend toward negativism' (Wilke and Reinemann, 2001: 291). Nor, apparently, are German journalists as interested in their British colleagues in 'exposing' the black arts of the spin doctors, possibly because they are less subject to direct pressure from them, which may in turn be because German parties (whose chancellor candidates are not always the undisputed leaders of their parties) have neither centralized their media operations to quite the same extent nor spent so much money on them (see Esser, Reinemann and Fan, 2000).

France, too, according to Kuhn (2004: 38) provides something of a contrast: not only does the media, as in most countries outside the UK, show little interest in the sexual misdemeanours of politicians (money, we should note, is another matter), but more generally 'there remains a strong journalistic culture of deference to politicians at the apex of the state apparatus'. Others have noticed the same thing: according to one UK journalist sent out to cover the 2002 presidential election in France, watching a key TV interview with the incumbent, Jacques Chirac (who, he claimed, would have been hounded out of politics years ago by the British press) 'was like watching an old man being gummed by a toothless spaniel' (Jeffries, 2002). Disdain there may be; as yet, however, it is still largely confined, at least in France, to satirical TV programmes and magazines. Not so in other countries. In both Poland and the Czech Republic, public broadcasters have had to combat accusations that they are too respectful to the governments, even if those governments did not necessarily share that view and (particularly in the mid-1990s) made fairly blatant attempts to interfere; but politicians had a notably less easy ride on the main commercial stations and some of their 'disrespect' began to rub off on their public service counterparts (see the contributions by Goban-Klas and Kettle to O'Neil, 1997). Some commentators, especially in the US where it has gone furthest, think that this style of journalism is contributing to falling trust and rising cynicism among voters (but see Norris, 2000, for an impressive rebuttal).

Bias and its effects

Many politicians in Europe would agree with the idea that their job is made more difficult by a media that promotes cynicism. On a day-to-day level, however, they are more worried about whether they are getting a fair deal compared to their opponents. So aware are they of the importance of media coverage, that they are acutely sensitive to, and often complain about, bias. It would be wrong to dismiss these complaints as predictable paranoia. This is especially the case when they come from smaller parties. These parties, sometimes on the extreme of the political spectrum, claim – with some justification – that they are squeezed out of mass coverage by their larger and possibly more mainstream competitors: the Liberal Democrats in the UK, the *Front National* in France, *Izquierda Unida* in Spain and the Czech Communists, for instance, routinely make this point. Mainstream parties, of course, will reply that coverage should be based on support and the likelihood of getting into government, not on some abstract idea of giving all voices an equal say. This may make sense between elections, but less so, perhaps, during election campaigns that should presumably be about everyone getting the chance to put their point across. Nevertheless, in many countries free election broadcasts are allocated according to party support: in Spain, for example, parties are allocated between 10 and 45 minutes in total, though they can divide this up between however many individual spots they like (see Sanders with Canel, 2004: 197). Interestingly, however, the media in general does devote more news time to so-called minor parties at election time, which conceivably could have the effect of boosting their vote by improving their visibility.

But smaller and/or extreme parties are not the only ones complaining. Larger, mainstream parties are also acutely concerned. We have already seen that public broadcasters in those states that have not created an arm's-length relationship between government and broadcasters are accused of bias (normally, in their case, in favour of the government of the day). But so, too, are privately owned media outlets – particularly those whose owners are said to exert undue influence on coverage, either directly or via the anticipated reactions of their journalists or even politicians themselves. For instance, French commercial broadcaster *TF1* allegedly promoted (though it has to be said unsuccessfully) the candidature of Edouard Balladur in the run up to the presidential election of 1995. It was said to have done so because the head of the company that controls it, Bouygues, had close links with other politicians in his camp (see Kuhn, 2004: 29). Accusations of bias and improper influence have been levelled at Rupert Murdoch in the UK (see Curran and Leys, 2000) and, before his empire went bust, Leo Kirch in Germany, both in relation to editorial interference and for allegedly using their large share of media markets to 'bully' politicians afraid of their influence on voters into granting them policy concessions and regulatory exemptions. And then, of course, there is Europe's one-man media-minefield, Silvio Berlusconi (see Box 7.10).

But is the influence of these 'moguls' – and the media in general – on voters really as great as it seems? Certainly, at first glance, it is logical to think that since, (as we suggested in Chapter 6) people are becoming less attached to particular parties and more volatile in their voting behaviour, their political choices at election time may be more and more open to influence through and by the media. But being convinced, for instance, that 'campaigns make a difference' is one thing (see Farrell and Schmitt-Beck, 2002); being able to actually prove 'media effects' on political behaviour is another. One noted expert on politics and the media (Mughan, 2000: 76), for instance, warns us that 'It must be remembered that a great deal of myth and hyperbole suffuses discussion of the political role of television. In truth, much remains shrouded in mystery' – so much so, in fact, that he quotes another authority to the effect that: 'The state of research on media effects is one of the most notable embarrassments of modern social science … [T]he scholarly literature has been much better at refuting, qualifying, and circumscribing the

BOX 7.10
Silvio Berlusconi

Acres of newsprint and thousands of hours of air time throughout Europe have been devoted to Silvio Berlusconi. This is not just because of his allegedly dubious business dealings. Nor is it simply because of his infamous 'gaffes' (comparing a German MEP to a concentration camp commandant, claiming that 'the war on terrorism' was a clash between Christian civilisation and the rest, and suggesting that he might introduce the photogenic Danish Prime Minister to his wife on the grounds that he was better-looking than the man with whom she was rumoured to be involved). It is also because of the conflict of interest inherent in his dual role as Prime Minister of Italy and owner of multiple media interests both in that country and abroad (see Ginsborg, 2004). Given the history of government interference and politicization of the public broadcasting system (RAI) in Italy, and the fact that Berlusconi dominates the commercial TV sector, becoming prime minister gave him potential control of 90 per cent of Italian television, in addition to the fact that he also has indirect control over a number of print media and advertizing outlets. He stands accused by opponents of using his position in government to protect and promote his business interests (including opening up the possibilities for cross ownership), of politically interfering (even more than they did!) in RAI's affairs by fixing its board, securing the silencing of critical journalists and the appointment of toadies, measurably reducing the airtime devoted to opposition politicians on both RAI and his own channels, and of using the latter to drive the supposed 'dumbing down' of political and other coverage. All this, plus the way Berlusconi was able to use his media power to leverage his overnight entry into politics in 1993, challenges comforting but perhaps outdated beliefs in a separation of powers between those who do politics and those who supposedly watch over them on our behalf.

thesis of media impact than supporting it.'

In short, while the common wisdom nowadays is that 'elections are won on television' or 'people vote the way they do because they believe what they read in the papers', we are a long way from knowing whether this is indeed the case. The fact

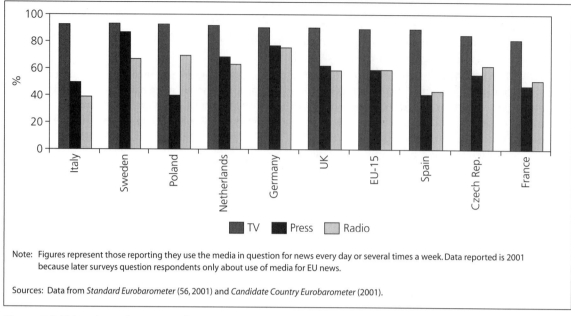

Note: Figures represent those reporting they use the media in question for news every day or several times a week. Data reported is 2001 because later surveys question respondents only about use of media for EU news.

Sources: Data from *Standard Eurobarometer* (56, 2001) and *Candidate Country Eurobarometer* (2001).

Figure 7.1 TV as the main source of news

that such sentiments are common wisdom – among political elites as well as the rest of us – may help drive the continuing mediatization of politics throughout Europe. But the evidence is very thin – especially for some kind of 'direct' effect like the conversion of what would have been, for example, a Socialist vote to a Conservative one. Against this scepticism, it must be said that the absence of proof for such effects may be down to the inability of political scientists to find convincing ways of measuring them and isolating them from all the other impacts on vote choice. This has not, however, stopped them trying – both for the print and for the broadcast media.

Few newspapers in Europe nowadays can be dismissed as no more than mouthpieces for particular parties. Although many have faced closure (the Italian Communist daily, *Unità*, is often on the brink), a few party organs (normally on the far left) still exist (such as the French Communist *l'Humanité*), but they sell very few copies. This is not to suggest, however, that European newspapers do not have their biases, even if those in the UK tend to be very much more strident about their partisan loyalties than most of their continental equivalents. But just because they are not diehard supporters of one party, and almost never 'announce for' one candidate or party in the way that British papers are expected to, does not mean that that in France and Germany, for example, both regional and national newspapers do not lean fairly obviously to the left or to the right. And because the bias is obvious, it is to some extent self-selected: a right-wing reader chooses a right-wing paper rather than the paper making her right-wing. It is also discounted, not least because trust in newspapers is not high (see Figure 7.2). This notwithstanding, there is some recent research from the UK which suggests, first, that newspapers may influence our outlook on the economy which may then feed through to voting (see Gavin and Sanders, 2003) and, secondly, that newspaper bias may have more electoral effect than we were previously able to detect, though only sufficient to make a difference in very close contests (see Newton and Brynin, 2001).

TV is potentially more of a problem for those worried about the impact of bias: it is clearly the major source of news for most Europeans (see Figure 7.1) and, except where partisanship in one branch of the media is a particular 'problem' (e.g. newspapers in the UK; television in Italy), generally more trusted than the press (see Figure 7.2). With regard to television, there is some limited

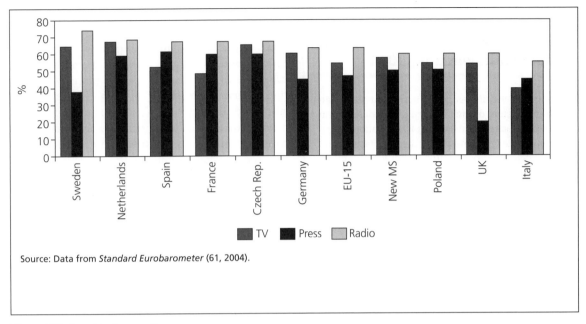

Source: Data from *Standard Eurobarometer* (61, 2004).

Figure 7.2 Trust in the media

research evidence of what are called 'indirect effects'. Most of the time, TV seems to reinforce partisanship (in short, the viewer has her prejudices confirmed whatever she watches), although some would argue for a stronger, short-term effect on the politically undecided and inattentive (for a summary of this more qualified position, see Curran, 2002: 133). However, given the fact, (as we saw in Chapter 6) that more and more people could be said to fit into these categories, this short-term effect on elections could become more and more important. It is also possible to argue, though not without qualification (e.g. Semetko, 2000: 362–3), that the media already has considerable 'agenda-setting power' and can 'prime' voters' sense of what is and is not important to think about when casting their votes (see Box 7.11) – all the more important if 'issue voting' (see Chapter 6) as well as personality preferences are indeed becoming more crucial to results (see Kleinnijenhuis *et al.*, 2001). More particularly, some claim that TV debates (and, importantly, media reporting of who won and who lost) can help shift votes if held sufficiently close to election day so that their effect does not wear off (see Denemark, 2002; also Gunther, Montero and Wert, 2000). Interestingly, given the developing

common wisdom surrounding the importance of 'presidentialization' in campaign coverage, the very latest work into 'leader effects' in elections (mainly in Europe) finds that, generally, individual leaders are not nearly so important to voters as everybody thinks (King, 2002).

There has been less research conducted on the agenda-setting power of the media when it comes to politicians themselves, despite the oft-voiced suspicion that the latter are increasingly driven by, say, the press into populist stances that they otherwise might eschew, particularly on immigration (see Chapter 10). Such effects may not be limited to the British tabloids. Writing on France, Raymond Kuhn, (2004: 29) notes that '*Le Monde* in particular has acquired the reputation of exerting independent, but also unaccountable, power through its capacity to support or undermine particular politicians and policy options'. The problem for political scientists, of course, is that, however well-connected or persuasive they are, they are unlikely to tempt politicians into admitting that this or that policy was pursued (or such and such a minister was dismissed) because of a press campaign.

This is a perennial difficulty in social and political science, particularly when it comes to media

BOX 7.11
Priming l'insécurité in the French presidential election, 2002

Liberals the world over reeled in shock at the results of the first round of the French presidential election when the leader of the far-right Front National, Jean-Marie Le Pen, emerged in second place ahead of the Socialist Prime Minister, Lionel Jospin, and earned himself a run-off election against the eventual winner, Jacques Chirac. But perhaps the result was more of a surprise than it should have been. After all, the media, in effect, decided that the central issue of the campaign would be *l'insécurité* (law and order) – an issue that the right (both mainstream and extreme) had made its own in the previous year and one on which the left was widely seen to be vulnerable. This does not mean, suggests one expert on both French politics and the media, that there was a conspiracy, expressly designed to favour one side over the other. As Kuhn (2004: 30) notes, a regular diet of crime may have helped make the latter an important criterion on which voters evaluated the candidates, but it did so largely because it conformed to conventional news values, suited TV's claims to be in touch with 'the people' and tapped into (as well as perhaps feeding) what opinion polls suggested were genuine concerns.

Researchers from a Marxist and/or cultural studies perspective would also suggest that the effect of the media simply cannot be traced over a short period, like an election. For them, the political power of the media has much more to do with the general legitimation of governments sitting atop (and doing very little about) pervasive structural inequalities. We might, the argument goes, struggle against some of these if our attention were not so distracted and our aspirations so limited by the 'non-political' product served up to us nightly by a corporate oligopolists, as well as by the public broadcasters increasingly forced to compete with them on their terms (see Curran, 2002).

These critics may have a point. For one thing, some argue (though not uncontroversially) that television militates against active involvement in society, political and otherwise (see Putnam, 2000). For another, it is hardly the stuff of crude conspiracy theory to suggest that the media, particularly the privately owned media, is unlikely to produce shows of any genre (current affairs or soaps) that routinely question and undermine the idea that liberal capitalism is the inevitable and best system, especially with advertisers breathing down their necks – evidence for which is plentiful in the US (see Campbell, 2004: 62–3) even if the topic is under-researched in Europe. Even if the media avoid systematically (though perhaps unconsciously) excluding those who question the consensus completely, it may well *frame* them negatively. It is not hard for journalists, if they want to, to present people as extreme (far-right or far-left organizations), disruptive (unions in industrial disputes or environmentalists taking direct action) or possibly violent (animal rights and anti-globalization protest groups).

Pressure groups and populists

But if this partial exclusion and negative framing is going on, it does not seem to have marginalized all the groups just mentioned. Indeed, as we shall see in Chapter 8, a number of them seem to be flourishing – something that is often put down (not least by their corporate opponents and by governments) to their skill in exploiting, of all things, the media! Rather than being a target for the media or

influence: because we cannot hope to measure or prove it, does that mean it is unimportant? Given the current state of our empirical knowledge, it would be more 'scientific' to say that the capacity of the media to help determine politicians' beliefs and behaviours is negligible; but would that be true? By the same token, it would be very hard to prove beyond doubt that politicians were able to influence the editorial line of the media; but it seems unlikely that, to use a recent example, governments' need for support at a time of crisis played no part whatsoever in the way most European newspapers swung in behind the supposed consensus on the need for military action to end Serbian aggression in Kosovo in 1999 (see Eilders and Luter, 2000 and Savarese, 2000). Equally, the extent to which those newspapers, by their actions, helped in some way to construct that consensus and build public support for it is very difficult, perhaps ultimately impossible, to judge.

running the risk of being ignored or sidelined by it, many pressure groups are an ideal source of stories. As a result, they can claim to play an important part in the agenda-setting 'issue-attention cycle' (see Downs, 1972) that politicians and governments may try to manipulate but – given the disdaining attitudes and the acceleration of news delivery – are possibly less and less able to control.

On a practical level, the groups' now-professionalized media staff do a lot of the investigative work news organizations cannot themselves afford to do, and go on to reproduce it in effective, easily digested formats that the organizations can rapidly turn into finished product. Their sometimes conflictual and often highly visual modes of engagement – mass protests, daring stunts, and so on – dovetail well with conventional news values, especially those of television. They also provide journalists with an alternative to more conventional news sources, such as governments, parties and corporations, to whom the public and journalists alike seem to afford less and less trust and respect. This is particularly the case where groups appear to be taking 'the public's' side against those other institutions in situations where the latter seem intent on ignoring popular feeling: hence the media 'sexiness' of protests against genetically modified (GM) crops.

All this brings some comfort to those on the progressive end of the political spectrum, seeming as it does to bear out Habermas's reformulation of the public sphere as a much more contested, congested and potentially transnational space in which civil society can use the media to transmit concerns to the political core and which thus acts as a countervailing power (see Curran, 2002: 135–6). But this also has what some would see as a darker side. 'Media-savvy' cause groups are undeniably attractive to a media keen to put itself onside with the public against a 'political class' that increasingly has to justify inclusion in coverage on news values alone. But so, too, are charismatic populists from the other end of the political spectrum. Prepared to say what 'everyone' is thinking in terms that anyone can understand, and launching attacks on 'the establishment' that 'no-one' likes or trusts in a style that resonates with almost universally-held news values, men like Jörg Heider in Austria, Jean-Marie Le Pen in France and the late Pim Fortuyn in Holland, are (or were) a news editor's dream. Little wonder that, in a public sphere increasingly dominated by media logic, their more mainstream opponents, constrained by the compromises inherent in responsible politics but condemned for 'spin' if they try to compete, are finding life harder and harder.

Cyberpolitics

It is not just trends in the conventional, 'mass' media that play into the hands of populists and promotional groups. By speeding up communication (including communication with the mass media), information technology (IT) has significantly cut the cost of starting from scratch. It also has the advantage of appealing to some who would otherwise by-pass politics, particularly the young. The internet is making a difference to politics, allowing non-conventional political actors rapidly to network their way to prominence and perhaps success (see Webster, 2001). It is also encouraging more conventional political actors across Europe – such as parties (see Gibson, Nixon and Ward, 2003, and Gibson, Römmele and Ward, 2003) and trade unions (see Ward and Lusoli, 2003) – to try and pull off the same trick, even if they are still at the stage of using the new technology simply to speed up and spruce up what they do already.

But the extent to which the web has blown (or will blow) 'politics-as-usual' out of the water can be overdone (see Norris, 2001). This is especially the case given different levels of penetration in different countries (see Figure 7.3) and the *digital divide* that seems set to separate, old and young, rich and poor and even English- and non-English-speaking (see Dahlgren, 2000, Hill and Hughes, 1998, and Norris, 2001). Just as in the world of commerce, there will be a few new entrants who do well by doing something no-one has done before (Microsoft, Apple, Amazon, Google, etc.). But most of the gains have been made and will be made by existing organizations who harness the new technology to allow them to do better what they have been doing reasonably successfully for years now. Big pressure groups that take an increasingly global (as opposed to purely domestic – or, indeed, European – view) of the causes they are interested in (see Chapter 8) – for instance, Greenpeace or Friends of the Earth or Amnesty International – are already finding the web helps them do what they have been doing for some time namely, mobilizing and aggregating otherwise passive and fragmented audiences whose feelings and/or purchasing power (see Bennie, 1998) can be used to outflank companies and, indeed, states (see Rodgers, 2003: chapters 4 and 5).

Just as there is a lot of hype and hyperbole surrounding the influence of the media more generally, especially on voters, there is a great deal of potentially unfounded speculation concerning the impact of new technology on how people use the media and how the media will interact with politics. This is not to say that things will not change significantly. Nor is it to assert that styles of communication that are now peripheral – 'blogging' by politicians is one example (see Ferguson and Howell, 2004) – will never catch on in ways that profoundly alter, say, the relationship between electors and elected. It is only to suggest that at the moment it is, to coin a cliché, too soon to tell. Future textbooks may well describe a politics and a media that are unrecognizable and even unimaginable from those described here. Yet, inertia is a powerful force in most cultures, and Europeans are just as likely as anyone else to adapt to novelty rather than adopt it wholesale. Certainly, anyone who assumes that the potential proliferation of spaces for political expression and activity offered by IT will be realized may be fooling themselves, especially when one considers the uses (largely commerical and leisure-based) to which the web is currently put by most citizens. And while it may well lead to what some would consider a welcome expansion of ideological diversity, the extent to which that expansion will be meaningful (in the sense of altering policy outcomes, for instance) is equally open to doubt.

To some, the fact that the impact of the net on politics may be oversold may not be such a bad thing. To them, the 'digital divide' between those who do and do not have access to the internet seems likely to perpetuate existing political inequalities and participation rates. Interestingly, however, one thing that Figure 7.3 indicates is that access to the net seems to vary as much, if not more, across European nations as it does across

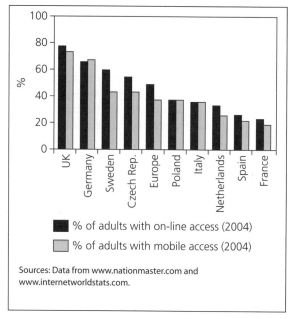

Figure 7.3 Usage of ICT in the EU

social classes. Figure 7.3 also shows figures for mobile phone penetration. This is not just for good measure; it is perhaps the case that if we are looking at the internet for the impact of ICT on politics, we may be looking in the wrong place. It could be that mobile telephony will have a far bigger impact.

The political impact of the mobile phone is becoming apparent in the activity of some of the protest groups we look at in Chapter 8. Both fuel protesters and environmental activists – and, indeed, the so-called 'anarchists' who have helped kick off violence at recent EU summits – use mobiles to organize. And they are not the only ones. European parties have already made huge advances in campaigning not via the net, but via call centres. Now, they are beginning to use text messaging on election day in order to get their known supporters out to vote. In some cases, governments have woken up to the potential, too. Predictably, perhaps, it was the Italian government run by Silvio Berlusconi which sent a text message to all Italians with mobiles reminding them to vote in the European elections of 12 and 13 June 2004. Unfortunately, it was a course of action that landed him in hot water with political opponents and those who wondered who had paid the estimated

€3 million cost: if it was the government, was it a waste of money and a breach of privacy; if it was *Forza Italia*, why did the message go through the government? Leaving aside these questions, however, it is perhaps significant that turnout in Italy (always high) was actually up in 2004 (73 per cent compared to 71 per cent in 1999), when across many other countries the decline was steep.

The media and 'Europe'

A certain amount of scepticism is warranted when it comes to considering the extent to which the media has affected politics in Europe by helping to construct a 'European' identity or promote a greater understanding of either other countries or the EU among its citizens. It is difficult to see its impact in these areas as much more than minimal, not least because there is as yet no genuinely pan-European media presence on the Continent. There is, as we have seen, a degree of Europeanization at the level of regulation and ownership. And there are clearly a handful of countries that have so much in common with their neighbours, not least linguistically, that they are happy to, say, watch their television and even read their news (see Box 7.12) – even if the flow tends to be one- rather than two-way.

Yet, there is as yet no genuinely European media market at the level of product. This is in spite of it being over a decade since the EU's 1991 *Television Without Frontiers* Directive came into effect (preventing member states from placing restrictions on the transmission of broadcasting from other member states) and despite the growth of cable and satellite television, to which getting on for a half of households in the Union now subscribe. Ultimately, European media integration faces a huge hurdle; namely, the cultural and language barriers that do so much to make the continent the diverse place it is (see Richardson and Meinhof, 1999). Attempts to create genuinely 'Euro-TV' have so far proved difficult: the audience share of pan-European channels 'rarely passes the 1 per cent mark' (Chalaby, 2002: 189). Programming with obvious cross-cultural appeal such as sport and music has achieved limited

BOX 7.12
Permeable borders: British media in the Irish Republic

Homegrown media and homegrown media businesses in Ireland are in rude health. Tony O'Reilly's *Independent* group may be based there, but it owns titles all over the English-speaking Commonwealth and in the United Kingdom itself. Even local newspapers retain a degree of political importance because of the 'pork-barrel' politics encouraged by the country's STV system, which allows voters to express preferences for particular candidates who therefore have an incentive to 'reward' voters with tangible achievements such as local roads, bridges and health centres. This media vibrancy, however, has done nothing to prevent penetration of the Republic's market by UK interests (see Collins and Butler, 2004). British tabloids are cheap compared to Irish papers and are quite popular – especially the *Sun* and the *Mirror*, customized Irish editions of which sell around 110,000 and 75,000, respectively. British papers in general make up a quarter of all daily sales and a third of all sales on a Sunday, when the broadsheet *Sunday Times* sells nearly 100,000 copies and the tabloid *News of the World* nearly 170,000. When it comes to broadcasting, the UK's Granada Media owns Ireland's terrestrial commercial broadcaster, TV3, while most homes in Ireland have no problem receiving, without satellite, British terrestrial television. Indeed, the importance of the latter should not be underestimated. In 1997, an Independent MP was elected to the Irish Parliament, the *Dáil*, on a ticket of preventing the removal of 'deflector' masts that, while legally dubious, ensured good reception of British TV throughout most of Ireland! Interestingly, getting rid of the masts would have delivered the distribution of the British channels (via a pay-TV system) to the owner of the *Independent*. Whether, though, this had anything to do with that paper's famous election-eve, front-page call for readers to vote against the incumbent government (which was dragging its feet on removal) we may never know. It certainly failed to persuade those who were elected in its place to act: the deflector masts remain to this day!

success, but even this – like the 'reality TV' concepts that turn into quite different shows when they are exported into foreign markets – has required skilful (and expensive) 'localization' or tailoring to different national audiences who, on balance, prefer domestically-oriented (even if foreign-inspired) programming (see Chalaby, 2002).

This preference, moreover, is supported by governments and parliaments who routinely insist on broadcasters showing a prescribed quota of domestically produced material as a condition of their licences. This insistence (mirrored by the EU Directives that insist on quotas for European programmes, apparently in order to stave off American hegemony) characterizes not just western but also central and eastern Europe. There, an acute awareness of the importance of the media in 'nation-building' (maintaining a sense of identity and community) has, in combination with the still widespread belief among elites that the media should reflect the views of the government, often trumped enthusiasm for market liberalization (see Sparks, 1997: 112–14).

All of this means that, with the possible exception of a few transnational 'top people in the Brussels micro-polity' of the EU and their interlocutors in government and business circles in Europe's capitals, there is no such thing yet as a 'European public sphere'. Apart from the *Financial Times* and a handful of upmarket satellite news broadcasters, there is no media space in which 'European citizenship' (see Meehan, 1993) can fully develop, certainly not without major inequalities in access and information (see Schlesinger, 1993 and Schlesinger and Kevin, 2000).

On the other hand, these kinds of analyses may be unduly pessimistic. For a start, the conception of a 'European public sphere' that they employ is arguably too ambitious. To pass their test, such a sphere would need to be truly supranational rather than (less ambitiously) simply multidimensional, encompassing multilevel linkages in mediated political coverage between the national and the European. In fact, with the exception of the UK (where the focus remains heavily internalized) these multilevel communication linkages are becoming more common. While political stories covered by the 'continental' media are still predominantly national, many of them also involve national figures commenting or 'making claims' about other European countries or the EU – espe-

cially where these 'European' actors can reasonably be expected to have an impact on policy (for instance, monetary policy and currency matters, rather than, say, pensions). As a result, the most thoroughgoing (and ongoing) comparative investigation argues that (with the exception of the UK) 'we can speak of a Europeanized public sphere to the extent that a substantial – and over time increasing – part of public contestation neither stays confined to the own national political space ... , nor extends beyond Europe without referring to it' (Koopmans, 2004).

This qualification notwithstanding, it remains true that a media beginning to Europeanize at the level of ownership and regulation seems unable to do much to Europeanize its product and, by implication, those who consume it. But can it at least improve their knowledge and their goodwill concerning the European Union itself? Bluntly, the answer seems to be 'no' – for several reasons. One former EU Commissioner, the UK's Chris Patten, probably put his finger on one of the key, but possibly intractable problems, at a conference held in London in February 2002 to discuss the British media's ignorance and negative treatment of European affairs: 'So much of what the EU does is, frankly, boring and technocratic. It does not lend itself to simple or attractive reporting.' But the media also share some of the burden of responsibility. Although there is evidence to suggest that European elections, for instance, do spark at least a modicum of interest in and information gathering on the EU by ordinary people, the effect very soon wears off – and it seems to be decreasing (along with turnout!) with each election (see Lord, 2004: 60–1). This should come as no surprise, however, given what research has revealed about media coverage – research summarized as part of Christopher Lord's admirable (and surely timely) 'democratic audit' of the EU (see Lord, 2004: 62–4; see also Kevin, 2003).

For a start, media coverage is 'sporadic' and 'events-based', often concentrating (unsurprisingly) on personalized conflict and bad news. It also varies across countries with regard to the amount of time and space devoted to EU matters, though there is no simple connection between lots of attention and enthusiasm in that member state for the EU. Secondly, while we should be careful not to forget that different media outlets in the same country will place their own meanings on the same piece of EU news (see, for example, the study of Italian portrayals of the launch of the euro in Triandafyllidou, 2003), the EU is nonetheless presented largely through national frames and filters. In other words, the focus is often on what 'it' (an external actor) is doing for or to 'us'. Not only is each nation therefore supplied with a different take on the same issue, but each is presented with a different notion of what the EU is about. For instance, if one compares German and British media coverage, the latter tends to present the EU as all of a piece whereas the former more often breaks it down into its component institutions; when the UK media does that, however, supranational institutions (the ones 'we cannot control' like the Commission) are four times more likely to be mentioned than the (arguably more powerful) intergovernmental ones. Lastly, the coverage of EP elections differs between countries, but only to the extent that some countries' media provide their publics with the most basic coverage while others fail to do even that. In the Netherlands in 1999, for instance, the EP elections 'took up only 1 per cent of total [TV] news coverage during the campaign', compared to the 27 per cent devoted to the general election campaign the year before – probably because those responsible for producing the news saw the EP elections (rightly or wrongly) as a 'non-issue' that meant nothing to voters (de Vreese, 2001: 168–9).

Hardly surprising, then, that the public throughout Europe confess in *Eurobarometer* surveys that they are not very knowledgeable about the EU (the average is around 4 on a scale of 1–10). This does not help support for the EU, which (as Table 7.3 suggests) seems to be correlated with thinking it is a good thing (though which way round the correlation runs is not clear). Clearly, this lack of support does little to boost participation in EP elections, and nor therefore can those elections boost interest in the EU. We should, though, qualify this gloomy picture by remembering that the issue of European integration may be becoming part of party political debate (see Chapter 5) and has recently featured in several European elections – something that is reflected in campaign coverage (see Semetko, de Vreese and Peter, 2000: 130–1). Whether this will be enough to stop what seems to be a vicious, rather than a virtuous, circle from turning, however, is a moot point. Certainly, the low level and poor quality of coverage of EU issues may well have major implications for any attempt to offset the relatively low level of European identification in some countries (see Chapter 1). But it also has more serious, less normative but more nitty-gritty implications. While the 'general public' of European countries is looking elsewhere, organized groups who, by definition, do not necessarily have 'the general interest' at heart are busy making their presence and their pressure felt. It is to these groups that we now turn.

Table 7.3 Support for EU membership and self-perceived knowledge about the EU			
My country's membership is …	*Knowledge Low (1–3) (%)*	*Knowledge Average (4–7) (%)*	*Knowledge High (8–10) (%)*
A good thing	37	55	64
Neither good nor bad	37	28	16
A bad thing	14	15	19
Don't know	12	3	1

Source: Data from *Eurobarometer* (60, 2003).

Learning resources

The literature on politics and the media is massive. A conveniently concise start would be Dahlgren (2000) or chapter 5 of Curran (2002). Anyone wanting a full-length comparative study should consult Hallin and Mancini (2004). Also useful is Gunther and Mughan (2000). On Europe and the media, see Kevin (2003). A piece that should stimulate argument and thought is Barnett (2002). So, too, should Norris, (2000). And of course, you should try out some newspapers and their websites. These are not confined to highbrow 'broadsheet' titles, although these sometimes have the advantage of publishing english-language editions (see, for example, http://www.faz.com or go to http://www.iht.com/global.html to get an English version of *El País* from Spain or *Kathimerini* from Greece). For a taster of what Europe's tabloids have to offer, try http://www.thesun.co.uk/ and (notwithstanding the language barriers!) http://www.bild.t-online.de/BTO/ and http://www.aftonbladet.se/. An absolutely 'must-visit' website for those interested in media ownership and the history of the media worldwide, allowing you to search by country, region, media group and keyword is http://www.ketupa.net/sitemap.htm. Anyone interested in the freedom of the press should also consult Freedom House's annual press surveys that can be found online at http://www.freedomhouse.org.

EXECUTIVE SUMMARY

- There are considerable variations between countries in media use, ownership and regulation, although all combine commercial systems with more or less independent public broadcasting.

- Politicians and the media enjoy a relationship characterized by mutual dependence and antagonism. The media environment is now more fragmented and political coverage possibly more personalized Parties have lost their uncontested right to access and their attempts to maintain control of the agenda have resulted, in some countries, in a media backlash.

- TV is indisputably the medium politicians care most about since it has the biggest reach and, like radio, is generally a more trusted source than the press.

- The evidence for media influence on election outcomes is thin (although not non-existent) and it could be that the media (and campaigning more generally) will become more important as voting becomes more volatile. The media's role in setting agendas and enhancing the salience of some concerns over others is probably more important than any direct effect.

- As yet, new ICTs do not appear to have had much of an impact on conventional politics, although there is some evidence that less traditional actors are making use of its potential. They are in any case at some advantage in as much as their activities are consonant with 'news values'.

- Even though European rules have an impact on regulatory regimes, which may have helped to boost cross-ownership between European countries, there remain considerable practical obstacles to a truly pan-European market, let alone a 'public sphere'.

Chapter **8**

Pressure politics: civil society, organized interests and new social movements

Pressure groups: different types, different opportunities

Pluralism and corporatism

Farming: a real-world example of power under pressure

There is (still) power in a union

Taking care of business

Rebels with a cause: NGOs and new social movements

'Venue shopping' and the Europeanization of pressure politics

The idea at the heart of representative democracy in Europe (see Chapter 6) is that citizens play a role in their own governance via the election of parliaments (and possibly presidents). It is also generally accepted that, like it or not, parties play a mediating role, helping to structure choices and aggregate interests, be they economic or cultural or religious (see Chapter 5). At the very least, according to the Austrian economist and political analyst Joseph Schumpeter – a man who thought too much citizen participation would be unworkable – parties provide competing teams of managers that we can choose between at the ballot box. But it would be a very 'thin' conception of democracy indeed that supposed citizens would – or, indeed, should – be content between elections to leave things to the politicians and the bureaucrats. After all, the policies initiated and implemented between those elections will rarely suit everyone and may even be seen as unfair by some people. As individuals, people are rarely so powerful that they can hope to influence policy on their own. They are therefore likely to band together in order to secure the introduction, prevention, continuation or abolition of whatever measures they feel are important to them – a tendency that, since de

Tocqueville, has been celebrated as one of the indicators and bastions of a healthy democracy.

It is this associative activity that constitutes a country's civil society (see Box 8.1) – something that, it is claimed, not only minimizes the risk of an over-mighty and unresponsive state, but also helps create (as well as draws on) the '**social capital**' that some see as essential for a genuinely participatory democracy and a healthy economy (see van Deth *et al.*, 1999, Hooghe and Stolle, 2003 and Putnam *et al.*, 2000). It is this kind of collective action and the political response to it that this chapter explores.

Definition

In the words of its most prominent supporter (Putnam 2000: 19):

Whereas physical capital refers to physical objects and human capital refers to the properties of individuals, **social capital** refers to connections among individuals – social networks and the norms of reciprocity and trustworthiness that arise from them.

The chapter begins by looking at pressure groups, the ways they have been classified and variations in which may explain variations in the way they work and in their relative success. It then moves on to look at two classic categories in which European states have been placed in relation to the role of organized interests – pluralism and corporatism – to see to what extent these 'ideal types' (used by social scientists to simplify analysis) tell us anything useful about the real world. It focuses in particular on two key real-world examples: first, a group that is often said to be very close to government and successful all over Europe – the

BOX 8.1
What is civil society?

Civil society is a term more often bandied about than defined. The best short definition is probably by the political theorist David Held (1987: 281), who sees it consisting of 'areas of social life – the domestic world, the economic sphere, cultural activities and political interaction – which are organized by private or voluntary arrangements between individuals and groups outside the direct control of the state'. A good longer definition is the one used by the London School of Economics' Centre for Civil Society (see http://www.lse.ac.uk/collections/CCS/). According to the Centre, civil society is:

the arena of uncoerced collective action around shared interests, purposes and values. In theory, its institutional forms are distinct from those of the state, family and market, though in practice, the boundaries between state, civil society, family and market are often complex, blurred and negotiated. Civil society commonly embraces a diversity of spaces, actors and institutional forms, varying in their degree of formality, autonomy and power. Civil societies are often populated by organizations such as registered charities, development non-governmental organizations, community groups, women's organizations, faith-based organizations, professional associations, trades unions, self-help groups, social movements, business associations, coalitions and advocacy groups.

BOX 8.2
New social movements

The label *new social movement* (NSM) is applied to pressure groups, many of which began to emerge in the 1960s, expressing a radical critique of mainstream societies, cultures and institutions for ignoring people and issues that did not fit conveniently or inexpensively into 'politics-as-usual'. Characteristic concerns include equality for women and for racial, ethnic and sexual minorities, the environment and animal rights, international peace and, more recently, globalization. Many observers see such concerns as typical of 'postmaterialism' and/or 'identity politics', wherein solidarity with a cause not directly associated with one's self-interest combines with a need for self-expression and self-realization to mean that 'the personal is political'. NSMs are also distinguished (at least, initially) by their commitment to more general anti-authoritarian and pro-egalitarian values – a commitment that also underpins the way they work: informal and fairly pluralistic networks, non-hierarchical structures and (what used to be thought of anyway as) non-conventional forms of protest, often involving (normally) non-violent direct action, such as marches, demos, sit-ins and boycotts.

agricultural lobby – and next one that many casual observers believe, we argue mistakenly, has been frozen out – the trade unions. It then looks, conversely, at business and discovers that it does not always 'win'. Both of these groups can be defined as 'interest groups' in the sense that they have something material to offer their members. To some theorists, this explains their success despite being outnumbered, if you like, by the general public. We question this idea by pointing to big national variations in the willingness of different nations to join groups and by looking at one of the most significant developments in Europe over the last three decades.

This is the mobilization of so-called *New Social*

Movements (Box 8.2) – groups that can offer people the chance to support a cause and, in so doing, express themselves and their values. We should not, though, be too naive. Many such groups have turned in to 'protest businesses'. Others are testament to the fact that the comfortable distinction between civil society (supposedly good) and not always non-violent direct action (widely regarded as bad) is not necessarily hard and fast. Finally, we look at the extent to which all the groups previously examined are operating at the European, transnational level.

Pressure groups: different types, different opportunities

Any organized attempt politically to promote a particular course of action or way of life which falls short of founding a party to contest elections can be labelled a 'pressure group'. But such groups take on many forms in twenty-first-century Europe. Some will clearly be based on self-interest on the part of those involved: these are sometimes labelled 'sectional' groups. Others may well be less self-regarding, and are known as 'cause' or 'promotional groups', though recently they may choose to call themselves NGOs (see Box 8.3).

Analysts have for some time found it useful to distinguish between what political scientist Wyn Grant labelled 'insider' and 'outsider' groups. The former had cosy, private and possibly more influential relationships with those in power, while the latter were excluded and therefore obliged to take a different, more public route that involved trying to shame rather than inveigle the government into action. More often than not, sectional interest groups were seen as insiders, providing the state with the information and the implementation infrastructure that otherwise it might have lacked in exchange for a degree of influence on policy. Cause groups, on the other hand, were seen as outsiders. These distinctions, which were never hard and fast (see Box 8.4), may be proving increasingly redundant. Governments have tried, in the spirit of 'the new public management' (NPM) to insulate themselves from the 'producer capture' (control of policy by insider groups) that too cosy a relationship with a pressure group may engender. And, as the structure of the economy has changed and economic growth weakened, they have also been less and less keen to provide the kind of payoffs that some of those groups might traditionally have expected. Conversely, the success of increasingly professional outsider groups at getting their issues onto the agenda has forced governments to take them more seriously and suggested to insider groups that they may have something to learn, particularly when it comes to using the media (see Chapter 7).

Nowadays, then, instead of particular strategies being associated with particular groups, they are best seen as a range of options which any group may exploit as it sees fit – bearing in mind, of course, that there may be a trade-off between, for example, a group embarrassing the government and how keen the government is to keep it in the

---

BOX 8.3

What's in a name? From pressure groups to NGOs

The leading British analyst of pressure group politics, Wyn Grant, has noted that:

> [A] new generation of pressure groups, typified by the environmental organization, Greenpeace ... would, of course, prefer to call themselves non-governmental organizations (NGOs) and regard themselves as part of something called 'civil society', beyond government but not part of the market economy. In politics, the way in which things are labelled is not an insignificant matter. If one disapproves of an organization, one calls it a vested interest. The term pressure group still carries negative connotations, while that of 'interest group' is more neutral, although might seem to apply only to sectional groups. The term NGO is now widely used, although mostly applied to environmental and other campaigning groups. In fact, traditional trade associations are just as much NGOs. The shift in terminology reflects, in part, a very favourable public perception of the new generation of NGOs ... This perception has been reinforced by the often-favourable attitude of the media towards such groups, in part because they provide the electronic media with good visual stories. (Grant, 2001: 337–38)

---

loop. Often, the decision of which path to pursue will be determined by circumstances or by what is sometimes referred to as the 'political opportunity structure' (Box 8.5) prevailing not just in each state but also, given the importance of the EU for some policy domains, Europe as a whole.

A good illustration of the point is provided by the extent to which (and the ways in which) pressure groups in different countries bother with parliament. Country studies gathered together by Philip Norton (1999) suggest that, for most, government is the main focus. However, they also suggest that the more chance the parliament has to modify and even make policy, the more effort groups put in to influencing it. Accordingly, the Italian parliament is seen not just as a channel to

BOX 8.4

The church: sectional or cause group, insider or outsider?

One of the most successful pressure groups in many European countries – even if it is not thought of as such – is the church. Given the precipitate decline in the number of devotees, the traditional religions have managed to retain many of their privileges and to maintain a possibly disproportionate influence on national life. Churches in Scandinavia and Germany for instance, still collect revenues, albeit on a voluntary basis, through the tax system. In Scandinavia, they have been instrumental in dissuading governments from liberalizing laws on alcohol consumption and opening hours. Meanwhile in other countries, including Spain, Ireland and especially Poland, they have managed not just to protect vast financial assets but also to exert a brake-like effect on political responses to social change, most obviously when it comes to education and, in particular, the abortion law.

BOX 8.5

Political opportunity structure

The idea of a *political opportunity structure* originates from research into social movements. It suggests that the strategies and the success of groups, while obviously dependent on contingency and on factors internal to the group, such as effective leadership or resources, also depend on more consistent institutional and even cultural factors. While there is considerable debate among scholars as to what it does and does not include (see McAdam, McCarthy and Zald, 1996), the following would seem to be important in the context of most European states:

▶ Supranationalism – is there an authority above the nation state?

▶ Governance – does federalism or decentralization mean there are 'multiple veto players', is parliament strong or weak, are groups expected to play a part in running the country and its economy? Do, for instance, civil servants and ministers traditionally consult with non-governmental actors and/or rely on them for implementation?

▶ Party system – is it fragmented and polarized, or restricted to just a few parties who are all relatively centrist?

▶ Media – is it centralized, is it populist, is it trusted, is it independent of the state?

▶ Other groups – is the market place of ideas and influence crowded?

▶ Public opinion – do people regard all or only some forms of direct action as acceptable in a democratic, civilized society?

get to where the real power lies, but a target in itself. Generally, pressure groups focused on committees, not only because they regarded this as the best way of getting their views on record – a particular attraction for 'outsider' groups – but also because this was where small, but perhaps significant, changes could be made. The country studies also suggested a significant difference in the relationships between groups and parliamentarians. In Germany and the Netherlands, the relationship is both formalized and in some ways incestuous: many MPs started off in pressure groups and maintain strong links with them, although, interestingly, this is now declining with the rise of the 'career politician'. Such a decline will make those countries rather more like the UK, where the relationship between pressure groups and parliamentarians has always been rather more indirect.

Pluralism and corporatism

Underpinning the political opportunity structure in each state are national traditions – not immov-

able, but nonetheless influential – concerning the extent to which groups, particularly groups representing employers and employees, are expected (and expect) to play a role in governance alongside the state. Some European states can be said to have a tradition of **pluralism**, while others are traditionally **corporatist**.

However, as is often the case in political analysis, these are ideal types. Even supposedly corporatist

Definition

In **pluralist** countries, the government may of course, take advice from and occasionally rely on groups, especially for implementation of its policies; generally, however, groups are supposedly kept at arm's length, granted access to make their case but given no special favours. Countries with a **corporatist** tradition, on the other hand, are those in which so-called 'peak organizations (such as the national federations of trade unions and employers) have an institutionalized role in the planning and the implementation of certain key state policies, notably on the economy and social policy. Traditionally, meeting with each other and with the government in so-called 'tripartite' bodies, groups make (and, crucially, stick to) trade-offs which are supposedly in the best interests of the whole country: a typical example would be unions agreeing to wage restraint in return for employers' efforts to maintain employment, with both trusting the government to do its best to maintain a stable and benign economic environment.

BOX 8.6
Sweden: the coexistence of corporatism and parliamentary democracy

The trade unions, via two federations – the massive LO (*Landsorganisationen*) and the smaller more white-collar TCO (*Tjänstemännens Centralorganisation*) – have an institutionalized place at all levels of Swedish governance. They have places on the boards of many of the agencies that play such an important part in the running of the country (see Chapter 3). The employers, via the SAF (*Svenska Arbetsgivareföreningen*) used to enjoy the same rights, but have recently argued that such bodies should be left to politicians alone. Despite this, and despite their criticisms of labour law and national wage bargaining, however, they continue to work with the unions and the government to maintain an 'active labour market policy', aimed less at creating employment and more at maintaining and improving 'employability' by facilitating training and mobility (geographical and between benefits and work). This helps to ensure that the economy, which is heavily export-oriented, retains its flexibility and capacity for low-inflationary growth despite the relatively high wages, taxes and benefits that are associated with what is sometimes called the 'Swedish model' (see Chapter 9). Yet none of this means there is no place for parliament. Indeed, the *Riksdag* is acknowledged to be one of Europe's most powerful legislatures (see Chapter 4). In fact, there is no 'zero-sum game' between corporatist-style concertation and parliamentary democracy. The *Riksdag*'s *remiss* system illustrates this nicely: each piece of proposed legislation is sent out to pressure groups (and to the wider public, if they wish) for comment before being formally introduced as a bill before the country's MPs.

European states have been wary of the degree of compulsion, monopoly, and (some would argue) economic sclerosis that full-blown corporatism might potentially entail; they can at best be labelled 'neo-corporatist'. In these countries there is, in certain sectors, a degree of 'concertation' between government and groups that other countries (and certainly neo-liberal right-wingers) might frown on. Indeed, as we suggest later, such concertation, far from disappearing, has made something of a comeback in recent years. But such concertation comes nowhere near undermining or replacing democratic government, as some critics of corporatism allege. Some of the countries in which this kind of sectorally-specific 'liberal corporatism' and 'tripartism' is especially strong also have strong parliaments: Germany is one, Sweden another (see Box 8.6). In any case, by no means all pressure groups or sectors are involved in, or benefit from, what tend to be framework agreements between what are routinely called in Europe (and in EU jargon) 'the social partners' (i.e. unions and employers or their 'peak associations'). Equally, as we shall see, there is no European state (and what-

ever its zealous advocates in the US might maintain, probably no state in the world) where pluralism is so pure that it does not systematically advantage some groups over others.

The way in which a group tries to exert influence depends on the political opportunity structure of the state or states in which it operates, but in all cases its success is likely to be based on its ability and willingness to:

▸ provide the state with something it needs but cannot or is unwilling to provide for itself in sufficient measure to allow it complete autonomy: financial/human resources; information/ expertise/knowledge;

▸ seriously put at risk the popularity either of the parties in government, or those that hope to be when that government is brought down.

To the extent that a group meets both of these criteria, and also to the extent that it is pressing a case to which there is little or only diffuse (rather than organized) opposition, it will tend to have a cosier relationship with those charged with the executive. Political scientists as we saw in Chapter 3, label the cosiest of these institutionalized relationships (or policy networks) 'policy communities', while at the other end of the spectrum are what they call 'issue networks'. Once again, of course, we have moved into the realm of the ideal type. In real-world Europe things are rather more messy and, indeed, changing over time, as we can see when we look, for example, at agricultural policy.

Farming: a real-world example of power under pressure

The archetypal policy community in many European states is often said to be agriculture. As we saw in Chapter 1, farming contributes less and less to European economies relative to other sectors. Yet it continues to attract vast subsidies from all European states, the bulk of which are now disbursed through the EU's CAP – a mechanism which, critics argue, allows the cost of subsidizing the sector to be hidden from voters at the domestic level. That may be true, but there are good reasons to suppose that even if it were not the case, agriculture would be relatively insulated from interference. For one thing, while European consumers do pay more for food than they need to, food nevertheless takes up a steadily declining proportion of family expenditure as increases in real wages have, over decades, outstripped increases in prices. Traditional notions about the rejuvenating simplicity, beauty and tradition of rural ways of life also continue to occupy an important place in

our conceptions of what it means to be, say, French, or Danish or Polish.

Taken together, this means that there is little opposition to what, if it were applied to industry, for example, might be seen as 'featherbedding' (making life so easy for producers, often via subsidies or protective measures, that they have no incentive to remain competitive). This makes for what political scientists refer to as an 'asymmetry of interests'. You have, on the one hand, a group of individual or family consumers who are not particularly bothered by subsidies just as long as food is reasonably cheap and plentiful. On the other, you have a highly organized group of farmers for whom the continuation of subsidies is a matter of the utmost importance, as well as politicians and bureaucrats who rely on them for their expert knowledge and their help in policy implementation. Given this asymmetry, the power of farming groups in every state – and just as importantly at the EU level, where they operate effectively under the umbrella of the the the Committee of Agricultural Organizations (COPA) – to extract money from governments with almost no questions asked by taxpayers is hardly surprising. Nor, of course, is it unique to Europe (see Smith, 1993).

Yet, the politics of agriculture also suggest that not even the tightest policy community can insulate itself entirely or for ever. First, this is because one sector invariably impinges on others. Secondly, once we dig a little deeper, we find that even the most well-organized pressure group contains within it a number of potentially conflicting interests. An illustration of the first point is the way in which the rather cosy relationship between farmers and governments has been disrupted in recent years by a number of food-scares whose trans-European implications are testimony to the extent of integration and interdependence. In such cases, the fear that practices in one sector, agriculture, may have negatively impacted on another (namely, health) meant that the policy community lost control over policy to the extent that political (though, interestingly, not agricultural) heads rolled (see Box 8.7). Common wisdom suggests that it sacrificed some long-term trust and legitimacy by being less than open about the issues involved. This can be overdone, however. In fact, levels of trust in food and farming in individual

European countries seem to be related more to levels of general political and personal trust than to whether or not a country has experienced food-scares or not: for example, the Italians, who have little experience of food-scares, are not very trusting compared to the British or even the Germans, who have had more than their fair share but appear to have been reassured somewhat by government reforms (see Poppe and Kjærnes, 2003).

Secondly, we need to realise that even the so-called 'agricultural lobby' is made up of many potentially conflicting parts. 'Feisty French farmers' are a common media stereotype across Europe, and especially in the UK, where their theatrical forms of protest – blocking roads, dumping manure, and so on – are guaranteed a place in the news. Interestingly, such antics are by no means an indicator that agriculture is an outsider group in a country that is still one of the largest exporters of food in the world. Indeed, they are testament to a political culture in which direct action has long been an acceptable (and effective) way of getting what you want and to the willingness – perhaps increasing willingness – of even well-connected pressure groups to pursue tactics that belie their categorization as 'insiders'. Yet, insiders is very much what they are. FNSEA (the French Farmers' Federation) for example, sends representatives to sit on state commissions responsible for setting both policies and prices, on ministerial advisory councils and on regional economic development bodies. Its former leaders have even held prominent political posts, particularly in administrations formed by the centre-right, which is particularly strong in the rural districts that some would say get a disproportionate number of seats in the National Assembly. In 1986, for instance, former FNSEA leader, François Guillaume was made agriculture minister in the 1986 Chirac government.

To some French farmers, however, 'insider' status has compromised their representatives, encouraging them into even more radical action: José Bové, who grabbed world headlines (and plenty of support) for an attack on a McDonald's franchise to protest at the plight of small farms in an increasingly globalized market, is one example. Similar protests about the agri-business domination of the National Farmers' Union (NFU) are

---

BOX 8.7
Pan-European food scares: the political fallout from economic integration

'Mad Cow Disease' or BSE first hits the headlines in the UK in 1998, just after a junior Health Minister is forced to resign when farmers' groups explode at her revelations about salmonella in British egg production. BSE peaks in the early 1990s, but British beef is subjected to a worldwide export ban by the European Commission when a link between BSE and a human equivalent (vCJD) is discovered in 1996. This does not prevent other countries suffering their own BSE outbreaks – including, most notably, Ireland, France, Portugal, Spain, Switzerland, and, in 2000, Germany, where the Social Democratic Minister of Agriculture (a farmer) resigns and is replaced by a Green.

In 1999, the political consequences are even more serious when Belgium reveals wide-scale poisoning of the country's poultry products by carcinogenic dioxins from inadequately cleaned feed storage tanks. Belgian and other European egg-based products are removed from supermarket shelves all over the world. Meanwhile, at home, the scare appears to be at least partly responsible not only for the resignations of the Health and Agriculture ministers, but also for a change of government in an election held in the midst of the storm. The Minister of Agriculture in the Netherlands also resigns after criticism that he failed to act swiftly enough.

In 2002, Germany is rocked by the news that chicken may have been contaminated by a banned carcinogenic herbicide (*nitrofen*) originating, as in Belgium, from inadequately cleaned feed storage tanks. At the same time, the agricultural policy community in the Netherlands is forced to cope with revelations that it has used and also exported pig feed contaminated (allegedly in Belgium via Ireland!) with a banned growth hormone, MPA – a serious situation because the country is the world's third largest exporter of pork. This time the authorities act very swiftly and with relative openness, and no resignations ensue.

occasionally heard in the UK, especially when times are tough (as they were, for example, in the foot and mouth outbreak in 2001). In Italy, the split is institutionalized: large- and small-scale farmers have traditionally organized in different groups, with the former's group, *Confagricoltura*, traditionally being less powerful than the latter's, *Coldiretti*, which historically controlled the para-public body, *Federconsorzi*, responsible with the Agriculture ministry for overseeing the sector.

There is (still) power in a union

Interestingly, Italy's farmers, whether large- or small-scale are not as powerful as their counterparts in France (or Britain, via the NFU, or Germany, via the *Deutscher Bauernverband*), which would seem to indicate that 'unity (especially when combined with the ability to recruit a majority of the potential members of a group) is strength'. The old adage certainly seems to hold good for one of the potentially most important pressure groups in any European country; namely, the trade unions. The patterned variation is very clear (Table 8.1). Countries where trade unions are fragmented by ideological and/or historical divisions and where they fail to recruit to their full potential take less account of the interests of labour, as opposed to those of business. In countries where the unions are concentrated (or at least willing to subordinate themselves to one 'peak' federation) and where they have high membership density (ie they recruit a large proportion of the workers available for recruitment) labour can expect to have its views taken into account. Often, indeed it will be institutionally involved in neo-corporatist economic and social management.

Once again, geography is not as good an indicator as history. True, Scandinavian unions (dense and concentrated) are powerful, but there is no typically 'Southern European' case. For instance, Italian unions may be fragmented but, even discounting for the large number of retired employees they continue to represent, they have far more members than unions in, say, France or Spain, where the importance of employee-elected works councils entering into binding deals with firms means that there is little incentive for workers thus represented (and bound) to join a union. And just as they were in the run-up to qualification for the single currency in the 1990s, Italian unions can be persuaded (at least, by centre-left governments) to dampen their demands for the supposedly 'greater good' of the country – something that is supposed to happen only in more corporatist countries.

Elsewhere in Southern Europe, Cyprus and Malta have density levels approaching those of Scandinavia, and Greece 'beats' Germany; the UK

Table 8.1 Union power

	Concentrated structure (%)	Loose structure (%)	Highly fragmented structure (%)
High membership density	Sweden (79)		
Medium membership density	Czech Rep. (30) Germany (30)	UK (29) Netherlands (27)	Italy (35)
Low membership density		Poland (15)	France (9) Spain (15)

Source: Data from European Industrial Relations Observatory, *Industrial Relations in the EU Member States and Candidate Countries*, 2002 (www.eiro.eurofound.eu.int).

and the Netherlands, where density levels match those of Portugal. Density varies considerably in Central and Eastern Europe, too: Slovenia and Slovakia (at around 40 per cent) are comparable with Ireland, while Hungary has only half as many unionized employees, and Lithuania, Latvia and Poland (see Box 8.8) even fewer. In the Czech Republic, workers disaffected with the communist regime infiltrated rather than (as in Poland) opposed the official trade unions, thereby enabling them, once democracy arrived, to benefit from their assets and organization (see Waller and Myant, 1994): this may explain why their density is on a par with that of the UK. Yet, clearly, unions are not perceived as worthwhile by most postcommunist workers, particularly younger people and those who work in the private sector. They may even be tainted by association with the 'official trade unions' of the Communist era. And they may suffer from what some see as a more general retreat into private life once 'people power' brought that era to an end (see Greskovits, 1998). Yet this variation should make us cautious about assuming some kind of uniform 'legacy effect'.

We should be careful, however, not to equate low union density and high fragmentation with complete and utter powerlessness. Just like their (rather more numerous but equally divided) Italian counterparts, France's trade unions have on several occasions, since the mid-1980s (most famously in 1995), employed direct action (strategic strikes and demonstrations) to derail plans by centre-right governments to make what they argued were much-needed labour market and pension reforms. And notwithstanding this kind of action (and the widespread belief that it is the only way to make France's supposedly aloof and elitist state listen), French unions are by no means absent from the dense undergrowth of advisory councils attached to all levels of the country's government. Conversely, we should remember that much of the power of the dense and concentrated (in the jargon 'encompassing') trade union movements may be more contingent than we think. True, their power is to some extent institutionalized through government consultation and (as in Sweden and Germany) membership of agencies and para-public bodies that help make and deliver welfare and labour market policies (see Chapter 3). But it also relies on

---

BOX 8.8
Poland's trade union movement: defeat from the jaws of victory

Poland's overthrow of Communist dictatorship was a triumph for the independent trade union, Solidarity (*Solidarność*), to whom some 60 per cent of Polish workers had belonged in the early 1980s and whose leader, Lech Wałesa, went on to be elected President of the newly created democratic republic. But any euphoria was short-lived. In contrast to its willingness to stand up to the old regime, Solidarity – legal once again – became an avid political sponsor of governments whose 'shock therapy' liberalization of the economy disadvantaged (at least, in the short term) many ordinary people. As a consequence, it never recovered its prestige – or, indeed, its membership. Taking into account the membership of Solidarity's rival, the OPZZ which has close affiliations with the social democrats, and a few much smaller unions, only 15 per cent at most of eligible Poles are union members; only in France is membership lower. As for those who do join, they tend to be older, poorer and much less likely to be employed in the go-ahead sectors of the economy that attract foreign capital, and whose owners seem determined to keep unions out. Such low density and fragmentation explains why most observers (not altogether fairly, see Iankova, 2002) write off Poland's 'Tripartite Commission on Socio-economic Issues' not as an indicator of incipient corporatism, but as a toothless 'talking shop' whose union delegates cannot possibly hope to deliver the co-operation of the Polish workforce – even if government and business organizations were of a mind to seek it.

Source: Data from European Industrial Relations Observatory, *Declining Trade Union Membership Examined*, European Industrial Relations Observatory (2002) (www.eiro.eurofound.eu.int).

---

their close relationship with social democratic parties. If the latter either lose office or, in office, are pushed by economic difficulties into taking 'tough decisions', then their trade unions allies may not appear quite so strong after all – especially if they simultaneously face rising unemployment. True, British trade unions were never able to embed corporatism in the same way as some of their continental and Scandinavian counterparts;

but their swift marginalization in the 1980s, after two decades or more of influence ('beer and sandwiches at Number Ten', etc.) are a case in point.

Looking outside the UK, however, it seems clear that corporatism – or at least government-facilitated 'concertation' between employer organizations and trade unions – has not gone away. If anything it has made a comeback recently – sometimes in the most unlikely places (supposedly liberal and pluralist Ireland being the most obvious example). Partly, this has been a response to exceptional circumstances. In the Netherlands, whose so-called 'poldermodel' (named after co-operative efforts needed to create and maintain land reclaimed from the sea) in some ways pioneered this new style of corporatism, co-operation between government, workers and employers came about in the 1980s in order to deal with fast-rising unemployment. In the 1990s, elsewhere in Europe, co-operation originated in the economic stability (and in some cases belt-tightening) that was required to ensure qualification for the single currency (see Chapters 1 and 9). Moreover, this new kind of corporatism is not necessarily (as, in fact, it is in Ireland) at a highly institutionalized national or 'macro' level. Instead it seems to be occurring at a more flexible, loosely-coupled, sectoral or 'meso' level, with success depending rather more than used to be the case on there being a social democratic presence in the government (see Baccaro, 2003, Blom Hansen, 2001, Compston, 1998 and Molina and Rhodes, 2002).

This kind of 'post-corporatist concertation' (O'Donnell, 2001), then, is more than a matter of cultural tradition: it is an instrumental and slightly more (party) political affair. Rather than creating obstacles to the growth that hopefully gets parties re-elected, government-enabled pacts between 'the social partners' have the potential to ensure that wage inflation does not undermine it. Getting unions on board also makes it easier for economies to promote active labour market strategies that enhance a country's human capital and workers' flexibility – the keys to competitiveness and productivity. Unions are also the key in many countries to governments pushing through pension reforms (see Anderson, 2001 and Baccaro, 2002) although, again, this is more likely to happen under centre-left governments (with whom the unions are more willing to work) than centre-right governments (whom they trust even less). Agreement between the social partners also helps to 'proof' policies against attempts to undo them by governments that may be composed of their opponents.

That said, as the examples of Sweden and especially Italy (see Vatta, 2001) suggest the support of the social partners, particularly the employers, is far more contingent than in the so-called 'golden age' of corporatism in the first three decades after the Second World War. We should also sound a note of caution about Central and Eastern Europe. There early moves toward setting up corporatist-style consultation between government, business and workers – the Polish 'Tripartite Commission on Socio-economic Issues' is a good example – produced (with the possible exceptions of Hungary and the Czech Republic; see Greskovits, 1998: 155–76 and Myant Slocock and Smith, 2000) little more than time-wasting 'talking shops'. Certainly, there seems to be little sign that any of the region's states will be emulating their western counterparts by experimenting with 'concertation' (see Bruszt, 2002: 135), although this could change when they, too, need to ensure economic stability in order to qualify for the euro. Even in western Europe, there is some doubt whether the attempt to blend supposedly 'neo-liberal' and 'corporatist' approaches to governing the economy really will allow some countries 'to continue having their cake and eating it too' (Boucher and Collins, 2003; see also Teague and Donaghey, 2003). But the fact that it is taking place at all strengthens the argument against the idea (discussed at greater length in Chapter 9) that Europe will and must eventually move in an 'Anglo-Saxon' or American direction.

Taking care of business

The power of farmers or unions in Europe, then, cannot be directly 'read off' from the quality or the extent or the coherence of its organization. And the same goes for the power of business. Take, for instance, the Spanish CEOE. The federation represents an impressive nine out of ten Spanish employers across a range of sectors. Yet, in the democratic era, and facing an ostensibly frag-

Poland (Polska)

Area: 7.9% of EU-25
Population: 8.5% of EU-25
GDP: 4.0% of EU-25
Joined EU: 2004
Capital city: Warszawa (Warsaw)

History: Poland was for centuries one of Europe's most disputed territories, its borders shifting time and time again as it fell victim to German and Russian imperial ambitions. For a time in the seventeenth century, it was one of the continent's largest states. Yet, between the end of the eighteenth century and the end of the First World War, Poland officially ceased to exist. It regained its independence in 1918 but democracy, always fragile and fractured by inordinately large numbers of parties, collapsed in 1926 when war-hero Marshal Pilsudski began a dictatorship that endured until 1935. Within four years, Poland had once again ceased to exist, initially carved up between Nazi Germany and Soviet Russia, and then occupied solely by the former after it invaded the latter in 1941, two years into the Second World War.

During the war, Poland lost around 6 million nationals or about one-fifth of its population, with half the victims Jews who perished in the Holocaust. Most, of course, were killed by the Germans. But the Russians, too, were brutal, massacring and secretly burying tens of thousands of Poland's military and civil elite at Katyn and other sites. And by failing to come to the aid of the Warsaw uprising in 1944, the Russians effectively allowed the Germans to kill hundreds of thousands of the city's population.

In the elections that followed the end of the war, the Russian-backed Communists took power and immediately began the process of dismantling democracy. Winning the hearts and minds of the people, however, proved far harder: both anti-Russian feeling and the Roman Catholic church remained strong. In 1978, Polish cardinal Karol Wojtyła was chosen as Pope Jean Paul II. His visit to Poland a year later, combined with industrial unrest in the country's important ship-building industry, saw the birth of the *Solidarność* (Solidarity) trade union, led by Lech Wałesa. Faced with the threat of a Russian invasion, the Communist authorities banned the union and imposed martial law in 1981. When, however, it became apparent some eight years later that the threat from the east no longer existed, the authorities began the round table process than led to the end of the Communist regime and the election of Wałesa as president. Since then, Poland has been governed by alternating coalitions led by a very fragmented centre-right or by the former Communist Party now standing as social democrats.

Economy and society: Initially touted as a shining example of 'shock therapy' (deregulation, currency reform and price liberalization), Poland's economy has recently given cause for concern: growth is back, but unemployment and state finances remain chronic problems. Poland's 38.6 million people have a GDP per capita of only 46% of the EU-25 average (2003). Although the importance of heavy industries such as coal and steel is declining as services begin to grow, the number of Poles working in what is a fragmented and inefficient agricultural sector is unusually high: whether it will drop with EU membership and any improved economic growth which follows will be interesting to watch. The Poles also stand out on account of their religiosity: Roman Catholic churches are well attended and remain an important influence on education, the media, and social mores and policy.

Governance: After flirting with the idea of a powerful president, Poland came down on the side of parliamentary democracy in its 1997 constitution, although even now the president (like the Senate in the country's bicameral legislature) has a veto over legislation. The veto can be overridden if the lower house (the *Sejm*) can muster a three-fifths majority – not always simple given that the country's proportional electoral system helps an unusually large number of personalized and antagonistic parties into parliament. The ability to build and sustain coalitions is therefore a key competence of the head of government, the prime minister, who is formally appointed by the president with the approval of the *Sejm*. There is a constitutional court, but it has not made many major interventions in Polish politics as yet, and neither the trade unions (including the once popular *Solidarność*), nor business associations are particularly powerful. Government in the countrys sixteen regions (*województwo*), however, is becoming more significant.

Foreign policy: The Poles have succeeded in achieving their two main priorities – protecting themselves from Russia and locking themselves into the European economy – by joining NATO (in 1999) and the European Union (in 2004). Cordial relations with Germany are accorded a particularly high priority by both countries. Relations with the US are also good: nearly 9 million Americans have Polish ancestry and many Poles remain grateful for the role the US played in defeating Communism in Eastern Europe; the country contributed forces to US-led missions in Afghanistan and Iraq.

Further reading: Millard (1999), Sanford (2002), Szczerbiak (2001) and Taras and Castle (2002).

mented union movement with few members, it has been unable to stave off labour market regulation which, while light compared to more corporatist countries, looks heavy compared to the regime in, say, Poland. There, in common with most CEE countries, civil society, at least as measured by associative activity, can hardly be described as burgeoning (see Howard, 2003). This is partly because many of those who might have taken an active leadership role were attracted instead by parliamentary politics. It is also because those who took over the old state enterprizes stuck with the personal and clientelistic *nomenklatura* (communist bureaucratic elite) networks they already knew. The fact that many new businesses were run by self-employed people or were very small also militated against associative activity (see Padgett, 2000). So, too (and this applies to pressure groups in general), did the desire of postcommunist governments of all stripes to avoid the creation of groups that could exercise countervailing power at a time when they were already concerned about their states' capacities to implement transitional reforms – concerns that probably led international organizations and, indeed, the EU, to do little or nothing to prod them into filling this 'institutional void' (see Bruszt, 2002). Over time, however, business associations are showing signs of institutionalizing and potentially becoming more influential, though often (and perhaps unfortunately) more through reputational and informal contacts than as-of-right formal processes (McMenamin, 2002). In the meantime, it must be said that Polish employers, relatively unencumbered as they are by government regulation, hardly seem to have been handicapped by the absence of powerful organized pressure groups fighting on their behalf.

Conversely, the vast majority of France's employers, accounting for some 800,000 firms, are represented by MEDEF (*Mouvement des Entreprises de France*), which since 1998, under the leadership of the combative Ernest-Antoine Seillière, has called for economic liberalization. It has not been entirely unsuccessful, but its influence has, first, been greater under conservative governments and, secondly, has not proved sufficient to budge them when they dig in their heels. For instance, France's centre-left government, elected in 1997, controversially introduced a maximum 35-hour week in order to 'share out jobs'. MEDEF managed to bring 30,000 businessmen out onto the streets to protest, albeit in vain, in 1999, but pressure on the centre-right government seems to have done the trick (see Chapter 9). Yet, the 'failure' of successive French governments to make it easier for bosses to hire and fire and to grasp the nettle on pensions and health costs belies MEDEF's claims to have put *l'entrepreneur au cœur de la société française* (the entrepreneur at the heart of French society). Similarly in Italy, the employers' organization, *Confindustria*, after a period of drift in the 1960s and 1970s (when individual firms such as Fiat exercised far more influence over policy than it ever could) has emerged as a dynamic advocate for liberal reforms. Indeed much was made of its partisan support for Silvio Berlusconi's *Forza Italia* party at the general election of 2001, particularly by Berlusconi himself. Yet the resulting centre-right government failed to deliver the pension reforms, tax cuts and labour market deregulation that the pressure group had demanded.

To some on the right of the political spectrum, the failure of business in some European countries to get government to deliver on its neo-liberal agenda is illustrative of the vestigial but nonetheless damaging influence of quasi-corporatist or statist arrangements. On the other hand, the fact that 'capital' in European countries cannot always get what it wants can be seen in positive terms: perhaps it reflects the vitality and value of pluralism in the face of criticisms from so-called 'neo-pluralists' (see Lindblom, 1977) that business is inevitably at a huge advantage, given the structural dependence of politicians on it to provide the economic growth that is normally vital to their re-election (see also Przeworski and Wallerstein, 1988). Of course, the fact that so many groups (unions being only the most obvious example) have a vested interest in a status quo that some regard as ultimately self-defeating can also be taken to illustrate the tendency of pluralism towards 'hyperpluralism' or 'overload' – a situation in which the sheer weight of groups forces goverments to take on more than they can handle and makes them unable to tackle serious problems (King 1975; see also Olson, 1982). This is precisely the interpretation that leant momentum to the 'new public management' (NPM) discussed in Chapter 3.

Rebels with a cause: NGOs and new social movements

Away from these arguments, however, there was traditionally a consensus that the prominence of business and unions, however qualified, proved that 'sectional' pressure groups which defend and promote the collective material interests of their members were likely to exert more influence in society than those that tried to do the same for so-called 'diffuse interests' – such as those of consumers – or for causes – such as 'the environment', 'peace' or 'developing countries'. This consensus was based on a theoretically persuasive explanation from what is labelled the *rational choice* school of political science (Box 8.9).

Sectional groups, the argument goes, tend to possess more of what government wants (in terms of resources, information and implementation). And, because they are more likely actually to pick up potential recruits in whichever sector they represent, they make it difficult for governments to appeal 'over their heads'. They recruit so well by offering what political scientists, following economists, call 'selective incentives' – largely material rewards that benefit only that group. Cause and even consumer groups, face a 'collective action problem' in that they have no significant selective incentives to offer a set of potential recruits. Even if material benefits exist, as they might for consumers if, say, price-fixing by a cartel of companies could be brought to a halt, recipients of those benefits are so numerous that any gain would be thinly spread and would be tiny compared to the gains of those doing the fixing – this is the 'asymmetry of interests' we referred to when discussing farmers. Additionally, if peace, an end to world-poverty and sustainability is achieved through the efforts of a cause group then everybody (aside, perhaps, from arms manufacturers and producers of pollutants!) will benefit. The fact that they can't be excluded from those benefits makes it rational for people to 'free-ride' on the efforts of a few activists.

That, of course, is the theory, but the reality – at least, in many European countries – is rather different. Domestic consumers, it has to be said, are still hard to organize, and pressure on prices and cartels tends to come from those businesses

BOX 8.9
Rational choice

Rational Choice is the name given to the idea, borrowed by political science from economics, that political phenomena can be explained by remembering that all actions are purposive, goal-oriented and 'utility-maximizing' within given constraints (see Elster, 1986 and Hargreaves Heap *et al.*, 1992). This allows the construction of formal models – often using 'game theory' – that enhance the study of politics' claim to be a science rather than a humanities subject, such as history. This has its downsides: in the wrong hands, it is capable of rendering the interesting uninteresting and the intelligible unintelligible; more profoundly, it relies on unrealistic assumptions about human behaviour and motivations, and can often be stronger theoretically than it is empirically (see Green and Shapiro, 1994). But it also has its upsides: in the right hands, it can cut through the detail to provide generalizations; in addition, proving why its hypotheses do not hold (or at least modifying them so that they accord with more realistic assumptions) can be an enormous boost to creative thinking and empirical research (see Dunleavy, 1991 and Friedman, 1996). Work on coalitions (i.e. why are there so many minority governments when a slim majority is surely the most rational option?) is one example (see Chapter 4). Work on groups and group members is another.

disadvantaged by them, rather than from the small consumer associations that do exist in Europe. The pressure also comes (as we shall see below) from the EU. However, the theory does little or nothing to explain why it is that the willingness to join groups – be they pressure groups or any of the other myriad social and cultural groups that make up civil society – is so different across Europe. Without going into too much detail, study after study has found that people in Scandinavian countries (and the Netherlands, possibly because of the tradition of church-based activity) are much more willing to join (and join several) groups, than are Southern Europeans, particularly those in Greece, Portugal, Spain, Italy (as a whole) and France, where activity is often more family- and friendship-based. Countries such as the UK, Germany, Belgium and Ireland sit somewhere in the middle. Eastern Europeans (see Howard, 2003) are very much in with their Southern counterparts. These variations can be partly explained by many factors (see Curtis, Baer and Grabb, 2001). Important ones seem to be differences in income, education, postmaterialist values – and possibly media consumption: put bluntly, the more television you watch, the less likely you are to get off the couch and go meet up to do things with other people in any kind of organized way, particularly if they are not already family or friends.

These regional differences are not the only reason to cast doubt on the theory. Notwithstanding the variation just mentioned, one of the major developments in Europe in the second half of the twentieth century was the growth of groups associated with what are sometimes labelled 'new social movements' (NSMs) (see Kriesi *et al.*, 1995). They are postmaterialist (see Chapters 5 and 6) in that they often focus on issues that, arguably, people struggling to make ends meet do not normally spend much time worrying about, especially if they lack the education that helps prompt or facilitate such thoughts in the first place. The spread of education and the comparative wealth that seem to have freed up so many Europeans (at least in the more prosperous west and north of the continent) to think about such issues has also given them the capacity to voice their concerns and to put their money where their mouths are. They also seem to have fuelled a concern with self-identity and the expression of that identity not just in consumption but in politics (see Della Porta and Diani, 1999). Simultaneously, the postwar growth of the electronic mass media (see Chapter 8) provided the ideal platform for the increasingly well-funded cause groups and non-governmental organizations (NGOs) to promote their ideals and exert pressure on both business and government.

NSMs have also been helped by, and might have done something to drive, the increased willingness (recorded in survey after survey) of people all over Europe to take political action that was previously seen as unconventional if not illegitimate (see Inglehart, 1999). While not necessarily rejecting conventional politics nor necessarily dissatisfied with democracy, people are less deferential. They

---

BOX 8.10

Different aims, similar tactics: direct action, old and new, in Germany

German anti-nuclear activists pioneered direct action tactics in the 1970s, so there was little that was new about the social movement-style protests that attempted to block the passage of a train carrying nuclear waste from France to a storage site in Gorleben in northwestern Germany in November 2001. Thousands of police officers, with dogs and helicopters and hundreds of metres of barbed wire, kept 1,000 protesters from disrupting unloading. Earlier, they had been forced to remove protesters who had chained themselves to railtracks. The shipment and the unloading went ahead, notwithstanding the government's commitment, long-term, to phase out nuclear power.

Just over a year before, in September, 2000, Germany, (as France, Italy, Spain and the UK) was hit by blockades mounted by lorry drivers, farmers and taxi drivers protesting against what they saw as unreasonably high petrol prices. Even though there were protests across Europe, they were not 'European' in the sense of being co-ordinated or targeted against the EU – in fact, their targets (and, in the end, the solutions they accepted) were domestic (see Imig, 2002: 917–18). In Berlin, more than 7,000 truck drivers brought the city centre to a standstill. This form of direct action had more effect, with the government (like other governments in Europe) announcing tax concessions to fuel users, notwithstanding its commitment to hiking eco-taxes.

---

will now demonstrate in the streets (and in the fields and trees!) in order to put their point across, be it idealistic or, as exemplified by the protests against high petrol prices that swept some countries in western Europe in 2000, utterly material (see Box 8.10). When it comes to idealism, the tendency to protest (in keeping with postmaterialist theory) is most associated with well-educated young people. In fact, though, it has been increasing since at least the 1960s. Indeed, there is even some suggestion that young people now, while still more likely than their parents to get involved in a demonstration, might not be quite as keen as those parents were when they were young. The fact that 'ordinary middle-class women', for instance, go on a demonstration is not, as the media suggest, simply a test of how much feeling there is about an issue but an indication of this 'cohort effect' (see van Aelst and Walgrave, 2001).

The need to transcend this 'normalization' of mass action may go some way to explaining what in recent years seems to have been a ratcheting up of those protests and groups that do attract young people in particular. Certainly, some kind of rioting seems to have become par for the course at meetings of the G-8 industrialized countries and, since 2001 when it met in Gothenburg, Sweden, the EU's European Council. On the other hand, it is easy to forget that European protest activity has often sparked violence in the past: the scenes in Gothenburg and in Genoa were as nothing, for instance, to the demonstrations in Paris in 1968. It is also easy to dismiss violence as ultimately counterproductive: a recent study of Germany (see Rucht, 2003) suggests it has to be seen, along with other unconventional 'social movement' tactics, as helping to provoke change and an increased sensitivity among conventional politicians towards the concerns of the less conventional. In other words, we might not like it but (in central and eastern Europe as well as in western Europe) it may be wrong to draw too hard and fast a distinction between civil society and what has been termed 'uncivil society': they are part of a continuum (see Kopecký and Mudde, 2002). On the other hand, it would be wrong to suggest that violence predominates in the 'anti-globalization' movement, which is not only extremely diverse but something that social and political scientists are only just beginning to get to grips with (see Poitras, 2003).

Despite its darker side, then, all this may give heart to those who believe that democracy is ultimately about 'the people' triumphing or at least controlling 'the interests'. But digging a little deeper suggests that this view is rather naive. This is because it fails to come to terms with the fact that groups like Greenpeace, Friends of the Earth, the Worldwide Fund for Nature or even Amnesty International, which are active in virtually every European country, and even some of the larger domestic cause groups, have so professionalized their operations that they are not by any stretch of the imagination 'bottom-up' or even democratic organizations. Rather, they are international 'protest businesses' (see Jordan and Maloney, 1997). Even groups that do not qualify as such now tend to join European or, very often in fact, worldwide federations in order to boost their presence – and, hopefully, their clout. For example (see Table 8.2), Birdlife International, a worldwide partnership of groups dedicated to the promotion and protection of birds and their habitats, provides a home for small groups that are little more than promoters of an interest in birds and birdwatching (such as the Swedish society), as well as groups which are quasi-commercial concerns (such as the Royal Society for the Protection of Birds [RSPB] in the UK). Even accounting for population differences, the latter has fifteen times as many members, as well as a much bigger profile and a larger role in actually managing projects in lieu of government – an 'insider' role, incidentally, which, critics suggest, prevents it from taking an effective (or, at least, publicly aggressive) stand against detrimental environmental practices

Much of the activity of traditionally 'outsider' transnational protest businesses such as Greenpeace is capital-intensive (as opposed to labour-intensive) and media-intensive. So, while membership is important for providing them with legitimacy, it is most important for providing them with the finance to carry on their occasionally stunningly successful campaigns (see Bennie, 1998). Most people who do join them do so for short periods and without expecting or desiring to actively participate beyond perhaps signing a petition, possibly joining a march and – most importantly to the group concerned – giving the cheque or credit card number that constitutes their donation to the cause. Some of this activity is counted by some political scientists as 'participation', but whether all such activities, simply because they go beyond turning up to vote every so often, really deserve to be included under the umbrella term of 'collective', let alone 'unconventional' action is a moot point. It is easy to overstate popular involvement in groups and other forms of pressure politics. When it comes to politics (and, indeed, the non-political group activity that some political

Table 8.2 Bird protection societies

Country	Society	Members	Staff
Czech Rep.	*Ceska spolecnost ornitologicka* (*CSO*)	1,800	5
France	*Ligue Pour La Protection des Oiseaux* (*LPO*)	30,600	89
Germany	*Naturschutzbund Deutschland* (*NABU*)	390,000	95
Italy	*Lega Italiana Protezione Uccelli* (*LIPU*)	42,000	95
Netherlands	*Vogelbescherming Nederland* (*VBN*)	125,000	45
Poland	*Ogólnopolskie Towarzystwo Ochrony Ptaków* (*OTOP*)	2,000	8
Spain	*Sociedad Española de Ornitología* (*SEO*)	8,000	50
Sweden	*Sveriges Ornitologiska Förening* (*SOF*)	11,000	24
UK	*Royal Society for the Protection of Birds* (*RSPB*)	1,011,000	1,200

Source: Data from Birdlife International (2004), http://www.birdlife.net/.

scientists believe may facilitate involvement in politics; see Bowler, Donovan and Hanneman, 2003), 'low-intensity participation' is certainly the keynote for most Europeans at the beginning of the twenty-first century.

The fact that groups campaigning for supposedly postmaterialist causes, such as human rights and the environment, do not necessarily have more spontaneous or 'flatter' structures than traditional sectional or interest groups does not, of course, mean that they play exactly the same role. Some of the functions of a campaigning environmental group outlined by a director of such a group (Box 8.11) would presumably not sit well with an 'insider' interest intent on maintaining the convenient insulation of its 'policy community'. 'Outsider' groups, of course, have to weigh up whether some of these functions are worth trading off in return for being kept in the loop by government. Conversely, they have to consider whether incorporation may also mean neutralization.

'Venue shopping' and the Europeanization of pressure politics

Traditionally, the activity of pressure groups in Europe went on at or below the level of the state. With the increasing importance of the EU, however, the activity of some groups has taken on an additional 'European' dimension. Business

---

BOX 8.11
Functions of a campaigning group

broker: carrying information between parties and actors

demonstrator: demonstrating new responses and solutions

educator: education of specialists, concerned parties and the public

ferret: digging for information and conducting investigations

innovator: developing new responses, solutions and policies

orchestration: engineering and manipulating events

scout: scanning for future problems

watchdog: monitoring legal processes and agreements

whistle blower: alerting the public, the government and other groups

Source: Burke, cited in Rawcliffe, 1998: 20–1.

interests, for instance, have had to adjust to the fact that the regulatory environment in which they operate – one which may well have a fairly direct impact on their 'bottom line', their investment decisions and their ability or willingness to compete in certain markets – is, depending on the sector, increasingly subject to European rather than simply domestic rules (see Majone, 1996; Young and Wallace, 2000).

Take competition policy and mergers and acquisitions (M&As). This issue is attracting ever-more attention from a European Commission determined to make a reality of the single or internal market. This clearly poses a threat to both firms and sectors that previously relied upon domestic rules to help maintain what some would argue are restrictive practices and/or cosy cartels – notorious examples would include the airline industry and (often highly subsidized) national carriers, or the automotive industry and its ability to restrict the sales of its products to franchized dealers. Since the Single European Act (SEA), the Commission has made efforts to liberalize such sectors. Trying to limit the damage, the big players in both sectors sought to lobby national governments, but also found it necessary to take their case direct to the Commission. The effect may have been to slow down the reforms, at the very least buying time either to work out an exit strategy or how to compete in the new environment. But liberalization, since it is part of the logic of the EU's single market and is backed up by European law (see Chapter 2), cannot be held off forever.

In any case, other groups that stand to benefit from entering the market or from the lowering of costs – and, indeed, governments who see liberalization as the key to faster growth through a more dynamic economy – will be lobbying in its favour. They may also, as a result of a better 'fit' between their domestic traditions and the EU's way of working, be better lobbyists. The inability in recent years, for instance, of state-owned companies and their government sponsors to prevent an EU-assisted attack on what were, in many mainland European countries, their virtual monopolies, may well have had something to do with the fact that, as Schmidt (1999: 164) notes more generally, the UK's 'larger, more fluid, more fragmented, horizontally integrated policy networks' do better

at promoting domestic interests 'in the multi-polar, competitive decision-making structure of the EU' than, for example, what she calls 'France's smaller, tighter, more cohesive, vertical, state dominated networks' or Italy's traditionally 'under-the-table' mode of business influence. Realizing this perhaps, French governments, far from being concerned at being outflanked abroad by groups it can more easily control at home, have, since the beginning of the 1990s, been encouraging its domestic interest groups to get active and involved at the European level (Szukala, 2003: 230).

Liberalization, however, is not inevitable across all sectors once responsibility for their regulation no longer resides solely with the state and takes on a supranational element. We shall discuss this further in Chapter 9. But, for the moment, one has only to think of the continuing support for agriculture as testimony to the capacity of some groups to maintain their grip even after the national state has lost (or voluntarily surrendered) its own. This is not surprising. Pluralism is no more 'pure' at the European than at the domestic level. Just as national governments are vulnerable to pressure because they rely on groups to provide them with information and help with implementation, so too are European institutions – perhaps even more so. Most obviously, the Commission – for all the talk of 'armies of Brussels bureaucrats' – has very few staff relative to its very large and very varied responsibilities. Even at the policy initiation stage, DGs (Directorate Generals) rely heavily on pressure groups to give them a sense of both what is needed and what is feasible. Given the limited time and resources available, the 'one-stop shops' provided by so-called 'Euro-groups' – groups often composed of the various national federations in a particular sector – are an attractive option. Bringing them on board, or at least getting them on-side, boosts the chances of an initiative being taken seriously and, if adopted, actually being implemented.

Implementation and enforcement is something which the Commission has great difficulty in ensuring, given its reliance on the member states. The fuss made (and law suits begun) by businesses and pressure groups (and individuals) whose interests or ideals are adversely affected by non-compliance on the part of member states (see Falkner *et al.*, 2004) are a good example of and a vital part of what have been called the 'horizontal enforcement' mechanisms (Neyer and Wolf, 2003) of the EU – an entity that ultimately depends not simply on rules but on the political willingness of states to follow them. Consulting with groups also provides a way – if not an entirely convincing one – round the so-called 'democratic deficit'. Even if the Commission cannot claim that its policies are subject to the will of the populace, the fact that some of the most well-informed and potentially vocal sections of it have been involved in the process provides them with at least some legitimacy.

So, whether pressure groups are campaigning to stimulate or to stave off change, the EU is now an important part of the political opportunity structure in which they operate. This explains why over a thousand lobby groups have offices in Brussels. In some ways, 'Europe' has obvious potential advantages over the state level for pressure groups. For a start, it affords the possibility of obliging (or at least giving an excuse to) domestic governments to make changes that might otherwise be difficult, either for electoral reasons or because there are plenty of institutions (corporatist structures, strong parliaments, active courts, etc.) that might combine to block reforms. The transnational firms that were active in lobbying the Commission to come up with the SEA (see Chapter 2) were certainly aware that it would be one way of getting governments and states that were reluctant (or, at least, claimed they were reluctant) to deregulate and privatise eventually to do just that once it came into effect in the early 1990s.

Likewise, for some interest groups, in marked contrast to cause groups, success depends in part on their ability to insulate their sector from the cut and thrust of mediatized and party politics. The EU provides a relatively benign environment where agendas can be set and deals cut in even more privacy than they are used to domestically. Depending on your point of view, what some have termed the 'network' governance of the EU (see Eising and Kohler-Koch, 1999) – multilevel and transnational 'problem-solving' between interested parties – either brings with it a much-needed maturity and flexibility to policy-making or effec-

tively depoliticizes it, putting it even further beyond the reach of democratic control. The chemical and pharmaceutical industries are often cited as examples of sectors that are prepared to swap the supposed limitations imposed by banding together as a 'Euro-group' (the European Chemical Industry Council, or *cefic*, and the European Federation of Pharmaceutical Industries and Associations, or EFPIA, respectively) in return for a fairly cosy relationship with the European institutions whose decisions could impact on their business. Whether this means, of course, that they, or any other interest group with similarly good access, actually get what they want – a charge frequently made not just by anti-globalization protesters but also by cause groups with objections to specific policies – is another matter.

In any case, some would say, cause groups can hardly complain about the 'business-friendly' nature or 'corporate domination' of EU policy-making because many of them, too, have found 'Europe' conducive to pursuing their goals. For one thing, getting changes made to EU rules and standards sometimes allows them to 'outflank' governments (and otherwise more powerful rival groups) at the domestic level (see Fairbrass and Jordan, 2001). For another, the EU provides them with considerable subsidies. For instance, it provides environmental groups with information via the European Environmental Agency (EEA) – information that can be used in campaigns, and the legitimacy of which is hard for opponents to question and for which otherwise campaigners would have to pay themselves. The Commission also makes a point of consulting such groups at all stages of the policy-making process as a counterweight to commercial interests. And they, too, can provide it with information (for example, on implementation failures by member states) and nudge it into action. Certainly, the Commission is already aware that environmental policy is one of the few areas where there is majority public support (even in supposedly 'Eurosceptic' countries) for a greater EU role. Moreover, some member states (e.g. in Scandinavia) are concerned that those that have lower environmental standards (in Southern and Central and Eastern Europe), for example, do not exploit them 'unfairly' to attract more foreign direct investment (FDI). Hence, there has been a perceptible increase since the 1990s in environmental legislation and action plans on matters such as air and water quality, and waste. Again, though, no one should come away with the impression that means, motive and opportunity necessarily add up to overwhelming influence for pressure groups, at least when it comes to environmental policy (see Jordan, 2001).

'Europe' also provides pressure groups with other opportunities to influence policy. Given the 'judicialization' of politics referred to in Chapter 3 and the potential power of the ECJ as well as the Court of Human Rights, it is hardly surprising that even supposedly 'counter-cultural' movements, such as those set up to promote gay and lesbian rights, have pursued a legal route to getting what they want. It is important, however, to realize that recourse to the courts often occurs alongside (rather than going on instead of) the strategies more commonly associated with NSM pressure groups, such as media campaigns or some kind of direct action – or, of course, more discrete lobbying. There is no necessary 'zero-sum' game between the various strategies on offer (see Hilson, 2002). Similarly, many of the large firms that are represented by sectoral interest groups and associations are increasingly willing to lobby simultaneously on their own behalf at both domestic and European levels (see Coen, 1998). Indeed, they are encouraged to do so by the Commission if not all the EU institutions (see Table 8.3). Meanwhile (as Table 8.3 suggests) national associations are often members of European associations (the so-called 'Euro-groups' referred to above), but this does not stop them lobbying EU institutions directly.

More generally, it would be mistaken to think that pressure groups, whether they represent causes or interests, have to choose between the domestic or the European stage. Many of them pursue their aims at both levels simultaneously. And being well or poorly connected at the level of the state does not mean they tend, in turn, to ignore or stress the EU level (see Beyers, 2002). In short, in an era of multilevel governance, pressure groups and their individual or corporate members – especially if they are well resourced – are happy to go be 'promiscuous'. As Richardson (2001) points out, with the possible exception of Germany, 'the EC/EU as a polity presents an American-style plethora of opportunity structures for interest groups, which respond accordingly by "venue shopping"' (see Richardson, 2001: 105–6). In other words, they will work both domestically and transnationally and tolerate a fair amount of duplication on the grounds that, on balance, it is better to risk wasting one's time and money (especially when it constitutes a tiny fraction of an annual turnover that may run into millions of euros) than miss a potential opportunity.

Given the activity of business interest groups at the European as well as at the state level, it may be hard to understand why some critics, especially in the UK, accuse the EU of introducing what former British Prime Minister Margaret Thatcher termed 'socialism by the back door'. What they really object to, however, is what they see as the institutionalization of corporatism in the EU system, symbolized by the so-called 'Social Chapter' of the Maastricht Treaty. Under the procedure it lays out, it is possible for legislation affecting the labour market – for example, the equal treatment of part-time workers or rules governing maximum working hours – to be agreed on by the so-called 'social partners' and then be simply rubber-stamped by the EU's normal legislative bodies, the Council and the EP. To (mainly British) critics of

---

Table 8.3 Who they like to see most: EU institutions and corporate lobbying

Commission	Council of Ministers	Parliament
(1) Individual large firms	(1) National associations	(1) European associations
(2) European associations	(2) European associations	(2) National associations
(3) National associations	(3) Individual large firms	(3) Individual large firms

Source: Adapted from Bouwen (2002: 383).

limitations on business, this is 'Europe' handing back unwarranted power to the trade unions just as they have been finally 'conquered' at home.

Many politicians in countries without a strong tradition of social partnership might have some sympathy. Governments in Central and Eastern Europe, for instance, will be hoping that accession to the EU does not provide the region's fragmented unions (or, indeed, its similarly poorly organized, if not utterly uninfluential, business groups) an opportunity to make up for their domestic weakness. Some observers, however, would point out that because the EU's policy-making process is so dependent on interest groups, such an attitude is naive: as a member state, better to risk having groups that can constrain you at the domestic level if it means they are also capable of exerting some influence on the country's behalf in Brussels (see Bruszt, 2002). In any case, there are politicians, even right-wing politicians, from more long-standing member states where 'concertation' between the government and economic interest groups is par for the course, and who therefore have few qualms about, at least, a limited reproduction of the process at the European level. In fact, social partner agreements are not that common, nor are they exactly rushed into; indeed, the ETUC (the trade union federation), and particularly UNICE and CEEP (the private and public sector employers) are often persuaded to take such a route only in order to stave off what might be even less welcome legislation made in the normal way (see Falkner, 2000b).

Institutions such as the Social Chapter, and the embedded respect for trade unions it seems to symbolize, help in part to explain why the latter have reconciled themselves to Europe (see Visser, 1998) – even in the UK, where Euroscepticism was and is unusually strong (Strange, 2002). In short, the EU has provided trade unions with a way of putting the brakes on, and even reversing labour market deregulation and 'anti-trade union legislation' at the domestic level.

When it comes to social movements, however, there is less evidence – outside the bigger, more organized lobby groups and 'protest businesses' –

of Europeanization. The existence of European federations to which national groups belong (environmental groups are a good example) can give a misleading impression of the extent to which they actually co-operate and/or work at the European level (see Rootes, 2004). This is partly a matter of resources. Even the larger environmental organizations, for instance, are nowhere near as well staffed as some of their corporate counterparts: for instance, Birdlife International has only three permanent staff in Brussels and fewer than ten at its European headquarters in the Netherlands. Campaigning organizations out of the mainstream, who may object, even violently, to some of what is done in their name (and in the name of the EU) are even less able to afford to 'venue shop'.

But this is also about focus. For instance, notwithstanding the increased competence of the Union in environmental policy, one of the most recent studies of environmental protest in western Europe stresses 'the extent to which both issues and forms of protests reflected the distinctive concerns and idiosyncratic dynamics of politics within each of the several states' it looked at (Rootes, 2003: 255). Other researchers have also found that most attention and direct action is directed at the domestic level, even when the target may (directly or indirectly) be the EU. And while the headlines surrounding violence at EU summits may suggest a Europeanization of contentious politics, the day-to-day reality for groups of, or representing, the powerless, is much less trans-national (see Balme, Chabanet and Wright, 2002 and Imig and Tarrow, 1999, 2001). In fact, and not perhaps surprisingly, most of the protests against the EU are carried out not by NSMs but by occupational interest groups, especially farmers and fishermen (see Imig, 2002), whose livelihoods are, of course, directly affected by its policies. For most Europeans, then, home is not just where the heart is but where they think, rightly or wrongly, that the power still lies. The problem, many argue, is that it no longer makes much difference which set of politicians, left or right, holds that power. This, and the common wisdom that surrounds it, is the focus of the Chapter 9.

Learning resources

On pressure group activity at the European (as well as the domestic) level, see Greenwood (2003) and Greenwood and Aspinwall (1997). On the revival of corporatism, see the excellent collection in Berger and Compston (2002). On groups and civil society, start with the informative Curtis, Baer and Grabb (2001). On social movements in Europe, see Della Porta, Kriesi and Rucht (1999), Imig and Tarrow (2001), Kriesi et al. (1995), and Rootes (2003). On civil society in Eastern Europe, see Howard (2003). Finally, virtually all groups now have some kind of web presence: even the supposedly inchoate fuel protesters of 2000 were said to be using the internet to get their point across. Many can be found at domain names such as .org and .net.

EXECUTIVE SUMMARY

- The traditional distinction between 'insider' and 'outsider' groups – while still useful – is beginning to blur, as governments have grown used to a more participatory policy process and groups employ a range of strategies according to the 'political opportunity structure' they inhabit and help shape.

- The even more traditional distinction between countries that are 'pluralist' (lots of competing groups in the 'market place of ideas') and 'corporatist' (more institutionalized consultation with the national associations of, say, employers and employees) is also breaking down.

- Groups that previously enjoyed privileged access to government in relatively enclosed 'policy communities' are having to reconcile themselves to a less insulated environment and follow multiple strategies.

- Trade union influence has been in long-term decline in Europe, but varies considerably – according to history more than geography. But even fragmented unions with low memberships can still disrupt governments.

- In any case, partly as a result of coping with the demands of the single currency and the single market, there is evidence to suggest a return to an albeit limited form of 'corporatism'.

- Business is at an advantage in any capitalist country because it creates the wealth citizens and governments rely on: the formal organizational capacity of business is no guide to its strength.

- The strength of 'new social movements' (NSMs) that push a more oppositional/alternative agenda is greater in the richer more northerly and westerly parts of Europe. The biggest of these campaigning groups are now as professional as they are participatory, becoming something akin to 'protest businesses'.

- More and more interest groups are operating on the European as well as at the domestic scene, since multilevel governance means that they are interrelated. National governments can be bypassed in this way, but they also recognize that national interests often benefit from such lobbying and involvement – a process encouraged by EU institutions.

- The EU also presents cause groups and NSMs with opportunities, although both finance and focus continue to mean that most alternative and protest activity still goes on at the national level.

Chapter 9

Politics over economics: enduring differences between left and right

Has politics ever really mattered?
Drifting to the right: the centre-left in Europe
Privatization
Flexible labour markets?
Bringing an end to 'tax and spend'?
The EU: deadweight or driving force?
Separating the facts from the hype
Why it still makes sense to be different
No easy explanations: the rise of the far-right

There are several easy assumptions about the current state of European politics and the European economy that, put together, constitute some sort of common wisdom. Perhaps the most prevalent is that 'left' and 'right' are becoming meaningless terms as governments and parties from both sides of the political divide are obliged to follow the same policies in order to cope with globalization and (less often mentioned in the media) Europeanization. Centre-left parties, the argument goes, may talk about a **Third Way** between old-fashioned **social democracy** and **neo-liberalism**, but this is supposedly little more than a fig-leaf to cover their retreat from the former and their embrace of the latter, even in those states (France and Germany are often cited) where the tradition of government intervention is strong. Apparently, the common wisdom continues, all mainstream politicians now believe that 'Anglo-Saxon' or 'American-style' capitalism (with its labour market flexibility, private ownership and a limited, low-spending role for the state) is the way of the future, anything else being seen as recipe for continued low growth, high unemployment, uncompetitiveness and international decline. Most of the EU's newest members will, it predicts, reinforce this trend. Accordingly, the EU, once it overcomes its vestigial support for economic interference, will – via the discipline

imposed by its new single currency – help ensure the triumph of more or less global neo-liberalism and the collapse of any serious social democratic alternative. Purveyors of the common wisdom also suggest that the absence of such an alternative is leading either to political apathy, reflected in ever-decreasing electoral turnout (see Chapter 6), or to the rise of populist politics which, especially on the xenophobic far right, sucks in the supposed 'losers' of globalization.

> *Definition*
> **Social democracy** traditionally describes the ideology of the (centre-) left and is associated with the promotion of equality and social and collective well-being via universal welfare and state intervention in the economy. **Neo-liberalism**, an ideology that has come to be associated with the conservative (centre-) right, is about 'shrinking' the state by lowering taxation and privatizing its assets, and about rewarding and encouraging individual responsibility and achievement. The **Third Way** represents an attempt by centre-left politicians, most famously Bill Clinton in the US and Tony Blair in the UK (and, to a lesser extent, Gerhard Schröder in Germany) to retool and update social democracy by learning some of the lessons of neo-liberalism without buying into it (or dumping social democratic values) completely.

This chapter aims to unpack what is really going on with Europe's centre-left and its political economy in order to problematize and, at least, qualify the common wisdom. Opinion poll evidence across Europe clearly shows that more and more voters claim to be able to tell little difference between right and left. But is the customer always right? The chapter begins by tackling one of the most exhaustively researched questions begged by the idea that European politics has moved 'beyond left and right': has politics ever really mattered that much, or have 'left' and 'right' never been much more than interchangeable management teams? It then goes on to explore the extent to which the contemporary left has gone over to the right in key areas such as privatization, labour market policy and 'tax and spend'. Each of these areas also allows us to look at the collapse or persistence of national regimes that seem to stand out against the supposedly uniform trend toward liberal capitalism. It also allows us comment on the extent to which postcommunist countries really have gone all the way from full-blown communism to capitalism 'red in tooth and claw'. The chapter continues by examining how European integration both hinders and hastens what the common wisdom would like to claim is a necessary drive toward liberalization, deregulation and 'sound' policies. It goes on to suggest that, once we separate the facts from the hype about the triumph of liberal capitalism and the decline of left and right, differences between ideologies (and nations) persist. The chapter ends by challenging the idea often put forward by media pundits that the supposed collapse of a political alternative to neo-liberalism in Europe has helped cause the rise of the far right.

Has politics ever really mattered?

Representative democracy in Europe assumes, and even relies on, political parties standing for a set of ideas-based policies rather than simply competing for the spoils of office. We should expect, then, that who governs (and, therefore, politics as a whole) matters. In other words, there should be some observable link between a party or parties being in power and public policy. In fact, the impact of parties is harder to measure than might be imagined: even the smallest 'ship of state' resembles an oil tanker rather than a speed boat – a small touch on the tiller or turn of the wheel takes a long time to register as a change of course, by which time the party or parties in question may be out of office. Nevertheless, political scientists have made some effort to make such measurements – and in a variety of ways. Few of them, however, are without problems.

One way of trying to find out whether parties

make a difference is to see to what extent parties' manifesto promises (the promises that they make in writing at election time) are translated into the formally announced programme of the governments they form or help to form. But this means of measurement is only talking about the translation of one form of words into another, not the translation of words into action. For this, we have to look at studies examining the extent to which governments actually redeem the pledges made in their programmes. Unfortunately, these studies are surprisingly rare, and tend to be confined to countries such as the UK and Greece, which are unusual in Europe in that they normally have one-party majority governments (see Chapter 4). The fact that they seem to show (see Kalogeropoulou, 1989 and Rallings, 1987) that over two-thirds of promises are kept – quite a high figure, given the contingencies of office – does seem to support the case for parties making a difference. But most European democracies are run by multiparty majority coalitions or either multiparty or single-party minority governments, making it much harder for a single party to see its ideas translated into deeds. This assumption is confirmed by one of the first comparative studies in this area involving the Netherlands and the UK (see Thomson, 2001), although the study, by showing that governing parties did most of what they said they would, also gives us some grounds for optimism that parties (and, by extension, politics) do make a difference.

Other studies aim to answer the question by looking at public spending – mainly on the grounds that left-wing parties (historically supportive of the welfare state and improved access to education) would be expected to spend more than right-wing parties (which historically have tended to worry more about, say, defence, and also where the money is going to come from). Again, taking these studies as a whole (see Alvarez, Garrett and Large, 1991; Blais *et al.*, 1996; Hicks, 1999; Imbeau *et al.*, 2001; Schmidt, 1996, 2002a) the verdict would seem to be a cautious 'yes', though it is important to note that a fair number of scholars would argue that 'politics hasn't mattered – much' (Caul and Gray, 2000: p. 234). Taking cross-national studies first, states that have experienced left wing government for a considerable time (in

Scandinavia and Austria) seem to have a bigger public sector than those for which the opposite is the case (Ireland, Switzerland and Germany). There also seems to be a link between left-wing government and more spending on education and welfare, though not health. Within-country studies (which can, of course, be added together to produce a cross-national conclusion) also seem to show a relationship between left-wing governments and higher spending and conservative governments and lower spending, although the effect is confined to majority as opposed to minority governments and is influenced by the size and strength of the opposition (as well as the existence of a strong trade union movement). On economic policy, there also appears to be a historical tendency for governments of the right to prefer lower inflation at the cost of higher unemployment and governments of the left to prefer the opposite. Income inequality also seems to be affected – going up when there are right-wing parties in government and down when their counterparts on the left are in charge.

Historically, then, there does seem to be at least some truth in the argument that 'politics makes a difference': that parties and governments of the left and right do different things and have different priorities. Indeed, politics may even make more difference than studies involving large-scale averages suggest. Such indicators cannot possibly hope to capture the myriad policy acts by an individual government that even the casual observer of politics would identify as being impossible under a government run by another party or parties. On the other hand, the fact that such studies are long-run comparisons should perhaps lessen the weight we should put on them now. If, as some argue, the differences between the main parties of the left and the right, and their effect on (say) welfare policy, has decreased rapidly in recent years (see Huber and Stephens, 2001) then studies like these may not accurately describe the present or persuasively predict the future.

Drifting to the right: the centre-left in Europe

The idea that Europe's centre-left parties have moved away from a traditionally social democratic

emphasis on government intervention, welfare spending and prioritizing full employment is commonplace. It does not come solely from crowing conservatives. But nor is it simply the catch-call of left-wingers torn between despair and trying to capitalize on the ensuing discontent of social democratic traditionalists. In fact, the abandonment of old-style socialism is also reflected in the rhetoric of some of social democracy's most prominent leaders, particularly in the UK and in Germany. In seeking to win office from centre-right parties who had been in power for over fifteen years, both Tony Blair and Gerhard Schröder insisted that they were pragmatic centrists. Their so-called 'Third Way' or *Neue Mitte* sought not to expand nor to 'shrink' the state, but to reconstruct it in order better to equip ordinary people to cope and compete in an increasingly global economy (see Green-Pedersen, van Kersberger and Hemerijck, 2001).

To devotees of the Third Way, globalization, voter resistance to tax rises and inflation, and market antipathy to profligate spending, were – rightly or wrongly – to be treated as givens. The state, whatever the evidence to the contrary (see Weiss, 1998), was no longer powerful. And populist preferences had to be accommodated rather than shaped. It was no longer a tiny minority that would be affected by, say, rises in taxation: the majority were now net contributors rather than beneficiaries and had a stake in the health rather than the hounding of capitalism. Their concerns about issues such as crime and immigration had to be taken seriously rather than dismissed as right-wing ravings. Governments of the left had to work with, not against, the grain. They had to admit that they had no monopoly on good policies, and that some of what their opponents had done needed doing: unions were important but they could not be allowed to run the show; welfare benefits should provide 'a hand-up not a handout'; sometimes the market did know better than the state, the consumer better than the civil servant. Ideology, they claimed, had to take a back seat: 'what counts is what works'.

But what also counts is what people (and parties) actually do, rather than simply what they say. In politics, discourse and rhetoric are undoubtedly important and arguably revealing (see Schmidt,

2001). But much of it – including the manifestos that political scientists have spent so much time studying (see Box 9.1) – is designed to reassure and reposition, rather than provide a blueprint for action. It may be fashionable to say there is no longer much difference between left and right. But it may not be true, or at least not wholly so.

For a start, the common wisdom relies on the assumption of some kind of postwar 'golden era' during which ideologically committed centre-left parties in Europe were conquering capitalism and building welfare states and economies safe from the depredations of international markets. The reality was rather different. The European centre-left spent most of the twentieth century trying not just to tame and humanize capitalism, but to make it work better, all the time operating within constraints imposed by both moderate voters and powerful international markets (see Pierson, 2001 and Sassoon, 1997). Recent developments are part of an ongoing story. Of course, one can compare contemporary and 'classic' social democracy 'now' and 'then', and find the latter wanting (see Thomson, 2000); but such comparisons not only risk caricaturing both periods but also downplaying the fact that social democracy has always been a particularly plastic ideology which varies over space as well as time (see Stammers, 2001). In any case, the sheer size and inertia of polities and economies has meant – and will mean – that the differences between right- and left-wing governments tend to be ones of degree rather than kind. It will also mean that they may be difficult to pick up in aggregate measures of, say, public and welfare spending.

Secondly, the extent to which countries plump for this or that policy has always been dependent on historical circumstances, be they material or ideational, to which parties – as representative institutions – have to adapt. For instance, the growth of welfare states throughout Europe had as much to do with the ratcheting-up of government intervention during the twentieth century's two world wars, and the resulting expectations of voters, as it did with 'socialism'. After all, many, if not most, of Europe's welfare states were built, at least in part, by conservative and Christian Democratic parties who otherwise might have been obliged to surrender power to their opponents.

BOX 9.1
Manifesto tracking

One of the longest continuous research projects in political science is the collection and coding of the manifestos of (western) Europe's political parties. One of the latest pieces of analysis from the project (Volkens, 2004; see also Volkens and Klingemann, 2002) explores the extent to which parties of the mainstream right and left have converged over time. Its findings are clear: in the 1940s–1960s, most centre-left parties moved to the left; but it also finds that they were followed in the same direction by almost all their centre-right opponents. From the 1970s onwards, the move was in the opposite direction: the centre-right moved right, and the centre-left, needing to keep in touch with the electorate, followed. Volkens' study cautions us, however, against exaggerating the extent of these shifts. Contrary to other scholars who use similar data (see Caul and Gray, 2000), Volkens also argues strongly against the idea of convergence: parties continued to maintain at least a semantic distance from each other. Interestingly, she also concludes that the 'policy shift to new Third Way issues ... is no recent development, but started as early as the 1950s'. Other analysts of the manifesto project data, including those, such as Caul and Gray, who do see more convergence, also make the point that it has been going on for four or five decades, rather than being a knee-jerk response to resurgent neo-liberalism.

Social democratic parties were booted out and blamed for the rising inflation and unemployment of the 1970s. By the same token, they knew that any chance of a comeback would rely on them publicly rejecting the semi-mythical 'tax and spend' and 'beggar-my-neighbour protectionist' policies that were supposed to have caused the problems their opponents claimed to have fixed. Their aim, like that of the centre-right after the Second World War, was to get into power and to stay there in order to do as much good (as they saw it) as possible. This often meant accepting things as they were rather than as they might have liked them to be. It also meant courting 'floating voters' who would sometimes be attracted by the arguments of 'the other side'. A certain amount of 'tacking to the right' by Social Democrats – and 'tacking to the left' by their opponents – was inevitable.

This is not to say that the parties doing the tacking did not to some extent genuinely share their opponents' (or the public's) analysis of their past mistakes. It seems clear that social democrats have indeed internalized the 'common sense' surrounding the advisability of, say, low inflation, balanced budgets and (to a lesser extent) the new public management (NPM). Moreover, they know that pursuing such policies earns them valuable credibility with finance markets. No doubt, some are also privately relieved that, when their political opponents carry out painful reforms, they may be doing social democracy a favour by doing what it would find difficult to do itself in the face of opposition from its own supporters. But none of this learning and adapting necessarily means that Europe's social democrats threw the baby out with the bathwater (see Green-Pedersen, van Kersberger and Hemerijck, 2001 and Martell, 2001). Part of the claim of leaders such as Schröder and Blair, after all, is that means can be de-coupled from ends, that values such as fairness and equality of opportunity (if not outcome) are best realized in up-to-date ways (Blair and Schröder, 1999). Utilitarianism and pragmatism has always been a strong streak in European social democracy: if the old ways of achieving the greatest good for the greatest number 'cannot be successfully implemented in the socio-economic and cultural environment of advanced capitalism' then they 'ought no longer be pursued' and swapped for something that might work better (Kitschelt, 1994: 7).

The same goes for European states. Simply because they take this or that headline policy on board may not mean that they have swallowed the neo-liberal prescription wholesale. Nor does it necessarily mean that they abandoned all that characterizes, say, the French, or the German – or, indeed, the Swedish – 'model'. Conversely, the evident, even proud, reluctance of some European states (including those just mentioned) to go all the way down the 'Anglo-Saxon' road need not mean that they have eschewed all the techniques and policies we have come to associate with it, such as privatization, flexible labour markets and cutting 'tax and spending'. When we look at each of these in turn, and in the light of the enthusiasm or

otherwise of both social democratic parties and individual states for them, we see a decidedly mixed picture – a continuation of the national variations in political economy that comparative research has long identified and which can, notwithstanding globalization, continue to exist (see Garrett, 1998a).

Privatization

State involvement in, or even public ownership of, certain key sectors of the economy was seen by many the *sine qua non* of socialism, as well as a characteristic of both corporatist and statist European countries. It is hardly surprising, then, that privatization has been taken as an indicator both of the ideological dilution of the left and of the willingness or reluctance of certain countries to 'get with the programme'. Beginning (somewhat more haltingly than many now remember) in the United Kingdom during the 1980s, the transfer of state assets into private hands has been going on all over the continent.

In the postcommunist countries, as we suggested in Chapter 1, privatization was a crucial part of the move away from the party-state past: outside Romania and Bulgaria (though they are now 'catching-up') most governments (even those run by communist successor parties) showed themselves to be reasonably keen 'systemic' privatizers (see Box 9.2). In the West, where public ownership was clearly far less important than it was in the Soviet bloc, privatization has not proceeded quite so rapidly and has often taken place in stages rather than as a 'big bang'. Nor, with some exceptions, has it been pursued with equal vigour by governments labelling themselves as 'left' or 'right'. In general, western Europe's socialist and social democratic parties have not been quite as enthusiastic as their opponents. On the other hand, critics point out that they have done nothing to reverse the trend. This, though, is hardly surprising given the huge costs of compensating shareholders, as well as the dim view international financial markets would take of any government going against what for them (and for organizations such as the IMF and the OECD) is now an unquestioned orthodoxy. It must also be said that this lack

BOX 9.2
Privatization as politics

Privatization can be motivated by politics rather than pure economic theory. These political motives are often mixed, but can be analytically separated as follows.

Systemic privatization hopes to alter a country's socio-economic and political environment fundamentally by reducing the state's role (and people's expectations of the state's role) in it. The privatization programmes of Central and Eastern Europe, and to a lesser extent those of Southern Europe before it, could be labelled 'systemic'. So, too, could those pursued towards the end of the 1980s and the early 1990s by the Thatcher and Major governments of the UK; they also aimed at the reduction of the power of organized labour, which is often at its strongest in the public sector.

Tactical privatization, by contrast, is mainly about achieving the short-term, often electoral, goals of parties, politicians and the interest groups that support them. The adoption of privatization by centre-right politicians in France during the late 1980s was driven by a desire to distinguish themselves from their Socialist opponents, as well as the need to reward key supporters. The revenue thus gained, however, allowed the government to finance measures to combat unemployment (and, ironically, to keep afloat other state-owned holdings) that otherwise it would have had trouble affording.

Pragmatic privatization is even more ad hoc and often crisis-driven: governments simply need the money to offset debt or public spending and are prepared to override even their own reservations in order to get it. The privatization which went on in European countries in the late 1990s, was one way of ensuring that countries such as Italy qualified for entry into the single currency – a process that required them to bring their budget deficits, their debt and their current spending into line with agreed norms. Privatizations carried out by centre-left governments in France and Germany also qualify as pragmatic.

Source: Based on discussion in Feigenbaum, Henig and Hamnett (1998).

BOX 9.3
Jospin: ni ..., ni ...

It was both surprising and disappointing to many that former French Prime Minister, Lionel Jospin, began his doomed campaign for the presidency in 2002 with an assurance that it was 'not a socialist one'. This, after all, was the man who introduced the 35-hour-week, spent millions on public schemes to reduce unemployment, upped welfare benefits, and was more than a little suspicious, not to say sniffy, about the 'Third Way' touted by his British and German counterparts. But Jospin was also the man who presided over what was the biggest sell-off of state assets in the country's history. Even though many of them were only part-sales (the state continued to hold majority stakes in France Télécom and Air France, for instance, and still owned a quarter of well-known car-maker, Renault), the Jospin government raised over €30 billion between 1997 and 2002 – a figure its centre-right successor will find it hard to surpass. Perhaps fewer people should have been surprised when Jospin argued in 2002 that his position was *ni, ... ni ...* ('neither nor')!

of enthusiasm has not prevented some very significant social democratic governments from selling state assets, most notably in France (see Box 9.3) and Italy. And even if we do not count the dismantling of state control in the former GDR, Germany has also begun privatizing.

That social democrats have sold off parts of the state points to the fact that the pursuit of privatization, especially (but not exclusively) on the left, has frequently been driven by instrumental rather than ideological motives (see Box 9.2). It has also had an EU dimension (Parker, 1998). One obvious example was the need for some states to lower debt or cover spending in order to meet the qualifying conditions for the single currency (see Chapter 2) without raising the tax burden to politically intolerable levels. This, more than a conversion to gung-ho neo-liberalism on the part of the left, does much to explain, for instance, the acceleration (and, in part, the falling away) of Italy's privatization programme under the social democrat-led *Ulivo* (Olive Tree) coalition in the late 1990s. Another reason was the need to respond to demands (expressed through the European Commission, but coming from corporations in countries that had already privatized such sectors) that states open up their telecoms and energy markets to competition. Such demands were designed to kick-start the so-called 'Lisbon process' by which European leaders – left and right – rather ambitiously promised at a summit in Portugal in March 2001 to make the EU economy the world's most competitive and dynamic economy by 2010!

In fact, privatization is rarely so thoroughgoing as media headlines might suggest or true believers might want. We noted in Chapter 1 that even in the keenest postcommunist states sales are still by no means always complete and often proceed in stages. The same is true for countries in western Europe. For instance, Norway seemed to stand out among Scandinavian countries as a keen privatizer, raising approximately €1.5 billion from the sale of shares in its fantastically wealthy *Statoil* company and almost €500 million from a massively over-subscribed sale of shares in *Den Norske Bank* in 2001. But even after the latter sale, the state continued to own 47 per cent of the shares and, in the case of the former, still controlled a full 80 per cent. The centre-right government that took over from the Labour government that sold those assets was not expected to go much further because both right- and left-wing politicians are sensitive to voter opposition to the foreign takeover of domestic firms – something a continuing controlling share on the part of the state can prevent.

This kind of 'economic nationalism' is still important in other European countries, notably France. But in other countries, too, governments supposedly keen to privatize surreptitiously left the state in *de facto* control by awarding it a 'golden share' that allowed it to intervene, for example, to block a takeover bid. Indeed, the technique originated in the 'home' of privatization, the UK, in the 1980s. Recently, however, the British government, and governments in Germany, Italy, the Netherlands and Spain, have been taken to task over the practice by the European Commission. In May 2003, the ECJ, in a decision that will undoubtedly affect other countries, ruled that both the UK and Spain, which had owned 'golden shares' in numerous companies that had supposedly been set free by privatization, would have to give them up. The only justification for such shares will henceforth be confined to enterprizes involving national security considerations – a definition which, judging by experience, will probably be stretched to the limit!

We should also note that there has been a considerable slowdown in privatization since the peak of the process in the late 1990s, both in the number of sales taking place and in terms of value. This is due, in part, to the economic slowdown that struck large parts of the world's economy (i.e. Asia and the US, as well as Europe) and sent share-markets downwards. Sensible governments postponed asset sales in the hope that they would find a better price in the future: Italy, for instance, delayed the sale of further stakes in the electricity company, ENEL, which it had begun selling off in 1999. But Italy, and its supposedly market-oriented Prime Minister, Silvio Berlusconi, was also criticized for lacking the political will to overcome another big barrier to privatization in some European countries; namely, the extent to which public ownership is not merely a matter of central but also of regional and local government. This is clearly the case in Germany, where many *Länder* own utility companies and regionally focused banks.

The slowdown in privatization in Europe is also due to the fact that much of what can easily be sold has in many countries already been offloaded. To coin a phrase, many of the 'cash cows' have gone and only the 'lame ducks' remain. European governments are also having to face the fact that some sectors may simply be too risky (strategically or financially) to privatize – at least, to privatize fully. True, this does not mean a complete halt to private sector involvement in previously state-run areas. For instance, the UK Labour government elected in 1997 initially disappointed those observers who hoped it would carry on where its pro-privatization Conservative predecessor had left off: the not-very-successful part-privatization of the air-traffic control system was about as far as it went. However, it has also angered left-wing critics with its enthusiasm for 'public–private' financing (PFI), whereby the private sector builds roads, transport systems, prisons and (increasingly) hospitals which are then leased back to the state. Yet, even under that government, one can argue that things have gone backwards. In 2001, for example, the UK government had to re-establish state ownership (albeit via a not-for-profit company) of the railway track operations that a Conservative government had privatized in the early 1990s. Interestingly, nobody suggested that this *de facto* 're-nationalization' was a sign that 'New' Labour was returning to its socialist roots. It may not be any more accurate, then, to see its plans to involve the private sector in public projects as proof that it has sold its soul to neo-liberalism.

By the same token, it is easy to pick up on head-lines that seem to suggest that, 'at last', privatiza-tion is embedding itself in countries that have a tradition of what neo-liberals would see as 'state meddling' in the business sector. Thus, much was made of Germany's social democratic Chancellor's apparent recommitment to privatization in 2001, when the federal government sold off its shares in Hamburg airport, diluted its holdings in other companies and promised to move on the sales of *Deutsche Telekom* and *Deutsche Post*. Similarly, the supposedly iconoclastic Nicolas Sarkozy, who was briefly France's Finance Minister in its centre-right government in 2004, created much excitement when he hinted at the privatization of France's *Electricité de France* (EDF) – an enterprize that, although a state-owned monopoly at home, has (to the extreme irritation of both the business sector and foreign governments) been gobbling up priva-tized utility companies in other European coun-tries! Perhaps predictably, Sarkozy's hints led to protest blackouts by its highly unionized work-force. But whether or not these promised reduc-tions of state ownership actually go ahead, they seem to have done little to change something that is arguably just as important; namely, the culture of state involvement.

This culture of state involvement and a wide-ranging *service publique* in France is by no means a thing of the past, notwithstanding the odd hint about privatization and the liberal hopes that the EU will see it off in the long term (see Cole, 1999 and Cole and Drake, 2000). A fortnight or so after declaring he would turn EDF into a public company, for instance, M. Sarkozy prevented the Swiss pharmaceuticals giant *Novartis* from gate-crashing a merger between *Aventis* and *Sanofi*, two French firms in the same field. The merger appeared to have been deliberately engineered to create a French 'national champion' to compete on the global stage. More was to come the following month when the government announced that it was bailing out *Alstom*, the trains, turbines and ship maker, by converting an €800 million loan it had granted into a government shareholding worth just over 30 per cent. This had apparently been squared with the European Commission (responsible for policing big takeovers and acquisi-tions) despite the fact that German industrial giant, *Siemens*, was hoping to buy parts of *Alstom* – and despite the Commission's supposedly strict rules preventing such blatant state aid! Germany could hardly complain, however. Not only did it do as much as possible in 2004 to prevent a rumoured American takeover of *Deutsche Bank*, it also had what liberals would see as an unenviable record of bailing out ailing industries of its own, beginning in 1999 with the rescue of engineering firm *Holzmann* in order to safeguard some 60,000 German jobs.

In fact, what in EU jargon is called 'state aid' is not confined to France and Germany, even though, on balance, it has declined in the last decade. A recent European survey (Curzon Price, 2004) notes that it is 'gradually being brought under control, but most governments find it diffi-cult to relinquish this instrument of policy'. It also notes that the European Commission 'still has problems enforcing discipline on member states' and that any decline could still be put at risk in an economic downturn – not just in France and Germany, but also in other big 'offenders' such as Spain and Italy.

Flexible labour markets?

One of the other key shifts in economic and social policy since the 1970s has been a de-emphasis of 'demand-side' solutions to unemployment toward 'supply-side' measures. The former attempted to use Keynesian government spending to smooth out the business cycle and offset recessions (see Chapter 1). Supply-side solutions, however, concentrate on removing rigidities in the labour market. These rigidities include 'excessive' worker protection or bureaucratic benefits systems that put people off taking up offers of work. Supply-side measures also focus on providing education and skills training better to equip firms and people to adjust to economic change. Generally, it is governments of the right that are most associated with a desire to move toward 'flexible labour markets'. For example, despite the general strike staged by Italian unions against such policies in April 2002, Silvio Berlusconi's centre-right administration could claim a mandate for trying to untangle the mass of laws and regulations that some would argue protect the rights of those with a job at the cost of those trying to get one.

There is no doubt, however, that some social democratic parties, though not all of them, have been part of this shift (see Box 9.4), or that much has been made (by both critics and fans) of their going with the flow instead of trying to stem the tide. Much to the chagrin of its union backers, for instance, the UK's Labour government made it clear on assuming office in 1997 that, like its Conservative predecessor, it would not allow the EU to re-regulate the country's comparatively unregulated labour market. Meanwhile, the SPD–Green government in Germany has at least tinkered with that country's heavily bureaucratic and heavily taxed labour market. Its *Agenda 2010* package, announced in the spring of 2003, was designed to make it more tempting for small and medium size businesses (SMEs) to take on workers and to ease rules on collective bargaining. Unfortunately, these changes (plus following the UK down the road of making it harder for unemployed people repeatedly to refuse offers of work) seem to have done little, as yet, to dent Germany's seemingly chronic high unemployment rate. This makes public spending difficult, if not impossible, to reduce – something which, incidentally, makes spending totals such an unreliable indicator of whether a government is right- or left-wing!

The adoption of supply-side measures, however, should not be taken as proof that differences between right and left have disappeared. The evidence suggests that the social democratic version of supply-side policies – which some see as the essence of the 'Third Way' (see Green-Pedersen, van Kersbergen and Hemerijck, 2001) can be quite different to the version preferred by the right. Unlike the centre-left, the centre-right has tended not to balance deregulation with more spending on

---

BOX 9.4
Bidding adieu to RTT

Réduction du temps du travail or RTT was, along with legislating to make the firing of workers even more difficult than it was already, one of the policies that saw Lionel Jospin's socialist-led government fêted by left-wingers who saw the so-called 'Third way' as little more than a sell-out (see Clift, 2001, 2002). As soon as the right returned to power in 2002, however, it began moves to erode the 35-hour-week. Interestingly, despite the fact that supporters claimed it had created something like 200,000 jobs, not everyone on the left was opposed to the idea. While unions mobilized to resist the government, some suggested that the only group to have really benefited were relatively well-paid (and relatively unionized) workers in the public sector. Many ordinary people, on the other hand, struggled under a regime that some say prevents them doing the overtime which – rightly or wrongly – was a vital addition to their weekly wage packet. Once you go behind the headlines, in other words, things are often ambiguous. Just as Jospin's pursuit of privatization seems to prove that differences between right and left are meaningless, his successors' actions seem to suggest their continuing relevance.

---

human capital (see Boix, 1998). Social democrats in countries such as the Netherlands might not grab the headlines like their counterparts in the UK or Germany, but they have long demonstrated there is nothing inherently 'right-wing' about a shift to supply-side policies (see Hemerijck and Visser, 2001). If there were, then we would have to re-write the record on what is widely acknowledged to be Europe's (not to say the world's) most persistently 'social democratic country' (Box 9.5).

In any case, even if we look at (say) Labour, in the UK, which has gone further than many of its centre-left counterparts in embracing deregulation, we see a government that extended trade union recognition, a government that for the first time ever brought in a minimum wage and a government that is regularly attacked by employers' organizations for introducing too much worker protection. We also see a government that signed

---

BOX 9.5

Supply-side social democracy in Sweden

Social democratic Sweden's relative economic success has long been underpinned by supply-side policies, and in particular an 'active labour market policy' through which the state provided a safety net, social services and skills development that would allow people and firms to adjust swiftly to changes in the international markets. This also had the considerable economic advantage of maximizing women's employability. In recent years, Sweden has looked less immune than previously to recession, and social democratic-led governments have had little compunction in slowing the growth of welfare spending, not least on pensions. They have also, like Labour in the UK, granted independence to the central bank to set interest rates. Indeed, they have gone further than their UK counterparts by cutting income tax and privatizing the Swedish postal service in order to allow it to compete more efficiently in Europe. The so-called 'people's home' may not be quite what it used to be, but few accuse Sweden, or the party that has run it for so long (the SAP), of a comprehensive or 'Blairite' betrayal of the ideals of social democracy.

BOX 9.6

Resisting the Anglo-Saxon 'hire and fire' culture

In March 2001, UK retailer *Marks and Spencer* (M&S) announced that its French stores were to shut, with the loss of hundreds of jobs. In the UK, such closures may be regarded as local tragedies, but they are also looked upon with a degree of fatalism: in business *c'est la vie*. Not so in France. There were condemnations by politicians, demonstrations in Paris and the company was taken to court and successfully prosecuted for breaking French labour law, which insisted on the right of workers to be consulted on such matters. Yet, the outrage was not wholly nationalistic. A few weeks after the M&S decision, French food manufacturer *Danone* announced the loss of over 2,000 jobs. Not only were there demonstrations, and even a consumer boycott, but the French government went so far as to tack on amendments to a bill already going through parliament: where over 1,000 people were to lose their jobs, businesses would have to offer retraining and enhanced severance pay. Meanwhile, at the EU level, the European Commissioner for Employment matters praised the French action. She insisted that workers and not just shareholders must be seen as 'stakeholders' in companies and used the affair to rally support for a proposal to extend to small firms' 'works councils' that would facilitate employee involvement in company strategy – plans that the UK insisted infringed the business freedom and flexibility that were vital to a dynamic European economy.

---

up to the EU's 'Social Chapter' – a measure that allows some EU labour law (examples so far include maximum working hours and rights for part-time workers) to be made by union-employer agreement (see Chapter 8). On the other hand, as if determined to make itself difficult to pigeonhole, the Labour government, since signing, has done its best to limit 'European interference' in labour market matters, claiming that 'light-touch' regulation is one of the keys to the UK's relatively low unemployment. The extent to which this stance – and opposition to it – is solely ideological (in a left–right sense) or in part cultural and national is a moot point (see Box 9.6)

Bringing an end to 'tax and spend'?

Social democrats in Europe, particularly in the UK, Germany and Italy, have been accused by critics to their left of trying to dismantle the welfare state. Rather than seeking to finance its expansion by maintaining or even ratcheting-up progressive rates of taxation, they have apparently been desperate to cut spending in order (now that they apparently no longer care about working people) to fund tax cuts for the middle class. In fact, beyond marginal changes (some of which admittedly impact harshly on those affected), there is little evidence for this. The reality is either more prosaic (little change and therefore few headlines) or even directly contradictory.

There is no doubt that most social democrats now buy into what, for them anyway, is a 'new macroeconomic consensus: fiscal stabilization = reduction in government debt burden = lower interest rates = more investment = increased economic growth = lower unemployment and stable inflation' (Teague and Donaghey, 2003: 110). But this does not mean that they do not tax and they do not spend. In Spain, for instance, social democratic PSOE may have been accused of selling out to market liberalism throughout the 1980s, but public expenditure, especially on health and education climbed relentlessly as the party, in power for the first time in over forty years, attempted to make up for decades of neglect under right-wing dictatorship (see Astudillo, 2002: 16–19 and Boix, 1998). More recently, the UK Labour government, supposedly keener than most to surrender social democracy to the market and the middle classes, presided from the late 1990s onwards over unprecedented rises in spending, particularly on youth unemployment, family support, education and (above all) on health, where by 2007–8 spending in real terms was to be double that of 1997. Moreover, it paid for this largesse not simply via economic growth and a decline in unemployment (which have always been social democrats' favourite sources). It also did it through tax rises – primarily via an early hit on the excess profits of privatized utilities and pension funds, and then via carefully disguised raids on personal income that have hit the middle classes hardest.

Little surprise, then, that at the same time as left-wing critics in Spain, the United Kingdom and elsewhere have been hounding social democrats for not doing enough, the centre-right in Europe continues to accuse them of doing far too much. According to conservatives, centre-left politicians remain addicted to pursuing 'tax and spend' policies and overprotecting a 'bloated' welfare state – all of which, according to them, creates inefficiencies, stifles initiative and swallows up resources that would be better employed in the private sector. Their criticisms seem to have resonance with some voters: at the turn of the twenty-first century, many social democratic governments were replaced by centre-right coalitions (see Table 9.1). And many of these coalitions promised – after elections if not always before them – to kick-start the economy by cutting public spending and 'slashing'

Table 9.1 Europe's short-lived centre-left 'hegemony'

EU countries with social democrats in government (1999)	Still in government (early 2005)	Date they lost office to the centre-right
Austria	No	1999
Belgium	Yes	
Czech Rep.	Yes	
Denmark	No	2001
Finland	Yes	
France	No	2002
Italy	No	2001
Germany	Yes	
Greece	No	2004
Netherlands	No	2002
Norway	No	2001
Portugal	No	2002
Sweden	Yes	
UK	Yes	

corporate and personal taxes. However, with the possible exception of Austria (where years of 'grand coalition' compromises between social and Christian democrats built a state that could, many claimed, afford to lose a little weight), their ability to deliver on these promises has been slightly disappointing.

This is not surprising. Historical evidence suggests that levels of taxation and public spending, while not utterly impervious to government action, are very 'sticky', making it difficult even for supposedly right-wing (let alone supposedly left-wing) administrations to do much 'dismantling of the welfare state' (see Green-Pedersen, 1999). This is partly because programmes create powerful constituencies with large numbers of votes. It is also because a great deal of public spending (and therefore taxation) is devoted to items which have been seen by most west Europeans – for good or ill – as rights rather than privileges. These include (above all) pensions, education, health-care and social security in the event of illness, accident, or unemployment. Many people also expect the state to supplement wages that no one can realistically live on, although there is more ambivalence throughout western Europe about helping the supposedly 'undeserving poor' who could do more to help themselves (see Wilensky, 2002: Chapter 10).

There is little to suggest that central and eastern Europeans (many of whom were, after all, brought up to believe that state provision of these things was automatic) view things very differently. Certainly, their political representatives seem to reflect those preferences, notwithstanding some initially radical rhetoric, reinforced by the recommendations of international bodies such as the IMF and the World Bank (see Ferge, 2001), about moving toward a more 'residual' or 'Anglo-Saxon' welfare state. Take healthcare, for instance, reforms in most postcommunist states 'have not been noteworthy for their emphasis on market competition or privatization' but were instead 'geared to securing universal access to health-care funded out of compulsory public or state-owned insurance schemes' and payroll taxes (Deacon, 2000: 155; see also Wagener, 2002).

In many of the areas just mentioned, in fact, there is an almost inbuilt pressure for spending increases right across Europe. Countries' government spending on education, for instance, varies between 4 and 8 per cent of GDP, with an average of around 5 per cent; but it is generally recognized that in order not to get left behind economically, a country's 'human capital' has to be constantly improved. Sweden and the UK, for instance, upped the numbers going into higher education between 1991 and 2001 by 85 per cent and 64 per cent, respectively. In health (see Figure 9.1), improvements in medical technology mean that people expect to be treated for conditions that previously would have been ignored and that might have served (as Charles Dickens's Mr Scrooge once put it) to 'decrease the surplus population'. As regards social security, there are several reasons why the state is more likely to spend in the future rather than save. These include the end of the concept of a 'family wage' (i.e. one big enough to support a non-working wife bringing up children) brought about by the entry of women into the labour force (see Chapter 1), the inability (or unwillingness) of governments to ensure full employment and the low wages paid to many in

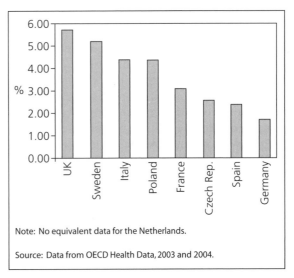

Note: No equivalent data for the Netherlands.

Source: Data from OECD Health Data, 2003 and 2004.

Figure 9.1 Average annual growth in public spending on health, 1997–2002

the (largely non-unionized) service sector economy – all situations that the state often ends up subsidizing through income support.

The other 'big-ticket item' – in some countries, the biggest ticket item – is old age pensions. We noted in Chapter 1 that Europe's ageing population was one of the biggest challenges facing its politicians. But, outside the UK (where governments of both right and left have made use of the highly majoritarian system to force through pension reform with little consultation) many have ducked it, or at least had to take things very slowly. Here is one issue on which there does seem to be a consensus among political elites, be they on the right or the left. Unfortunately, however, the consensus often seems to unite those that are in government rather than in opposition. An obvious exception to this rule has been Sweden, where a commission involving stakeholders and five political parties in the 1990s managed to produce a package which essentially supplemented the state earnings-related scheme with private provision and went some way to means-testing the basic pension. Elsewhere, the situation has, sadly, been very different. In office, most governments in Europe have at least attempted to tackle the problem by a combination of the following: by reining back entitlements, most obviously by indexing to inflation rather than average wages; by raising the retirement age and by de-privileging public sector employees on particularly generous schemes (a real problem in France and Italy); and by encouraging or mandating private provision. In opposition, however, many parties have opportunistically supported (or, at least, declined to criticize) protests.

In some countries, reform has been forced through despite the lack of cross-party consensus: the social democratic government in Germany, for instance, managed in 2001 to bring in a phased reduction of entitlements in the face of criticism from the Christian Democrats, who seemed to have departed from a long-running agreement on such matters. In other countries, however, the lack of consensus, especially when combined with popular protest, makes it difficult, and even impossible, for those supposedly in power to act decisively. Of course, this is not always the case: Austria's right-wing government faced mass protests and strikes over its planned pension reforms in the summer of 2003, but promised to soldier on – partly perhaps because the country has no recent history of such events bringing down governments. Elsewhere, however, things are different. The right-wing Italian government of Silvio Berlusconi, for instance, almost forfeited office in the summer of 2004 when – in the face of mass public protests reminiscent of those that had brought it down in the mid-1990s – it just managed to pass relatively minor changes to a pension system that swallows up a large proportion of GDP and current spending by the state. Similarly, the French government has had to undertake only piecemeal reform, and that almost by stealth, lest it spark off a repeat of the 1995 demonstrations that led to the downfall of the last centre-right administration that tried to force the pace on pensions. This is a serious problem because both countries (like the UK) operate 'pay-as-you-go' systems, where pensions are paid by taxes on those currently working: since the size of that group is going to shrink relative to pensioners, it will face an increasing (and perhaps politically intolerable) tax burden unless something is done.

It is clear from these examples that the capacity or willingness of parties and governments to make these 'hard choices' (Pierson, 2001) does not seem to vary according to whether they can be described as 'left' and 'right'. This is just as true in central and eastern Europe, where governments have taken the opportunity offered by majority acceptance that there needed to be at least some reform to put in place multitiered (Swedish-style) pension systems that many of their western counterparts are struggling to implement (see Wagener, 2002: 162–8). In Hungary, for instance, it was the ex-communist Social Democrats who, in the mid-1990s, radically reformed the country's pension system, introducing mandatory second-tier private provision (see Deacon, 2000).

Again, this does not necessarily mean that 'right' and 'left' have no meaning. But because Europe's voters seem to want to have it all (for instance, low taxes and early retirement on generous pensions) they have helped create a new division that does, indeed, threaten to go 'beyond left and right'. This is the division between parties and politicians who, however reluctantly, force voters to face up to the impossibility of 'having it all' (and are often – as in Hungary – thrown out at the next election) and those who are prepared to pretend for the sake of office that 'hard choices' can be avoided. Unless voters change, it may be facile (even if very fashionable) to put all the blame for 'the state we're in' on politicians. After all, they are simply trying to make the 'least worst' trade-offs they can between what Europeans want and what they need (see Kitschelt, 2000: 160–6). What they are not doing, however, is taxing or spending much less (see Table 9.2).

The EU: deadweight or driving force?

We have already observed that the EU has played a role in privatization and the debate over flexible labour markets. In fact, it is a key factor in any discussion of the triumph (or otherwise) of liberal capitalism and the constraints on governments, especially of the centre-left. Not only does it provide a framework of binding legislation and decision rules within which both economic and political activity in European countries must take place, it provides an arena in which politicians and the representatives of interest groups articulate their views and attempt to move that framework in their desired direction. It also – and this should

Table 9.2 Total tax revenue as a percentage of GDP, 1973–2001

Country	1973	1981	1986	1995	2001
Sweden	38.8	47.4	49.3	48.5	51.4
France	34.0	40.9	43.4	44.0	45.0
Italy	24.4	31.6	35.9	41.2	42.0
Netherlands	39.8	43.0	43.4	41.9	39.5
Czech Rep.	n/a	n/a	n/a	40.1	38.4
UK	31.4	36.7	38.2	34.8	37.3
Germany	33.0	34.2	34.0	38.2	36.8
Spain	18.0	24.3	29.6	32.8	35.2
Poland	n/a	n/a	n/a	39.6	33.6
EU-15	31.0	36.5	39.2	40.1	41.2
US	26.9	27.5	25.9	27.6	28.9

Note: Years before 2001 are dates of EU enlargement.

Source: Data from *OECD Revenue Statistics, 1965–2002*, p. 74.

never be forgotten amid all the talk of globalization – helps constitute what for all European countries has become by far their biggest market (see Chapter 1).

Like social democracy, the EU seems to get it in the neck from both sides. On the one hand some neo-liberals see it as a pathetic, self-delusionary refuge from the bracing winds of globalization. They also see it as a bastion of 'continental corporatism' (see Chapter 8), whose support for labour and environmental standards and excessive product regulation risks clogging up still further the arteries of an already ailing European economy. On the other hand, their opponents see the EU as a potentially anti-democratic (and anti-social democratic) attempt to embed or institutionalize neo-liberalism that has taken on its own momentum – a momentum that the largely domestic focus of Europe's centre-left is likely to prevent it doing much about, even assuming it wanted to (see McGowan, 2001). To these radical critics, the EU is the creation of politicians who are convinced that there is no alternative, yet sceptical about their own ability (or the ability of their counterparts in other countries) to persuade their voters of the case. The key to this project is the single market,

and the single currency. These will apparently encourage capital, among other things, to relocate to where labour is cheapest, regulation is lightest and taxes are lowest and, in so doing, force governments to 'shrink' the state in order to ensure that their country remains an attractive place in which to do business.

More explicitly, the run-up to joining the euro was supposed to oblige Europe's overspending governments to tighten their belts by forcing them to meet 'convergence criteria' (set levels of debt, deficit and inflation) in order to qualify. And, when the single currency was adopted, it meant governments surrendering control of interest rates to the European Central Bank (ECB) (see Chapter 2), thus depriving them of an important tool of economic policy and control. At the same time, their new-found inability to devalue their currencies in order to adjust to balance of payments problems was designed to force them into structural measures (such as lowering real wages and taxes and introducing supply-side measures) to regain international competitiveness. Moreover, in order to ensure that all countries in the 'Eurozone' (the name given to the collection of states that have adopted the euro) play the game and preserve the credibility of the new currency, they have to sign up to the Stability and Growth Pact (SGP), policed by the Commission (see Box 9.7, Heipertz and Verdun, 2003 and Howarth, 2004). This is supposed to stop them building up debts and deficits by, for example, countercyclical spending to offset a Eurozone ('one-size-fits-all') interest rate that might be set so high that it risks choking off their economic growth.

We should be careful not to portray all these obligations as externally imposed by the EU on unwilling victims in the member states: clearly, there were many conservative interests in many of them who were keen that their politicians swallow the medicine, and many politicians willing to use EMU – as they use EU compliance more generally – to help them do what they wanted to do anyway (see Dyson and Featherstone, 1999 and Radaelli, 1997). But we should also be careful before assuming that the need to qualify for the single currency in the first place did, in fact, force European countries into swingeing cutbacks: as Rhodes (2002: 44) puts it:

[i]n reality, 'getting in shape for EMU' did nothing to prevent even the most debt-ridden and poorly managed European economies from reducing their deficits and debts while also boosting spending on social and employment policy. Higher taxes, privatization and lower interest payments, facilitated by falling interest rates on smaller national debts, all allowed welfare states to keep on growing.

Now that the euro is in use, it would appear that the will of politicians has proved far stronger than the rules they (or, rather, their predecessors) designed in order to constrain themselves. So far, anyway, European governments have responded to the limitations of the interest rate regime simply by breaching the SGP – and so far earned nothing more than a scolding for so doing (Box 9.7). Nor, as yet, is there much sign of them trying to exert significant downward pressure on real wages. In fact, real wages continue to grow throughout Europe and are one reason why, for instance, the EU's bloated agricultural budget, which adds considerably to the price Europeans pay for food, is more an issue for the 'chattering classes' than it is for ordinary consumers.

Of course, these are still early days, and one important part of the supposedly neo-liberal single market jigsaw is yet to fall into place. This is the idea of 'tax harmonization' – the bringing into line of all member states' tax rates and policies that is argued for on two grounds. First, from a neo-liberal point of view, national differences in tax regimes and rates represent inefficient and trade-distorting barriers to genuine competition. Secondly, there are those who believe there must be European control of tax and fiscal policy in order to offset the ECB's control of interest rates and monetary policy – something that some neo-liberals might support if they could believe (which, interestingly, few can) that rates would, as a result, be lower rather than higher. There are few signs, however, that either Europe's politicians or their electorates are listening to such arguments. Opinion polls show next to no support for tax harmonization. Consequently rates of VAT, of corporation tax and excise duty continue to vary (though, especially in the case of the first two, less so once necessary statistical adjustments are made to the standard or headline

---

BOX 9.7

Big stick or big joke? The EU's Stability and Growth Pact

Under the terms of the SGP, Eurozone countries are not supposed to run budget deficits of more than 3 per cent of GDP. If they do, they are eventually liable to fines payable to the European Commission. However, it is not the Commission but the other member states, acting through the Council of Ministers, that decide on punishment. So far, they have proved reluctant to allow the Commission to do anything other than issue warnings and reprimands. One of these, issued in 2001, was enough to make Portugal cut spending in order to keep below the ceiling in 2002. Since then, however, the failure to take action against Germany and France, the most persistent offender, has rendered the Pact something of a laughing stock – so much so that, in 2004, six of the twelve Eurozone countries (Germany, France, Italy, Greece, the Netherlands and a rather bitter Portugal!) looked set to breach the rules. The Commission responded by taking the Council of Finance Ministers to the ECJ for failure to act. In July 2004, the ECJ found in favour of the Commission, although this 'moral victory' may well be rendered redundant by a review of the Pact, at which some of its rules may be relaxed. Nevertheless, to dismiss the pact too lightly would be a big mistake: the fact that the Eurozone's supposedly sovereign nations have agreed to permanent surveillance (and potential sanctioning) of their governments' spending and borrowing by a supranational institution represents a major development in the political economy of Europe and European integration (see Jones and Verdun, 2004).

---

rates always quoted in the media). And whether these variations really make much of a difference to business decisions, or whether they really are used by governments as means of enticing firms to set up or stay in their countries, is very difficult to judge (see Radaelli, 2004).

But if the EU has 'failed' to get compliance and harmonization on tax and spending, does it matter? Perhaps not, if it means that there ends up being a balance between what Scharpf (1998) neatly characterizes as 'negative integration' (the EU attempting to prevent governments from doing things such as protecting industries or running deficits) and 'positive integration' (EU regulations, social policies and subsidies). By the same token, the apparent preservation of welfare and labour relations systems at the national level means that the absence of such institutions at the EU level may not actually matter as much as some – particularly those who insist such a capacity has to be developed as a counterweight to the EU's liberal agenda – think it does (see Rhodes, 2002). Moreover, we should not understate the level of aid to backward regions, let alone to farmers. Structural funding to these regions between 2000 and 2006 totals €183 billion (Molle, 2001), much of which is devoted to 'supply-side measures' such as retraining and not simply job-creating infrastructure projects. Nor should we forget the fact that by enlargement, the EU, irrespective of whether its institutions increase their power over national governments, has expanded both the opportunities and the options available to businesses in Europe – both of which they can use to their advantage. In 2004, for instance, German-owned industrial concerns, *DaimlerChrysler*, *Siemens* and *Bosch*, were able to force longer working hours in factories in Germany and France partly by threatening to re-locate plants to the Czech Republic and Hungary, where wages are lower.

How much longer that wage differential will last, however, is debatable. Clearly, it will not close in the next decade, but it is unlikely to last for ever. For one thing, the economies of the new member states are growing much faster than their western counterparts – and the continuation of such growth is not only likely but clearly in the interests of the EU and all its member states (see Gros, 2002). For another, the gradual institutionalization of welfare states in the postcommunist countries (see below) is likely in the long term to lead to higher-wage economies. Nor is it something that the EU, as an institution, seems to want to do anything, or to be capable of doing anything, about. Member states, after all, have been so determined to prevent the EU from having any say about how they organize social provision that they have expressly denied it competence in the field in recent treaties. As a consequence, the EU can neither enforce 'European' models of welfare (see

Chapter 1) on the region nor, as seems on balance more likely, prevent its governments adopting them, albeit in hybrid fashion (see Kovács, 2002 and Wagener, 2002).

Separating the facts from the hype

Comparative scholar Martin Rhodes provides a recent concise, no-nonsense but authoritative attempt to separate the European facts from the globalized hype about the triumph of neo-liberalism and the apparently concomitant 'end of the nation state' or at least its capacity to help determine the economic fate of its people (see Ohmae, 1996 for an example). He notes the following (Rhodes, 2002: 41–2):

▸ 'European welfare states remain large, expensive and highly redistributive and their systems of labour market protection both generous and extensive'.

▸ '[T]here is no necessary correlation between welfare-state size/redistribution and the competitiveness of a country's companies in export markets' – something that markets are well aware of.

▸ '[A]nalyses of transnational investments patterns provide no support for the argument that multinationals are exploiting the differences in labour-market standards and regulatory institutions' between European countries (i.e. engaging in what is called 'social dumping').

▸ Broadly speaking, richer European countries are preserving levels of social spending while poorer ones tend to increase it in order to catch up. Meanwhile, 'permanent contracts remain dominant (and highly regulated by collective agreements and statute), and although there has been a spread of new contract forms (short-term, part-time work) in Europe, countries with high levels of social protection have also extended that protection to these "new" forms of work'.

▸ Because companies base their location decisions on myriad factors and governments find it hard to estimate the gains from tax competition with other countries, little such competition (and, therefore, downward pressure on revenues) has taken place.

Rhodes is not alone (see, for example, van Kersbergen, 2000) and his general conclusions are backed up not just by the findings of large quantitative projects (see Stephens, Huber and Ray, 1999), but by country studies and cross-national studies of particular policy areas. Studies of both types point to the continued persistence not just of welfare states but of national differences, most of which continue to correspond to Esping-Anderson's (1990) regime types outlined in Chapter 1. Three recent examples should suffice.

In the first example, Virpi Timonen outlines some of the changes made to the welfare states of Finland and Sweden – changes which include more private delivery of publicly funded services and a trend towards means-tested pensions – but nevertheless concludes that, because they continue to cover almost everyone and are therefore supported by almost everyone, they have not changed fundamentally, even when confronted with globalization and recession (Timonen, 2003).

The second example is central and eastern Europe. True, there is considerable debate between those (e.g. Ferge, 2001) who see the regions' governments, pressured by the need to persuade the World Bank and the IMF that they have really changed, heading down the Anglo-Saxon route and those (e.g. Deacon, 2000) who see a more 'European model' beginning to bed down. But, on balance, a mixture of institutional inertia, electoral constraints, and reasonably intelligent picking and mixing on the part of politicians (see Kovács, 2002 and Wagener, 2002), has seen to it that (Kovács, 2002: 198–9)

> The 'communist welfare state' is being transformed *but* its relatively tightly knit safety net (including traditional protecting ropes) has not disappeared. At the same time, transformation is not excessive, the institutional experiments do not go much beyond their counterparts in Western Europe.

In our third example, researchers focused on maternity benefits and child care programmes across Europe (and North America) and found, firstly, continued support (despite some limited convergence) for the idea of different countries belonging to different welfare regimes, secondly, that 'reports of the welfare state's demise do not hold true in these areas', and, thirdly, that while cultures and past patterns and choices influence current provision, 'the specific decisions that governments make' were just as vital (see Henderson and White, 2004). A similar conclusion is reached, incidentally, by a recent study (Mahler, 2004) which supports the idea that domestic politics plays a bigger role than globalization in determining the level of income inequality and redistribution in advanced countries. In other words, because politics still matters (and matters as much, if not, more than markets) Europe's welfare states – still largely protected from EU 'interference' – remain distinctive and, though not unchanged, relatively intact.

Why it still makes sense to be different

Just as Europe's welfare states are still welfare states, its social democrats can still claim, with some justification, to be social democrats, though not perhaps without qualifications. The biggest of these is that they have largely abandoned their goal of a more equal society – a goal that survived even long after most social democrats had embraced (more or less grudgingly) a role for the market as well as the state. This does not necessarily mean they are happy to let the poor get poorer. But it does mean that they are less concerned than previously about the gap between rich and poor which, as we saw in Chapter 1, has got wider all over Europe (largely as a result of the rich being allowed to get richer). Instead, they are now more preoccupied with *horizontal redistribution* (between old and young, sick and healthy, employed and unemployed) than with *vertical redistribution* (between rich and poor) (see Bonoli, 2004). Europe's social democrats have also admitted the difficulty of maintaining full employment via demand management and shifted their focus onto maximizing employment via supply-side measures that are often labelled 'active labour market policies'. They have also gone beyond the idea that 'more is (necessarily) better' when it comes to state involvement and public spending, and admitted the

The Netherlands (Nederland)

Area: 0.9% of EU-25
Population: 3.6% of EU-25
GDP: 4.2% of EU-25
Joined EU: founder member 1957
Capital city: Amsterdam

History: After breaking free from Habsburg and Spanish rule by the mid-seventeenth century and French rule by the beginning of the nineteenth, the Netherlands assumed its present status as a constitutional monarchy in 1848. Even though much of its Roman Catholic-dominated south became part of Belgium in 1839, the Netherlands remained a religiously divided society, with profound cultural and social differences not just between Catholics and Protestants' but also between different branches of the latter. These differences were both maintained and contained by the *verzuiling* ('pillar') system: social groups marked off from each other by their denomination or ideological affiliation led largely separate existences, with their own welfare services, unions, business groups, political parties and media. From 1958 to 1973, all coalition governments were dominated by the centrist Christian Democrats. By the 1970s, however, the declining importance of religion and the consequent crumbling of the pillar system, allowed more governing flexibility. After a period of 'grand coalitions' with the Christian Democrats, the social democratic Labour Party finally got together with the economically liberal VVD and the more centrist D'66 party to form what became known as 'the purple coalition'.

The Christian Democrats finally made it back into office in 2002, but not without the help of the far-right List Pim Fortuyn (LPF) – a collection of political novices put together by a media-savvy maverick who was assassinated by an animal rights activist just before the election. After it, the LPF – and, consequently the government, fell apart. At the election of 2003 something like 'normal service' was resumed, but the Labour Party's recovery proved insufficient to oust the Christian Democrats, who formed a second centre-right coalition with VVD and D'66.

Economy and society: The Netherlands may be one of the most densely populated countries in the world, but its population is still only 16.3 million. Nevertheless, the Dutch economy has for some time been regarded as one of the strongest in Europe, resulting in a per capita GDP that in 2003 was around 20 per cent higher than the EU-25 average. Rotterdam, half of whose population are said to be immigrants or from immigrant families, is the continent's biggest port, but the country as a whole is strong in road transportation, petrochemicals, consumer electronics and banking. It also has a highly efficient agricultural sector. This export-oriented economy may be vulnerable to downturns in big markets such as Germany, but it has helped the Dutch build one of the world's most developed welfare states; indeed, the supposedly successful combination of the two became known as the 'Dutch miracle'. Recently, however, more attention has been paid to its downsides, not least the extent to which sickness benefit and part-time work masks unemployment. And, while the Netherlands' (or at least its cities') famously tolerant attitude to drugs and alternative life-styles continues, its embrace of multiculturalism appears to be under strain especially after episodes of religiously motivated violence. This may make life more difficult for the country's 650,000 Muslims.

Governance: The Netherlands is a parliamentary democracy, elected under a PR system affording seats in the legislature to parties that gain just two-thirds of 1 per cent of the national vote. This low 'threshold' facilitates a large number and spread of parties in the more powerful, popularly elected *Tweede Kamer* (Second Chamber). The less powerful First Chamber is chosen by the councils of the country's twelve provinces. Majority coalitions are very much the norm, even if two or three months of hard bargaining elapses between election night and the government being sworn in by the Queen. Notwithstanding this preference for majorities, the policy process is typically consensual – indeed, some say getting anything done takes too long (the so-called 'Dutch disease'). The Supreme Court (the *Hoge Raad*) is a comparatively weak institution since, unlike its counterparts in other countries, it cannot pronounce upon the constitutionality of laws passed by parliament, nor subject the actions of politicians and public servants to full judicial review.

Foreign policy: The Second World War put paid to the Netherlands' century-old policy of trade-boosting neutrality, as well as to its empire in South America and the Dutch East Indies (most of which is now Indonesia). It was a founding member of NATO, and worked hard to maintain a good relationship with the USA, as well as the UK, despite the fact that the latter was initially cagey about joining the EEC, which the Netherlands helped found in 1957. This traditionally 'Atlanticist' outlook came under strain in the 1980s, following huge public protests against the siting of US nuclear missiles in the country. Some observers also argue that the Netherlands, one of the biggest net financial contributors to the EU, is also cooling in its enthusiasm for further European integration. This would seem to be borne out in recent European Parliament elections.

Further reading: Andeweg and Irwin (2005) and Keman (2002).

private sector into areas that previously might have been thought to be public sector preserves.

Such an agenda might not be what some radical critics want; but it may be sensible (even superior) in the light of increasing evidence that, in the real world, individuals slip in and out of need over their lifetimes far more than we previously imagined – and far more than media-sexy terms like 'under-class' or 'middle-England' (and their European equivalents) imply (see Goodin *et al.*, 1999). But simply because social democracy is not what it was (what political ideology or institution or policy regime is?) need not mean that it is no longer social democracy. The latter has never been interested in being a prophet crying in the wilderness. Indeed, it has left that role to Europe's 'left parties', many of whom, incidentally, are in the forefront of opposition to the supposedly 'neo-liberal' side of the EU (see Dunphy, 2004).

In fact, these left parties are far from impotent or unimportant. In many countries, their presence makes it all the more unlikely that social democrats will ever take what their critics call 'betrayal' too far: if they did, then many of the votes of the disillusioned and the disadvantaged might accrue to the more radical alternative, which would probably swing the centre-left back to the left. This happened at the 1998 election in Sweden, when the Social Democratic SAP lost significant support to the Left Party and was henceforth distinctly more cagey about rationalizing the welfare state. Likewise, the existence of the Greens (and more liberal or libertarian variants of the left) relies on social democrats failing – at least, in the eyes of their critics – to defend core values (in this case, civil liberties and the interests of developing countries). But the presence of alternative parties on the social democrats' left flank also ensures that, looking over their shoulders, they do not completely forget such things.

Of course, the 'anchoring' effect of Green and Left potential depends in part on the extent to which this potential is likely to seriously damage the capacity of the social democrats to get into and dominate government. In some countries – Germany and Sweden are the most obvious examples – the social democrats can, in effect, afford to 'contract out' at least part of the conscience vote to smaller parties to their left, banking on the fact that

the latter will probably join them in a progressive bloc that should prove capable of amassing more parliamentary seats than the bloc on the other side. The Swedish SAP can count not only on the Greens, but also on the Left Party, notwithstanding its concern not to cede it too many of its voters. The German SPD, however, is stuck with the greens alone, since it would be reluctant to cede voters to the former communist PDS or a planned new party of the left. This, along with its union links, rather limits its ability to move too far into *die neue mitte* (Chancellor Gerhard Schröder's equivalent of 'the Third Way', literally translated as 'the new middle'). So, too, we should add, does the need to avoid being seen to be too close to the centre-right Christian Democrats – something that can happen all too easily in a country where cross-party co-operation is so institutionally necessary that it has been labelled the 'Grand Coalition State' (see Schmidt, 2002b). In other countries, the centre-left has to be even more careful about not allowing too much space to open up on its left flank. France is the best example, though Italy and the Netherlands, to cite just two more examples, also have party and electoral systems that consistently deliver up small, radical parties to whom unwary 'centrists' can lose votes if they stray too far. The French socialist's candidate for the presidency in 2002, Prime Minister Lionel Jospin, is widely thought to have blown his chances by taking too centrist a stance, leading some on the left either to abstain or vote for no-hopers who wore their radical hearts on their sleeves.

There is, of course, one country in Europe where the electoral system's power to squeeze out smaller parties presents no such constraints – the UK. Yet, even there, social democracy's supposedly rightward drift is more contestable than New Labour's opponents on both the left and the right (and in the media) sometimes acknowledge. For instance, a 'state of the nation' report by a leading UK think-tank (Paxton and Dixon, 2004) observed that inequality had risen slightly under the Labour government that took office in 1997, largely as a result of the rich continuing to get richer. It also observed that, in 2001, just over 20 per cent of children in Britain were living in households earning below 60 per cent of median income: this compared favourably with Spain and Italy (around

25 per cent), but less well with Sweden (around 10 per cent), Germany and the Netherlands (around 15 per cent) and France (just under 20 per cent). Yet, the report also noted that the rise in inequality had begun to level off under Labour, and that Labour's policy of targeted assistance to working families and children had contributed to it going from bottom of the EU-15 table in 1998 to eleventh in 2001. Defenders of Labour's continued centre-left credentials can also argue that, by focusing on (and delivering) economic growth and employment, and concentrating government help on working families, the UK government has pursued a 'classic postwar' social democratic strategy – even if, by 'talking right and acting left', it has done it by stealth. In any case, the radical rhetoric that characterized Labour before the party began its 'modernization' in the mid-1980s was always rather unconvincing given what (with the exception of 1945–8) was its very modest style of socialism in government.

European social democracy, then, has always been accommodating and has always operated in diverse institutional, cultural and competitive settings. These have, of course, increased as the end of communism in central and eastern Europe has produced a new bunch of parties that have adopted – some would say simply pasted on – the 'social democratic' label. This is problematic because, as we suggested in Chapter 5, the differences between left and right do not as yet (and may never exactly) replicate traditional western distinctions (see Sitter, 2003). The latter are rooted in the extent of state involvement in the economy and welfare provision. Distinctions in some postcommunist democracies have more to do with attitudes to the communist past, moral and family values and, indeed, to European integration, with 'social democrats' in central and eastern Europe being generally more favourable to the EU than their slightly more 'sceptic' right-wing opponents. These different bases for distinguishing the two sides are particularly the case in Poland, although the left and right in the Czech Republic and Hungary could possibly claim to be more like their western counterparts (see Millard, 2004). They, too, hope to make moderate use of the power of the state to enhance citizens' quality of life and to maximize their equality of opportunity and their access to

decent and hopefully helpful support whenever markets fail. But they, too, have stopped trying to pretend that they have either the will or the means to prevent those markets failing in the first place.

So, the supposed collapse in the distinction between right and left, and the concomitant weakening of the welfare state, is, to say the least, an idea in need of severe qualification. It is also one that offers us little purchase on one of the defining features of party politics since the 1990s and perhaps longer. This is the 'bipolarization' of politics we referred to in Chapter 5 – the fact that far from tending toward politics that advantages centre parties and 'grand coalitions' between large left- and right-wing parties, many of Europe's party systems appear to be structured by competition between blocs of parties, cleaving to either the left or the right. The left bloc generally contains Left parties, Greens, social democrats and some progressive or social liberals. Its counterpart on the right includes Christian Democrats, conservatives and market liberals. It also includes, increasingly, the far right (see Bale, 2003) – a force whose rise is also blamed by some on the presumed decline of difference between right and left and reforms to the state that apparently make it incapable of protecting people from the predations of globalization.

No easy explanations: the rise of the far right

It is common wisdom that a combination of political convergence and economic dislocation has led inexorably to the rise of apathy and more extreme alternatives. We have already suggested in Chapter 6, that apathy and 'disconnect' can be overdone at least when measured by turnout at general elections. Declines in the latter have not yet gone on long enough, nor are they uniform enough, to constitute a definite trend. Likewise, the rise of protest politics on the left, and the tendency for what appear to be increasingly large numbers of young people to become alienated from conventional politics and attracted to postmaterialist alternatives (see Chapter 8) may turn into something more permanent than, say, the hippie and street-fighting movements of the late 1960s and early

1970s. Rather more concrete, though still a little hyped, is the rise of the far-right (see Chapter 5) – something which pundits and politicians themselves often put down to what they claim is 'the lack of clear alternatives' presented by the political mainstream.

This explanation for the impressive performance of far-right parties since the 1990s has some merit. Class-based appeals, overt or even covert, have declined, and media-oriented, leader-focused campaigns may not have encouraged the far-right to claim all the parties are the same (they have always done that) but they may have made that claim easier to believe. Also, one of the keys to their electoral fortunes in recent years has been the success those parties have enjoyed in recruiting young, poorly educated working-class men (although we should note that support for the far right is by no means confined to them). These are the sort of people who in previous generations would have been expected to vote for left-wing or centre-left parties. Perhaps it is the case that those parties (or, at least, the economies they 'run') are no longer providing these people with the standard of living or, more particularly, the job security that they were brought up to expect. Equally, by emphasizing equality of opportunity (often based on educational ability) and by tolerating more inequality of outcome than previously, the centre-left may have helped the 'winners' in society to pull more obviously away from the 'losers'. Perhaps social democratic parties, along with a shrinking trade union movement, are also failing to supply these 'losers' with the class-conscious comradeship that their fathers (or at least their grandfathers) may have enjoyed.

Ultimately, however, the 'decline of difference'/'victims of globalization' explanation is just too pat. Things are more complicated than that (see Norris, 2005). Indeed, as an explanation it is deeply flawed and inadequate. It is flawed because it relies on what we have seen is a partial reading of social democracy's past and present orientation and an overly pessimistic impression of economic change and welfare decline. It also relies on a model of voting (i.e. class-based) that, as we noted in Chapter 6, many analysts are sceptical about. We should therefore be careful about blaming the centre left for supposedly letting down and losing what 'should' be 'their' voters. It is inadequate

because it does not explain why, when large numbers of voters claim to have trouble telling the difference between the parties, only some of them plump for the far-right. Nor does it explain why the far-right is much more successful in some countries rather than others. This variation appears, incidentally, to have little to do either with how, or how well, those countries have adjusted to economic change: the far-right has done particularly well in top-performing, low-unemployment, welfare states such as Austria, Denmark, Norway, and the Netherlands, and hopelessly in countries whose economies are either in much worse shape (e.g. Germany) or have much bigger differences between rich and poor (e.g. Spain and the UK). Moreover, and rather depressingly for the social democratic parties, the loss of office many of them experienced in the late 1990s–early 2000s – losses that could be blamed on the far-right helping the centre-right back into power (Bale, 2003) – occurred even though nearly all of them that lost office did so after presiding over economies that were performing pretty well.

In other words, things just are not as conveniently simple as the 'decline of difference'/'victims of globalization' explanation makes out. Moreover, those who buy into it also make the mistake of assuming that support for the far-right is simply a protest vote – something the other parties could do something about if they were somehow more responsive and less convergent. Yet, research shows that far-right voters are far less likely to be protest voters than is widely assumed: they vote for extremist parties because they are convinced by their populist arguments – arguments that may include, but go way beyond, the hardly novel suggestion that the 'old parties' are 'all the same' (see Mény and Surel, 2002). Those arguments also have less to do with left-right competition on the socio-economic dimension, where centre-left and centre-right are supposed to have converged, than they have with 'values', where the evidence of convergence between the largely liberal left and the more conservative right is even thinner. In particular, people voting for the far-right are worried about an issue that has come to dominate populist discourse – the growing presence of immigrant minorities in what they consider to be 'their' countries. It is to this issue that we now turn.

Learning resources

A usefully reflective literature review on twenty-first century social democracy is provided by Powell (2004) and an accessible, subtle and refreshingly balanced attempt to link developments in the European and international economy with the words and deeds of centre-left governments is provided by Hall (2002) in a volume that also contains useful contributions on the UK, Italy and France. Anyone interested in a long-term comparative political economy and its links to politics should also dip into Wilensky (2002). A stimulating read on the survival or otherwise of the welfare state in particular and national choices more generally in the face of globalization is Garrett (1998b). As for the far right, see Chapter 10.

EXECUTIVE SUMMARY

- Politics – or at least the occupation of office by one party rather than another – can and sometimes does make a difference, if not a huge one.

- The oft-heard assertion that the social democratic centre-left, and indeed Europe as a whole, is drifting towards policies that are traditionally associated with the more neo-liberal centre-right needs qualifying. Evidence for it on several key indicators – privatization, labour market policy and the supposed end of 'tax and spend' – presents a decidedly mixed picture.

- The equally familiar assertion that the EU's economic governance and its single market and currency will 'lock-in' neo-liberalism may also be wide of the mark, as are suggestions from the other side of the ideological spectrum that European integration necessarily promotes corporatist sclerosis.

- The facts about European political economy and the state in Europe need to be separated from the hype: for instance, welfare provision is not in terminal decline in the West and has survived the postcommunist transition in the East; its systematic varieties, like those of capitalism, still seem to exist. Politics continues to engage with, if not necessarily to trump, economics.

- There are sound political (and more specifically electoral) reasons why the centre-left is unlikely to 'meld' or 'morph' into the centre right.

- The idea that such 'melding' and 'morphing' explains the rise of far-right parties across Europe is deeply flawed, however attractive it may seem to pundits and politicians alike.

Chapter 10

Not wanted but needed: migrants and minorities

Migration into Europe: then and now
Europe's immigrants: who they are, where they come from and where they live
Political responses: populism, priming and catch-22s
Defusing Europe's 'demographic time bomb'?
Policy responses: towards 'Fortress Europe'?
Integrating citizens
The Roma: Europe's oldest ethnic minority
No settled future

We observed in Chapters 2 and 3 how European states were devolving power, sometimes to the extent that traditional distinctions between unitary and federal states seem less and less useful. We also observed that these moves were often, at least in part, a response to claims for autonomy or even independence made by minorities who feel they constitute a nation or even a race apart. But those who feel that they are somehow trapped in the wrong body politic are not, however, the only minorities in Europe. The population of most, if not all, European countries is now made up not just of the descendents of those who lived there centuries ago, but also of those who have arrived much more recently – and, indeed, are still arriving. Whether these minorities are distinctive through **race** or only **ethnicity**, their presence, and the fact that they are being joined by more immigrants every day, is the source of considerable anxiety and friction in many European countries – to an extent that it is not always appreciated in a country such as the USA which is (comparatively speaking anyway) more relaxed about the issue.

But the newly arrived are not the only group to find that Europe is not always as welcoming as they

might have hoped. Discrimination, be it outrageous or petty, can still be an everyday occurrence even for black, Asian, Chinese and Arabic people whose grandparents came to Europe five decades ago. It is also very much a reality for one of the continent's oldest minorities – people who have lived in Europe for centuries, but nevertheless continue to inspire misunderstanding, mistrust and sometimes outright hostility from the ethnic majorities whose states they share. They are the Roma – better (though arguably more pejoratively) known as gypsies.

Definition
Although frequently (and often very reasonably) used interchangeably, the terms race and ethnicity do have different origins and connotations. **Race** is essentially about visually obvious physical characteristics that mark out some individuals from others, even if advances in genetics seem finally to have put paid to the notion – at least, at the level of science if not popular culture – that such differences were somehow immutable and/or more than skin-deep. **Ethnicity** is to do with belonging to a social group that is tied by shared background, culture and language (and perhaps race, as well) and that may see itself (and be seen as) distinctive from the wider society. Inasmuch as it is ever really possible, one can perhaps escape or mask one's ethnicity, should one choose to do so. Persuading others, particularly if they are prejudiced, to ignore one's race may well be more difficult.

This chapter begins with an account of patterns of migration into Europe, explaining why so many people have chosen and been able to make the place their home in the past, and why so many are joining them. It then looks at who Europe's newest arrivals are, what they do and where they live, before going on to examine some of the less-than-edifying public, political and media responses to their coming, particularly in the light of fears surrounding Islamic terrorism. Next, the chapter looks at the ways in which European countries have begun, via the EU, to co-operate on immigration. It asks whether this is just one more surrender of sovereignty or yet another way to help preserve it, along with their historically determined immigration regimes. The chapter ends by exploring the situation of the Roma minority that has been around in Europe for nearly a thousand years, but is still at the bottom of the heap.

Migration into Europe: then and now

Most of Europe's minorities have always lived there – or, at least, their ancestors have. But Europe is also home to millions of people who came, or whose ancestors came, from other places. Immigration is nothing new in Europe. It has been going on for centuries. Indeed, if one supports the evolutionary hypothesis that the first Europeans came 'out of Africa', it has been going on since the beginning of human history. And even as the state system whose development we traced in Chapter 1 created national borders, they were rarely impermeable. European countries might not have encouraged immigration as much as 'settler' societies such as the US. But they often relaxed their restrictions when the labour market was tight and (perhaps more reluctantly) when claims were made upon them by citizens of their former colonies – Arabs from French North Africa, Afro-Caribbeans from the British Commonwealth or Surinamese from the Dutch East Indies (see Box 10.1)

Sometimes the flow of people into Europe has been a gradual, barely contested process, with intermarriage making a scientific nonsense of the idea of racial purity and bouts of emigration from Europe to the Americas and Australasia balancing out the numbers coming in. At other times, immigration has been more high-profile. Periodically, it has become the kind of influx that – especially when whipped up by the media – causes widespread anxieties about 'overcrowding', about competition for jobs, housing, welfare and sexual

partners and about cultural practices (such as forced marriage, honour killing and female circumcision) that many Europeans regard as alien, even barbaric. Migration, like European integration and especially eastern enlargement, has the capacity to both undermine and reinforce people's notions of where they come from, who they are and where they are going (see Spohn and Triandafyllidou, 2002).

For centuries, then, people have moved in and out of Europe without attracting much attention or doing much to alter, at least visibly, the ethnic balance. But there have also been several waves of immigration, often into particular countries, that have skewed the distribution of the continent's minorities, sometimes temporarily, sometimes permanently. For instance, by the late nineteenth-century, Jews had lived in Europe for centuries – mostly, though not always, without experiencing too many problems. But then the Jewish populations of several countries were swollen by others fleeing nineteenth-century 'pogroms' (organized massacres and expulsions that today we might call 'ethnic cleansing' or even genocide) in the Russian empire. East Central Europe and Germany were the obvious places to escape to. Tragically, however, they were also those most afflicted by the Nazi Holocaust of the 1940s (see Chapter 1), once again reducing, in the most terrible way imaginable, the previous expansion.

After the Second World War, waves of immigration were experienced first by nations that were victorious and/or possessed colonies in Africa and the Caribbean: the 1950s and 1960s saw West Indians coming to the UK and Moroccans, Algerians and Tunisians coming to France. In both countries, they came because labour shortages created demand for (often unskilled) workers at wages that seemed princely compared to what they could earn at home. The same was true, especially from the early 1960s on, in (West) Germany. There, *Gastarbeiter* (guestworkers), often Turkish, poured in to do the relatively low-paid jobs that (in the days of full employment we described in Chapter 1) Germans turned their noses up at, but that needed doing if the country's 'economic miracle' was to be sustained. The UK, Germany and France also took in large numbers of Spanish, Portuguese and Italians. They were either leaving

---

BOX 10.1
Out of Africa, but not necessarily everywhere else: European decolonization

France, after almost eight years of fighting, left the Americans to try and sort out Vietnam after 1954. After another eight years of fighting, it left Algeria in 1962, having long disposed of its colonies further south in Africa. It continues, however, to hang on to territorial possessions in the Caribbean, Indian Ocean and in Polynesia – the so called DOM-TOMs. The DOMs (*Départements d'Outre-Mer*) – Guadaloupe, Martinique, French Guyana and Réunion – are fully integrated into France politically. The TOMs (*Territoires d'Outre-Mer*) are still effectively colonies: they are Wallis and Fortuna, French Polynesia (including Tahiti) and the nickel-rich island of New Caledonia, where in recent years an independence movement has forced France into granting it more autonomy.

The UK got out of India and Burma (Myanmar) reasonably peacefully, and out of Palestine, as it was then called, rather more violently just after the Second World War. During the 1950s, the British fought limited armed conflicts (but eventually saw the installation of friendly governments) in places such as Malaya, Cyprus, Kenya and southern Arabia. In the 1960s, it not only got out of Africa – rather too hurriedly, some say, given the instability its sudden departures engendered – but also withdrew from a major defence presence in South East Asia. On the other hand, it fought a war to re-take the Falkland Islands that Argentina decided to occupy in 1982. Fifteen years later in 1997, the UK handed Hong Kong back to China.

The Netherlands withdrew from Dutch East India in 1949, when it became Indonesia. It granted independence to Surinam, next to French Guyana in the northern part of South America, in 1975.

Belgium was forced out of the Congo in 1960 by nationalist movements, with the chaos surrounding the withdrawal doing much to convince British policy-makers that they, too, must accelerate their own withdrawal from Africa.

Portugal pulled out of the African countries of Mozambique and Angola in 1975 when, partly as a result of the strains imposed by trying to hang on to them, there was a peaceful (and eventually democratic) overthrow of the authoritarian regime that had ruled Portugal since the 1930s. It handed over Macau to China in 1999.

Italy and **Germany** both had limited colonial empires, based mainly in Africa, which they were forced to surrender after the Second World War ended in 1945.

Spain lost the last of its South American and Caribbean imperial possessions in the nineteenth century, but continues to hold on to its African outposts of Ceuta and Melilla in what is otherwise Morocco.

---

dictatorships (in the case of the first two) or (in the case of all three) the poverty of their native lands. Greeks and Greek Cypriots came for similar reasons, though in smaller numbers. The only countries relatively unaffected by these waves of essentially primary migration (see Box 10.3, p. 231) were in Scandinavia and the Soviet bloc. In the case of the former, this was because they were too hard to get to and had no historic, colonial links. In the case of the latter it was because, quite simply, nobody wanted to go there.

Before the end of the Cold War in 1990, then,

Europe's minorities came largely because it made economic sense for those directly concerned. It still does, given the numbers of foreigners in the labour force of most European countries (see Table 10.1). It did not always benefit the underdeveloped countries from which immigrants came: they lost skilled, or at least potentially skilled, labour. On the other hand, the remittances they sent back home were useful in economies starved of cash and, in the case of poorer European countries, the consumer durables that were increasingly taken for granted in the richer north.

Table 10.1 Where they are: foreign population as a percentage of total population

Country	% foreign-born residents	% non-national residents	% non-nationals in labour force
Sweden	11	6	5
Netherlands	10	4	3
Germany	n/a	10	9
France	10	6	6
UK	8	4	4
Italy	3	3	2
Spain	3	3	2
Czech Rep.	2	7	n/a
Poland	n/a	1	n/a

Sources: Data from the European Migration Centre (http://www.emz-berlin.de/Statistik_2/index_stat.htm) and Eurostat, *Population Statistics*.

Since then, however, the situation has become considerably more complicated. A more unsettled geopolitical environment has increased the numbers of people in Africa and the Middle East desperate to flee persecution and civil war, some of whom attempt officially to claim asylum (see Box 10.2). Meanwhile, the economic situation has gone from bad to worse. The insistence on the part of developed countries (often via the multinational agencies that they dominate, such as the IMF and the World Bank) that developing nations pursue what some see as a counterproductive conversion from subsistence to cash economies that will help them to honour overseas loans, has made it very difficult for ordinary people. This is particularly the case when, at the same time, critics say, the EU's highly subsidized, highly protected, agricultural sector is allowed to dump its products in their markets without having to face free and fair competition from their producers. Even where people can manage to feed their families, they have little hope that they can attain a standard of living that comes close to what, with the advent of global brand advertizing and media, they see being enjoyed – apparently by all – in the prosperous parts of the world. Little wonder, then, say some critics of the developed countries, that more and more people than ever before will do what ever it takes to make a new life for themselves and their families.

All this means that European countries with a history of immigration are finally having to come to terms with the fact that those who have come are unlikely ever to want to go 'home'. It also means that those countries with no history of immigration – often countries, in fact, that supplied immigrants to those that did – are having to adjust to the fact that they, too, are now destinations rather than points of departure (see Box 10.3).

Europe's immigrants: who they are, where they come from and where they live

Given the role of civil and international conflict in pushing people into migration, we should be forgiven if we often concentrate more on where immigrants come from than who they are. But the latter matters, too. Sociological research suggests that they tend to cluster at either ends of the educational spectrum. This is not necessarily a problem. It may be easier for European politicians to make a case for bringing in university graduates to fill skill shortages in particular sectors, but Europe also needs unskilled workers: they are willing to do menial jobs, especially in the expanding service sector, and they are likely to make a positive contribution to birth rates which, as we pointed out in Chapter 1, are below replacement rates and making pension reform a priority. In this last respect, in fact, it seems that they are already doing their bit: one in five births in Switzerland is to a

---

BOX 10.2

Immigration types and terms: legal, illegal, primary, family reunion, asylum, residency, citizenship and amnesties

Immigration can be legal (i.e. people enter countries according to the rules set down by states for accepting them) or *illegal* (i.e. people enter illicitly without permission). Legal immigration can be split into a number of categories. *Primary immigration* occurs when an individual (perhaps with his or her immediate family) moves to another country, having got its permission to do so, for economic reasons – in other words, to work. *Family reunion* occurs when individuals move to another country (again, with permission) in order to join their relations who are already there, often, but not always, as a result of primary immigration. It is also possible for people to move legally to another country because they are a refugee with well-founded fear of persecution (commonly, though not necessarily, by the state) in their own country – this is known as seeking or claiming *asylum*. It is often the case with such applications, of course, that the person arrives prior to his or her claim being accepted and, in fact, it may turn out to be rejected (possibly because he or she is, in fact, an economic migrant trying to avoid the need for prior permission to enter the labour market). This leaves the individual with the choice of returning home (and he or she may be obliged to do so by the receiving country) or evading the authorities and becoming an *illegal immigrant*. In reality, the application process and any attendant appeal may take time, and the decision of the authorities may be to deny someone refugee status but still allow him or her to stay on other (humanitarian) grounds. In the long term, this might allow the individual concerned to apply for *residency* (the permanent right to remain) or even *citizenship* (the adoption of the receiving country's nationality). This is also a possibility when, as happens in many southern European countries, *amnesties* are granted to illegal immigrants who are offered the chance to 'regularize' their status in return for making themselves known to the authorities (and therefore paying tax and insurance contributions!).

---

foreign-national mother, one in eight in Germany and the UK.

Research – and common sense – also suggests that immigrants are rarely the poorest of the poor. Most not only come from countries where there is already some economic development, but have had to amass funds to get themselves, legally or otherwise, to Europe in the first place: in Kurdistan, it costs about twice as much (€6,000) to buy illegal entry into Europe as it does to build an average family home. Many media stories about the plight of asylum-seekers ('bogus' or otherwise) feature women and children, either to elicit our sympathy or provoke our outrage. Far more commonly, in fact, Europe's immigrants are single men in their twenties and thirties, chosen by the families who help to get that money together because they are seen to have the best chance of making it to, and in, the promised land.

Although some use kinship connections and aim for a particular destination, many have only the vaguest idea of where they might end up. Nor do they necessarily want to come forever – indeed, some experts think that stricter immigration regimes actually trap people into not leaving what might otherwise have been a temporary home. Given the restrictive climate, people quite justifiably fear not getting back in again should the planned return home not work out. On the other hand, if they do stay, it is often because they find it easy (legally or illegally) to get work. This is one of the reasons why the UK is a relatively popular European destination (and why, by the same token, immigrants there make a positive contribution to GDP and state revenue). Once they do find work, and as long as they regularize their status, many immigrants send for their relations and, in some cases, pick up a new spouse from overseas. In Europe, just as in the US, family reunion is by far the biggest source of legal migration – and not necessarily one that contributes skilled or even able-bodied immigrants.

Many immigrants in Europe do badly paid work, just as they do in the US. Unlike the US, however, European countries have high unemployment and more generous welfare systems. Immigrants there are many times more likely to be unemployed than non-immigrants. Their children thus often grow

BOX 10.3
Spain: from sender to receiver

Spain used to export labour northwards and tourists southwards. It still does the latter, but the former was coming to an end even before the country joined the EU in 1986. As is predicted to occur in the newest member states, catching-up economically soon means that only the most adventurous and best qualified bother to leave their native land to look for work elsewhere. Nowadays, Spain imports not just tourists from the north, but immigrants from the south, particularly from sub-Saharan Africa (SSA), many of whom work in what has become known as 'polyculture', the mass cultivation of fruit and salad crops under plastic in Southern Spain. Until recently, the favoured, but highly dangerous route – best guesses put drownings at around 750 per year – was across the Straits of Gibraltar from northern Morocco. That was until Spain spent well over €100 million on high-tech radar and night vision equipment for the most vulnerable parts of its southern coast near Algeciras and Tarifa. Since then, the Canaries have taken over as the main destination for immigrants, with the well-known resort island of Fuerteventura – the nearest to the African coast – proving particularly popular. Unlike the bulk of tourists, however, immigrants tend to arrive not by plane but by boat – this time put on a ferry to the islands' principal city, Las Palmas, where they sleep rough and try to cobble together the fare to get to the mainland. Neither trip, of course, requires a passport since the Canaries are fully a part of Spain.

Spain (like next-door neighbour Portugal) is still exceptionally homogeneous, with a foreign population of only 3 per cent, half of whom are in any case affluent northern Europeans taking advantage of its relatively low cost of living and superb climate. Surveys suggest that its population is also less prone to xenophobia and racism than that of many other European countries. Spain (like Italy) has also tolerated a degree of illegal immigration, which it has regularized through amnesties (or the introduction of quotas for which those currently working illegally could apply). All this may change. Although its agricultural industry continues to suck in cheap migrant labour, Spain has recently tightened its immigration regime, not least as a response to pressure from other EU governments to better police what is now, in effect, a common border. The centre-right government that ran the country between 1996 and 2004, also supported Britain's calls for tougher measures by other member states. And while there are few signs yet of the kind of mass concern, bordering on hysteria, evinced further north in Europe, there have been incidents of racially motivated crimes and even riots.

up poor. They also underperform at school. This becomes a vicious circle of deprivation, in which crime – particularly street crime – soon enters. For instance, in Rotterdam, in the Netherlands, it has been calculated that nearly eight out of ten who are jailed for such offences are from ethnic minorities. Little wonder, perhaps, that it was the platform for the meteoric rise of the populist politician Pim Fortuyn, who was murdered just before his eponymous new party did so well in the Dutch election of 2002 (see Chapter 5).

The performance of Pim Fortuyn and populist politicians in some other European countries suggests that, just as more and more people want to come to the continent, they are less and less welcome. In fact, although over 1 million people per year still enter the EU legally, the barriers to primary (i.e. economic) immigration were first raised in Europe during the recessions of the 1970s and

1980s. These troubled economic times marked the end of the postwar boom and, partly as a result of the sometimes counterproductive policies pursued to improve matters, saw unemployment return to levels not seen since the 1930s (see Chapter 1). Neither the barriers nor the recessions did much to reduce the push factors for people in developing or conflict-ridden countries: anything was better than where they were, and would-be immigrants were simply driven into increasingly desperate and unlawful measures to get around restrictions. Currently, illegal immigration into the EU is put at about half a million people per year, with many paying thousands of dollars to 'people-smugglers' or traffickers to help them make it, if not to the European mainland, then to some of its remote islands, often with tragic results. Bodies being washed up on the beaches of Southern Spain and Sicily hardly bear a mention in the news nowadays, so common are they.

Table 10.2 Where Europe's asylum-seekers come from

Country	Share of EU-24* in 2003 (%)	Change 2002–3 (%)
Russian Federation	9.2	+73
Serbia and Montenegro	7.0	−23
Iraq	6.9	−50
Turkey	6.4	−20
China	4.3	+15
Afghanistan	3.9	−46
Somalia	3.7	+9
Nigeria	3.5	−2
Iran	3.1	+8
India	3.1	−5
Democratic Rep. of Congo	2.8	−22

Note: * EU-24 is EU-25 excluding Italy.

Source: Data from UNHCR, *Asylum Levels and Trends (2003)* http://www.unhcr.ch.

This estimate of half a million per year for illegal immigrants covers those who, on arrival, simply disappear, having no contact with the authorities, often melting into the communities already established by their (legal) forerunners, although some of them, of course, make the headlines by being discovered or dying either *en route* or while working illegally. A similar number of immigrants, however, make it to Europe every year and then claim asylum. It is this half a million or so people per year who are also a political issue throughout much of the continent. Like 'illegals', some will be economic migrants pure and simple, and therefore 'bogus'. But – like Jews from Germany in the 1930s, who also had difficulty persuading authorities in liberal democracies that they were genuinely in need of a place of safety – many will be fleeing for their lives.

Notwithstanding the views of media pundits, populist far-right politicians, or perhaps many ordinary people, the number of asylum applications is – on the face of it – largely a function of civil conflict or the likelihood of human rights violations (see Table 10.2). For instance, the fact

that the total number of asylum applications to EU countries in 2001 (when there were 385,000) was less than half the total in 1992 (when there were 765,000) is attributed by experts to the end of the conflict in the former Yugoslavia. That conflict in the early 1990s generated huge numbers of refugees, the bulk of whom flooded into Germany, and then produced another blip as ethnic Albanians escaped Slobodan Milosevic's second round of 'ethnic cleansing' in their native Kosovo. Similarly, promises by Turkey to improve the conditions and treatment of its Kurdish minority and hoped-for improvements on the same issue in 'the new Iraq' are likely to sharply reduce numbers. Iraqis (mainly Kurds), after all, accounted for around 7% of asylum-seekers in Europe before the American-led invasion of 2003. A more secure situation in Afghanistan, where millions fled the *Taliban* regime, and in Sri Lanka, where fierce ethnic conflict has been creating refugees for decades, would also help. A more settled Somalia, Sudan and Congo would also do much to reduce numbers of people desperate to get away from those countries. By the same token, particular European countries would 'benefit' from improvements in the human rights situation of particular countries with whom they have a colonial, geographical or pre-existing migration connection, and are therefore a natural destination for those fleeing (see Table 10.3)

On the other hand, the putative end of conflict and human rights abuses in these regions and countries will not put an end to the furore surrounding immigration and ethnic minorities in many European countries. International and civil conflict shows little sign of drying up altogether. This means that other countries will simply take their place as suppliers of refugees, be they genuine or (as was the case with Albanian nationals who presented themselves as coming from Kosovo) simply jumping through a window of opportunity to make a journey they always wanted to make, war or no war. In any case, those opponents of immigration who are prepared to note that numbers of asylum seekers have dropped in recent years, observe that they have dropped further and faster in non-European countries, some of which (such as Australia) have taken a very tough line. They can also point to the fact that the political economy of

Table 10.3 Connections and asylum seekers*

Receiving country	Sending country	% of all receiving country's asylum applications (2003)
Belgium	DR Congo	20
Czech Rep.	Former USSR	75
France	Algeria	10
Germany	Turkey	20
Poland	Former USSR	90
UK	Zimbabwe	10
	India	10
	Pakistan	5

Note: * Rounded to nearest 5 per cent.

Source: Data from UNHCR, *Asylum Levels and Trends*, (2003) http://www.unhcr.ch.

BOX 10.4

Islamophobia

It is the extent rather than the existence of European Islamophobia (fear or hatred of Muslims) that is novel. The threat posed by Muslim militancy has long been a familiar tune sung by Europe's far-right politicians, particularly in Denmark and Italy, where there have also been several orchestrated campaigns against the building of mosques. But more people are prepared to listen nowadays. Take the Netherlands, where something approaching a moral panic occurred in 2002. Media reports (backed up by undercover recordings) suggested some of the religious leaders of the country's 800,000 Muslims (who make up 5 per cent of the population) routinely railed against 'the West' and 'western values' such as gender equality and tolerance of homosexuality. The panic not only resulted in a crash course in Dutch language and anti-discrimination being made mandatory for any newcomer wanting to practice as an *imam*. It also gave rise to the rather impractical suggestion that only Dutch be spoken in the country's mosques. Meanwhile, across the border in Germany, the opposition Christian Democrats attempted (unsuccessfully, it turned out) to make last-minute electoral capital in 2002 from a promise to expel some 4,000 (out of a total of 30,000) Muslim fundamentalists who were 'suspected of belonging to foreign terrorist organizations' and therefore 'ready for violence'. While few European politicians would go quite this far, many are concerned at the spread of *Salafism* or radical Islam, and governments (and their security forces) have begun to take an increasingly public interest in the *imams* who supposedly preach it.

Europe also seems likely to produce a continued demand for workers who can be employed casually and, because they are either illegal or supposedly temporary, with little regard for the regulations and social security costs that apply to EU citizens. At the same time, xenophobia in those countries where immigration has been highest (or, at least, most visible) in recent years has been taken to new levels with the rise of concern about Islamic terrorism after the September 11 2001 attacks on New York and Washington and the March 2004 attack in Madrid (see Box 10.4)

Unfortunately, 'giving it time' does not seem to be the solution to cultural, racial and religious prejudice, especially when people can point, as they can after September 11 (and March 11) to a genuine threat to their safety and security. In France, large numbers of Muslim Arabs from North Africa (and some from the middle East) have been living – and, of course, raising families – for around fifty years. Now constituting up to 7 per cent of France's population, they are still routinely subjected to discrimination, have difficulty (like their co-religionists throughout Europe) in getting permission to build places of worship, and are overrepresented in all the negative statistics. Meanwhile, opinion polls show again and again that the majority thinks there are far too many of them. A few popular professional footballers of North African extraction cannot change the reality on the ground.

Possibly, if today's immigrants did not look so different, were more widely dispersed, and did not insist on their human right to hold on to their religion and culture, it would be easier. European countries might be able to muddle through and let hypocrisy – and, of course, the immigrants themselves and those who live directly alongside them –

take the strain. But the problem is one of visibility, of concentration and of an apparent 'failure' of **integration** or **assimilation** that is subjected to increasing media and political attention. Many of Europe's biggest cities (particularly in western Europe) are now multicultural. They are not, however, always 'melting-pots': different communities live alongside each other but often share little in common. To the middle-class liberal this may be a cause for celebration, bringing welcome diversity in the arts, in cuisine and in the economy. Others, whether they live in the city and resent the changes and the differences or, instead, live outside them and see them as modern-day dens of iniquity, are less welcoming, perhaps distrustful and even downright hostile. Both as a cause and an effect of this negative reaction, Europe's ethnic minorities congregate in particular parts of particular cities. It is also obvious that newly arrived immigrants will set up where they have family and friends, and where there may

---

Definition
Assimilation involves minorities and/or migrants adopting the practices, customs, language, manners and even the mores of the host country. That they do so is often a demand of those who dislike immigration or minorities more generally. This is partly, their critics suggest, because they fear difference, partly because they think it causes problems and partly they know very few migrants would ever pass such a rigorous test! Most European governments demand rather less, but are increasingly vocal about promoting the **integration** of migrants and minorities into society. They want them, notwithstanding the preservation of their own culture (especially, although not exclusively, in the private sphere), to live easily and productively alongside the majority population – which more often than not comes down to an ability to communicate in the host country's language and a realization that one's behaviour has to be tailored to one's new circumstances. If assimilation is about swallowing the host culture, integration is about respecting and sharing enough of it to get by and cause as little concern to the majority population as possible.

BOX 10.5
Determined integration or indefensible discrimination? Bans on religious dress

French public education has for hundreds of years insisted on a secular approach: the state must be kept separate from religion. In recent years, this has caused problems with France's five million Muslims, many of whom argue that girls should be allowed to cover their heads in accordance with their religion. After a series of court rulings, French President Jacques Chirac announced in December 2003 that, in the light of a commission report, not just ostentatious and provocative but all obvious symbols of religion be prohibited in schools, that he would seek a legal ban on the wearing of 'conspicuous' religious symbols, by pupils. Although the ban covers all religions and seemed to have the support of around two-thirds of the French public (and according to some opinion polls about half of all Muslim women), it was seen by some Islamic groups as deliberately targeting Muslim schoolgirls who wished to wear traditional dress. Many commentators compared what they saw as the 'over-the-top' reaction of the French with the much more relaxed attitudes to the question in other European countries. However, in June 2004, the UK High-Court upheld an English school's ban on a pupil wearing the *jilbab* (a long flowing robe covering everything but feet and face), claiming that its already liberal, culturally-sensitive dress-code was sufficient to guarantee the girl's human rights under the European Convention on Human Rights.

---

be jobs. For instance, foreigners constitute, at most, 8 per cent of the population of the Netherlands, but in Rotterdam they make up around 30 per cent.

There is nothing new in this concentration, perhaps. Anyone familiar with the US will know that certain neighbourhoods in certain cities are often associated with a particular ethnic group. But in the US, the strong sense of American identity, the stress on English and the drive toward upward mobility, all reinforced by an education system that stresses citizenship and an economic system that makes such mobility possible for so many, tends to work against the establishment of ghettos from which there is no escape. At least, this is the

Table 10.4 Far-right electoral performance and parliamentary status, 2004[1]

	Previous vote % (date)	Latest vote % (date)	Parliamentary status
Austria (FPÖ)	26.9 (1999)	10.2 (2002)	Coalition partner
Belgium (VB)	9.9 (1999)	11.6 (2003)	Opposition
Denmark (DF)	7.4 (1998)	12.0 (2001)	Support party
France (FN)	14.9 (1997)	11.3 (2002)	No seats
Italy[2] (AN)	15.7 (1996)	12.0 (2001)	Coalition partner
(LN)	10.1 (1996)	3.9 (2001)	Coalition partner
Netherlands (LPF)	17.0 (2002)	5.7 (2003)	Opposition
Norway (FrP)	15.3 (1997)	14.7 (2001)	Support party
Portugal (CDS/PP)	8.3 (1999)	8.8 (2002)	Coalition partner
Switzerland (SVP)	22.5 (1999)	26.6 (2003)	Coalition partner

Note: 1 Party names are given in full on p. xvi ff.

2 The inclusion of AN as a far-right party in 1996 would be uncontroversial, but by 2001 its leadership (if not all its followers) had moved to a more 'respectable', conservative position; in contrast, the LN's inclusion in 1996, when its main appeal was regionalist and it had not yet moved so clearly into xenophobic territory, is disputable.

case for people who, whatever their creed, could pass as 'white' (something that has never been true for African-Americans and, at the moment, seems difficult for Latinos and some Asians). In Europe, the state – with the exception of France (see Box 10.5) – is rather more reluctant to force the issue in schools, where minority languages are often protected by law. Welfare can also more easily become a way of life – albeit not a very comfortable one. And many immigrants (and even their children) have little hope of passing as 'white'. Therefore, reassurances that all this is 'just a phase' that has to be gone through every so often are, perhaps understandably, met with rather more scepticism and distrust.

Political responses: populism, priming and catch-22s

Attitudes to minorities do differ considerably between European countries. Indeed, levels of tolerance may be surprisingly high, given the niggardly spin often put on public opinion by the media, especially in the UK (see Figure 10.1). But there is no doubt that large numbers of Europeans

– among elites as well as the so-called masses (see Lahav, 2004: 105–6) – are very worried by the situation. Predictably, Europe's populist politicians have not been slow to pick up on – or even to help drive – these concerns. But the mainstream has had to respond to them, and to some extent has also had a hand in driving them, too.

In the 1990s, parties of the far right scored some notable successes, especially in western Europe (see Table 10.4). We should note, however, that perceptions of immigration being a problem or there being too many foreigners in a country – a perception that is not unrelated, incidentally, to the actual number of foreigners there (see Lahav, 2004: 120) – is by no means a guarantee that the far right will do well. Take Greece: attitudes to immigrants there are among the most hostile in Europe according to most surveys (see, for instance, Figure 10.1). Yet, there is little evidence of a far-right breakthrough: the only party that one could label a far-right party, the populist Orthodox Rally (LAOS) took only 2 per cent of the vote at the 2004 election. Meanwhile, countries with high foreign populations can go for years without the far right making an impact. This suggests that while their success can, in part, be put down to their

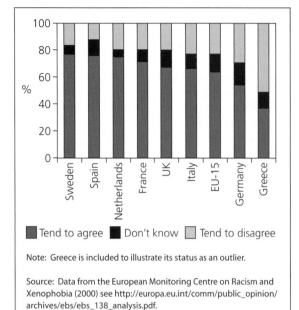

Tend to agree ■ **Don't know** ☐ **Tend to disagree**

Note: Greece is included to illustrate its status as an outlier.

Source: Data from the European Monitoring Centre on Racism and Xenophobia (2000) see http://europa.eu.int/comm/public_opinion/archives/ebs/ebs_138_analysis.pdf.

Figure 10.1 'It's good for society to be made up of people from different races, religions and cultures'

strongly anti-immigrant stance, it also has to do with the media-friendliness (see Chapter 8) and organizational skills of certain far-right leaders (van der Brug, Fennema and Tillie, 2000 and Lubbers, Gijsberts and Scheepers, 2002).

There is also another important but often forgotten point to make about far-right success. This is that, in terms of getting into government, it has harmed the centre-left more than the centre-right. Unlike its counterpart on the left, the mainstream right has fewer dues to pay to progressive values such as liberalism and tolerance, and less compunction about getting together in government with more extreme parties on platforms that emphasize their need – and their willingness – to 'do something' about a 'crisis' they themselves have done more than a little to talk up in preceding years (see Bale, 2003). Both mainstream and extreme politicians, in other words, have, along with the media, helped to 'prime' immigration as an issue, increasing its salience among voters (see Chapter 8). The common wisdom that it is in those countries that maintain what is pejoratively labelled by pundits a 'conspiracy of silence' on the issue that the far right do best is inaccurate: take Scandinavia, where immigration has been talked about quite openly

BOX 10.6
Sweden: still immune?

Sweden is often held up as unusual in that far-right populist parties have – with one temporary exception in the early 1990s – fared miserably at the polls (see Rydgren, 2002); this is in spite of the fact that polls suggest public concern about immigration (which, after peaking at the time of the war in the former Yugoslavia, now runs at about 40,000 per year, most of whom arrive to join family members). It is also in spite of a worrying degree of organized racist violence. The poor performance of the far right stands in marked contrast with Sweden's Nordic neighbours, Denmark and Norway, where such parties perform well. At the 2002 election, however, the populist mantle was taken on, a little surprisingly, by the Liberal Party. Arguing that theirs was not a racist party and that – primarily for economic reasons – they did not want to limit immigration, the Liberals focused on welfare dependency among newcomers – symbolized by the infamous Rinkeby township near Stockholm where almost three-quarters of the mainly immigrant residents are on benefit. The Liberals also argued that those unable to find work should, after a short period, be repatriated. They also made a big issue of the apparent failure of migrants (who make up some 7 per cent of the population) to 'integrate' into Swedish society. This they promised to tackle with language and citizenship classes – even though these are already quite extensive. It seemed to work as an electoral strategy: in a matter of months, the Liberals went from being a party in danger of slipping below Sweden's 4 per cent threshold to 13.4 per cent, trebling its score at the previous election. Time will tell whether the genie is out of the bottle or whether we will see a re-establishment of the cross-party consensus which seems to have succeeded – contrary to so much common wisdom elsewhere in Europe concerning the dangers of a 'conspiracy of silence' – in damping down the vote for the far-right

and quite vituperatively for years in Norway and especially Denmark, but not in Sweden (see Box 10.6).

Interestingly, neither Europe's extreme nor mainstream politicians now justify their hard (some would say hostile) line on immigrants on the explicit grounds of racial difference or superiority. Instead, they talk of 'a clash of cultures', of ways of life that cannot be reconciled when immigrant minorities refuse to 'assimilate' and adopt the dress, customs and ideologies of their host country (see Eatwell, 2000: 411). They also talk about the links between immigration and rising crime and chronic abuse of the welfare state – both issues that the right has traditionally owned. The left is vulnerable on these issues because, as was Lionel Jospin's defeated Socialist Party at the French elections of 2002, it is seen as soft, as 'out of touch' with how things really are for ordinary people.

Certainly, many social democrats rightly fear a loss of working-class support to the far right on this issue, notwithstanding the easily forgotten fact that an individual's views on immigration and minorities are in part structured by an individual's left-right orientation (see Lahav, 2004: 127–35). But the left faces a catch-22. If it adopts a more hard-line attitude in order to appear responsive to public concerns, and therefore lower support for more extreme parties, it risks rendering legitimate (rather than squeezing out) the very xenophobia its strategy is designed to contain – xenophobia that may then boost support for those parties it is trying to defeat. Take the UK Labour government which, in the face of a xenophobic press and a mainstream Conservative Party willing to score points off it for

being 'soft' on immigration, began ratcheting up its already hard-line rhetoric on the issue from 1999 onwards. It could hardly be surprised, then, when opinion polls in 2002 suggested that most British people think that their country takes in around a quarter of the world's refugees when in fact the figure is nearer 2 per cent. Polls also showed that the issue has come to be seen as one of the most pressing problems facing the UK, apparently displacing more familiar bread-and-butter issues such as unemployment and rising prices, and even the perennial health, education and 'law n' order'. Yet figures suggest that, in terms of asylum applications per head of population, the UK does not even appear in the top ten when ranked alongside other European states (see Figure 10.2).

Part of the reason for the gap between appearance and reality may be down to the news media. But the problem is not all in the fevered imaginings of editors and their supposedly gullible readers. In terms of absolute numbers recorded by the UNHCR, the UK, for instance, began to receive more and more applications for asylum from the late 1990s. In 2002, it received (counting dependents) over 100,000 – far more than most other European countries, including Germany, and more than any other country in the industrialized world. In fact, 2002 saw a 12 per cent increase on the previous year, while across the North Sea in the Netherlands and in Denmark, which both tight-

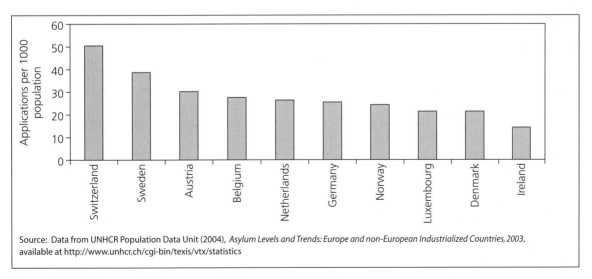

Source: Data from UNHCR Population Data Unit (2004), *Asylum Levels and Trends: Europe and non-European Industrialized Countries, 2003*, available at http://www.unhcr.ch/cgi-bin/texis/vtx/statistics

Figure 10.2 Asylum applications per capita, Europe, 1990–2003

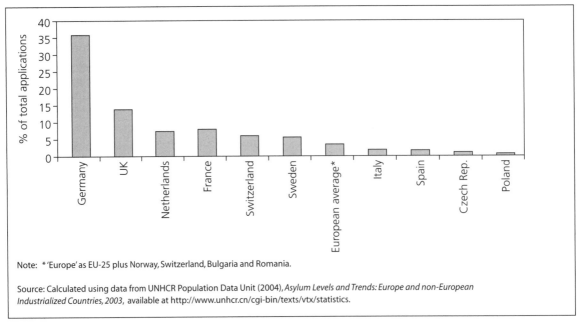

Note: * 'Europe' as EU-25 plus Norway, Switzerland, Bulgaria and Romania.

Source: Calculated using data from UNHCR Population Data Unit (2004), *Asylum Levels and Trends: Europe and non-European Industrialized Countries, 2003,* available at http://www.unhcr.cn/cgi-bin/texts/vtx/statistics.

Figure 10.3 Asylum-seeking, 1990–2003: who shouldered the burden?

ened their regimes as far-right populist parties began to influence policy, asylum applications dropped by 57 per cent and 48 per cent, respectively! London alone played host to over 200,000 asylum seekers and refugees. Meanwhile, the annual cost of processing and supporting asylum seekers in the UK in 2002 was said to be running at almost €2.5 billion – much of it going not simply on welfare benefits, but to landlords and lawyers and the like catering especially for such people. Just over 40 per cent of those applying for asylum were granted permission to stay on one ground or another. The others simply helped to clog up the system, contributing to massive delays in processing genuine cases. Moreover, as all European states find, it has been one thing to turn down an application and another to actually return the person concerned to their country of origin (real or imagined). Many remain regardless of a decision going against them, either because they simply escape the supervision of the authorities or because nowhere else will agree to take them back.

What the media does not tend to do, however, is to reflect the reality of the ebbs and flows. It tends to focus on numbers going up but rarely on them going down, which from 2002 onwards they appear to be doing all over Europe (with the possible exception of France). This means that few people would have realized the sharp decline in applications from Iraq, Afghanistan and Sri Lanka, and the tightening of security at ports, which helped reduce the flow by 2003. Nor does the media spend much time on the positive side of immigration. This is not necessarily because all media sources are anti-immigrant; they are not. But, as we noted in Chapter 8 when we touched on news values, good news is no news. But news or not, it is important that Europe's voters be reminded that without foreign workers, many of their basic services would collapse – not only garbage collection or street sweeping or transport (or for that matter fast-food outlets), but also healthcare.

Centre-left governments who ignore this apparent 'good news' story and insist on taking a tough line on immigration are also certain to infuriate their liberal (often better-educated and middle-class) supporters. They will argue that the far-right threat is hyped beyond all proportion (especially in countries where it does not perform well, perhaps because of the electoral system) and that multiculturalism is as beneficial as it is inevitable in a glob-

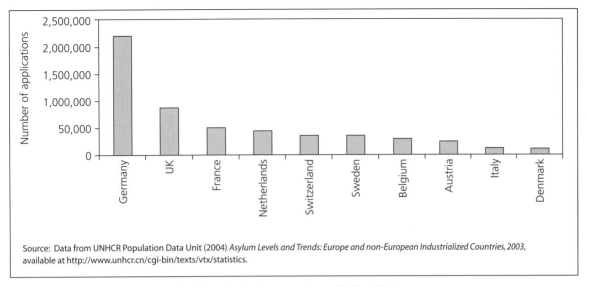

Figure 10.4 Top ten asylum destinations in absolute numbers, 1990–2003

alized world. They will also argue that the total number of people, illegal and otherwise, coming into the EU as a whole every year amounts to only about one thousandth of its population (about the same proportion, incidentally, as enter the US). In other words, they will claim that the absolute numbers coming, which the media always likes to use because they are inherently more alarming, actually matter less in terms of the numbers arriving and staying relative to countries' existing population. The UK, Germany and France, in other words, should, according to this line of reasoning, both expect and accept hundreds of thousands of refugees because, in terms of population, they are big countries.

But the liberal, progressive argument that the numbers coming in, or trying to come in, are proportionately small may be a little disingenuous, given the unequal burden shouldered by some countries (see Figure 10.3) and the absolute numbers involved (see Figure 10.4). First, given the tendency of migrants to concentrate in certain cities and regions, it may well be that it is absolute rather than relative figures that really matter. Secondly, the figures are quite high – especially for asylum seekers. Thirdly, like it or not, some of these will be 'bogus', which means they are an easy target for the populist press and politicians.

Fourthly, research suggests that numbers do have a significant impact on attitudes. It is all too easy simply to caricature those people, and indeed those countries, who are worried as 'intolerant racists' (see Box 10.7). Some certainly are; but most are just afraid that their way of life, their standard of living and now their safety, is under threat: the question of migration has become a question of *security* (see Huysmans, 2000). Whether or not these fears are rational or irrational, they are unlikely to be allayed by statistical sophistication. The governments who compile the statistics, after all, are also busy introducing 'tough, new' (as they are always labelled) policies designed to 'crack down' on 'illegals' and 'bogus asylum seekers'. It is this rhetoric and these reactions that arguably serve to support the stereotype of immigrants as people who cannot wait to swamp and then swindle the 'ordinary, hard working people' of Europe.

Defusing Europe's 'demographic time bomb'?

Governments – of all political stripes – in Europe are faced with a dilemma over immigrant minorities. Their majority populations, it seems clear, are

---

BOX 10.7
Historic and hysterical? Switzerland's asylum debate

Switzerland is famous for its direct democracy (see Chapter 6), and also quite well known in Europe for having one of the continent's most popular far-right parties, the Swiss People's Party, whose leader (the controversial Christoph Blocher) was appointed Justice and Home Affairs Minister in December 2003. Just a year before, in a referendum in November 2002, Swiss voters had to decide on a proposal that the country automatically expel anybody claiming refugee status who had arrived via a state that was itself free from persecution. They rejected the proposal but only by the thinnest margin in Swiss history – 50.1 per cent against, 49.9 per cent for. Coming on the back of Switzerland's continued ambivalence about its having providing a safe home for wealth plundered by the Nazis from the victims of the Holocaust, the narrow result attracted the opprobrium of liberal commentators all over Europe for demonstrating just how xenophobic it was.

But how many other countries in Europe have had to cope with the numbers of asylum seekers that Switzerland has experienced since 1990 (see Figures 10.2–10.4)? And how many could put the issue to a vote and feel confident they would get the 'right' result? And how different was the Swiss plan from the EU's own 'Dublin Accord' that tries to prevent asylum seekers 'shopping around' by insisting they make their claim in the first EU member state they enter? Certainly, Switzerland has been no less likely than other European countries to grant refugee status to applicants: between 10 and 15 per cent of those who make a claim are recognized (see http://www.unhcr.ch/cgi-bin/texis/vtx/statistics for details for each country). On the other hand, concern has mounted as numbers applying have increased dramatically in recent years. Some would argue it has occasionally reached hysterical, and even sinister, proportions. In December 2002, Swiss media revealed the plans of one town (Meilen near Zurich) which has a holding centre for asylum seekers, to ban them from places such as schools and sports grounds, to prevent them from congregating in public places, and to forbid them from using the municipal swimming pool unless accompanied by a local resident or local official. According to media reports, this *apartheid*-style regime was based on a map showing no-go areas, indicated on the key by four black men with a line through them!

---

anxious about, not to say hostile toward, any increase in their numbers. And there is political capital to be made out of this anxiety and potential risks in not being seen to respond. On the other hand, experts are telling them that short-term labour shortages, combined with the ageing of majority populations whose fertility rates are way below replacement levels (see Chapter 1), make immigration more and more necessary. Some, of course, will choose to side with 'the people' against the experts – this after all is one of the essences of populism (see Taggart, 2000). Some would say, however, that this is the height of irresponsibility or a derogation of democratic leadership – something that means trying to lead (or even stand out against) public opinion instead of following and even inflaming it.

Take Italy. Commenting in June 2003 on the tragic fate of small, often unworthy, vessels transporting immigrants and asylum seekers across to Italy from Africa via the Sicily Channel, Italian cabinet minister and leader of the xenophobic Northern League, Umberto Bossi, shocked liberals when said he wanted 'to hear the roar of the cannon. The immigrants must be hunted down for better or for worse ... At the second or third warning – boom! Fire the cannons at them! Otherwise this will never stop.' To his critics, this gung-ho attitude completely ignored the predicted crisis facing his country when, in fifty years time, its population has shrunk so much that there will be only one-and-a-half workers for every well-paid pensioner. Nor, they pointed out, would it do much for the enterprizes in his beloved Lombardia (the industrial region in the north of Italy) which are crying out for labour, skilled or otherwise. As long as their workers do their jobs, Northern Italy's employers are understandably none too fussy about where they come from, what colour their skin is and which god they worship.

Bossi's critics can certainly claim that the statistics, as well as the employers, are on their side. The

UN Population Division Report released in the spring of 2000 made it clear that Italy, and, indeed, the whole of Europe, was going to have to think very seriously about *increasing* immigration in order to cope with its shrinking and ageing population. It estimated that, while the world's total population would grow from 6 billion at the beginning of the new century to 9 billion by 2050, the population of the newly expanded EU would fall from 729 million to 628 million. This, it pointed out, would pose big problems if countries were to maintain the same level of provision for the non-working, especially the elderly. In Italy, for example, there are currently around four working people for every retired person. By 2050, the United Nations estimates that over 40 per cent of Italians will be sixty-plus. In order to maintain the present 4:1 ratio, Italy will either have to raise the retirement age to 77 or it will need to take in 2.3 million immigrants per year.

As a whole, the EU will need to admit millions of immigrants over the next fifty years to keep its worker:pensioner ratio constant. Yet the chances of it, or any individual member state, being willing to bring in so many people seem remote in the extreme. For example, the government in Germany – a country that has been praised by many liberal commentators as being more willing to 'grasp the nettle' than others in recent years – caused uproar when it introduced an equivalent of the US Greencard scheme in order to attract a paltry 20,000 IT professionals from India. And in 2002, its plans to make more general economic immigration easier were derailed by the Federal Constitutional Court (see Chapter 3) – much to the delight of the Christian Democrats, who, like many centre-right parties, seem willing to reflect (some would say pander to) the xenophobia felt by many Europeans. In view of the latter, it may not be surprising that there was no stampede to snap up the German 'Greencards'.

In short, say some observers, political attitudes and action, and not just bureaucracy, will have to change if Europe is to compete for the kind of migrants it needs most. Even if they do, however, nobody should assume that immigration is the answer to defusing Europe's (or at least Southern Europe's and Germany's) 'demographic time bomb' – the nickname given to the crunch that will come when the needs of the aged will begin to swamp the capacity of the rest of the population to support them. Research and common sense suggest that immigrants, like all of us, have a nasty habit of getting older sooner or later. It also suggest that they (or at least their offspring) will soon follow more established Europeans in having fewer and fewer children!

Policy responses: towards 'Fortress Europe'?

During the 1990s, the EU's member states have begun to co-operate more closely on immigration. They have been spurred on by its salience as a domestic political issue and by the knowledge that, since Europe's internal borders have come down under the *Schengen Agreement* (see Box 10.8), it is much easier for illegal immigrants and asylum seekers to move around the continent and select the country of their choice. Realizing that it would

---

BOX 10.8
The EU's Schengen Agreement

Although signed in 1985, the provisions of this multilateral agreement designed to promote the free movement of people (primarily as consumers and labourers) first came into force in 1995. By it, EU countries (minus the UK and Ireland), along with Norway and Iceland, commit themselves to allowing citizens and those who are legally resident in the 'Schengen' countries to pass between them without needing to show a passport. The *quid pro quo* for this freedom of movement is supposed to be strengthened security at the external borders of the EU. Also important is police co-operation, information-sharing (using the computerized Schengen information system or SIS) and the establishment of a common visa policy. Non-citizens coming into the *Schengen area* as visitors are limited to a three-month stay, will almost certainly need a visa and may need to show means of support. Schengen was incorporated into the Union's *acquis communautaire* (with derogations – get-out clauses – for the UK, Ireland, and also Denmark) by the Amsterdam Treaty in 1997.

The Czech Republic (Česko)

Area: 2.0% of EU-25
Population: 2.2% of EU-25
GDP: 1.6% of EU-25
Joined EU: 2004
Capital city: Praha (Prague)

History: The present-day Czech Republic (occasionally referred to as Czechia) began life in January 1993, after seventy-five years as part of a federal state known as Czechoslovakia. The latter was created when the Austro-Hungarian Empire was broken up following the First World War. For hundreds of years before that both 'the Czech lands' of Bohemia and Moravia, and what in 1993 was eventually to become the Slovak Republic, had been a thorn in the side of the Habsburg dynasty, resisting German culture and language as well as Roman Catholicism. The exception was the German-speaking area of the Sudetenland. Claims of discrimination against its inhabitants (nearly a fifth of Czechoslovakia's population) gave Hitler's Germany an excuse to annexe part of what, by the mid-1930s, was one of Europe's most prosperous democracies. With the infamous 'Munich Agreement' of 1938, France and Britain's 'appeasement' policy effectively handed over the country to Hitler. When he occupied the capital, Prague (*Praha*), in 1939, Slovakia, already chafing against the Czech-dominated federation, declared itself independent.

Following Hitler's defeat in the Second World War, a reunified Czechoslovakia seized the opportunity to expel 2.5 million ethnic Germans, tens of thousands of whom died on forced marches into Germany. Elections in 1946 brought the Communist Party to power and by 1948 it had effectively put an end to democracy. Over the next four decades, the country developed into a repressive regime, especially after an attempt at liberalization (known as 'the Prague Spring') was crushed by Russian-led military intervention in August 1968. In the next two decades, the Russian-backed regime had little trouble overcoming an intellectual dissident movement such as Charter '77, but found itself unable to resist massive demonstrations (quickly labelled 'people power') which accompanied the collapse of other Communist governments around Europe in November 1989.

After a virtually bloodless hand-over of power to democratic reformers, dubbed the 'velvet revolution', came the 'velvet divorce' with Slovakia. This happened against the wishes of founding president (and former leader of Charter '77) Václav Havel, whose petition signed by 1 million Czechoslovak citizens for a referendum was ignored by parliamentary politicians on both sides. Since then, the Czech Republic has been ruled by coalitions led initially by the centre-right Civic Democrats and then, following corruption scandals in the late 1990s, by the centre-left Social Democrats. The latter, though, have found it hard to find a majority, not least because they cannot work with a largely unreformed Communist Party that is still capable of garnering up to a fifth of the vote. This has resulted, some critics maintain, in an unhealthily cosy relationship with the centre-right opposition: before the 2002 election, for instance, something of a disguised 'grand coalition' ran the country.

Economy and society: The country's 10.2 million people have one of the highest standards of living in Central and Eastern Europe: in 2003, its GDP per capita was around 69 per cent of the EU-25 average. This is due not just to tourism but to industry – Czech car makers and defence manufacturers have, like banking and property, proved attractive to foreign investors for whom the country's proximity to the huge German market is an obvious plus. A reasonably comprehensive welfare state and fairly moderate economic policies have helped ease the strains of transition on a population which (with the possible exception of some in the Moravian region who would like more autonomy) sees itself as largely homogeneous.

Governance: The Czech Republic is a parliamentary democracy whose government is led by a prime minister appointed, at the suggestion of the speaker of the parliament, by the president. The latter – a largely ceremonial head of state – is elected every five years by both chambers of the bicameral parliament. The more powerful lower house, the Chamber of Deputies, is elected every four years by proportional representation. Members of the upper house, the Senate, serve longer, six-year terms, and, in contrast, are elected in single-member constituencies under a majoritarian electoral system, with one-third of the members up for re-election every two years. Their job is primarily to scrutinize legislation, as well as to appoint the Constitutional Court, whose members are nominated by the president.

Foreign policy: The Czechs have devoted themselves to returning to the heart of Europe by achieving membership of NATO, which they joined in 1999, and the EU, of which they became part in May 2004. Other objectives include establishing a reputation for reliability and stability in order to attract foreign investment, especially from Germany. Relations with the latter are accorded a high priority in spite of (or perhaps because of) continuing sensitivities on both sides over the Sudetenland and the German occupation.

Further reading: Fawn (2000) and Hanley (2004).

not be enough to nag vulnerable 'gatekeepers' such as Spain and in particular Italy (with its 8,000 km coastline) to improve security, they began to put in place collective agreements such as the *Dublin Accord* (which insists that asylum seekers must make their claim in the first EU country they arrive in and can be returned there if necessary).

More recently, EU member states have taken collective action and built collective institutions – joint sea patrols in the Mediterranean and an EU-wide finger print database (*Eurodac*) are good examples. So, too, are ongoing attempts to bring migration issues into the dialogue the EU has with third countries under the Common Foreign and Security Policy (CFSP), as well as into negotiations on development aid, focusing in particular on North Africa and, to a lesser extent, the middle East (see Chapter 11). There was, however, little support in 2002 for a UK government suggestion that the EU consider reducing aid to poorer countries who failed to do enough to stop their citizens emigrating. Nor was support forthcoming when, the following year, the UK (backed again by Spain) suggested that the EU consider Australian-style detention camps outside its borders to which would-be refugees could be deported and then processed. However, a watered-down (and arguably more sensible, as well as more ethical) suggestion that the EU manage facilities in other parts of the world closer to the flashpoints which produce refugees, and co-operate more with sending and transit countries (Boswell, 2003), was greeted more sympathetically.

This kind of co-operation has been accompanied in the EU by recent moves to erode the national veto on so-called Justice and Home Affairs (JHA) issues by bringing as many as possible under the first or EC pillar of the EU's three-pillar structure (see Chapter 2). On the face of it, then, migration policy is being Europeanized. But, in fact, most informed observers remain convinced that member states have pooled their resources only on those aspects of policy that they believe will support their main aim, which is to ensure they maintain national control in an area that goes to the heart of sovereignty and which their voters obviously care so much about (see Geddes, 2003 and Lahav, 2004). European states, in other words, are in effect 'contracting out' responsibility for immigra-

tion only where it would make little or no sense for them to try to do the job themselves and/or where collective action helps in the construction of a 'first line of defence'. This line began to move outward (via subsidies toward the cost of improved border protection) even before CEE states were formally admitted to the EU in 2004. Indeed, it can be argued that the need for secure borders was one of the drivers for enlargement. It is certainly noticeable that co-operation on immigration has been far more fulsome from countries that look like being allowed to join the EU (such as Romania and Bulgaria) than from those (such as Albania or Morocco) who do not, at least in the short to medium term, have a hope of joining (see Joppke, 2002: 272).

Just as importantly, European states have also followed each other in 'contracting out' responsibility to private actors, such as airlines and shipping companies, by making them financially liable for bringing in passengers without appropriate documentation. Many of them have also introduced an expanded 'white list' of those countries from which applications for asylum will be assumed to be unfounded and added countries to their lists of countries from which visas will be required. Many have also made it tougher for asylum seekers to get state benefits. This is an example of states learning from each other – of Europeanization via best practice, if you like. But this is not full harmonization because learning and co-operation goes only so far and there is no surrender of sovereignty. There may be superficial similarities, but states are unwilling, for instance, to harmonize the way they either treat or make decisions on immigrants, asylum and citizenship. Each European country, then, continues to operate its own immigration regime with respect to non-EU nationals. These regimes have developed, in a 'path-dependent' manner (see Hansen, 2002), in response to individual states' immigration priorities, history and institutional structure (see Box 10.9).

European states, then, have preserved their competence when it comes to controlling the numbers coming into their countries. If policy fails to restrict those numbers, it will not be because states have somehow surrendered competence to the EU. Rather, it is because they themselves find it difficult to construct controls that will meet

---

BOX 10.9
Europe's path-dependent immigration regimes

Germany's attitude to immigration and citizenship (see Green, 2004) is rooted in the fact that its main postwar aim was to encourage, or at least leave the door open for, ethnic Germans who, as a result of the Second World War and the Cold War, were left stranded outside the Federal Republic. This commitment, and the related conception of citizenship as being limited to those with blood links rather than being based on birth and residence, meant that until the 1970s it refused to contemplate offering German nationality to the immigrants that its powerful economy sucked in. Moreover, Germany maintained the fiction that these 'guestworkers' would and could return 'home'. At the same time, it was determined to demonstrate its liberal credentials by running a relatively relaxed asylum regime. Consequently, the German population (and some German politicians) had severe difficulties with the idea that Germany had a large but also permanent (and mainly Turkish) minority population. In the early 1990s, they also experienced a huge influx of refugees from the former Yugoslavia, which even if many of those people return home, will be seen by some as a problem. German policy-makers already operate in a federal and consensual system that gives many 'veto players' a say (see Chapters 3 and 4). This arguably encourages immobilism, making it hard to make changes. Germany has had difficulty getting domestic legislation on matters like citizenship and immigration past voters, legislators, state parliaments and the Federal Constitutional Court. Any attempt to do it by the back door (i.e. via the EU) would almost certainly be noticed and blocked.

France, on the other hand, has – since the nineteenth century – had a hang-up about underpopulation. Partly as a consequence of this, and partly as a consequence of its tendency to incorporate its overseas possessions directly into the French state, it has historically made it very easy for immigrants to come to France (even *sans papiers* i.e. illegally), as well as for foreigners to gain French citizenship. This, along with the decolonization process in North Africa and the country's relative economic strength in the postwar period, resulted in a large minority population which, even if it feels alienated, has every right to be there, whatever the arguments of the far-right *Front National*. On the other hand, France's (compared to Germany's) relatively unencumbered state has found it easy – though not wholly so (see Hollifield, 1999) – to crack down (at least formally) on immigration. And it would probably regard Europeanization of policy as a threat to what it sees as its unquestionable domestic competence on the issue.

---

sometimes contradictory objectives and all at the same time. First, a regime will have to cope with the sheer unpredictability of migrant flows. Secondly, states continue to want to run broadly humane asylum, family re-unification and relatively generous welfare arrangements. Thirdly (and relatedly), they want to insulate those arrangements from legal challenge, especially given the ever-increasing role of the courts, national and supranational, in human rights (broadly defined). Fourthly, they want enough 'wiggle room' to allow them – either formally, or (especially in Southern Europe), informally – to make room for migrants who add to the skills base and/or the flexibility of their domestic labour markets (see Favell and Hansen, 2002 and Geddes, 2003). In as much as 'Fortress Europe' (or Fortress Britain, Fortress Germany, Fortress France, etc.), exists, those who

man its ramparts are aware that it has to have a drawbridge – not just for humanitarian and legal reasons, but in the knowledge that they can, if needs be, let it down to allow people to trip across.

Integrating citizens

As a response to the 'failure' to achieve 'zero immigration' which is inherent in these contradictory strands in their immigration regimes, and partly as a response to fears about the threat to security (cultural and physical) posed by the separatism supposedly inherent in multiculturalism, many have put an additional premium in recent years on the integration, if not the full-blown assimilation, of minorities. Each European country allows resident foreigners to naturalize in different ways and

Table 10.5 Citizenship and naturalization rates, 2000

	Basic citizenship requirements	*Numbers naturalized per year (2000)*
Czech Rep.	Descent[1], birth or residence (5 years)	7,309[2]
France	Birth or residence (5 years)	94,002
Germany	Birth or residence (8 years) and language ability	186,688
Italy	Descent or birth	7,442[3]
Netherlands	Birth or residence (5 years), naturalization test	49,968
Poland	Descent, birth or residence (5 years)	under 1000
Spain	Descent, birth or residence (time-varying according to nationality)	16,743
Sweden	Birth, residence (5 years), or (limited) descent	43,474
UK	Birth or residence (5 years) and some language and citizenship knowledge	82,210

Notes: 1 Descent represents qualification because parent/grandparent is/was a citizen.
2 1999.
3 1995.

Sources: Data on citizenship from the following:
http://www.psp.cz/cgi-bin/eng/docs/laws/1993/40.html#5
http://www.southern-cross-group.org/anothercitizenship/france.html http://www.southern-cross-group.org/anothercitizenship/uk.html
http://www.germany-info.org/relaunch/info/consular_services/citizenship/generalinformation.html
http://www.legislationline.org/view.php?document=55311
http://www.netherlandsconsulatevancouver.ca/?file=RWN#Naturalization_test
http://www.polskiinternet.com/english/info/polishcitizen.html
http://www.iom.int/DOCUMENTS/PUBLICATION/EN/5_SPA.pdf
http://www.migrationsverket.se/english.jsp
Data on naturalization from Eurostat, *Statistics in Focus: Population and Social Conditions, Theme 3 – 3/2004.*

at different rates, each having its own citizenship requirements (see Table 10.5). But in increasing numbers of them, these requirements are now moving beyond simply birth and/or residence to include familiarity with the country and its language that is tested before citizenship is granted.

Politicians all over Europe, then, have been calling for and putting into place measures that they claim are designed to improve the integration of immigrants, most notably language and citizenship classes. Again, this is Europeanization, but by learning and following best practice (if that is what it is) rather than driven by the EU. As to the practical results of such measures, beyond providing a measure of reassurance to 'host' populations, it may be too early to tell. Critics on both sides see such attempts as symbolic sops that will make little or no difference. To ardent multiculturalists, they represent a pointless attack on their 'live and let

live' approach. To those who believe that integration should mean nothing less than complete assimilation into the culture and belief system of the receiving country (assuming for the moment that countries of several million individuals can be said to possess a uniform set of practices and values), the odd citizenship and language class cannot possibly hope to deliver what they want.

The Roma: Europe's oldest ethnic minority

Unlike other European minorities with claims to nationhood, the claim by some Roma (or Gypsies) that they constitute a nation is based not on territory but on identity. Even then, it is greeted with some scepticism. This is understandable perhaps in view of a widespread tendency among the Roma to see themselves in terms of families or possibly clans rather than a people as a whole. That they do so is not surprising in view of their origins: they came in dribs and drabs. While there is evidence to show that their ancestors had begun arriving in Eastern Europe from India in the eleventh century, possibly as mercenaries, there is no recorded mass influx. What we do know is that from very early on (possibly because they were associated with the non-Christian Ottoman empire) they were subject to vicious, often murderous, prejudice. This prejudice, along with restrictions on their liberty (up to and including slavery in Romania until the mid-nineteenth century), made it very difficult for them to integrate into the mainstream economy and society. Integration would not have been easy in any case, given their own desire to preserve their language and their physical separation from *gadje* – the non-Roma majority.

This separation continues to a greater or lesser extent in whichever country Europe's 4–5 million Roma find themselves living. As Table 10.6 shows, they are widely but not evenly distributed. Roma are concentrated in Southern and (despite Nazi attempts to exterminate them along with the Jews) in Central and Eastern Europe. Few nowadays are nomadic, but their more settled life has not meant they have caught up in socio-economic or, indeed, political terms with the majorities around them (see Barany, 2002). Living, as many do, a ghetto-style existence on the margins of society, and sometimes on the margins of legality, Roma are much more likely than others to suffer ill-health, to have bigger families and to be uneducated, unemployed, on welfare and in prison. They are also frequently the victims of racially motivated attacks. Their participation in electoral politics is at best minimal. The few political parties that have organized to represent them have found it hard going, not least because they find it difficult to overcome the fragmentation and in-fighting that some argue characterizes Roma culture more generally.

At a transnational level, however, organization has proved somewhat more successful. The International Union Romani (IRU) was given advisory committee status at the UN in 1993 and has now celebrated three decades of work. At its fifth World Congress in Prague in 2000, the IRU demanded the world recognize Roma as a non-

Table 10.6 Where most Roma live in Europe

Country	Estimated number of Roma living in the country	Roma as proportion of total population %
Romania	1,500,000	6.5
Spain	600,000	1.0
Hungary	482,000	4.7
Bulgaria	700,000	8.5
Slovakia	500,000	9.5
Czech Rep.	200,000	2.0

Source: Data on Central and Eastern Europe from Barany (2002: 160); data on Spain from Spanish government delegation working with UNHCR – see UN press release March 2000, available at http://www.unhchr.ch/huricane/huricane.nsf/newsroom.

territorial nation. It also declared that it would henceforth attempt to organize not just 'embassies' in other countries, but also a parliament or parliaments – something that may be more possible than one might think, given the successful running of such institutions by the *Sami* people (sometimes called Lapplanders) who are spread across four countries in northern Scandinavia and Russia (see Myntti, 2002). It also attempted to progress its claims for compensation for Roma murdered in the *Porajmos* (as they call the Holocaust).

Interestingly, the sponsor of the congress was the Czech government – something which prompted considerable criticism among west European Roma. They single out that country – or, at least, its population – as being one of the worst offenders against Roma rights (see Box 10.10). Certainly, the Czech Republic seems to have started putting its house in order only as a condition of joining the EU (see Ram, 2003) and after pressure from existing member states complaining that poor treatment encouraged asylum seeking by Roma in their countries. Such cynicism may be warranted but, on the other hand, it begs the question. Is not one of the positive sides of EU expansion its capacity to oblige applicant states to conform to liberal democratic norms, be they in the commercial or the civil rights sphere? As long as the EU, via information provided by its own monitoring and that done by pressure groups, ensures such norms are main-

BOX 10.10

Back to the ghetto: Roma in the Czech and Slovak Republics

Partly because it seems to contrast so sharply with its reputation (or, at least, the reputation of its liberal former president, Václav Havel), the Czech Republic's treatment of its small Roma population has attracted widespread attention in the European media. The new state's beginning was marred by its insistence in 1993 that some 100,000 Roma were, in fact, Slovaks, despite the majority having been born, apparently, in Czech territory. Fast forward five years, and there were regular reports of police and officials displaying not just blatant discrimination towards, but actually ignoring criminal attacks on, Roma. Then came the news that the town of Usti, on the Elbe river, was planning to construct 4 m-high walls around what, in effect, would become a closed compound or ghetto patrolled by security guards and police. Hardly surprising then, if many Czech Roma, much to the disquiet of some western Europeans (and their populist newspapers), were keen to leave the country and claim asylum elsewhere on the continent. On the other hand, things were certainly no better for the Roma of Slovakia who, owing to a fertility rate that is more than double that of other Slovaks, are predicted by some demographers to become the majority by the end of the twenty-first century. Both republics made conspicuous efforts to improve in the run-up to EU accession – especially with regard to education, health and even housing. But how effective such measures will be in the long term, let alone the short term, is hard to predict. However earnest the intentions of politicians may be, they cannot turn around centuries of popular prejudice in a few short years.

ties, even though they can claim to have been in some European countries longer than many of those who now consider themselves part of the 'native' majority. Interestingly, Roma can claim to be the prototypical postmodern European citizens, scattered throughout a continent and possessing several identities – ethnic, state and European – simultaneously. Yet in other ways, they are more like sub-Saharan Africans: according to a UN development report released in January 2003 (which made the comparison) one in six of the estimated 5 million Roma in Europe goes constantly hungry, and only two-thirds even make it through primary school.

Given this, it hardly comes as a surprise to find Roma trying to migrate – often by claiming asylum from persecution – in order to make a better life elsewhere in Europe. Increasingly, their claims are treated with scepticism. Indeed, it is difficult to see how it can be otherwise: the west European nations they try to get into, after all, can hardly accept that Roma face persecution in the very same countries they have just agreed to admit as functioning liberal democracies to the EU. In some ways, the Roma plight symbolizes the complex difficulties Europe – or, at least, some countries in it – face with regard to all minorities. According to many in their native countries, they do not belong there since they exist outside the mainstream majority of 'the nation'. If they manage to make it out to other countries, they suffer and present similar difficulties to other immigrant minorities. Hanging on to their language and their culture, refusing to 'marry out' of it, means they will retain their identity, which may be essential to human happiness. The flipside, however, is their visibility – one of the things that makes it so hard for them to gain acceptance (or at least indifference) rather than hostility.

tained and more than cosmetic – then does it really matter that they did not originate out of the goodness of Czechs' (or Slovaks' or Hungarians' or Romanians') hearts?

While clearly the Roma receive a raw deal in the EU's new member states and current applicants, they have long been subject to serious discrimination in those western countries in which they have a presence, including most obviously Spain and (to a lesser extent) Greece. Certainly, they are rarely accorded any more respect than immigrant minori-

No settled future

Those who are sympathetic to the plight of migrants and minorities argue that politicians and governments in Europe could and should behave in ways that make the situation less combustible – as could the media. Collectively, they argue, those politicians might also spend a little less time constructing a 'Fortress Europe' and a little more time on dismantling the protective tariffs and subsidized agriculture that deny 'Third World' countries the chance to trade their way out of poverty (see Castles, 2004). Joint sea patrols around the Mediterranean and a continental fingerprint database like *Eurodac* may sound impressive. Along with other restrictions, they help to send a 'not welcome' message to potential immigrants, which may (especially in some Nordic countries) be helping to stem the flow. But they are unlikely to stem it completely, dealing as they do with symptoms rather than causes. Rather more helpful, perhaps, are suggestions that more be done to help the UNHCR provide for and protect refugees in or just outside the countries from which they are fleeing, possibly in tandem with moves toward a quota system. Support may be forthcoming from rich European states for this redirection of their asylum-related spending: it will not only help those genuinely in need, but also justify their tougher treatment of those applicants arriving on their soil. Those who think that either redirection or restriction will put an end to the problem, however, may be fooling themselves – unless, of course, civil wars suddenly come to a halt all over the globe.

Learning resources

Any of the following will provide food for thought and plenty of information on the issues discussed here: Geddes (2003) Harris (2000, 2001), Joppke (2002) and Lahav (2004). See also Castles (2004). Well worth reading, too, are Favell and Hansen (2002) and Geddes (2000) and, for colour, Fraser (2000) and Harding (2000). Schuster (2000) provides an overview of Europe's various asylum regimes in a special issue of a journal devoted to the subject. Anyone interested in the far right should read Eatwell (2000) and the rest of the special issue of which his article is a part, as well as Norris (2005) and Rydgren (2004). They should also go to http://www.politik.uni-mainz.de/ereps/ and http://www.bath.ac.uk/esml/ecpr/. On the Roma, see Barany (2002); for a more journalistic but still useful portrait, 'Gypsies: The World's Outsiders', *National Geographic*, April 2001.

EXECUTIVE SUMMARY

- Driven by a combination of human need, labour demand and continued colonial ties, immigration has long been a fact of life in Europe, even if governments, responding to public concerns, have been trying to limit it since the 1970s.

- Partly as a result of these restrictions, but also because of the relative wealth of Europe, improvements in transport and a possible increase in global conflict since the end of the Cold War, more migrants have begun arriving either illegally or as asylum seekers. Numbers have also been swollen by comparatively unrestricted family reunion. These patterns, plus the historically constituted regimes and relationships of individual states, mean that the 'burden' of immigration has been unequally distributed.

- Immigration poses problems for politicians because of public antagonism (some of which they, along with the media help create), but also because it might help offset the negative affects of Europe's ageing population.

- Although countries maintain their own distinctive immigration regimes, they also cooperate at European level where they believe it will help them maintain control. Recently governments have put a premium not just on restricting entry but also on improving the integration of those migrants already in Europe.

- Europe's record on integrating minorities is not always good: problems for the Roma, for example, persist. Immigration and the dilemmas it poses are likely to continue in the future.

Chapter 11

Making the world a better place? Europe's international politics

Security and defence
Foreign policy
Europe in the developing countries
Europe and the global environment
Europe as a global trader
Lest we forget: the domestication of
  international politics in Europe

No exploration of the politics of a continent is complete without an assessment of how the states within it handle – both jointly and severally – their relations both with each other and with the rest of the world. This chapter begins that assessment by looking at security and defence. It moves on to look at foreign policy – clearly a related area but one in which European states have, on the face of it, been rather more prepared to compromise. Next, it looks at an area in which co-operation is often thought to be even more comprehensive; namely, aid to the developing countries. Finally, after a brief examination of another field apparently characterized by co-operation – the environment – it focuses on one in which European co-operation and compromise is said to have gone furthest; namely, trade. As the chapter moves progressively through the themes, it moves the focus further and further into the world; but it makes no apology for taking as its starting point Europe itself, believing that it is all too easy to forget particularly when it comes to security, that this is where governments have over the years concentrated most of their efforts and scored most of their achievements. The focus at all times is on the interaction between individual state concerns and instruments and the collective action of the EU.

Security and defence

Long before the attacks of September 11 2001 in New York and Washington and 11 March 2004 in

Madrid, it was fashionable to suggest that the end of the Cold War between 1948 and 1989 (see Chapter 1), far from ushering in a 'new world order' to be overseen by 'the international community', might paradoxically have made the world a more dangerous place. As the director of the US Central Intelligence Agency (CIA) told the Senate in February 1993: 'We have slain a large dragon, but we live in a jungle filled with a bewildering variety of poisonous snakes.' These include the 'rogue states', terrorists, or WMD (weapons of mass destruction) that threaten our way of life and the raw materials on which such weapons depend, or drug and people trafficking by organized crime, or civil wars spilling thousands of refugees across vulnerable borders – all of which blur the boundaries between 'external defence' and 'internal security'.

Yet, the CIA director's warning had more than a little amnesia about it. As one analyst acerbically observed (Mueller, 1994: 358), the Cold War itself was 'a jungle filled with at least two dragons and poisonous snakes, some of whom were variously, changeably, and often quite ambiguously, in devious complicity with one or other of the dragons'. Moreover, the relatives of hundreds of people who lost their lives as a result of 1970s bombings and shootings in West Germany, Italy and the UK could have reminded him that there was nothing new about terrorism. So, too, could the survivors of the aeroplane hijackings that first became fashionable in that decade. Europe has known for a long time that, in a world where extremes of material wealth and spiritual values continue to co-exist, its democracy and its peace and prosperity cannot be taken for granted, but have to be promoted and protected, not least within the continent itself (see Box 11.1).

Security is about perception, about the absence, or at least the minimization, of unacceptable risk

---

BOX 11.1
Europe's democracy promoters: the OSCE and CoE

The Organization for Security and Co-operation (OSCE) was finally established as a permanent body in 1949. With the end of the Cold War, the OSCE was used as a framework in which arms reduction negotiations could take place. Now with a membership of fifty-five nations that includes Europe, most of the former Soviet Union (FSU) and the US and Canada, it has its headquarters in Vienna, but is governed by an annual meeting of member states' foreign ministers. Its main activities are election monitoring (eg Ukraine in 2004), and the resolution and policing of border disputes in the new democracies of Europe, the Balkans and Eurasia.

The Council of Europe (CoE), founded in 1949, was one of the forerunners of the EU. However, it involved the UK (which did not join the EU until the 1970s) and other countries such as Switzerland and Norway that have never joined. Also, it was always a forum for political, legal and cultural co-operation rather than economic integration. From the early 1990s, its membership swelled to encompass most of postcommunist Europe. Like the OSCE, it is governed by foreign ministers, but it also has a parliamentary assembly. It was set up to promote parliamentary democracy, human rights and the rule of law, and if possible to set pan-European standards for them. To that end, it has overseen almost 200 binding treaties and conventions, most famously the European Convention for the Protection of Human Rights and Fundamental Freedoms (known as ECHR) that most European countries (including most recently the UK) have incorporated into their domestic law. The convention is overseen by the European Court of Human Rights, a body that is completely distinct from the EU's Court of Justice (ECJ). The ECHR sits in Strasbourg and can be appealed to from member states. The CoE is now tasked with assisting postcommunist countries to integrate human rights and the protection of minorities into their reform programmes.

---

not just to life, but to those things that are thought to make it worthwhile; or at least easier – freedom and prosperity via access to essentials like food and water and to the raw materials and friendly fellow nations that make trade possible (see Wyllie, 1997). Providing it, and providing for the defence of the realm, is one of the most fundamental functions of the state: it is both a responsibility to its people and the guarantor of its own survival. Maintaining the armed forces that are traditionally thought of as the ultimate upholders of security, and holding on to the right to deploy them, is not only one of the symbols of sovereignty, it is also a crucial part of its substance. It is, then, hardly surprising that governments do not give up such things lightly, if indeed they are willing to give them up at all. They are, however, realistic. They know that they are unlikely to be able to protect their people unless they combine their own efforts with those of other states.

In Europe, this knowledge is reinforced by often bitter historical experience. But the history of the hundred and fifty years prior to 1945 also presented Europe with something of a catch-22.

Clearly, maintaining some kind of 'balance of power' between various alliances of states was ultimately insufficient to prevent the outbreak of armed conflict (see Chapter 1). Yet the gap in military potential between France and Germany could not be effectively offset either by Britain (an island) or Russia (which had huge ambitions of its own), meaning that peace and some kind of stability could be achieved only with the help of an extra-European power – the US – that might one day prove unwilling to assist. The only feasible way out of this *impasse* was to enmesh the continental powers of Germany and France and their smaller allies in an indigenous institution that would effectively ensure their economic interdependence, making them realize that their best interests lay in peaceful co-operation rather than armed conflict. Whatever the criticisms of this institution – now known as the EU – few would deny that it has achieved what, beneath both the grand rhetoric and the less edifying wheeling and dealing, was always its primary purpose; namely, to bring stability and security to a continent that otherwise seemed destined periodically to tear itself apart.

Yet the EU and its forerunners were only a necessary rather than a sufficient condition of peace in Europe after 1945. In fact, the absence of war also relied, in depressingly familiar fashion, on a balance of power – this time between the two nuclear-armed superpowers, the Russian-dominated Soviet Union and the US, with European countries as members either of the Russian-led Warsaw Pact or the US-led NATO (see Chapter 1). To Europe's political and military leaders, concerned about a possible return of US isolationism ushering in either Soviet domination or a return to western European rivalry, NATO had three basic purposes, pithily summed up by its first Secretary General: to 'keep the Russians out, the Germans down, and the Americans in' (see Lundestad, 1998a, 1998b). While the definition of European security and the instruments used to strive for it have expanded in recent years, European states have, by and large, not lost sight of those three basics. And for many of the states that have 'rejoined Europe' after first Nazi and then Russian Soviet repression, those basics remain as relevant as they ever were for their western counterparts.

'Old' and 'New' Europe

The 2003 war in Iraq is often said to have brought into sharp relief two competing visions for European security and defence. For many, these rival visions were symbolized in the row over the public letter of support for the US hard-line signed in January 2001 by the prime ministers of Denmark, Hungary, Italy, Poland, Portugal, Spain and the UK, as well as the president of the Czech Republic. This group of countries apparently shared a perspective that during the Cold War was labelled 'Atlanticist'. This perspective holds that European states must implicitly acknowledge their limitations and therefore do nothing which endangers a security relationship with what is now the world's only superpower, the US. This is then contrasted with the perspective of what American Defense Secretary Donald Rumsfeld (in a manner designed to infuriate those countries so labelled) called 'old Europe' – especially France and Germany. The leadership of the latter came in for particular criticism because it had, claimed

Washington, allowed its desire to cosy up to anti-war voters in the general election of 2002 to override its responsibilities to the 'transatlantic alliance' and the US-led 'War on Terror'.

Rumsfeld had a point. There is an 'old Europe' perspective that holds that the continent is capable of pursuing – and, indeed, should make moves to pursue – a more independent course. Such thinking is partly motivated by objections in principle to a 'unipolar' world dominated by a US 'hyper-power' that some Europeans have always held in cultural contempt (see Markovits 2004, 2005) and that now seems more determined than ever to use its military might to back up its considerable economic advantages. It may also have something to do with the fact that European countries cannot as yet, and may never wish to, project power to the same extent or in the same way as the Americans (see Kagan, 2002, 2004). Instead, they place more weight on the value of diplomacy and on the ideas of **soft power** and **security community**.

Definition
Soft power comprizes trade and aid, cultural links and institutionalized 'political dialogue' through a web of sometimes overlapping international organizations (such as the OSCE and possibly NATO) that, at least within Europe itself, constitutes what some call a **security community** – an area characterized by such a high level of transactions and communication that conflicts are always resolved peacefully.

But some of these distinctions are too simplistic. 'Old Europe' is not simply a collection of introverted pacifists and appeaser countries who habitually shy away from confrontation. In fact, some of those European countries most closely associated with 'old Europe', not least France, argue that both a European security community and European autonomy should be reinforced by a measure of 'hard' (i.e. military) power. And, interestingly, other countries that would escape US criticism, primarily the UK, have some sympathy with this idea. They are, though, more ambivalent about achieving it by bringing security and defence more firmly into the provenance of the EU by, for example, making available sufficient forces and instituting majority voting for ESDP, the

---

BOX 11.2
European Security and Defence Policy: key dates and events

1992 EU's Maastricht Treaty makes possible moves towards not just a common foreign and security policy (CFSP), but also towards 'the progressive framing of a common defence policy, which might in time lead to a common defence'. Meanwhile the 'Petersberg Tasks' outlined by ministers of the Western European Union (WEU) – set up just prior to and then rather overshadowed by NATO – included humanitarian search and rescue missions, peace-keeping, crisis management and 'peace-making' by combat forces, often in co-operation with the United Nations.

1997 EU's Amsterdam Treaty enables European Council to 'avail' itself of the WEU in order to carry out missions of the sort outlined in the 'Petersberg Tasks', which were incorporated into the treaty. The new 'High Representative' appointed to oversee CFSP (ex-head of NATO, Javier Solana) would (in 1999) become the head of the WEU, which would in effect be incorporated into the EU (basically confirmed by the Nice Treaty of 2000).

1998 France and the UK sign 'St Malo Declaration', outlining the need for more effort on defence by the EU countries (the UK emphasis) and greater autonomy for the EU to carry out missions without NATO (the French emphasis).

1999 Cologne and Helsinki summits of EU leaders. The first notes that 'the Union must have the capacity for autonomous action, backed up by credible military forces, the means to decide to use them, and a readiness to do so, in order to respond to international crises without prejudice to actions by NATO'. The second sets 'head-line goals' including the creation by December 2003 of an EU 'Rapid Reaction Force' (RRF), made up, note, of national forces from member states, not an EU army, of 50,000–60,000 deployable within sixty days for a year on 'Petersberg Task'-style missions. It also sets up military planning/liaison bodies in the Council. Meanwhile Poland, Hungary and the Czech Republic join NATO

2001 Laeken summit of EU leaders declares ESDP 'operational', but ...

2002 Delays in deploying EU peace-keeping force to Former Yugoslav Republic of Macedonia (FYROM) because countries other than France and Belgium insist that ESDP operate on a 'Berlin-plus' basis – i.e. with the ability to call on NATO assets if needed. Delays and disputes also arise because of difficulties raised by NATO (but non-EU) member Turkey, and because of suspicions of smaller EU countries about pretensions to leadership by a *directoire* of France, the UK and Germany, who themselves are in dispute concerning the French desire to stress the autonomy of ESDP from NATO.

2003 France, UK and Germany fall out further over the Iraq war. France, Germany, Belgium and Luxembourg hold their own summit meeting on ESDP, hinting at closer integration on defence by core countries and a possible NATO-style 'mutual defence clause' for the EU, obliging them to come to each other's aid militarily if attacked. The US and the UK are furious, so too are other EU member states. Realizing their error, the mischievously labelled 'Chocolate-makers' back down and re-stress their commitment to NATO. Henceforth the 'Berlin-plus' basis (i.e. ESDP has the ability to call on NATO assets if needed) becomes the consensus. EU 'Operation Concordia', keeping the peace in FYROM, begins in April, with 250 EUFOR troops from fifteen member states. June sees the start of 'Operation Artemis', keeping the peace in part of the Congo, involving 1,500 troops (most of them, as with Artemis, French) – the first EU mission outside Europe. At the end of the year, Rome summit agrees to an advanced strategic planning capability for EU, but one that will liaize closely with NATO, which announces the entry in 2004 of the former Soviet states Estonia, Latvia and Lithuania, as well as Slovenia, Slovakia, Bulgaria and Romania.

2004 NATO hands responsibility for peacekeeping in Bosnia to EU.

European Security and Defence Policy, (see Box 11.2). This is because such a policy could complement American efforts, but it might sometimes diverge from them: theoretically, at least, Europe could decide on some issues not to stand 'shoulder to shoulder' with the US – something which the UK, keen to maintain its 'special relationship' with the Americans (see Dumbrell, 2001), still wants to do.

On the other hand, just like other Europeans, the British have to at least consider the possibility that the US may not always be there to keep the peace in Europe. This is especially true in the light of America's declared intention, after coming to Europe's aid on several occasions in the 1990s when it proved unable to end civil wars in the former Yugoslavia, to focus less US time, men and money on the defence of a continent that many in Washington believe should start looking after itself. The question for the UK, and for other European nations, is whether attempts to show that they are more willing than previously to shoulder the burden of their own defence will fuel or forestall US impatience. And could it, in the very long term, even begin to worry the US that Europe may try to match it militarily, as it is trying to match it politically, economically and diplomatically (see Haseler, 2004)?

There are some who believe, especially after the arguments over Iraq, that a European challenge to US hegemony and hyper-power is not just inevitable but perhaps even desirable if that is what it takes to finally force people into thinking of themselves as 'European' (see the pundits cited in Markovits, 2004: 25–7). Fortunately perhaps, the idea that any such challenge is imminent, however, is laughable. Most European countries (especially those that had to meet the strict convergence criteria for monetary union) spent the 1990s cashing in on the post-Cold War 'peace dividend' of lower defence spending. As a result, they are nowhere near matching or even approaching US defence spending (see Box 11.3). But, just as significant as spending totals, is the way armed forces are organized. The UK, and to a lesser extent, France, because they were global powers, have more mobile forces that can be deployed overseas reasonably rapidly. Most other European states, however, constructed rather static, conscript-based forces

---

BOX 11.3
Europe's 'meagre' defence spending

The USA has by far the biggest defence budget of any single state on the planet: its spending amounts to around 45 per cent of global defence spending and, if one were to take the top ten spenders, the Americans spend more than the other nine combined. This is not altogether surprising: as a continental power surrounded by vast oceans on either side, the US necessarily requires a huge navy and air force to defend itself and project its power abroad. Its high spending is also due in part to its desire to maintain an edge in technology and, of course, to the upkeep and development of its still-extensive nuclear arsenal.

Europe as a whole spends less than two-thirds of what the USA spends, and spending as a proportion of GDP is much lower by comparison: this is true as a whole and of individual countries, although there are considerable differences in this respect.

	Defence spending 2002 as % of GDP	Defence spending 2002 in $US billion
France	2.5	30.7
UK	2.4	36.6
Czech Rep.	2.1	1.4
Italy	1.9	20.2
Poland	1.9	3.5
Sweden	1.7	4.3
Netherlands	1.6	6.9
Germany	1.5	25.1
Spain	1.2	7.8
EU-25	1.9	154.4
US	3.4	362.1

Source: Data from Schmitt (2004).

---

that are far less suitable for today's flexible power projection and 'crisis management' scenarios: the US has over 250 large transport planes, the EU countries put together possess fewer than fifteen! Defence analysts also argue that research and development (R&D) makes up such a low proportion of spending, and is so fragmented between countries, that European forces risk losing out to technologically superior opposition or remaining forever reliant on American hi-tech equipment that is either expensive to buy or could be denied them should the US not support their actions.

Still the 'German Question'

But it is not just the US that is crucial to the calculations of Europe's biggest defence players, France and the UK. The question of Germany is just as important as ever – perhaps even more important than it has been for decades. On the one hand, Germany had to be persuaded (and to persuade its people) that it could and should contribute more and more practically to European defence. On the other, any increased contribution must not allow it to slip the bonds that had seen it safely locked into, rather than dominating, the continent. Germany, since reunification, has been trying to come to terms with this dilemma itself. Since the 1950s, it had been used to thinking of itself as a 'civilian power' (see Hyde Price, 2003 and Maull, 1990) – a polity that, like Japan and perhaps also the EU, sought multilateral and non-military solutions to international problems – if necessary, through what critics sometimes labelled 'chequebook diplomacy'.

Germany's re-birth as Europe's biggest (and still richest) nation in 1990, however, gave it the confidence to go against its so-called 'co-ordination reflex' (the tendency not to act without consulting and getting the consent of its EU partners) and recognize Croatia and Slovenia when they declared independence from Yugoslavia. This move was regarded with some concern on the part of other member states, especially France and Britain, who (rightly, it turned out) feared it would ignite a war in the Balkans – one in which none of them wanted to intervene. Ironically, it was this war – or, more precisely, the genocidal atrocities that accompanied it – that (with the help of Federal Constitutional Court rulings in 1994 declaring 'out-of-area' deployment of German armed forces legal) allowed Germany's leaders to persuade enough of its people that it should henceforth play a more active, assertive and military role in world affairs. This new role was symbolized not just by peace-keeping missions in the former Yugoslavia,

but by German participation in NATO bombing raids in Kosovo in 1999 and the removal of the *Taliban* regime in Afghanistan that had provided a safe haven for *al Quaeda* (the Islamic 'terrorist network' that carried out the September 11 2001 attacks on the World Trade Center in New York and the Pentagon in Washington).

Indeed, the negative reaction of the German government to the invasion of Iraq has to be seen in the context of the potential of such an unpopular action to undermine its painstaking (and painful) attempt to convince a still sceptical German public that military action abroad is not inherently wrong. Meanwhile, Germany's support for ESDP has to be seen in the light of that same desire to move toward being a 'normal' country and away from being one that forswears the full range of instruments to protect and promote its considerable economic interests. Europeanizing security and defence policy offers Germany a way to do this at the same time as reassuring its partners that it will not seek to do anything more than return to normality. The fear that it may do – notwithstanding Germany's leading role in facilitating EU enlargement (see Tewes, 2001 and Thompson, 2001) – also helps to explain why so many of Europe's new democracies sided with the US (and the UK, Spain, and Italy) over Iraq.

Russia: Eurasia's (ex)superpower

Reassurances concerning Germany's continued commitment to a future within (rather than above and beyond) Europe are also vital to the continent's relationship with the other state that, along with the US, is regarded as vital to its security; namely, Russia.

Not least because of its energy exports and its 143 million consumers, Russia represents considerable, and as yet under-realized, trade opportunities for Europe. But it also represents a considerable security threat. This is not because there is much likelihood (certainly in the short to medium term) of it precipitating interstate conflict with European nations (see Mangott, 2000). In fact, the problem is more to do with Russia's weakness than its strength, as well as with its historical 'failure' to develop from an empire into one or more nation states, as happened in most of Europe (see Chapter 1).

Russia's economy is still performing so poorly and is still so prone to corruption that it is failing to recreate, let alone, surpass the standard of living provided by Soviet communism to its people, among whom wealth and income are very inequitably distributed. Meanwhile, the Russian Federation contains a number of republics which would like to break away (most notoriously, Chechnya). It also borders a number of former Soviet and now 'newly independent states' that, in addition to being geographically close and potentially economically important to the EU, contain very big Russian minorities: examples include Belarus (1 million Russians or 11 per cent of the population), the Ukraine (11 million or 22 per cent) and Kazakhstan (4.5 million or 30 per cent). A number of these states, as well as Russian republics, also harbour their own ethnic conflicts, as well as religious extremists who may respond to global faith-based terrorism. All this creates potential instability not just in Russia itself, but also in Europe's eastern 'near abroad'. It also creates problems further afield. Russia (like the UK and France, we should note) is still one of the world's biggest arms producers and sellers, and has continued to provide several Middle Eastern countries with weapons, and more besides: the nuclear technology which some fear Iran will use to develop WMD was sold to them by a Russia desperate to maintain and increase its trade in 1995.

The most obvious way in which Europe deals with this potential instability to its east is the continuation and expansion of NATO, as well as its extension into a forum for dialogue with Russia in what is called the NATO–Russia Council, established in May 2002. NATO therefore operates both as a workable military alliance but also as part of a system of 'multilateral security governance' wherein institutionalized dialogue with potential adversaries can be conducted and their potential risks thereby scaled down (see Smith, 2000). In so doing, it complements European (and US) attempts to involve and enmesh Russia in the institutionalized 'international community' that have cleared the way to its membership of non-security bodies such as the G-8 meetings of the leaders of the world's industrialized countries and the World Trade Organization (WTO). On the other hand, Russian dialogue with NATO and its members does not extend to its being granted a say (or even to its being consulted) on military operations that they deem necessary, such as airstrikes in Kosovo in 1999.

The second way Europe deals with the security risk that Russia potentially presents is somewhat old-fashioned, hardly savoury, but, for all that, possibly necessary. It is to allow the Russian Federation what amounts to a 'sphere of influence' over much, though (as the dispute over Ukraine in 2004 showed) not all, of the territory formerly presided over by the Soviet Union (see Chapter 1). This policy, for example, involves the tacit acceptance (despite formal scoldings) that Russia can do what it likes in the breakaway republic of Chechnya – important to Russia not only in symbolic but also economic terms, since it is the main route for oil from Kazakhstan to Russia's big Black Sea port of Novorossiysk. This tacit acceptance of Moscow's hard-line risks offending Islamic extremists; but it also has the considerable advantage – especially in the wake of the massacre of schoolchildren in Beslan in September 2004 – of allowing Europe, the US and Russia to feel, rightly or wrongly, they have something in common in the 'War on Terror'.

The third way Europe has attempted to reduce the risk to its security from Russia and the other countries of the FSU is to provide substantial financial and development assistance, accompanied by political dialogue and promises of improved access to the European single market. EU funding is significant, beginning with the establishment in the early 1990s of the TACIS (Technical Assistance to the CIS) programme. But much of the assistance has been bilateral. German aid to Russia, for instance, is particularly significant – something that may also have something to do with the fact that the country is by far Russia's biggest trading partner. On a political level, the EU and Russia agreed to two summits per year and, at the 2003 St Petersburg summit, it was decided to establish a 'Permanent Partnership Council' (PPC) to promote ministerial contact between member states and Russia. Combined economic and political co-operation between the EU and Russia is also being built on with the announcement at the end of 2003 of the so-called 'European Neighbourhood Policy' (ENP). Reduced to its essentials, this will see a number of states bordering the EU offered the prospect not of membership but of 'a stake in the EU's internal market'. Russia is not strictly a part of the policy but, significantly, will share in the economic benefits on offer. If, like the other 'neighbours', it can demonstrate progress (or, at least, no slippage) on items such as respect for borders, markets, the rule of law and human and minority rights, it stands to benefit from free trade with the EU. The latter represents a pretty big carrot, especially for Russia, for whom over half of its trade is already with EU member states.

Europe's Mediterranean 'neighbours'

The idea of a European 'neighbourhood', and the potential economic benefits that may flow from 'neighbourly' behaviour is also an important part of Europe's attempt to handle the security risks posed by countries to its immediate south and east; namely, the Southern Mediterranean (Map 11.1). Those affected include Morocco, Algeria, Tunisia (which historically have been intertwined with France, and to a lesser extent Spain, and which are often collectively referred to as the *Maghreb*), as well as Libya, Egypt, Israel, Palestine, Jordan, Lebanon and Syria. Many of them are economically troubled and politically unstable. They are experiencing a population explosion in spite of the poverty that pervades the majority of them, and in many of them there is significant opposition to the governing regimes. At the same time, they are a significant source or at least a conduit for the energy resources on which Europe relies. Whether they be 'failed', 'rogue' states or simply troubled states, they therefore represent a fertile ground for almost everything Europe worries about (see Coulombis and Veremis, 1999): maritime pollution, illegal immigration and drug trafficking, and terrorist threats to mainland Europe or, just as seriously, to its energy supply.

Although France maintained postcolonial links with some pretty unsavoury regimes in the region (see Meyrede, 1999), there was surprisingly little collective thought about the Southern Mediterranean until Spain joined the EU in 1986 (see Gillespie, 2000). Spain, like France has a complicated mesh of bilateral security and economic agreements with a number of North African states to its south, and for some time they

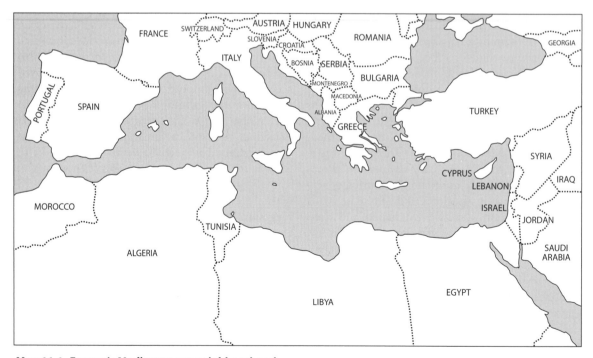

Map 11.1 Europe's Mediterranean neighbourhood

have played a much bigger role in both its trade and its foreign policy than have states that are often (but wrongly) assumed to matter more to Spain for cultural reasons, such as those in South America (see Kennedy, 2000: 122). In the early 1990s, Spain began a concerted attempt (with the French and Italians) to draw the EU's attention to the need to 'do something' for the Mediterranean. Its efforts finally paid off in the so-called 'Barcelona Declaration' of 1995, by which the states were offered a much bigger and more comprehensive package of EU assistance – accompanied by political dialogue aimed at securing improvements in human rights (although not at the cost of stability!). Via the Barcelona Declaration, France, Spain and Italy, all of whom had to work very hard to limit spending in order to qualify for the single currency, were able to put the EU's money where their mouths were (for more details see Gillespie, 1997, Stavridis *et al.* 1999 and Xenakis and Chryssochoou, 2001).

EU development assistance to the Southern Mediterranean amounted, according to the Commission, to €2.4 billion between 2000 and 2003. Free trade, too, is supposed to be an important part of the package on offer, although the extent to which the countries in the region actually trade with the EU varies considerably – all the way from Libya and Tunisia (which do 80 per cent of their trade with the EU), through Morocco and Algeria (70 per cent) and Syria (60 per cent) to Israel, the Lebanon and Egypt (25–30 per cent), and finally Jordan (less than 5 per cent). The ENP, then, builds on efforts already in place, but adds political conditions to the prospect of a bigger economic gain via closer integration with the EU's internal market. However, if one regards poverty as the main source of instability, then simply encouraging trade and providing development assistance (and attaching strings to both) is unlikely to prove a quick fix to the security risks posed by the Southern Mediterranean: Israel's GDP per capita may reach 80 per cent of the EU average, but (with the exception of Lebanon, where it is 20 per cent), not one of the Southern Mediterranean countries can claim to reach even 10 per cent.

This is why many would argue that 'soft power' instruments such as trade and aid have, in the end, to be backed up by 'hard power' – military threats or even actual force. In fact, when it comes to the Middle East, Europeans probably need to be as much if not more interested in that particular commodity than the nation many of them like to think of as the 'bad guy', the US. In fact, Europe consumes over three times the amount of oil it produces and is more reliant on Arab energy suppliers than the Americans. Along with the need to keep onside what in some countries is a sizable Muslim population (see Chapter 1), this is why European countries have been so keen to try to counterbalance US backing of Israel in the drawn-out Palestinian peace process (see van Dosenrode and Stubkjær, 2002). This is also why even those governments critical of America's policy in the Middle East have to help clear up the mess they believe it has created in places such as Iraq. In any case, their doing so, some wryly observe, fits nicely into the pattern created after the US interventions in FYROM whereby 'America fights and Europe does the dishes' by providing the bulk of men and money for peacekeeping.

Back to defence

In fact, one can question how hard and fast this putative division of labour really is. True, European countries did indeed provide most of the 'stabilization force' that came in once the Americans had cleared the *Taliban* out of Afghanistan and promised to provide hundreds of millions of euros to help get the country back on its feet; but not all observers dismiss the initial warfighting role of French and British forces in Afghanistan as insignificant (see Menon, 2004a). And, even assuming it does exist, can that division of labour – between a US specializing in 'hard power' and a Europe that is better at 'soft power' – go on for ever? The question raises once again the extent to which Europe is willing to both share the burden with the US (the UK emphasis) and/or assume some degree of autonomy from it (the French emphasis).

This, as we have seen, is what ESDP, at least in part, is about. Whether Europe actually needs or finds it convenient to use it in an operational as well as a symbolic sense, however, remains to be seen. For one thing, however much commentators talk about Sweden, Finland, Austria and Ireland supposedly moving toward 'postneutrality' in what seems to be a more dangerous world there seems little prospect of them surrendering their neutrality soon. This means that they may pick and choose missions, preferring perhaps to contribute to the non-military side of putative European operations (see Menon, 2004a). For another, experience also suggests that the key to things working is as much political as institutional: unless big players, big contributors and big strategic thinkers such as France, Germany and Britain form some kind of informal trilateral *directoire* (and are allowed to do so by the other member states), things just will not happen (see Crowe, 2004: 41–2; and Menon, 2004b).

Experience also suggests that – especially in times of crisis – institutions will not stop the formation of ad hoc 'coalitions-of-the-willing' making use of national rather than multinational military assets (see Duke, 2000: 29). This is true whether they involve countries outside Europe, as in Iraq, or inside, as in the little remembered Italian-led intervention in Albania in 1997, undertaken in order to prevent a breakdown in state control turning into complete anarchy (see Foster, 1998 and Silvestri, 1997). Nor will institutional membership prevent those states in Europe with global pasts and global pretensions projecting their power (albeit in ways that they think are for the best) in smaller conflicts well away from Europe. The sending of British troops to Sierra Leone to shore up a UN force in trouble is one example. The (possibly less successful) French intervention of 2002 in Ivory Coast (where France has a permanent military base) is another.

What ESDP is certainly *not* about – at least in the foreseeable future – is establishing EU control over the defence capability of its member states, forcing them to say 'yes' to what other states want them to do or preventing them from saying 'no'. True, there now exists a *Eurocorps*, based on 900 dedicated soldiers from France, Germany, Spain, Belgium and Luxembourg (see http://www.euro corps.org), but this was set up separately from ESDP. It is also important to note that the decision-making basis for ESDP is intergovernmental (see Chapter 2): it may now be possible for some states to go ahead with a mission should others who do not support it choose to let them to

get on with it; but if they want to, they can still veto any operation. Nor, we should note, does the supranational Commission, which is at least consulted on and can make suggestions in EU foreign policy, have any formal role in ESDP.

In any case, a report on ESDP approved by all heads of state and government at the EU's Nice summit in 2000 (see UK House of Lords, 17 January 2002, *Hansard*, Column 1210) made three things crystal clear. First, that 'NATO remains the basis of the collective defence of its members. Second, that '[t]he development of the ESDP will contribute to the vitality of a renewed transatlantic link'. And, third, that it 'does not involve the establishment of a European army. The commitment of national resources by Member States to [its] operations will be based on their sovereign decisions.' It is difficult to see how in the short to medium term this can be got around. Moreover, significant numbers of European people do not want it to be got around, especially in western European countries and particularly in Scandinavia and the UK (see Figure 11.1). Nor, one suspects, do their leaders, civil and military. As one US ambassador to the EU put it in the early 1990s (see Duke, 2000: 188):

Until the major European nations, including Germany, are prepared to send their young men abroad to fight, and to die if necessary, in a European cause, under a European flag, and within a European command, no amount of planning for a European security identity will field a single battalion.

This, of course, is the ultimate test. But even on rather less ambitious criteria, there is precious little evidence of Europeanization when it comes to the impact of the EU on defence policy. The most recent comprehensive attempt to find it, wisely looking country-by-country, uncovered some indirect effects: the single currency may have forced member states to spend even less on defence than they might have done; there are moves towards a rationalization of European defence industries and procurement; and, most interestingly, German policy-makers used the need to be good Europeans to ease their country out of its relatively passive stance. But the same study found that 'big

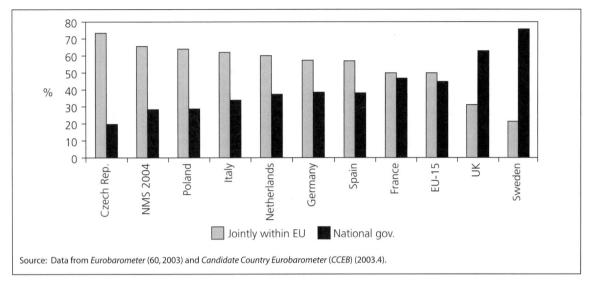

Source: Data from *Eurobarometer* (60, 2003) and *Candidate Country Eurobarometer* (*CCEB*) (2003.4).

Figure 11.1 'Should decisions on defence be made by national government or jointly within the EU?'

decisions are still national' and that, for all the rhetoric about interdependence, 'the EU itself has exercised little or no direct impact over shifts in national defence policy' (see Freedman and Menon, 1997: 156ff).

Foreign policy

The right to determine their own defence policies is clearly something European states are keen to protect. When it comes to foreign policy – often a rather less highly-charged area – there is a similar concern to preserve their sovereignty. But there is also, too, more of a recognition that co-operation with other states, particularly if they are also in the EU, can be beneficial. This recognition applies at the level of ordinary citizens: opinion polls indicate that, except in postcommunist countries where people seem more worried about foreign policy than they do about defence, there is greater support for European consultation on foreign policy decisions than there is on the defence side (see Figure 11.2). It is also true on the elite level. Even before the formal declaration in the Maastricht Treaty signed in 1992 that the EU would establish (albeit intergovernmentally rather than supranationally) a 'Common Foreign and Security Policy' (widely known as CFSP), member states were engaging in

what had become known as 'European Political Co-operation' or EPC (see Nuttall, 2000).

Yet much of the potential afforded by the CFSP for common action – and for the EU to assert its 'presence' and its 'actorness' (see Allen and Smith, 1998, Bretherton and Vogler, 1999 and Hill, 1993) – remains unrealized, as various audits undertaken by academic observers, more or less ruefully note (see for example Holland, 2004a). There are many reasons for this. At the level of process, the insistence by EU member states on a clear distinction between the EU's foreign policy, on the one hand, and its trade and aid policies, on the other, means that many of the instruments that they themselves routinely use to support their bilateral aims cannot be brought to bear by the EU. This, plus the fact that, as yet, the EU lacks a constitutionally and internationally recognized 'legal personality' that would allow it to act more cohesively in global forums, too often means that it has to be content with 'declaratory diplomacy'. Yet, even when it manages to go further, and (say) impose sanctions on a foreign regime abusing human rights, the hard-won consensus for that action soon frays under pressure from contradictory national interests. The relations between Europe and Zimbabwe are a case in point (see Weiland, 2004). In early 2003, France bowed to pressure from other African countries and invited

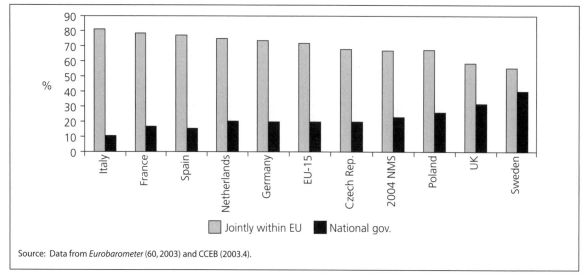

Figure 11.2 'Should decisions on foreign policy be made by national government or jointly within the EU?'

President Robert Mugabe to a summit in Paris that was conveniently due to start the day after the EU's 'smart sanctions' on the Mugabe regime expired, forcing the other member states to grant France a temporary 'opt-out' lest it refuse to renew the sanctions for another year! As long as state interests remain so diverse and potentially contradictory, then no amount of institutional tinkering can compensate for the lack of political will that, ultimately, lies behind what some see as the failure of the CFSP.

That said, we should think twice before portraying the national interest vs CFSP as some sort of simple zero-sum game. Indeed, it is clear that European co-operation offers individual states or groups of states opportunities better to pursue their national interests, at least where they are perceived to coincide with those of the rest. For instance, states such as France, the UK, Portugal and Belgium can use the CFSP to speak and act on African questions without necessarily drawing attention to (and fire for) supposedly 'neo-colonial' attitudes. Meanwhile, states such as Ireland, Austria, Finland and Sweden can use participation in the CFSP to at least finesse, if not necessarily to transcend, their non-aligned or neutral stances (see Manners and Whitman: 2000: 247–8).

Nor should we think of European countries' foreign policy elites as somehow insulated from each other. Far from it: observers draw attention to the effect of Europeanization on the tendency of states in Europe to consult each other almost as a reflex and often before their traditional allies. For example, Scandinavian policy makers will tend to think 'European' rather than simply 'Nordic', while those in the UK may now think of consulting their partners across the Channel rather than going across the Atlantic first (see Manners and Whitman: 2000: 249). On the other hand, the extent to which socialization into collective habits, norms and identities has taken place is easily overdone, especially with regard to policy-makers from larger member states such as France, Germany and the UK. This is irrespective of the fact that they have been in the Community as long (or in some cases longer) than some of the member states in which that socialization is more noticeable (Manners and Whitman, 2001: 251–2).

This points to a more general pattern among EU member states. States with more global interests, such as France and Britain, tend to be rather more reticent about foreign policy convergence than often (but not always smaller) states with a more exclusive European focus, such as (prototypically) Belgium or Italy. The latter realize that Europe may afford them far more say in world affairs than they could ever hope to get acting alone, and that the less intergovernmental the process, the less likely a putative European policy is likely to reflect mainly the interests of the larger member states. Located somewhere between these two extremes are three groups. First, there are the states with a more 'Atlanticist' focus but that also like to think of themselves as good Europeans (Spain, Portugal, Denmark and the Netherlands). Secondly, there are states with a particular regional focus and/or a tradition of neutralism (Ireland, Austria, Sweden and Finland) or at least multilateralism (Germany). Thirdly, there are the postcommunist states: they are concerned to be good Europeans and, to some extent, share the anxieties of other smaller states that a purely intergovernmental 'European foreign policy' will be dominated by larger states; but they are also determined to preserve the sovereignty that they have only just won back after years of Soviet domination.

It is also important to remember that Europeanization, and the variation in the extent to which it seems to have affected the foreign policy-making of EU member states, is by no means the only factor impacting on such policy-making. Any list would have to include the following questions (many of which are posed by Manners and Whitman, 2001: 252–61). How important is parliamentary oversight on foreign policy: practically unimportant as in France and the UK, or a potential constraint, as in the Nordic countries? To what extent do subnational governments get involved: not at all, as in most states, or increasingly often as in the federal states such as Belgium or Germany? Do parties make a difference: who would argue with the assertion that the election of a Socialist government in Spain in 2004 very swiftly reoriented Spain back to a more 'European' as opposed to 'Atlanticist' foreign policy orientation? Does this indicate that foreign policy – traditionally rather an elitist forum (a policy community rather than an issue network, to use the language of Chapter 8) – is becoming more generally politicized and even rising in salience among voters? Does this explain how the German SPD, by departing from its traditional acquiescence and criticizing the US over Iraq in the autumn of 2002, managed to stave off electoral defeat that, given difficulties on the home front, it otherwise deserved? How influential are pressure groups: do defence industry lobbies push some countries (France and Britain) in one direction, while internationalist trade unions try to push other governments (Sweden, Germany) in another? How extensive is prime ministerial (or, in the case of France, presidential) intervention in foreign policy: is the foreign minister and his department very much in charge (as in, say, the Netherlands) or do they have to work hand in hand with the head of government (as in the UK, France, Germany and, increasingly, Italy)? And what about the bureaucratic politics and foreign ministries (see Hocking and Spence, 2002): to what extent are they under pressure financially and losing exclusive competence over foreign (and especially European affairs) to a whole range of departments who find themselves consulting with their opposite numbers in other member states?

Most of these issues, of course, pertain to foreign policy-makers 'at home' in Europe. There is less research on the Europeanization of those who carry out those policies 'in country' outside Europe. What work there is (see Bale, 2000, 2004) suggests a familiar pattern: by and large, diplomats from smaller states are keener on co-operation with their fellow ambassadors than those from larger states; meanwhile, all states see the multilateral approach as a more or less useful addition to, rather than as a substitute for, their primarily bilateral approaches. Material, and not merely symbolic, obstacles remain in the way of any moves toward some kind of integrated, 'European' diplomacy. It might make sense in terms of up-front cost savings, but individual European countries would lose the considerable commercial benefit of their own flag-waving public diplomacy. It would demand changes from a group of relatively insulated and privileged civil servants. And, in the end, it is hard to see a European diplomatic service until there is a clear 'European' interest to represent. In as much as there is one already – on aid and trade (our next topics) – it is already well represented by the European Commission's own external service which runs over 120 diplomatic delegations throughout the world (see Bruter, 1999).

None of this makes it any easier for Europe to 'speak with one voice' in or to the rest of the world, notwithstanding the appointment, following the Amsterdam Treaty, of a 'High Representative' who is supposed to do just that – a High Representative who, interestingly, was almost completely by-passed by both 'old' and 'new' Europe in the intra-European row in the run-up to the Iraq war in spite of his widely acknowledged qualities as a networker and credible mover and shaker (Crowe, 2004: 37). None of this means that European foreign policy is necessarily a mess, but it is necessarily messy. As the pre-eminent analyst of European foreign policy, puts it (Hill, 1998: 48–9):

> We cannot know where the European foreign policy system is heading ... What is clear, however, is the interplay taking place between the national and the collective ... This has produced a pattern of multi-level diplomacy in which the various elements sometimes, compete, sometimes reinforce each other, and sometimes merely co-exist.

Europe in the developing countries

Europe may spend less than two-thirds of what the US spends on the military, but it prides itself in spending at least twice as much on development assistance – indeed, Europe provides around a half of the $60+ billion per year that governments around the world give in aid to developing countries – a figure which is due to rise to some $75 billion by 2006 (see Table 11.1). Much of this overseas development assistance (ODA) is still provided on a bilateral basis to particular countries, often those with colonial links (as Table 11.1 also shows), but a significant proportion now comes through the EU.

In 2002, the EU spent €7.9 billion on development assistance world-wide, including Europe. €6 billion of this went through the EU budget, mainly to FSU countries, Asia, Latin America, North Africa and the Middle East, as well as to pre-accession countries. The remaining €1.9 billion is

Table 11.1 Who spends how much on aid and where and how they spend it

Country	ODA (% GNI) (2003)	ODA (US$ billion) (2003)	% of ODA spent bilaterally (2002)	Top three recipients (2002)
Netherlands	0.81	4.059	73	Indonesia, India, Tanzania
Sweden	0.70	2.100	63	Tanzania, Mozambique, Russia
France	0.41	7.337	66	Ivory Coast, French Polynesia, New Caledonia
UK	0.34	6.166	71	India, Serbia and Montenegro, Tanzania
Germany	0.28	6.694	63	Serbia and Montenegro, China, Bolivia
Spain	0.25	2.030	58	Nicaragua, El Salvador, China
Italy	0.16	2.393	43	Mozambique, Tanzania, Eritrea
Czech Rep.	0.10	0.087	n/a	n/a
Poland	n/a	n/a	n/a	n/a
EC	–	8.147	–	–
EU-15 countries total	0.35	36.825	–	–
Average donor country	0.41	–	–	–
US	0.14	15.791	80	Egypt, Russia, Israel

Notes: GNI is gross national income and the UN target is that donor countries should be giving 0.7 per cent of their GNI.

Sources: Data from OECD, *Net Official ODA in 2003* (preliminary figures) and Donor Aid Charts.

funded more directly by the member states, with each negotiating its own commitment every five years. This is managed on their behalf by the Commission as the 'European Development Fund' (EDF) and goes to some 650 million people living in seventy-seven African, Caribbean and Pacific nations – the so-called ACP countries – under an agreement signed at Cotonou in June 2000 that came into force in April 2003 for a twenty-year period, subject to five-yearly reviews.

The Cotonou Agreement is the latest in a long line of agreements under which the EU and its forerunners have provided ODA and preferential access to European markets to countries which, more often than not, are former colonies of member states. Unfortunately, while the assistance provided to the ACP should not be sniffed at, the Commission itself noted prior to Cotonou that the results were pretty meagre in terms of the overall EU development goals (namely, to reduce poverty and produce sustainable socio-economic development in the countries helped) to facilitate their integration into the world economy and to support democracy and human rights. According to European Commission figures, per capita GDP in sub-Saharan African (SSA) – where most EU help goes (see Figure 11.3) – grew on average only 0.4 per cent per year between 1960 and 1992, compared to 2.3 per cent for developing countries as a whole. Only 6 per cent of African trade is intra-African: most African nations (indeed most ACP nations) are still exporting and importing to Europe instead of, as it were, building indigenous (and possibly economically more rational) trade networks. And yet ACP countries' share of the EU market was not only overconcentrated in a few commodities (60 per cent of trade was in only ten products), but between the mid-1970s and the late-1990s it actually halved.

Irrespective of outcomes, there has been considerable criticism of the way in which, over the years, Europe's development assistance has been managed. Firstly, there is the overlap and duplication between EU programmes, the bilateral efforts of member states and the work of non-European governments, other international organizations and non-governmental organizations (NGO)s. Secondly, there is the corruption and misspending in the developing countries themselves. These crit-

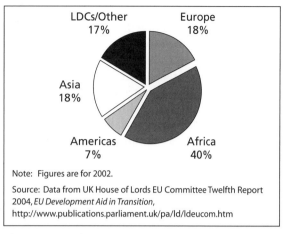

Note: Figures are for 2002.

Source: Data from UK House of Lords EU Committee Twelfth Report 2004, *EU Development Aid in Transition*, http://www.publications.parliament.uk/pa/ld/ldeucom.htm

Figure 11.3 Where overseas development assistance channelled through the EU goes

icisms led to the recent establishment of *EuropeAid*, an EU agency tasked with co-ordinating and implementing the EU effort – an arrangement that appears to be improving matters considerably. Co-ordination will always be an issue, of course, but most analysts believe that a 'mixed economy' of donors is healthy, even if there is some risk of overlap. They also point to the fact that the EU has considerable advantages over bilateral providers. For instance (although this could change with an increased security and foreign policy presence), it is seen by most receiving countries as 'neutral' rather than 'neo-colonial'. In addition, the fact that the EU, via the Commission, is responsible for negotiating multilateral trade agreements (see below) means it is in a better position than single countries to ensure coherence between these agreements and aid packages. On the other hand, European countries continue to run with bilateral trade agreements and often (all too often, say critics) tie aid to a commitment on the part of the recipient to buy their goods and services. One advantage of EU action in this area is that this kind of 'tied aid' is much reduced, even if it is not eliminated.

The other big change that has come about in recent years is the increasing 'conditionality' attached to development assistance coming from European countries (see Holland, 2004a). While some of the conditions have to do with promoting economic reform, most of them are to do with good governance (transparency and accountability) and, increasingly, human rights and gender equality. This is part of an overall trend toward including a political dimension in the aid relationship. Also important, but rather less trumpeted, is the encouragement of trade liberalization. This has to happen so that most, if not all, ACP countries, and their trade relationships with European countries that are still inclined to grant them non-reciprocal, special treatment, are to meet ever-stricter WTO rules. The downside of this will be that their markets will be open to the advanced industrialized countries. The upside of this is the granting to the least developed countries (or LDCs) practically free access to European markets. The fact that free access will apply only to the poorest of the poor raises the critical question of coherence. Put bluntly, European countries give with one hand but take away with the other by continuing to protect markets – particularly agricultural markets – in which developing countries may well enjoy a comparative advantage. Whether this will change with the announcement in early 2001 that the EU will within a decade allow free access to its markets for around fifty of the world's (LDCs) – the so-called 'Everything but Arms' (EBH) proposal – is a moot point (see Holland, 2002: 225–31).

Another, recent criticism is that Europe is increasingly using aid as a tool of foreign and security policy, meaning that its 'near abroad' will get an unfair share compared to those far-away countries who need it more. Those concerned with security are of course right to point to the fact that, as a strategy paper *A Secure Europe in a Better World* (European Council, 2003) (endorsed by European heads of government in December 2003) put it, 'security is a precondition of development'. But many in the development community suspect that the security to be protected is less that of the developing countries than that of Europe itself. Only the naive would expect or demand no linkage between development assistance and foreign and security policy, but many would argue it would be misguided if long-term goals such as poverty reduction (which might eventually contribute to a more secure world) were made subordinate to immediate security priorities. In any case, controlling and/or reducing the flow of migrants into Europe (see Chapter 10) can also be seen as a security priority, which aid to the sending countries (espcially if made conditional) might address (Boswell, 2003).

Critical voices in the development community also argue that the newer member states (whose commitment to and capacity for helping the poorest countries is probably lower than that of their richer counterparts in western Europe) should not deflect EU efforts even further away from the far-away poor to the non-EU countries of Eastern Europe. This would be understandable – they have closer trading relationships and obvious security concerns – but would be a very negative consequence of enlargement. Those concerned with the far-away poor are probably also right to worry that the security focus of the EU as a whole on Islamic North Africa, and the Middle East also risks diverting its attention from the ACP. On the other hand, it has long been a criticism of EU assistance policy that (at least as far as EDF financing goes, and owing in no small part to the initial influence of the French) it has been over-concentrated on the ACP, leaving out massive areas of poverty in Asia and, to a lesser extent, in Latin America.

These criticisms notwithstanding, few would begrudge the EU making the most of its aid role. Admittedly, its efforts are far from perfect and it has a nasty habit, firstly, of forgetting that much of 'its' spending is actually done by individual member states and, secondly, of making comparisons with the US only on publicly provided aid when the Americans spend almost four times as much on privately provided aid as the Europeans. Nevertheless, the EU is clearly a major player in the developing world, and it does seem to be the case that Europe's aid and development policies have been subject over the years to Europeanization. Almost every country still handles most of its ODA bilaterally: some of them, indeed, give such substantial amounts that they come close to matching the EU's own efforts (though much – sometimes up to a third – of their help is still tied to trade). Yet, increasingly, all of them try to help LDCs in a way that attempts not to cross-cut or duplicate EU efforts. This would seem not only to make sense, but also to be in keeping with the wishes of most of their citizens (Figure 11.4). This does not mean, however, that individual European countries will eventually

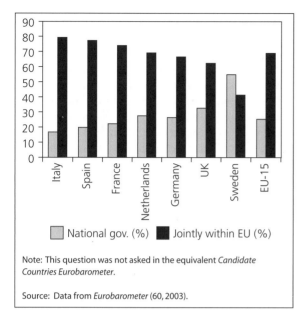

Note: This question was not asked in the equivalent *Candidate Countries Eurobarometer*.

Source: Data from *Eurobarometer* (60, 2003).

Figure 11.4 'Should decisions on humanitarian aid be made by national government or jointly within the EU?'

subsume their development spending into the EU effort: as with diplomacy, there are both symbolic and bottom-line reasons for continuing to maintain a national presence in the world.

Europe and the global environment

Europe leaves a big footprint in the world. Its citizens, its industries (and its highly subsidized farm animals!) are responsible for billions of tons of sometimes toxic waste, for depleting fish stocks, eroding soil and for 15 per cent of world emissions of greenhouse gases (GHGs). With the growing realization that the latter, in particular, are contributing to global warming, European countries have, in recent years, come to realize that environmental policy cannot be pursued simply at a national, nor even just a regional, EU-wide level. Of course, they still have a lot to learn and a lot to do at those levels (see McCormick, 2001), even though they have taken the opportunity offered by EU enlargement to force the relatively high standards of the northern part of the continent onto the southern and eastern parts. But the EU has also

turned its attention further afield. As Bretherton and Vogler (1999: 96) note, it is 'the clear aspiration of the Commission and Member State governments to move well beyond ... essentially regional concerns and to adopt a global leadership and [an] "agenda-setting-role"'.

It, and they, have pursued this role in spite of manifold and manifest difficulties caused by the 'mixed competence' (between the EU and the member states) that characterizes policy and the capacity to make international agreements in this area, as well as the big inconsistencies in European countries' taxation and energy regimes (see Bretherton and Vogler, 1999: 103). This is partly due to the seriousness of the situation, and partly due to the fact that European unity is seen as the only way of (a) governments persuading their own populations and business sectors to make sacrifices; and (b) getting foreign powers (not least the US and Japan) to agree to do so. But whatever its causes, this unity was crucial in getting the agreement to cut GHG emissions that was affirmed in the UN-based Kyoto treaty negotiated in 1997. Along with what was widely perceived as the intransigence of the US during the negotiations, this may well have contributed at least a little to the 'presence' – or, at least, the recognition – of the EU in the world. For instance, an opinion survey carried out by Gallup in the US in May 2004 (published on 7 June) may have made depressing reading for the EU: 77 per cent of Americans admitted to knowing very little or nothing about it (not least that its population is larger than that of the US). On the other hand, although the US was rated more positively than the EU on promoting peace and economic growth and fighting poverty and terrorism, the EU was rated by Americans as better on 'protection of the environment'.

Unfortunately, say critics, what has happened to the Kyoto Treaty may have demonstrated the truth of this impression, but it has also demonstrated European weakness. Leaving aside the fact that a number of countries within Europe look set to miss their target contributions to the overall EU reduction of 8 per cent (as the US said would happen all along), the EU has been able to do nothing to prevent the US from refusing to ratify an agreement that needs ratification from states that produce 55 per cent of GHGs in order to force the hand even of those states that have signed but did not ratify. Yet, interestingly, such criticism may be premature. It does not take into account the fact that Europe's relations with other states may be enough to make the difference, in the sense of getting Kyoto (inadequate though it may be) over the 55 per cent hurdle. By far the most important relationship in this respect is with Russia, whose ratification would by itself clear the hurdle. In this respect, things begun to look hopeful at the end of May 2004 – and in a way that provides proof positive of the interdependence of 'high' and 'low' politics and the different spaces in which Europe needs to act in the world. Announcing, to the surprise of many commentators, that 'We will speed up Russia's movement toward the Kyoto Protocol's ratification', Russian President, Vladimir Putin, noted that 'The EU has met us half way in talks over the WTO and that cannot but affect positively our position on the Kyoto Protocol.'

Europe as a global trader

Europe is able to exert this kind of leverage (and, indeed, provide so much aid) because it is one of the wealthiest places on the planet. Europe may only contain 5 per cent of the world's population; but it produces nearly one-third of the world's economic output, accounts for about one-fifth of all trade flows (indeed, nearer a half if one includes intra-EU trade), and at least one-third of the world's foreign direct investment (FDI). Not only this, but trade is the one area in which the EU has really got its act together. Member states allow the European Commission to act as its single negotiator (at least, when it comes to goods, if not services) in world trade forums such as the WTO. Consequently, its voice has to be listened to, even by a country such as the US; which in other areas can think and act relatively unilaterally.

If even the US has to listen, so, too, do less powerful countries. Many of these like to present themselves to their publics as doing battle with 'Fortress Europe'. This apparently protectionist behemoth seems to them determined to protect the interests of its producers (particularly, via the hated CAP, its agricultural producers), even if it means denying its consumers access to the cheap imports that third countries are dying to provide. This may be a misleading impression: even though things continue to move slowly on agriculture, the EU is (relatively speaking) no longer so bent on protection – indeed, some would say quite the opposite (see Woolcock, 2000). But it is a persistent impression. In many countries, especially, for instance, Australia and New Zealand (see Chaban, Holland and Benson-Rea, 2003 and Murray, 2003), the EU (in as much as it is thought of at all) has a pretty poor reputation – in marked contrast, it should be said, to many of the member states who are happy to let the Commission do their dirty work for them!

These impressions notwithstanding, the trade and investment links between the EU and other advanced industrial and rapidly industrializing countries are highly significant. For instance, China and Europe are each other's second biggest trading partners: according to European Commission merchandize figures for 2003, China made up 12 per cent of the EU-25's imports and was the destination for 5 per cent of its exports. For Japan, the figures were 8 per cent and 5 per cent, respectively, although for both countries the trade in services was much lower (China accounting for just 1.5 per cent of the EU-15 in 2002 and Japan 4.2 per cent). In Australia and New Zealand, EU countries account for 15–20 per cent of trade, and in Canada they account for 10 per cent of its imports and 6 per cent of its exports. It is these kinds of volumes that guarantee Europe – or, at least, European countries – a significant 'presence'. So, increasingly, will the fact that many overseas financial institutions now hold currency reserves in euros. Indeed, it may well be the case that the € sign is as familiar to non-Europeans as the blue flag with twelve gold stars – a symbolic advantage not lost on advocates of the single currency.

Trade between the country whose currency is presently the world leader, the US, and countries belonging to the European Union is highly significant. Just as importantly, for those who worry on both sides of the Atlantic about balance of payments deficits, it is also relatively even. This in marked contrast to the dealings of both America and Europe with, say, China and Japan. Both the US and the EU countries account for around 20

Sweden (Sverige)

Area: 11.3% of EU-25
Population: 2.0% of EU-25
GDP: 2.2% of EU-25
Joined EU: 1995
Capital city: Stockholm

History: Sweden's early history was bound up with that of the other Nordic countries. It conquered Finland in the thirteenth century, but was then subsumed into the kingdom of Denmark. It regained its independence in the early sixteenth century under a king elected by its parliament, the *Riksdag*. For the next hundred and fifty years, it went from strength to strength, conquering territory in modern-day Estonia, Latvia, Russia, Germany and Poland, and even making incursions into what is now the Czech Republic during the high point of its power, the Thirty Years War (1618–48). After this, it began to lose out to other powers, most notably Russia, to which it was forced to cede Finland in 1809. Things looked up soon after when the *Riksdag* elected a high-ranking French soldier as regent and then king, creating the line of Bernadotte, which still reigns in Sweden today. As a reward for siding with Britain and Prussia (now part of Germany) against the French dictator, Napoleon Bonaparte, Sweden was granted effective control over the kingdom of Norway – a situation that lasted until 1905 when the Norwegians peacefully regained their independence. The nineteenth century saw Sweden adopt, first, a liberal constitution, then (in the 1860s) parliamentary government and finally a fully-fledged democracy after the First World War (1914–18).

Sweden did not take part in that conflict and likewise remained neutral in the Second World War (1939–45), managing to escape the occupation endured by its Nordic neighbours and to develop its economy by trading with the combatants. If neutrality was the first defining feature of the twentieth century for Sweden, the second was the unparalleled political hegemony of its Social Democratic Party (SAP). The SAP effectively ran Sweden from 1932 to 1976. During this period it pioneered anti-recessionary public spending and then went on to construct the third defining feature of Sweden in the twentieth century, its highly comprehensive welfare state. Even since wresting power from the SAP in the mid-1970s, the so-called 'bourgeois' parties of the centre-right, led by the conservative Moderates, have only managed to govern Sweden twice – once between 1976 and 1982, and then between 1991 and 1994, since when the SAP has again been continuously in office with the support of the smaller, more radical Left Party and the Greens.

Economy and Society: Sweden's 8.9 million citizens are some of the richest in Europe, with a per capita annual income of around 15 per cent above the EU-25 average for 2003. Much of that income is swallowed up by taxes to pay for the welfare state, although the universal nature of many of the benefits it offers (in both cash and in kind) means that support for it remains high, even amongst those who pay most. This is despite the fact that recent pension reforms will see the introduction of an element of means-testing that for some goes against the fiercely egalitarian grain. Sweden can afford its welfare state because it has a very competitive international trading sector which, although privately owned, seems to benefit from the stable economic environment, industrial harmony and active labour market policies facilitated by the state. Things are not perfect, of course: there is unemployment, much of it disproportionately affecting Sweden's half

a million or so immigrant population, many of whom arrived only in the 1980s–1990s from places such as the former Yugoslavia and the Middle-East. Until their arrival, Sweden was unusually ethnically homogeneous – a homogeneity that also applied to religion: over nine out of ten Swedes still identify, even if only minimally, with the state Lutheran (Protestant) church which is financed through the tax system.

Governance: Sweden is a parliamentary democracy and a constitutional monarchy. Its unicameral legislature reflects the relatively consensual nature of Swedish political life. Its procedures, like policy-making more generally, encourage consultation with outside interests, especially the powerful unions (to which most people belong) and employers' organizations, although the latter have cooled somewhat toward government-facilitated economic planning in recent years. Responsibility for many state functions is exercised by agencies, often at the regional or county level. Strong respect for due process has not precluded adaptation and innovation: Sweden undertook a major overhaul of its constitution as recently as the mid-1970s, and was the pioneer of the *ombudsman* system designed to help citizens redress grievances against public bodies without expensive recourse to the law – a system that has since spread to other countries.

Foreign policy: Sweden put off joining the EU until 1995. By then, the end of the Cold War had calmed concerns about membership undermining its neutral, non-aligned stance. Nevertheless, the country rejected adopting the euro in a referendum in 2003. Sweden still declines to join NATO, but is active in a non-combat role in humanitarian interventions all over the world.

Further reading: Arter (1999), Aylott (1999), Hancock (2003) and Miles (2000).

per cent of each other's trade – around €1 billion per day. The US accounts for over a third of European trade in services, and also exports significant amounts of energy to the EU countries, which in return run a balance of payment surplus with the US on machinery, and especially cars. Some 60 per cent of foreign investment in the US is from Europe, which in turn derives 50 per cent of its foreign investment from the US. Moreover, trading and investment relationships are growing as multinational companies on each continent buy into, takeover and merge with each other. It is not just a relationship *à deux*, either. Between them, the EU and the US are easily the world's most successful capitalist economies; as such, they go some way to determining, via the various rounds of WTO negotiations, the trading framework for the rest of the world.

Partly because of this, and partly because of the media's preference for conflict (see Chapter 7), the very healthy trading relationship between Europe and the US can sometimes get subsumed in tales of sporadic (though sometimes long-running) disputes. Sometimes these occur at world trade talks: during the negotiation of the so-called Uruguay Round of GATT, the WTO's predecessor, which basically ran from 1986 to 1993, there were huge arguments over Europe's refusal to allow services (and particularly cultural matters) to be opened up to US firms, as well as over agriculture. These arguments saw the French emerge as a convenient fall guy for all concerned – a pattern that seems to have become a permanent feature of transatlantic relations more generally. They also rather undermined the notion of the Commission as 'Europe's' sole negotiator not needing to look over its shoulder at individual countries: it was clear that many aspects had to be cleared by individual member states before the Commission could sign off on them. Outside of these multilateral trade talks, there have also been big bilateral rows between the US and Europe over steel tariffs (in 2002), GM crops and animal growth hormones (ongoing), Cuba (also ongoing) and, strange but true, bananas.

Amid these very public spats, it is easy to see why the media, and therefore citizens, lose sight of things like the 'New Transatlantic Agenda', signed by Bill Clinton and EU representatives in 1995 – an agreement designed to provide some wordy reassurance (and institutional infrastructure) to back up continued political co-operation (and hopefully enhanced trade co-operation) in the post-Cold War era. Things are not helped either by accusations by American commentators and policy-makers that Europeans are rather keener than they should be to see 'the flag following trade' rather than using economic clout to achieve foreign policy objectives or to reward good behaviour on the part of foreign regimes.

The American critics have a point. What they see as Europe's intransigence goes right back to the reluctance among European states to support Israel in the 1973 war with Arab countries, partly (though not purely) because they feared a backlash by oil-producing states. Americans were also enraged by European states' refusal to stop importing gas from the Soviet Union following its role in suppressing the 1981 liberalization of the then communist regime in Poland. Europe's determination to ignore the US boycott of Cuba, with which it has trade, tourism and (Spanish) cultural links, has also been a problem (see Byron, 2000). And, much to the irritation of some in the US, European states, both collectively and individually, continue to attempt a constructive dialogue with the Islamic regime in (oil- and gas-rich) Iran and not to allow 'local difficulties' in Tibet and Taiwan to interfere in relations with the economic powerhouse that is China.

But things are changing. It would be naive to think that European pragmatism is ever likely to give way to idealism. But European governments, particularly acting together as the EU, are beginning to realize that their collective interests (in the trade as well as the security field) may well lie in investing more political content in what previously have been very much economic relationships, perhaps via bilateral forums or perhaps via contacts with Asian regional cooperation organizations like ASEAN and ASEM (see Forster, 2000). This is especially true in East and South East Asia, (see Bridges, 1999, Edmonds, 2002, Gilson, 2000 and Wiessala, 2002). If anything, given heightened fears concerning migration and WMD in North Korea, collective diplomacy in those regions may well increase.

But we should be careful. EU specialists are bound to stress the role of collective as opposed to bilateral diplomacy between individual member states and the countries concerned. Similarly, it is all very well for the EU to claim that it accounts for a large chunk of world trade and therefore enjoys massive presence; but it is a little misleading. Obviously, the EU helps provide the framework for those trade flows; but it is individual member states and the companies within them that actually do the business. It is rather like UEFA (the body which regulates soccer in Europe) claiming credit for all the goals scored and wins notched up by European countries in the World Cup finals that, via its association with FIFA (the world governing body), it goes some way to helping stage every four years. Clearly, at least some of the audience will recognize the collective brand; but many more of them will be aware of the nations of which it is composed.

Lest we forget: the domestication of international politics in Europe

'Europe' in the world, then, is a complex mix of individual states and the European Union of which the majority are a part. And it is about the interaction between national foreign policies, CFSP (and ESDP), and the 'external relations' of the EU when it operates in the trade (and increasingly perhaps) the aid and the environmental field (see Knodt and Princen, 2003). There is no reason to think this will change any time soon. Certainly, we should be careful not to presume that foreign policy in Europe is somehow on an inevitable evolutionary progress toward eventual integration. Doing so will only disappoint, since the gap between expectations and capability is unlikely to disappear (see Hill, 1993). As Smith (2004) argues (see also Hill, 1998), it could be that the 'part-formed foreign policy' of the EU will always be expressed as much by supposedly non-foreign policy instruments such as trade and aid, and that it is pointless, in the absence of a collective 'European interest' to expect it to take on the forms we traditionally associate with states – states that, in any case, wish to cling on to those forms even in the 'postmodern' or 'postsovereign' age.

But whatever 'Europe's' place in the wider world, the biggest success story with regard to defence,

foreign policy and even development aid, has been Europe itself. Prior to the founding and development of what is now the EU, most European countries regarded their immediate neighbours as part of the rest of the world. That is no longer the case: within Europe, international politics have been substantially 'domesticated'. It is not just that European states – even those states that retain global interests and/or wish to maintain a close relationship with the US – no longer consider armed conflict between themselves as even an outside possibility. It is also that, at the very least, they reflexively think about the mutual consequences of their following their own interests and, in some, cases hesitate even to define those interests without or before consultation (Aggestam, 2000: 71). And even where those interests would appear to differ, they will often lay them aside for what they consider as more important in the long term; namely, a security and a prosperity that they recognize is best guaranteed collectively. The EU, probably more even than organizations such as the OSCE, contributes to a European security community.

The most obvious recent example of this, of course, is EU enlargement. This was achieved not just because of the long-term; economic potential of expanding the single market. It also fitted with the even longer-term foreign policy goal – albeit not one always very consciously or consistently pursued (see Zielonka, 1998) – of 'securing' the 'near abroad' by 'locking-in' democracy, just as it was locked-in in Spain, Portugal and Greece in the 1980s and in the previously non-democratic states of western Europe after the Second World War. Even the prospect of membership, it seems, is enough to persuade potentially troublesome states, especially in the Balkans, to 'behave themselves' – witness the progress of Croatia, officially declared a candidate for EU membership in June 2004.

The enlargement that took place in 2004, we should also note, was achieved – particularly as accession became a reality – without the support of the majority in some of the biggest countries of what was then the EU-15. *Eurobarometer* 61, conducted just a month or so before the accessions of May 2004, found support for enlargement running at just 28 per cent in Germany, 31 per cent in the UK and 37 per cent in France. Even in highly enthusiastic Spain, Italy and Sweden, the

---

BOX 11.4
Talking Turkey at last?

Turkey has been formally associated with the EU since 1963 and first applied to join in 1987. After a customs union took effect in 1996, Turkey was finally accepted as a candidate country in 1999, since when it has accelerated economic and political reforms. There remain, however, several obstacles to membership. The first is its sheer size – people-wise. Within ten years Turkey's population, which is young and growing fast, will be equal to that of Germany, and is already bigger than the combined population of the ten states that joined the EU in 2004. This would give Turkey a big say in EU institutions, while its poverty (its per capita income is only around a quarter of the EU average and very unevenly distributed) would ensure that it swallowed up large amounts of EU regional funding. Meanwhile, the prospect of Turks being granted free movement and the right to work in Europe is a terrifying prospect to some: Germany would be particularly concerned, since nearly 2 million Turks already live there, and these concerns are allied to fears all over Europe about importing Islamic terrorism.

Turkey's Islamic culture means that for many European politicians (notably in France and Germany), it simply does not belong in Europe. This downplays the fact that (as we saw in Chapter 1) Turkey has been an integral part of European history for centuries and has grown closer and closer to Europe in recent times (see Müftüler-Bac, 1997). This negative attitude angers other European politicians, especially the British. They point to the fact that Turkey is an assertively secular state. They also worry that, by denying it entry, the EU would send a signal to the Islamic world that its support for the 'War on Terror' is really little more than a Judeo-Christian crusade. Turkey, they note, has been a loyal member of NATO for half a century, and (given its land borders with Syria, Iran and Iraq, as well as with several states of the FSU) would provide a buffer zone against, and a bridgehead into, potentially unstable, but also potentially lucrative, parts of the world. Incorporating Turkey into the EU would, in any case, help consolidate democracy there and improve its economy, meaning that the country itself would present less of a risk to its European neighbours (see Hughes, 2004).

'don't knows' and those against were 41 per cent, 45 per cent and 46 per cent, respectively, while in the more ambivalent Netherlands they outnumbered supporters by 12 per cent. Hopefully, experience will show that their leaders really did 'know best'. However, they may be less able to insulate themselves against public opinion – and, indeed, their own prejudices – when it comes to enlarging the EU to include countries whose claim to be part of 'us' rather than 'them' is less secure (see Neumann, 1998). But while thinking twice about

Turkey (see Box 11.4) and other countries may be democratic, and may be realistic, the problem with putting limits on enlargement is that, by fixing what are declared to be finite borders, the EU may lose some of its capacity – amply demonstrated in the case of Central and Eastern Europe (see Grabbe, 2003) – to exert leverage over the behaviour of aspirant states. On the other hand, if the widespread apathy that greeted the accession of 2004 is anything to go by, Europeans do seem a little tired of making history.

Learning resources

Must-reads on individual countries' foreign policies (and their interaction with the EU) are Christiansen and Tonra (2004), Hill (1996) and Manners and Whitman (2000). On postcommunist states' foreign policies, see Fawn (2003). On defence, see Howorth and Keeler (2003). Obvious first ports of call on the issue of Europe (and the EU) in the world are Bretherton and Vogler (1999) and Piening (1997). Those interested in CFSP should start with Soetendorp (1999), though Hill (1993) and Sjursen (2001) are stimulating shorter pieces. On development and aid, see Holland (2002, 2004b). Those interested in Europe in particular parts of the world should consult the following texts: on the transatlantic relationship, Peterson and Pollack, (2003); on Asia, Wiessala (2002); on the Middle East, van Dosenrode and Stubkjær, (2002); on the Mediterranean, Youngs (2003); on China, Edmonds (2002); on Russia, Stent and Shevtsova (2002) and Webber (2000); on Africa, Brown (2002) and Olsen (2002); and on South America, Youngs (2002).

EXECUTIVE SUMMARY

- For all the new challenges presented by the post-Cold War world, and notwithstanding the growth of the EU, European countries continue to face some perennial security and defence dilemmas.

- Obvious examples include the need to ensure that a potentially more assertive Germany remains locked – into a European 'security community', and to minimize potential risks coming from the former Soviet Union (FSU) – largely by granting Russia leeway in its own backyard and by further boosting trade.

- Another obvious – and internally most contentious – instance is Europe's reliance on the US. But whether this continues or not, Europe will have to spend and, as it has already begun to do, co-operate more on defence. Such co-operation is unlikely to lead to full integration of Europe's armed forces.

- A new challenge – dealt with mostly through aid but increasingly through conditional offers of trade, too – is Europe's 'Mediterranean neighbourhood' in North Africa and the Middle East.

- Foreign policy co-operation is institutionalized, but individual European states – particularly the large ones – guard their right to promote and protect their national interests. Domestic influences on foreign policy are still important.

- European governments, bilaterally and via the EU, are big aid donors especially to their former colonies, though their spending is often tied to trade and their markets still protected. The co-ordination and efficiency of aid has improved recently.

- Co-operation between countries via the EU is most obvious in the environmental field and in setting the terms of world trade through the WTO. High-profile disputes with the US and the EU's protectionist reputation disguise the enormous contribution to world trade made by European countries.

- All these global roles should not be allowed to mask Europe's main achievement: ensuring fifty years of peace and prosperity within the continent itself by building and expanding the EU. Perhaps, though, that expansion has reached its limits.

References

A

Aberbach, J.D., Putnam, R.D. and Rockman, B.A. (1981) *Bureaucrats and Politicians in Western Democracies* (Cambridge, MA: Harvard University Press).

van Aelst, Peter and Walgrave, Stefaan (2001) 'Who is that (Wo)man in the Street? From the Normalisation of Protest to the normalisation of the protester', *European Journal of Political Research*, 39(4), pp. 461–86.

Aggestam, Lisbeth (2000) 'Germany', in Ian Manners and Richard G. Whitman (eds), *The Foreign Policies of European Union Member States* (Manchester: Manchester University Press).

Agranoff, Robert (1996) 'Federal Evolution in Spain', *International Political Science Review*, 17(4) pp. 385–401.

Allen, David and Smith, Michael (1998) 'The EU's Security Presence: Barrier, Facilitator, or Manager?', in Carolyn Rhodes (ed.), *The European Union in the World Community* (Boulder, CO: Lynne Rienner).

AlSayyad, Nezar and Castells, Manuel (eds), (2002) *Muslim Europe or Euro-Islam: Politics, Culture, and Citizenship in the Age of Globalization* (Latham: Lexington Books).

Alter, Karen (2001) *Establishing the Supremacy of European Law: The Making of an International Rule of Law in Europe* (Oxford: Oxford University Press).

Alvarez, Michael R., Garrett, Geoffrey and Lange, Peter (1991) 'Government Partisanship, Labor Organization, and Macroeconomic Performance', *American Political Science Review*, 85(2), pp. 539–56.

Anckar, Carsten (1997) 'Determinants of Disproportionality and Wasted Votes', *Electoral Studies*, 16(4), pp. 501–15.

Anderson, Benedict (1991) *Imagined Communities: Reflections on the Origin and Spread of Nationalism* (London: Verso).

Anderson, K.M. (2001) 'The Politics of Retrenchment in a Social Democratic Welfare State: Reform of Swedish Pensions and Unemployment Insurance', *Comparative Political Studies*, 34(9) pp. 1063–91.

Andeweg, Rudy B. (2000) 'Ministers as Double Agents? The Delegation Process Between Cabinet and Ministers', *European Journal of Political Research*, 37(3) pp. 377–95.

Andeweg, Rudy B. and Irwin, Galen A. (2005) *Governance and Politics of the Netherlands*, 2nd edition (Basingstoke and New York: Palgrave Macmillan).

Arter, David (1999) *Scandinavian Politics Today* (Manchester: Manchester University Press).

Arter, David (ed.) (2001) *From Farmyard to City Square: The Electoral Adaptation of the Nordic Agrarian Parties* (Aldershot: Ashgate).

Arts, Will, Hagneaars, Jacques and Halman, Loek (2004) *The Cultural Diversity of European Unity: Findings, Explanations and Reflections from the European Values Survey* (Leiden: Brill).

Asp, Kent (1983) 'The Struggle for the Agenda: Party Agenda, Media Agenda and Voter Agenda in the 1979 Swedish Election Campaign', *Communication Research*, 10(3), pp. 333–55.

Astudillo Ruiz, Javier (2002) 'The Spanish Experiment: A Social Democratic Party–Union Relationship in a Competitive Union Context', Harvard Centre for European Studies, Working Paper, 83.

Auer, Andreas and Bützer, Michael (eds) (2001) *Direct Democracy: The Eastern and Central European Experience* (Aldershot: Ashgate).

Aylott, Nicholas (1999) *Swedish Social Democracy and European Integration: The People's Home on the Market* (Aldershot: Ashgate).

B

Baccaro, L. (2002) 'Negotiating the Italian Pension Reform with the Unions: Lessons for Corporatist Theory', *Industrial and Labour Relations Review*, 55(3) pp. 413–31.

Baccaro, L. (2003) 'What is Alive and What is Dead in the Theory of Corporatism?', *British Journal of Industrial Relations*, 41(4), pp. 683–706.

Badinger, Harald and Breuss, Fritz (2003) 'What has Determined the Rapid Post-war Growth of intra-EU Trade?', IEF Working Paper,48, Wirtschaftsuniversität Wien.

Bale, Tim (2000) 'Field-level CFSP: EU Diplomatic Cooperation in Third Countries', *Current Politics and Economics of Europe*, 10(2), pp. 187–212; also available at http://www.lse.ac.uk/Depts/intrel/pdfs/EFPU%20Working%20Paper%204.pdf.

Bale, Tim (2003) 'Cinderella and her Ugly Sisters: The Mainstream and Extreme Right in Europe's Bipolarising Party Systems', *West European Politics*, 26(3), pp. 67–90.

Bale, Tim (2004) 'Business as Usual? Europe's Overseas Diplomacy in the Age of CFSP', in Martin Holland (ed.), *Common Foreign and Security Policy: The First Ten Years* (London: Continuum).

Bale, Tim and Bergman, Torbjörn (forthcoming) 'Captives no Longer, but Servants Still? Contract Parliamentarism and the New Minority Governance', *Government and Opposition*.

Bale, Tim and Kopecký, Petr (1998) 'Can Young Pups Teach an Old Dog New Tricks? Legislative Lessons for Britain from Eastern Europe's New Constitutional Democracies', *Journal of Legislative Studies*, 4(2) pp. 159–78.

Balme, Richard, Chabanet, Didier and Wright, Vincent, (eds) (2002) *L'action collective en Europe* (Paris: Presses de Sciences Po).

Barany, Zoltan (2002) *The East European Gypsies: Regime Change, Marginality, and Ethnopolitics* (Cambridge: Cambridge University Press).

Barnett, Steven (2002) 'Will a Crisis in Journalism Provoke a Crisis in Democracy?', *Political Quarterly*, 2(4), pp. 400–8.

Barrett, David B., Kurian, George T., Johnson, Todd M. (2001) *World Christian Encyclopedia: A Comparative Survey of Churches and Religion in the Modern World*, 2nd edition (New York: Oxford University Press).

Batory, Agnes and Sitter, Nick (2004) 'Cleavages, Competition and Coalition-building: Agrarian Parties and the European Question in Western and East Central Europe', *European Journal of Political Research*, 43(4), pp. 523–46.

Baudino, Claudie (2003) 'Parity Reform in France: Promises and Pitfalls', *Review of Policy Research*, 20(3), pp. 385–400.

Bekke, Hans A.G.M. and van der Meer, Frits M. (eds) (2000) *Civil Service Systems in Western Europe* (Cheltenham: Edward Elgar).

Bell, David S. (2002) *French Politics Today* (Manchester: Manchester University Press).

Bennie, Lynne G. (1998) 'Brent Spar, Atlantic Oil and Greenpeace', *Parliamentary Affairs*, 51(3). pp. 397–410.

Berger, Stefan and Compston, Hugh (eds) (2002) *Policy Concertation and Social Partnership in Western Europe* (Oxford: Berghan Books)

Bevir, Mark, Rhodes, R. A. W. and Weller, Patrick (2003) 'Comparative Governance: Prospects and Lessons', *Public Administration*, 81(1), pp. 191–210.

Beyers, J. (2002) 'Gaining and Seeking Access: The European Adaptation of Domestic Interest Associations', *European Journal of Political Research*, 41 (5), pp. 585–612.

Beyme, Klaus von (2003) 'Constitutional Engineering in Central and Eastern Europe', in Stephen White, Judy Batt and Paul G. Lewis (eds), *Developments in Central and East European Politics 3* (Basingstoke: Palgrave Macmillan).

Bielasiak, Jack (2002) 'The Institutionalization of Electoral and Party Systems in Postcommunist States', *Comparative Politics*, 34(2), pp. 189–210.

Billig, Michael (1995) *Banal Nationalism* (London: Sage)

Birch, Sarah, Millard, Frances, Popescu, Marina and Williams, Kieran (2002) *Embodying Democracy: Electoral System Design in Post-Communist Europe* (Basingstoke: Palgrave Macmillan).

Blair, Tony and Schröder, Gerhard (1999) *Europe: The Third Way/Die Neue Mitte*, available on numerous websites, e.g. http://www.iedm.org/library/blair_en.html

Blais, A., Blake, D. and Dion, S. (1996) 'Do Parties Make a Difference? A Reappraisal', *American Journal of Political Science*, 40(2), pp. 514–20.

Blom Hansen, J. (2001) 'Organized Interests and the State: A Disintegrating Relationship? Evidence from Denmark', *European Journal of Political Research*, 39(3) pp. 391–416.

Blondel, Jean and Müller-Rommel, Ferdinand (eds), (1997) *Cabinets in Western Europe* (Basingstoke: Palgrave Macmillan).

Blondel, Jean and Müller-Rommel, Ferdinand (2001) *Cabinets in Eastern Europe* (Basingstoke: Palgrave Macmillan).

Blondel, Jean, Sinnott, Richard and Svensson, Palle (1998) *People and Parliament in the European Union: Participation, Democracy and Legitimacy* (Oxford: Clarendon Press).

Boix, Charles (1998) *Political Parties, Growth and Equality: Conservative and Social Democratic Economic Strategies in the World Economy* (Cambridge: Cambridge University Press).

Bomberg, Elizabeth (2002) 'The Europeanisation of Green Parties: Exploring the EU's Impact', *West European Politics*, 25(3), pp. 29–50.

Bonoli, Giuliano (2004) 'Social Democratic Party Policies in Europe: Towards a Third Way?', in Giuliano Bonoli and Martin Powell (eds), *Social Democratic Party Policies in Contemporary Europe* (London: Routledge/ECPR).

Borraz, O. and John, P. (2004) 'The Transformation of Urban Political Leadership in Western Europe', *International Journal of Urban and Regional Research* , 28(1), pp. 107–20.

Börzel, Tanja A. (2002) 'Pace-setting, Foot-dragging and Fence-sitting: Member State Responses to Europeanization', *Journal of Common Market Studies*, 40(2), pp. 193–214.

Boswell, C. (2003) 'The "External Dimension" of EU Immigration and Asylum Policy', *International Affairs*, 79(3), pp. 619–38.

Boucher, G. and Collins, G. (2003) 'Having One's Cake and being Eaten Too: Irish Neo-liberal Corporatism', *Review of Social Economy*, 61(3), pp. 295–316.

Bouwen, Pieter (2002) 'Corporate Lobbying in the European Union: The Logic of Access', *Journal of European Public Policy*, 9(3), pp. 365–90.

Bowler, Shaun, Donovan, Todd and Hanneman, Robert (2003) 'Art for Democracy's Sake? Group Membership and Political Engagement in Europe', *Journal of Politics*, 65(4), pp. 1111–29.

Brants, Kees and Siune, Karen (1998) 'Politicization in Decline', in Denis McQuail and Karen Siune (eds), *Media Policy: Convergence, Concentration and Commerce* (London: Sage).

Bretherton, Charlotte and Vogler, John (1999) *The European Union as a Global Actor* (London: Routledge).

Brettschneider, Frank (1997) 'The Press and the Polls in Germany, 1980–1994: Poll Coverage as an Essential Part of Election Campaign Reporting', *International Journal of Public Opinion Research*, 9(3), pp. 248–65.

Bridges, Brian (1999) *Europe and the Challenge of the Asia Pacific: Change, Continuity and Crisis* (Cheltenham: Edward Elgar).

Broughton, David and Donovan, Mark (eds), (1999) *Changing Party Systems in Western Europe* (London: Pinter).

Broughton, David and Ten Napel, Hans-Martien (2000), *Religion and Mass Electoral Behaviour in Europe* (London: Routledge).

Brown, William (2002) *The European Union and Africa: The Restructuring of North–South Relations* (London: I.B. Tauris).

Brug, W. van der, Fennema M. and Tillie, J. (2000) 'Anti-immigrant Parties in Europe: Ideological or Protest Vote?', *European Journal of Political Research*, 37(1) pp. 77–102.

Bruszt, László (2002) 'Making Markets and Eastern Enlargement: Diverging Convergence', *West European Politics*, 25(2), pp. 121–40.

Bruter, Michael (1999) 'Diplomacy without a State: The External Delegations of the European Commission', *Journal of European Public Policy*, 6(2), pp. 183–205.

Budge, Ian, Crewe, Ivor, McKay, David and Newton, Ken (2003) *The New British Politics* (London: Longman).

Budge, Ian and Keman, Hans, (1990) 'New Concerns for Coalition Theory: Allocation of Ministries and Segmental Policy-making; A Comparative Analysis' *Acta Politica*, 90(2) pp. 151–85.

Buller, James and Gamble, Andrew (2002) 'Conceptualizing Europeanization', *Public Policy and Administration*, 17(2), pp. 4–24.

Burchell, John (2001) 'Evolving or Conforming? Assessing Organisational Reform within European Green Parties', *West European Politics*, 24(3), pp. 113–43.

Byron, J. (2000) 'Square Dance Diplomacy: Cuba and CARIFO-RUM, the European Union and the United States', *European Review of Latin American and Caribbean Studies*, 68, pp. 23–45, available at http://www.cedla.uva.nl/fs_top.htm?60/60_publications61_en_infoeurrev.htm

C

Campbell, Vincent (2004) *Information Age Journalism: Journalism in an International Context* (London: Arnold).

Carty, R. Kenneth (2004) 'Parties as Franchise Systems: The Stratarchical Organizational Imperative', *Party Politics*, 10(1), pp. 5–24.

Cassese, Sabino (1999) 'Italy's Senior Civil Service: An Ossified World', in Edward C. Page and Vincent Wright (eds), *Bureaucratic Elites in Western European States* (Oxford: Oxford University Press).

Castells, Manuel (1997) *The Power of Identity, Volume II: The Information Age: Economy, Society, and Culture* (Oxford: Blackwell).

Castles, Stephen (2004) 'Why Migration Policies Fail', *Ethnic and Racial Studies*, 27(2), pp. 205–27.

Caul, Miki L. and Gray, Mark M. (2000) 'From Platform Declarations to Policy Outcomes: Changing Party Profiles and Partisan Influence over Policy', in Russell J. Dalton and Martin P. Wattenberg (eds), *Parties without Partisans: Political Change in Advanced Industrial Democracies* (Oxford: Oxford University Press), pp. 208–37.

Chaban, Natalia, Holland, Martin and Benson-Rea, Maureen (2003) *External Perceptions of the European Union: A Survey of New Zealanders' Perceptions and Attitudes towards the European Union*, NCRE Research Series, No.1, University of Canterbury, New Zealand, available at http://www.europe.canterbury.ac.nz/research/nc/survey_identity_nz.pdf

Chalaby, Jean K. (2002) 'Transnational Television in Europe: The Role of Pan-European Channels', *European Journal of Communication*, 17(2), pp. 183–203.

Chondroleou, Georgia (2004) 'Public Images and Private Lives: The Greek Experience', *Parliamentary Affairs*, 57(1), pp. 53–66.

Christiansen, Thomas and Tonra, Ben (eds) (2004) *Rethinking EU Foreign Policy: Beyond the Common Foreign and Security Policy* (Manchester: Manchester University Press).

Chu, Jeff (2003) 'O Father, where art thou' *Time Magazine*, 16 June, 2003, see http://www.time.com/time/europe/archive/

Church, Clive H. (2004) *The Politics and Government of Switzerland* (Basingstoke: Palgrave Macmillan).

Clark, David (1998) 'The Modernization of the French Civil Service: Crisis, Change and Continuity', *Public Administration*, 76(1), pp. 97–116.

Clift, Ben (2001) 'The Jospin Way', *Political Quarterly*, 72(2), pp. 170–9.

Clift, Ben (2002) 'Social Democracy and Globalisation: The Case of France and the UK', *Government and Opposition*, 37(4), pp. 466–500.

Closa, Carlos and Heywood, Paul (2004) *Spain and the European Union* (Basingstoke: Palgrave Macmillan).

Coen, David (1998) 'European Business Interests and the Nation State: Large Firm Lobbying in the European Union and Member State', *Journal of Public Policy*, 18(1), pp. 75–100.

Cole, Alistair (1999) 'The *service publique* under Stress', *West European Politics*, 22(4), pp. 166–84.

Cole, Alistair and Drake, Helen (2000) 'The Europeanization of the French Polity: Continuity, Change and Adaptation', *Journal of European Public Policy*, 7(1), pp. 26–43.

Coleman, Stephen (2003) *A Tale of Two Houses – The House of Commons, the Big Brother House and the People at Home* (London: Hansard Society).

Collins, Neil and Butler, Patrick (2004) 'Political Mediation in Ireland: Campaigning between Traditional and Tabloid Markets', *Parliamentary Affairs*, 57(1), pp. 93–107.

Colomer, Josep M. (2002) 'Spain and Portugal: Rule by Party Leadership', in Josep Colomer (ed.), *Political Institutions in Europe* (London: Routledge).

Compston, Hugh (1998) 'The End of Policy Concertation? Western Europe Since the Single European Act', *Journal of European Public Policy*, 5(4), pp. 507–26.

Compston, Hugh (ed.) (2004) *Handbook of Public Policy in Europe: Britain, France and Germany* (Basingstoke: Palgrave Macmillan).

Conceição, Pedro, Ferreira, Pedro and Galbraith, James K. (2001) 'Inequality and unemployment in Europe: The American Cure', in James K. Galbraith and Maureen Berner (eds), *Inequality and Industrial Change: A Global View* (Cambridge: Cambridge University Press).

Conradt, David P. (2004) *The German Polity* (London: Addison-Wesley).

Cook, Timothy E. (1998) *Governing with the News: The News Media as a Political Institution* (Chicago: University of Chicago Press).

Corbett, Richard, Jacobs, Francis and Shackleton, Michael (2003) *The European Parliament* (London: John Harper).

Cordell, Karl and Wolff, Stefan (eds) (2004) *The Ethnopolitical Encyclopaedia of Europe* (Basingstoke: Palgrave Macmillan).

Cowles, Maria Green and Dinan, Desmond (eds) (2004) *Developments in the European Union 2* (Basingstoke: Palgrave Macmillan).

Coulombis, Theodore and Veremis, Thomas (1999) 'Introduction: The Mediterranean in Perspective', in Stelios Stavridis, Theodore Coulombis, Thomas Veremis and Neville Waites (eds), *Foreign Policies of the EU's Mediterranean States and Applicant Countries in the 1990s* (Basingstoke: Palgrave Macmillan).

Cowles, Maria Green, Caporaso, James and Risse, Thomas (eds) (2001) *Transforming Europe: Europeanisation and Domestic Change* (Ithaca: Cornell University Press).

Crewe, Ivor and Thomson, Katarina (1999) 'Party Loyalties: Dealignment or Realignment?' in Geoffrey Evans and Pippa Norris (eds), *Critical Elections: British Parties and Elections in Long-term Perspective* (London: Sage).

Crouch, Colin (1999) *Social Change in Western Europe* (Oxford: Oxford University Press).

Crowe, Brian (2004) 'A Common European Foreign Policy after Iraq?', in Martin Holland (ed.), *Common Foreign and Security Policy: The First Ten Years* (London: Continuum).

Crowley, P.M. (2002) 'The Stability and Growth Pact: Review, Alternatives and Legal Aspects', *Current Politics and Economics of Europe*, 11(3), pp. 225–44.

van Cuilenburg, Jan and McQuail, Dennis (2003) 'Media Policy Paradigm Shifts: Towards a New Communications Policy Paradigm', *European Journal of Communication*, 18(2), pp. 181–207.

Curran, James (2002) *Media and Power* (London: Routledge).

Curran, James and Leys, Colin (2000) 'Media and the Decline of Liberal Corporatism in Britain', in James Curran and Myung-Jin Park (eds), *De-Westernizing Media Studies* (London: Routledge).

Curtis, James E., Baer, Douglas E. and Grabb, Edward G. (2001) 'Nations of Joiners: Explaining Voluntary Association Membership in Democratic Societies', *American Sociological Review*, 66 (4), pp. 783–805.

Curzon Price, Victoria (2004) 'Industrial Policy' in Ali M. El-Agraa, (ed.) *The European Union: Economics and Policy*, 7th edition (London: Prentice-Hall/FT).

D

Dahlgren, Peter (2000) 'Communication and Democracy in Late Modernity', in Barrie Axford and Richard Huggins (eds), *New Media and Politics* (London: Sage).

Dalton, Russell J. (1996) 'A Divided Electorate?, in Gordon Smith, William E. Paterson and Stephen Padgett (eds), *Developments in German Politics* (Basingstoke: Palgrave Macmillan).

Dalton, Russell J. (2000) 'The Decline of Party Identification', in Russell J. Dalton and Martin P. Wattenberg (eds), *Parties without Partisans: Political Change in Advanced Industrial Democracies* (Oxford: Oxford University Press).

Dalton, Russell J., McAllister, Ian and Wattenberg, Martin P. (2000) 'The Consequences of Partisan Dealignment' in Russell J. Dalton and Martin P. Wattenberg (eds), *Parties without Parisans: Political Change in Advanced Industrial Democracies* (Oxford: Oxford University Press).

Dalton, Russell J. and Wattenberg, Martin P. (eds) (2000) *Parties without Partisans: Political Change in Advanced Industrial Democracies* (Oxford: Oxford University Press).

Davies, Norman (1998) *Europe: A History* (London: Harper Collins).

Davis, Rebecca Howard (1997) *Women and Power in Parliamentary Democracies: Cabinet Appointments in Western Europe, 1968–1992* (Lincoln, NE: University of Nebraska Press).

De Bens, Els, and Østbye, Helge (1998) 'The European Newspaper Market', in Denis McQuail and Karen Siune (eds), *Media Policy: Convergence, Concentration and Commerce* (London: Sage).

De Winter, Lieven (2002) 'Parties and Government Formation, Portfolio Allocation, and Policy Definition', in Kurt Richard Luther and Ferdinand Müller-Rommel (eds), *Political Parties in the New Europe: Political and Analytical Challenges* (Oxford: Oxford University Press).

Deacon, Bob (2000) 'Social Policy in Eastern Europe: The Impact of Political Globalisation', *Journal of European Social Policy*, 10 (2), pp. 146–61.

Della Porta, Donatella and Diani, Mario (1999) *Social Movements: An Introduction* (Oxford: Blackwell).

Della Porta, Donatella, Kriesi, Hanspeter and Rucht, Dieter (eds) (1999) *Social Movements in a Globalizing World* (Basingstoke: Palgrave Macmillan).

Denemark, David (2002) 'Television Effects and Voter Decison Making in Australia: A Reexamination of the Converse Model', *British Journal of Political Science*, 32(4), pp. 663–90.

Deschouwer, Kris (2003) 'Political Parties in Multi-layered Systems', *European Urban and Regional Studies*, 10(3), pp. 213–26.

van Deth, Jan and Janssen, Joseph (1994) 'Party Attachments and Political Fragmentation in Europe', *European Journal of Political Research*, 25, pp. 87–109.

van Deth, Jan, Maraffi, Marco, Newton, Kenneth and Whiteley, Paul (1999) *Social Capital and European Democracy* (London: Routledge).

Díez Medrano, Juan and Gutiérrez, Paula (2001) Nested Identities: National and European Identity in Spain', *Ethnic and Racial Studies*, 24(5), pp. 753–78.

Dimitrakopoulos, Dyonissis, G. (2001) 'Incrementalism and Path Dependence: European Integration and Institutional Change in National Parliaments', *Journal of Common Market Studies*, 39(3), pp. 405–22.

Dogan, Mattei (2001) 'Class, Religion, Party: Triple Decline of Electoral Cleavages in Western Europe', in Lauri Karvonen and Stein Kuhnle (eds), *Party Systems and Voter Alignments Revisited* (London: Routledge).

Donsbach, Wolfgang and Klett, Bettina (1993) 'Subjective Objectivity: How Journalists in Four Countries Define a Key Term of their Profession', *Gazette*, 51, pp. 53–83.

Döring, Herbert (ed.) (1995) *Parliaments and Majority Rule in Western Europe* (New York: St Martin's Press).

van Dosenrode, Soren and Stubkjær, Anders (2002) *The European Union and the Middle East* (London: Sheffield Academic Press/Continuum).

Downs, Anthony (1972) 'Up and Down with Ecology: "The Issue Attention Cycle"', *The Public Interest*, 28, pp. 38–50, available at http://www.anthonydowns.com/upanddown.htm

Duke, Simon (2000) *The Elusive Quest for European Security: From EDC to CFSP* (Basingstoke: Palgrave Macmillan).

Dumbrell, John (2001) *A Special Relationship: Anglo-American Relations in the Cold War and After* (Basingstoke: Palgrave Macmillan).

Dunleavy, Patrick (1990) 'Mass Political Behaviour: Is There More to Learn?', *Political Studies*, 38(3), pp. 453–69.

Dunleavy, Patrick (1991) *Democracy, Bureaucracy and Public Choice: Economic Explanations in Political Science* (Hemel Hempstead: Harvester Wheatsheaf).

Dunleavy, Patrick, Gamble, Andrew, Heffernan, Richard and Peele, Gillian (2003) Developments in British Politics 7 (Basingstoke: Palgrave Macmillan).

Dunphy, Richard (2004) *Contesting Capitalism? Left Parties and European Integration* (Manchester: Manchester University Press).

Duverger, Maurice (1954) *Political Parties: Their Organization and Activity in the Modern State* (London: Methuen).

Dyson, Kenneth and Featherstone, Kevin (1999) *The Road to Maastricht: Negotiating Economic and Monetary Union* (Oxford: Oxford University Press).

E

Eatwell, Roger (2000). 'The Rebirth of the Extreme Right in Western Europe', Parliamentary Affairs, 53(3), pp. 407–25.

Edmonds, Richard Louis (ed.) (2002) 'China and Europe Since 1978', Special Issue of *China Quarterly*, 169.

Eilders, C. and Luter, A. (2000) 'Germany at War: Competing Framing Strategies in German Public Discourse', *European Journal of Communication*, 15(3), pp. 415–28.

van der Eijk, C. and Franklin, M. (eds) (1996) *Choosing Europe? The European Electorate and National Politics in the Face of Union* (Ann Arbor: University of Michigan Press).

Eising, Rainer and Kohler-Koch, Beate (1999) 'Introduction: Network Governance in the European Union', in Beate Kohler-Koch and Rainer Eising (eds), *The Transformation of Governance in the European Union* (London: Routledge/ECPR).

Elazar, D.J. (1997) 'Contrasting Unitary and Federal Systems', *International Political Science Review*, 18(3), pp. 237–51.

Elgie, Robert (ed.) (1999) *Semi-presidentialism in Europe* (London: Frank Cass).

Elgie, Robert (2003) *Political Institutions in Contemporary France* (Oxford: Oxford University Press).

Elster, Jon (1986) 'Introduction' in Jon Elster (ed.), *Rational Choice* (Oxford: Blackwell).

Ericson, Richard, Baranek, Patricia and Chan, Janet B.L. (1989) *Negotiating Control: A Study of News Sources* (Toronto: University of Toronto Press).

Esping-Andersen, Gøsta (1990) *The Three Worlds of Welfare Capitalism*, (Cambridge: Polity Press).

Esser, Frank (1999) '"Tabloidization" of News: A Comparative Analysis of Anglo-American and German Press Journalism', *European Journal of Communication*, 14(3), pp. 375–405.

Esser, Frank, Reinemann, Carsten and Fan, David (2000) 'Spin Doctoring in British and German Election Campaigns: How the Press is being Confronted with a New Quality of Political PR', *European Journal of Communication*, 15(2), pp. 209–39.

European Council (2003) *A Secure Europe in a Better World – A European Security Strategy*, available at http://ue.eu/uedocs/cmsUpload/78367.pdf

Evans, Geoffrey (1999) *The End of Class Politics?: Class Voting in Comparative Context* (Oxford: Oxford University Press).

Evans, Jocelyn A.J. (ed.) (2002) *The French Party System* (Manchester: Manchester University Press).

Evans, Jocelyn, A.J. (2003) *Voters and Voting: An Introduction* (London: Sage).

Evans, Jocelyn A.J. (2004) 'Ideology and Party Identification: A Normalisation of French Voting Anchors?', in Michael Lewis-Beck (ed.), *The French Voter* (Basingstoke: Palgrave Macmillan).

F

Faas, T. (2003) 'To Defect or not to Defect? National, Institutional and Party Group Pressures on MEPs and their Consequences for Party Group Cohesion in the European Parliament', *European Journal of Political Research*, 42(6) pp. 841–66.

Fairbrass, J. and Jordan, A. (2001) 'Protecting Biodiversity in the European Union: National Barriers and European Opportunities', *Journal of European Public Policy*, 8(4), pp. 499–518.

Falkner, Gerda (2000a) 'How Pervasive are Euro-politics? Effects of EU Membership on a New Member State', *Journal of Common Market Studies*, 38(2), pp. 223–50.

Falkner, Gerda (2000b) 'The Council or the Social Partners? EC Social Policy between Diplomacy and Collective Bargaining', *Journal of European Public Policy*, 7(5), pp. 705–24.

Falkner, Gerda, Treib, Oliver, Hartlapp, Miriam and Leiber, Simone (2004) 'Non-Compliance with EU Directives in the Member States: Opposition through the Backdoor?', *West European Politics*, 27(3), pp. 452–73.

Farrell, David M. (2001) *Electoral Systems: A Competitive Introduction* (Basingstoke and New York: Palgrave Macmillan).

Farrell, David M. and Schmitt-Beck, Rüdiger (2002) *Do Political Campaigns Matter? Campaign Effects in Elections and Referendums* (London: Routledge).

Farrell, David M. and Webb, Paul (2002) 'Political Parties as Campaign Organisations', in Russell, J. Dalton and Martin P.Wattenberg (eds) *Parties without Partisans: Political Change in Advanced Industrial Democracies.* (Oxford: Oxford University Press).

Favell A. and Hansen R. (2002) 'Markets against Politics: Migration, EU Enlargement and the Idea of Europe', *Journal of Ethnic and Migration Studies*, 28(4), pp. 581–601.

Fawn, Rick (2000) *The Czech Republic: A Nation of Velvet* (London: Routledge).

Fawn, Rick (ed.) (2003) 'Ideology and National Identity in Postcommunist Foreign Policies', Special Issue of the *Journal of Communist Studies and Transition Politics*, 19(3).

Featherstone, Kevin and Radaelli, M. Claudio (eds) (2003) *The Politics of Europeanization* (Oxford: Oxford University Press).

Feigenbaum, Harvey, Henig, Jeffrey and Hamnett, Chris (1998) *Shrinking the State: The Political Underpinnings of Privatization* (Cambridge: Cambridge University Press).

Ferge, Zsuzsa (2001) 'Welfare and "Ill-fare" Systems in Central and Eastern Europe', in Robert Sykes, Bruno Palier and Pauline M. Prior (eds), *Globalization and European Welfare States: Challenges and Change* (Basingstoke: Palgrave Macmillan).

Ferguson, Ross and Howell, Milica (2004) *Political Blogs – Craze or Convention?* (London: Hansard Society), available at http://www.hansardsociety.org.uk/assets/Final_Blog_Report_.pdf.

Forster, Anthony (2000) 'Evaluating the EU–ASEM Relationship: A Negotiated Order Approach', *Journal of European Public Policy*, 17(5), pp. 787–805.

Foster, Edward (1998) 'Ad hoc in Albania: Did Europe Fail?', *Security Dialogue*, 29(2), pp. 213–18.

Franklin, Mark N. (2001a) 'How Structural Factors Cause Turnout Variations at European Parliament Elections', *European Union Politics*, 3(2), pp. 309–28.

Franklin, Mark N. (2001b) 'European Elections and the European Voter', in Jeremy Richardson (ed.), *European Union: Power and Policy-making*, 2nd edition (London: Longman).

Franklin, Mark (2002) 'The Dynamics of Electoral Participation', in Laurence LeDuc, Richard Niemi and Pippa Norris (eds), *Elections and Voting in Global Perspective 2* (Thousand Oaks, CA: Sage).

Franklin, Mark N. (2004) *Voter Turnout and the Dynamics of Electoral Competition in Established Democracies since 1945* (New York: Cambridge University Press).

Franklin, Mark N., Mackie, Thomas T. and Valen, Henry (1992) *Electoral Change: Responses to Evolving Social and Attitudinal Structures in Western Countries* (Cambridge: Cambridge University Press).

Fraser, Nicholas (2000) *The Voice of Modern Hatred: Encounters with Europe's New Right* (London: Picador).

Freedman, Lawrence and Menon, Anand (1997) 'Conclusion: Defence, States and Integration', in Joylon Howorth and Anand Menon (eds), *The European Union and National Defence Policy* (London: Routledge).

Freeman, J. (2002) 'Women in the European Parliament', *Parliamentary Affairs*, 55(1), pp. 179–88.

Friedman, Jeffrey (ed.) (1996) *The Rational Choice Controversy: Economic Models of Politics Reconsidered* (New Haven, CT: Yale University Press).

Fuchs, Dieter and Klingemann, Hans-Dieter (2002) 'Eastward Enlargement of the European Union and the Identity of Europe', *West European Politics*, 25(2), pp. 19–54.

G

Gabel, Matthew J. (2000) 'European Integration, Voters and National Politics', *West European Politics*, 23(4), pp. 52–72.

Gabel, Matthew J. and Anderson, Christopher J. (2002) 'The Structure of Citizen Attitudes and the European Political Space', *Comparative Political Studies*, 35(8), pp. 893–913.

Gaffney, John (ed.) (1996) *Political Parties and the European Union* (London: Routledge).

Gains, Francesca (2003) 'Executive Agencies in Government: The Impact of Bureaucratic Networks on Policy Outcomes', *Journal of Public Policy*, 23(1), pp. 55–79.

Gallagher, Michael, Laver, Michael and Mair, Peter (2001) *Representative Government in Modern Europe* (New York: McGraw-Hill).

Gallagher, Michael and Uleri, Pier Vincenzo (eds) (1996) *The Referendum Experience in Europe* (Basingstoke: Palgrave Macmillan).

Gamble, Andrew (2003) *Between Europe and America: The Future of British Politics* (Basingstoke: Palgrave Macmillan).

Garrett, Geoffrey (1998a) *Partisan Politics in the Global Economy* (Cambridge: Cambridge University Press).

Garrett, Geoffrey (1998b) 'Global Markets and National Politics: Collision Course or Virtuous Circle', *International Organization*, 52(4), pp. 787–824.

Gavin, Neil and Sanders, David (2003) 'The Press and Its Influence on British Political Attitudes under New Labour', *Political Studies*, 51(3), pp. 573–91.

Geddes, Andrew (2000) *Immigration and European Integration* (Manchester: Manchester University Press).

Geddes, Andrew (2003) *The Politics of Migration and Immigration in Europe* (London: Sage).

Gibson, Rachel and Harmel, Robert (1998) 'Party Families and Democratic Performance: Extraparliamentary vs Parliamentary Group Power', *Political Studies*, 46(3), pp. 633–50.

Gibson, Rachel, Newell, James and Ward, Stephen (2000) 'New Parties, New Media: Italian Party Politics and the Internet', *South European Society and Politics*, 5(1), pp. 123–43.

Gibson, Rachel, Nixon, Paul and Ward, Stephen (eds) (2003) *Political Parties and the Internet: Net Gain?* (London: Routledge).

Gibson, Rachel, Römmele, Andrea and Ward, Stephen (2003) 'German Parties and Internet Campaigning in the 2002 Federal Election', *German Politics*, 12(1), pp. 79–108.

Giddens, Anthony (1990) *The Consequences of Modernity* (Stanford, CA: Stanford University Press).

Giddens, Anthony (1994) *The Third Way: The Renewal of Social Democracy* (Cambridge: Polity Press).

Gijsberts, M. and Nieuwbeerta, P. (2000) 'Class Cleavages in Party Preferences in the New Democracies in Eastern Europe: A Comparison with Western Democracies', *European Societies*, 2(4), pp. 397–430.

Gillespie, Richard (ed.) (1997) *The Euro-Mediterranean Partnership: Political and Economic Perspectives* (London: Frank Cass).

Gillespie, Richard (2000) *Spain and the Mediterranean: Developing a European Policy towards the South* (Basingstoke: Palgrave Macmillan).

Gilson, Julie (2000) *Japan and the European Union: A Partnership for the Twenty-First Century?* (Basingstoke: Palgrave Macmillan).

Ginsborg, Paul (2003) *Italy and Its Discontents 1980–2001: Family, Civil Society, State* (Harmondsworth: Penguin).

Ginsborg, Paul (2004) *Silvio Berlusconi: Television, Power and Patrimony* (London: Verso).

Goetz, K.H. (2001) 'Making Sense of Post-communist Central Administration: Modernization, Europeanization or Latinization?', *Journal of European Public Policy*, 8(6), pp. 1032–51.

Goodin, Robert, Headey Bruce, Muffels, Ruud and Dirven, Henk-Jan (1999) *The Real Worlds of Welfare Capitalism* (Cambridge: Cambridge University Press).

Grabbe, Heather (2003) 'Europeanisation Goes East: Power and Uncertainty in the EU Accession Process', in Kevin Featherstone and Claudio Radaelli (eds), *The Politics of Europeanization* (Oxford: Oxford University Press).

Grant, Wyn (2001) 'Pressure Politics: From "Insider" Politics to Direct Action', *Parliamentary Affairs*, 54, pp. 337–8.

Gray, Pat and t'Hart, Paul (eds) (1998) *Public Policy Disasters in Western Europe* (London: Routledge).

Green, Donald P. and Shapiro, Ian (1994) *Pathologies of Rational Choice Theory: A Critique of Applications in Political Science* (New Haven: Yale University Press).

Green, Simon (2004) *The Politics of Exclusion: Institutions and Immigration Policy in Contemporary Germany* (Manchester: Manchester University Press).

Green-Pedersen, Christoffer (1999) 'The Danish Welfare State under Bourgeois Reign', *Scandinavian Political Studies*, 22(3), pp. 243–60.

Green-Pedersen, Christoffer (2001) 'Welfare-state Retrenchment in Denmark and the Netherlands, 1982–1998: The Role of Party Competition and Party Consensus', *Comparative Political Studies*, 34(9), pp. 963–85.

Green-Pedersen, Christoffer and van Kersbergen, Kees, 'The Politics of the "Third Way": The Transformation of Social Democracy in Denmark and the Netherlands', *Party Politics*, 8(5), pp. 507–24.

Green-Pedersen, Christoffer, van Kersbergen, Kees and Hemerijck, Anton (2001) 'Neo-liberalism, the "Third Way" or What? Recent Social Democratic Welfare Policies in Denmark and the Netherlands', *Journal of European Public Policy*, 8(2), pp. 307–25.

Greenwood, Justin (2003) *Interest Representation in the European Union* (Basingstoke: Palgrave Macmillan).

Greenwood, Justin and Aspinwall, Mark (1997) *Collective Action in the European Union: Interests and the New Politics of Associability* (London: Routledge).

Greskovits, Béla (1998) *The Political Economy of Protest and Patience* (Budapest: Central European University Press).

Gros, Daniel (2002) 'Health not Wealth: Enlarging the EU', *West European Politics*, 25(2), pp. 141–51.

Grzymala-Busse, Anna and Innes, Abby (2003) 'Great Expectations: The EU and Domestic Political Competition in East Central Europe', *East European Politics and Societies*, 17(1), pp. 64–73.

Guibernau, Montserrat (1999) *Nations Without States* (Oxford: Blackwell).

Gulyás, Agnes (2003) 'Print Media in Post-Communist East Central Europe', *European Journal of Communication*, 18(1), pp. 81–106.

Gulyás, Ágnes (2004) 'Public Images and Private Lives: The Case of Hungary', *Parliamentary Affairs*, 57(1), pp. 67–79.

Gunther, Richard and Mughan, Anthony (eds) (2000) *Democracy and the Media: A Comparative Perspective* (Cambridge: Cambridge University Press).

Gunther, Richard, Montero, José Ramón and Linz, Juan J. (2002) *Political Parties: Old Concepts and New Challenges* (Oxford: Oxford University Press).

Gunther, Richard, Montero, José Ramón, and Wert, José Ignacio (2000) 'The Media and Politics in Spain: From Dictatorship to Democracy', in Richard Gunther and Anthony Mughan (eds), *Democracy and the Media: A Comparative Perspective* (Cambridge: Cambridge University Press).

Guyomarch, Alain, Machin, Howard, Hall, Peter A. and Hayward, Jack (2001) *Developments in French Politics 2* (Basingstoke: Palgrave Macmillan).

H

Habermas, Jürgen (1989) *The Structural Transformation of the Public Sphere.* (Cambridge: Polity).

Haddad, Yvonne Yazbeck (2002) *Muslims in the West: From Sojourners to Citizens* (Oxford: Oxford University Press).

Hall, Peter A. (2002) 'The Comparative Political Economy of the "Third Way"', in Oliver Schmidtke (ed.), *The Third Way Transformation of Social Democracy: Normative Claims and Policy Initiatives of the New Social-Democratic Left at the End of the 21st Century* (Burlington, VT: Ashgate).

Hall, Peter A. and Soskice, David (2001) 'An Introduction to Varieties of Capitalism', in Peter A. Hall and David Soskice (eds), *Varieties of Capitalism: The Institutional Foundation of Comparative Economic Advantage* (Oxford: Oxford University Press).

Hallin, Daniel C. and Mancini, Paolo (2004) *Comparing Media Systems: Three Models of Media and Politics* (Cambridge: Cambridge University Press).

Halman, Loek (2002) *The European Values Study: A Third Wave: Source Book of the 1999/2000 European Values Study Surveys* (Tilburg: University of Tilburg).

Halman, Loek and Riis, Ole (2002) *Religion in a Secularizing Society: The Europeans' Religion at the end of the 20th Century* (Leiden and Boston: Brill).

Hancock, M. Donald (2003) 'Sweden', in M. Donald Hancock *et al.*, *Politics in Europe* (Basingstoke: Palgrave Macmillan).

Hanley, David (ed.) (1994) *Christian Democracy in Europe: A Comparative Perspective* (London: Pinter).

Hanley, Seán (2004) 'Blue Velvet: The Rise and Decline of the New Czech Right', *Journal of Communist Studies and Transition Politics*, 20(3), pp. 28–54.

Hansen, R. (2002) 'Globalization, Embedded Realism, and Path Dependence: The Other Immigrants to Europe', *Comparative Political Studies*, 35(3), pp. 259–83.

Harcourt, Alison J. (2003) 'Europeanization as Convergence: The Regulation of Media Markets in the European Union', in Kevin Featherstone and Claudio Radaelli (eds), *The Politics of Europeanization* (Oxford: Oxford University Press).

Harding, Jeremy (2000) *The Uninvited: Refugees at the Rich Man's Gate* (London: Profile).

Hardt, Michael and Negri, Antonio (2000) *Empire* (Cambridge, MA: Harvard University Press).

Hargreaves Heap, Shaun, Hollis, Martin, Lyons, Bruce Sugden, Robert and Weale, Albert (1992) *The Theory of Choice: A Critical Guide* (Oxford: Blackwell, 1992).

Harris, Nigel (2000) 'Should Europe End Immigration Controls? A Polemic', *European Journal of Development Research*, 12(1), pp. 80–106.

Harris, Nigel (2001) *Thinking the Unthinkable: The Immigration Myth Exposed* (London: I.B. Tauris).

Harrison, J.L. and Woods, L.M. (2001) 'Defining European Public Service Broadcasting', *European Journal of Communication*, 16(4), pp. 477–504.

Haseler, Stephen (2004) *Super State: The New Europe and its Challenge to America* (London: I.B. Touris).

Hay, Colin (2000) 'Contemporary Capitalism, Globalization, Regionalization and the Persistance of National Variation', *Review of International Studies* 26(4), pp. 509–31.

Hayward, Jack (1982) 'Mobilising Private Interests in the Service of Public Ambitions: The Salient Element in the Dual French Policy Style' in Jeremy J. Richardson (ed.) *Policy Styles in Western Europe* (London: George Allen & Unwin).

van Hecke, Steven and Gerard, Emmanuel (eds) (2004) *Christian Democratic Parties in Europe since the End of the Cold War* (Leuven: Leuven University Press).

Heidar, Knut and Koole, Ruud (2000) *Parliamentary Party Groups in European Democracies: Political Parties Behind Closed Doors* (London: Routledge).

Heinderyckx, F. (1993) 'TV News Programmes in Western Europe', *European Journal of Communication*, 8(4), pp. 425–50.

Heipertz, Martin and Verdun, Amy (2003) *Ruling Europe: Theory and Politics of the Stability and Growth Pact, Draft Report* (Cologne: Max Planck Institute), available at http://www.mpi-fg-koeln.mpg.de/people/hz/Dokumente/hz-av_gesamt.pdf

Held, David (1987) *Models of Democracy* (Stanford: Stanford University Press).

Held, David, McGrew, Anthony, Goldblatt, David and Perraton, Jonathan (1999) *Global Transformations: Politics, Economics and Culture* (Cambridge: Polity Press).

Hemerijck, Anton and Visser, Jelle (2001) 'Dutch Lessons in Social Pragmatism', in Stuart White (ed.), *New Labour: The Progressive Future?* (Basingstoke: Palgrave Macmillan).

Henderson, Ailsa and White, Linda A. (2004) 'Shrinking Welfare States? Comparing Maternity Leave Benefits and Child Care Programs in European Union and North American Welfare States, 1985–2000', *Journal of European Public Policy*, 11(3), pp. 497–519.

Hendy, David (2000) *Radio in the Global Age* (Cambridge: Polity Press).

Héritier, Adrienne, Kerwer, Dieter, Knill, Christopher, Lehmkuhl, Dirk, Teutsch, Michael, Douillet, Anne-Cécile (2001) *Differential Europe: The European Union Impact on National Policy Making* (Lanham, MD: Rowman & Littlefield).

Hicks, Alexander (1999) *Social Democracy and Welfare Capitalism: A Century of Income Security Politics* (Ithaca: Cornell University Press).

Hill, Christopher (1993) 'The Capability–Expectations Gap, or Conceptualising Europe's Global Role', *Journal of Common Market Studies*, 31(3), pp. 305–28.

Hill, Christopher (ed.) (1996) *The Actors in Europe's Foreign Policy* (London: Routledge).

Hill, Christopher (1998) 'Convergence, Divergence and Dialectics: National Foreign Policies and the CFSP', in Jan Zielonka (ed.), *Paradoxes of European Foreign Policy* (London: Kluwer).

Hill, Kevin A. and Hughes, John E. (1998) *Cyberpolitics: Citizen Activism in the Age of the Internet* (Lanham, MD: Rowman & Littlefield).

Hilson, C. (2002) 'New Social Movements: The Role of Legal Opportunity', *Journal of European Public Policy*, 9(2), pp. 238–55.

Hirst, Paul and Thompson, Grahame (1999) *Globalization in Question: The International Economy and the Possibilities of Governance*, 2nd edition (Cambridge: Polity Press).

Hix, S. (2002) 'Parliamentary Behavior with Two Principals: Preferences, Parties, and Voting in the European Parliament', *American Journal of Political Science*, 46(3), pp. 688–98.

Hix, Simon (2004) *The Political System of the European Union*, 2nd edition (Basingstoke: Palgrave Macmillan).

Hix, Simon and Goetz, Klaus (2000) *Europeanized Politics? European Integration and National Political Systems* (London: Frank Cass).

Hix, Simon, Kreppel, Amy and Noury, Abdul (2003) 'The Party System in the European Parliament: Collusive or Competitive?' *Journal of Common Market Studies*, 41(2), pp. 309–31.

Hix, Simon and Scully, Roger (eds) (2003) 'The European Parliament at Fifty', Special issue, *Journal of Common Market Studies*, 41(2).

Hocking, Brian and Spence, David (2002) *Foreign Ministries in the European Union* (Basingstoke: Palgrave Macmillan).

Holland, Martin (2002) *The European Union and the Third World* (Basingstoke: Palgrave Macmillan).

Holland, Martin (2004a) 'When is Foreign Policy not Foreign Policy? Cotonou, CFSP and External Relations with the Developing World', in Martin Holland (ed.), *Common Foreign and Security Policy: The First Ten Years* (London: Continuum).

Holland, Martin (2004b) 'Development Policy: Paradigm Shifts and the "Normalization" of a Privileged Partnership', in Maria Green Cowles and Desmond Dinan (eds), *Developments in the European Union 2* (Basingstoke: Palgrave Macmillan).

Hollifield, J. (1999) 'On the Limits of Immigration Control in France', in Grete Brochmann and Tomas Hammar (eds), *Mechanisms of Immigration Control* (Oxford: Berg), pp. 59–95.

Holtz-Bacha, Christina (2004) 'Germany: How the Private Life of Politicians got into the Media', *Parliamentary Affairs*, 57(1), pp. 41–52.

Holzhacker, R. (2002) 'National Parliamentary Scrutiny over EU Issues: Comparing the Goals and Methods of Governing and Opposition Parties', *European Union Politics*, 3(4), pp. 459–80.

Hooghe, Liesbet and Marks, Gary (2001) *Multi-level Governance and European Integration* (Lanham, MD: Rowman & Littlefield).

Hooghe, Liesbet, Marks, Gary and Wilson, Carole J. (2002) 'Does Left/Right Structure Party Positions in European Integration?', *Comparative Political Studies*, 35(8), pp. 965–89.

Hooghe, Marc and Stolle, Dietland (2003) *Generating Social Capital: Civil Society and Institutions in Comparative Perspective* (Basingstoke: Palgrave Macmillan).

Hopkin, Jonathan (1999) *Party Formation and Democratic Transition in Spain: The Creation and Collapse of the Union of Democratic Centre* (Basingstoke: Palgrave Macmillan).

Hopkin, Jonathan (2003) 'Political Decentralization, Electoral Change and Party Organizational Adaptation: A Framework for Analysis', *European Urban and Regional Studies*, 10(3), pp. 227–37.

Hopkin, Jonathan and Paolucci, Caterina (1999) 'The Business Firm Model of Party Organisation: Cases from Spain and Italy', *European Journal of Political Research*, 35(3), pp. 307–338.

Hopkins, Thomas D. (1998) 'The Czech Republic's Privatization Experience', in Demetrius S. Iatridis and June Gary Hopps (eds), *Privatization in Central and Eastern Europe: Perspectives and Approaches* (London: Praeger).

Howard, Marc Morjé (2003) *The Weakness of Civil Society in Post-Communist Europe* (Cambridge: Cambridge University Press).

Howarth, David (ed.) (2004) 'The Stability and Growth Pact', special issue of the *Journal of European Public Policy*, 11(5).

Howorth, Joylon and Keeler, John T.S. (eds) (2003) *Defending Europe, NATO and the Quest for European Autonomy* (Basingstoke: Palgrave Macmillan).

Huber, Evelyne and Stephens, John D. (2001) *Development and Crisis of the Welfare State: Parties and Policies in Global Markets* (Chicago: University of Chicago Press).

Hug, Simon (2002) *Voices of Europe: Citizens, Referendums, and European Integration* (Lanham, MD: Rowman & Littlefield).

Hughes, Kirsty (2004) *Turkey and the European Union: Just Another Enlargement? Exploring the Implications of Turkish Accession* (Brussels: Friends of Europe Working Papers, June, available at http://www.friendsofeurope.org

Huysmans, J. (2000) 'The European Union and the Securitization of Migration', *Journal of Common Market Studies*, 38(5), pp. 751–77.

Hyde-Price, Adrian (2003) 'Defence and Security Policy', in Stephen Padgett, William E. Paterson and Gordon Smith (eds), *Developments in German Politics 3* (Basingstoke: Palgrave Macmillan).

I

Iankova, Elena A. (2002) *Eastern European Capitalism in the Making* (Cambridge: Cambridge University Press).

Iatridis, Demetrius S. and Hopps, June Gary (eds) (1998) *Privatization in Central and Eastern Europe: Perspectives and Approaches* (London: Praeger).

Ignazi, Piero (2003) *Extreme Right Parties in Western Europe* (Oxford: Oxford University Press).

Imbeau, L.M., Pétry, F. and Lamari, M. (2001) 'Left–right Party Ideology and Government Policies: A Meta Analysis', *European Journal of Political Research*, 40(1), pp. 1–29.

Imig, Doug (2002) 'Contestation in the Streets: European Protests and the Emerging Euro-polity', *Comparative Political Studies*, 35(8) pp. 914–33.

Imig, Doug and Tarrow, Sidney (1999) 'The Europeanisation of movements? Contentious Politics and the European Union', in Donatella della Porta, Hanspeter Kriesi and Dieter Rucht (eds), *Social Movements in a Globalizing World* (Basingstoke: Palgrave Macmillan).

Imig, Doug and Tarrow, Sidney (2001) *Contentious Europeans: Protest and Politics in an Integrating Europe* (Lanham, MD: Rowman & Littlefield).

Inglehart, Ronald (1999) 'Postmodernization, Authority and Democracy', in Pippa Norris (ed.), *Critical Citizens: Global Support for Democratic Government* (Oxford: Oxford University Press).

Inglehart, Ronald F. and Baker, Wayne E. (2000) 'Modernization, Cultural Change, and the Persistence of Traditional Values', *American Sociological Review* 65, pp. 19–51.

Inglehart, Ronald and Rabier, Jacques-René (1986) 'Political Realignment in Advanced Industrial Society: From Class-based Politics to Quality of Life Politics', *Government and Opposition*, 21, pp. 456–79.

Ishiyama, John T. and Breuning, Marijke (1998) *Ethnnopolitics in the New Europe* (Boulder, CO: Lynne Rienner).

J

Jakubowicz, Karol (2004) 'Ideas in Our Heads. Introduction of PSB as Part of Media System Change in Central and Eastern Europe', *European Journal of Communication*, 19(1), pp. 53–74.

Jeffries, Stuart (2002) 'How the French Lost their Cleavage', *Guardian*, 15 April 2004.

Jenkins, Bryan and Sofos, Spyros (1996) *Nation and Identity in Contemporary Europe* (London: Routledge).

Johansson, Karl Magnus and Zervakis A. Peter (eds) (2002) *European Political Parties between Cooperation and Integration 2002* (Baden-Baden: Nomos Verlag).

Jones, Erik (2002) *The Politics of Economic and Monetary Union: Integration and Idiosyncrasy* (Lanham, MD: Rowman & Littlefield).

Jones, Erik and Verdun, Amy (eds) (2004) *The Political Economy of European Integration: Arguments and Analysis* (London: Routledge).

Joppke, Christian (2002) 'European Immigration Policies at the Crossroads', in Paul Heywood, Erik Jones and Martin Rhodes (eds), *Developments in West European Politics* (Basingstoke: Palgrave Macmillan).

Jordan, Andrew (ed.) (2001) *Environmental Policy in the European Union: Actors, Institutions and Processes* (London: Earthscan).

Jordan, Grant and Maloney, William (1997) *Protest Businesses? Mobilising Campaigning Groups* (Manchester: Manchester University Press).

Judge, David and Earnshaw, David (2003) *The European Parliament* (Basingstoke and New York: Palgrave Macmillan).

K

Kagan, Robert (2002) 'Power and Weakness', Policy Review (Hoover Institution), 113, available at http://www.policyreview.org/JUN02/kagan.html

Kagan, Robert (2004) *Paradise and Power: America and Europe in the New World Order* (New York: Atlantic Books).

Kalogeropoulou, Efthalia (1989) 'Election Promises and Government Performance in Greece: PASOK's Fulfilment of its 1981 Election Pledges', *European Journal of Political Research*, 17(3), pp. 289–311.

Katz, Richard and Mair, Peter (1995) 'Changing Models of Party Organization and Party Democracy: The Emergence of the Cartel Party', *Party Politics*, 1(1), pp. 8–28.

Kaufman, Bruno and Waters, M. Dane (2004) *Direct Democracy in Europe: A Comprehensive Reference Guide to the Initiative and Referendum Process in Europe* (Durham, NC: Carolina Academic Press).

Keating, Michael (2000) *The New Regionalism in Western Europe: Territorial Restructuring and Political Change* (Aldershot: Edward Elgar).

Keating, Michael (2001) *Nations Against the State: The New Politics of Nationalism in Quebec, Catalonia and Scotland* (Basingstoke: Palgrave Macmillan).

Keating, Michael and Liesbet, Hooghe (1996) 'By-passing the Nation State? Regions and the EU Policy Process', in Jeremy Richardson (ed.), *European Union: Power and Policy Making* (London: Routledge), pp. 216–29.

Keman, Hans (2002) 'The Low Countries: Confrontation and Coalition in Segmented Societies', in Josep M. Colomer (ed.), *Political Institutions in Europe* (London: Routledge).

Keman, Hans (2003) 'Explaining Miracles: Third Ways and Work and Welfare', *West European Politics*, 26(2), pp. 115–35.

Kennedy, Paul (2000) 'Spain', in Ian Manners and Richard G. Whitman (eds), *The Foreign Policies of European Union Member States* (Manchester: Manchester University Press).

van Kersbergen, Kees (1995) *Social Capitalism: A Study of Christian Democracy and the Welfare State* (London: Routledge).

van Kersbergen, Kees (2000) 'The Declining Resistance of Welfare States to Change?', in Stein Kuhnle (ed.), *Survival of the European Welfare State* (London: Routledge/ECPR).

van Kersbergen, Kees, Hemerijck, Anton and Manow, Philip (2000) 'Welfare without Work? Divergent Experiences of Reform in Germany and the Netherlands', in Stein Kuhnle (ed.), *The Survival of the European Welfare State* (London: Routledge).

Kevin, Deirdre (2003) *Europe in the Media: A Comparison of Reporting: Representation and Rhetoric in National Media Systems* (Mahwah, NJ: Lawrence Erlbaum and Associates).

King, Anthony (1975) 'Overload: Problems of Governing in the 1970s', *Political Studies*, 23(2–3), pp. 284–96.

King, Anthony (1976) 'Modes of Executive–Legislative Relations: Great Britain, France and West Germnay', *Legislative Studies Quarterly*, 1(1), pp. 11–36.

King, Anthony (1994) '"Chief Executives" in Western Europe', in Ian Budge and David McKay (eds), *Developing Democracy: Comparative Research in Honour of J.F.P. Blondel* (London: Sage).

King, Anthony (ed.) (2002) *Leaders' Personalities and the Outcomes of Democratic Elections* (Oxford: Oxford University Press).

Kirchheimer, Otto (1966) 'The Transformation of the Western European Party System' in Joseph La Palombara and Myrah Weiner (eds), *Political Parties and Political Development* (Princeton: Princeton University Press).

Kiss, Csilla (2002) 'From Liberalism to Conservatism: The Federation of Young Democrats in Post-Communist Hungary', *East European Politics and Societies*, 16(3), pp. 739–63.

Kitschelt, Herbert (1994) *The Transformation of European Social Democracy* (Cambridge: Cambridge University Press).

Kitschelt, Herbert (2000) 'Citizens, Politicians, and Party Cartellization: Political Representation and State Failure in Post Industrial Democracies', *European Journal of Political Research*, 37, pp. 149–79.

Kitschelt, Herbert, Mansfeldova, Zdenka, Markowski, Radoslaw and Tóka, Gábor (1999) *Post-communist Party Systems: Competition, Representation and Inter-party Cooperation* (Cambridge: Cambridge University Press).

Klich, Jacek (1998) 'The Concept of Mass Privatization in Poland: Theoretical and Practical Considerations', in Demetrius S. Iatridis and June Gary Hopps (eds), *Privitization in Central and Eastern Europe: Perspectives and Approaches* (London: Praeger).

Kleinnijenhuis, Jan, Maurer, Kepplinger, Hans Mathias and Oegema, Dirk (2001) 'Issues and Personalities in German and Dutch Television News: Patterns and Effects', *European Journal of Communication*, 16(3), pp. 337–59.

Knodt, Michèle and Princen, Sebastiaan (2003) *Understanding the European Union's External Relations* (London: Routledge).

Knutsen, Oddbjørn and Scarbrough, Elinor (1995) 'Cleavage Politics' in Jan W. Van Deth and Elinor Scarbrough (eds), *The Impact of Values* (Oxford: Oxford University Press).

Koopmans, Ruud (2004) 'Integrated Report: Cross-National, Cross-Issue, Cross-Time', Project report for the EU-funded project *The Transformation of Political Mobilisation and Communication in European Public Spheres*, available at http://europub.wz-berlin.de/project%20reports.en.htm.

Kopecký, Petr and Mudde, Cas (2002) *Uncivil Society: Contentious Politics in Post-communist Europe* (London: Routledge).

Kopecký, Petr (2003) 'Structures of Representation: The New Parliaments of Central and Eastern Europe', in Stephen White, Judy Batt and Paul G. Lewis (eds) *Developments in Central and East European Politics 3*, (Basingstoke: Palgrave Macmillan).

Kostadinova, Tatiana (2003) 'Voter Turnout Dynamics in Post-communist Europe', *European Journal of Political Research*, 42(6), pp. 741–60.

Kovács, János Mátyás (2002) 'Approaching the EU and reaching the US? Rival Narratives on Transforming Welfare Regimes in East-Central Europe', *West European Politics*, 25(2), pp. 175–204.

Kreppel, A. (2000) 'Rules, Ideology and Coalition Formation in the European Parliament: Past, Present and Future', *European Union Politics*, 1(3), pp. 340–62.

Kreppel, A. (2002) *The European Parliament and Supranational Party System* (Cambridge: Cambridge University Press).

Kriesi, Hanspeter, Koopmans, Ruud, Duyvendak, Jan Willem and Giugni, Marco G. (1995) *New Social Movements in Western Europe: A Comparative Analysis* (London: UCL Press).

Kriesi, Hanspeter (1998) 'The transformation of cleavage politics', *European Journal of Political Research*, 33, pp. 165–185.

Kriesi, Hanspeter, Armingeon, Klaus, Siegrist, Hannes and Wimmer, Andreas (eds) (2003) *Nation and National Identity: The European Experience in Perspective* (West Lafayette, IN: Purdue University Press).

Kselman, Thomas and Buttigieg, Joseph A. (eds) (2003) *European Christian Deomocracy: Historical Legacies and Comparative Perspectives* (Notre Dame: University of Notre Dame Press).

Kuhn, Raymond (2004) '"Vive la différence"? The Mediation of Politicians' Public Images and Private Lives in France', *Parliamentary Affairs*, 57(1), pp. 24–40.

L

Ladrech, Robert (2000) *Social Democracy and the Challenge of European Union* (Boulder, CO: Lynne Rienner).

Ladrech, Robert (2002) 'Europeanization and Political Parties: Towards a Framework for Analysis', *Party Politics*, 8(4), pp. 389–403.

Lahav, Gallya (2004) *Immigration and Politics in the New Europe: Reinventing Borders* (Cambridge: Cambridge University Press).

Laitin, David D. (2002) 'Culture and National Identity: "The East" and European Integration', *West European Politics*, 25(2), pp. 55–80.

Lauf, Edmund (2001) 'The Vanishing Young Reader: Socio-demographic Determinants of Newspaper Use as a Source of Political Information in Europe, 1980–1998', *European Journal of Communication*, 16(2), pp. 233–43.

Lavigne, Marie (2000) 'Ten Years of Transition: A Review Article', *Communist and Post-Communist Studies*, 33(4), pp. 475–83.

Levy, Mark R. (1981) 'Disdaining the News', *Journal of Communication*, 31(3), pp. 24–31.

Lewanski, Rudolf (1999) 'Italian Administration in Transition', *South European Society and Politics*, 4(1), pp. 97–131.

Lewanski, Rudolf (2000) 'The Development and Current Features of the Italian Civil Service System', in Hans A.G.M. Bekke and Frits M. van der Meer (eds), *Civil Service Systems in Western Europe* (Cheltenham: Edward Elgar).

Lewis, Paul G. (ed.) (2001) *Party Development and Democratic Change in Post-Communist Europe* (London: Frank Cass).

Lindblom, Charles (1977) *Politics and Markets* (New York: Basic Books).

Lijphart, Arend (1999) *Patterns of Democracy: Government Forms and Performance in Thirty-six Countries* (New Haven, CT: Yale University Press).

Lipset, Seymour Martin and Rokkan, Stein (1967) 'Cleavage Structures, Party Systems and Voter Alignments: An Introduction' in Seymour Martin Lipset and Stein Rokkan (eds) (1967) *Party Systems and Voter Alignments: Cross-National Perspectives* (New York: Free Press).

Lohmann, Susanne, Brady, David W. and Rivers, Douglas (1997) 'Party Identification, Retrospective Voting, and Moderating Elections in a Federal System: West Germany, 1961–1989', *Comparative Political Studies*, 30, pp. 420–49.

Lord, Christopher (2004) *A Democratic Audit of the European Union* (Basingstoke: Palgrave Macmillan).

Lubbers, Marcel, Gijsberts, Merove and Scheepers, Peer (2002) 'Extreme Right-wing Voting in Europe,' *European Journal of Political Research*, 41(3), pp. 345–78.

Lundestad, Geir (1998a) *Empire by Integration: The United States and European Integration, 1945–1997* (Oxford: Oxford University Press).

Lundestad, Geir (1998b) *No End to Alliance. The United States and Western Europe: Past, Present and Future* (Basingstoke: Palgrave Macmillan).

Luther, Kurt Richard and Müller-Rommel, Ferdinand (eds) (2002) *Political Parties in the New Europe: Political and Analytical Challenges* (Oxford: Oxford University Press).

M

MacIver, Don (1999) *The Politics of Multinational States* (Basingstoke: Palgrave Macmillan).

Magone, José M. (2004) *Contemporary Spanish Politics* (London: Routledge).

Mahler, Vincent A. (2004) 'Economic Globalization, Domestic Politics, and Income Inequality in the Developed Countries: A Cross-National Study', *Comparative Politics*, 37(9), pp. 1025–53.

Mair, Peter (1996) 'Party Systems and Structures of Competition', in Lawrence le Dine, Richard G. Niemi and Pippa Norris (eds), *Comparing Democracies: Elections and Voting in Comparative Perspective* (London: Sage).

Mair, Peter (2000) 'The limited impact of Europe on national party systems', *West European Politics*, 23 (4), pp. 27–51.

Mair, Peter (2001) 'The Green Challenge and Political Competition: How Typical is the German Experience?', *German Politics*, 10(2), pp. 99–116.

Mair, Peter (2002) 'In the Aggregate: Mass Electoral Behaviour in Western Europe, 1950–2000', in Hans Keman (ed.), *Comparative Democratic Politics: A Guide to Contemporary Theory and Research* (London: Sage).

Mair, Peter (2004) 'The Europeanisation Dimension', *Journal of European Public Policy*, 11 (2), pp. 337–48.

Mair, Peter and van Biezen, Ingrid (2001) 'Party Membership in Europe, 1980–2000', *Party Politics*, 7(1), pp. 5–21.

Mair, Peter and Mudde, Cas (1998) 'The Party Family and its Study', *Annual Review of Political Science*, 1, pp. 211–29.

Mair, Peter, Müller, Wolfgang and Plasser, Fritz (eds) (2004) *Political Parties and Electoral Change* (London: Sage).

Majone, Giandomenico (1996) *Regulating Europe* (London: Routledge).

Malgin, Artem (2002) 'The Commonwealth of Independent States: Summary of a Decade', *Russian Politics and Law*, 40(5), pp. 43–54.

Mangott, Gerhard (2000) 'Farewell to Russia: The Decline of a Global Power', in Heinz Gärtner, Adrian Hyde-Price and Erich Reiter (eds), *Europe's New Security Challenges* (Boulder, CO: Lynne Rienner).

Mann, Michael (1997) 'Has Globalization Ended the Rise and Rise of the Nation State?', *Review of International Political Economy*, 4(3) pp. 472–96.

Manners, Ian and Whitman, Richard G. (eds) (2001) *The Foreign Policies of European Union Member States* (Manchester: Manchester University Press).

Markovits, Andrei (2004) 'European Anti-Americanism (and Anti-Semitism): Ever Present though always Denied', Harvard Centre for European Studies Working Paper, 108, available at http://www.ces.fas.harvard.edu/working_papers/Markovits.pdf

Markovits, Andrei (2005) *European Anti-Americanism and Anti-Semitism in a Changing Transatlantic Relationship* (Princeton: Princeton University Press).

Marks, Gary and Wilson, Carole J. (2000) 'The Past in the Present: A Cleavage Theory of Party Response to European Integration', *British Journal of Political Science*, 30(3), pp. 433–59.

Martell, Luke (2001) 'Capitalism, Globalization and Democracy: Does Social Democracy have a Role?' in Martell (ed.) *Social Democracy: Global and National Perspectives* (Basingstoke: Palgrave Macmillan).

Martinez-Herrera, Enric (2002) 'From Nation Building to Building Identification with Political Communities: Consequences of Political Decentralisation in Spain, the Basque Country, Catalonia and Galicia, 1978–2001', *European Journal of Political Research*, 41, pp. 421–53.

Mateju, P. and Vlachova, K. (1998) 'Values and Electoral Decisions in the Czech Republic', *Communist and Post-Communist Studies*, 31(3), pp. 249–69.

Mattila, Mikko (2004) 'Contested Decisions: Empirical Analysis of Voting in the European Union Council of Ministers', *European Journal of Political Research*, 43(1), pp. 29–50.

Maull, Hanns W. (1990) 'Germany and Japan: The New Civilian Powers', *Foreign Affairs*, 69(5), pp. 91–106.

Maurer, Andreas and Wessels, Wolfgang (2001) *National Parliaments on their Ways to Europe: Losers or Latecomers?* (Baden-Baden: Nomos) (an updated edition is planned for 2005).

Maurer, Andreas, Mittag, Jürgen and Wessels, Wolfgang (2003) 'National Systems' Adaptation to the EU System: Trends, Offers, and Constraints', in Beate Kohler-Koch (ed.), *Linking EU and National Governance* (Oxford: Oxford University Press).

Mazower, Mark (1998) *Dark Continent: Europe's Twentieth Century* (London: Allen Lane).

Mazzoleni, G. (1987) 'Media Logic and Party Logic in Campaign Coverage: The Italian General Election of 1983', *European Journal of Communication*, 2(1), pp. 81–103.

McAdam, Doug, McCarthy, John D. and Zald, Mayer N. (eds) (1996) *Comparative Perspectives on Social Movements: Political Opportunities, Mobilizing Structures, and Cultural Framings* (New York: Cambridge University Press).

McCormick, John (2001) *Environmental Policy in the European Union* (Basingstoke: Palgrave Macmillan).

McCormick, John (2005) *Understanding the European Union*, 3rd edition (Basingstoke: Palgrave Macmillan).

McGowan, Francis (2001) 'Social Democracy and the European Union: Who's Changing Whom?', in Luke Martell (ed.), *Social Democracy: Global and Local Perspectives* (Basingstoke: Palgrave Macmillan).

McMenamin, Iain (2002) 'Polish Business Associations: Flattened Civil Society or Super Lobbies?', *Business and Politics*, 4, pp. 299–315.

McNair, Brian, Hibberd, Matthew and Schlesinger, Philip (2002) 'Public Access Broadcasting and Democratic Participation in the Age of Mediated Politics', *Journalism Review*, 3(3), pp. 407–22.

McQuail, Denis (1998) 'Commercialization and Beyond', in Denis McQuail and Karen Siune (eds), *Media Policy: Convergence, Concentration and Commerce* (London: Sage).

McQuail, Denis (2001) 'The Media in Europe', in Montserrat Guibernau (ed.), *Governing European Diversity* (London: Sage).

Meehan, Elizabeth (1993) 'Citizenship and the European Community', *Political Quarterly*, 64(2), pp. 172–86.

Menon, Anand (2004a) 'The Foreign and Security Policies of the European Union', in Maria Green Cowles and Desmond Dinan (eds), *Developments in the European Union 2* (Basingstoke: Palgrave Macmillan).

Menon, Anand (2004b) 'From Crisis to Catharsis: EDSP after Iraq', *International Affairs*, 80(4), pp. 631–49.

Mény Yves and Surel, Yves, (eds) (2002) *Democracies and the Populist Challenge* (Basingstoke: Palgrave Macmillan).

Merkel, Wolfgang (1992) 'After the Golden Age', in Christiane Lemke and Gary Marks (eds), *The Crisis of Socialism in Europe* (Durham, NC: Duke University Press).

Messmer, William B. (2003) 'Taming Labour's MEPs', *Party Politics*, 9(2) pp. 201–18.

Meyer-Sahling, Jan-Hinrik (2004) 'Civil Service Reforms in Post-Communist Europe', *West European Politics*, 27(1), pp. 71–103.

Meyrede, Laurant (1999) 'France's Foreign Policy in the Mediterranean', in Stelios Stavridis, Theodore Couloumbis, Thanos Veremis and Neville Waites (eds), *Foreign Policies of the EU's Mediterranean States and Applicant Countries in the 1990's* (Basingstoke: Palgrave Macmillan).

Michels, Robert (1962) *Political Parties: A Sociological Study of the Oligarchical Tndencies of Modern Democracy* (New York: Free Press), Also available at http://religionanddemocracy.lib. virginia.edu/library/tocs/MichPoli.html

Miles, Lee (ed.) (2000) *Sweden and the European Union Evaluated* (London: Continuum).

Millard, Frances (2004) *Elections, Parties, and Representation in Post-communist Europe* (Basingstoke: Palgrave Macmillan).

Millard, Frances (1999) *Politics and Society in Poland* (London: Routledge).

Molina, Oscar and Rhodes, Martin (2002) 'Corporatism: The Past, Present and Future of a Concept', *Annual Review of Political Science*, 5, pp. 305–31.

Molle, Willem (2001) *The Economics of European Integration: Theory, Practice, Policy* (Aldershot: Ashgate).

Moravcsik, Andrew (2001) *The Choice for Europe: Social Purpose and State Power from Messina to Maastricht* (Ithaca: Cornell University Press).

Mueller, J. (1994) 'The Catastrophe Quota', *Journal of Conflict Resolution*, 38(3), pp. 355–75.

Müftüler-Bac, Meltem (1997) *Turkey's Relations with a Changing Europe* (Manchester: Manchester University Press).

Mughan, Anthony (2000) *Media and the Presidentialization of Parliamentary Elections* (Basingstoke: Palgrave Macmillan).

Müller, Wolfgang C. and Saalfield, Thomas (eds) (1997) *Members of Parliament in Western Europe: Roles and Behaviour* (London: Frank Cass).

Müller, Wolfgang C. and Strøm, K. (eds) (2000) *Coalition Governments in Western Europe* (Oxford: Oxford University Press).

Murray, Philomena (2003) 'An Asia Pacific Response to the European Union: Australian Elite Perceptions', *Asia-Europe Journal*, 1, pp. 103–19.

Murschetz, P. (1998) 'State Support for the Daily Press in Europe: A Critical Appraisal', *European Journal of Communication* 13(3), pp. 291–313.

Myant, Martin, Slocock, Brian and Smith, Simon (2000) 'Tripartism in the Czech and Slovak Republics', *Europe-Asia Studies*, 52(4), pp. 723–40.

Myntti, Kristian (2002) 'The Sami Cultural Autonomies in the Nordic Countries', in Kinga Gál (ed.), *Minority Governance in Europe* (Budapest: Local Government and Public Service Reform Initiative/Open Society Institute).

N

Nassmacher, Karl-Heinz (ed.) (2001) *Foundations for Democracy: Approaches to Comparative Political Finance* (Baden-Baden: Nomos).

National Geographic (2001) 'Gypsies: The World's Outsiders', April.

Negrine, Ralph (1998) *Parliament and the Media: A study of Britain, Germany and France* (London: Pinter).

Negrine, Ralph and Lilleker, Darren (2002) 'The Professionalization of Political Communication: Continuities and Change in Media Practices', *European Journal of Communication*, 17(3), pp. 305–23.

Neumann, Iver B. (1998) *Uses of the Other: 'The East' in European Identity Formation* (Minneapolis: University of Minnesota Press).

Newell, James (2000) *Parties and Democracy in Italy* (Aldershot: Dartmouth).

Newton, Kenneth and Brynin, Malcolm (2001) 'The National Press and Party Voting in the UK', *Political Studies*, 49(2), pp. 265–85.

Neyer, Jürgen and Wolf, Dieter (2003) 'Horizontal Enforcement in the EU: The BSE Crisis and the Case of State Aid Control', in Beate Kohler-Koch (ed.), *Linking EU and National Governance* (Oxford: Oxford University Press).

Nielsen, Jorgen (2004) *Muslims in Western Europe* (Edinburgh: Edinburgh University Press).

Nieuwbeerta, Paul and De Graaf, Nan Dirk (1999) 'Traditional

Class Voting in 20 Postwar Societies', in Geoffrey Evans, *The End of Class Politics?: Class Voting in Comparative Context* (Oxford: Oxford University Press).

Norris, Pippa (2000) *A Virtuous Circle: Political Communication in Postindustrial Societies* (Cambridge: Cambridge University Press).

Norris, Pippa (2001) *Digital Divide: Civic Engagement, Information Poverty and the Internet Worldwide* (Cambridge: Cambridge University Press).

Norris, Pippa (2005) *The Rise of the Radical Right* (Cambridge: Cambridge University Press).

Norris, Pippa and Inglehart, Ronald (2004) *Sacred and Secular: Religion and Politics Worldwide* (Cambridge: Cambridge University Press).

Norton, Philip (ed.) (1999) *Parliaments and Governments in Western Europe* (London: Frank Cass)

Norton, Philip (ed.) (1990) *Parliaments and Pressure Groups in Western Europe* (London: Frank Cass).

Nugent, Neill (2004) *European Union Enlargement* (Basingstoke and New York: Palgrave Macmillan).

Núñez, Xosé-Manoel (2001) 'What is Spanish Nationalism Today? From Legitimacy Crisis to Unfulfilled Renovation (1975–2000)', *Ethnic and Racial Studies*, 24(5), pp. 719–52.

Nuttall, Simon J. (2000) *European Foreign Policy* (Oxford: Oxford University Press).

O

O'Brien, Robert and Williams, Marc (2004) *Global Political Economy: Evolution and Dynamics* (Basingstoke and New York: Palgrave Macmillan).

O'Donnell, R. (2001) 'Towards Post-corporatist Concertation in Europe', in Helen Wallace (ed.), *Interlocking Dimensions of European Integration* (London: Pinter).

O'Leary, Brendan (2003) 'What States Can Do with Nations: An Iron Law of Nationalism and Federation?' in T.V. Paul, G. John Ikenberry and John Hall, *The Nation-state in Question* (Princeton: Princeton University Press).

O'Neil, Patrick H. (ed.) (1997) *Post-Communism and the Media in Eastern Europe* (London: Frank Cass).

Ohmae, Kenichi (1996) *The End of the Nation State: The Rise of Regional Economies* (London: HarperCollins).

Olcott, Martha Brill, Åslund, Anders and Garnett, Sherman W. (2000) *Getting It Wrong: Regional Cooperation and the Commonwealth of Independent States* (Washington, DC: Carnegie Endowment for International Peace).

Olsen, G.R. (2002) 'Promoting Democracy, Preventing Conflict: The European Union and Africa', *International Politics*, 39(3), pp. 311–28.

Olson, Mancur (1982) *The Rise and Decline of Nations: Economic Growth, Stagflation, and Social Rigidities* (New Haven, CT: Yale University Press).

P

Padgett, Stephen (2000) *Organizing Democracy in Eastern Germany: Interest Groups in Post-Communist Society* (Cambridge: Cambridge University Press).

Padgett, Stephen, Paterson, William E. and Smith, Gordon (2003) *Developments in German Politics 3* (Basingstoke: Palgrave Macmillan).

Pagden, Anthony (ed.) (2002) *The Idea of Europe: From Antiquity to the European Union* (Cambridge: Cambridge University Press).

Page, Edward C. and Wouters, Linda (1995) 'The Europeanisation of the National Bureaucracies', in Jon Pierre (ed.), *Bureaucracy in the Modern State: An Introduction to Comparative Public Administration* (Aldershot: Edward Elgar).

Page, Edward C. and Wright, Vincent (1999) *Bureaucratic Elites in Western European States: A Comparative Analysis of Top Officials* (Oxford: Oxford University Press).

Palmer, Jerry (2002) 'News Production: News Values', in Adam Briggs and Paul Cobley (eds), *The Media: An Introduction* (London: Longman).

Panayi, Panikos (2000) *An Ethnic History of Europe since 1945: Nations, States and Minorities* (London: Longman Pearson).

Panebianco, Angelo (1988) *Political Parties: Organisation and Power* (Cambridge: Cambridge University Press).

Papadopoulos, Yannis (2001) 'How Does Direct Democracy Matter? The Impact of Referendum Votes upon Politics and Policy-Making', *West European Politics*, 24(2), pp. 35–58.

Papathanassopoulos, S. (2001) 'The Decline of Newspapers: The Case of the Greek Press', *Journalism Studies*, 2(1), pp. 109–23.

Papatheodorou, E. and Machin, D. (2003) 'The Umbilical Cord that was Never Cut: The Post-dictatorial Intimacy Between the Political Elite and the Mass Media in Greece and Spain', *European Journal of Communication*, 18(1), pp. 31–54.

Parker, David (ed.) (1998) *Privatisation in the European Union: Theory and Policy Perspectives* (London: Routledge).

Pasquino, Gianfranco (2002) 'Italy: A Democratic Regime under Reform', in Josep M. Colomer (ed.), *Political Institutions in Europe* (London: Routledge).

Pauly, Robert J. (2004) *Islam in Europe: Integration or Marginalization?* (Aldershot: Ashgate).

Paxton, Will and Dixon, Mike (2004) *The State of the Nation: An Audit of Injustice in the UK* (London: IPPR).

Pennings, Paul (2002) 'Voters, Elections and Ideology in European Democracies', in Hans Keman (ed.), *Comparative Democratic Politics* (London: Sage).

Péteri, György (2000) 'Between Empire and Nation-state: Comments on the Pathology of State Formation during the "Short Twentieth Century"', *Contemporary European History*, 9(3), pp. 367–84.

Peters, B. Guy (2001) *The Politics of Bureaucracy* (London: Routledge).

Peters, B. Guy and Pierre, Jon (2000) *Governance, Politics and the State* (Basingstoke: Palgrave Macmillan).

Peters, B. Guy and Wright, Vincent (2000) *Administering the Summit: Administration of the Core Executive in Developed Countries* (Basingstoke: Palgrave Macmillan).

Peterson, John and Pollack, Mark (2003) *Europe, America, Bush* (London: Routledge).

Pfetsch, B. (1996) 'Convergence through Privatization? Changing Media Environments and Televised Politics in Germany', *European Journal of Communication*, 11(4), pp. 427–51.

Piening, Christopher (1997) *Global Europe* (Boulder, CO: Lynne Rienner).

Pierre, Jon (ed.) (1995) *Bureaucracy in the Modern State: An Introduction to Comparative Public Administration* (Aldershot: Edward Elgar).

Pierson, Christopher (2001) *Hard Choices: Social Democracy in the Twenty-First Century* (Cambridge: Polity Press).

Pissarides, Christopher, Garibaldi, Pietro Olivetti, Claudia, Petrongolo, Barbara and Wasmer, Etienne (2004) 'Women in the Labour Force: How Well is Europe Doing?', in Tito Boeri, Daniela Del Boca and Christopher Pissarides (eds), *Women at Work: An Economic Perspective. A Report for the Fondazione Rodolfo Debenedetti* (Oxford: Oxford University Press).

Plasser, Fritz and Plasser, Gunda (2002) *Global Political Campaigning: A Worldwide Analysis of Campaign Professionals and their Practices* (Westport, CT: Greenwood/Praeger).

Poguntke, Thomas and Webb, Paul (eds) (2004) *The Presidentialization of Politics: A Comparative Study of Modern Democracies* (Oxford: Oxford University Press).

Poitras, Guy E. (2003) 'Resisting Globalization: The Politics of Protest in the Global Political Economy', *International Politics*, 40(3), pp. 409–24.

Pollitt, Christopher and Bouckaert, Geert (2000) *Public Management Reform: A Comparative Analysis* (Oxford: Oxford University Press).

Poppe, Christian and Kjærnes, Unni (2003) *Trust in Food in Europe: A Comparative Analysis* (Oslo: National Institute for Consumer Research).

Powell, Martin (2004) 'Social Democracy in Europe', in Giuliano Bonoli and Martin Powell (eds), *Social Democratic Party Policies in Contemporary Europe* (London: Routledge/ECPR).

Procházka, Radoslav (2002) *Mission Accomplished: On Founding Constitutional Adjudication in Central Europe* (Budapest: Central European University Press).

Przeworski, Adam and Wallerstein, Michael (1988) 'Structural Dependence of the State on Capital', *American Political Science Review*, 82: 11–29.

Putnam, Robert D. (1988) 'Diplomacy and Domestic Politics: The Logic of Two Level Games', *International Organization*, 42(3), pp. 427–60.

Putnam, Robert D. (2000) *Bowling Alone: The Collapse and Revival of American Community* (New York: Simon & Schuster).

Putnam, Robert D., Leonardi, Robert and Nanetti, Raffaella, Y. (2000) *Making Democracy Work: Civic Traditions in Modern Italy* (Princeton: Princeton University Press).

Q

QAA (2000) *Politics and International Relations Subject Benchmark Statement* (Gloucester: Quality Assurance Agency for Higher Education), available at http://www.qaa.ac.uk/crntwork/benchmark/politics.pdf

Qvortrup, Mads (2002) *A Comparative Study of Referendums: Government by the People* (Manchester: Manchester University Press).

R

Radaelli, Claudio (1997) 'How Does Europeanization Produce Domestic Policy Change?', *Comparative Political Studies*, 30(5), pp. 553–75.

Radaelli, Claudio (2004) 'The Puzzle of Regulatory Competition', *Journal of Public Policy*, 24(1), pp. 1–23.

Rallings, Colin (1987) 'The Influence of Election Programmes: Britain and Canada, 1945–79', in Ian Budge, David Robertson and Derek Hearl (eds), *Ideology, Strategy and Party Changes: Spatial Analysis of Post-War Election Programmes in 19 Democracies* (Cambridge: Cambridge University Press).

Ram, M. (2003) 'Democratization through European Integration: The Case of Minority Rights in the Czech Republic and Romania', *Studies in Comparative International Development*, 38(2) pp. 28–56.

Ramadan, Tariq (2003) *Western Muslims and the Future of Islam* (Oxford: Oxford University Press).

Raunio, Tapio and Hix, Simon (2000) 'Backbenchers Learn to Fight Back: European Integration and Parliamentary Government', *West European Politics*, 23(4), pp. 142–68.

Rawcliffe, Peter (1998) *Environmental Pressure Groups in Transition* (Manchester: Manchester University Press).

Reeves, Minou (2003) *Muhammad in Europe: A Thousand Years of Western Myth-Making* (New York University Press).

Rhodes, R.A.W. (1997) *Understanding Governance: Policy Networks, Governance, Reflexivity and Accountability* (Buckingham: Open University Press).

Rhodes, R.A.W. (2002) 'Globalization, EMU and Welfare State Futures', in Erik Jones Hayward and Martin Rhodes (eds), *Developments in West European Politics* (Basingstoke: Palgrave Macmillan).

Rhodes, R.A.W. and Weller, P. (eds) (2001) *The Changing World of Top Officials: Manderins or Valets* (Buckingham: Open University Press).

Richards, David and Smith, Martin (2002) *Governance and Public Policy in the UK* (Oxford: Oxford University Press).

Richardson, Jeremy (2001) 'Policy-making in the EU: Familiar Ambitions in Unfamiliar Ssettings', in Anand Menon and Vincent Wright (eds), *From the Nation State to Europe?* (Oxford: Oxford University Press).

Richardson, Jeremy, Gustafsson, Gunnel and Jordan, Grant (1982) 'The Concept of Policy Style' in Jeremy Richardson (ed.), *Policy Styles in Western Europe* (London: George Allen & Unwin).

Richardson, Kay and Meinhof, Ulrike H. (1999) *Worlds in Common? Television Discourse in a Changing Europe* (London: Routledge).

Rodgers, Jayne (2003) *Spatializing International Politics: Analysing Activism on the Internet* (London: Routledge).

Roncarolo, Franca (2004) 'Mediation of Italian Politics and the Marketing of Leaders' Private Lives', *Parliamentary Affairs*, 57(1), pp. 108–17.

Rootes, Christopher (2003) *Environmental Protest in Western Europe* (Oxford: Oxford University Press).

Rootes, Christopher (2004) 'Is There a European Environmental Movement?', in Brian Baxter, John Barry and Richard Dunphy (eds), *Europe, Globalisation and Sustainable Development* (London: Routledge).

Rosamond, Ben (2000) *Theories of European Integration* (Basingstoke: Palgrave Macmillan).

Rose, Richard (2001) *The Prime Minister in a Shrinking World* (Cambridge: Polity Press).

Ross, George, Hoffman, Stanley and Malzacher, Sonja (1987) *The Mitterrand Experiment* (Cambridge: Polity Press).

Rouban, Luc (1995) 'Public Administration at the Crossroads: The End of French Exceptionalism', in Jon Pierre (ed.), *Bureaucracy in the Modern State: An Introduction to Comparative Public Administration* (Aldershot: Edward Elgar).

Rucht, Dieter (2003) 'The Changing Role of Political Protest Movements', in *West European Politics*, 26(4), pp. 153–78.

Rydgren, Jens (2002) 'Right Wing Populism in Sweden: Still A Failure But for How Long?', *Scandinavian Political Studies*, 25(1), pp. 27–56.

Rydgren, Jens (ed.) (2004) *Movements of Exclusion. Radical Right-wing Populism in the Western World* (Hauppauge, NY: Nova Science).

S

Saggar, Shamit (2000) *Race and Electoral Politics in Britain* (London: UCL Press).

Sanders, Karen with Canel, María José (2004) 'Spanish Politicians and the Media: Controlled Visibility and Soap Opera Politics', *Parliamentary Affairs*, 57(1), pp. 196–208.

Sanford, George (2002) *Democratic Government in Poland: Constitutional Politics Since 1989* (Basingstoke: Palgrave Macmillan).

Sartori, Giovanni (1997) *Comparative Constitutional Engineering: An Inquiry into Structures, Incentives and Outcomes* (Basingstoke: Palgrave Macmillan).

Sassoon, Donald (1997) *One Hundred Years of Socialism: The West European Left in the Twentieth Century* (London: Fontana).

Savarese, Rossella (2000) '"Infosuasion" in European Newspapers: A Case Study of the War in Kosovo', *European Journal of Communication*, 15(3), pp. 363–81.

Scarrow, Susan E. (1994) 'The "Paradox of Enrolment": Assessing the Costs and Benefits of Party Membership', *European Journal of Political Research*, 25(1), pp. 41–60.

Scharpf, Fritz (1998) 'Negative and positive integration in the political economy of European welfare states', in Martin Rhodes and Yves Mény (eds) *The Future of European Welfare: a New Social Contract* (Basingstoke: Palgrave Macmillan).

Schlesinger, Philip (1993) 'Wishful Thinking: Cultural Politcs, Media and Collective Identities in Europe', *Journal of Communication*, 43(2), pp. 6–17.

Schlesinger, Philip and Kevin, Deirdre (2000) 'Can the European Union become a Sphere of Publics?', in Erik Oddvar Eriksen and John Erik Fossum (eds), *Democracy in the European Union: Integration through Deliberation?* (London: Routledge).

Schmidt, Manfred G. (1996) 'When Parties Matter: A Review of the Possibilities and Limits of Partisan Influence on Public Policy', *European Journal of Political Research,* 30(2), pp. 155–83.

Schmidt, Manfred G. (2002a) 'The Impact of Political Parties, Constitutional Structures and Veto Players in Public Policy', in Hans Keman (ed.), *Comparative Democratic Politics* (London: Sage).

Schmidt, Manfred (2002b) 'Germany: the Grand Coalition State', in Josep M. Colomer (ed.), *Political Institutions in Europe* (London: Routledge).

Schmidt, Manfred (2003) *Political Institutions in the Federal Republic of Germany* (Oxford: Oxford University Press).

Schmidt, Vivien A. (1999) 'National Patterns of Governance under Seige: The Impact of European Integration', in Beate Kohler Koch and Rainer Eising (eds), *The Transformation of Governance in the European Union* (London: Routledge/ECPR).

Schmidt, Vivien A. (2001) 'The Politics of Adjustment in France and Britain: When Does Discourse Matter?', *Journal of European Public Policy*, 8(2), pp. 247–64.

Schmitt, Burkhard (2004) *Defence Expenditure*, updated July 2004 (Paris: European Union Institute for Security Studies [EUISS], available online at http://www.iss-eu.org/esdp/ll-bsdef.pdf

Schmitt, Hermann and Sören Holmberg (1995) 'Political Parties in Decline?', in Hans-Dieter Klingemann and Dieter Fuchs (eds), *Citizens and the State* (Oxford: Oxford University Press).

Schmitter, Phillipe C. (1996) 'If the Nation-state Were to Wither away in Europe, What Might Replace It?', in Sverker Gustavsson and Leif Lewin (eds), *The Future of the Nation-State* (London: Routledge).

Scholte, Jan Aart (2001) *Globalization: A Critical Introduction* (Basingstoke: Palgrave Macmillan).

Schöpflin, George (1995) 'Nationalism and Ethnicity in Europe, East and West', in Charles A. Kupchan (ed.), *Nationalism and Nationalities in the New Europe* (Ithaca: Cornell University Press).

Schudson, Michael (2003) *The Sociology of News* (New York: W. W. Norton).

Schuster, L., (2000) 'A Comparative Analysis of the Asylum Policy of Seven European Governments', *Journal of Refugee Studies*, 13(1), pp. 118–32.

Sciarini, Pascal, Fischer, Alex and Nicolet, Sarah (2004) 'How Europe Hits Home: Evidence from the Swiss case', *Journal of European Public Policy*, 11(3), pp. 353–78.

Semetko, Holli A. (2000) 'Great Britain: The End of News at Ten and the Changing News Environment', in Richard Gunther, and Anthony Mughan (eds), *Democracy and the Media: A Comparative Perspective* (Cambridge: Cambridge University Press).

Semetko, Holli A., de Vreese, Claes H. and Peter, Jochen (2000) 'Europeanised Politics – Europeanised Media? European Integration and Political Communication', *West European Politics*, 23(4), pp. 121–41.

Setälä, Maija (1999) *Referendums and Democratic Government: Normative Theory and the Analysis of Institutions* (Basingstoke: Palgrave Macmillan).

Silvestri, Stefano (1997) 'The Albanian Test Case', *International Spectator*, 32(3–4), pp. 87–98.

Sitter, Nick (2003) 'Cleavages, Party Strategy and Party System Change in Europe, East and West', in Paul Lewis and Paul Webb (eds), *Pan European Perspectives on Party Politics* (Leiden: Brill).

Siune, Karen, Svensson, Palle and Tongsgaard, Ole (1994) 'The European Union: The Danes Said "No" in 1992 but "Yes" in 1993: How and Why?', *Electoral Studies*, 13(2), pp. 107–16.

Sjursen, Helene (2001) 'The Common Foreign and Security Policy: Limits of Intergovernmentalism and the Search for a Global Role', in Svein Andersen and Kjell Eliassen (eds), *Making Policy in Europe,* 2nd edition (London: Sage).

Sklair, Leslie (2002) *Globalization: Capitalism and its Alternatives*, 3rd edition (Oxford: Oxford University Press).

Smeeding, Timothy M. (2002) 'Globalisation, Inequality and the Rich Countries of the G-20: Evidence from the Luxembourg Income Study (LIS)' (Canberra: Reserve Bank of Australia), available at http://www.rba.gov.au/PublicationsAndResearch/Conferences/2002/smeeding.pdf

Smith, Anthony D. (1991) *National Identity* (Harmondsworth: Penguin).

Smith, Anthony D. (1992) 'National Identity and the Idea of European Unity', *International Affairs*, 68(1), pp. 55–76.

Smith, Mark (2000) 'NATO Enlargement and European Security', in Lisbeth Aggestam and Adrian Hyde-Price (eds), *Security and Identity in Europe: Exploring the New Agenda* (Basingstoke: Palgrave Macmillan).

Smith, Martin J. (1993) *Pressure, Power and Policy: State Autonomy and Policy Networks in Britain and the United States* (New York: Harvester Wheatsheaf).

Smith, Michael (2004) 'CFSP and ESDP: From Idea to Institution to Policy', in Martin Holland (ed.), *Common Foreign and Security Policy: The First Ten Years* (London: Continuum).

Soetendorp, Ben (1999) *Foreign Policy in the European Union: History, Theory and Practice* (London: Longman).

Sotiropoulos, Dimitri A. (2004) 'Southern European Public Bureacracies in Comparative Perspective', *West European Politics*, 27(3), pp. 405–22.

Sparks, Colin (1997) 'Post-communist Media in Transition', in John Corner, Philip Schlesinger and Roger Silverstone (eds), *International Media Research: A Critical Survey* (London: Routledge).

Sparks, Colin (2000) 'Media Theory after the Fall of European Communism: Why the Old Models from East and West won't do Anymore', in James Curran and Myung-Jin Park (eds), *De-Westernizing Media Studies* (London: Routledge).

Spohn, Willfried and Triandafyllidou, Anna (eds) (2002) *Europeanisation, National Identities and Migration: Changes in Boundary Constructions between Western and Eastern Europe* (London: Routledge).

Stammers, Neil (2001) 'Social Democracy and Global Governance', in Luke Martell (ed.), *Social Democracy: Global and National Perspectives* (Basingstoke: Palgrave Macmillan).

Stanyer, James and Wring, Dominic (eds) (2004) *Public Image, Private Lives: The Mediation of Politicians Around the Globe*, Special Issue of *Parliamentary Affairs*, 57(1).

Stavridis, Stelios, Theodore Couloumbis, Thanos Veremis and Neville Waites (eds) (1999) *Foreign Policies of the EU's Mediterranean States and Applicant Countries in the 1990's* (Basingstoke: Palgrave Macmillan).

Stent, Angela and Shevtsova, Lilia (2002) 'America, Russia and Europe: A Realignment?' *Survival*, 44(4), pp. 121–34.

Stephens, J.D., Huber, E. and Ray, L. (1999) 'The Welfare State in Hard Times', in Herbert Kitschelt, Peter Lange, Gary Marks and John D. Stephens (eds), *Continuity and Change in Contemporary Capitalism* (Cambridge: Cambridge University Press).

Stevens, Anne (2003) *Government and Politics of France* (Basingstoke: Palgrave Macmillan).

Stone Sweet, Alec (2000) *Governing with Judges: Constitutional Politics in Europe* (Oxford: Oxford University Press).

Strange, Gerard (2002) 'British Trade Unions and European Integration in the 1990s: Politics versus Political Economy', *Political Studies*, 50(2), pp. 332–53.

Stråth, Bo (ed.) (2001) *Europe and the Other and Europe as the Other* (Various: Peter Lang).

Strøm, Knaare (1990) *Minority Government and Majority Rule* (Cambridge: Cambridge University Press).

Strøm, K., Budge, I. and Laver, M. (1994) 'Constraints on Cabinet Formation in Parliamentary Democracies', *American Journal of Political Science*, 38(2), pp. 303–35.

Szczerbiak, Aleks (2001) *Poles Together? The Emergence and Development of Political Parties in Postcommunist Poland* (Budapest: Central European University Press).

Szczerbiak, Aleks (2003) 'Old and New Divisions in Polish Politics: Polish Parties' Electoral Strategies and Bases of Support', *Europe-Asia Studies*, 55(5), pp. 729–46.

Szczerbiak, Aleks and Bale, Tim (2005) 'Why is there no Christian Democracy in Poland', unpublished manuscript.

Szczerbiak, Aleks and Taggart, Paul (2005) *Opposing Europe: The Comparative Party Politics of Euroscepticism, I and II* (Oxford: Oxford University Press).

Szukala, Andrea (2003) 'France: The European Transformation of the French Model', in Wolfgang Wessels, Andreas Maurer and Jürgen Mittag (eds), *Fifteen into One? The European Union and its Member States,* 2nd edition (Manchester: Manchester University Press).

T

Taggart, Paul (2000) *Populism* (Buckingham: Open University Press).

Taras, Ray and Castle, Marjorie (2002) *Democracy in Poland* (Boulder, CO: Westview Press).

Teague, Paul and Donaghey, James (2003) 'European Economic Government and the Corporatist quid pro quo', *Industrial Relations Journal*, 34(2), pp. 104–18.

Tesser, L. (2003) 'The Geopolitics of Tolerance: Minority Rights under EU Expansion in East-Central Europe', *East European Politics and Societies*, 17(3), pp. 483–532.

Tewes, Henning (2001) *Germany, Civilian Power and the New Europe* (Basingstoke: Palgrave Macmillan).

Thompson, W.C. (2001) 'Germany and the East', *Europe-Asia Studies*, 53(6) pp. 921–52.

Thomson, Robert (2001) 'The Programme to Policy Linkage: The Fulfillment of Election Pledges on Socio-economic Policy in the Netherlands, 1986–1998', *European Journal of Political Research*, 40(2) pp. 171–97.

Thomson, Stuart (2000) *The Social Democratic Dilemma: Ideology, Governance and Globalization* (Basingstoke: Palgrave Macmillan).

Tilly, Charles (1975) 'Reflecting on the History of European State-making', in Charles Tilly (ed.), *The Formation of the National State in Western Europe* (Princeton: Princeton University Press).

Tilly, Charles (1993) *Coercion, Capital and European States, AD 990–1992* (Oxford: Blackwell).

Timonen, Virpi (2003) *Restructuring the Welfare State: Globalization and Social Policy Reform in Finland and Sweden* (Cheltenham: Edward Elgar).

Trappel, Josef and Meier, Werner A. (1998) 'Media Concentration: Options for Policy', in Denis McQuail and Karen Siune (eds), *Media Policy: Convergence, Concentration and Commerce* (London: Sage).

Triandafyllidou, Anna (2003) 'The Launch of the Euro in the Italian Media', *European Journal of Communication*, 18(2), pp. 255–63.

Tsebelis, George, Jensen, Christian B., Kalandrakis, Anastassios and Kreppel, Amie (2001) 'Legislative Procedures in the European Union: An Empirical Analysis', *British Journal of Political Science*, 31(4) pp. 573–99.

Turner, Barry (2005) *Statesman's Yearbook 2005: The Politics, Cultures and Economies of the World* (Basingstoke: Palgrave Macmillan).

Tworzecki, Hubert (2003) *Learning to Choose: Electoral Politics in East-Central Europe* (Stanford: Stanford University Press).

Vatta, A. (2001) 'Concertation and Employers' Organizations in Italy: The Case of Confindustria', *South European Society and Politics*, 6(3), pp. 103–22.

Verheijen, Tony (ed.) (1999) *Civil Service Systems in Central and Eastern Europe* (Cheltenham: Edward Elgar).

Visser, Jelle (1998) 'Learning to Play: The Europeanization of Trade Unions', in Patrick Pasture and Johan Verberckmoes (eds), *Working Class Internationalism and the Appeal of National Identity: Historical Debates and Current Perspectives* (Oxford: Berg).

Vlachová, Klára (2001) 'Party Identification in the Czech Republic: Inter-party Hostility and Party Preference', *Communist and Post-Communist Studies*, 34(4), pp. 479–99.

Volkens, Andrea (2004) 'Policy Changes of European Social Democrats, 1945–1998', in Guiliano Bonoli and Martin Powell (eds), *Social Democratic Party Policies in Contemporary Europe* (London: Routledge).

Volkens, Andrea and Klingemann, Hans-Dieter, (2002) 'Parties, Ideologies, and Issues. Stability and Change in Fifteen European Party Systems 1945–1998', in Kurt Richard Luther and Ferdinand Müller-Rommel, (eds) *Political Parties in the New Europe: Political and Analytical Challenges,* (Oxford University Press, Oxford).

de Vreese, Claes H. de (2001) 'Election Coverage: New Directions for Public Broadcasting', *European Journal of Communication*, 16(2), pp. 155–80.

W

Wagener, Hans-Jürgen (2002) 'The Welfare State in Transition Economies and Accession to the EU', *West European Politics*, 25(2), pp. 152–74.

Wallace, Helen (2000) 'Europeanisation and Globalisation: Complementary or Contradictory Trends', *New Political Economy*, 5(3), pp. 369–82.

Wallace, Helen and Wallace, William (2000) *Policy-Making in the European Union* (Oxford: Oxford University Press).

Waller, M. and Myant, M. (1994) *Parties, Trade Unions and Society in East-Central Europe* (London: Frank Cass).

Ward, Stephen and Lusoli, Wainer (2003) 'Dinosaurs in Cyberspace?: British Trade Unions and the Internet', *European Journal of Communication*, 18(2), pp. 147–79.

Ware, Alan (1996) *Political Parties and Party Systems*, (Oxford: Oxford University Press).

Waters, Malcolm (2001) *Globalization* (London: Routledge).

Weaver, D.H. (1998) 'Journalists around the World: Commonalities and Differences', in D.H. Weaver (ed.), *The Global Journalist: News People around the World* (Cresskill, NJ: Hampton Press).

Webb, Paul, Farrell, David M. and Holliday, Ian (eds) (2002) *Political Parties in Advanced Industrial Democracies* (Oxford: Oxford University Press).

Webber, Mark (ed.) (2000) *Russia and Europe* (Basingstoke: Palgrave Macmillan).

Webster, Frank (ed.) (2001) *Culture and Politics in the Information Age: A New Politics* (Routledge: London).

Weiland, Heribert (2004) 'EU Sanctions against Zimbabwe: A Predictable Own Goal?', in Martin Holland (ed.), *Common Foreign and Security Policy: The First Ten Years* (London: Continuum).

Weiss, Linda (1998) *The Myth of the Powerless State: Governing the Economy in a Global Era* (Cambridge: Polity).

Weller, Patrick, Barkis, Herman and Rhodes, R.A.W. (eds) (1997) *The Hollow Crown: Countervailing Tends in Core Executives* (Basingstoke: Palgrave Macmillan).

Wessels, Wolfgang and Maurer, Andreas (eds) (2001) National Parliaments on their Ways to Europe: Losers or Latecomers (Baden-Baden: Nomos Verlag).

Wessels, Wolfgang, Maurer, Andreas and Mittag, Jürgen (eds) (2003) *Fifteen into One? The European Union and its Member States*, 2nd edition (Manchester: Manchester University Press).

Wheeler, Mark (2004) 'Supranational Regulation: Television and the European Union', *European Journal of Communication*, 19(3), pp. 349–69.

Whitefield, Stephen (2002) 'Political Cleavages and Post-communist Politics', *Annual Review of Political Science*, 5, pp. 181–200.

Wiessala, Georg (2002) *The European Union and Asian Countries* (London: Sheffield Academic Press/Continuum).

Wilensky, Harold, (2002) *Rich Democracies: Political Economy, Public Policy, and Performance* (Berkeley: University of California Press).

Wilke, Jürgen and Reinemann, Carsten (2001) 'Do the Candidates Matter? Long Term Trends of Campaign Coverage – A Study of the German Press Since 1949', *European Journal of Communication*, 16(3), pp. 291–314.

Wilson, David and Game, Chris (2002) *Local Government in the United Kingdom* (Basingstoke: Palgrave Macmillan).

Wincott, Daniel (1999) 'The Court of Justice and the Legal System', in Laura Cram, Desmond Dinan and Neill Nugent (eds), *Developments in the European Union* (Basingstoke: Palgrave Macmillan).

Wolinetz, Stephen (ed.) (1997) *Party Systems* (Aldershot: Ashgate).

Wolinetz, Stephen (ed.) (1998) *Political Parties* (Aldershot: Dartmouth).

Woolcock, Stephen (2000) 'European Trade Policy' in Helen Wallace and William Wallace (eds) (Oxford: Oxford University Press).

Wright, Vincent and Hayward, Jack (2000) 'Governing from the Centre: Policy Co-ordination in Six European Core Executives', in R.A.W. Rhodes (ed.), *Transforming British Government, 2: Changing Roles and Relationships* (Basingstoke: Palgrave Macmillan).

van der Wurff, Richard (2004) 'Supplying and Viewing Diversity: The Role of Competition and Viewer Choice in Dutch Broadcasting', *European Journal of Communication*, 19(2), pp. 215–37.

Wyllie, James H. (1997) *European Security in the New Political Environment* (London: Longman).

Wynn, Terry (2004) *The EU Budget: Public Perception and Fact. The European Union – How Much does it Cost, Where does the Money Go and Why is it Criticised so Much?* (Brussels: Land Use and Food Policy Intergroup), available at http://www.terrywynn.com/

X, Y, Z

Xenakis, Dimitris K. and Chryssochoou, Dimitris, N. (2001) *The Emerging Euro-Mediterranean System* (Manchester: Manchester University Press).

Yanai, Nathan (1999) 'Why do Political Parties Survive? An Analytical Discussion', *Party Politics* 5(1), pp. 5–18.

Young, Alisdair and Wallace, Helen (2000) *Regulatory Politics in the Enlarging European Union: Weighing Civic and Producer Interests* (Manchester: Manchester University Press).

Youngs, Richard (2002) 'European Union and Democracy in Latin America', *Latin American Politics and Society*, 44(3), pp. 111–39.

Youngs, Richard (2003), 'European Approaches to Security in the Mediterranean', *Middle East Journal*, 57(3), pp. 414–31.

Zeff, Eleanor E. and Pirro, Ellen B. (2001) *The European Union and the Member States: Cooperation, Coordination and Compromise* (Boulder, CO: Lynne Rienner).

Zielinksi, Jakub (2002) 'Translating Social Cleavages into Party Systems: The Significance of New Democracies', *World Politics*, 54(2), pp. 184–211.

Zielonka, Jan (1998) 'Policies without Strategy: The EU's Record in Eastern Europe', in Jan Zielonka (ed.), *Paradoxes of European Foreign Policy* (London: Kluwer).

Ziller, Jacques (2001) 'European Models of Government: Towards a Patchwork with Missing Pieces', *Parliamentary Affairs*, 54, pp. 102–19.

Index